PROPAGANDA AND COMMUNICATION
IN WORLD HISTORY

PROPAGANDA AND COMMUNICATION
IN WORLD HISTORY

VOLUME I  The Symbolic Instrument in Early Times

VOLUME II  Emergence of Public Opinion in the West

VOLUME III  A Pluralizing World in Formation

# PROPAGANDA AND COMMUNICATION IN WORLD HISTORY

## VOLUME I

The Symbolic Instrument
in Early Times

*edited by*

Harold D. Lasswell
Daniel Lerner
Hans Speier

*AN EAST-WEST CENTER BOOK* 天
Published for the East-West Center by
The University Press of Hawaii
Honolulu

Manufactured in the United States of America

"Egyptian Civilization" by John A. Wilson is reprinted by permission of The
University of Chicago Press from *The Intellectual Adventure of Ancient Man*
by H. and H. A. Frankfort et al. Copyright 1946 by The University of
Chicago.

"Judaism: The Psychology of the Prophets" by Max Weber is reprinted by
permission of Macmillan Publishing Co. from Max Weber's *Ancient Judaism*,
translated by Hans Gerth and Don Martindale. Copyright 1952 by The Free
Press of Glencoe.

Library of Congress Cataloging in Publication Data
Main entry under title:

The Symbolic instrument in early times.

  (Propaganda and communication in world history ; v. 1)
  Includes bibliographical references and index.
  1.  Communication—Social aspects—History—Addresses,
essays, lectures.  2.  Public opinion—History—Addresses,
essays, lectures.  3.  Communication (Theology)—Ad-
dresses, essays, lectures.  4.  Symbolism in communication
—History—Addresses, essays, lectures.  I.  Lasswell,
Harold Dwight, 1902–     II.  Lerner, Daniel.
III.  Speier, Hans  IV.  Series.
HM258.P74    vol. 1 301.14s [301.14]    78–23964
ISBN 0-8248-0496-1

These three volumes are dedicated to
  JEAN LERNER
our indispensable collaborator
who, with insight, skill, and good cheer,
did whatever needed to be done
through the years of these studies

# CONTENTS

Preface                                                                    xi

1. Introduction                                                             1
   *The Editors*

2. Continuities in Communication from Early Man to
   Modern Times                                                            21
   *Margaret Mead*

3. Early Mesopotamia, 2500–1000 B.C.                                       50
   *Jacob J. Finkelstein*

4. Neo-Assyrian and Neo-Babylonian Empires                                111
   *A. Leo Oppenheim*

5. Egyptian Civilization                                                  145
   *John A. Wilson*

6. Indian Civilization                                                    175
   *R. S. Sharma*

7. On the Spread of Buddhism to China                                     205
   *Arthur F. Wright*

8. Chinese Civilization                                                   220
   *Arthur F. Wright*

9. Classical Civilization                                                 257
   *John Ferguson*

10. Judaism: The Psychology of the Prophets                     299
    *Max Weber*

11. Christian Missions in the Ancient World                     330
    *Charles W. Forman*

12. Communication in Classical Islam                            348
    *George Kirk*

THE OTTOMAN EMPIRE: A COLLOQUY

13. The Modernization of Social Communication                   381
    *Şerif Mardin*

14. Ottoman Political Communication                             444
    *Bruce McGowan*

15. Propaganda Functions of Poetry                              493
    *Talat Sait Halman*

16. Communication Patterns in Centralized Empires               536
    *S. N. Eisenstadt*

17. Western Civilization: The Middle Ages                       552
    *Robert Brentano*

Contributors                                                    597
Index                                                           601

VOLUME II: Emergence of Public Opinion in the West

THE ENLARGING SYMBOLIC OF THE MODERN WEST

1. The Renaissance and the Broadening of Communication
   *William Bouwsma*
2. The Impact of the Reformation Era on Communication and
   Propaganda  *Nancy L. Roelker*
3. The Enlightenment as a Communication Universe  *Peter Gay*
4. The Modern History of Political Fanaticism: A Search for the
   Roots  *Zev Barbu*

THE SYMBOLIC IN WORLD REVOLUTIONARY PROCESSES

5. The Rise of Public Opinion  *Hans Speier*
6. Millenarianism as a Revolutionary Force  *Guenter Lewy*
7. Karl Marx—The Propagandist as Prophet  *Saul K. Padover*
8. Communist Propaganda  *William E. Griffith*

SYMBOL MANAGEMENT IN THE CONTINUING SPREAD OF
   CRISIS POLITICS

9. The Communication of Hidden Meaning  *Hans Speier*
10. The Truth in Hell: Maurice Joly on Modern Despotism
    *Hans Speier*
11. From the Dialogue in Hell Between Machiavelli and Montes-
    quieu
    *Maurice Joly*
12. Deception—Its Decline and Revival in International Conflict
    *Barton Whaley*

MOBILIZATION FOR GLOBAL DEVELOPMENT AND SECURITY

13. The Revolutionary Elites and World Symbolism  *Daniel Lerner*
14. Changing Arenas and Identities in World Affairs
    *Harold R. Isaacs*
15. Communication, Development, and Power  *Lucian W. Pye*
16. Rhetoric and Law in International Political Organs
    *Oscar Schachter*

NUCLEAR POWER: A COLLOQUY

17. War Department Release on New Mexico Test, 16 July 1945
18. Thoughts on Progress, Peaceful Coexistence and Intellectual
    Freedom  *Andrei D. Sakharov*
19. The Chances for Peace  *Hans Speier*

VOLUME III: A Pluralizing World in Formation

THE MULTIVALUE CONTEXT

 1. Must Science Serve Political Power?   *Harold D. Lasswell*
 2. The Marriage of Science and Government   *Jerome B. Wiesner*
 3. Rising Expectations: Frustrations   *Joseph J. Spengler*
 4. The Respect Revolution: Freedom and Equality   *Lewis M. Killian*
 5. Love and Intimacy: Mass Media and Phallic Culture
    *Arnold A. Rogow*

THE MULTIVARIATE PROCESS

 6. The Language of Politics: General Trends in Content
    *Ithiel de Sola Pool*
 7. The Media Kaleidoscope: General Trends in the Channels
    *W. Phillips Davison*
 8. The Moving Target: General Trends in Audience Composition
    *L. John Martin*
 9. The Effects of Mass Media in an Information Era
    *Wilbur Schramm*
10. The Social Effects of Communication Technology
    *Herbert Goldhamer*

THE SYMBOLIC INSTRUMENT—RETROSPECTS AND PROSPECTS

11. The Historic Past of the Unconscious   *Andrew Rolle*
12. Social Science and the Collectivization of Hubris
    *Joseph J. Spengler*
13. The Emerging Social Structure of the World   *Alex Inkeles*
14. The Future of World Communication and Propaganda
    *Harold D. Lasswell*

# PREFACE

The idea of this series originated twenty-five years ago at Stanford in the course of a research project on the world revolution of our time. Lasswell and Lerner were then, respectively, senior consultant and research director of this project. Speier was then head of the social science division at RAND; he joined Lasswell and Lerner as coeditor in 1967. Although the editors have since lived through changes of venue, they have not suffered a change of heart.

Our purpose, then as now, has been to fill the great void in our knowledge of the historical contexts from which our present preoccupation with communication and propaganda evolved. The literature in this field is barren save for the unique book entitled *Die öffentliche Meinung in der Weltgeschichte* by Wilhelm Bauer, which proved to be fertile but not seminal—without offspring. This book has never been translated. Published in 1929, it antedated the rise of Nazism and its "propaganda state," the subsequent global diffusion of "psychological warfare" in World War II, and the "cold war" that shaped the postwar quarter century. Beyond its isolation in a language no longer lingua franca, Bauer's book broached a subject that has since grown beyond the reach of a single scholar.

This led to our first important editorial decision—that our projected study would be the work of many minds from many lands. We next decided that we should try to enlist the very best scholars available to take a fresh look at each historical period and analytical issue we selected. A glance at our table of contents will reveal that these editorial aims have, in the main, been realized.

No editorial strategy, however, can survive so many years without adapting its tactics. In a few instances, where enlisted contributors proved to be mortal or otherwise vulnerable to time's arrow, we have reprinted the best paper extant that was relevant to our editorial aspirations. Two such papers are included in volume I. Surely no apology is needed for reprinting here the papers on ancient Judaism by Max Weber and on ancient Egypt by John Wilson.

Originally we planned for two volumes in which every paper would integrate the historical and analytical modes of exposition within its own framework. This plan has been executed with the happy results presented in the first two volumes. However, it turned out to be impossible to encompass contemporary research within the confines of a few concluding chapters in volume II. Accordingly, we added a third volume to this study and trust that the publication delays this entailed will reward the reader's patience with enhanced enlightenment.

Volume III shifts the expository mode of the first two volumes from historical focus within a conceptual framework to analytical focus within a historical context. We believe this mode will be rewarding to many readers, particularly those who have been afflicted by the crippling conception that the development of communication and propaganda in our own time is a sort of historical "sport"—a "spontaneous" creation of Stalin, Mussolini, Hitler, and the like. It is rewarding—and perhaps reassuring—to be reminded that contemporary communication is a societal phenomenon with a long past and with a future.

Volume I spans human history from its recorded beginnings in primitive and tribal communities through the formation of centralized empires (the Great Society of the ancient world) to the medieval system of Western Europe. We have not sought to cover this vast stretch of historical experience in encyclopedic or textbook fashion. Rather we have been guided by the work of modern scholars, whose painstaking labors among ancient records and relics have reconstructed for us the form and content of societies that contributed significantly to shaping the symbolic instrument.

Thus, after a review of earlier societies, we turn to the great valley-empires in which, for the first time in available records, social communication was not only practiced but codified and transmitted to posterity. Our contributors pass in review the riverine societies that arose and flourished for a time, along the Tigris-Euphrates, the Nile, and the Indus Valleys. Out of these beginnings, and sometimes parallel to them, grew the great and durable social systems that did not rely exclusively upon conquest and commerce. These systems built the continuing stateways and lifeways that have earned them, among scholars, the sobriquet "civilization"—here exemplified by the Mesopotamian, Babylonian, Egyptian, Indian, Chinese, and the classical (Graeco-Roman) civilizations of ancient Europe.

A major force in shaping the symbolic instrument, in the context of early civilization, was the codification of belief and behavior in the great religions that originated in the Mediterranean basin. We examine here the roles played by Judaism, Christianity, Buddhism, and Islam in this historical process. The focus on these codes implies no editorial parochialism. It is a plain historical fact that these particular codes, for reasons that may or may not be related to their virtues as theology and ritual, did diffuse far beyond their original time and space confines to become world religions. Although the mode of diffusion was different in each case—Judaism by diaspora, Christianity by propaganda, Buddhism by transfer, Islam by conquest—all played significant roles in the evolution of world communication. Other major religions such as Hinduism and Shintoism did not, despite their inherent virtues, achieve this degree of global diffusion. Moreover, our editorial efforts to enlist for volume I scholars specialized in other religions came to nought.

If some opportunities were lost, however, others were gained. We are fortunate to include three convergent studies of the Ottoman Empire that illuminate the unique communication system developed under this aegis—studies that converge from diverse social, political, and aesthetic starting points. Volume I concludes with a retrospective analysis of communication in the ancient empires and a perspective on the medieval transformations that shaped the symbolic instrument for future epochs and arenas. The story continues in volume II. Each volume contains its own introduction, notes on contributors, and index.

# PROPAGANDA AND COMMUNICATION
# IN WORLD HISTORY

# 1

# INTRODUCTION

## *THE STUDY OF COMMUNICATION— THEORY AND CONTEXT*

The study of communication has become more versatile and thorough in recent years as new methods of investigation are tested and incorporated as part of the standard equipment of the scholars and scientists who work in the field. An army of technicians has been trained to plan and to execute the propaganda campaigns mounted by the thousands of official and unofficial organizations that operate inside and across national boundary lines.

An example of innovation is "survey research," which is widely used to describe the attitudes of large populations. Another technique is "content analysis," which has a long history of evolution from textual criticism and cryptography. It is often employed to summarize in quantitative form the messages that are brought to the attention of mass audiences by television, radio, film, print, and other media of communication.

Technical virtuosity notwithstanding, all is not well with the study of communication. It must be acknowledged that talented minds, preoccupied with perfecting new instruments of inquiry, often allow themselves to become excessively engaged with the here and now.

## *The Neglect of History*

The present symposium was initiated in agreement with those critics who allege that the shortcomings of an otherwise impressive field are usually related to the neglect of history. *Propaganda and Communication in World History* is a step toward overcoming these limitations.

To neglect the past is to encourage an exaggerated estimate of the uniqueness of many contemporary occurrences and developments. The dissolution of colonial empires in the wake of World War II led to dramatic and often tragic conflict among the legal and ethical norms prevailing in different parts of the globe. Surely it is not irrelevant to recall that similar contradictions have been lived through whenever the boundaries of the "known world" or of an international system were rather suddenly enlarged.

Paradoxical though it may seem, neglect of the past entails imperfect understanding of the present. The genuine novelties of the current scene may be belittled or overlooked if they are not perceived against a backdrop of comparative history. In our time it is doubtful that we are fully aware of the consequences of the fact that the earth is no longer perceived as open to discovery and colonization and that our planet may be facing oblivion.

It is not always recognized that a dim view of the past impoverishes science. The crippling of science follows from the fact that the details of history are potential data for science. Neglect of historical research cannot fail to impose a significant deprivation on scientific knowledge and understanding. It is generally agreed that the historian's primary obligation is to "tell it like it was" in "actual" time. "Actual" time is described, for instance, when a scholar of communication tells us how many magazine articles were published on various topics in the nineteenth century. The content of public media is generalized in "potential" time when a scientific formulation covers all possible situations in which the requisite conditions occur.

Failure to identify some of the factors that may significantly affect communication is a consequence of vaguely perceived history. Awareness of contrasting past situations is a corrective to the experience of anyone who feels at home only in his own society and period. A humble instance is the investigator who, living in a society where domestic servants are rare, greatly underestimates the role of servant gossip in other social systems.

The main effect of insufficient historical knowledge is the practice of presuming the universality of forces whose impacts are culture-bound in the present. It was never difficult for operators to confuse the propaganda of *this* war with the propaganda characteristics of *all* wars.

Among the more subtle consequences of inadequate mastery of the past are the constraints that are imposed on the invention and use of theoretical models to guide research. In recent years, for example, historical comparisons have been too sparingly used to supplement and to improve findings that have depended on micro-models for the study of communication in small groups. There is no doubt of the importance of the researches guided by micro-models. For instance, the workings of conflict and accommodation have been identified and made subject to intensive scrutiny. However, it seems likely that recent research has relied too exclusively on results that are unrelated to larger configurations in space and time. If macro-models had been available and applied, probably they would have drawn attention to long-term changes whose presence cannot be recognized in small-group investigation.

In many areas of contemporary public policy, specialists in communication are in lively demand. They often find themselves at a disadvantage from lack of comparative knowledge because few completed studies have explored the complexities of the communication component of public policy. For example, an adequate analysis must lay bare the multiple forces—political, legal, economic, religious, ethical, and so on—that affect the process.

Nor is lack of relevant knowledge altogether one-sided or restricted to those who specialize in communication. Many scholars of history and prehistory have failed to keep in touch with communication analysis, and consequently have neglected to deal thoroughly with the periods for which they have primary responsibility. Partly in view of these limitations the present enterprise includes relatively specific descriptions of some modern scientific procedures, and calls attention to topics of policy promise, which can be useful in historical research as well.

## THE PLAN OF THE THREE VOLUMES

The foregoing paragraphs summarize the considerations that led us to initiate *Propaganda and Communication in World History*. We were encouraged when we found that our point of view struck a responsive chord among distinguished colleagues in every pertinent field. We are especially grateful to contributors who laid aside other urgent commitments and joined in completing the project.

A preview of the plan of the three volumes may be serviceable. A dual emphasis is present throughout. At one pole is concern for temporal order; at the other is formal and technical analysis. Neither emphasis is exclusively exemplified in any chapter, because in varying degrees each author takes both sets of considerations into account. Casual inspection will confirm that the first two volumes follow a loose temporal sequence, and that the third is mainly analytic and refers almost exclusively to the recent past.

### The Prevalence of Propaganda

The present undertaking has benefited from convergent conceptions of the two key terms in the title, *communication* and *propaganda,* and from common recognition of the importance of certain questions. We adhere to customary usage by distinguishing between *communication* as an inclusive process and *propaganda* as deliberately manipulated communication. Insofar as human communication is a relatively specialized mode of interaction, its distinctiveness lies in the employment of "signs" to mediate between subjective events. A sign is therefore a sound (or some other physical event) that is elicited by a subjective (symbolic) event or that elicits a subjective (symbolic) event. The most familiar example of a sign is a word that connects sound with sense (meaning) in a natural language. Word equivalents cover an enormous range that includes gestures, letters, pictures, sculptures, monuments, drumbeats, and other objects or events (for example, marches, state funerals, public executions).

Propaganda is closely related to other modes of communication. It does not sufficiently discriminate to define propaganda as an act of premeditation. We must connect it with a social setting in which there is controversy. Propaganda can be identified as a deliberate effort to influence outcomes of controversy in favor of a preference. In this way propaganda is differentiated from the deliberate transmission of information, or from either ceremonial or purely expressive acts. Jacob Finkelstein draws attention to the point that in the early history of Chaldea and Assyria, although a public communication might be a polemic, it was not addressed to a mass audience. Inasmuch as the same statement may be noncontroversial in a local setting and controversial in a larger context, it is essential to delimit the boundaries of the situations pertinent to any specific analysis.

Those who have discussed the question agree that it is often puzzling to decide whether the chief communicators of an epoch stand far enough outside the common culture to comprehend their relationship to it. Do they know what they are doing when they gain personal advantage by manipulating the faiths, beliefs, loyalties, and routines of society?

In answering such questions, our colleagues often have shown exceptional ingenuity in piercing a veil of inadequate documentation and establishing a set of irresistible presumptions. A. Leo Oppenheim accomplishes this in his original interpretation of a letter by Esarhaddon, indicating that it was actually addressed to the elite of Assur, a privileged city, and was written to justify imperial policy during a period of general discontent.

We know that human history covers the range from conscious awareness of communication management on the part of leaders to situations in which awareness is almost wholly absent. The depth of insight into primary process in the sense of depth psychology remains problematic where private and intimate sources are not open to scholars. The problems that appear in this connection recur through many essays and in the end receive systematic treatment from Andrew Rolle.

### Communication as End and Means

We find that communication often is valued for its own sake as an exercise in expressive skill. More commonly it is used in pursuit of other values, notably enlightenment. Some measure of enlightenment—of factuality—is an indispensable means of attaining any desired outcome. In consequence, expressive and matter-of-fact styles of communication are both involved when the symbolic instrument is employed in the shaping and sharing of a value. A wide range of variation in relative emphasis can be demonstrated if we investigate the place that is given to comparable values in different societies.

Consider political power outcomes, understood as the giving or receiving of support in the making of important decisions. Wherever wars, elections, or their equivalents occur, we expect to find some reliance on matter-of-fact communication by administrators and on evocative proclamations by leaders. In the conduct of economic activities science-minded agriculturalists operate on the basis of matter-of-fact information about water, soil, seed, and markets. On the other hand, farmers in primitive societies rely on ceremonies as they plough, plant, cultivate, and harvest their crops. The pursuit of well-being (safety, health, comfort) involves communications that vary from solemn rites of exorcism to a pharmacist's prescription. The ceremonial component is relatively high in religious and ethical matters (rectitude), and in culminating moments of glory and infamy (respect). Evocativeness is a prominent characteristic of the language of individual love or of group loyalty.

In referring to value outcomes above we usually mentioned or implied a positive example of value indulgence. As deprivations occur in connection with every value, it is not surprising that every natural language provides a vocabulary associated with gestures to make these distinctions with different degrees of intensity. Various means are available to identify the powerless, ignorant, poor, defective, clumsy, unloveable, contemptible, and the impure, as well as to designate elite groups in a community.

### The Dimensions of Communication

We circulated among our colleagues a brief outline of the process of communication. At the same time we underlined the advantages to each writer of staying within the analytic framework and the conventional usages with which he felt most comfortable. The following revised outline is intended to assist the reader in discovering his equivalent conceptions of the communication process. It is a translation device whose possible standardizing influence on usage is incidental.

A well-known list of questions can be raised about single and collective acts of communication. *Who / says what / in what channel / to whom / with what effect?* The queries emphasize the initiators of a message, the message content, the network of channels, the audience, and the impacts of the process. Convenient as a starting point, these questions must be amplified if they are to provide an explicit guide to some aspects of communication.

*Who initiates a message?* The initiation of a message is one of several roles that may be played by anyone who participates in a given process of communication. When we describe a conversation or monitor the inflow and outflow of communications to a message center, it may be found that everyone initiates about the same number of messages in a given period. In extreme contrast is the movement of messages in some hierarchies where the flow is from top to bottom, and critical or rebellious demands originating at the bottom are directed at the top.

*What is the content of messages?* We may be interested in the manifest or latent content, or in the style. Style refers to the arrangement of the signs and symbols used in a communication.

*With what intentions are messages initiated?* We referred above to the controversial intentions that distinguish propaganda from nonpropaganda statements. Attention was also called to the level of conscious awareness on the part of a communicator. For many purposes it is useful to consider the communicator's value demands. Is he absorbed in communication as an end in itself, or does he perceive it as a means for affecting political power, wealth, or other valued outcomes? What expectations does he entertain about the probable effectiveness of a message? With what role does he identify himself (for instance, is he speaking as an official or as a private individual, as an expert or as a layman)?

*In what situations do communications take place?* In spatial terms we recognize many forums in which messages are given and received. The forum may include visitors to the moon as well as millions of viewers on earth. Or its boundaries may be narrowly circumscribed. In temporal terms we identify ephemeral pairs and clusters at one extreme; at the other, we note the chain of participants in legends that persist as cultural legacies through thousands of years.

*What channels and other assets are available to communicators?* It is generally understood that messages are transmitted as information in channels that utilize the sensory-motor equipment of man and a variety of resources in the environment. Because of the enormous role of technology we shall presently comment upon it at some length. It is important to take into account the point that, in addition to technological facilities, a communicator may be able to mobilize other value-assets (political power, prestige, and so on) to influence results. In particular he may facilitate or impede the access to channels of communication. Conversely, to ensure attention to his own communication a power holder may censor or suppress competing messages.

*What strategies render the assets effective in accomplishing a communicator's purpose?* Strategies must be employed to assemble and manage available capabilities in ways that expedite the results sought. For instance, the possession of money is not enough. If a world audience is to be reached, money must be transformed into the control of communication satellites, and the satellites must be competently managed.

*What audiences are reached?* As implied above, the role of audience member may or may not alternate with the role of initiator of communications. The audience may be small and well known to the communicator, or large and anonymous. It may differ from the communicator also in any number of attributes —power, knowledge, age, beliefs, and so on.

*With what effects?* Immediate impacts of a message or a channel can be described according to the attention received from an audience. More fundamentally, it is possible to appraise the degree to which values are positively or negatively affected. It is also relevant to explore the effect of communication on the invention, diffusion, and restriction of specific patterns that constitute the practices of a personality or a culture.

The preceding outline of communication can be adapted to all the problems relating to the process. There is the question of *goal:* What value outcomes are sought? Of *trend:* To what extent has the direction of change been toward or away from the preferred goals? Of *condition:* What factors have conditioned the direction and magnitude of trends? Of *projections:* What is the probable sequence of future events? Of *alternatives:* What policies are most likely to optimize values?

In the concluding chapter of the third volume we provide an indication of our overriding goals. The aim is very different from that of the scholarly monks of the Middle Ages who wrote the lives of the saints to show the hand of God in history and, if facts were missing, prayerfully filled in the gaps. Our value commitments are such that we welcome the discipline of data obtained by scholarly and scientific procedures. We have, however, used our concern for human dignity to influence results in a fundamental manner. We have sought for light on the role of the common man as both subject and object of manipulation. Therefore such an explicit inquiry as that of Arthur Wright into the history of ancient China is especially pertinent.

As the contributors demonstrate, historical trends can be accounted for in varying degrees at different times and places. It seems premature to attempt to apply a common framework of scientific explanation to identify and appraise the impact of conditioning factors.

In the closing chapter we outline some projections and draw policy-relevant inferences from the historical record. No doubt history will be drawn upon in coming years to stimulate and justify any number of policy alternatives.

## THE CHANGING FUNCTION OF COMMUNICATION

As a glimpse of some fundamental aspects of the findings to come, we offer a brief presentation of the changing function of communication.

In one of Pieter Bruegel's paintings, dated 1560, more than eighty different children's games are depicted. Almost all of them are still familiar to us. We used to play them ourselves when we were young. We learned the games from other children who transmitted them to us, as they had been transmitted to them and as we in turn handed them on, along with rhymes and riddles and nonsense verse, in face-to-face contact with younger children. Thus a long chain of communication extends backward for many centuries and, hopefully, forward into the distant future. The games live on without the aid of writing and reading.

From the dawn of history to this day, most communication has been by word of mouth. Oral communication without the help of technical devices, such as loudspeakers, wireless transmitters, and telephones, occurs not only among children but in many other relationships: in the household among family members, among neighbors and friends; in schools, court-houses, barracks, jails, and churches; in the marketplace, bar-bershops, coffeehouses, and the theater; in factories and offices; on pilgrimages, stage coaches, riverboats, trains, and airplanes; in taverns and at court; in parliament and other meeting places. Much of language itself, a great deal of the information needed for meeting the demands of everyday life, our manner and mor-als—all these depend largely on oral communication. So do religious beliefs and rites, and the lore about nature, folksongs, folktales, proverbs, and many other parts of practical wisdom.

Although oral communication with each new generation can keep pace with time, *continuous* relays of both message and memory are required to bring the past up to the present ever anew. Once the chain of communication is broken, tradition fades with the passage of time unless memory is stored and can be retrieved at will. There must be writing and reading for such *discontinuous* communication to occur. Thus today, we can return to the immediate and distant past by reading what was recorded for future use a short or a long time ago.

Similarly, the reach of oral communication in space is bound-ed by the range of the human voice. This limits the transmis-sion of information over long distances to the speed with which messengers can travel. We tend, perhaps, to underestimate the speed of disseminating news in times when its transmission altogether depended on a spontaneously operating human relay system. A famous instance in this regard is the fact that the news of the victory of Macedonicus over Perseus at Pydna in Macedonia in 168 B.C. took only four days to arrive in Rome.

Certain ancient regimes employed a technique, known also from primitive societies, of posting men as links in a chain of oral communication capable of outpacing fast riders. The ancient Persians are credited with the ability to transmit important news at the speed of fifty miles a day. To be sure, only news relevant to the exercise of government was handled in this manner, and it could not travel across the sea. Even in modern times, until fairly recently, diplomats overseas were dependent on the packet boat for receiving instructions from the home center and sending intelligence back. As late as the beginning of the nineteenth century, a diplomatic despatch posted in London took sixty days to reach Washington, D.C. The situation changed drastically only with the invention of telegraphy. By the momentous increase in the speed of transmission it became possible for the diplomat abroad to inform the home center promptly of changes occurring in the host country and for the center to control more tightly the activities of its diplomatic representatives in foreign countries.

In modern times, messages characteristically travel faster than messengers, but this is only secondarily the result of advances in the technology of transmission; it is primarily the consequence of the dissociation of the message from the messenger, that is, the ability to encode messages in such a way that they can be seen rather than heard. Beginning with the invention of writing and ending with the modern revolution in communication that owes so much to the transistor and to the computer (as Herbert Goldhamer describes in volume III), technological advances have enabled man to surmount the natural barriers to oral communication in four principal ways: by storing messages for retrieval, by speeding up the transmission of messages far beyond the performance of messengers, by bridging virtually any spatial gap, and by ensuring simultaneous reception at widely separated locations.

Technological progress in the field of communication must not be envisioned as linear advance, in which each later phase, marked by increased speed or range or by lower cost, renders earlier technologies altogether obsolete. At any point in time, there is room for some overlapping use of simple and advanced techniques. Such overlapping may obtain for different reasons.

First, although an advanced technology may be available, simpler forms may persist for purely social reasons. For example, in Cicero's age Roman literature was produced to be read out loud to friends, but much of it was preserved by the *bibliopola* to whom the author gave his work for copying and distribution to buyers who were unknown to the author. The same situation had prevailed in Athens since the fifth, and in Alexandria since the third, century. Written copies of ancient literature thus survived the long period from the fifth to the tenth century when no literary public existed in the West. Similarly, the poetry of the troubadours, largely produced for oral delivery to illiterate listeners, flourished at a time when clerics were capable of writing and reading.

Second, different technologies of communication may overlap because of a lack of centralization in society. Parochial modes of communication, for example village gossip, may coexist with fairly sophisticated networks controlled by the government reaching distant areas by printed documents issued to subordinate local authorities.

Third, different technologies of communication may overlap in a given society for political reasons. Just as nonmilitary counterelites in the modern state lack means of violence as efficient as those controlled by the legitimate government, so the means of communication employed by counterelites often are woefully inferior to the dominant ones. This is particularly, but by no means exclusively, true of illiberal regimes. Prior to Hitler's seizure of power, Nazi propaganda operated without the help of press and radio. It scored its successes despite the fact that control over these media was exercised by political and economic groups whose power Hitler wanted to usurp. He succeeded in his propaganda by means of the spoken word, mass meetings, and terror in the street. Similarly, opposition to repressive regimes is regularly forced to use a backward technology of communication for conveying intelligence information and all other messages and for its propaganda. In fact, usually this is one of the major handicaps the opposition must overcome when bidding for power. More generally speaking, the control by totalitarian governments of news appearing in the mass media and the suppression of public dissent typically entails the resurrection of earlier, more primitive, modes of communication: dissenters resort to graffiti, rumors, inefficient ways of duplicating and disseminating news, and so on.

Finally, the introduction of an advanced technology of communication may reinforce the use of earlier technological means instead of rendering them obsolete in practice. It has been claimed that the Hussite revolt might have spread in Europe like the Lutheran Reformation, had its religious propaganda been able to benefit, as did Luther and Calvin, from the invention of the printing press. But as Nancy L. Roelker points out in her essay in volume II of this series, the astonishing increase in religious pamphleteering in the Reformation era triggered an equally notable growth of reformist preaching. In analytical perspective the case is similar to the increase in newspaper reading as a result of the introduction of the wireless distribution of news in this century.

At all stages of development, communication is embedded in the form society has assumed, its religious, political, military, and economic life, its given social differentiation, and its territorial organization. What are the requirements in the field of communication for the population to participate in the political life of the community? Above all, there must be no monopoly on learning held by a privileged and socially closed minority, be they a class of priests in command of esoteric knowledge or a political class in possession of politically relevant information withheld from the population at large. Such minorities may even serve supreme political power holders who are themselves illiterate. Charlemagne vainly tried to learn how to write while attracting from afar monks who were responsible for the cultural renaissance under his reign.

Generally speaking, for politics actively to involve large parts of the population, the political language must be a common tongue and public records must be widely accessible. Those who speak the common tongue must be able to read and write. They must also be interested and educated enough to reflect upon political life and powerful enough to act. In a word, they must be literate citizens. It is not necessary, however, for the citizenry to be unilingual. In ancient Rome, both Greek and Latin were spoken, just as modern Switzerland has four official languages and many other countries have polyglot populations without loss to political integration. Although multilingualism contains the potential of divisiveness if nationalist feelings are associated with each tongue, it is more important to note that a monopoly on any language for magical, religious, or political use necessarily precludes the idea of common citizenry and institutionalizes instead through the medium of language the rule of an active minority over an illiterate or ignorant mass of subjects condemned to passivity.

From the vantage point of communication and its social functions, the main requirements of political participation in Western society were the ascendency of the vernaculars over Latin, widespread literacy and the rise of free markets for printed information on politics, a market, that is, to satisfy the needs of the impecunious as well as the rich.

In volume II, W. J. Bouwsma details how the replacement of Latin as an exclusive language by the vernacular as a dignified medium of learning and literature was initiated in the West by humanists in the period of the Renaissance. This momentous shift away from Latin as the language that unified a small educated stratum across geographical and linguistic boundaries contributed to the later rise of national consciousness and pride. It might even be argued that a high price was ultimately exacted for this progress: the division of the formerly unified culture of the West. But this happened only in the era of nationalism, ushered in by the French Revolution, when large masses in peacetime and in war passionately embraced, or recoiled from, the political causes their governments espoused.

Another impetus toward the replacement of Latin by the vernacular and, ultimately, toward the formation of a literate public came from the religious reformers. They insisted on the study of God's word without the help of priestly intermediaries and preached in the mother tongues of the faithful who did not know Latin. John Wyclif (1328–1384) preached at Oxford and London in the vernacular. So did John Milíč (circa 1325–1374), the father of Czech Reform, a forerunner of John Hus, and Matthew of Janov (circa 1355–1393), his immediate successor, at Prague. Toward the end of his life, Milíč preached every day in three different churches in Latin, Czech, and German. And

Matthew, like Wyclif, translated the Bible into his mother tongue. In the fifteenth century the Lollards extended the use of the Wyclifite translation, and in 1500—seventeen years before Luther published his ninety-five theses—no less than thirty Bible translations had been printed in vernacular versions. After 1522, the Scriptures were available to every European nation in its mother tongue.

The literature inspired by the religious reformers was devotional and edifying in the first place. For the modern political public to arise, additional forces had to change the fabric of society. The secularization begun in the Renaissance was brought to fruition in the period of the Enlightenment. Now education was expected to ensure freedom from superstition and prejudice, and the dignity of man's reason to replace the dignity of tradition. Among the middle classes moral and political concerns began to attract more attention, while purely edifying literature lost ground. But the philosophies of the Enlightenment were "elitists," to use a modern term. Their interest was not the liberation of the masses but the liberation of the mind, and modern public opinion as a force in political life would not have asserted itself had it not been for the vital concern on the part of economic innovators, usually referred to as the modern bourgeoisie, with fiscal and budgetary matters. Once the government yielded to demands that these matters no longer be kept secret, the solid foundation for public opinion and public information on politics was laid.

On the moral and philosophical plane in the same era, the ardent faith in the rights of men to govern themselves as free and equal brothers became the great modern utopia. It spawned momentous institutional changes in society as well as liberal, radical, and communist ideologies and the associated propaganda efforts that still are an integral part of modern civilization.

## THE PROMISES AND THREATS OF COMMUNICATION TECHNOLOGY

The social functions of communication, as we have seen, are no simple, invariant consequences of technological innovation. Nonetheless, the promises and threats to any established order of any revolution in the media are so far-reaching that analytic and policy considerations justify the added emphasis that we propose to give, especially to print, film, and radio/television.

Technology is the history of man's learning to rearrange his environment. Our knowledge of this history is rudimentary. Man learned to make fire, then he learned to make a wheel, next he learned to "walk on water." Exploration of the seas was to the fifteenth century what exploration of the planets is to the twentieth century. Christopher Columbus is the established hero of that maritime venture that made Europe the center of the world then known.

Twenty years or so before Columbus "discovered" the New World, Johann Gutenberg "invented" movable type—perhaps a more important event in human history than the geographical accident of Columbus. For, movable type made possible the diffusion of writing and reading, resulting in the three Rs— "reading, ritin, rithmetic"—which became the distinctive feature of Western civilization and may yet become the premise of human survival on this planet.

After the invention of writing, print was thus the next momentous technological event in communication history. The studies reported in these volumes, particularly in volume I, alert us to the importance of Aramaic tablets and Chinese characters in the "prehistory" (if we may borrow a Marxist expression) of communication. Movable type—print—starts the "history" because it was this piece of technology that made it possible for large parts of the population to become literate.

Literacy is a major clue to human history as the story of communication. The ancient Hebrews regarded themselves as "people of the books." Every major religion created thereafter in the Western world—Catholicism, Islam, and all the varieties of Protestantism—relied on a "book." But to repeat, through most of human history people at large could not read the book, and the monopoly on reading held by a privileged few was broken only a few centuries ago. Indeed, it is only in the present century that the Catholic church relaxed the proscription against its communicants reading the Bible alone.

What literacy did was give people ideas and opinions, first of religious dissent and reform, then of political dissent, reform, and revolution. Some learned that literacy was an instrument of power. Others learned that literacy as an outcome of aspiration could become a source of frustration. What literacy taught in this often harsh way was the perception of alternatives to the impoverished lives of people in towns and villages who wanted to better themselves. The diffusion of literacy became a major rearranger of the human environment as people learned that the shaping and sharing of values was manageable.

But this learning was long in coming. Gutenberg invented his movable type in Mainz in the fifteenth century, and we have mentioned the influence of printing upon religious propaganda in the age of the Reformation. But it was not until the eighteenth century that this piece of technology entered deeply into secular activities—when the British devised the "penny press." During those three centuries Europe was building an audience and a market for print—people who could read, who had an extra penny, and who cared enough about "the news" to spend that extra penny on a broadsheet rather than on cakes and ale. That it took Europe three centuries to move from the technological innovation of movable type to the institutional innovation of the penny press is a clue to the acceleration of history that has been associated with the subsequent impact of communication technology upon the rise of public opinion, the reshaping of human personality, and the remaking of social institution.

In capsule form, the next two centuries—nineteenth and twentieth—are foreshadowed by the great events that ended the eighteenth century. In 1776, the thirteen colonies of America wrote the Declaration of Independence, which, appealing to the opinions of mankind, animated the American Revolution and formed what has been aptly called "the first new nation." Its motto was: Life, Liberty, and the Pursuit of Happiness. Our historians have taught us to appreciate the titanic struggles that went on in Independence Hall as that last great phrase "the pursuit of happiness" was superimposed over the simple word "property." Most Americans could not read then, but "the news" interpreted in print by Thomas Paine and Samuel Adams spread rapidly from those who could to those who could not.

A similar process was activated by the French Revolution of

1789. By then, "the press" was clamoring for its own voice in public affairs as the Fourth Estate. Not just Marat, but even Danton. As Hans Speier's essay in volume II reminds us, the rise of public opinion as a force in public policy was foreshadowed in a confidential memorandum from the Comte de Vergennes to his king rejecting Jacques Necker's proposal to *publish* the royal budget. The radical Necker believed that he could raise taxes by telling people what their money would be used for—issues about which the French people were consentient. The conservative Vergennes was skeptical about the cost-benefit relationship involved, because he cared more about politics than economics. He therefore cautioned that, if Necker's appeal to public opinion was institutionalized, his king would have to witness a reversal of roles between those who command and those who obey.

Vergennes, a perspicacious man, was right in his forecast. There has been a reversal of roles between those who command and those who obey. In the "consensual" societies of the Western world today—that is, in societies that are neither pre- nor post-democratic—no governor dares to "command" and none of the governed feel obliged to "obey."

To understand this, we must go to the technology that has made modern communication potentially operative in the lives of all people on our planet. The next great step after print was film. All who have looked at Brady's photographs of the Civil War will appreciate that the camera did then what television did in the Vietnam War. Together, the technology of camera and film brought the visual dimension into the communication network with an impact far wider than that of the woodcuts in the religious propaganda of the Reformation.

The third great communication revolution—after print and film—brought the audio dimension into operation. This was radio, based on the technology of the vacuum tube and the wireless broadcast of voice signals. With the coming of radio, only a half-century ago, the basic audiovisual technology was available for the creation of mass media. And, in accelerating tempo and bewildering profusion, the past half-century has been creating them.

Many Western people alive today recall vividly what happened to them in the 1920s and thereafter as the mass media entered their lives. Later generations need to be reminded. "Movies" became "talkies"; Charlie Chaplin and Theda Bara were supplanted by Clark "Hot Lips" Gable and Marlene "Legs" Dietrich; the cinema pianist, who had helped us to thrill and chill as the inaudible buzz saw approached the heroine, was replaced by Vitaphone; the small frame of black and white gave way to the spectacular Panavision of Technicolor.

Radio, a challenging problem of building his own "crystal set" to a boy in the 1920s, became a commercial product— reduced in cost by mass production of vacuum tubes and therefore readily available to the masses. Radio went first into the home, next into the automobile, then into the pocket. But, with transistors, we are running a bit ahead of the story because transistors and plastics—and all the rest of the new technology —enter into human history only after World War II.

Having run ahead of the story, let us end this sketch of communication technology in human affairs—and the end is not yet—before we return to the more important question: So what? During World War II, men learned to breach the earth's gravity and reach for the stars. This produced awesome weapons of destruction—missiles of many shapes and sizes. It also produced an instrument of great constructive potential for life on this planet—the communication satellite. This piece of technology, wedded to all that went before and came with it (such as transistors, computers, and plastics), has made possible the first operational world communication network in human history. What have we done with it? What should we do with it?

This is the great "So what" question that arises from this review of communication and propaganda in world history as perceived by scholars from many disciplines in many countries. When, where, why did communication—the exchange of subjective meaning, an exclusive ability of Homo sapiens—become mass media? We do not pretend to answer this question in this introduction. We stress only the importance of raising it in historical and analytical perspectives. Future generations will have to seek a viable answer. We reserve our own comments on this momentous question for the concluding remarks in volume III.

Consider the acceleration of history by communication technology. It took three hundred years for movable type to become a penny press as the Western world became literate and monetized. It took one hundred years for camera and film to produce standard visual equipment. It took fifty years for radio to make the audio dimension an inescapable part of our lives. Then came television, less than twenty-five years ago, which became the first complete audiovisual mass-medium by moving communication into our homes—the transition, for Americans, from FDR's fireside chats on radio to "the first television war" in Vietnam.

Now, with television satellites, the spread of communication around the world is upon us. Americans created this new world and are still the only producers of communication satellites—their efforts being abetted by Japanese skill in producing low-cost transistor receivers that are widely consumed.

The new technology that creates the first operational world communication network poses drastic problems for students of communication and propaganda as shaping forces in world history. How will poor people in poor countries who cannot read, but can see and hear, understand this new world that is not at all Jeffersonian—where only those with a stake have a voice? How will the rising expectations promoted by the mass media be prevented from producing rising frustrations? How can we rearrange the environment created by communication technology and reshape it to satisfy the human values needed by people?

# 2

## CONTINUITIES IN COMMUNICATION FROM EARLY MAN TO MODERN TIMES

MARGARET MEAD

Consideration of the earliest forms of communication among members of the human species, including species that preceded Homo sapiens (Pfeiffer 1969), is usually valued for throwing light upon human evolutionary processes (Alland 1967) and sometimes for suggesting biological limits within which human communication has operated and may be expected to operate in the future (Roe and Simpson 1958). Under such enquiries we may place discussions of the origins of speech (Hockett and Ascher 1964), of the growth of the human articulatory apparatus, and of the growth of the brain itself, in ways responsive to the needs of conceptualization. In the second category we may place discussion as to man's need for immediate relationships to others, in terms of touch, taste, and smell, and the

This chapter is based chiefly upon fieldwork by the author between 1925 and 1971. Where work by other fieldworkers or writers is drawn on, where there are extensive discussions of the culture of a people referred to, or where a point has been discussed extensively in print, these will be noted. All other statements are based upon the personal experience of the author, either in communications from informants or colleagues whose accuracy she has reason to trust, or upon her own field observations. These will not be noted. The second section draws heavily upon the author's article ''Public Opinion Mechanisms among Primitive Peoples'' (Mead 1937b).

possible impairment of communication when the distance re-
ceptors of sight and sound take preeminence in the communication process (Montague 1971; Ruesch and Kees 1956). Both of
these approaches are valuable and each would require voluminous documentation.

In this chapter I plan to stress: (1) the modes of communication that may be inferred—from the study of contemporary
primitive peoples and from the study of living primates (Premack 1970; Brown 1970) and other less closely related creatures
—to have characterized early man, and the way in which all of
these still obtain to some extent today (Mead 1964a); (2) the
way in which comparative studies among different kinds of preliterate and exotic cultures may illuminate our understanding of
contemporary communication processes (Mead 1937a) and so
provide material for culture building and for the development
of new institutionalized forms of communication (Mead 1965);
(3) the consequences of juxtaposing very old traditional cultural
practices and the most modern forms of communication, print,
radio, and TV, when recently contacted primitive peoples,
village dwellers of traditional cultures, or the currently culturally disadvantaged meet. These three approaches must not be
thought of as exhausting the contributions that anthropology
can make to contemporary studies of propaganda and communication, but only as a selection from a vast field that I hope
will be congruent with the stated aims of this series.

## EARLY FORMS OF COMMUNICATION

All the primitive peoples that exist on the planet today have
highly developed forms of language; whatever other and presumably earlier modes of communication they also use must be
considered as already modified by the existence of language
itself. For example, mimetic behavior seldom occurs alone; apprenticeship in a manual skill will be accompanied by a running
commentary that may or may not be related to the actions being
performed; gestures may be highly patterned and related to the
rhythm of speech, to the meaning embodied in a communication, or to the relative status of the two speakers (Birdwhistell
1970). No one of these can give us information on what such
patterned gesture behavior would have been in the absence of

speech. What research does is simply to uncover layers of behavior, the relative age of which can be inferred from such methods as distribution mapping, or from comparative studies of apes and monkeys who have various degrees of kinship with man (Pfeiffer 1969). So Alan Lomax, in his worldwide comparative studies of dance, song, and instrumental music, can make the assumption that dance may be older than song, and so provides us with a correspondingly older clue to the behavior of early man. But the dance forms he studies coexist with song, instrumentation, and language. Similarly, assumptions about early man's capacity to use tools before he had language, and possible primacy of changes in the brain over changes of the articulatory apparatus, are again inferential.

With these qualifications in mind, we may assume there was a period in the life of early man when speech had not yet been developed and all communication depended upon the visible presence of the communicators, or upon some visible and tangible object. We may assume there was no way for one individual to communicate to another individual how to make or to use a tool, how to find the right path, how to track a particular animal, or how to perform a particular ritual, except by demonstration. The demonstration might be literal, as when every step of a process is demonstrated for the learner, or condensed, as when some part or parts of a process represent the whole—as we find in hunting ceremonials when an animal may be represented by some condensed reference—its pace or gait, or a mask representing its outline. A tool, without an owner, might also communicate some information to a finder as he attempted, without other information, to infer its use, a use that could be fully communicated immediately by one of its habitual users. It is possible also that concrete objects were used to bridge distances—as they still are extensively in primitive societies—for example, a spear or arrow might represent threat, challenge, or danger if placed in a spot where another group would find it; a fire that had been left conspicuously unquenched might also be a message. The line between reading such messages, as when a human being tracks an animal by observing bent leaves, or tracks in the sand or mud, and the purposeful utilization of such tracks to convey a message between human beings was, and is, blurred. So today, human beings leave objects or arrays in particular ways to signal to others what they have done or mean to do, but a detective will still use the method of the hunter tracking his prey to read unintended messages in the way artifacts have been discarded or arranged.

It is only one further step to the use of objects to convey symbolic messages, as certain leaves or feathers are used as emblems of social groups, or to convey messages either held in the hand of a human messenger, left where paths will cross, or placed in designated spots. Such are the hieroglyphic taboos of the Pacific, signs fabricated or constructed of a diversity of natural objects that are placed on property, typically fruit-bearing trees, to warn a would-be trespasser that a charm carrying specific disease-bearing qualities has been placed on that particular tree or garden. The use of smoke signals, originally developing out of the ability to identify the smoke from the fire of others, has a long line of descendants. Today we find special flares used by trucks travelling on lonely roads, or carried by planes that possibly may come down in strange and uninhabited places. Shouting across valleys sometimes develops into a special form of pronunciation or change in the language—as among the Arapesh—and semaphoring, for example, may be regarded as a similar form of communication when language and spelling out the language replace the sound of the shouted words. Drum signals range all the way from simple signals that mean distress or an alarm to gather a group together, a kind of signal from a suspended wooden gong still used in Balinese villages, to elaborately coded messages in West Africa, and descriptive rhythmical arrangements to accompany ceremonies function in the same way as verbal narration, but with greater ambiguity. Disguised communication, as when hunters in the jungle—as among the Siriono (Holmberg 1951)—imitate the call of a jungle bird in communicating with each other without alerting their prey to their presence (Mead 1953), has its counterpart today in coded messages sent in wartime, which can be overheard, intercepted, but not decoded.

Forgery also occurs among primitive peoples, as when one village will forge a message—a composite of leaves and weapons, mnemonically arranged—and, attributing it to a village that they wish to attack, send it to a village of whom they wish to make allies, saying it had been sent by the village that is the intended victim (Bateson 1936). Public notices or public statements of particular states are also found, so that a man may set up a collection of materials in front of his wife's house—a shaped piece of bark from which pigs are fed, with a couple of spear points and a bunch of mnemonic plants—as a public notice that he considers his wife unfit to feed pigs. (Mead 1964a, Plate 2). This in turn may precipitate complicated relationships with his wife's clan or, if she comes from another village, with his wife's village. One modern version of such behavior is the practice of "publishing" in which a husband declares in a newspaper that he will not be responsible for his estranged wife's debts. A political analogue is the public dismissal of an official from public office, or his published forced resignation.

Communication by omission also occurs frequently: a failure to recognize a visitor in proper sequence of priority in a ceremonial greeting, substitution of some other title—as in kava ceremonies in Samoa—the omission of some small formal act of courtesy, was, in earlier times in Samoa, the possible signal for an outbreak of hostilities between two villages (Mead 1930). In the Eastern European countries today, the presence or absence of important public figures at important ceremonies—such as pall bearers at a state funeral—is intently scanned by the public, who are fully aware that such presences or absences are politically communicative (Mead 1952).

The human messenger who carried a message between two groups, separated by distance, was a necessary form of communication if any sort of concerted action, such as for feasting, for war, or for large-scale cooperative hunting, was to be taken. He was frequently given some mnemonic device, a notched stick, for example, to indicate the number of days, or the number of pigs, or the number of men involved. These mnemonic devices sometimes would be preserved and displayed later to validate some political claim or counterclaim, much as letters between responsible officials are invoked today. The letter, even though it could be forged, and can be disowned, is felt to be somehow more convincing than anyone's word. In the case of *United States* v. *Alger Hiss,* finding the typewriter on which some of the papers in dispute had been typed changed the degree of validity of the case, even though the typewriter was found by the defense but later used by the prosecution (Hiss 1957).

But reliance upon a human messenger for the communication of any complicated information was essential up to the time that writing was developed, and some such information was conveyed in complex forms like the *quipu* (knotted string devices) carried by messengers in the ancient Inca empire, which was managed without any form of script (Locke 1923). The messenger developed into the courier who carries the document and may be replaced by the diplomatic pouch, in which written communications can take place between public officials of different groups at great distance. But for delicate negotiations the human messenger is still found, either carrying the written communiqué in his hand from one embassy to another, or in conspirational groups; and in governments that continue to ape conspirational behavior there are still many interchanges in which no writing is involved and no written memoranda are kept. In primitive societies, for example, the Iatmul (Bateson 1936) or the Manus (Mead 1937a), what someone really said, when there is only the word of one of the two who have communicated, is a matter of continuous dispute. This situation is continued today when there is a mixture of private conversations, private written communication, and public accounts of such communication at variance with what actually occurred. However, in societies without script, there is usually also a much higher degree of expected and traditional behavior, and individuals often substitute imputed expected behavior for behavior that actually occurred. So, in response to a question as to what a shouted interchange at the other end of the village is about, a bystander, or even an informant sent up to find out, will reply that so and so has come from village Y to berate a man of village X for not having fulfilled his promised contribution to a feast in which both villages are involved. Upon later enquiry, it will be denied that a man from village Y was there at all, but the informant confronted by this denial will merely answer: "Oh wasn't he? Well, if he had been, that is what he would have said."

Comparisons of individual memories of events that had been objectively recorded in the past show how important a part the assumption of culturally regular behavior plays in the subsequent account of any event, and how confused the reporting becomes as soon as events depart from cultural expectations. They also throw light upon the communicative importance of small event-specific details embedded in a mass of conventional behavior, where the change of one leaf or the alteration of one emblem may convey an enormous amount of information. Most traditional religious ceremonials, with their variation of costume, music, and ritual objects, or acts, depend upon this alteration of details in expected and ritualized behavior. Forms of communication that occur in the modern world only if some new recurrent event, such as the safe return of the astronauts from the moon, are sufficiently ritualized so that the omission of some familiar detail—for example, the special cake for which there is a special baking pan, or the failure of the president of the United States to throw out the first ball of the baseball season, or the annual parade in the People's Republic of China— can have meaning. The relative permanence of the validating material detail, the notched stick, the knotted string, also is important. Stone monuments, even if they are actually three or four standing stones, unshaped, but obviously set up by man, may be used to validate long past historical events and are paralleled by the later habit of rulers to carve their accomplishments and decrees in stone. The very fact that stone or masonry or pottery has both permanence and can be forged lends a particular political efficacy to such records. It is exceedingly common in preliterate societies for the truth of some myth of origin or migration to be validated by pointing to some feature of nature —a promontory, a mountain, a pool—that could not have been forged as the ultimate proof of what the narrator is saying.

Degree of ambiguity of messages also exists at all levels, from a drummed communication of "trouble" in Arapesh or Manus, on which the listeners put their own interpretations in terms of their knowledge of probable events, through the ambiguous replies of the oracle at Delphi to the vagueness and ambiguity of contemporary political messages. So in Arapesh (Mead 1935) a group of people will listen to a slit gong rhythm that is simply a vague statement of distress and decide that an old man in another village—in the direction from which the sound comes—has died; they pack up and start for the funeral observance, only to be met half way with the news that the sound came from a different hamlet and meant something quite different. Political leaders can play upon these ambiguities, sending ambiguous messages that later can be denied or, where writing exists, couching their messages with deliberate ambiguity, later to be denied or elaborated as occasion demands. Most discussions of communication stress the importance of conveying accurate information, about individual intentions, political plans, or organizational or bureaucratic arrangements. But the ability to make any commitment tentative or vague, to temporize, to suggest to two contending groups that one is on the side of each, is a political skill that is well developed, and easily implemented when there are no written records of any kind (Schwartz 1962).

In fact, one of the significant characteristics of preliterate societies is the ease with which the past is edited and the record altered (Mead 1970). There are no books to burn, no chronicles to alter, no steles or carved stone records to tear down. Usually in these small communities there are just a few individuals who, by ability, interest, or explicit social role, are the custodians of records of past events, former ownership of land, genealogical connections, validating religious events, and so on. In Samoa, in 1926, where I had access to records that had been collected decades before, and also could compare the versions that the official heralds in each village had of the protocol pronouncements of other villages (Churchill n.d.), it was possible to trace the changes that the official heralds had made, as they augmented the power of one official title, occupied by a strong man whose rank they wished to enhance, and demoted another title, whose holder could not play an important role (Mead 1930). But ordinarily such methods of checking up are not available, and however much the people of each village may assert that their version of an event or a social form is accurate, there is no proof. In the absence of such comparisons, new customs may be very rapidly transmuted into ancient custom, and the young of each generation may be given a feeling of immutability, of the complete absence of change, as in Polynesia

(Mead 1967), or technology and custom may remain steady over very wide areas, as among the Eskimo.

The way in which the conservatism or flexibility of custom is institutionalized will in turn affect the distribution of power in a preliterate society. If, for example, there are official heralds, as among the Samoans (Mead 1930), or official record keepers, as among the Maori (Tregear 1904), the power to manipulate, to preserve, or to destroy lies in very few hands. Where the knowledge necessary for the exploitation of the environment and the ceremonials necessary for the continuance of economic life are lodged in the old men, this may establish a gerontocracy or, in the case of an epidemic or famine in which the old die, be responsible for tremendous hiatus in the transmission of social forms. But among the Eskimo, where children are taught very early the necessary subsistence skills, and where each man must be able to orient his visitors to the local terrain, there is no such social predominance of the old, and instead institutionalized self-immolation of the old when they cease to be physically useful is expected behavior (Freuchen 1931). In modern societies the rewriting of textbooks and the falsification of historical films are cases where the changes, introduced by those in power, can be studied in detail so that individuals become conscious of such falsifications and revisions of historical events. But in preliterate societies, without records, the appearance of immutable custom can be maintained side by side with continuous revision.

I think it can be maintained that all of our modern methods of communication amplify, expand, or contract earlier methods of communication but never have wholly displaced them, and that every one of these earlier methods of communication not only still exists today but provides a kind of template on the basis of which new methods of communication can be elaborated. When the radio voice replaced print and public appearances of messengers and emissaries, there was a great increase in the size of the audience for whom the message of a political leader had high credibility. From the beginning of political radio—as used by the great Euro-American leaders in the 1930s and 1940s—this tremendous extension of credibility, as a voice came directly from the leader to the people, was slowly eroded by stories of how sounds on radio were fabricated and by films in which the appearance of the leader was in great contradiction to the sound of his voice, so that by the time the health of Chairman Mao was questioned in the 1960s, a very primitive form of communication, pictures of the chairman swimming, had to be produced, a form of communication which attempts to replicate full face-to-face evidence (*New York Times* 1966). It may well be that live television, in which it is clear that the events could not be controlled or manipulated, as for example with the return of the American astronauts from the exploration of space, a political assassination on the screen, a sinking vessel aflame at sea, is responsible for the failure of television to produce the kind of partly fabricated charismatic leadership to which the heard voice, unaccompanied by a palpable visual presence, lent itself in the mid-twentieth century. Deception is far less possible. It is in this sense that McLuhan's phrase a "global village" (McLuhan and Fiore 1967) can be best understood, for on a world scale, as on the scale of the primitive preliterate or nonliterate village, those events that are witnessed by the whole village are the only events with this special kind of credibility.

It is probable that before language was developed, pre–Homo sapiens creatures communicated with each other with a combination of genetically controlled and learned types of behavior—the kind of behavior that the term *nonverbal* is used to describe today. Analysis with the use of film and video tape, and microanalysing equipment, shows that the same kind of messages, now in the context of speech, occur today, so that posture and gesture, approach and retreat, tensing and relaxing of the body serve to reinforce or negate verbal messages (Birdwhistell 1970; Hall 1961, 1966), and that this can even be carried over into handwriting, so that a handwriting expert can detect falsification as expressed in the form of the writing.

Members of the same small community, members of a family, members of tightly knit communities of adults such as religious orders will pass on such forms of communication, nonverbally, and without bringing them into conscious awareness. When such groups come into contact with each other, then misunderstanding or heightened consciousness results. We can hypothesize that language had its origins when two groups, each with adequate communication based upon partly genetic, partly learned meagre communication forms, came in contact with each other (Mead 1964a). Materials on the learned behavior of small groups of monkeys and primates and on the capacity of primates to learn how to perform complicated acts of comprehension suggest that the capacity to learn may have far preceded the capacity to teach, and that the kind of communication upon which all human groups depend, however simple or however complex their technology or their social organization, is based on the capacity to conceptualize and to convey to others information about something that is not present, something at a distance in time or space that can be referred to and invoked (Mead 1964b). However, the capacity for human speech, pan-human as it is, is not only the framework within which all other forms of communication take place; it also makes possible the shrinkage of communication into attenuated, linear, and skeletal forms, as in written communications that lack rhythm or imagery. Such communications when they survive from an earlier age can form the basis for new elaborations of religion and philosophy, or contemporaneously can narrow human communication so that all paralinguistic phenomena fall well below the conscious level. On the other hand, any face-to-face contact between groups who speak different languages and employ different paralinguistic styles may again raise the other types of communication into consciousness. It remains to be seen whether our new methods and conceptualizations of these other kinds of communication, by touch, degree of distance, posture, gesture, and so on, may introduce a permanent change in the nature of human communication. One such change has been introduced by the institution of the small conference, which articulately and consciously provides for the type of communication of many-to-many that occurs in a small primitive or village community when the members meet face-to-face to discuss some matter of local policy (Mead and Byers 1968). In such gatherings, silence is as communicative as words; yawns, stretching, scratching, inattention may be as significant as words. In the centuries since large political aggregations and cities have made it impossible for all those concerned with any policy to meet and talk face-to-face, most inventions have been matters of bridging distance, sending messages from one place to another, providing stadiums and podiums from which one person, in a commanding position and with amplified voice, could address and control many, and finally means by which a single leader could address, by radio and television, millions of others, who have no way to respond. The present search for greater consciousness of other means of communication may restore, technologically, some of the kinds of multisensory communication characteristic of small primitive groups and village-dwelling people.

### SIMPLER SOCIETIES AS PROVIDING CLARIFYING MODELS

Preliterate or nonliterate societies tend to have greater coherence than modern complex societies. As such societies also can be described much more completely than is possible for our great complex societies, it is possible to use brief, condensed descriptions as models of different kinds of communication all of which occur, in various forms, in modern societies.

In making the following brief analyses I refer only to societies on which there is quite complete ethnographic material, societies in which I have worked actively and through the native language: Mountain Arapesh of New Guinea in 1931–1932, the Iatmul of the Sepik River in 1938, and Bali in 1936–1938 and 1939.

The Mountain Arapesh represent a society that depends upon the continuing response of individuals for impetus or inhibition of community action, in the manner defined by Floyd Allport (1937).

> The term public opinion is given its meaning with reference to a multi-individual situation in which individuals are expressing themselves, or can be called upon to express themselves, as favoring or supporting (or else disfavoring or opposing) some definite condition, person, or proposal of widespread importance, in such a proportion of number, intensity, and constancy, as to give rise to the probability of affecting action, directly or indirectly, toward the object concerned.

The Arapesh (Mead 1935, 1937a, 1937b, 1938, 1940, 1947a, 1949a; Fortune 1939, 1942) are a Papuan-speaking people of New Guinea who occupy a mountainous country stretching between the seacoast and an inland plain. They are without any institutionalized political forms, they have no chiefs, priests, sanctioned soothsayers, or hereditary leaders. They live in small communities in which residence is exceedingly shifting, that are loosely classified for ceremonial purposes into geographical districts. Between the hamlets of each district, and between adjacent hamlets of different districts, there are numerous interrelationships based on present and past marriages, trade friendships, economic cooperation, and so on. Any communal work is done by temporary constellations of affiliated persons based on the various ties of blood relationship, marriage, and residence. No man's allegiance to any group—his patrilineal kin, his patrilineal clan, his hereditary hamlet, his district, his ceremonial feasting division—is either fixed enough over time, or binding enough at any given moment, to prevent his following his own immediate impulses of helpfulness or of hostility, his tendency to avoid trouble or to plunge into it when occasion offers. The smallest event—the slaughter of a pig, the presence of a festering sore on the foot of some unimportant person, the death of an infant, the elopement of a woman—may become a political issue, and may lead to the formation of new alliances or to the declaration of new hostilities. Both alliances and hostilities, however, are equally short-lived because, owing to the lack of political organization, they cannot be maintained over time; a new issue will realign everyone tomorrow.

Let us take the instance of the trespass of a pig owned by a resident in one hamlet on the gardens of a member of another hamlet. There is in existence a mode of procedure in such cases. The man whose garden has been trespassed upon kills the pig, and—if he feels friendly toward the owner of the pig, or is a quiet man and anxious to avoid trouble—sends word to the owner to come and get his pig. This results in a minimum of bad feeling, as the meat still can be used to discharge debts among a meat-hungry people. If, however, the owner of the land is angered by the trespass and his feeling of outrage is not assuaged by killing the pig, he not only kills the pig but he eats it. But such an act may lead to hostilities from the pig's owner and is therefore an act of political significance upon which he will not venture without first sounding out public opinion. While the pig continues to root in his garden, or while it lies freshly bleeding from his spear, he consults his nearest age-mates and immediate associates, his brother, his brother-in-law, his cousin. If they are against eating the pig, the matter goes no further. But if they approve, the matter is carried to a slightly higher authority, the fathers and uncles who happen to be in the immediate vicinity. Finally, to clinch the matter, a Big Man, a man who has shown some rather reluctant ability to take responsibility in the organization of social life, is consulted. If he says yes also, the pig is cut up and all who have given their consent to the venture share in eating the pig, and thus affirm their willingness to share in any unpleasant consequences—an immediate scrap, a longer battle of black magic, or the severance of existing peaceful feasting relationships with the pig-owner's group. An Arapesh has an opinion *for* or *against* every course of action proposed, and upon the nature of these expressed opinions, who is *for* and who is *against*, depends the fate of the issue. Such a society may, perhaps, be said to represent the political importance of public opinion at its maximum, a society that depends upon personal attitudes and relies upon aggregations of emotionally involved persons to produce action.

The Iatmul people of New Guinea are a tribe of headhunters who live in large, independent villages on the Sepik River (Bateson 1932, 1936; Mead 1941, 1947a, 1947b, 1949a). Without any form of chieftainship or centralized authority, they are able to integrate for peaceful community living and action against outsiders as many as a thousand people. The Arapesh district seldom included more than two hundred persons, a hamlet averaged about forty. Iatmuls depend upon a system of cross-cutting groups in terms of which individuals act as members of patrilineal clans, as members of matrilineal groups, as members of opposed age grades, as members of one of two opposed totemic moieties. Considerations of intergroup relationships, of defending one's mother's clan against all others, or of always meeting a challenge from the opposing age grade, supersede the merits of actual issues. The communities are held together only by the fact that these various loyalties overlap and contradict each other so that the man who is one's formal foe today—*qua* group membership—is one's formal ally tomorrow.

Let us consider, then, examples of the functioning of public opinion among the Iatmul, in the play of group attitudes. The elder age grade of Moiety A* were initiating the novices from Moiety B. Initiation ceremonies among the Iatmul are marked by a series of irresponsibly executed brutalities. On this particular occasion, an innovator, a member of the elder group of Moiety A, proposed that one bullying episode should be omitted from the series. This was an occasion upon which public opinion could be expressed. A member of the elder age grade of Moiety B, the group that would presently initiate the novices of Moiety A, immediately turned the proposal into an occasion for ceremonial hostility, completely ignoring the issue at hand, and accusing Moiety A of being afraid of what *his* Moiety, B, would do later when they had to initiate the A novices. Moiety A, in response to this taunt, carried out the rite with particular cruelty. The fact that the proposed change would have softened the fate of their own children was ignored by Moiety B in favor of the chance to make a point of ceremonial hostility.

Here it is necessary to recognize a peculiarity of Iatmul culture. Any rite once neglected is regarded as gone forever. If the proposed omission had been carried through, the initiatory system would have been impoverished by one episode. Had the member of Moiety B been interested in preserving an item of ceremonial he could have chosen no more effective method than to invoke the rivalry feeling between the two groups. So an Iatmul who wished to organize a headhunting raid in which other people were not yet interested, might start a proposal for the raid with a taunt to the other side about the paucity of heads that they had taken in the past year. This taunt would be flung back with interest, and in the end the jealous pride of each moiety would be involved in going on the same raid.

Thus in societies so organized, the impetus to action is given

*I have considerably simplified this statement. The more intricate details may be found on p. 135 of *Naven* (Bateson 1936). I have translated Ax3 as "elder brother grade of Moiety A''; Ay3 as "elder age grade of Moiety B''; By4 as "novice group of Moiety B,'' and so on.

not by an appeal to the direct opinion of individuals on an issue, but indirectly through the invocation of group loyalties and group rivalries. Where an individual is a member of a series of concentric groups—so that, as a member of his family, of his household, his clan, his village, his dual organization, his district, he is consistently associated with the same people— there is danger of these group attitudes hardening into hostilities that will split the society. Unless there is a central authority at the head to which all are bound, this danger is especially great if opinions become organized instead of fortuitous. This condition hardly obtains among the Iatmul because the cross-cutting of loyalties prevents the formation of permanent antithetical attitudes within the community.

The Balinese (Bateson and Mead 1942) are not a primitive people; they have shared for hundreds of years in the civilization and religion of India as mediated through the Buddhist and Hindu cultures that spread into Indonesia. However, the mountain villages, which maintain many of their ancient social forms and over which the immigrant Javanese aristocracy and later the Dutch colonial government maintained a very distant surveillance, are good representatives of remote peasants in a feudal society.

In this third type of society the individual is not emotionally involved with the immediate issue, or in his loyalty to a group or to series of groups with overlapping and cross-cutting memberships. The community is composed not of political individuals but of a certain number of house sites, seats in the council houses, recurrent duties to the temple. Into these cubbyholes in a spatially and calendrically defined social organization individuals are fitted as occasion dictates. Their whole dependence is on the preservation of the impersonal pattern.

In a Balinese mountain village, all able-bodied men are members of the village council and progress in turn toward greater and greater official importance until at last they are superannuated and replaced. In this scheme each human unit is a cipher; he fits into a cubbyhole that is successively filled by a series of human beings, each one of whom has been trained from childhood to feel that his whole safety depends upon the continuance of the pattern. Whereas in societies like the Arapesh, the question is: "How do I feel about it?" and "How do A, B, and C feel about it?" and in societies like the Iatmul, the question is "Does my group support this?" or "Does the opposite group oppose it?"—and the issue itself becomes irrelevant except to a few individuals who may consciously or unconsciously exploit these loyalties to produce results—in societies like the Balinese, the question is only: "What is the place of this new proposal in our pattern of decreed and traditional behavior?" This question is asked as seriously and as self-consciously as the constitutionality of a proposed act of Congress might be discussed by a professor of jurisprudence. The process of rejection or acceptance, however, is as colorless as the placing of a name in a decreed alphabetical order.

For example, a new form of incest is committed in a village; a man impregnates his first cousin twice removed, his classificatory grandmother. In this village it is not permitted to marry a first cousin. In other villages of which the people have heard, it is forbidden to marry a person reckoned as two generations removed. The council meets and deliberates. The head men hesitate and demur; they do not know the answer. Relatives of the girl and of the boy are called before them and say merely: "We will follow whatever decision is made." The village law about first-cousin incest is that both persons shall be expelled from the village and placed on "Land of Punishment" to the south of it and forbidden to participate in village ceremonies or worship other than the Gods of Death. No one pleads the cause of the boy or the girl. No one speaks of the outrage. Neither family attempts to gather adherents and form a party. The calendrical expert, who is the greatest authority on village law, points out: (1) that they might consider whether a first cousin twice removed is nearer than a plain second cousin, with whom marriage is permitted; and (2) that if the couple are expelled the village will have to undergo a taboo period of forty-two days and that such and such of the various feasts that are scheduled will have to be postponed and such and such feasts will have to be omitted entirely. The day drags on. Occasionally someone points out to the head men: "You are the heads. It is your business to decide what the law is." Finally it is decided that, no matter how far removed, a first cousin is a *first* cousin, and the law of the village is clear. The villagers are apportioned and half are sent to each house to lift the house and set it outside the village. The relatives of the girl worry about the cost of the purification ceremonies; the relatives of the boy weep a little quietly at home. No one takes sides; they follow the law, and for forty-two days no one may pray to the gods or consult a soothsayer about his illness. In Allport's sense there is no public opinion situation. No one can be said to "favor or support" or to "disfavor or oppose . . . some definite condition, person, or proposal of widespread importance." The only political feeling the people possess is in favor of the preservation of the pattern. Not, How do I feel? or How does my group feel?, but How does this issue fit in? That is the only question.

It is as if the body politic to which a new issue had to be referred in each of the three types of society might be likened to three types of officials to whom one applied for some relaxation of a regulation. The first type would act as he felt, according to whether he liked or disliked the applicant, whether he wished to appear to be a jolly good fellow, whether he feared the consequences in terms of a rebuke from a superior, and so forth. The second type would refer his behavior to such considerations as that he and the applicant were both Masons or both Catholics, or to a difference of race, nationality, or class. The third type of official merely looks up the code book to find whether or not the law which he is administering permits the granting of the request, and quite impersonally and coolly he replies that it can or cannot be done. He is involved in neither permission nor refusal; he merely administers the law.

An innovator or importer among the Arapesh must suit the new item to the feeling of the people. There is no body of law to which an innovation may be referred. The people are so easygoing that they are quite ready to accept as already customary an act that has occurred twice. There is no group sufficiently powerful and organized to defend an innovation or to impose it on the community. There is no group pride that can be invoked to support an innovation otherwise unsupported. There is nothing whatsoever to determine the issue except the congruence of the proposed innovation with the feeling of the individual Arapesh who are immediately concerned.

In 1932, a new ceremony was being purchased by an Arapesh village (Mead 1935), a ceremony that had been brought from afar. It contained new masks, new songs, new dances, new styles of clothing, and bits of associated magic. One of these bits of magic provided that the owners would become so desirable that all the women within many miles would run away to them. Now the village of Kobelen had paid a great deal for the ceremony, straining village resources to the utmost. But this last observance they rejected; they refused even to hear this charm. The idea of being pursued by strange and amorous women was thoroughly discordant with the mild, highly domesticated love ideals of the Arapesh. They said: "You may keep that spell. It would only bring us trouble."

An examination of Arapesh importations from surrounding cultures shows that this is typical; every importation is pruned and toned down until it is congruent—not with the articulate form of the culture, but with the feeling of individuals.

On the other hand, in the Iatmul village of Komindimbit (Bateson 1936), a strange wooden mask was introduced into the initiatory ritual. A group of men from the village had found it resting as a trophy of war in a foreign village and had stolen it and taken it home with them. They decided to make it into one more symbol in terms of which they could score off the other moiety. At the next initiation, the mask was duly treated as a mystery, housed in a special house, the novices of the other moiety were all whipped before they could see it. After this it was duly entrenched as part of the initiatory system.

As a third contrast, consider this problem arising in a Balinese mountain village: Can the village priestess wear black-and-white-striped velvet? She is a sacred person, surrounded with taboos concerning what she may dare to wear, eat, carry, whom she may safely visit, under what type of roof she may safely sleep. It is a good piece of cloth, but can she wear it? The matter is referred to those who are wise in the law, and their decision takes into account that (a) all black cloth is forbidden to religious functionaries in that village, (b) silk is forbidden, (c) this cloth is neither all black nor exactly silk. Can she wear it? Once the problem is settled, legalistically, in terms of how much black makes a piece of cloth black, how much softness may be

assumed to be analogous to silk, she is still free to wear it or not.
But if the decision is incorrect, she herself—not the village, not
her kin, but she herself—will be punished by the gods, and in
any case no one else will be interested. The slightest break in the
pattern must be viewed with great caution and if adopted must
be rationalized.

So a Brahman priest in Bali has been forbidden from time
immemorial to walk under running water, and Balinese roads
are frequently crossed by irrigating aqueducts. As motor roads
were built and priests fared further afield, getting out and
climbing steep road banks became more and more of a nuisance. And now one famous priest has decided that he may sit
in a closed car and not get out when the car goes under an
aqueduct, because the car is really his house, and he is not on
the road at all.

It may be objected that these instances are curiously incomparable; in one case I describe the rejection of an im-
ponderable bit of magic, in the second case the incorporation of
an alien religious object, and in the third a decision about wearing a piece of cloth. But I can plead, in extenuation, that I am
following here the facts as I know them. Societies like the Arapesh that depend upon the emotional organization of their
members to integrate their institutions can afford to risk the importation of whole institutions, whereas more tightly organized
societies have to find a formal place for the importation, while
the Balinese habitually deal with items of culture in small discrete bits.

A third form of illumination from the study of primitive and
traditional village societies comes from instances where peoples,
members of small isolated societies who owe the preservation of
their social forms primarily to isolation, respond to the introduction of new forms of communication, script or radio or
television. The first encounter of a New Guinea people with any
of these media is only a more dramatic form of a process that
has been going on throughout human history, but as the contrasts between the most technologically advanced and the most
primitive peoples widen, in these last hours of the accomplishment of worldwide experience with modern media of com-

munication, we have an opportunity to study this process that may not come again.

The use of script often does not carry with it the same meaning that it had in the contact culture, where the relationship between reading and writing is fully understood (Mead 1971). Writing may be introduced without any books, so that the phonetic transcription of a native language or, in Papua New Guinea, of Neo-Melanesian (Pidgin English) may become a method of sending messages at a distance without providing any access to the printed materials of the civilization from which writing was borrowed. Often first experienced in the form of tax lists or censuses or, today, electoral rolls in the hands of governmental officials, it also can be seen primarily as a form in which the conduct of a nonliterate people can be controlled by the literate. Under conditions of rapid change, this experience can be translated, as it was in an election in Bunai village in Manus in 1953, into resentment against the few literate members of the community.

Script may come to stand primarily for a means of letter writing, and letters may become so highly stylized that the single message, sandwiched in between long elaborate phrases, may be one that could have easily been carried by a child messenger or even a mnemonic device. This was the status of letter writing in Samoa in 1925; yet interisland boats always carried many, many letters. But among the Dobuans, in 1927, letters were used almost exclusively for forging attacks on individuals, a modified form of the sorcery practices that pervaded the community (Fortune 1932). Forged letters were placed on footpaths to be found and reacted to.

On the other hand, script may be experienced primarily as an activity to facilitate the handling of sacred texts, people may be taught to pronounce sections of another language, the Bible or the Koran, and to read these texts accurately, without any idea that anything they produce themselves by writing is in any way comparable to a book. I found in 1953 that the Manus people, who had been exposed to a little distant schooling and had seen typewriters for more than twenty-five years, nevertheless had never grasped the idea of printing. When they saw five paperback copies of the same book, *Growing Up in New Guinea,* their sudden understanding of the way printing could replicate material so entranced them that a group of men sat up for many hours finding their own names in the index. After a large number of men, but no women, had learned to write in the village of Pere, Manus, in 1953, the leading men began keeping records in the courts, which had been introduced by the Australian administration (Mead 1942). Notes would be kept on the evidence given by women, and then they would be requestioned and challenged because the evidence they gave was not exactly identical. Illiterate, they had no recourse, and the whole procedure exacerbated their sense of helplessness, already raw from the rules the men had introduced that the only valid evidence was when "you see it with your eye, you hold it with your hand." This rule barred both hearsay evidence—the rule from which it had been derived—and also any evidence based on sound. Women, convinced of the delinquencies that they could not prove, felt doubly entrapped and infuriated. So, either reading or writing may become a political weapon or a source of power for a local individual, or of one group against another.

Elections also present occasions when plans made on the basis of a society used to writing can go far astray. In Pere, in 1967, a balloting spot was set up, made by a high table and two three-sided booths, made of cardboard, placed back to back. Men voted on one side, and women on the other. The illiterate were allowed to have the help of any interpreter they chose, to whom the voter, facing into the booth with back to the village, whispered his or her choice. No one realized what the consequences would be when all the women, most of them still illiterate, chose the same interpreter, who therefore was in a position to know how the vote was going. The interpreter also heard the whispers of the illiterate men on the other side of the voting booth. These are subtler contretemps that escape the attention of those who are considering the need to publish photographs of the candidates for territory-wide elections.

One of the most studied and revealing sets of communication contacts between people widely separated in the technology of communication has been in nativistic cults: cults in which a people, still only partly understanding the more complex culture to which they have been exposed, attempt to obtain at once some of the benefits or promises of the higher culture. These attempts vary through a wide spectrum. There are the promised return of the ancestors, the destruction or the eviction of the white man, and the return of the buffaloes as in the well-known Northern American Indian Ghost Dance movement (Mooney 1898). There are attempts at a new moral organization, usually with many elements from the missionizing religions, and a revitalization of a people shattered by alien contact, as in the Handsome Lake Movement (Wallace 1970). There are movements where large groups will plan self-immolation as part of hastening the coming of the Day of Judgment—instances of this have appeared in Africa—and the peculiar form that such cults take in Oceania where they are called Cargo Cults (Lawrence 1964; Linton 1943; Berndt 1952; Schwartz 1962; Mead 1942; Worsley 1957). Throughout Papua New Guinea, since the end of the nineteenth century, these cults have appeared with rather monotonous frequency: a prophet arises who promises that the ancestors, angels, other mythological figures, and sometimes, Jesus Christ, will arive laden with desirable goods of the white man's world—kerosene, soap, and canned meat in 1932, and cargo planes and ships after World War II. The means of hastening the arrival is to discard all the old, kill the pigs, root up the gardens, and often to imitate various forms of the contact culture: sit at tables and "read" newspapers, put a white tablecloth on a table, and build a fictional aerial to receive wireless messages. These cults have recently taken a turn that is more perplexing to the administration, as a leader will announce that a human sacrifice is necessary to bring about the desired millennium, "for it needs be that one man should die for the people." These combinations of ancient literalness of belief with misunderstood parts of Christian doctrine—sometimes vividly presented to them with pictures of the dead rising from their graves—often are very intractable. The cult, which may have appropriated the name of some real figure, as the "Johnson Cult" in New Hanover, which was said to have been triggered by an American GI suggesting—as a joke—that all the natives vote for President Johnson or a character like King Berra (a misinterpretation of Canberra, the Australian capital from which political decrees emanate) or John Brown from the song "John Brown's Body" resurrected from the American Civil War.

These cults, woven together from fragments of old and new, products of an intense desire to bridge the gap between the very superior technology and power of the white man and the inferior technology and powerlessness of the local peoples, may occasionally serve as precursors of new political movements, as one did in the case of the Southcoast Manus led by Paliau, now a member of the elected House of Assembly (Schwartz 1962). But more often, such cults are counterproductive, drawing intense energy into waiting for promised cargo that does not come and nourishing the kind of recurrently stimulated millennial hope that becomes the more urgent the more it is disappointed. Such political movements, although most dramatic when they occur among an isolated primitive people waiting for planes or ships manned by angels and spirits of ancestors, nevertheless also occur when some part of a political program, developed in a center of high technology, is partially and incompletely communicated to the less literate, more remote, or less sophisticated sections of the population. There seems to be no reason to believe that this will not continue to be a part of the political process in modern states for a very long time. The revolution of rising expectations all over the world is very largely the result of a failure to comprehend the complex, tedious, and long-term efforts that are necessary to acquire the social status and the material culture of the privileged, whether those privileged be members of another race or simply the wealthier members of society. The possibility of the substitution of some magical and immediately efficacious remedy, of prizes and lotteries and get-rich-quick schemes, of successful brigandage or kidnapping that bridge the gap between rich and poor, are comparable in function to the ghost-manned cargo ships of New Guinea cult beliefs and use the same psychological mechanisms and present some of the same problems to administrators and the same temptations to demagogues. Versions of Marxism, versions of bilateral and multilateral technical assistance as well as versions of Christianity are now available all over the world, with the same implicit command: "Stop your everyday activities, make a final commitment by destroying all of your meagre resources. The millennium must come because it is now unthinkable that it should not."

Primitive men, village dwellers in traditional and exotic societies, poorly educated and depressed rural migrants to the cities, and the oppressed poor in cities all experience the same kind of distance from the manifestations of the technically advanced and highly desirable material culture with which they are summarily presented—from the first white explorer who shows them a steel axe to the television set in an unsealed cabin in the mountains of the American Southeast, the same mechanisms of hope and denial come into play. As the psychological mechanisms are the same, although the cultures involved may be so different, intensive study of some of the more bizarre and dramatic events that inaugurate and characterize nativistic cults is exceedingly revealing of a kind of political process that is likely to be with us for a long time (Mead and Schwartz 1960). There have been serious and well-meaning attempts to take leaders of recently acculturated New Guinea groups to Australia or Indonesia to see how things are really made. But a carefully planned demonstration that white men do physical work and that their possessions are not produced by magical formulas— very possibly stolen from the people of New Guinea in mythological times—and that motor cars are fabricated in factories will then be defeated by a visit to a mint, which does not dispel the belief in the primitive visitors as it does not in many other unsophisticated visitors that the government has the secret of simply manufacturing money and that all evils will be solved by mastery of this magical secret. In our technology-dominated age, careful cross-cultural studies of such phenomena may have the effect of general educational illumination that political satire once had in establishing political sophistication or revolutionary political change in other periods.

BIBLIOGRAPHY

(If more than one edition, date of first is given in parentheses.)

Alland, Alexander, Jr. 1967. *Evolution and Human Behavior*. New York: Natural History Press.

Allport, Floyd H. January 1937. "Toward a Science of Public Opinion." *Public Opinion Quarterly* 1, no. 1: 23.

Bateson, Gregory. 1932. "Social Structure of the Iatmul People of the Sepik River." *Oceania* 2: 245–291, 401–453.

———. (1936) *Naven*. 2d ed. Stanford: Stanford University Press, 1966.

Bateson, Gregory, and Mead, Margaret. (1942) *Balinese Character: A Photographic Analysis.* "Special Publications of The New York Academy of Sciences" 2. New York: New York Academy of Sciences. Reissued 1962.

Berndt, Ronald M. 1952. "A Cargo Movement in the Eastern Central Highlands of New Guinea." *Oceania* 23: 40–65, 137–158, 202–234.

Birdwhistell, Ray L. 1970. *Kinesics and Context.* Philadelphia: University of Pennsylvania Press.

Bowlby, John. 1951. "Maternal Care and Mental Health." *Bulletin of The World Health Organization* 3, no. 3: 355–534.

Brown, Roger. 1970. "The First Sentences of Child and Chimpanzee." In *Psycho-Linguistics,* pp. 208–231. New York: Free Press.

Churchill, William. n.d. *Fa'alupega IV, Manua.* Manuscripts on Samoa in Bernice P. Bishop Museum.

Eiseley. Loren C. 1955. "Fossil Man and Human Evolution." In *Yearbook of Anthropology-1955,* edited by William L. Thomas, pp. 61–78. New York: Wenner-Gren Foundation.

Fortune, Reo F. (1932) *Sorcerers of Dobu.* New York: Dutton, 1963.

_____. 1939. "Arapesh Warfare." *American Anthropologist* 41, no. 1: 22–41.

_____. August 1942. *Arapesh.* "Publications of the American Ethnological Society" 19. New York.

Freuchen, Peter. 1931. *Eskimo.* Translated by A. P. Maerker-Branden and E. Branden. New York: Grosset and Dunlap.

Hall, Edward T. 1961. *The Silent Language.* New York: Fawcett.

_____. 1966. *The Hidden Dimension.* Garden City, N.Y.: Doubleday.

Hiss, Alger. 1957. *In the Court of Public Opinion.* New York: Knopf.

Hockett, Charles F., and Ascher, Robert. June 1964. "The Human Revolution." *Current Anthropology* 5, no. 3: 135–168.

Holmberg, Allan R. 1951. *Nomads of the Long Bow.* Publications of the Institute of Social Anthropology, Monograph 10. Washington, D.C.: Smithsonian Institution.

Lawrence, Peter. 1964. *Road Belong Cargo.* New York: Humanities Press.

Linton, Ralph. 1943. "Nativistic Movements." *American Anthropologist* 45: 230–240.

Locke, L. Leland. 1923. *The Ancient Quipu or Peruvian Knot Record.* New York: American Museum of Natural History.

McLuhan, Marshall, and Fiore, Quentin. 1967. *The Medium Is the Massage.* New York: Random House.

Mead, Margaret. (1930) *Social Organization of Manu'a.* Bernice P. Bishop Museum Bulletin 76. Honolulu: Bishop Museum Press, 1969.

_____. (1935) *Sex and Temperament in Three Primitive Societies. Part I,*

*The Mountain-Dwelling Arapesh,* pp. 3–165. New York: Morrow, 1963.

———, ed. (1937a) *Cooperation and Competition Among Primitive Peoples.* Boston: Beacon Press, 1961.

———. 1937b. "Public Opinion Mechanisms Among Primitive Peoples." *Public Opinion Quarterly* 1, no. 3: 5–16.

———. (1938) *The Mountain Arapesh. I. An Importing Culture.* "Anthropological Papers of the American Museum of Natural History," 36, pt. 3. New York: American Museum of Natural History, pp. 139–349. Reprinted as *The Mountain Arapesh II. Arts and Supernaturalism.* Garden City, N.Y.: Natural History Press, American Museum Science Books, 1970.

———. (1940) *The Mountain Arapesh. II. Supernaturalism.* "Anthropological Papers of The American Museum of Natural History," 37, pt. 3. New York: American Museum of Natural History, pp. 319–451. Reprinted as *The Mountain Arapesh II. Arts and Supernaturalism.* Garden City, N.Y.: Natural History Press, American Museum Science Books, 1970.

———. 1941. "Administrative Contributions to Democratic Character Formation at the Adolescent Level." *Journal of the National Association of Deans of Women* 4, no. 2: 51–57.

———. (1942) *New Lives for Old: Cultural Transformation, Manus 1938–1953.* New York: Morrow, 1956.

———. (1947a) *The Mountain Arapesh. III. Socio-Economic Life,* and *IV. Diary of Events in Alitoa.* "Anthropological Papers of The American Museum of Natural History," 40, pt. 3. New York: American Museum of Natural History, pp. 163–419. Reprinted as *The Mountain Arapesh III: Stream of Events in Alitoa.* Garden City, N.Y.: Natural History Press, American Museum Science Books, 1971.

———. 1947b. "The Implications of Culture Change for Personality Development." *American Journal of Orthopsychiatry* 17, no. 4: 633–646.

———. (1949a) *The Mountain Arapesh. V. The Record of Unabelin with Rorschach Analyses.* "Anthropological Papers of The American Museum of Natural History," 41, pt. 3. New York: American Museum of Natural History, pp. 285–390. Reprinted as *The Mountain Arapesh, I.* Garden City, N.Y.: Natural History Press, American Museum Science Books, 1968.

———. (1949b) *Male and Female.* New York: Morrow, Apollo Editions, 1967.

———, ed. 1952. *Studies in Soviet Communication,* vols. 1 and 2. Cambridge, Mass.: Center for International Studies, MIT.

———. (1953) "The Tiv of Nigeria." In *Cultural Patterns and Technical*

*Change,* edited by Margaret Mead, pp. 96–126. New York and Toronto: New American Library, 1955.

———. (1964a) *Continuities in Cultural Evolution.* New Haven and London: Yale University Press, 1966. "Plate 2. A symbolic statement, Arapesh, 1932." In *Continuities in Cultural Evolution,* following p. 324.

———. 1964b. Comment on "The Human Revolution," by Charles F. Hockett and Robert Ascher. *Current Anthropology* 5, no. 3: 160.

———. 1965. "The Future as the Basis for Establishing a Shared Culture." *Daedalus* (Winter), pp. 135–155.

———. 1967. "Homogeneity and Hypertrophy: A Polynesian-Based Hypothesis." In *Polynesian Culture History: Essays in Honor of Kenneth P. Emory,* edited by G. A. Highland and others, pp. 121–140. Honolulu: Bishop Museum Press.

———. 1970. *Culture and Commitment: A Study of the Generation Gap.* Garden City, N.Y.: Natural History Press/Doubleday.

———. 1971. "Early Childhood Experience and Later Education in Complex Cultures." In *Anthropological Perspectives on Education,* edited by Murray L. Wax, Stanley Diamond, and Fred O. Gearing, pp. 67–90. New York and London: Basic Books.

Mead, Margaret, and Byers, Paul. 1968. *The Small Conference.* Paris and The Hague: Mouton.

Mead, Margaret, and Schwartz, Theodore. 1960. "The Cult as a Condensed Social Process." In *Group Processes, Transactions of the Fifth Conference, 1958,* edited by Bertram Schaffner, pp. 85–187.

Montague, Ashley. 1971. *Touching: The Human Significance of the Skin.* New York: Columbia University Press.

Mooney, James. (1898) *The Ghost-dance Religion and the Sioux Outbreak of 1890.* Chicago: University of Chicago Press, Phoenix edition, 1956.

*New York Times.* 1966. Picture of Mao Tse-tung, swimming, 26 July, p. 2, col. 4; article, 25 July, p. 4, col. 5.

Pfeiffer, John. 1969. *The Emergence of Man.* New York: Harper & Row.

Premack, David. 1970. "A Functional Analysis of Language." *Journal of Experimental Analysis of Behavior* 14: 107–125.

Roe, Anne, and Simpson, George G., eds. 1958. *Behavior and Evolution.* New Haven: Yale University Press.

Ruesch, Jurgen, and Kees, Weldon. 1956. *Nonverbal Communication.* Berkeley: University of California Press.

Schwartz, Theodore. 1962. "The Paliau Movement in the Admiralty Islands, 1946–1954." *Anthropological Papers of the American Museum of Natural History* 49, pt. 2, pp. 207–422. New York.

Tregear, G. 1904. *The Maori Race.* Wanganui, N.Z.: Willis.

Wallace, Anthony F. C., and Steen, S. C. 1970. *The Death and Rebirth of* the Seneca: The History and Culture of the Great Iroquois Nation, their Destruction and Demoralization, and their Cultural Revival at the Hands of the Indian Visionary, Handsome Lake. New York: Knopf.

Worsley, Peter. 1957. *The Trumpet Shall Sound*. London: MacGibbon and Kee.

# 3

## EARLY MESOPOTAMIA, 2500–1000 B.C.

### JACOB J. FINKELSTEIN

From the standpoint of chronological priority it is inevitable
that a world-historical survey focused on a given set of social institutions or phenomena will begin with a look toward ancient
Mesopotamia. What have the ancient Sumerians and Babylo-
nians to tell us about this or that set of phenomena in the
organization of a society and a polity? That the earliest surviving evidence for social communication derives from ancient
Mesopotamia is a commonly known fact. Yet, it is less commonly known or, perhaps, understood that the *kinds* of written
remains from ancient Mesopotamia—and especially from the
third and second millennia B.C.—rarely lend themselves to a
satisfying response to questions and themes of a general nature
as formulated by social scientists. The overabundance of evidence for all manner of inquiry constrains them to formulate
themes and questions in such a way as to subsume as much of
the particular as possible within the general. For ancient Mesopotamia the situation is quite the reverse. Our written sources
are painfully finite and, above all, accidental.

When called upon by social science or by disciplines other
than humanistic—and even there the response will be selective
—to present the Mesopotamian evidence with respect to any
given theme, it will usually be found that a single body of

source material will be invoked, almost whatever the theme. The Mesopotamians chose to preserve in written form only a minute fraction of what transpired in their daily lives, whatever the social level on which each might have lived and whatever the realm of activity in which they participated, whether political, social, economic, or spiritual. It is, of course, true that continued excavation certainly will yield additional written documentation. But if the past experience is any guide, a safe prediction is that any such new evidence will constitute in overwhelming proportion little more than quantitative accretions toward the documentation of phenomena about which we are as informed as we are ever likely to be from the evidence already at hand. In short, there is small chance that the yield of further written remains will open up new vistas for inquiry, especially in these areas that are likely to engage the attention of social scientists. This is not to assert that the evidence already available has been adequately exploited toward such ends; the situation is most nearly the reverse. It is important, however, to offer an initial caveat, lest the student of society expect from Mesopotamian sources adequate responses to set questions in a measure that he has come to expect from experience with civilizations of other ages and places.

Writing began in ancient Sumer toward the beginning of the third millennium B.C. with concise and laconic records of a more or less fiscal character written on clay tablets. This was followed shortly by brief votive inscriptions of rulers and noblemen on stone objects or tablets, and immediately thereafter by the beginning of the systematic tabulation of the objects of "material culture" and nature in what became the characteristic tradition of the scribal schools down to the end of cuneiform writing in the Hellenistic Era. However, little of the written remains of the first half of the third millennium B.C. can qualify as usefully relevant to the theme of "communication and propaganda"—even placing the broadest possible interpretation on these terms, particularly on propaganda, which one presumes is the narrower focus of this survey. Obviously, communication is an antecedent and necessary precondition for propaganda.

From material written during the first half of the third mil-

lennium B.C., and in the latter part of the fourth millennium as
well, it is certain that we are dealing with well-organized polities, conventionally denominated as "city-states" of relatively
circumscribed territorial dimensions. The remains of large
architectural structures, for the most part to be identified as
temples supported by a surrounding complex of dwellings,
storehouses, and workshops, all of it often circumscribed by a
protective city-wall, certify the existence of some form of hierarchically organized society. The ruling segment of which,
whether dominated by a leader of a more or less theocratic cast[1]
or of a more distinctly temporal or "secular" character, that is,
a "king,"[2] would have had to depend on at least a rudimentary
bureaucracy for the enforcement of its policies and measures. By
the same token, some form of communication would have been
resorted to in order to justify the maintenance of its dominant
position (or its acquisition thereof) vis-à-vis contending or
potentially challenging elements from within the society and
from without the political entity. Although we have no direct
information as to the methods by which information publicly
was disseminated in this early period, it is to be noted that in
the lists of professions that were being compiled as early as the
middle of the third millennium B.C. the "courier" was already
known.[3]

From the same period and from similar sources we have also
the first occurrences of the sign that denotes "herald, crier,"[4]
an official who, despite his relatively specific title, exercised a
variety of functions, among which was that of palace official, in
the different periods of Mesopotamian history. There is sufficient evidence, in short, that the Sumerian ruler in the first half
of the third millennium B.C. already disposed of formal and
regular channels through which to communicate any information he wanted to have disseminated throughout the territories
under his authority as well as the means to transmit dispatches
to particular officials and individuals.

At this point it might be well to discuss the question of the
physical means of such communication. The fastest and most
reliable medium, as already suggested by the professional terminology mentioned above, was the foot runner, and it is to be
presumed that for longer distances such persons were utilized in

relays. It is true that recent research has made it almost certain that not only the true horse, but also horseback riding, was known in Mesopotamia at a far earlier age than had been traditionally believed.[5] There is good lexical, pictorial, and skeletal evidence that the horse was known in the third millennium, and equestrianism early in the second millennium B.C.[6] Textual evidence, however, provides no support for any suggestion that the horse might have been used as a "pony express" at this early date: the documentary evidence is strongly to the contrary. Indeed, there appears to be no ground for supposing the horse to have been employed for rapid communication until well into the first millennium, and more particularly in the Persian period.

Before coming directly to grips with the evidence bearing on our theme from the middle of the third millennium onward, it would be helpful to state at the outset that "propaganda" as used in ancient Mesopotamia played a comparatively minor role in maintaining or enhancing the authority of the rulers and ruling classes. As is of course well known, the term itself is of relatively recent coinage. It presumes a situation or context where a number of competing ideologies or sources of authority seek the allegiance or loyalty of large masses of persons. "Propaganda" in such a context seeks to persuade the members of the audience to which it is addressed of the legitimacy of the authority on whose behalf it is issued, and of the unique "truth" of the ideology or principles set forth within it. This is always within a context wherein the source of a particular stream of propaganda recognizes explicitly or implicitly the existence of alternative and competing ideologies or powers whose authority and legitimacy it denies. Even apart from the consideration that in ancient Mesopotamia the fraction of the population that was literate was even more minute than that of Europe in the seventeenth century, the target of what we might properly consider as instances of "propaganda" was an audience that consisted, at best, of that segment of the population that was a real or potential threat to the political authority at any given moment. At no time did this target include the great mass of the population, who may be presumed to have had little concern over the question of legitimacy of political authority. With few exceptions, then, these manifestations that we shall treat as examples of propaganda would, by modern criteria, fall rather under the rubric of polemic, or epigraphic effort which, in one form or another, may be thought to have a tendentious purpose or function.

## THE ROLE OF PUBLIC OPINION

The implication should not be drawn from the absence of any need on the part of the ruling elites to create propaganda in the modern sense that these rulers were free to exercise their authority in any unrestrained or arbitrary manner. The literary tradition about protohistorical times (before 2500 B.C.) as redacted from about 2200–1700 B.C. speaks frequently of the important place held by the council of "elders" and the assembly of all free male adults whom the king felt obliged to consult before embarking on major undertakings, such as wars, although he was not constrained to abide by their views if they conflicted with his own.[7] By the time these traditions assumed literary form, that is, when the early city-state polity had given way to larger entities embracing relatively broad territories, the scope of these institutions for "popular political participation" had long since been restricted to matters of purely local concern, primarily the dispensing of justice and the supervision of purely local administrative affairs. But the ruling power, that is, the king (and his palace officialdom) nevertheless might indulge in willful and arbitrary displays of power only at the risk of popular rebellion and the price of his own head and the future of his dynasty. "Public opinion" was something a ruler could ignore only at his peril.

For this there is eloquent evidence from the palace archives of the kingdom of Mari of the early eighteenth century B.C. An outstanding case involved a secret directive by the king to a local governor to have a particular individual residing within the latter's jurisdiction secretly liquidated and buried at whatever time and place would prove opportune. We are not told what the intended victim had done to deserve this, but the context could be only political, because the king's main aim was to have him done in in secrecy: "Whether he go up to heaven, or go down to hell—no one is ever again to see him."[8] The governor, in his response, informs his lord that he has not found the right time and place to carry out the king's order. It is clear, however, that this was deliberate procrastination, not necessarily out of a sense of squeamishness or of the immorality of the order, but because of the fear of adverse popular repercussions, and the governor concludes by pointedly, if respectfully, telling his king: "Let my lord ponder upon his kingship before I execute the order of my lord."[9] In another instance, the same governor who protested against the king's order in the last case had himself demanded from another district officer the extradition of certain persons to face (unspecified) charges. In reply the recipient declares that, having made the accused testify before local agents of the former, and finding their declarations irrefutable by these agents, he is in all decency unable to comply with the extradition request. As his reason, he concludes, rhetorically: "Would it be at all proper for me to tie up these free citizens and deliver them to you? I would thereby only shatter my authority in my own district."[10] It is clear from these instances that popular opinion and civil obedience could be substantively alienated by flagrant violation, on the part of the king and his bureaucracy, of the elementary standards of justice.

Not only in matters of private justice but also in the area of traditional economic rights and privileges there was marked sensitivity to popular feeling about arbitrary governmental decisions. In another letter from the Mari archives, Shamshi-Adad the king of Assyria (1815–1782 B.C.) writes to his son Yasmakh-Adad, his viceroy at Mari,[11] warning him in the strongest terms against the latter's intended measure of reapportioning and redistributing the crown land allotments of the local inhabitants of the Euphrates region. To proceed with such an injudicious measure surely would provoke "loud public outcry." In the same letter, Yasmakh-Adad is warned against recognizing claims for exemption from corvée by certain tribal groups on the ground that other similar groups would be very resentful and might defect altogether by deserting their territories.[12]

Although the Mari records are unusually rich in providing examples of the restraint that public opinion could exert on the exercise of the central political authority, it would be incorrect to consider the phenomenon isolated or atypical. The expressions used to denote "public opinion" and "protest" as found in the Mari archives[13] are paralleled in sources of other provenience and from earlier ages in Mesopotamia. We shall have occasion below to discuss from another vantage point those documents emanating from the royal court that are now commonly designated as "reform" texts and edicts. The explicit or implied motivation for all such promulgations is the prior existence of certain economic imbalances in the society and the abuse of authority, primarily for unfair economic advantage, by those in a position to do so. The preambles and the epilogues to the documents of this type—and they may also at times include the better-known documents we are wont to identify as "law-codes," including the "Code" of Hammurapi—often will be found to contain explicit allusion to popular dissatisfaction, dissension, and even hints at violent internal strife, which the substantive measures outlined in the "reforms" were designed to curb. The key phrases used to describe such measures were "the establishment of equity" and the "establishment of freedom from (economic and personal) injustice." Ur-Nammu, the founder of the Ur III dynasty (2111–2094 B.C.) tells, in the prologue to his enactment of laws—the earliest document of this type to have thus far survived—that by freeing (through his measures) the citizens of Sumer and Akkad from certain abuses and by the "establishment of equity" he curbed public hostility, violence, and armed strife.[14] Almost two hundred years later, Lipit-Ishtar of the Isin dynasty (1934–1924 B.C.) echoed the same words in the prologue and epilogue to his own law collection, adding explicitly, as one of the aims of his reforms, that they were designed to curb public outcry and protest against oppressive conditions.[15]

One of the most striking descriptions of an instance of public protest against official policy and its consequences comes not from "real life" but from the Old Babylonian epic of Atrahasis, which is devoted to the early history of mankind from Creation to the Flood and its aftermath. In the initial episode of this story, it was the gods—before mankind was created—who were forced to perform all the heavy manual labor as their corvée duty under the direction of the seven major gods led by Enlil. After forty years of forced labor digging the great rivers and canals they not only set up a loud protest against their oppression,[16] they organized what was in effect a violent strike, burning their working tools, marching against the dwelling-place of Enlil (the chief deity of the pantheon, whose shrine was the city of Nippur) in the middle of the night, surrounding it, and threatening war against him. The menace is avoided only as a result of the intercession of other gods who manage to persuade Enlil of the justice of the laborer-gods' grievances.[17] It is hardly to be doubted that this episode must have been inspired, at least in part, by a real-life precedent involving real people and a real monarch or other political authority; it is not the sort of event that a writer could have invented out of whole cloth without such an occurrence having taken place either within the writer's own experience or out of knowledge of some such incident in the past, even if the details might have been embellished in this mythological context.

Oppressive and unjust corvée are perennial grounds for public protest against the king from the earliest times down to the end of the Neo-Babylonian period in 539 B.C. The epical and mythological literature of Mesopotamia constitutes a valuable source for attitudes and phenomena that reflect real-life situations that are otherwise undocumented in the more prosaic kinds of sources, and the incident just described is far from unique in this respect. The very fact of its being set in a mythological framework may even be said to enhance its reliability as evidence that in policy toward the society at large a Mesopotamian ruler was not—because even Enlil, the chief god of the pantheon was not—a free-handed, unrestrained tyrant. The people, as already suggested earlier, were fully cognizant of their individual rights, for limited though they were, they were sanctioned by immemorial tradition. It would have been a foolish monarch who would have embarked on a policy that entailed any serious infringement or curtailment of these hallowed rights. Rather, as most of the inscriptions of the kings—particularly in connection with their law promulgations and their "reform" edicts—repeatedly emphasize, the aim of the ruler is to persuade the public (as well as posterity and the great gods) that his primary obligation is to ensure the well-being of the population. The metaphor most widely appealed to is that of "the faithful shepherd" (that is, the king) who is ever attentive to the well-being of his flock, seeing to it that they graze contentedly and safely in green pastures.[18]

It must be reiterated by way of conclusion, however, that apart from the caution indicated where the traditional prerogatives of the citizenry were concerned, and the danger of public odium entailed by brazen disregard of elementary standards of justice, a king—or any other ruling authority—was not in historical times answerable to the general population for approval of any policy he might pursue, particularly in his conduct of foreign affairs[19] or in his rivalry with the power of the temple organizations. It is always to be understood, of course, that when such ventures met with failure instead of success, a revolt —or, in modern terms more precisely, a coup—by the elite might relieve the king of both his crown and his head. The omen canons, from their earliest to their last formulations, concern themselves with this theme to a far greater extent than with any other subject. Like predictions of natural calamities, military defeats, and regicide, popular uprising and rebellion comprise one of the regularly recurring *topoi* in the vast corpus of divination literature. Only the contemplation of such potential consequences of royal policy could serve as a restraint against a ruler's unbridled ambitions and impel him to heed the advice of the more prominent elements in the palace and temple hierarchies.

### THE TWO FOUNTAINS OF PROPAGANDA

There were two distinct sources of propaganda, the king, that is, the "secular" authority, and the cultic establishment, that is, the great temple-complexes of the urban centers and their staffs who—especially in the period with which our documentation begins, in the middle of the third millennium B.C.—rivalled the royal authority in both economic and political power. The tension between these two powerful forces in Mesopotamian social life was never completely relieved in the course of Mesopotamian history, and it periodically broke into open hostility. Indeed, the end of native Mesopotamian political rule in 539 B.C., when Cyrus entered Babylon, was brought about in large part by disaffection of the local priesthood who considered their own king, Nabonidus, a traitor to their own and to Babylonian interests. Then, and at various earlier points, tracts of a more or less polemical nature would issue from either of these sources against the other. Inasmuch as, over the many centuries, the power of the royal authority increased at the expense of that of the temples, it is the literature emanating from these latter sources that betrays the greater propagandistic cast, whereas in the earliest periods the reverse would appear to be true only in isolated instances. For the most part, however, the inscriptional material and the school-tracts of the earlier periods, where they addressed themselves to the themes of the king and kingship, are content to extol the virtues of the subject and of the office in an increasingly formal and stylized way, emphasizing the king's piety toward the gods, his concern for social welfare, as well as his military prowess; antagonisms and rivalries between the king and the cultic establishment remain muted.

## THE ROYAL COURT
### King Lists

It was thought at one time that the compilation in the scribal centers of ancient Sumer, Babylonia, and Assyria of lists of kings extending backward many millennia in time, even to the legendary times "before the Flood," had as its purpose little more than the pursuit of knowledge for its own sake, and that it exemplified one aspect of the multifaceted scholarly proclivities of the scribal schools. With the critical edition of the great Sumerian King List by Jacobsen in 1939[20] it became clear that its author had a purpose in mind that must be viewed as tendentious from its very inception. It fostered the ideology that recast the entire earlier historical record of dynastic rivalries between the different city-states of early Sumer into the mold of a single legitimate "kingship" whose special quality was vouchsafed for by the fact that it "descended from Heaven," and this, the only "true" or legitimate kingship, was vested in only one king and in only one city at any given time.

This ideology appears to have arisen in reaction to the domination of most of the territory of Sumer and Akkad by the alien hordes of the Guti, a mountain people from the highlands east of the Mesopotamian plain, who, around 2200 B.C., began to ravage the territory of the riverine cities and sack them. They brought about the fall of the dynasty of Akkad and ruled these ancient lands, including the holy city of Nippur, according to the tradition of the King List, for approximately a century. With a new feeling approaching something of a "national consciousness," the yoke of the Gutians was broken by a revolt led by Utu-Khegal, a local dynast in Uruk, the events of which are described in a vivid literary manner by a text from later times, but which is thought to be at least an echo of a commemorative inscription composed in Utu-Khegal's own time (circa 2116–2110 B.C.). In any case, Utu-Khegal adopted in his own surviving inscription the epithet "King of the Four Regions (of the World)," which had been coined first by Naram-Sin the great ruler of the Akkad dynasty (circa 2260–2223 B.C.), who had indeed subjugated and ruled almost all of ancient Mesopotamia from Eastern Asia Minor and the Kurdish Mountain regions to the Persian Gulf, and had been adopted only once—with less justification—by one of the Gutian rulers in apparently conscious emulation of Naram-Sin. Utu-Khegal himself hardly merited the epithet in the literal sense in view of his short reign, but in the period that was inaugurated immediately upon his death—often denoted as the "Sumerian Renaissance"—the dynasts, now centered upon Ur, the neighboring city of Uruk, made good upon this boast, and for a full century efficiently administered a truly unified Mesopotamia.

It was probably early in this period—according to Jacobsen already in the time of Utu-Khegal—that the Sumerian King List was composed, with the manifest purpose of demonstrating that even as now (that is, under Utu-Khegal or under the kings of the Ur III dynasty) it has been ever since the dawn of history: there was only one "true" ruling dynasty at any one time, when the home city of that dynasty was also in the ascendant, and that through military defeat—the implication that such defeat was the result of divine displeasure must be assumed, as in later tradition this motif rises to the surface in increasingly insistent and even strident terms—and by the choice of the great gods, the "kingship" devolved legitimately to the current incumbent dynasty. This conception thereafter held firm even when the facts no longer justified it, as in the period immediately following that of the Ur III dynasty (following 2003 B.C.), which is known as the Isin-Larsa period.

The kings of Isin considered themselves the legitimate successors to the Ur III dynasty, and under them the scribes at Nippur, then under the rule of Isin, which lay only about twenty miles to the south, incorporated the kings of the Isin line within the successive editions of the King List. Contemporaneous with the inauguration of the Isin dynasty by Ishbi-Erra[21] another dynasty was founded at Larsa, only about twenty-five miles to the north of Ur and about fifty miles south of Isin. This dynasty was to remain independent and intact until it was overthrown by Hammurapi of Babylon over two hundred years later (circa 1763 B.C.) in the course of the great unification accomplished by that monarch, ephemeral as it proved to be. Larsa itself was to dominate the south, by its takeover of Ur from the Isin dynasts before the twentieth century B.C. was out. Moreover, the Isin dynasts exercised virtually no authority in the north of Babylonia and east of the Tigris, where many petty city-states assumed independence after the fall of the Ur III dynasty and its efficient administration. Yet the assertion by the Isin dynasts of their titular rule over "the Four Regions" was never challenged, even after the beginning of the nineteenth century B.C., when Larsa intermittently gained control of the holy city of Nippur ruled by the Enlil, chief deity of the Sumerian pantheon, by virtue of which a monarch might have legitimately claimed suzerainty over all of Sumer and Akkad.[22]

The Larsa kings were not incorporated into the King List, nor did they ever adopt the epithet of rulers of "the Four Regions." Even more striking is the fact that the most complete manuscript of the Sumerian King List,[23] which was apparently written at Larsa well after that dynasty had superseded the Isin kings in territory and influence, ends with the latest completed reign of the Isin kings[24] but makes no attempt to add further to the scheme. This stands in contrast to another tablet from Larsa of approximately the same date[25] that records only the names of the legendary kings before the flood, and—in a gesture that can only be interpreted as a display of local patriotism—inserts a Larsa dynasty of two kings (whose names are imperfectly preserved) in second place when the scribe knew full well that in the common tradition there were only five dynastic cities before the flood and that Larsa had no place among them.[26] The Isin dynasts, and the scribes working under their aegis, appear therefore to have successfully insinuated themselves into the programmatic scheme of the single line of a historically legitimate kingship, and with them the canon of this linear history of the kingship was closed.

As far as our sources indicate, it appears that not only the Larsa dynasty but also the dynasty of Babylon accepted their exclusion from the line without demurrer. We have no evidence that Hammurapi, who did in fact unite all of Mesopotamia under his authority and styled himself king of the Four Regions (together with even more ambitious epithets), ever attempted to integrate his line into this transcending historical scheme, even though some of the manuscripts of the King List were executed in about his time.[27] It was only many centuries later, when the programmatic nature of Sumerian King Lists had long since been forgotten, that the Babylonian school scribes began to extend the list to include the kings reigning in Babylon down into the first millennium B.C.

Thus the author of the Sumerian King List, in conformity with the thesis of the single kingship that he was propounding, arranged his sources in such a way that what were in fact contemporary dynasties ruling in different cities in Sumer and in Akkad—and it must be assumed that at least in some instances the fact of their contemporaneity was known to the author—were placed one after the other, and in some instances a single continuous line of kings ruling in a single city was wrenched apart in order to accommodate a line of kings from another city that the author felt had to be fitted in at that point. In other instances, early kings known from original sources to have exercised wide territorial authority, and even entire known and important dynasties, find no place at all in the scheme. The most glaring example is the omission of the great Early Dynastic line of Lagash which, under Eannatum (circa 2470 B.C.), was certainly the most powerful in all of Sumer and Akkad.

It now appears that this omission was deliberate, and although the specific reasons for the omission are not known they may be reasonably guessed. For a scribe in Lagash, writing about the middle of the Old Babylonian Period, when the "canonical" Sumerian King List was gaining currency, composed an independent king-list of the Lagash rulers extending in a direct line from the time immediately following the great Flood to the reign of Gudea (circa 2144–2124 B.C.). But this was not meant as a true historical reconstruction, as it is replete with the kinds of exaggerated reigns, not just of earliest kings (many of whose names seem to be contrived and artificial) as in the canonical king-list, but also of very late rulers the true lengths of whose reigns were surely known to the scribe. From this and other features of the text, the conclusion has been drawn that this was a "politico-satirical work" contrived as a deliberate response to the canonical Sumerian King List, and a mocking parody of it, whereby the writer sought to show that the Lagash rulers, although slighted by the "orthodox" arbiters of history, could boast of an unbroken tradition of kingship the equal or superior of any city that was accorded the distinction of hosting the "legitimate" kingship by the author of the canonical King List.[28]

The discovery of the Lagash text provided the needed perspective in which better to assess the motivation of the canonical King List in its presentation of the line of the Isin kings as *the* legitimate dynasty that inherited the linearly bequeathed kingship from the time it was first granted by the gods to mankind, as against the implied illegitimacy of all the other kingships that arose in Sumer and Akkad with the downfall of the Ur III dynasty.[29] The tendentiousness of the Sumerian King List now stands out much more clearly than had previously been appreciated.

### The Assyrian King List

The great Assyrian King List is not, as was believed for a long time, a wholly reliable and objective record of the kings of Assyria extending from the late third millennium B.C. to the seventh century B.C. Although it ultimately came to be regarded in ancient Assyria as the authentic canon of Assyrian kings, it seems to have had its inception during the dynasty of Shamshi-Adad (1813–1781 B.C.),[30] a foreign (Amorite) usurper who, while presenting his own, essentially non-Assyrian, pedigree linked it with the older and native royal line of Assyrian kings as a way of legitimizing his seizure of the throne. Because he had been an extraordinarily successful monarch his claim of legitimacy ultimately gained acceptance: four later Assyrian kings adopted his name, and one took the name of his son Ishme-Dagan. What began, at least in part, as a propaganda effort ended as the accepted orthodoxy. To add to the irony, there is preserved the inscription of a later king who drove the great-great-grandson of Shamshi-Adad from the throne, still calling the family "alien seed," and took the throne himself. But despite the fact that this new ruler, Puzur-Sin, seems to have been a scion of the native line of the older Assyrian kings—this is implied by his inscription—his name (and possibly the names of his immediate successors in his direct line) was expunged from the canonical list of kings at some later date (or might never even have been admitted to the canon) and his name does not appear in any extant copy of the King List. This appears to have been a deliberate act of "censorship" by which an authentic native king or dynasty was simply excised from the Assyrian historical tradition.[31]

### The King

As already intimated at the outset of this chapter, there is extant almost nothing at all emanating from the court chancery of any Mesopotamian ruler which we may rightfully classify as "propaganda." As far as the ruler's relationship to the vast majority of his subjects is concerned, there was no need to elicit their favorable opinion with regard to any policy he might pursue, nor even in regard to the more fundamental questions of the general acceptance of his authority. Externally, it was the aim of every monarch to expand the territory under his rule, or at least to defend as far as possible that which he already ruled. From different periods we do have isolated documents that, if they cannot be classified as propaganda, do attest the use of polemic, either to justify the taking of military measures against a foreign opponent or to denounce the actions of an opponent. Internally, it was the aim of the monarch to impress upon the population, as well as the gods—rhetorically at least—his faithful execution of the duties incumbent upon him as their ruler. These duties were to relieve the oppression of the weak by the wealthy classes, to mitigate social and economic injustices, to curb the rapacity of officials and priests, to protect the citizenry by the construction of walls, to ensure the productivity of the land by the maintenance and expansion of the irrigation system, to ensure the support of the temple organizations by the perpetual rebuilding and expansion of the temples and the erection of new ones, as well as to keep the priesthoods well supplied with quantities of large and small cattle for offerings as well as for their consumption, together with every other conceivable variety of foodstuffs.

The so-called Reform text of Urukagina, the last ruler of the pre-Sargonic dynasty of Lagash (circa 2350 B.C.), already bears many of the motifs and features that were to be characteristic of a whole genre of such royal testaments and inscriptions down to the end of independent Mesopotamian rule.[32] The first section enumerates the king's building activities, which include temples to different deities, a canal, and a city wall. The largest and central part of the text is devoted to a description of the tyranny of the previous royal establishment—not explicitly of the rulers themselves but of their bureaucracy—over the prerogatives of the temples and their assets as well as over the ordinary citizenry,[33] with a whole range of oppressive taxes, imposts, and plain extortions and confiscations. One is entitled to believe that a considerable part of this description is exaggeration, designed to set into bolder relief the series of "reforms" instituted by the new "saviour"-king. The passages first recapitulate the entire series of oppressive practices in the context of the enactment of their complete abolition, and then go on to describe additional reforms designed to advance the cause of social justice and welfare. We have—probably for the first time in recorded human history—the rhetorical flourish of the king protecting the widow and the orphan against the encroachments of the rich, a motif that echoes in royal pronouncements throughout the remainder of Mesopotamian history, most noticeably in the prologues and epilogues of the law "codes" of later rulers, such as Ur-Nammu (2111–2094 B.C.) the founder of the Ur III dynasty,[34] Lipit-Ishtar (1934–1924 B.C.) of the Isin dynasty,[35] and Hammurapi.[36]

In Urukagina's text one easily detects an extraordinary solicitude for the welfare and integrity of the temple organizations and their personnel. By contrast with the palace bureaucracy almost no criticism at all is levelled at the oppression of the populace—or any large sector of it—by the priesthoods and the officialdom that ran these organizations, even though such practices could not have been significantly less onerous than those of the palace organization. Apparently this was still an age when it was vital for the secular authority to pay heed, both in word and deed, to the interests of the temple organizations. In later times, these were to fall completely under the political domination of the rulers, who increasingly began to style themselves as the builders and sustainers of the great temples. The royal epigraphical rhetoric, designed to demonstrate the ruler's concern for the welfare of the temples and their personnel, began to increase in eloquence in almost direct proportion to his increasing domination of their fortunes. This might have been designed to have some tranquilizing effect on the population, or that sector of it whose interests or fortunes depended on the continued prosperity and independence of the temples; but, looking at the picture from the perspective of some two millennia of subsequent history, it is not difficult to note the increasing concern emanating from the priestly sources over the royal prerogatives. The literature of the first millennium provides some striking examples of open criticism of the monarchical relationship to the temples, and even of concerted efforts to undermine the royal power and to betray it to foreign conquerors.[37]

But it is not difficult to detect the beginning of such criticisms, in a somewhat more veiled form, at the beginning of the second millennium, and possibly even earlier. We shall return to this subject shortly. As far as the efforts of Urukagina are concerned, one must concede that his reform, at least insofar as it aimed to restore the rights of the temple organizations and to curb the incursions of the palace establishment into their precincts and prerogatives, must have had some real effect. After the defeat of Urukagina by Lugalzagesi of Umma—the archrival city of Lagash from the earliest times—the priesthood of Ningirsu (the tutelary deity of the Lagash city-state) inscribed a text that is as unique in its way as Urukagina's own reform text was precedent setting. It describes the enemy's sacking of their own city, the destruction of its temples, the desecration of its shrines, the plunder of its treasures, and—in what can only be understood as a rejection of the conventional orthodoxy whereby a city's destruction was to be laid at the doorstep of its ruler for whose presumed cultic transgressions the angry god decreed the calamity—defiantly asserts Urukagina's blamelessness. Instead they called down the wrath of Ningirsu upon the head of the triumphant enemy, and dared to assert that even Lugalzagesi's own goddess, Nisaba (the tutelary deity of Umma), would make him pay for his sins.[38]

The self-praise of Sumerian and Babylonian kings took many forms. Most explicit were the sacred hymns composed to their glory, a genre that appears to have reached its greatest popularity with the Ur III kings but was continued in much the same vein for the kings of the Isin dynasty.[39] Once again, it would not be appropriate to denominate such literature as "propaganda." It would probably be more correct to think of it as the then current stock-in-trade of those elements in the royal court and in the scribal centers entrusted with the monarch's "public relations." Their purpose was to extol the virtues of the kings, all of whom had been accorded the status of gods and even had shrines erected in their honor, where offerings were made to them as to the nonmortal deities.[40] Most of these paeans of praise portray the king variously in the role of military hero, public benefactor, and consort of Inanna, supreme goddess of love and fertility.

A most strikingly individualistic composition of this genre is a self-praising hymn of Shulgi (2093-2046 B.C.), the son and successor of Ur-Nammu and the most powerful ruler of the Ur III dynasty.[41] The main theme of this extraordinary piece is the king's unusual running ability. Shulgi, speaking of himself, describes his incomparable feat of having run in one day from Nippur to Ur, where he offered appropriate sacrifices, feasted, bathed, and rested, and then raced back to Nippur—the distance between the cities is about one hundred miles!—all accomplished before the marvelling and applauding throngs that lined the road, and in the face of a fierce thunderstorm on the return run.[42] From the number of surviving manuscripts (of a late period) of this composition, it is certain that it was one of the most popular and most widely circulated stories about Shulgi, and we have direct evidence that it was current in the Ur III period and was almost certainly composed in that king's own lifetime.[43]

There was yet another way in which the good name of the king was broadcast throughout the realm, which, if not as spectacular as the fulsome royal hymns, nevertheless reached every segment of the population in a more subtle manner. This was the use of royal year names. Down to the middle of the second millennium B.C. the kingdoms in Sumer and Babylonia used a dating system whereby each year was identified by a formula that commemorated an act of the king—usually one that had occurred in the previous year, but sometimes also in that same year[44]—considered to be of special significance. Examples include a military victory over a foreign enemy, the construction or dedication of a temple or an important statue of the king erected within some temple, the installation of a high priest or priestess in a major sanctuary, the construction of a city wall, or the proclamation of a remission of debts or tax arrears and the release of persons indentured for debt. All documents, whether recording transactions in the private sector or of public administration, were obliged to record their date (at the end of the text) by utilizing a more or less abbreviated version of the royal formula identifying that year, and it became a growing practice to precede the formula itself by recording the name of the king explicitly.

In this manner, a device that served the primary purpose of accurate record keeping[45] at the same time served as an effective means of keeping the name of the reigning monarch and his most praiseworthy deeds, whether unadorned or embellished,[46] in the mind of the general public.[47] The view has indeed been expressed that the proclamation of the regnal year name was closely linked to the royal hymns, inasmuch as there is evidence of a correlation of the royal deeds that form the theme of the hymns on the one hand and the subject of the year name on the other.[48] There is sufficient ground, therefore, to suggest that the practice of naming years after events or deeds involving the monarch served a deliberate political purpose that, in addition to its practical function, may also, by our classification, be deemed "propagandistic."[49]

An entirely separate category of royal propaganda is represented by the heroic military epic. As far as the sources are preserved, this particular genre appears to have been created only toward the close of the period with which this chapter is concerned and derives from Assyria rather than Babylonia. The rise of this genre apparently coincided with the renascence of Assyrian military might in the middle of the fourteenth century B.C. and the ambition of its kings to share in the hegemony over the ancient Near East together with the other three leading "international" powers of the time, Egypt, the Hittites, and the Mitanni Empire of Northwest Mesopotamia. The prime obstacle in the path of this aspiration was the Kassite dynasty that had been ruling in Babylonia for two and a half centuries and which was, at this time, at the zenith of its international prestige. Ashur-uballit I of Assyria (1365–1330 B.C.), who is generally credited with effectively reviving Assyria's fortunes, first began to intervene in Babylonia on the pretext of protecting family interests; he had given a daughter in marriage to the Kassite crown prince, after the manner of the age. Nevertheless, the understanding, affirmed by treaty, was that Babylonia was the superior, and Assyria the subject power, and the boundaries between the two kingdoms were specifically demarcated. Assyrian ambition, however, was not to be reined, and internal palace intrigue in the Kassite kingdom—in which the Assyrian royal family played a role—finally led to Assyrian military intervention. A series of wars began under Ashur-uballit's son and successor, Enlil-nirari (1329–1320 B.C.), which culminated in the sacking of Babylon by Tukulti-Ninurta I (1244–1208 B.C.), who took the chief statue of Marduk (the patron god of Babylon), together with much of the temple treasures, back to Assyria, and had himself proclaimed king of Babylonia and all of Sumer and Akkad[50] after taking captive to Assyria his Kassite rival, Kashtiliash IV (1242–1235 B.C.).[51]

This entire sequence of events was accompanied by a staccato of propagandistic literature cast in the form of epic poems. The earliest of these was composed by Adad-nirari I (1307–1275

B.C.) and relates to his wars with Nazimaruttash, the contemporary Kassite king (1328–1298 B.C.). Only small fragments of this composition survive, but these are sufficient to suggest its structure and style, which are better perceived in the parallel epic of Tukulti-Ninurta, composed a half-century or more later. This text also survives only in part, but it is known to have consisted of at least seven hundred long lines. The opening sections comprise a narrative indictment of the Kassites for having transgressed against divine oaths (presumably relating to prior treaties between Babylonia and Assyria), in consequence for which grave transgressions the gods desert the Kassite king and ordain his punishment. There then follows an extravagantly laudatory hymn to Tukulti-Ninurta, the extant part of which stresses his military accomplishments. Much of the remainder is set in the form of vivid "enactment" of the specific "events" that culminated in the great military triumph of the Assyrian king, with passages giving ostensibly the very words spoken by the two antagonists. Included also are direct "quotations" of the soliloquies of Kashtiliash, and of his discussions with his advisors and his military leaders. The Kassite is depicted as conscious of his own wrongdoing by the fact that the gods do not respond to his enquiries through divination, which in itself amounts to a premonition of the fate in store for him and his troops. At various points, the Assyrian casts taunts in his direction to arouse him to do battle. The enemy is not deprecated; the Kassite king is given the epithet "mighty" and the power of his armies is not minimized, the more gloriously to characterize the Assyrian victory. The Kassite king, however, is taunted and challenged to the final engagement, which he then joins only to be defeated and to be taken captive to Assyria.

Tukulti-Ninurta, on the other hand, is depicted as not only pious and loyal to the treaties but also magnanimous. When the emissaries of Kashtiliash are brought in fetters before him bearing the hostile message of their king, he sets them free and accords them proper hospitality. He then lays the evidence of his rival's treachery before Shamash, the god of justice, thus observing all the proprieties and civilities and not setting off immediately to war. He responds at first by sending a message to Kashtiliash recounting the history of the relations between their respective predecessors, as a demonstration of his forbearance. The Kassite, as already noted above, reflects sadly at his requital of the Assyrian king's kindnesses with hostility, but nevertheless persists in carrying the aggression further. The burden of the entire episode is the demonstration that Tukulti-Ninurta went to war reluctantly and at the urging of his own officials, because of the unrelenting defiance and aggression of the Kassite king. However, once that active war had begun, it was carried to its inevitable and triumphant conclusion. The gods themselves participate in the battle to assure that its outcome will leave the Assyrian king as the victor.

It is not surprising that, apart from the fact of the wars themselves and the final outcome, there is no evidence from Tukulti-Ninurta's own historical inscriptions or from any other sources that the story as embroidered in this epic had any basis in fact. There is every reason to believe the contrary: that these embellishments were for popular consumption, and that the epic was intended for oral recitation before large (and illiterate) audiences. It is one of the few literary compositions in cuneiform that have been plainly denominated as "propaganda."[52] Again, it is not to be supposed that the Assyrian king was seeking to justify his conduct before the masses of his subjects; the epic was composed well after all the events described in it, although still during the reign of the victorious king. The purpose of the composition was the magnification of Tukulti-Ninurta as a peerless military hero, but also as a pious, just, and humane sovereign, concerned with the advancement of learning. Among the treasures of Babylonia that he is described in the epic as having carried back to Assyria as gifts to the gods were collections of tablets dealing with learned and cultic subjects. He desires to create for himself the image of the sage as well as the conqueror in the eyes of his contemporaries and for posterity. He may have succeeded in both, even though his renown in later ages, which extended into the Bible in the figure of Nimrod, and into Hellenistic Greek sources under the name of Ninos, rested primarily on his theretofore unprecedented conquest and rule of Babylonia.[53]

Assyria relapsed into relative insignifance with the assassination of Tukulti-Ninurta in 1208 B.C., not reemerging as a mighty imperial power until almost a century later under the rule of Tiglath-Pileser I (1115–1077 B.C.). The genre of the heroic royal epic disappeared at the same time. Nothing in the area of literary creations magnifying the king's achievements that was developed in the succeeding centuries can be said to resemble that epic form. Tiglath-Pileser, after spending much of the earlier years of his reign conquering the lands to the north and west of Assyria, turned his attention to Babylonia and sacked much of it, including the royal palace of Babylon itself, carrying back to Assyria much booty—very much in the manner of Tukulti-Ninurta, with the difference that the later king did not (and presumably was not able to) attempt to incorporate the southern kingdom into his own empire.

His accomplishments were nevertheless of the stuff of which epics could have been made, especially his extravagant hunting expeditions on land and in the Mediterranean Sea, the proportions of which one need not doubt and which set a precedent for all subsequent Assyrian monarchs seeking to establish great reputations for daring, bravery, and power. All of this is related in proud but largely prosaic detail in his surviving annals and inscriptions. Like Tukulti-Ninurta, apparently he included in his booty from Babylonia quantities of cuneiform tablets; although these are not mentioned in his inscriptions, almost all the surviving Middle Assyrian literary and religious tablets derive from the library accumulated and transcribed under his aegis, a most impressive collection, the remains of which were discovered in the ruins of the old capital city of Ashur.[54] Yet among this collection only two short hymns are devoted to the magnification of Tiglath-Pileser,[55] and these are couched in largely stereotyped hymnic terms without specific historical references. They bear far closer relationship to religious psalmody and epic associated with gods, and to the ancient Sumerian hymns to kings, than they do to the epic of Tukulti-Ninurta. They must nevertheless be mentioned here as a possible form of propagandizing the glories of the king among the general public, for one of them closes with the instruction: "Let the present [generation] hear [this hymn] and recite it to the later."[56]

Only the briefest word need be said here about the foremost

literary achievement of the Assyrians, namely, the development of the genre of royal annals—the systematic recording of the royal deeds in yearly sequence—the earliest surviving example of which dates from the closing years of the fourteenth century B.C.[57] The annalistic form was from a very early date utilized in a general way that might be characterized as "propagandistic," in the same sense that the tendency was always to magnify the king's successes, if not to exaggerate them, in a blatant way, and to mask in relatively favorable words reverses of events whose outcome was not totally to the Assyrian king's advantage. But the form ultimately was utilized for more immediate self-serving and even apologetic purposes, and hence came to be used as a vehicle for royal propaganda in the narrower sense in which the term has been construed here. This tendency, however, manifested itself most fully only with the kings of the Neo-Assyrian Empire, and must therefore be left out of consideration in this chapter.

## THE TEMPLE ORGANIZATIONS

There can hardly be any doubt that, viewed in the perspective of continuous interaction between temple and palace over the span of more than two thousand years of independent Mesopotamian recorded history, the authority and sheer economic and political power of the temples and the highest echelons of their hierarchies—which, at the emergence of the city-states of Sumer early in the third millennium B.C., may be conceded parity with the authority of the temporal ruler (insofar as his duties could be separated in this way from the theocratic nexus in which it was exercised)—suffered a steady decline. This trend is to be attributed not so much to arrogation and expropriation of temple power and wealth by the temporal monarchs in individual and calculated confrontations with the temple hierarchies— such as were implied in the reform text of Urukagina discussed above—as to the gradual but palpable changes that took place through the centuries as consequences of continuous political, economic, and commercial activity, encompassing ever broader geographical horizons, that could not but affect the political, economic, and even the religious and spiritual conditions prevailing within any given autonomous state entity.[58]

Nor can it be doubted that the personnel who administered the manorial estates and enterprises of the temples sensed the diminution of their authority and influence; they had a better grasp of the past of their organizations—the chief scribal centers were, after all, attached to the several temple establishments—than modern scholars have been ready to credit them with. And they were not averse to utilizing their scribal cadres for purposes of overt or thinly veiled polemic directed toward the temporal authority in implied protest against what they perceived as their reduced estate. This tendency reached its peak (or nadir) in the time of the First Dynasty of Babylon and later when they resorted even to outright forgery of monuments and documents purporting to establish the antiquity of certain economic prerogatives they sought to assert.

The most notorious document of this kind is the "Cruciform" monument of Manishtusu (2269–2255 B.C., the son and second successor to Sargon of the Akkad dynasty), a curious stone object (of twelve sides in the shape of a "cross" if viewed from above or below) containing almost four hundred lines of writing. In it the king, speaking in first person, and in gratefulness for certain military victories, donates a long and detailed series of gifts, perpetual offerings, and incomes to the priesthood of the temple of Shamash (the sun-god) at Sippar. Despite the archaic form of the script and of the language, there were certain clues arousing the suspicion that this was not an authentic early Akkadian inscription. Apart from certain lapses in both the writing and the grammar that betrayed a later origin, the text concludes with an oath by the gods that is introduced by the unprecedented statement that "This is not a lie, it is indeed the truth," which, as a gratituous "protest," should have been enough to arouse suspicion as to its origin. It was not until 1949, however, that the fraudulent nature of this document was exposed by I. J. Gelb, who concluded that its time of composition was the period of the First Dynasty of Babylon, when the Shamash temple at Sippar was an economically powerful institution.[59] On the basis of fragmentary duplicates of the same text, however, which are clearly datable to the first millennium B.C., the document has more recently been assigned to the Neo-Babylonian period, that is, well into the first millennium.[60]

Apart from orthographic indications, however, the content of the text reflects some knowledge of the affairs of the Shamash temple (named Ebabbar) at Sippar as we know it from thousands of contemporary documents, and the possibility must therefore still be reckoned with that the time of the original forging of this document was the period of the First Dynasty of Babylon, that is, before the middle of the second millennium B.C. We are of course ignorant of the effect that this text aimed to achieve; probably it was to no avail. Nor need it be assumed that the contemporary temporal ruler to whose attention it was directed ignored it out of recognition of its fraudulent nature. One may presume rather that the conditions that prompted the concoction of claims to such lavish endowments were such that the contemporary monarch would not have been disposed, or possibly even able, to recognize them even if the document had been authentic. Appeals to history in support of contemporary economic rights and privileges, even when fully justified by the documentary record, rarely outweigh the exigencies and conditions of the time when the claims are presented.[61]

But the "Cruciform" monument forgery, although the most blatant of its kind,[62] was not wholly unique. At least two other documents, dating from the first millennium B.C., pretend to be inscriptions of earlier kings of the Kassite dynasty of Babylonia, one of which, ascribed to Agum II (early sixteenth century B.C.), is little more than a long list of votive offerings of objects and furnishings, made of precious materials, to the great temples of Marduk and his consort in Babylon, and the other, ascribed to Kurigalzu (early fourteenth century B.C.), an endowment text comprising lists of lands and offerings to the goddess Ishtar.[63] Both of these documents are written in the form of a first-person testament, much in the manner of the "Cruciform" donation, which is not in any way typical of other land-grant documents of the Kassite period. While it is not universally agreed among scholars that these two documents are forgeries—although there is no doubt that the texts themselves were written in the first millennium—the larger consensus is that they are in fact "pious frauds," and hence of the same genre as the "Cruciform" donation.[64] Once again, there is no way of ascertaining the degree of veracity in these documents— that is, whether or not they contain some elements of truth about the facts of the alleged endowments even if the texts themselves are forgeries—or how successful they were in achieving the ends that prompted their composition.

But the genre may be traced back still further, at least to the period of the First Dynasty of Babylon, from which we have what is unquestionably an apocryphal inscription of a king, Lugalannemundu, of the protohistorical dynasty of Adab as preserved in the Sumerian King List.[65] This inscription[66] bears all the characteristics of the "apocryphal" or "forged" documents previously described, except for the fact that it is written in Sumerian instead of Akkadian.[67] It is composed as a first-person narrative, the primary burden of which—after the standard recording of the king's victories over his foes and the establishment of peaceful and prosperous conditions—is the recounting of the king's devoted reconstruction, the outfitting of a new temple complex, its walls and gates, and the ceremonies of its dedication.[68] The genre we are reviewing here would therefore appear to have a long history, going back to a period far earlier than the first millennium B.C. As to its purpose, the most obvious conclusion would be that the compositions were created, or at least inspired, by partisans of the temple establishments who, by thus presenting "testimony" of the pious acts of earlier kings, thereby "hint" to the contemporary sovereign of the blessings that would flow from the favor of the great gods if he would emulate such ancient examples.

Even greater antiquity, however, is documented for the genre that might justifiably be characterized as "cautionary stories" related of earlier rulers. These, in a sense, should be grouped together with the "exemplary stories" we have just reviewed. But, whereas this class consists of apocryphal stories of ancient kings who record therein their worthy and pious deeds that heralded prosperous and successful reigns, the cautionary legends and apocryphal inscriptions of similar vein concentrate on the iniquities and sins of such ancient kings. They particularly deal with their cultic transgressions and neglect of their pious responsibilities toward certain important cult centers, and the calamities that proceeded therefrom as a result of the wrath of the gods. This genre, or more precisely, compositions centered on this theme, probably because of its greater forcefulness and the unambiguity of its "message," enjoyed a longer popularity and more varied forms of expression in the never-ceasing polemic of the temple organizations against the crown. It is to be observed in its boldest manifestations in the propaganda of the first millennium B.C.,[69] but we now have direct proof of its existence at least as early as the time of the Ur III dynasty.

Probably the most popular of the early compositions of this genre is the text that has been conventionally entitled "The Curse of Agade (Akkad)."[70] The burden of this long Sumerian poem[71] is that the ruin and permanent desolation of Agade— the capital city of the great Akkad dynasty founded by Sargon circa 2340 B.C.—was brought about by the great gods to avenge the plunder, sacking, and desecration of the E-kur, the central temple of Nippur and the abode of Enlil, alleged to have been perpetrated by Naram-Sin, Sargon's grandson (2260–2223). The composition was certainly the creation of the priests and partisans of the Nippur temple organization.[72] The text itself reveals that the priestly authorities of Nippur[73]—for reasons, and in circumstances, of which we are ignorant[74]—had trans-ferred their allegiance to a puppet rival by the name of Man-sium and crowned him in the temple of Ninurta (the "vizier" of Enlil) in Nippur.

Naram-Sin, as the poem relates, having at first relapsed into consternation and mourning at the instant reversal of his for-tunes and those of his city, then launched an all-out attack against Nippur, displaying contempt for its most sacred shrine as if it were worth "a mere thirty shekels of silver."[75] Whatever the truth of all this, it is almost beyond question that at some time during the reign of Naram-Sin there was internal strife in Sumer, and that a puppet named Mansium (or Mansum) was enthroned as a challenge to Naram-Sin. This event is laconically mentioned in the omens with historical allusions—a genre we shall discuss below—where this Mansium is referred to as "like a butterfly . . ."[76] with the implication that his moment of glory was as ephemeral as that of the butterfly, and that Naram-Sin, who surely could not have been expected to stand idly by, made short shrift of him and his supporters in a concerted strike at the rebellious cities of Sumer.[77] But, according to the poet (who makes no further mention of the puppet king or even hints at his fate), Naram-Sin proceeds to wreak total destruction upon the E-kur and to despoil its treasures.

For this crime Enlil calls down upon all the land of Sumer and Akkad the terrible mountain hordes of the Gutians, "who, unlike civilized nations, know no restraints; who, although human in form, give forth speech like a dog,"[78] and who thereupon wreak terrible devastation throughout the land. The author cannot refrain from expressing the horror and contempt felt by the Sumerians for the barbarians of the mountains,[79] in the same tone as they are referred to in the Sumerian King List and in the Utu-Khegal text discussed earlier. In order to curb and appease Enlil's justified but unrestrained wrath[80] the great gods vow that Akkad will be devastated and levelled.[81] They pronounce a series of the most terrifying curses against it, decreeing that it will never again be fit for human habitation, that its soil will turn permanently saline, and that even the physical evidence of its existence will be erased from the memory of man. The composition concludes with the doxology: "For the destruction of Akkad, praise be to Inanna."[82]

This work is but the earliest example of what developed into an almost distinct genre of its own that persisted to the end of the cuneiform literary tradition, and in modified form spread elsewhere into the ancient Near East. This is the series of vaguely related apocryphal stories and pseudo-epigraphs telling of the spectacular rise and glory of the dynasty of Akkad and its even more spectacular destruction, the latter attributed to the alleged sins of Naram-Sin. One can hardly doubt that this "historiosophic" outlook was originally inspired by the priesthoods of the ancient Sumerian cities, led mainly by the temple establishment in Nippur, the precise circumstances of which remain unknown to us. It may be surmised, however, that they were less than enthusiastic over the theretofore unexampled dominance of a dynasty with a north Babylonian base[83] that set about to fashion a political and economic unity such as had not been experienced before in the heartland of Sumer.

There is a unanimity of opinion in the historiographic literature of later times that this policy was openly resisted in virtually all of the old Sumerian city-states as evidenced by the reports of the revolts that occurred against Sargon himself in his later years and against every one of his successors as each, in turn, ascended the throne in Akkad. Sargon's two sons, Rimush and Manishtusu, who followed each other on the throne, enjoyed only brief reigns (twenty-five years between them), both apparently having been assassinated by their own courtiers in the context of internal strife about which we remain otherwise ignorant. One might easily surmise that powerful but disaffected elements from the Sumerian cities had a hand in these intrigues; the bare facts themselves are preserved only in historical allusions in the omen texts, and these would appear to have been inspired by the priestly personnel, particularly by those who were specialized in divination techniques and the "learning" upon which it depended.

Nor can there be any doubt that the polemic against the Akkad dynasty, with its focus mainly upon the figure of Naram-Sin, bore fruit as soon as Sumer and Akkad were liberated from the Gutian interregnum.[84] The rulers of the Ur III dynasty remain silent about the Akkadian precedent that had in fact pioneered the foundation of a Mesopotamian political unity upon which their own successful unified administration of virtually all of Mesopotamia was firmly based. This also despite the fact—which we now better grasp—that the "Sumerian Renaissance," which the Ur III dynasty is conventionally thought to represent, was presided over by rulers who were themselves "Semites," that is, their spoken language, as that of the majority of the population they governed, was Akkadian.[85]

Instead, the formal royal rhetoric as well as the cultic pageantry allied the dynastic line with Gilgamesh and the latter's divine ancestry as it had been formulated in the mythological and epical traditions—Shulgi, the most powerful dynast of the line, audaciously calls himself Gilgamesh's brother. Thus they quite pointedly demonstrated loyalty to the ideal form of polity exemplified by the hegemony of Uruk in Early Dynastic times (about five centuries before their own) but with which they in fact had almost nothing in common. Indeed, it was Shulgi who began to style himself a deity, by the placement of the divine determinative before his name in all his inscriptions, a conceit then emulated by all his successors including the kings of the Isin and Larsa dynasties. But the precedent for this presumption was none other than Naram-Sin, the first Mesopotamian king to apply to his own name (and person, if it was more than merely honorific) the divine determinative. It will therefore not do to attribute the execration of Naram-Sin by the literary-priestly establishment to any alleged sense of outrage on the part of the latter for Naram-Sin's blasphemous usurpation of divine prerogatives and "the belief that such presumption could not go unpunished by the offended gods,"[86] inasmuch as they responded to the same act by Shulgi with nothing short of unrestrained adulation.[87]

The early polemic against Naram-Sin, exemplified by the "Curse of Akkad" composition, became a point of departure for a variety of interrelated genres of literature such as apocryphal inscriptions, apocalypses and "prophecies," omens, and "religious chronicles," all of them closely interrelated thematically and in idiom, most of the exemplars of which, however, date to the first millennium B.C. and hence beyond the scope of the present chapter.[88] Not all of these are uniformly vitriolic. The omens with explicit allusions to Naram-Sin recall his victories, not any alleged setbacks. But the frequent allusions in the omen literature to the portents that marked the downfall of the Akkad dynasty, which ultimately become archetypal for the more generalized prediction of the violent end of dynasties, suggest that the literary traditions engendered in priestly circles at a very early date were not without effect. We shall return to this subject below in considering the omen traditions separately.

As for early pseudohistorical testaments about the reverses suffered by Naram-Sin, there exists an apocryphal "inscription" in which this king, writing in first person, relates in detail a widespread and concerted revolt against him by many city-states, including the kings of Umma, Uruk, and Nippur, and even a usurper in Kish, at the very center of the Akkad ruler's territory. Despite the fact that there seems to be a kernel or two of historical fact woven into this text,[89] the composition may certainly be regarded as essentially a fabrication and exaggeration, inspired at least in part by the accumulated negative traditions about Naram-Sin. The text had also gone through some redactional history, as it is in considerable degree already corrupt, and—as far as the surviving material indicates—ends inconclusively; the outcome of the revolt, which surely would have disclosed its successful suppression by Naram-Sin, is not reported.[90]

Closely related in purpose to the types of works emanating from temple sources just described is the peculiar genre of the apocryphal testamentary "confession" of a king of the distant past. This is commonly known by the modern designation "*narū*-literature," after the Akkadian term that means "stela," an inscribed stone monument.[91] The conceit of compositions of this genre—at the beginning or at the end of the text, or in both places—is to have the subject (the long-dead king) state that the experiences he is about to relate (or already has related) be inscribed on a stone monument so that future generations, and especially future kings, should be able to read it. The purpose was to benefit from the bitter experiences of the narrating king, to learn how he overcame them (if he did), so as to avoid falling into similar predicaments themselves. The genre is not to be confounded with the pious but calculatingly fraudulent "inscriptions" discussed earlier, inasmuch as the *narū* composition is designed as a work of outright fiction and was not intended to be passed off as an authentic work of the king who was its subject. There is no attempt to cast it in ancient dialect or early orthography or in archaic script, and it is never in fact inscribed on stone. It is written on clay tablets in the cursive script and language of the time in which it is composed or copied.[92]

It is not fortuitous that Sargon and Naram-Sin of Akkad—and especially the latter—are the most important subjects of the *narū* legends. The Akkad dynasty, and these two leading royal figures in particular, became the favorite exemplars for whatever cautionary tales were to be concocted in later times with the purpose of driving home some particular message with greater or lesser subtlety to the contemporary royal authority. Naram-Sin was the favorite figure especially for demonstrating the tragic consequences of conduct displeasing to the gods. He is the subject of a series of stories and episodes recorded in this literary form in almost all periods of Mesopotamian history, and also in Asia Minor where the scribes in the Hittite capital of Hattusas transcribed them in both the Akkadian and the Hittite languages. The stories are all closely linked together, and from provenance and age it is clear that there is only a single tradition at work, which extends even to identity of phraseology extending over many lines. All add up to a common central motif, presented in a single tone. The experience by Naram-Sin and his armies of a series of calamitous defeats at the hands of foreign tribes and hordes from the mountains who, in the Hittite and in the Neo-Assyrian versions, take on monstrous appearance, with doubt being voiced (in the Hittite version) even as to their mortal nature. These defeats prompt Naram-Sin to soliloquize remorsefully about his own conduct, his errors of judgment, and the misfortunes brought on by them upon his own realm, the responsibility for which he acknowledges as his own.

While the question remains somewhat disputed whether or not the late Assyrian version ends on a note of salvation,[93] there is no mistaking the dark and pessimistic tone of the whole. The main burden of the story is that Naram-Sin inscribed this testament of his experience on a stone stela so that future kings might read it and take heed for their own conduct. He adjures them to devote their energies to peaceful and productive pursuits for the benefit of their subjects, to avoid war at almost any price—even at the cost of letting the enemy roam at will through the countryside—to be ever humble and modest, and "to turn the other cheek."[94] It need hardly be stressed that such advocacy of pietism and even of a variety of quietism as the appropriate temper for a monarch could have no basis in the real experience of Naram-Sin or any other ruler in ancient Mesopotamia. This is not to discount the pious manifestations and expressions of Mesopotamian kings toward the gods and the temples as reflected in countless original inscriptions and in pictorial representation as evidence of the sincere submissiveness of the kings to the gods themselves. But these manifestations are of a different order; they exemplify the king's earthly role as the mediator between the spheres of the gods and of mankind, and they cannot be said to bear in any significant way upon the kinds of sentiments expressed in the *narū*-literature. For all their awareness of the inscrutability of the will of the gods, and their willing or unwilling submission to its consequences, Mesopotamian kingship did not—and probably could not—produce a Marcus Aurelius.

The genre of the *narū*—the fictional royal inscription particularly in its self-chastizing form—was but another weapon in the ongoing polemical campaign of the temple establishments against the overweening (as they saw it) authority of the royal palace. That it was couched in the form of an apparently harmless fiction of a testament of a famous king from the distant past should not permit one to regard it as a genre of "belles-lettres" pure and simple. This it might have been as well; but that it was meant to serve an immediate political purpose as well, and that it might have been originally designed deliberately to serve this purpose, even if ultimately it became just a part of the inherited accumulation of traditional literature, must always be borne in mind. This aspect will probably stand out in bolder relief upon consideration of the unique genre of text to be reviewed immediately below.

### Divine Prophecies

The genre to be reviewed here comprises a relatively small group of compositions, all extant copies of which were executed in the first millennium B.C. and would therefore, at first sight, appear to fall beyond the chronological scope of this chapter. It will become apparent, however, that on internal evidence some of the more important of them can be shown to arise out of a historical context toward the end of the second millennium B.C., with the likelihood that the time of their composition was contemporaneous with the latest of the events alluded to within the body of the texts themselves.

It will also become apparent after a brief review of the "prophecy" texts of a literary nature that the genre is very closely related to the apocryphal "inscriptions" of the type we have just discussed. For certain of these texts a valid case could be made even for grouping them together with these pseudoinscriptions. But before proceeding further, it would be helpful to define more precisely what is meant by "prophetic" texts in the Mesopotamian context, inasmuch as the words *prophet* and *prophecy* are peculiarly "Western," conjuring up, as they are bound to do, the biblical range of personages and authors to whom these terms are characteristically applied, and to the literary works ascribed to them.

In the first instance, Mesopotamian prophecy[95] is always oblique in its relationship to the contemporary political scene, and in this it stands in sharp contrast to the classical forms of biblical prophecy that name names and offer criticism and advice in direct and unambiguous terms. A typical Mesopotamian "prophetic" text will begin with events of the near or more distant past, often presenting them as if they are still to occur in the future, carrying the sequence down to the time in which the author is writing, but disguising this as the final stage of events and conditions in a future still far off. Thus even events already past as well as contemporary conditions are cast in the form of predictions, that is, "prophecies."

Typically again, the names of the personalities who were the central figures in these events are never stated, but the essential details are presented in such a way that the allusions are unmistakable. The contemporary monarch—for whose benefit these works were composed—would have had no difficulty in identifying the allusions and the message intended by their juxtaposition, whether or not he was disposed to heed the advice implied. Modern scholarship, where documentation has been available from more or less trustworthy historical sources, has equally been able to identify the past allusions as well as the exact period in which the "prophecy" itself is to be situated. It will be evident from these features that the phenomenon under consideration bears a closer relation to the late biblical genre of apocalyptic and revelation, and to such sections in the works of the classical Hebrew prophets that are themselves visionary or apocalyptic in character, but which in fact might be viewed as *vaticinia ex eventu*. Obliquity and implicitness are, in general, characteristic of Mesopotamian thought and expression, and in their own subtle way enhance the effectiveness of propaganda couched in such forms.

We may now turn to a series of compositions that best illustrate the features just outlined. Most individual of all is a lengthy work that may most appropriately be characterized as the "Autobiography of Marduk."[96] After a brief invocation of the major gods of the pantheon to pay attention to his narrative, the god begins his tale with the words "I, Marduk." In this composition, the narrating patron god of Babylon relates in deliberately cryptic diction three occasions in his earlier "life" when he abandoned Babylon and took up residence in the foreign lands of the Hittites, Assyria, and Elam (southwestern Iran). Historically, these occasions allude to (1) the destruction of Babylon circa 1595 B.C. by the invading Hittites, which brought to an end the First Dynasty of Babylon, (2) the victory of Tukulti-Ninurta I and his control of Babylonia circa 1227 B.C. (already discussed above), and (3) the Elamite invasion of Babylonia circa 1160 B.C. that put an end to the long-lived Kassite dynasty. On each of these occasions, the main cultic statue of Marduk was carried off to the enemy lands where it remained for a longer or shorter period, but was ultimately returned to its homeland. In this text, however, the god is made to say that these periods of exile were self-imposed, and that by virtue of his stay in these lands their fortunes prospered (while those of Babylon languished).[97]

It is apparent, although not explicitly stated, that his decisions to go into exile were prompted by the sins and misdeeds of the Babylonian king reigning at the time of each exile. Similarly, his decision to return to his capital was occasioned by the rise of a new king in Babylon who, with a manifestation of proper reverence for the god, thereby inaugurates a new period of prosperity. The moment in which the composition is set is the end of the time of his exile in Elam, obviously of very recent memory to the writer, for he goes into great detail—using stock descriptions known from other texts—about the suffering of Babylon during his exile in Elam.[98]

At this point the god is made to state that having "fulfilled the days and years" of his self-imposed exile, his "heart yearned" for Babylon, and it is this juncture that serves as the present moment of the entire narrative. What follows is cast as a prophecy of what lies in the future, although it must be presumed that the main events, centering around the triumph of Babylonia over Elam, and the consequent return of the statue of Marduk from its place of captivity amid great rejoicing and celebration, had in fact already occurred. The prophecy begins with the prediction that a new king of Babylon will arise who will rebuild the chief temple of Marduk in Babylon to an unrivalled height and unprecedented splendor. He will order that Babylon thenceforth be exempt from all levies and imposts (a clue to the source and inspiration of the narrative). He will "take my hand" (that is, of Marduk)[99] and proceed to reconstruct the shrines and the ceremonial equipage of Marduk and the other gods, "he will gather together the dispersed," and his reign will inaugurate a long period of peace, domestic tranquility, prosperity, and abundance. The penultimate preserved section of the text is devoted to a prophecy of the destruction of Elam by the unnamed saviour-king, which must, beyond doubt, also be viewed as a *vaticinium ex eventu*.[100] The prophecy then concludes with a carefully detailed list of monthly, daily, and annual temple offerings and sacrifices that the "future" saviour-king is to make in the god's behalf to ensure the continued enjoyment of Marduk's favor.

The saviour-king who is the human hero of this composition is now easy to identify: it is Nebuchadnezzar I of Babylon (1124–1103 B.C.), who inflicted an important defeat upon the Elamites and did in fact return the revered statue of Marduk from its Elamite exile and re-install it in Esagila, the great temple of Marduk in Babylon, amid great celebration. These facts are known from independent and contemporary sources. It is gradually becoming clearer to modern scholarship that the reign of this king is one of the major watersheds of Mesopotamian religious and intellectual history, and that it was recognized as such through all subsequent periods in Assyria as well as in Babylonia.[101] The true historical context of this work was promptly identified by its recent editor, who also correctly observed the propagandistic, or at least self-serving, purpose of its priestly author(s),[102] which is to be particularly noted in the passages that "prophesy" the enactment of the tax-exemption of Babylon, and especially the detailed program of offerings with which the king was to endow Marduk's temple. Here we may surely see more of a request than a fulfillment—all couched in the form of an oracle by Marduk himself.

Whether or not Nebuchadnezzar I received this message as a truly divine oracle, and whether he responded favorably to all the specific requests it contained, cannot be ascertained. Considering the highly flattering terms in which he is portrayed in it, it would not be surprising if he did grant the Marduk priesthood all that it pleaded for, whatever he may have thought about the real authorship of the prophecy. The composition itself entered the mainstream of cuneiform religious literature; the texts extant represent at least three separate manuscripts of it dating to the period of the Neo-Assyrian Empire (eighth to seventh centuries B.C.) when its original historical setting might have been already lost to memory.[103] For at this later time, the Marduk prophecy was combined into a text series, in which sequence it is followed by another apocryphal prophecy attributed to Shulgi, the great king of the Ur III dynasty who had been apotheosized,[104] and was thereafter venerated as a deity.[105]

The late and altogether fictitious attribution of this composition to Shulgi immediately ranges it alongside the apocryphal *narū*-literature surrounding the figures of Sargon and Naram-Sin discussed earlier. As in the latter, it begins with a brief and highly stylized autobiography in which Shulgi recalls his great accomplishments in general terms and in more or less cryptic language (as in the Marduk text), stressing the fact that he was favored with direct oracles and visions by the Sun-god and Ishtar, also that his triumphs were all the direct results of his having responded promptly to the wishes and commands of the gods. The remainder of the composition, insofar as it is preserved,[106] consists of oracular prophecies set in the future, but which—like the Marduk text—alludes to the Elamites, Hittites, and Assyrians in the context of the rise and fall of Babylon's fortunes.[107]

The scheme of the future seen by the author—it may even be characterized as his vision of history in general—is a regular alternation of calamitous and prosperous reigns under a succession of kings in Babylon, which affect all the ancient centers of Sumer and Akkad. The description of conditions in the periods of adversity parallels that of the Marduk text and of similar compositions. It is implied throughout (and is at one juncture explicit) that the calamitous periods, which entail the downfall of the dynasty through defeat by enemy forces, are brought about by divine will, presumably prompted by displeasure with the king's conduct, both in social and in cultic matters. Like the Marduk text, the Shulgi prophecy ends on a note of salvation. A new king will arise (in Babylon) who will rebuild all the great shrines of the gods in the ancient cultic centers of southern Mesopotamia and will re-institute their proper routine of offerings and sacrifices.

The compositions just discussed have been selected not only because the historical setting of the first of the two falls within the range of time to which this chapter is limited, but also because among the prophetic or apocalyptic literature in cuneiform they display a broad historical sweep viewed from a well-defined perspective. This is particularly noticeable in the Marduk narrative. It is messianic in tone, but immediate in purpose.[108] Other prophetic and didactic compositions, including pseudochronicles that boldly set out to "rewrite" all of Babylonian history from the standpoint of concern for (or neglect of) the cultic shrines of Marduk on the part of a succession of Mesopotamian rulers, may be grouped into a series of closely interdependent genres or subgenres of which the Marduk narrative might have been the archetype.[109] All of these, however, cannot be proved to have a historical setting before the first millennium B.C.—insofar as one may assume that they were intended to reflect the political context of a particular time—and thus fall outside the scope of the present chapter.

### Divination

As suggested by the very term used to denote this activity, it has as its essential purpose the foretelling of events, that is, the foreseeing of the concomitants in the realm of human affairs of observations drawn from the realm of natural phenomena— "nature" here being understood in its broadest sense. It is an activity engaged in primarily by those specialized elements in any population who are presumed to have the requisite background and expertise necessary for the identification and reliable interpretation of all manner of manifestations that are thought to provide the clues to what the "fates" or the "gods" have in store for the "client," that is, the party in search of such advance knowledge.

It is characteristic of Mesopotamian professional terminology that the element of "divinity" is absent in the native Akkadian term, *barū*, which denotes in a specialized but neutral way the act of "observing, inspecting, and so forth." There is no explicit evidence that persons identified by the title *barū* were attached exclusively to the temple organizations or that they owed their "loyalty" to such organizations. It would therefore be misleading to refer to these persons as "divination-priests" (as is often done), because this amounts to an intrusion of a connotation alien to the native context. The experts in this craft were nevertheless organized into "guilds" (to be understood here in a broad rather than a strict sense), and such groups, or "guilds," could be attached to the palace as well as to the temples, and to the armies. They could also be consulted by private individual clients, but it is not clear whether a *barū* thus serving the general public was engaged in independent "private practice" or was attached to one of the larger organizations. It is more likely that the latter was the case, inasmuch as the practice of divination required long learning and training for attaining an adequate level of proficiency, and elaborate ritual purification and other preparatory acts were required of the diviner to ensure direct divine cooperation in the central activity that was to follow if his efforts were to yield results that were unambiguous and reliable. This was all the more necessary if the inquiry at hand concerned matters of great moment, such as the affairs of state.[110]

For the earlier period, with which this chapter is concerned, the activities of the diviner appear to have been in large part preempted by inquires falling within what we should designate as the "public sphere," which means the fortunes of the king, the royal family, and—by implication or indirection—the welfare of the entire country. By far the most popular form of divination in the earlier period was extispicy, that is, the examination of all the entrails *(exta)* of a sacrificial lamb or kid in an orderly sequence, with particular attention given in greatest detail to the liver and gallbladder. When the latter set of organs constitute the sole area of attention of the diviner—which would appear to have been the case in the earliest periods for which we have direct evidence—the procedure is referred to as hepatoscopy. Overwhelmingly, hepatoscopy was invoked in the interests of state and public policy. Our special concern here is with any evidence bearing on the possible use of the techniques of such divination by its practitioners to exert some influence over royal policy and decisions. It should be stated forthwith that there is no evidence that diviners at any time offered deliberately misleading or false information, that is, advice affecting royal policy that was in contradiction with what—by their canons—was indicated by their observations; indeed, we would be in no position to suspect such fraud even if we had all the necessary facts about any single instance for, by the nature of this entire ''science'' or art, ambiguity is of its very essence.

It is, however, of great interest to our theme that the diviners, as an ongoing profession throughout Mesopotamian history, were always conscious of their indispensable role—which at times could amount almost to a veto power—in the determination of royal policy.[111] While they were not typically the initiators of policy, some, as in the Mari administration, held governorships of great territories, or other high offices, under the king. That their political powers are not to be ascribed to personal relationships with the dynastic line but rather to their professional importance is suggested by the case of one Itur-Ashdu, a diviner who held high office both during the Assyrian interregnum and then under the native dynasty (the two dynasties having been bitter enemies), when he was the viceroy of one of the northern regions of the kingdon.[112] It was thus inevitable that, granting the conscientiousness and honesty in the practice of their divinatory art, the conclusions and recommendations they reported to the king (who was their primary client) always had, at least as a secondary purpose, the protection and advancement of their own interests whether as a special group or as individuals.

As suggested earlier, the *ratio operandi* of the diviner's art was the principle that a complex of observations—such as the peculiarities and anomalies found in the internal organs of a sacrificial animal—pointed in a particular or more general way to some prospect in affairs of state: for example, defeat in battle, assassination of the king, palace uprising, famine, popular rebellion, or the favorable converse of these.[113] The ground for such correlations—which came to be elaborated in the greatest detail—was the belief that in the past identical complexes of observations were accompanied or closely followed by political or social events that were especially fateful for the future of these past rulers and their dynasties. Overwhelmingly, these historical allusions were centered on the kings of the dynasty of Akkad, which may properly be said to have served as the paradigmatic base for the prognostic element in all public or state-centered divination practice, even where no specific historical personage is mentioned.[114] There is no ground for suspecting that these historical allusions were deliberately falsified or fabricated by the diviners for their immediate ends. Indeed, in contrast to the unending polemic against the figure of Naram-Sin in the literary output of the temple-oriented elites, the historical references to the fortunes of Naram-Sin in the omens are invariably favorable.

With this record one therefore turns with some wonder to the passage in the "Legend of Naram-Sin" discussed above, where the king is made to lament the fact that, prior to his disastrous defeats, he had consulted the diviners and the oracles, had been given uniformly the advice that he should not engage the enemy, and had then contemptuously dismissed their warning, saying: "What lion ever took note of oracles; what wolf ever consulted the interpretress of dreams? I shall go, like a bandit, wheresoever I please." Here Naram-Sin is made out to be a virtual blasphemer, and by his own imagined confession.[115] We thus see that, even while the core of objective information in the corpus of omen texts reports nothing unfavorable in connection with Naram-Sin, the temple-inspired tradition once again falls back upon its favorite bête noire as the archetypal scoffer at the authority and potency of the diviners' arts. This too must be seen as a thinly veiled warning to contemporary royal patrons that to disregard the advice of the diviners is to court disaster just as surely as Naram-Sin's hubris of old brought about his undoing.[116]

### The Babylonian Creation Epic

We cannot close our survey of the propaganda of the religious organizations of early Mesopotamia without reviewing what might in some respects be considered the greatest piece of pro-

pagandizing literature that emerged from the entire output of
the cuneiform world, namely, the composition that has come to
be known as "The Babylonian Epic of Creation" or, more
simply, "The Epic of Creation." The very title we have conferred upon it implies that the cosmology and theology advanced in it were more or less normative for all of Mesopotamia
and representative of the religious thought of Mesopotamians
throughout the greater part of two millennia. In part this conception of the composition is a result of the purely fortuitous accident that it was the best preserved text of its genre preserved
in the remains of the great cuneiform library of Ashurbanipal at
Nineveh of the seventh century B.C. It was recovered in the early years of Assyriological discovery about a century ago and is
now in the British Museum. But at a distance of a century, and
with the recovery of many thousands of additional cuneiform
literary tablets from many sites in Mesopotamia, from ages
reaching back almost two thousand years before Ashurbanipal,
we are now in a position to characterize and assess the "Babylonian Epic of Creation"—or, to refer to it by its native title
*Enuma Elish*[117]—with greater accuracy.

Far from reflecting a typical or "orthodox" Mesopotamian
cosmology, we now may see that in certain fundamental respects it might even be characterized (in modern terms) as
"heretical," or at least aberrant. Even the most cursory reading
of the text would reveal that the dominating theme of the entire
composition is the assertion of the supremacy of Marduk among
the gods, emphasizing particularly, and at greatest length, the
course of cosmological and mythical events culminating in Marduk's achievement of this uniquely exalted status.[118] The portion of the text devoted to the creation of the visible universe (as
seen and sensed by the Mesopotamians) is relatively brief, and
quite clearly subservient to the major theme.[119]

It is vital to our present theme to stress that the "heterodoxy" that characterizes much of *Enuma Elish* was conscious
and deliberate. The pantheon of great gods, as the story un-
folds, was confronted by a terrible threat of destruction at the
hands of the primeval forces of Chaos (personified by Tiamat—
the power of the great salt waters—and her supporting host).
For no explicable reason, the great gods were paralyzed with
fear; Ea (the god Enki in Sumerian)—the progenitor of Marduk

in the author's scheme—the hero of the first encounter against the forces of Chaos in earlier cosmic time, proved ineffective in the present situation, as did Anu, the erstwhile king of the pantheon. They then turned to Marduk—whose birth and physical appearance are described earlier in the epic in the most extravagantly glowing terms—to be their hero and saviour. Marduk, with great self-assurance, and with disdain for the enemy that had so immobilized his elders, agrees to undertake the battle, but only on condition that the entire pantheon of great gods relinquish in his favor all of their independent authority, and this they must do before he goes off to face Tiamat:

> If I am indeed to be your avenger—
> Am to smite down Tiamat and rescue your lives,
> Convoke ye the Assembly; proclaim supreme my destiny.
> When ye in Upshukinna have happily convened,
> Let my utterance, instead of yours, determine the fates.
> Nothing I devise shall ever be altered,
> Nor revoked nor distorted the command of my lips.[120]

The bold demand for divine supremacy is unexampled in previous Mesopotamian theology. It has been aptly described as a form of "religious imperialism" alien to the theological pluralism characteristic of early Mesopotamian thought.[121] In the epic itself, the great gods are described as having happily agreed to the bargain: they of course had no choice. The end of Tablet 3 describes the scene:

> Entering the Assembly, they kissed each other,[122]
> Falling into conversation, they sat down to the banquet.
> They partook of bread, poured forth fine beer.
> Dipping their drinking-tubes in the sweet liquor.
> As they drank the intoxicant, their bodies expanded;
> Growing ever more languorous, their mood became carefree.
> For Marduk, their avenger, they fixed his decrees.

Considering the momentousness of the action they were called upon to take, would it be too far-fetched to suspect that the gods could not have been envisaged as willingly divesting themselves of all their authority in such a light-hearted manner if they had been cold sober?[123]

The new theology was not limited, however, to the exaltation of Marduk; nor was it intended to establish for him a mere religious primacy. In conformity with ancient Mesopotamian cosmic thought, the rank of a god reflects and is reflected in the significance of the temple that is his abode, and the city that it symbolizes. From earliest historical times in Mesopotamia the most exalted rank was occupied by Enlil and reflected in the cosmic significance of his shrine E-kur[124] and the city of Nippur in which it was located. There was no integral relation of this rank with the political power exerted by the city thus exalted: Nippur was not the seat of any significant political authority in historical times. Throughout the largest segment of Mesopotamian history, the Enlil-Ekur-Nippur complex retained its primacy in normative Mesopotamian theology and cosmology, even through long periods when the terrestrial city of Nippur was outside the political control of the ruling dynasty, as, for example, the period of the First Dynasty of Babylonia after the reign of Hammurapi.

The author(s) of *Enuma Elish* set about deliberately and unabashedly to change this scheme. The aim of the composition, quite simply, was to effect a total reorientation of Mesopotamian religious and cosmological thought, that is, to transfer religious and cosmological primacy from the older complex to Marduk-Esagil-Babylon (the name of the temple complex in Babylon). The crowning episodes in *Enuma Elish,* in Tablets 5 and 6, are those in which the gods, at Marduk's behest, are portrayed as building with their own labor the city of Babylon and its sacred precincts[125] to serve as their "homes."[126]

In contrast to the older cosmology set down in the Epic of Atrahasis, where the gods are described as building Nippur, the Ekur, and the Twin Rivers, as the unwilling and rebellious slaves of Enlil, they are here portrayed as going about their labor with boundless joy and in sycophantic adulation of their newly enthroned lord. Enlil, who otherwise had played no part in the story—inasmuch as Marduk had tacitly replaced his persona throughout the epic—also joins the tribute at this juncture. Babylon, which less than a millennium earlier had been only an obscure hamlet, thus becomes the primeval "Jerusalem" not only for the people but for all the gods themselves.

Perhaps the ultimate wonder is that this bold and grand conception was so completely victorious. It appears to have quickly superseded all preceding or "rival" cosmologies throughout Mesopotamia, including Assyria.[127] In the native Mesopotamian tradition about the antediluvian age, Babylon now assumed the rank of the first earthly city where kings ruled in the age "before the Flood."[128] From all indications, this crowning achievement of priestly propaganda in ancient Mesopotamia was, like the Marduk prophecy discussed above, a product of the age of Nebuchadnezzar I.[129] The triumphant return of Marduk's statue from its Elamite captivity appears to have occasioned this "Exaltation of Marduk"—a title that would more accurately reflect the purpose and content of *Enuma Elish* than "The Babylonian Epic of Creation"—more than the military defeat of the Elamites. The latter, gauged purely in terms of its political effect, appears to have been negligible, and the military achievement itself of relatively minor consequence.[130] Tiglath-Pileser I, who came to the throne of Assyria only a few years after the rise of Nebuchadnezzar in Babylon, soon overshadowed the latter's achievements in every direction.[131]

Indeed, both kingdoms very soon were to lapse into relative obscurity and weakness under the impact of the invasion of the Aramaean tribes from the western desert that neither was able to contain. Babylonia was in fact not to become an international power of any consequence until the rise of the Chaldean (Aramaean) dynasty of Nabopolassar and Nebuchadnezzar II toward the end of the seventh century B.C. We note these facts only to forestall the implication that it was the political achievement of Nebuchadnezzar I that was mother to the exaltation of Marduk and the city of Babylon, so that the latter phenomenon might be viewed as a political and ex-post-facto program inspired by the crown rather than the priesthood. Although Nebuchadnezzar may have had some active part in this expression of resurgent "nationalism"—he was in any event its immediate beneficiary—it is clear that the major force in bringing it about was of priestly character and inspiration, with roots planted in the religious establishment of the Kassite age, well antedating the time of Nebuchadnezzar.[132] It is largely the result of the theological and ideological achievement toward the close of the second millennium B.C. that from the beginning of the first millennium B.C. down to our own day, "Babylon" and "Babylonia" are the names that have come to signify—just as "Jerusalem" did in another area, and at a somewhat later time—the total intellectual and spiritual achievement of the various peoples who shared the three millennia of ancient Mesopotamian civilization.

NOTES

1. Sumerian *EN* in the later literature, or *ENSÍ(K)*, the first of which later denotes more specifically the cultic leadership, and the latter term, the stewardship or "governorship" of a polity whose true "lord" or "proprietor" was believed to be a deity.

2. Sumerian *LUGAL*, which by literal understanding of the compound logogram means only "great man," later rendered in Semitic Akkadian by *šarrum*, which more exactly denotes "king" in approximately our own understanding of this title. It is not certain how far the attributes of "kingship" as a station of secular authority and as the supreme cultic representative of the deity and of the city or state as they are known from the later historical periods may be retrojected to the latter part of the fourth and the earlier part of the third millennium B.C. Inasmuch as the term *LUGAL*, even in the earliest periods of writing, may denote also the simple idea of proprietorship, that is, "owner," the stress upon the secular aspect of the position, in contrast to the cultic one, would appear justified.

3. Sumerian *KAS₄*: Akkadian *lāsimu(m)*, a sign compounded of two separate signs, the one denoting "foot, to go" and the other denoting "road, journey." The Akkadian is the active participle of the verb "to run."

4. Sumerian *NIMGIR* : Akkadian *nāgirum*.

5. The traditional view had been that the horse was first introduced into the Near East with the coming of the Kassites in the first half of the second millennium B.C., and that it was to be associated—on the basis largely of the name, *anshe-kur-ra* in Sumerian "ass of the mountain region (that is, foreign)" : *sisū* in Akkadian—with intrusive Indo-European elements.

6. See P. R. S. Moorey, "Pictorial Evidence for the History of Horse-riding in Iraq before the Kassite Period," *Iraq* 32 (1970): 36 ff.; and M. A. Littauer, "The Figured Evidence for a Small Pony in the Ancient Near East," *Iraq* 33 (1971): 24 ff.

7. See, on this subject in general, T. Jacobsen, "Early Political Development in Mesopotamia," *Zeitschrift für Assyriologie* 52 (Neue Folge 18, 1957): 91 ff. For a somewhat different view, see A. Falkenstein, "Zu 'Gilgamesh und Agga,' " *Archiv für Orientforschung* 21 (1966): 47 ff.

8. See J. R. Kupper, "L'Opinion Publique à Mari," *Revue d'Assyriologie* 58 (1964): 79 ff.

9. The preceding line is partially lost, but it speaks of "the whole country," and both the immediate contexts and parallel situations in other documents assure the sense of a danger of a popular reaction that would go against the king.

10. See the translation of this letter in A. L. Oppenheim, *Letters from Mesopotamia* (Chicago, 1967), p. 103.

11. For a brief period, the Mari territory on the Middle Euphrates was under the control of Assyria, but shortly after the death of Shamshi-Adad it was again under the rule of the native dynasty that Shamshi-Adad had ousted. After about thirty years Hammurapi put an end to its independence.

12. See Oppenheim, *Letters*, p. 96 ff. For other examples in the Mari archives of the fear of popular indignation at preferential treatment for certain persons in the realm of economic life, see the article by Kupper cited in note 8 above.

13. The typical ones are *pī mātim* "the mouth of the land," and *pī ālim*, "mouth of the city."

14. See the translation by the present writer in J. B. Pritchard, ed., *Ancient Near Eastern Texts Relating to the Old Testament*, 3rd ed. (Princeton, N.J. 1969), p. 523 ff.

15. For a translation, see S. N. Kramer in Pritchard, ed., *Ancient Near Eastern Texts*, p. 159 ff. The word for "public outcry, protest, etc." is the Sumerian *i.Utu*, which is literally the cry "O Sun-god," the sun, *Utu* (*Shamash* in Akkadian), being the god whose primary area of concern is that of justice. The Akkadian for *i.Utu* is *tazzimtum*, which specifically denotes the public outcry against oppression and injustice and is the term used in the letter from Shamshi-Adad discussed above.

16. The word *tazzimtum* is used to describe their outcry.

17. The solution to these grievances is the creation of man, who is destined thenceforth to take the burden of which the gods will be relieved. For the entire sequence, see W. G. Lambert and A. R. Millard, *Atrahasis: The Babylonian Story of the Flood* (Oxford, 1969).

18. See, for example, Hammurapi's epilogue to his code, in Pritchard. ed., *Ancient Near Eastern Texts*, p. 177 f. The appropriate lines, after his reference to his putting an end to wars, should be rendered: "I made the land prosperous; I enabled the people to lie down in green pastures, allowing none to frighten them." The extended metaphor, which is so close to that made famous in Psalm 23, goes back to a time even earlier than that of Hammurapi.

19. That is, including inter-city-state relations, as well as military and commercial ventures of greater ambitious scope in geographical terms.

20. Thorkild Jacobsen, *The Sumerian King List*, Assyrilogical Studies No.

11 (Oriental Institute of the University of Chicago, 1939). The "Sumerian" of the title is to be understood mainly as denoting the language in which the text was composed, as the Semitic Dynasty of Akkad, whose founding, at around 2340 B.C., marks the end of the Early Dynastic Period, is included within it, as are also many rulers with Semitic names in much earlier dynasties, as for example, the early kings of Kish, given as the first dynasty after the Flood, the earlier dynasts of which bore Semitic names.

21. Who had been a governor of Mari on the Upper Euphrates under the suzerainty of the last king of the Ur III dynasty, and who took possession of Isin before the final overthrow of that dynasty.

22. The first Larsa king to gain at least temporary control of Nippur was Sumu-ēl, 1894–1866 B.C.

23. The Weld-Blundell Prism, W-B. 444, first published by S. Langdon in *Oxford Editions of Cuneiform Texts*, vol. 2, 1923; it served as the mainstay of Jacobsen's critical edition of the King List.

24. Sin-magir, 1827–1817 B.C., whose successor Damiq-ilishu was the last of the line, having been defeated by Rim-Sin, king of Larsa in 1794 B.C., when Isin was incorporated into the Larsa realm.

25. W-B. 62, published by Langdon in the same volume cited in note 23.

26. In no other list of the antediluvian dynasties is Larsa to be found.

27. The Sumu-abum found in an extant fragment of a king-list does not appear to be identical with the founder of the Babylon dynasty who bore the same name.

28. See E. Sollberger, "The Rulers of Lagaš," *Journal of Cuneiform Studies* 21 (1967): 279 ff. Among all the old Sumerian city-states, Lagash appears to have been unique in that it continued to flourish and to have reached even the zenith of its prosperity during the period of the Gutian supremacy. This was achieved under a series of rulers who apparently made their peace with the Gutian suzerains, in token of which they refrained from claiming the title of "king," contenting themselves instead with the somewhat less exalted but nevertheless highly charged and ancient title of *ensi,* "viceroy, governor, prince, etc."—with the connotation that they were the stewards of the domain whose true king was the tutelary deity—but who enjoyed in every tangible respect the status of independent rulers with a territory encompassing probably the greater part of the heartland of ancient Sumer. This was particularly true of Gudea (circa 2144–2124 B.C.), probably the best-known ancient Sumerian in the modern world, by virtue of the number and quality of his surviving statues, inscriptions, and architectural achievements. His domains seem to have included even the city of Ur. It might well be suspected, therefore, that the elites of the other Sumerian cities harbored resentments against the Lagash rulers for enjoying their prosperity only as "traitorous collaborators" of the hated Gutians. Utu-Khegal (circa 2116–2110 B.C.), the "liberator" of the Sumerians from the Gutian yoke, appears to have been

recognized as king in Lagash after his victory, and seems at one point to have settled a border dispute between Ur and Lagash in the latter's favor. Ur-Nammu, the founder of the Ur III dynasty, however, retained a deep animus against Lagash, which he indulged after the brief reign of Utu-Khegal in Uruk (he also might have been instrumental in cutting short the reign of his superior and rival), not only by promptly going to war against Lagash and killing its last *ensi*, Nammahani (circa 2109 B.C.)—as he himself relates in the prologue to his law-"code"—but also systematically defacing the latter's monuments, an otherwise unprecedented act in Mesopotamian political rivalry (see W. W. Hallo, "The Coronation of Ur-Nammu," *Journal of Cuneiform Studies* 20 [1966]: 138). The consequence of this entire chain of events may therefore have been the excision of all references to Lagash in the Sumerian King List that was then beginning to take shape. By this act of censorship even the great Lagash kings of the pre-Sargonic era also were deprived of their share in the divine patrimony of "kingship" in the scheme formulated by the authors of the King List.

29. The existence of a number of separate summaries of the reigns of the kings of Isin in which they follow the list of the kings of Ur III dynasty without interruption bears out this intention. See E. Sollberger, "New Lists of the Kings of Ur and Isin," *Journal of Cuneiform Studies* 8 (1954): 135 ff.

30. See B. Landsberger, "Assyrische Königsliste und 'Dunkles Zeitalter'," *Journal of Cuneiform Studies* 7 (1954): 109.

31. See Landsberger, "Assyrische Königsliste," p. 37.

32. It exists in a number of somewhat variant copies, all of the time of Urukagina. For an English translation, see S. N. Kramer, *The Sumerians* (Chicago, 1963), p. 317 ff.

33. It is commonly believed that Urukagina, if not altogether a usurper, was not a lineal descendant of the dynastic family that had reigned over Lagash and much of Sumer from at least early in the twenty-sixth century B.C. to shortly before his own time.

34. See the translation by the present writer in Pritchard, ed., *Ancient Near Eastern Texts*, p. 523 ff.

35. For translation, see Kramer in Pritchard, ed., *Ancient Near Eastern Texts*, p. 159 ff.

36. See the translation by J. T. Meek in Pritchard, ed., *Ancient Near Eastern Texts*, p. 163 ff.

37. See chapter 4 this volume, on the first millennium B.C., by A. L. Oppenheim.

38. See Kramer, *The Sumerians*, p. 322 f. Of course, it is not impossible, and it is even probable, that this text was composed not immediately upon the sacking of Lagash by Umma, but with hindsight of the overthrow of Lugalzagesi soon afterward by Sargon of Akkad circa 2340 B.C. The text would then have constituted an expression of gloating satisfaction over seeing

the destroyer of their city destroyed in his turn; they might not have dared record their feelings in this vein while Lugalzagesi was still in the position of suzerain. See also, H. Hirsch, "Die 'Sünde' Lugalzagesis" in *Festschrift für Wilhelm Eilers* (Wiesbaden, 1964), p. 99 ff. Thus too, the priesthood of Marduk in Babylon did not give full vent to their hatred of Nabonidus, as they did in their villifying "Verse Account" (see the translation by Oppenheim in Pritchard, ed., *Ancient Near Eastern Texts*, p. 312 ff.), until *after* he was overthrown by Cyrus the Great in 539 B.C. and entered Babylon without resistance.

39. The extant manuscripts of this genre date mainly to the period of the First Dynasty of Babylon, from about 1900 to 1700 B.C., but there is sufficient evidence to prove that their composition occurred during the reigns of the kings who were the subject of these adulations.

40. For some reason still unknown, Ur-Nammu was not accorded such status in his lifetime, that is, the determinative for deity does not appear before his name in contemporary inscriptions, but in all other respects he was accorded the same honors as his successors.

41. In later ages the entire period came to be denoted as the Shulgi dynasty.

42. One cannot help being reminded of the extraordinary swimming exploits ascribed to Mao Tze-tung.

43. See W. W. Hallo, "On the Antiquity of Sumerian Literature" *Journal of the American Oriental Society* 83 (1963): 173. The text itself offers the clue to the "Sitz im Leben" of the composition: the inauguration of a new highway between the two cities with well-appointed inns erected at appropriate intervals for the comfort of weary travellers. For a translation of the text, see Kramer in Pritchard, ed., *Ancient Near Eastern Texts*, p. 584 ff.

44. In such instances, that is, where no royal act in the early part of the year had as yet been accomplished that was deemed appropriate for this honor, the first month or two of the new year continued to use the formula of the previous year to which there was prefixed the phrase "Year After etc."

45. At the close of a reign, a list of the regnal year names was normally drawn up giving their proper sequence, and at longer intervals a sequence of reigns was drawn up in similar fashion for archival purposes; copies of most of these have been preserved and are the primary source for our knowledge of the chronology and even of events for most of the period between the beginning of the Ur III dynasty and the end of the First Dynasty of Babylon in about 1595 B.C.

46. Perhaps even altogether fictitious, although this would probably have been the exception rather than the rule.

47. Beginning with the Kassite dynasty (after the end of the First Dynasty of Babylon), this custom was abandoned in favor of dating by giving the name of the king and the year number alone, for example, King N, Year 1, 2, 3,

and so forth. The Assyrians, from the earliest times to the end of the independent existence of Assyria in 509 B.C., employed a system whereby each year was identified by an eponym, that is, the name of a high official (including the king himself, who usually took this honor in his second year) who was accorded this honor for a period of exactly one year. Dating in cuneiform documents by an era from a fixed point in time was instituted only with the Seleucids in 311 B.C.

48. See W. W. Hallo, "The Cultic Setting of Sumerian Poetry" in *Actes de la XVII*e *Rencontre Assyriologique Internationale* (Ham-sur-Heure, Belgium, 1970), p. 118 ff.

49. In this respect, as in many others, the Mari archives provide the most vivid glimpse of the way these names were adopted. In one instance, the official who was apparently charged with promulgating the year names had decided that the current year was to be called "The year (after that) in which king Zimrilim presented a great throne to the god Dagan." He was informed, by the respondent, however, that the throne had not yet been presented. (It might not yet have been completed.) The latter then suggests an alternative name, "Year in which Zimrilim went in military support of Babylon (that is, of Hammurapi), on the second campaign to the country of Larsa," and requests that it be submitted to the king for approval. See the translation in Oppenheim, *Letters from Mesopotamia*, p. 104 ff.

50. Apart from the Mitanni Empire, which was at the point of disintegration through internal strife that culminated in the assassination of its last independent ruler, Tushratta, around 1360 B.C.

51. Tukulti-Ninurta actually ruled over Babylonia for seven years before the local officials managed to elevate a local dynast, but the Babylonian traditions refused to recognize the fact officially, in contrast to their response in the Neo-Assyrian period, when, after the conquest of Babylon by Sennacherib, both he and Esarhaddon were formally acknowledged as kings of Babylonia.

52. The translation of the main pieces of the text by E. Ebeling was done under the title *Bruchstücke eines politischen Propaganda-gedichtes aus einer assyrischen Kanzlei, Mitteilungen der altorientalischen Gesellschaft*, vol. 12, pt. 2 (Leipzig, 1938).

53. See E. A. Speiser, "In Search of Nimrod," *Eretz-Israel* 5 (1958): 32-36. For another discussion of the Tukulti-Ninurta Epic proper, together with the publication of additional fragments of it, see W. G. Lambert, "Three Unpublished Fragments of the Tukulti-Ninurta Epic," *Archiv für Orient-forschung* 18 (1957–1958): 38 ff. It is to be noted that almost all scholars who have studied or commented upon this composition have noted its similarities to the Iliad both in technique and in the motifs employed.

54. At the contemporary site named Qalat Sherqat, about one hundred miles downstream on the Tigris from the modern town of Mosul.

55. He is mentioned by name in only one of them, a poorly preserved piece

that has not yet been edited. The other, presumed, but not certainly to be so identified, has been translated by E. Ebeling, "Ein Heldenlied auf Tiglathpileser I, etc.," *Orientalia* 18 (1949): 30 ff.

56. This is strikingly similar to one of the closing instructions in *Enuma Elish*, the so-called Babylonian Epic of Creation: "Let the father, by reciting, teach it to his son." Although the latter composition—after the Epic of Gilgamesh perhaps the best-known literary creation of ancient Mesopotamia—is by no means devoid of propagandistic motivation (and we shall have occasion to refer to it again in discussing the propaganda of the religious organizations), the theological didactic element is uppermost, and the parallel closing instruction in the two pieces here discussed underscores the general affinities of the Tiglath-Pileser hymn with literature of this kind rather than with the very personal kind of text represented by the Tukulti-Ninurta Epic.

57. This is a fragment of the reign of Arik-den-ilu (1319–1308 B.C.). It is thought by some that the genre was adopted from the Hittites, yet the first Hittite king who utilized the annalistic form in its strict definition—and is credited with having created the form—is Mursilis II (circa 1344–1314 B.C.), who invoked the form not only for his own reign but also to record the achievements of his father Suppiluliuma, the greatest of the Hittite rulers of the empire period. But the Hittites are also known to have developed at an early period (circa eighteenth to seventeenth centuries B.C.) court chronicles and royal testaments, some examples of which have survived. These not only deal with great military achievements but also offer glimpses of domestic political affairs and of palace intrigue, in a style unknown either in Babylonia or Assyria.

58. See, in general, F. R. Kraus, "Le rôle des temples depuis la troisième dynastie d'Ur jusqu'à la première dynastie de Babylone," *Cahiers d'Histoire Mondiale* 1 (1954): 518–545; and A. Falkenstein, "La cité-temple sumérienne," ibid., pp. 784–814. For a criticism of the conventional conception of Mesopotamian economy in the third millennium B.C. as being alternatively temple- or state-controlled, see I. J. Gelb, "On the Alleged Temple and State Economies in Ancient Mesopotamia," *Studi in Onore di Edoardo Volterra*, vol. 6 (Pavia, 1969), pp. 137–154.

59. *Journal of Near Eastern Studies* 8 (1949): 346–348.

60. E. Sollberger, "The Cruciform Monument," in *Jaarbericht Ex Oriente Lux* (1968), pp. 50–70, where a full edition and translation of the text are to be found.

61. The liberal reparations paid by the West German government to victims of the Nazi era cannot be cited as an example, as this was prompted by the desire of a defeated nation to be "rehabilitated" into the community of nations, and was indeed a prerequisite toward this end imposed by the victorious nations. More apt and more typical has been the fate of the reparations

and related types of claims entered by American Indian and Mexican-American groups against the federal and several state governments in modern times, the legitimacy of which is rarely open to doubt.

62. It is a striking prototype of the better-known "Donation of Constantine" concocted in the eighth century A.D. in support of the primacy of the See of Rome, which in its early history was given little credence, but which from the later Middle Ages until the eighteenth century was periodically appealed to by popes and other defenders of papal authority.

63. It is not clear from the text to which temple(s) of Ishtar these endowments were assigned. It appears that the land allotments were located in two different sections of Babylonia.

64. See Gelb, *Journal of Near Eastern Studies* 8:348 n. 12. B. Landsberger, speaking of the Agum inscription, calls it "apocryphal," *Journal of Cuneiform Studies* 8 (1954): 67.

65. No inscriptions of this king are thus far known, but in the light of earlier experience in Assyriology—where names in the early part of the King List that had been thought only legendary (largely because of the absurdly long reigns often ascribed to them) were ultimately attested by authentic contemporary inscriptions brought to light by excavation—it would be rash to suggest that Lugalannemundu did not exist, even though the King List assigns him a reign of ninety years. But there is no way of ascertaining with any precision the time in which he reigned; somewhere between the twenty-eighth and twenty-seventh centuries B.C. might be a fair estimate. The location of the city of Adab is known, having been briefly excavated at the end of the nineteenth and in the early years of this century. It lay about thirty miles southeast of Nippur and yielded inscriptions of rulers in the last part of the Early Dynastic era.

66. Preserved in two fragmentary copies from the reigns, respectively, of Abi'eshuh (1711–1684) and Ammisaduqa (1646–1626).

67. This suggests the likelihood that the extant manuscripts are themselves but copies of a manuscript of even earlier date, when the Sumerian language was the normal vehicle for such creative efforts, possibly as early as the period of the Ur III dynasty.

68. The text was edited by H. G. Güterbock, in *Zeitschrift für Assyriologie* 42 (Neue Folge 8, 1934): 40 ff.

69. See chapter 4 in this volume by A. L. Oppenheim.

70. It is well to note here that the titles by which Mesopotamian literary creations are identified in the modern literature have been coined by the Assyriologists themselves. The ancients always identified a composition by its opening words.

71. It consists of 282 lines, and as a result of the presence of parts of at least twenty-seven separate copies, the text as now known is almost completely

restored. It was edited with a translation, by A. Falkenstein, in *Zeitschrift für Assyriologie* 57 (Neue Folge 23, 1965): 43 ff. For a full summary of the text, see also Kramer, *The Sumerians,* pp. 62–66.

72. The twenty-seven manuscripts utilized by Falkenstein for the reconstruction of the text were all from Nippur. Later excavations in the temple precincts of Nippur turned up additional copies, including a fragment written during the Ur III dynasty (all other copies being of later date), compare Falkenstein, *Zeitschrift für Assyriologie,* p. 44.

73. Nippur, the sacred city par excellence of the Sumerians, by virtue of its being the residence of Enlil, the effective head of the pantheon, was administered by authorities closely linked with the temple organization. The city therefore never had a "dynasty" of its own and was never the formal capital of the temporal ruler. It was, however, crucial to the establishment of any king's legitimacy that he recognize the Nippur cultic ascendency, by enacting there at least part of the ceremonial of his inauguration, by the sponsorship of building efforts, and by the establishment of enormous endowments to its offerings and to its treasures. The temple establishment in Nippur, boasting (as far as we know) the largest scholarly and literary community in ancient Sumer, was thereby in a position to turn out paeans of praise to the glory of monarchs who zealously courted the favor of the Nippur establishment and to excoriate (usually, after he had disappeared from the scene) and even villify such monarchs who, for whatever reasons, incurred their displeasure.

74. The text merely alludes, darkly, to the disenchantment of Inanna, the great goddess, with Agade of which she had been made patroness by Sargon.

75. Line 107. This is the earliest known example of the idiom ultimately made famous in the betrayal of Jesus by Judas Iscariot, by which time the original force of the idiom had been forgotten. E. Reiner, in her article "Thirty Pieces of Silver," *Journal of the American Oriental Society* 88 (1968): 186 ff., traces the history of the idiom in the light of the Sumerian passage and shows conclusively that the true sense is the same as the English "not worth a farthing."

76. The allusion is not completely preserved.

77. See Falkenstein, *Zeitschrift für Assyriologie,* p. 89.

78. Thus, even when invoking the Gutians as an instrument of punishment by Enlil.

79. Almost in the same way that the biblical prophets treat the foreign enemies such as Assyria and Babylonia as mere instruments of Yahweh for the punishment of the iniquitous Israelites.

80. This is a *topos* in a great deal of Sumerian and Akkadian mythological and epical literature.

81. As in other occurrences of this motif, the idea is to focus the punish-

ment on the precise culprit, thereby diverting the indiscriminate fury of Enlil from the innocent. With the annihilation of the real offender, the god will be appeased and the rest of the land will be spared the worst.

82. Inanna (that is, Ishtar in Akkadian) is the heroine deity, because it was she who first turned her back on Akkad (according to the author of this text, lines 55–60). Sargon had dedicated his dynasty to her, and she was thereafter its patroness. It must be assumed too that it was with her approval that the great gods—she is numbered among them—decreed its destruction.

83. The rivalry between the northern political center of Kish (the main seat of Sargon's realm) and Uruk, the earlier main center of Sumerian political power, is strongly reflected in the early historical inscriptions and in the epical traditions of later times.

84. In actual fact, the dynasty of Akkad continued to rule in very circumscribed territory contemporaneously with the Gutian kings, who were formally recognized by the King List. Its line was not finally extinguished until about fifty years or even less before the liberation under Utuhegal in about 2116 B.C.

85. Of the five kings of the dynasty only the first two, Ur-Nammu and Shulgi, bear Sumerian names, while the last three are pure Akkadian.

86. See C. J. Gadd, *Cambridge Ancient History,* vol. 1, chap. 19 (1963), p. 27.

87. It is true, of course, that priestly attitudes might have undergone a change in this regard in the two centuries between Naram-Sin and Shulgi, but the imputation of divine punishment for hubris, as suggested by Gadd, strikes one as a characteristically Classical and Western notion, that is, not distinctive of Mesopotamian thought, at least in the earlier ages. It would be more characteristically Mesopotamian that practical considerations of political and economic power underlay the antagonism displayed by the priestly establishment and the elites of the old city-states of Sumer against the policies of the Akkad kings in general and of Naram-Sin in particular.

88. See A. K. Grayson and W. G. Lambert, "Akkadian Prophecies," *Journal of Cuneiform Studies* 18 (1964): 7 ff. See also chapter 4 in the present volume by A. L. Oppenheim.

89. The name of the king of Uruk, one Lugalanna, is also known from a diatribe against him and his city in the poem "The Exaltation of Inanna" attributed to Enheduanna, the daughter of Sargon (and hence the aunt of Naram-Sin) who had been appointed by her father as high-priestess of the moon-god at Ur. See W. W. Hallo and J. J. A. van Dijk, *The Exaltation of Inanna* (New Haven, 1968), pp. 2, 25 ff., 56 ff. Arad-Enlilla, who is mentioned as the king of Umma, is almost certainly to be equated with the king whose name is written as TE-Enlilla (the signs in question are very similar), who occurs in one of the historical allusions in the omens of the Old Babylo-

nian period. See A. Goetze, "Historical Allusions in the Old Babylonian Omen Texts," *Journal of Cuneiform Studies* 1 (1947): 263.

90. The king of Nippur is given as one Amar-Enlilla, which must surely be a corruption, as it is uncommonly similar to Arad-Enlilla, already identified in the text as the king of Umma. In any case, the name can in no way be related to Mansium, whom the "Curse of Agade" text (discussed above) had given as the one elevated to the kingship of Nippur by the local priesthood. The name is very likely therefore an artificial creation. More certainly artificial is the figure identified in the text as the king of Kish, one Iphur-Kish; the name means "Kish assembled," which is nothing but a play on the preceding line of the text that related the fact that "the city of Kish assembled" (in revolt). The text was last translated and discussed by A. Poebel, *Assyriological Studies* vol. 14 (Chicago, 1946), p. 23 ff.

91. From the Sumerian *NA.RÚ.A,* "an erected (inscribed) stone monument."

92. Indeed, the final version of the Epic of Gilgamesh is set in precisely this frame. In his proëmium, the writer and narrator—imagining himself, as it were, as a local guide to tourists visiting the city of Uruk—conducts his listeners around the walls and squares of Uruk, telling them of these building accomplishments of the hero whose experiences he is about to relate, and telling them also that this hero, Gilgamesh, after returning to his native city from his long travels, his experiences, and his unsuccessful quest (for immortality, or at least for eternal youth) "inscribed all his travail" upon a stone stela (Sumerian *NA.RÚ.A,* as above), the implication being that this was the source from which later generations, including that of the narrator, learned the details of these ancient exploits.

93. Even at best, the redemptive aspects are insignificant in proportion to the catastrophic component of the legend. The fragmentary condition of the Old Babylonian and Hittite versions of the story leave us no clue as to whether they concluded on any kind of redemptive note.

94. The Neo-Assyrian version of this tale was last edited by O. R. Gurney, "The Cuthean Legend of Naram-Sin," *Anatolian Studies* 5 (1955): 93 ff. It is by far the most complete of the versions extant. A fragment of an Old Babylonian version was published by the present writer in *Journal of Cuneiform Studies* 11 (1957): 83 ff. The Akkadian version from Boghazkoy (the site of the Hittite capital) has only recently been published in copy, but has not yet been edited. For the fragments in the Hittite language, see H. G. Güterbock, *Zeitschrift für Assyriologie* 44 (1938): 49 ff., and H. A. Hoffner, Jr., in *Journal of Cuneiform Studies* 23 (1970): 17 ff. It should be emphasized that the total material extant is not yet sufficient to establish the precise literary affinities among the different versions.

95. We must ignore here the phenomenon of prophets and prophetesses

who appear in the archives of Mari. While, to be sure, we find recorded in these texts certain of their brief messages to the king—usually messages or oracles these prophets say they have received directly from one or another of the deities especially revered in Mari—they are typically quite brief and are concerned with immediate matters. As has been conceded by all who have studied the material more closely, the affinities of Mari prophecy are not with Mesopotamia, but rather with certain aspects of biblical and even West Semitic prophetic phenomena. In any case, the light shed by these documents on the subject of the present chapter is too meagre and indirect to require our special attention.

96. The text—far from being complete even now—has been restored from many fragments, some of them previously known, by R. Borger, in *Bibliotheca Orientalis* 28 (1971): 3 ff., under the title "Gott Marduk und Gott-König Šulgi als Propheten." The Shulgi narrative will be discussed below.

97. This notion is omitted, however, in the case of the Elamite "exile," because the event was too recent—as we shall see—and the writer could not bring himself to allow such favorable recognition to the current prime enemy.

98. "I caused livestock and grain to ascend to the sky [that is, disappear]; I caused the beer to sicken the land [that is, made it unpotable]; the corpses of the dead blocked the gates; brother consumed brother [that is, cannibalism]; friends smote each other with weapons; the well-born lay rapacious hands on the poor; the [royal] sceptre is short [that is, authority is ineffective]; ill fortune keeps the country in thralldom; usurping kings diminish the country; lions impede the use of the highways; mad dogs bite the people—those who are bitten do not survive but die."

99. This is the standard idiom for the formal and ceremonial obeisance of a monarch to the patron deity.

100. Just as over a thousand years before the imprecations of the Lagash priests against Lugalzagesi for his destruction of their sanctuaries must have been composed after he was himself defeated by Sargon, see above note 38.

101. See W. G. Lambert, "The Reign of Nebuchadnezzar I: A Turning Point in the History of Ancient Mesopotamian Religion," in *The Seed of Wisdom,* W. S. McCullough, ed. (Toronto, 1964), p. 3 ff. For a full review of the reign of this ruler and its documentation, see J. A. Brinkman, "A Political History of Post-Kassite Babylonia," *Analecta Oriental* 43 (Rome, 1968), p. 104 ff.

102. Borger, "Gott Marduk," p. 21 ff., cited in note 96 above.

103. This would not conflict with the fact that the accomplishments of Nebuchadnezzar I as the saviour-king who delivered Babylon from the Elamites were remembered and recalled in other cuneiform documents well into Hellenistic times.

104. See above pages.

105. The title of this composition is "I, Shulgi," after its incipit, which occurs also as the "catch-line" at the close of the Marduk prophecy. The latter is titled "O Haharnin, O Hayashum," the first two gods named in Marduk's invocation, after which the narrative proper begins with "I, Marduk."

106. The text is in a more fragmentary state than the Marduk "autobiography."

107. It should be remembered that in the age of Shulgi, that is, during the Ur III dynasty, the city of Babylon was of no account whatever. It did not become a center of any political consequence until the founding of the First Dynasty of Babylon (of which Hammurapi was the sixth in succession) just after 1900 B.C.

108. There are striking analogues between this composition and certain types of biblical prophecy, for example, Jeremiah, chapters 31–32, and 49:34–39, which is a dire oracle against Elam, this at a time when Elam had long since ceased being an independent power of any consequence. One suspects that there may be more than a coincidental similarity between such prophetic utterances and the Marduk text. The overall structure of the Book of Kings similarly reflects a tendentious purpose and a tone similar to this and to other cuneiform "historiosophic" compositions of the first millennium B.C.

109. It may be noted at this point that before the true scope and character of the Marduk narrative became known through the recent edition by Borger (see note 96 above), the composition was referred to in the scholarly literature as the "Marduk *narū*," that is, it was thought to belong to the same genre of apocryphal and autobiographical inscriptions as the Naram-Sin Legend, the Birth Legend of Sargon, and some of the others already discussed above. See H. G. Güterbock, *Zeitschrift für Assyriologie* 42 (1934) p. 79 ff.

110. For the centrality of "the arts of the diviner" in the Mesopotamian learned tradition, its importance to statecraft, and its influence beyond the borders of Mesopotamia, see the summary essay by A. L. Oppenheim in *Ancient Mesopotamia* (Chicago, 1964), p. 206 ff. For more varied studies and assessments of the role of the diviners in Mesopotamia see the series of essays by different scholars in *La Divination en Mésopotamie Ancienne* (Paris, 1966).

111. Here again, the most informative sources for the period before the first millennium are the royal archives of Mari, both under the native dynasty and in the Assyrian interregnum. See A. Finet, "La Place du Devin dans la Société de Mari" in *La Divination en Mésopotamie Ancienne*, p. 87 ff., and especially p. 92 ff.

112. Ibid.

113. Of course, as in all ages, the principle holds that "good news is no news," so that the aim of divination for affairs of state was to keep close watch

on unfavorable portents. In practice, however, the diviners appear to strive to report favorable portents (with hedging precautions) in order to remain in good grace with the royal client. It therefore was usual, when the portents were unmistakably unfavorable, for the diviners to repeat their efforts until the obstacle to what they perceived to be the royal intention was overcome, for example, by suggesting a more propitious moment for the royal undertaking.

114. See J. J. Finkelstein, "Mesopotamian Historiography" in *Proceedings of the American Philosophical Society* 107 (1963): 461 ff.

115. The tradition that Naram-Sin received unfavorable omens is also present in the curse of Akkad composition discussed above, but the king's reaction there was to proceed to pillage the shrines in Nippur, and it was only after this sacrilege that the great military disasters ensued.

116. In the first millennium there is more explicit admonition by the diviners to Esarhaddon about the latter's failure to heed their advice. See Oppenheim, *Ancient Mesopotamia,* p. 227, and W. von Soden, "Religiöse Unsicherheit, Säkularisierungstendenzen und Aberglaube zur Zeit der Sargoniden," in *Analecta Biblica* 12, *Studia Biblica et Orientalia* 3 (Rome, 1959): 356 ff. By far the greatest amount of direct information about the activities of the diviners and their relation to the king and royal household, particularly of those who may be called the "astrologers" (in a very broad definition of the term), derive from the Assyrian palace archives of the first millennium B.C. The evaluation of these sources from the standpoint of our present theme must be reserved for chapter 4.

117. "When Above. . . .", the two opening words of the composition.

118. One must note here that there is evidence from older Mesopotamian cosmological sources that suggests the Marduk partisans did not construct their scheme altogether out of whole cloth. There can be detected in it, for example, some echoes of a much older theology centering on the god Enki who, as Ea, is made the father of Marduk by the author of *Enuma Elish*. But the differences between this older composition (it exists only in Sumerian manuscripts dating to the early second millennium B.C.) and the strikingly "totalitarian" outlook of *Enuma Elish* are of a magnitude that compels one to consider the latter as a fundamentally new conception.

119. Of approximately eleven hundred lines (divided over seven tablets), little more than about one hundred can be said to deal with the creation theme in the strict sense, and even within these sections the aim of the author is not so much to provide explanations for the major phenomena of the cosmos as to further exemplify the matchless power and wisdom of the hero-god, Marduk. To this end, the author utilizes only so much of the full repertory of creation motifs as will satisfy this aim, neglecting the rest. Thus, apart from the creation of man (which occupies the first forty lines of Tablet 6) there is no mention at all of the creation of organic life on earth, either in the sea or on

land, such as one finds in other creation stories in cuneiform as well as in Genesis, chapters 1 and 2. There is of course no question but that the author was familiar with these other traditions, for he draws on them and at times even paraphrases them when they fill his needs, as in the section on the creation of man.

120. Tablet 2: 123–129. *Upshukkina,* the name of the divine assembly hall, is of Sumerian origin and is based on the literal term for "assembly."

121. Lambert, "The Reign of Nebuchadnezzar I," p. 7 ff., cited in note 101 above.

122. In greeting.

123. There is even a suggestion that the banquet was part of the plan to win the unanimous consent of the gods. At the beginning of Tablet 3, Anshar, the presiding officer of the assembly, to whom Marduk had stated his conditions, advises his messenger, who is to be sent out to round up the gods for the meeting, that the decision will be made after the gods had sated themselves with food and drink. But this was not to be part of the message, carried to all the gods, which set forth the reasons for the call to the assembly.

124. Lit: "mountain house."

125. Including the Tower mentioned in Genesis, chapter 11.

126. The text itself offers this as the meaning of the name Babylon: "Residential quarters of the Gods."

127. The replacement of the name of Marduk in the Assyrian editions of *Enuma Elish* by the Assyrian national god Ashur, is purely formalistic, and does not affect intrinsic belief. Nor did the final and great sacking of Babylon by Sennacherib in 689 B.C., and his removal of the Marduk statue once more to Assyria, materially alter Babylon's cultural and cultic primacy even temporarily.

128. Displacing, in this context, not Nippur—which was not included in this tradition because it was not a seat of human "kingship" (among other reasons)—but Eridu, in the far south of Sumer, which Mesopotamian tradition credited with being the first site at which the civilized arts had flourished.

129. See Borger, "Gott Marduk," p. 22; Lambert, "The Reign of Nebuchadnezzar I," p. 6 ff. implies a similar view.

130. Brinkman, "Political History," p. 108 ff.

131. Ibid.

132. Lambert, "The Reign of Nebuchadnezzar I," p. 6 ff.

# 4

## NEO–ASSYRIAN
## AND NEO–BABYLONIAN EMPIRES

### A. Leo Oppenheim

In Mesopotamia the institution of kingship was the prime mover and the sustaining nucleus of all large-scale political structures, from city-state to empire. When we focus attention on the first millennium B.C., the Assyrian Empire looms high in our view, overshadowing contemporary Babylonia, which reaches a similar preeminence in the ancient Near East only after the downfall of Assyria in 612 B.C.[1] Both empires entered the first millennium encumbered with the legacies of many previous state structures. They endured repeated and complex political, social, and economic changes along with a history filled with catastrophes and drastic reverses, most of which are only vaguely known to us. An attempt to trace this development and its effects within the arbitrary delimitation of the first millennium—which is my task here—cannot possibly do justice to the subject and is bound to bear the stigma of superficiality.

To function effectively, Mesopotamian kingship had to wield its inherent political power in two ways, or, as one could also phrase it in the context of this volume, the king had to communicate meaningfully in two directions: with his own subjects and with the outside world, which means with his enemies. In both areas the communications were either organizational, that is, bureaucratic, or sign-producing, that is, symbolic.

The organizational systems were set up with the purpose of ensuring the proper functioning of the state through structured chains of command. They were to deal with the levying of services, taxes, and other dues; with internal security; with the administration of justice (although not with the entire judicial system); and with the maintenance of adequate armed forces and of certain religious institutions, typically temples. A systematic study of these internal communication arrangements would be very valuable. Such investigations, however, should concern more than the nomenclature and hierarchy of the officialdom that implemented these internal communications and more than its spatial organization designed to cover the entire realm.[2] It would probably prove quite interesting and revealing to bare the underlying attitudes of these officials toward individual responsibility, their conflicts over royal interference, the ethics of the "civil" service (normative versus factual), and the extent to which royal directives could penetrate administrative layers against the resistance of previously established local authorities. Material for such investigations is actually available in the numerous administrative documents and letters written to and by officials during most of this period.[3]

In the present chapter I will be concerned with the sign-producing—symbolic—systems, insofar as they originate in the person of the king. To make known the importance and power of his office, often enhanced by his personal relationship to the gods,[4] the king behaved in certain symbolic ways that were geared to communicate his power to subjects and enemies alike. In this way the king assured his subjects of his protection and care in exchange for submission to be expressed in appropriate acts and attitudes, and also kept his enemies at bay, repulsing them when they were aggressive, impressing and subduing them whenever they were not in a position to be aggressive. Thus the state as a political unit within the interplay of similar units was held together and kept functioning by its central symbol, the king, who represented it both to the outside world and to his own subjects.

For such purposes the king used linguistic and nonlinguistic sets of signs as well as physical constructs, monuments, and monumental buildings. The linguistic signs are accessible to us to the extent that they are preserved in writing; the nonlinguistic are either described or referred to in writing, depicted in figural representations, or have left traces in certain buildings and other structures. Special ceremonial forms are likewise nonlinguistic, such as those set up for the king's contacts with his entourage, his army, his people, and his enemies, characteristic royal attire, behavior meant to express the special cultic status that endowed the king with a unique position in relation to gods and his subjects. All this served to establish the divine right of the king to claim respect, loyalty, obedience, services, taxes, and tribute—whatever the specific situation required.

Of the two main sources of information we have for all this, documents and monuments, I will discuss the latter first. Monuments seem to present fewer problems, and they do not seem to show such a complex variety of coexisting traditions as written sources, let alone nonlinguistic signs.

Monumental and extensive palace constructions, as well as impressive fortifications protecting the capital and other cities of the realm, bespoke most directly the might of the ruler. That impression was sustained and reinforced by the nature of the decorations (murals, reliefs) applied to certain essential buildings such as city gates, the throne hall, and the main courtyard of the palace.[5] These decorations mirror iconographic traditions whose topical contents vary greatly. Such representations may be in a more or less naturalistic style, illustrating the king's warlike exploits by showing battle scenes, pictures of the siege and capture of enemy cities, the submission of defeated kings, prisoners of war, tribute bearers, and the like. Apparently on another level are representations of imaginary events such as the king appearing before or with his gods, or protected by divine apparitions; their function can well be characterized as basically apotropaic. Purely symbolic designs of a particular nature are especially abundant in the palaces of the Sargonids (the Assyrian rulers from Sargon II to Assurbanipal, that is, from 721 to 627 B.C.); they show what we choose to call "divine spirits" engaged in a variety of obviously ritual activities, of which the religious meaning and emotional impact still remain beyond our reach.[6] With equal eloquence, yet on a more practical level, the size and contents of treasury, armory, and harem[7] proclaimed the fact that the king had found favor in the eyes of his gods and was respected if not feared by other kings.

The entire array of physical arrangements (buildings, decorations) and ceremonies enacted therein were readily understood by the king's subjects, and by the ambassadors of foreign rulers when they entered capital and palace, where they came to bring messages to the royal chancellery, either to inquire after the health of the king or to ask for help, which was to be bought with presents, homage, and submission. The fame of these kings, their palaces and cities spread easily through the kingdoms of the Near East and even beyond, attesting to the effectiveness of such display.[8]

To further publicize their claims, the kings availed themselves of the essentially royal privilege, traditional for Mesopotamian rulers dating from the empire of Akkadi (twenty-third century B.C.): the erection of stelae.[9] These elongated rectangular stone slabs, typically with rounded tops, show representations of the king himself in full regalia, alone or with his god, with divine symbols or with a subjected enemy king, and are often covered with lengthy inscriptions. At times, pictures and writings arranged so as to form a stela-like composition were hewn into live rock. The setting up of such monuments is recorded with pride in contemporary royal inscriptions as the exercise of a royal privilege.

The emplacement of the stelae is noteworthy; we find them at city gates and inside sanctuaries, also in border regions, in mountain passes, and on or near prominent topographical features where they were clearly situated for the purpose of communicating their messages—designs as well as inscriptions—to a maximum number of viewers. In a considerable number of instances, however, the locale of a stela was selected with quite obvious disregard for the apparent function of these monuments as a means of communication between king and viewer. To assess the significance of the observation that stelae were not always provided with that degree of accessiblity we would deem essential for disseminating their message (the fame and power of the king who erected them), one has to resort to somewhat complex considerations, which will take us from the discussion of monuments to that of the literary sources.

A very old Mesopotamian tradition required that any object —especially a precious object—dedicated to a god and deposited in his sanctuary, either in fulfillment of a vow or coming from booty obtained in war, had to carry a formal inscription indicating at least the names of the deity and the king. Quite often reference was made in the text of the inscription to the act of dedication itself and to the circumstances accompanying the pious deed.[10] The same practice was applied to temples newly built or repaired, and, in the first millennium, even to the palaces erected by the king. In the case of buildings, however, the dedications were inscribed on metal, stone or clay tablets, clay cylinders or prisms, that were always deposited in the foundations of such buildings at certain traditional spots and protected by brick boxes, and so forth.[11] Such inscriptions, which— especially in the first millennium—reach a considerable length and show under the various kings a remarkable variety in subject matter and degrees of complexity, are called by Assyriologists "royal inscriptions," "building inscriptions," or "foundation documents." They were written first in Sumerian (which in Babylonia was used for that purpose even in the first millennium)[12] and later in nearly all the dialects of Akkadian. This body of textual material represents a considerable section of the literary effort of the Mesopotamian scribes, ranking in size and importance with the literary production pertaining to what I have called in my book *Ancient Mesopotamia* the "stream of tradition."

In these compositions a limited number of specific topics appear with impressive regularity, and always in more or less the same sequence. The pivotal topics are the dedication proper, that is, the identification of king and deity by means of elaborate titularies (see below) and of hymnic addresses, and the identification of the building itself. The circumstances of the inauguration of the temple or palace, often described in conjunction with extensive reports on the king's military activities up to that point in his rule, and a terminal section addressing any future ruler who might discover the inscription, are likewise essential. Apparently the scribe often was granted a measure of freedom to indulge his artistic aspirations and was at liberty to emphasize certain topics and neglect others, for reasons that most likely were connected with the actual concerns of his "public."

I have used the word "public" purposely because I think that inscriptions of this kind, important as they are for today's historians, from the point of view of intent and formulation, should be considered literary creations written for the king's glorification and his courtiers' edification. This is particularly evident in the long and elaborate compositions written for the Assyrian and Babylonian rulers of the first millennium B.C. There is ample evidence that, much earlier, royal inscriptions of that genre were likewise vehicles for both artistic expression and political pronouncements. As a matter of fact, the Mesopotamian scribes were well aware of the exemplary quality of some of these early texts, as is shown by the fact that many of them were incorporated into the curricula of the scribal schools with the result that numerous phrases and specific expressions taken from texts of the second millennium were echoed in the royal inscriptions of the first millennium with surprising exactness.

An important stylistic feature of all these inscriptions is the often lengthy and quite formalized "self-predication" of the king, consisting of a string of short sentences with parallel structure: his titulary, in the Assyriological parlance. Predications of this kind were used from the Sumerian period on, not only as a means for poetic elaboration but occasionally, and rather sophisticatedly, to serve theological and political ends although the wording of royal titularies need not always be in accordance with political realities.

The self-predication of the king begins with his regnal name,[13] often as carefully chosen as the name of a pope. The titles, standard and ad hoc epithets, and other courtly designations of the king—apart from references to individual achievements—show the same blend of traditional rigidity and elaborate quasi-hymnal redundancy as does the entire literary genre of royal inscriptions.[14]

Within the remarkable amplitude of regional, temporal, and accidental or individual variations in style and content of the royal inscriptions, it was always the court of the ruler that provided the social and political milieu in which this genre of literature originated and developed. At such courts scribes and poets vied with each other to glorify their lords in words and songs, and so created the literary forms for their outpourings to king and courtiers, their public.

These documents are meant not so much to reflect actual ("historical") events—although we are compelled to use them as a source of information in this respect—as they are to serve as a mirror of how these kings saw themselves, and what they wanted their "image" to be in the eyes of their subjects and enemies. The texts convey to us, at least in a general way, the tenor and mood of the politics of the court that influenced royal decisions and thus reflect the social and economic conditions prevalent in the country at a given period. The scribes seem to have been as conscious of their own historic traditions (as one can readily infer from their use of old and nearly forgotten Sumerian and Akkadian titularies) as they were of the political aspirations and dreams of their lords and of the social and economic pressures of the day. The texts produced under these circumstances represent in many respects the result of a complex feed back, exhibiting the scribes' influence on the king's ideas as they strove to justify the latter's personal ambitions and to fit them into ancient patterns and examples manipulated by them to this very end. Despite all the typical adulation of court poetry and the hyperbole inherent in a literature created under such conditions, the "royal inscriptions" of Mesopotamia have to be admitted as evidence for the ideological trends and preferences of their period and setting—quite apart from their value for historians and philologists.

The easy accessibility of these texts, first to those scholars who were merely interested in their language and then to those who were concentrating on their historical data, has for some time prevented us from realizing that they are indeed literary creations and that they should be studied as such. The entire text category should be subjected to whatever literary critcisms can be justifiably applied to them. A hermeneutic approach will have to be evolved, requiring an intellectual confrontation of the student and the text. The kind of understanding achieved by such an approach is necessarily dependent on the personality of the investigator and is affected by his social conditioning and by the ideas of the time which he lives; it is therefore unstable, but productively so. This, however, is true of any philological and historical "understanding," a fact that is often conveniently overlooked.

Yet all we know and can know of the intellectual and artistic achievement embodied in this type of literature as a living and effective whole is what we find in building inscriptions and on stelae.[15] Songs, legends, and stories circulating at court or in certain segments of the population in praise of king and country form part and parcel of that same tradition. They are lost to us save for a few quotations that happen to have been written down.[16]

Under similar circumstances, the Mesopotamian courts of the second millennium produced, apart from royal inscriptions, another literary genre: the royal hymns of the Neo-Sumerian and subsequent periods,[17] either written for the ruler in praise of a deity or addressing the king himself.[18]

The outstanding fact concerning the royal inscriptions is that they were normally written on objects that were buried beneath the buildings constructed by the king and were destined to be read—apart from the gods they addressed—only by a later ruler who would discover them one day when undertaking to rebuild the temple or palace. Moreover, the documents say explicitly that the king who might discover them should use them for identifying the original purpose of the ruin and the name of its builder.[19] Consequently, we are faced with a situation essentially similar to that which we have observed (see above) concerning the stelae; just as the monuments often were placed so as to be inaccessible to a viewer, or rather, a reader, so the foundation documents typically were placed in a position that prevented any reader from taking cognizance of their content.

Both types of texts are therefore basically ceremonial writings, rather than messages meant for communication. In their substance, however, they reflect a dialogue that took place continuously at the court of the king between the ruler and those who helped him determine the policies of the realm and to reconcile political and economic realities with the traditional aspirations of Mesopotamian rule over an ever-expanding empire.

There remains a difference between the two text types,

building insciptions and inscribed stelae; the former, buried as they were, are patently not meant for publication, while the latter, the stelae, appear to have fulfilled their purpose of making their king's achievement public merely by their existence and their pictorial representation. The stela of Nabonidus, king of Babylon (555–539 B.C.), erected in Harran in Upper Mesopotamia, seems to offer a pertinent illustration.[20] Although it is obvious that the inscription on that stela, written in Akkadian, could hardly have been read and understood in that Aramaic-speaking region save by some temple scribes, Nabonidus saw fit to report in it the crucial events of his reign, the civil war, and also his prolonged absence from his capital, Babylon, in careful and circumspect wording. There are veiled allusions to the internal social and religious crisis that Babylonia went through during Nabonidus's rule and the text indeed reads as if it had been composed as a public document in the modern sense of the term, as if it were to be subjected to critical scrutiny. However, the publicity function of the stela was considered achieved *ex opere operato* rather than through actual communication from written text to reader.[21]

We now come to the one aspect of the nonlinguistic behavior of the Mesopotamian king that is easily discernible: that of his contacts with the enemies of the kingdom. It is more difficult to trace the other channels of communication through which the king strove incessantly to impart to his own country, and to his allies, his claim to power and the divine sanction—if not order—for all his activities. We may learn here and there from texts, and especially from monuments, about regal attire and the paraphernalia of royal office, about certain ceremonies performed at court and abroad involving the king's contacts with courtiers, ambassadors, and subjects, about rituals he had to perform because of his relationship with the gods, about his coronation and his participation in festive occasions (in Assyria, typically banquets).[22]

The information concerning that aspect of the symbolic behavior of the king which we call warfare is abundant and explicit. The Assyrian sources are by far more elaborate and direct in this respect than those from Babylonia, where the "internal" aspect of the symbolic behavior of the king, such as his relationship to the gods and their sanctuaries, is given more space in royal inscriptions, and where references to warfare are pointedly restricted to allusions, much to the chagrin of the modern historian.

From the time of the Assyrian king Arik-dēn-ili (1319–1308 B.C.), if not earlier,[23] Assyrian royal inscriptions evolved a pattern for referring to warlike activities in the form of either reports on specific campaigns or annalistic accounts. The older way of enumerating the king's victories within the phraseology of his titulary (by calling him the victor over this or that enemy or the conqueror of specific cities, or by indicating in geographical terms the ever-extending borders of the empire) continued in use, although it was less in evidence than the annalistic reporting that began with Tiglath-Pileser I (115–1077 B.C.).

The new style seems to express a new attitude toward warfare. War during this era was apparently waged specifically against the enemies of the god Aššur, rather than overtly for booty; it was undertaken to proclaim and demonstrate the glory of the king and his god rather than to extend the empire, although the empire came more and more to rely on conquest as an essential prerequisite for its very existence. A calculated cruelty against the defeated, the sack and destruction of cities and fortresses, and the relocation of entire populations[24] made the threat of war with Assyria so dreaded that diplomatic means often were as successful as military ones in achieving the submission and eventual incorporation of a continuously enlarging circle of neighboring kingdoms.[25] The destruction wrought served as an object lesson for all enemies of Assyria. The deliberate use of terror tactics and the ruthless enforcement of treaties stipulating annual tribute payments were successful only when directed by an energetic king. Whenever the driving force of such a ruler disappeared, the imperial superstructure was likely to disintegrate speedily and the conquered provinces to revert to their former regional and economic separation.

When one reads through the royal inscriptions of that period one can hardly fail to gain the impression that for the high officials who made and applied the policies of the empire, waging war and winning battles was the raison d'être of kingship, the core of the king's relationship to the world outside Assyria, and

the ultimate goal of the organization of the realm and its subjects. Victory is presented as the patent and final proof of divine
support[26] and ultimately of royal legitimacy.[27] It was therefore
the only topic suitable for royal inscriptions and provided the
major incentive for their authors. In reality, trade and commerce were as important for Assyria as the profits derived from
its ceaseless wars,[28] as we know through unmistakable allusions
to be gleaned from many public and private documents. This,
by the way, is in need of an essential qualification: it seems—to
put it bluntly—that the urban centers profited by trade, and the
"military establishment" by war. The tension that such a situation is bound to have created within the economic structure of
the empire will be discussed below.

The victory over the enemy, regardless of what actually happened on the battlefield, constitutes in the royal inscriptions
only one step in an established sequence of *topoi*. With much
ritualistic punctilio, a series of well-defined activities is recorded, beginning, as an Old Testament phrase so concisely states,
"at the time that kings go out to battle" (1 Chronicles 20:1).
Three steps can be discerned: the marching out of the king and
his army; the battle, which necessarily culminates in victory;
and the triumph, including the punishment inflicted on the defeated army, followed by the report of the victory to the king's
god.

In the first place the immediate causes of the war are usually
given, except in instances in which the annual departure of the
military expedition had become so ritualized that the coming of
the appropriate season was reason enough to go to war. Wars are
consistently presented as defensive or punitive actions, undertaken because tribute or homage were denied, or to reconquer
lost territory. Occasionally some episodic embellishments—such
as the arrival of a messenger and the king's reaction to his
news—are included, or prayers and acts of divination are mentioned.[29]

The second phase, the description of the battle, is often provided with an introduction giving the itinerary and recounting
the difficulties surmounted en route. The actual battle, or
rather the particular encounter of the campaign that the author
wishes to present as the decisive engagement, is at times in-

troduced by the mention of royal prayers, of divination performed, and, occasionally, of dreams and even divine apparitions to encourage king and army.[30] The incidents of the battle
itself are more shrouded in an elaborate quasi-hymnic phraseology than is any other phase in the recorded sequence. Military
strategy is hardly ever mentioned.[31] The sole significant event of
the battle is the attack led by the king personally and the ensuing rout of the enemy. During this attack the mysterious and
awe-inspiring phenomenon that the king shares only with the
gods becomes effective—an irresistible, unearthly, terrifying
luminosity that spreads fear, consternation, and panic in the
ranks of the enemy. The light shining forth from the person of
the ruler and the terror emanating from his weapons, which are
those of his god, Aššur, result in the annihilation or surrender
of his adversaries.[32]

An unsuccessful enagement or an indecisive outcome can be
reported only as a victory, if it is mentioned at all. This, however, does not mean that factual events are willfully distorted or
misrepresented—only that in the frame of reference applied
such incidents do not matter. We see here the emotion-charged
symbolic rendering of a historic event and not the recording of a
reality in time and place. The works of the Egyptian artists that
show an oversized Pharaoh overpowering his enemies through
his mere onrush, and the well-known paintings of the last half
millennium in the Western world depicting kings, popes, and
generals rising victoriously over their foes shown dead, wounded, fleeing, or in fetters offer suggestive parallels.

The triumph over the defeated enemy is realized on two separate levels: the quantities of men killed, cities destroyed,
prisoners and booty taken, and the conquest or reconquest of
land, on the one hand; the solemn reporting of the king's success to the god or gods who inspired, encouraged, and assisted
the royal victor, on the other. Such reports form an intrinsic
part of the war ritual and are not meant to be records of facts.
They may and in fact do, of course, contain important historical, religious, social, and political information. We are indeed
often able to cull evidence of that nature from booty lists, from
the disposition of the conquered land and its inhabitants, from
the punishment imposed upon them, and the like. Such in-

formation is, however, only incidental and not recorded for its own sake, just like the geographical facts upon which the itineraries and other data are based. These details are, certainly, quite reliable, inasmuch as the inscriptions were royal pronouncements and their substantive content must have been known as the official version of the reported events, so that facts of common knowledge could not easily be falsified.

At this point I propose to consider the material presented so far as a background study for an inquiry that is to show the *Sitz im Leben* of the presupposed "dialogue" (see above). The data arrayed in the preceding pages have been known in substance to Assyriologists and interested laymen for quite some time, although I readily plead guilty to having rearranged the spotlights occasionally in such a way as to throw into sharper relief those features I deem more relevant than others.

I shall focus now on a new interpretaton of a document long known—a letter of Esarhaddon to the god Aššur. It reveals, in my opinion, opposition within the ruling circles of Assyria to the harsh treatment of the king's enemies, or at least of certain enemies. As a matter of fact, evidence for internal dissent in Mesopotamia should not surprise us per se. Dire predictions are mentioned quite frequently in second-millennium omens referring to impending changes in the mood and the attitudes of the country. Such forecasts provide an illuminating contrast with the importance certain contemporary royal inscriptions place upon having the country unanimous (literally "of one mouth"), indicating contentment with the king's leadership and his administration of the realm.[33] These allusions should be emphasized; they alter, if not invalidate, the picture of a despotic monarchy so easily presupposed for Mesopotamian states. The lavishly used image of the king as shepherd obviously has two applications:[34] the ruler is supposed to make all political decisions for his country, and he is responsible not only for the physical well-being but also the happiness of his wards. Although he likes to present himself in his titulary as beloved and favored by the gods, approval and consent within his own country are essential to him; however, this side of his need is much less "publicized" in the royal inscriptions.

Accident has preserved for us several examples of royal communications addressed to the god Aššur, written in the form of letters at the conclusion of victorious campaigns. Two of them are preserved well enough for a detailed study: one written by Sargon II (721–705 B.C.), the other by his grandson Esarhaddon (680–779 B.C.). The first is almost completely intact and has been the subject of many investigations; the second is available only in two fragmentary tablets that contain less than half of the original text; it has not found the interest it deserves, as will be shown. Of one other such document only a fragment exists, too small to be worthy of investigation.[35]

In a paper entitled "The City of Assur in 714 B.C." I discussed the letter of Sargon at some length as to its content, style, and purpose. The letter—written and most likely also forwarded and read by the king's chief of chancellery—is addressed to the god Aššur and to the lesser gods and goddesses of the city, as well as to the city itself, the ancient capital of the Assyrian empire abandoned by the Assyrian kings after 883 B.C. in favor of capitals that they built for themselves. I contended in this paper that subject matter as well as stylistic peculiarities suggest that the letter of the king to the god Aššur and the city of Assur was written under conditions fundamentally differing from those that determined content and form of the typical historical or royal inscriptions of the period. The key to the understanding of the document is given us when we realize that it is not only styled as a letter but is actually functioning as such; it represents a communication of the king intended to be read to the addressees. It is therefore written in a way purposefully designed to engage the attention of a listening audience and not only to record events—although the letter does this in a splendid way—or to sing the praises of king and god, which task it by no means neglects. In short, the letter is a communication from Sargon to the citizens of Assur; their pantheon headed by the god Aššur is mentioned solely for reasons of courtesy.

To capture the attention of its audience, the Sargon letter introduces topics of general interest not directly related to its main subject matter. In my paper I pointed out two such topics: descriptions of foreign mores, and references to the marvels of nature encountered in the mountain region. Obviously the king's scribe not only knew the literary arts consonant with the ancient traditions of his craft but he was also able to write for an audience of contemporaries whom he wanted to interest. This scribe could certainly write "histories" in the sense of Herodotus' "Introduction."

However, the purpose of Sargon's letter was basically political. It strives to defend an action of the king that approached sacrilege: the sack of Muṣaṣir, the capital of Urartu, and the carrying off of the image of its god. This lightning raid into Urartu and the resulting rape of its capital must have been considered outrageous either because it was contrary to war practices among civilized states or because it was offensive to the citizenry of Assur for some reason (a suggestion is offered below). The very fact that the image of Haldia, the national god of Urartu, was returned a few years later speaks for the bad conscience of Sargon. In Mesopotamia divine images obtained from enemies in this manner were usually kept by the victor, who would only give them back under pressure of dire political or military necessity. For some reason Sargon felt compelled to convince the citizens of Assur of the appropriateness of his behavior, and he charged his chief scribe with the task of writing a letter calculated to impress and appease the citizenry.

Compared with the range of diction, the sophisticated style of presentation, and the amount of military, political, and technological information yielded by the letter of Sargon, the letter of Esarhaddon appears to be much less interesting and to be concerned with an apparently unimportant episode reported in a redundant phraseology—at least to the extent that the text is preserved.[36] For the purpose of the present investigation, however, the letter of Esarhaddon to the citizens of Assur turns out to be a rather important document, relevant to the problem of communication between king and subjects inasmuch as it reveals, unexpectedly, the tensions that beset the relationship between the king and the old capital, Assur.

The nature and background of the incident told in that document are relatively clear in broad outline, although the state of preservation of the tablet places severe limitations on our ability to understand certain essential details. It appears that a considerable number of rather prominent Assyrian civil and military officials had deserted and taken refuge in the neighboring country of Šubriya,[37] along with persons referred to summarily as "murderers and criminals," which in such a context means politically involved Assyrians who fled their home country. For some reason Esarhaddon found it necessary to send an emissary to the king of Šubriya to offer these refugees a written amnesty and a safe-conduct in order to induce them to return to Assyria. At this point the text becomes quite fragmentary, but this much is clear: the king of Šubriya must have refused to comply with Esarhaddon's request, and he must have done this in a form that Esarhaddon considered unpardonably offensive.

After a gap in the tablet the story is taken up at the point when the Assyrian army under Esarhaddon had already reached the borders of Šubriya, and when the unfortunate ruler of that country tried desperately to appease the anger of the Assyrian king. The balance of the document is to a great extent a report on the former's repeated but belated attempts to obtain pardon from Esarhaddon. With unusual explicitness the letter describes each of these attempts and its rejection, quoting in full the arguments offered by both sides. Twice, speeches—or messages, the text is not quite clear on this point[38]—were exchanged at the very walls of the capital of Šubriya, then under siege. There the king of Šubriya performed or had performed symbolic acts with the obvious purpose of demonstrating to Esarhaddon and to his own people, as well as to the entire Assyrian army, his utter humiliation.

One cannot help being reminded by such dramatic scenes, enacted at the wall of the besieged city, of two well-known parallel episodes that took place under identical conditions and are reported respectively in the Old Testament and in Thucydides' History of the Peloponnesian War. It seems to me to be worth a short digression to discuss these curious and heretofore unnoticed parallelisms.[39]

In all three instances the scene takes place before the walls of a city about to be besieged, and the protagonists are the attackers and the defenders, represented by their spokesmen. In every case a dramatic dialogue occurs, with content transcending the accidental political or military situation of the episode, thus elevating the confrontation to an existential level. The dialogue does not consist merely of the challenge to surrender and the refusal by the city's defenders, although this constitutes its situational origin; it presents a serious and well-reasoned discussion on such eternal topics as war and its ideology, and the nature and morals of power, and, emerging from these topics, a discussion of the meaning of history. It is somewhat startling that the same problems are broached and discussed with searching intensity under externally similar circumstances in Hebrew, Assyrian, and Greek texts.

Let me characterize the individual dialogues as succinctly as possible, because the Hebrew and Greek examples have often been investigated and discussed.

The city of the first episode is Jerusalem under Hezekiah, and the besieging army that of Sennacherib (704–681 B.C.), the father of Esarhaddon, led in this instance not by Sennacherib but by high royal officials. These officials parley with the officials of Hezekiah and not with the king himself. They demand the surrender of the city to the superior power of Assyria. Their arguments are partly rational, partly emotional: no help will come from Egypt, and Judah's own god is not going to deliver his besieged city because of their king's sin—Hezekiah had taken away the altars and "high places" where the god was traditionally worshipped, and had restricted the cult exclusively to Jerusalem. They terminate their arguments with the bold assertion that the Lord himself had given the Assyrians the command to destroy the city.

Obviously the reasoning offered in that speech is meant to impress the officials of Hezekiah; it is no less evident—and more important to realize—that its arguments touch upon topics that must have been seriously discussed within the city itself. The religious reform movement that changed an essential cult practice seems to have created much antagonism, and the presence of the Assyrian army was bound to increase apprehension. The failure or success of the siege had apparently come to be considered by the "movement" and its antagonists as expressing divine approval or rejection. The burning actuality of the issues involved was obviously the reason why the Judean officials asked the Assyrians to speak Aramaic so that the soldiers on the wall witnessing the discussion would not understand what was said.

At this point, the tenor and substance of the Assyrian officials' speech change abruptly. Instead of a dialogue in statesmanlike terms between representatives of equal status, the emissary addresses the soldiers directly, realizing that he has an issue that might effectively crack the defense of the city. He harangues the soldiers, asking them to turn against their king because their god cannot and will not save them. They should submit to Assyria and let themselves be settled in another country under similar living conditions. Jerusalem cannot expect to be saved by its god, just as other cities—protected as they were by their own gods—could not escape Assyrian military power. The dialogue at the wall ends abruptly and no reply is given, but the prophet Isaiah, to whom the king turns in despair, promises that the Lord will defend Jerusalem and the Assyrians be made to depart. Whatever the underlying realities of that episode may have been, the story is told to present a divine and miraculous solution of a severe internal religious and political conflict in the garb of the traditional challenge and rejection that mark the beginning of a siege.

The second such incident takes place much later, in 416 B.C., at Melos, an island in the Aegaen Sea. An expeditionary force sent by the Athenians has just landed to compel the inhabitants of Melos to submit to the Athenian empire. Before resorting to arms the Athenians and the representatives of Melos meet for a discussion, reported by Thucydides as a dialogue styled as if written for the stage. This is the only instance in which the great historian uses this form of presentation.

The "Melian Dialogue" begins with a curious exchange of arguments reminiscent of the incident at the walls of Jerusalem. The Athenian envoys are not allowed to speak before the people, but have to negotiate solely with the magistrates and the "chief men"; this, as the Athenians are clever enough to point out immediately, is intended to prevent the people from being influenced by what they call "seductive and unanswerable arguments." Just as was the case before the walls of Jerusalem, the leaders of the besieged city do not want its inhabitants to know about such negotiations.

First the Athenians and the Melians agree to dispense with the orations customary in such a situation; instead the Athenians will make specific statements to which the Melians are to express their reaction. Thus the stage is set for the dialogue. As is well known, the arguments of the Athenians constitute a masterful exposition of the mentality of the aggressor. To a great extent they parallel those of the Assyrian officials: outside help is a vain hope—the Lacedaemonians (like the Egyptians in the Bible) cannot deliver the city; and the power of the aggressor— the Athenian (like the Assyrian) Empire—cannot be withstood. It is vital to the very existence of both empires that no enemy be allowed to withstand their attack.

What makes the Melian dialogue unique and exciting is not that power prevails where no miracles interfere, but that the Athenians have the intellectual audacity to dispense with what they call "fine words," and to speak of "necessity" and "expediency" rather than of what is right. When the Melians raise the question of what is "righteous" or pleasing to the gods, this is summarily dismissed, and Athens' "right" is based squarely on the fact that the rule of the stronger is natural for mankind.

Through all this speaks, of course, the historian Thucydides. He voices his aversion to imperialism and his detached view of power, exactly as the prophet Isaiah, in the scene at the wall of Jerusalem, expounds his belief in the supreme power of the Lord over the realities of history, and—as will be shown presently—exactly as the court poet and scribe of Esarhaddon propounds the "hard-line" imperialistic policy of his king in the face of an opposition that we cannot yet trace. In all three instances, actual events are deliberately utilized to carry a political or ideological message addressed to the listener. Of course, by its very nature the encounter between assailant and defender at the wall readily lends itself to a dramatic exposition of contrasting points of view.

Let us now return to the letter of Esarhaddon and to the symbolic acts performed by the king of Šubriya to demonstrate his submission. The unfortunate king appears atop his capital's wall, dressed like a penitent, with the demeanor of a slave, and, kneeling, offers the submission of his country. He asks for an Assyrian governor and promises to pay tribute and to pay damages for each refugee withheld. He accuses himself of having broken the oath of allegiance and declares himself a sinner pleading for mercy. His lengthy utterance (lines 8 to 24 of column 1) is rather summarily rejected by Esarhaddon (lines 29 to 32). The latter points out that he had summoned the rebel three times without success, which he considers to be a display of wanton disobedience. Nothing can stop the "weapons of Aššur" once they have set out to punish the god's enemies.

A siege wall is built around the capital of Šubriya and the countryside is laid waste in the meantime, a typical Assyrian strategy. Then we read about a second confrontation, during which the two sons of the king of Šubriya bring out an effigy of their father, again clad as a slave, in fetters, and shown working a millstone to demonstrate his complete loss of social status. In the short message of complete surrender relayed by them (lines 24–26 of column 2), the king of Šubriya offers himself, if spared, to serve as an example of how Assyria punishes a crime against it by being exhibited in this very attire to all those who do not fear and obey Esarhaddon. The Assyrian king answers this time in a letter of rather unusual style (lines 28 to 39). It exhibits Esarhaddon's love for proverbial sayings and dwells with much display of synonyms on the impending and inevitable doom of the king of Šubriya, ending with an explicit denial of any pardon.

The fall of Šubriya itself and the punishment meted out its king are lost in another break of the text. The booty taken there was apparently quite sizable and was distributed, as the tablet informs us, to the king's palaces and their officials, and to the citizens of Nineveh, Calah, Kakzu, and Arbela, all the great cities of Assyria. The omission of the ancient capital of Assyria, Assur, in this enumeration is certainly not accidental, and will be discussed presently. A special point is made concerning the fate of the refugees whom the king of Šubriya had given asylum and for whom he had risked his kingdom and his life. Their lives were spared but they were punished by mutilations of all kinds and taken back to Assyria. Here we learn a new and perhaps important fact: not only Assyrians but also natives of Urartu had found refuge in Šubriya, and these, too, as Esarhaddon sees fit to stress, were sent back to their home country. Then the city was rebuilt and given a new, Assyrian name.

At this point one must ask why this seemingly trivial campaign was considered worth recording so explicitly, inasmuch as similar happenings must have occurred time and again during the centuries of relentless attacks by Assyrian kings upon neighbors near and far. And why was the punishment meted out by Esarhaddon to the king of Šubriya made the topic of a letter directed to the god Aššur, that is, in reality to the citizenry of Assur? To take the attack of Sargon against Urartu and the conquest of its sacred city Muṣaṣir as the subject of such a communication seems more logical to us, because the attack constituted an outstanding military achievement and, moreover, an act that seems to have met with criticism.

I propose that the answer—or at least one of the answers—lies in the mood of Esarhaddon's letter, which is much too consistent to be accidental. Its elaborate political rhetoric, the intransigent and ever-repeated formulation of Assyrian imperial policies, the stress placed on the sanctity of the oath of a vassal, the demand for absolute obedience to the king's commands, and the eloquent phraseology of humiliation and submission (as well as the cruelty of the punishment recorded, most likely, in the lost parts of the text) all point in the same direction. The letter must have been meant to counteract a spirit of dissent and criticism against such procedures, and the letter's explicitness was to bring home the message that the king did not intend to soften his attitude in these respects.

The following observations provide some corroboration for my interpretation. It is certainly not accidental that the *casus belli* was furnished by fugitives from Assyria who found refuge in a small neighboring kingdom. It is no less important that Esarhaddon was quite anxious to grant safe-conduct and pardon to the person whom the letter characterizes as robbers, thieves, criminals, and murderers, although he has to concede that there were royal officials, governors, overseers, commanding officers, and law enforcement agents among them. The fact that Šubriya harbored refugees not only from Assyria but also from Urartu might likewise be meaningful, especially because Esarhaddon explicitly reports their repatriation after the fall of Šubriya. The Assyrian king's willingness to return them to Urartu, thus appearing to help the king of Urartu, remains a problem, however.

One gains the impression that we have here indications of widespread opposition to royal policies in Assyria. It looks as if a political or even a social movement—in order to avoid the term "religious"—was at work, possibly fomented or at least supported by Šubriya, affecting individuals of importance in both Assyria and Urartu. The offer of amnesty made by Esarhaddon indicates that he considered these persons essential to Assyria by virtue of either their technical knowledge or certain personal qualities. Yet, one is bound to ask, why did the king of Šubriya find it appropriate to defy Assyria (and perhaps also Urartu) in order to protect these exiles? Were they natives of his own country, did they share his ideological attitudes? Obviously the circumstances underlying the behavior of all persons involved, kings and fugitives, are too complex to be established solely on the basis of the evidence of our broken tablet. Still it adds another piece of evidence for one of those grave internal stresses that repeatedly beset the Assyrian empire and contributed to its instability.

What matters in the present context is that Esarhaddon must have had a clear purpose in mind when sending this letter. The message it conveys is addressed to the citizens of Assur, and clearly constitutes a solemn warning. The citizens were made to hear the terrible fate of a city that dared to refuse obedience to the orders of the king of Assyria. This interpretation fits in with the pointed omission of Assur from the list of major Assyrian cities that, as the letter states, received a share of the booty taken at the sack of the capital of Šubriya. One could suggest that some or even most of the refugees who had fled to Šubriya came from the old free city of Assur.

Šubriya, however, also harbored fugitives from Urartu, whom Esarhaddon repatriated. Of course, their designation as refugees is not necessarily to be taken as accurate. It is quite possible that the Assyrian king removed these natives of Urartu from his newly acquired province, Šubriya, just because they represented or professed the same attitudes as the Assyrian refugees, attitudes that he rejected, although they were acceptable to Urartu. This could possibly mean that dissent in Assur—perhaps also in other cities of the realm that enjoyed the same privileged status —was not solely an urban phenomenon but was in some way connected with political concepts valid both in Urartu and in the kingdom of Šubriya, concepts considered inadmissible within the framework of the empire structure powered and maintained by the Assyrian kings.

If we admit this interpretation as possible, the background of the entire incident would appear illuminated by more rational motives. The fugitives from Assyria had to take refuge in countries where their political or other dissident attitudes were favored; the wrath of Esarhaddon was directed much more against the king Šubriya and what he stood for than against the individual Assyrians, for whom the Assyrian king showed an unwonted interest as expressed in the offer of amnesty and in their relatively "mild" punishment. What was done to the capital of Šubriya Esarhaddon apparently did not dare to do to an Assyrian city. And this might be the reason for the elaborate rhetoric of the letter that so pointedly displays the political thinking of the king and his entourage.

The citizens of the old capital Assur seem to have been always opposed, if not to the imperialistic aspirations of the Assyrians, at least to some of the ways in which they were implemented. Not without reason did the Assyrian kings move out of the capital after Assurnasirpal II (883–859 B.C.) and resort to building their own new royal cities, cities in which no civil opposition could hamper them. The power of the ancient capital, however, was hardly affected: Sargon II (721–705 B.C.) himself had to side with Assur in his fight for the throne and was therefore compelled to reaffirm the city's old privileges. He also felt the need to explain the raid of Muṣaṣir to the citizens of Assur. His grandson Esarhaddon (680–669 B.C.) was apparently obliged to restrict himself to the veiled threats in the letter we are discussing, in the face of what might be termed a growing opposition to his policies, probably actively supported by the free citizens of Assur.

One might now inquire to what extent the Assyrian kings of the first millennium (and earlier, beginning with Tukulti-Ninurta I, 1244–1208 B.C.) were able to achieve their goal of communicating effectively with subjects and enemies (see above).

The terrifying mask that was deliberately turned toward the

outside world was undeniably effective. The Old Testament reflects in numerous poignant passages the fear inspired by Assyrian military might and by the ruthless aggressiveness directed against all those nations that found themselves in the path of Assyrian expansion. No less eloquent is the song of savage triumph in Isaiah 14:4–21 over Assyria's downfall. Whenever the mask had to be dropped by a king whose military power was insufficient—the reasons for such internal reverses in Assyrian history are still far from clear—it was taken up again by a later ruler who was either more energetic or who had a larger and more aggressive army. The motivations for such behavior are probably impossible to discover today. Because of the peculiar power structure of the Assyrian Empire, which will be discussed presently, the self-interest of the kings themselves seems to provide a motive both strong and persistent enough to have led Assyria along the course it actually took.

It is far more difficult to gauge the effectiveness of the king's communication apparatus directed toward his own subjects, to whom are addressed the solemn assurances of royal protection and good shepherdship and the recurring stress on the special relationship between the king and all the deities of the native pantheon. The political structure and the social texture of Assyria under kings with imperial ambitions is hard to trace and to evaluate, not only because of the lack of documents but also because the basic facts underlying the very existence of the state are taken for granted and therefore do not fall within the areas of the scribe's, or rather poet's, interests. The following attempt at a dissection of the Assyrian body politic is admittedly quite crude and tentative, and is not offered here *ut aliquid diceretur* but *ne taceretur.*

There is first, of course, the king and what may well be called his "services," namely, the palace (including the temple), the army, and the fiscal administration of the realm. Here belong also the king's cities, the capital itself, fortresses, and newly conquered cities, all either founded by the king or rebuilt by him, and settled by the officials of his administration, by craftsmen and soldiers whom he had taken prisoner in his campaigns, and the displaced populations moved there from far-off conquered lands. Then come the old privileged cities of the empire —prominent among them Assur, the ancient capital—which obviously represent an alien growth within that body politic, protected as they were by tradition, religion, and their own economic might. Last but by no means least in importance is that very variable power element consisting of the hard-to-trace category of "vassals" or high royal officials (Assyrian *rabûti*), who are mentioned at times as being in conflict with the king. Their influence, based on their extensive domains and other holdings of land and people, seems to have varied with the king's ability to keep his top administrative hierarchy in line and to prevent the governors of larger provinces from more or less overtly assuming royal privileges.

This was the more necessary as a native tradition of long standing was directed against certain essentially royal privileges. There is, first of all, the aversion to the very title "king" (Akk. *šarru*, Sum. *lugal*), avoided by the rulers of the city of Assur and its territory up to the last quarter of the second millennium. Then the right of the governors of certain provinces to act as eponyms, that is, to participate, on the level of the king himself, in the ceremonial casting of lots that determined the *heros eponymos* who was to give his name to the calendar year. However standardized the sequence of such officials became later on, the procedure itself characterizes the king originally as *primus inter pares*. The right of governors to erect stelae (see note 9) in their own realms as well as in Assur could well be connected with this tradition. The inevitable tension between the rulers of the capital city and the high officials of the realm must have necessarily influenced the internal history of Assyria. The empire thus presents the achievement of a series of able and ambitious kings striving through many centuries to create a strong kingdom in the Babylonian tradition, even though there was a native resistance to such a political structure.

There is an undeniable lack of cohesion between the separate parts of the whole just enumerated, although, theoretically at least, the freedom of the cities was protected and guaranteed—by tradition or special treaty—by the king himself, and the *rabûti* were by definition his vassals or servants. Of course the king's political, religious, and military position was preeminent. His entire machinery of communication was geared to bring that very message across to subjects and enemies alike. And, as a matter of fact, the sanction of the gods and the economic fact of the extent of his "Hausmacht," that is, his own cities and provinces with their yield in taxes and soldiers, could well have furnished a reliable basis for a consolidated rule. The king's army, however, proved a liability in time of peace; it had to be fed, housed, trained, provided with the indispensable horses for the chariotry and later cavalry, and, above all, supplied with new recruits. The obvious sources for replacement of men and horses were tribute, booty, and prisoners of war, but this in turn required new raids, new wars or, at least, relentless exaction of stipulated tribute deliveries. Although the palace organization was supposed to produce such necessities as garments, weapons, and tools for the needs of the king, his court, and the entire army, it was obviously much easier and more effective to rely on tribute and spoils of war for these purposes. The increasing size of the empire in any case must have outstripped the industrial facilities of the palace. Thus again, as is the case with military personnel, the continuity of warfare or, at least, the enforced regularity of full annual deliveries of tribute, was essential for the very functioning of the military machine, if not for the existence of the empire as such. The king of Assyria was thus not only the head and symbol of the state but at the same time completely dependent on the functioning of the interlocking institutions of palace, army, and royal land.

With regard to the functioning of the royal "services," we know only a few details about the chain of command, the delegation of royal power, special proclamations made by the king *(amat šarri),* and the correlated feedback of intelligence obtained through special officials and their reports. The archives of the last Assyrian kings have given us about two thousand letters sent to or dispatched by the rulers, some of which are quite revealing in these respects.

The free cities and often the provinces held by certain royal officials were not structurally integrated into the "services" headed by the king, but were linked to the state merely through the person of the ruler, who thus occupied in a very real sense the key position in the overall power structure. In his ability to coordinate these discrete institutions and substructures was bound up the fate of the empire.

We might, then, sum up this cursory survey of the internal communication system centered in the king of Assyria—we know even less about Babylonia—by stating that it was much less effective and stable than the system geared toward the outside world. And yet the latter was based exclusively on the effectiveness of the former. The repeated collapses of the power of Assyria during the history of the empire that extends over roughly seven centuries perhaps then could be interpreted—with that measure of exaggeration pardonable only in a concluding statement—as the result of breakdowns in internal communication.

NOTES

1. Certain more or less technical terms used in this chapter will be defined here. The designation "ancient Near East" is meant to cover the several civilizations that arose during the last four millennia B.C. in the region between the Persian Gulf and the Mediterranean Sea and, bordered by a line extending from Anatolia in Central Asia Minor, to the southwest of the Iranian Plateau and from the western reaches of the Arabian Peninsula to the First Cataract of the Nile. "Mesopotamia" denotes the alluvial plains of southern Iraq and the highlands of Upper Syria within, but also at times beyond, the limits of the two rivers, including the piedmonts of the Zagros chains. At the beginning of the first millennium B.C. Babylonia (with its capital Babylon on the Euphrates) occupied the southern reaches of Mesopotamia from the shores of the Persian Gulf, extending at times into the northwest along the two rivers, while the Assyrian heartland straddled the middle course of the Tigris with such capitals as Assur on the Tigris, Calah (Nimrud), Nineveh, Dūr-Šarrukīn (Khorsabad), and so on, all between the river and the foothills of the Zagros. The range of the empires ruled from these capitals varied considerably, incorporating at times nearly the entire region of the ancient Near East.

For the history of the period, see Fischer Weltgeschichte, *Die altorientalischen Reiche,* vol. 3 (Frankfurt a.M., 1967), sect. 1; R. Labat, "Assyrien und seine Nachbarländer (Babylonien, Elam, Iran) von 1000–617 v. Ch., Das neubabylonische Reich bis 539 v. Chr.," pp. 9–111; J. M. Munn-Rankin, "Assyrian Military Power 1300–1200 B.C.," in *The Cambridge Ancient History,* vol. 2, rev. ed., chap. 25 (Cambridge, 1967) (and its extensive review by J. A. Brinkman in *Bibliotheca Orientalis);* and J. A. Brinkman, *A Political History of Post-Kassite Babylonia, 1158–722 B.C.* (Rome, 1968).

2. There are very few books dealing with this topic, and they are all more or less obsolete by now. E. Klauber, *Assyrisches Beamtentum nach den Briefen*

*aus der Sargonidenzeit* (Leipzig, 1910); E. Forrer, *Die Previnzeinteilung des assyrischen Reiches* (Leipzig, 1920). See also the article "Assyrische Zeit" by D. Opitz under "Beamter" in *Reallexikon der Assyriologie,* vol. 1 (Berlin and Leipzig, 1928), pp.457b–466a.

The dictionaries currently published contain much material bearing on the designations of officials, but as a rule such presentations are concerned with semantic and diachronic considerations, whereas meaningful studies of this topic must give prime consideration to the synchronic and functional aspects and the relationships between the spheres of power of individual officials.

3. The raw material is presented in R. F. Harper, *Assyrians and Babylonian Letters* (London and Chicago, 1892–1914, 14 vols.); and C. H. W. Johns, *Assyrian Deeds and Documents* (Cambridge, 1898–1923, 4 vols.); also *American Journal of Semitic Languages and Literatures* 42 (1926): 170–275, to which may be added R. C. Thompson, *The Reports of the Magicians and Astrologers of Nineveh and Babylon* (London, 1900; 2 vols.) and also C. H. W. Johns, *An Assyrian Doomsday Book, or Liber Censualis of the District Around Harran in the Seventh Century* B.C. (Leipzig, 1901). It is not feasible to cite here even a representative selection of the scholarly work (books and articles) done in the last seventy years on the material contained in these and related sources. I restrict myself to mentioning three recent books: J. N. Postgate, *Neo-Assyrian Royal Grants and Decrees* (Rome, 1969); G. Van Driel, *The Cult of Aššur* (Assen, 1969); and M. Dietrich, *Die Aramäer Südbabyloniens in der Sargonidenzeit (700-648)* (Kevelaer, 1970).

4. No study dealing principally with the concept of Mesopotamian kingship more recent than R. Labat, *Le caractère religieux de la royauté assyro-babylonienne* (Paris, 1939), can be listed here. For the material collected by M.-J. Seux, see below, note 14.

5. See B. Hrouda, *Die Kulturgeschichte des assyrischen Flachbildes* (Bonn, 1965).

6. Related to this problem, which a few decades ago was quite popular and still is as far from any solution as ever, I will cite only Franz Hančar, "Das urartäische Lebensbaummotive, Eine neue Bedeutungstradition," *Iranica Antigua* 6 (1966): 92–108.

7. The Old Testament, which quite often gives us a much more direct insight into the realities of historical settings than does the extremely formalized Mesopotamian literature, tells a revealing episode concerning the prestige value of royal treasuries. From Isaiah 39:2 we learn that Hezekiah, upon receiving the messengers of the king of Babylon (Merodach-baladan), who brought a letter and presents, "showed them the house of his precious things, the silver, and the gold, and the spices, and the precious ointment, and all the house of his armor, and all that was found in his treasures." For a similar display of riches, see the visit of the Queen of Sheba (especially 1 Kings 10:3

ff.), which is reported on a more naive level. See also S. Morenz, *Prestige Wirtschaft im Alten Ägypten* (Bayerische Akademie der Wissenschaften, Phil.-Hist. Klasse, Sitz. Ber. 1969, Heft 4), pp. 26 ff.

8. As to the fame—which reached to the Mediterranean Sea (Ugarit)—of the palace of the king of Mari, see the letter given in G. Dossin, "Le royaume d'Alep au XVIII^e siècle avant notre ère d'après les 'Archives de Mari,' " *Bulletin de l'Académie royale de Belgique, Classe des lettres* (1952) pp. 63–69. For first-millennium evidence illustrating the westward spread of the fame of Mesopotamian capitals, we have a verse (Fragment No. 7) of the mid-sixth-century elegiac poet Phocylides, "A prudent little city riding over a rock is better than stupid Nineveh that has been destroyed," and the passages about the wondrous size of Nineveh, in Jonah 3:3, and of Babylon, in Aristotle, *Politics* 3,3. One also could mention E. Edel, "Ein neuer Beleg für 'Nineveh' in hieroglyphischer Schreibung," *Orientalia Nova Series (Or NS)* 37 (1968): 417–420.

The use of Greek mercenaries all over the ancient Near East beginning with the mid-third of the first millennium, was of course, a contributing factor in that spread of information. For descriptions of Greek and Carian mercenaries in the ancient Near East, see M. M. Austin, *Greece and Egypt in the Archaic Age* (Proceedings of the Cambridge Philological Society, Supplement No. 2, 1960), pp. 14 ff. and n. 5 on p. 15.

9. In spite of the book by H. Genge, *Stelen neuassyrischer Könige, Eine Dokumentation und philologische Vorarbeit zur Würdigung einer archäologischen Denkmalgattung,* Teil 1: Die Keilinschriften (Dissertation, Universität zu Freiburg im Breisgau 1965), much work remains to be done on these monuments. From Mesopotamia proper two groups of royal stelae require special mention: first, those made by the Assyrian provincial governors (cf. E. Unger, *Die Stele des Bel-Harran-beli-ussur, ein Denkmal der Zeit Salmanassars IV* [Konstantinopel, 1916]; and Stephanie Page, "A Stela of Adad-Nirari III and Nergal-Ereš from Tell al Rimah," *Iraq* 30 [1968]: 139–153) and by a Babylonian official of that rank (F. H. Weissbach, *Babylonische Miscellen* [Leipzig, 1903], No. 4, Das Relief und die Inschriften des Šamaš-rêš-uṣur); and second, the stelae found in Assur, erected in two long rows, which were, as a rule, provided with quite short inscriptions arranged in a very characteristic way, and lacking figural representations. For the latter, cf. W. Andrae, *Die Stelenreihen in Assur* (Leipzig, 1913). It might also be mentioned that *entu*-priestesses (typically of royal descent) erected stelae when installed in their high priestly office; see Brinkman, *Political History,* p. 112 and n. 532. All persons who had the privilege of erecting such monuments, the governors, the princesses of *entu*-rank and, possibly, the eponyms who might have been responsible for the stelae in the two rows of Assur, exercised a royal privilege.

10. The history of this literary genre remains to be written. Many new texts have been published since S. Mowinckel, "Die vorderasiatischen Königs- und Fürsteninschriften, eine stilistische Studie," in *Eucharisterion H. Gunkel* (Göttingen, 1923), pp. 278–322; and W. Baumgartner, "Zur Form der assyrischen Königsinschriften," *Orientalistische Literaturzeitung (OLZ)* 27 (1924): 313–317. The strands of local traditions and regional developments are so complex and interwoven that it will require a major effort to investigate this part of the Mesopotamian literary tradition.

11. See R. S. Ellis, *Foundation Deposits in Ancient Mesopotamia* (New Haven, 1968), pp. 94–124.

12. For Sumerian and bilingual texts of this type, see Brinkman, *Political History*, pp. 5 and 7, also n. 55; bilingual texts from the reign of Šamaš-šuma-ukīn (668–648 B.C.) are also extant.

13. The role and importance of genealogies often added to the royal names seems to depend on the length of the rule of the dynasty. Thus Samsuiluna, the son of Hammurapi, speaks with pride of his five royal grandfathers (*VAS* 1 33 iii 10), and the Assyrian kings of the first millennium love to name at least two generations of their royal ancestors; they also stress their descent from Adasi, a very early king of Assur. See in this context, F. R. Kraus, *Könige, die in Zelten wohnen: Betrachtungen über den Kern der assyrischen Königsliste* (Amsterdam, 1965); and J. J. Finkelstein, "The Genealogy of the Hammurapi Dynasty," *Journal of Cuneiform Studies (JCS)* 20 (1966): 95–118; also W. G. Lambert, "Another Look at Hammurabi's Ancestors," *JCS* 22 (1968): 1–2.

14. The study of this rich source of historical and political information still has not progressed much beyond the alphabetic listing of the words and phrases. See M.-J. Seux, *Épithetes royales akkadiennes et sumériennes* (Paris, 1967).

15. To praise famous kings of the past, Mesopotamian poets used the characteristic form of inscriptions on stelae for creating a literary genre called by H. G. Güterbock "*narû*-literature." See his presentation, "Die historische Tradition bei Babyloniern und Hethitern," *Zeitschrift fur Assyriologie (ZA)* 42 (1934): 19–66, also *ZA* 44 (1938): 49–149.

16. A well-known quotation is preserved in a letter addressed to the king that the (unnamed) writer ends as follows: "as it says in a song of Akkadi (i.e., Babylonia): 'All people listen to you, my shepherd, on account of your sweet voice' " (R. F. Harper, *Assyrian and Babylonian Letters* 435 r. 10 ff.).

17. See W. H. Ph. Römer, *Sumerische Königshymnen der Isin Zeit* (Leiden, 1965), and W. W. Hallo, "Royal Hymns and Mesopotamian Unity," *JCS* 17 (1963): 112–118.

18. An interesting and as yet little-known literary genre seems to have flourished at the courts of the victorious kings toward the end of the second millennium: epic poems using and elaborating upon contemporary events,

specifically royal victories. Apart from a longer text of which copies were found in Assur as well as in Nineveh, published by E. Ebeling, *Bruchstücke eines politischen Propagandagedichtes aus einer assyrischen Kanzlei* (Leipzig, 1938) and see W. G. Lambert, "Three Unpublished Fragments of the Tukulti-Ninurta Epic," *Archiv für Orientforschung (AfO)* 18 (1957-58): 38-51, there are other fragments, see E. F. Weidner, "Assyrische Epen über die Kassiten-Kämpfe," *AfO* 20 (1963): 113-115.

19. The future ruler is asked to replace the document after having anointed it in the foundation of such a building. The practice of anointing sacred objects is quite atypical in Mesopotamia.

20. The text was published by C. J. Gadd, "The Harran Inscriptions of Nabonidus," *AnSt.* 8 (1958): 35-92, with corrections by W. L. Moran, "Notes on the New Nabonidus Inscriptions," *Or NS* 28 (1959): 130-140. See also the article by W. Röllig cited in note 21, below.

21. For the historic situation, see W. Röllig, "Erwägungen zu neuen Stelen König Nabonids," *ZA* 56 (1964): 218-260; also H. Tadmor, "The Inscriptions of Nabunaid: Historical Arrangement," *Assyriological Studies* 16(1965): 351-364.

22. This characteristic feature of Assyrian royal ceremonials has not received the attention it deserves. We have a rather elaborate description of a royal meal in a text published by K. F. Müller, *Das assyrische Ritual, Teil I, Texte zum assyrischen Königsritual* (Leipzig, 1937), especially pp. 59-67, and a number of references exist in royal inscriptions and letters to banquets given by the king for his officials at special occasions (called *qarītu, tašīltu*). Of the banquet given by Aššurnasirpal II (883-859 B.C.) for the inhabitants of the new royal city of Calah and many other guests, we even have a list of the foods served; see D. J. Wiseman, "A New Stela of Aššur-naṣir-pal II," *Iraq* 14 (1957): 24-44.

The role of the king's meal in Babylonia proper remains to be investigated. For Mari customs that may well reflect those of Babylon, although this should not be taken simply for granted and allowances made for the difference in cultural background, see Madelaine Burke, "Une réception royale au palais de Mari," *Revue d'assyriologie et d'archéologie orientale* 53 (1959): 139-146. For a suggestion concerning the royal meal in the Babylonia of the late first millennium, cf. my *Ancient Mesopotamia* (Chicago, 1964), pp. 192 ff.

The Assyrian kings invited not only officials and subjects to such commensal ceremonies, but also the deities of the pantheon of the city of Assur. Such an occasion (called a *tākultu*) is likewise described in some detail in a document published by R. Frankena, *Tākultu de sacrale maaltijd in het assyrische ritueel* (Leiden, 1954), with additions by the same author in *Bibliotheca Orientalis* 18 (1961): 199-207. It might be noted that this custom has a curious parallel in the Roman practice of inviting Jupiter (and other important gods of the pantheon) to a banquet (called *Iovis epulum*) in the Senate. See

G. Wissowa, *Religion und Kultur der Römer,* 2d ed. (München, 1912), pp. 127 and 421 ff.

23. Very few royal inscriptions are preserved of the period that precedes the quite fragmentary document (*BRM* 4:49).

24. The twentieth-century attitude toward warfare (as well as toward trade, see my *Ancient Mesopotamia,* p. 356, n. 6 to chap. 2) precludes any adequate understanding of earlier attitudes. Two articles, published as papers of the twelfth *Rencontre Assyriologique Internationale,* represent the traditional approach to a topic that may well require a new one: W. von Soden, "Die Assyrier und der Krieg," *Iraq* 25 (1963): 131–144; and H. W. F. Saggs, "Assyrian Warfare in the Sargonid Period," ibid.: 145–154. See also, E. Cassin, "Techniche della guerra e strutture sociali in Mesopotamia nella seconda metà del II millennio," *Rivista Storica Italiana* 77 (1965): 445–455.

The "economic" aspect of Mesopotamian warfare, by which I mean the distribution of booty by the king, must not be neglected. There are apparently several practices to be distinguished: distribution among the troops participating in the victory (well-known from the Assurbanipal passage about the distribution of the camels captured in the war against the Arabs), among cities, and among the temples and palaces. Typically, the booty distributed consisted of prisoners of war, exceptionally of domestic animals; metal, treasure, and manufactured objects (whenever they could be recovered) were apparently not distributed.

The relocation of entire populations as a pacification measure is apparently Sumerian in origin, as will be shown by M. Civil in the forthcoming publication of an inscription of Šu-Sin, king of Ur (2037–2029 B.C.).

25. For the first and crucial phase of Assyrian imperialism, see J. M. Munn-Runkin, *Assyrian Military Power, 1300–1200* B.C. (CH² XXV).

Treaties between Assyrian kings and western rulers at this period are quite rare, attested only for Aššur-nirari VI (754–745 B.C.), (see E. F. Weidner, *AfO* 8 [1932–33]: 17–34 and Esarhaddon (680–669 B.C.), (see R. Borger, *Asarhaddon* [Graz, 1956], pp. 107–109), while references to such arrangements (called *adû*) with vassal states are frequently mentioned in first-millennium Assyrian inscriptions. For an interesting example of a long and well-preserved *adû*, see D. J. Wiseman, *The Vassal-Treaties of Esarhaddon* (London, 1958).

26. Such an incident as the death of Sargon II (721–705 B.C.) in battle represents therefore a crucial problem in terms of royal propaganda, not to say royal "theology." On this we have some information in a few fragmentary tablets, of which one was published by H. Tadmor, *Eretz Israel* 5 (1958): 150–163 (in Hebrew), and others that will be dealt with by the same author. It is of interest to point out that the scribe who wrote the "Bull-inscription" for Sargon II (published by H. Winckler, *Die Keilinschriften Sargons nach den Papierabklatschen und Originalen* [Leipzig, 1889], pp. 44 ff.) seems to have

given some thought to the successes of Merodach-Baladan (II), king of Babylon (721–710 B.C.) in view of the "godlessness" of his rule. He writers in line 31: "Merodach-Baladan, king of Chalde who exercised kingship over Babylon against the will of the gods and (nevertheless) was victorious."

27. Sargon II himself avoids mentioning his father in nearly all his inscriptions. This has been shown by E. Unger, *Sargon II von Assyrien der Sohn Tiglathpilesers III* (Istanbul Asariatika Müzeleri Nesriyati IX; Istanbul, 1933), pp. 16–20.

28. In my article "Essay on Overland Trade in the First Millennium B.C.," *JCS* 21 (1967, published in 1969): 236–254, especially pp. 246 ff., I had occasion to point out one such instance. More material can be readily assembled to show the continuity of Assyrian interest in trade from the Old to the Neo-Assyrian period.

29. The acceptance of divination was not invalidated by a rarely attested but persistent strain of skepticism, as I have pointed out in my *Ancient Mesopotamia*, pp. 226 ff.

30. For incidents in which dreams and "visions" play the main role, see my book, *The Interpretation of Dreams in the Ancient Near East* (Philadelphia, 1956), pp. 187 and 199 ff.

31. Quick movements of troops and unexpected attacks by smaller contingents in unorthodox strategic situations account for a number of spectacular Assyrian military successes. Attention here should be called to the ceremonial way in which battles between armies were arranged among the mountain peoples as described in Sargon II's letter, *Textes cunéiformes du Louvre* 3 111. This brings out the fact that Assyrian warlike behavior was contrary to the mores of the period also in this respect.

32. For a publication on this topic, see H. Cassin, *La splendeur divine: Introduction a l'étude de la mentalité mésopotamienne* (Paris and La Haye, 1968).

33. The pertinent terminology deserves an investigation based on such key words as ṭēm māti, milik māti, mitgurtu, etc. As a sample of the euphemistic terminology used, consider the term *tēšītu*, which, derived from *ešû*, "to be in confusion," actually means "civil war," exactly as our *war*, French *guerre*, etc., comes via late Latin *gwerre*, from German *Wirren* (see O. Brunner, *Land und Herrschaft* [Vienna, 1970], pp. 38 ff.). As a matter of fact, there is no word for *war* in Akkadian, just as there is no word for *peace* in the postmedieval sense of this "Western" term.

34. Compare lately Ilse Seibert, *Hirt-Herde-König, Zur Herausbildung des Königstums in Mesopotamia* (Berlin DDR, 1969).

35. For such a letter written by Shalmaneser IV (782–772 B.C.), see A. Ungnad, "Der Gottesbrief als Form assyrischer Kriegsberichterstattung," *OLZ* 21 (1918): 72–75. To complete the picture of this very special aspect of communication between king and god, one should mention a letter addressed

by a deity, most likely Aššur, to the king of Assyria; see E. F. Weidner, "Ein Gottesbrief über den fünften Feldzug Šamši-Adads V," *AfO* 9 (1933–34): 101–104. For a quite atypical prayer of Assurbanipal to the god Aššur that the subscript describes as "message *(šipirti)* of Assurbanipal to Aššur residing in (the temple) Ehursaggalkurkurra in order to grant his prayer, overthrow his enemy, kill [his adversaries(?). . . ], see *Cuneiform Texts from Babylonian Tablets* 35 44 ff. and Theo Bauer, *Das Inschriftenwerk Assurbanipals,* vol. 2 (Leipzig, 1933), pp. 83 ff.

36. The text is preserved on two fragments, both from the second tablet of a two-tablet draft. The first fragment (*K.* 7599) contains fourteen lines of the top (upper right corner) of the second of a two-tablet sequence, and the second fragment (*K.* 2852 + *K.* 9662) gives us another second tablet of such a sequence. The latter is written in two columns with the end of the obverse and the beginning of the reverse broken off and considerable gaps in cols. i and ii. The original size of tablet *K.* 2852 + can only be guessed at—probably fifty to sixty lines per column, hence four hundred to four hundred fifty for the entire composition (on two tablets), comparable with the four hundred thirty of the letters of Sargon. The text itself is obviously an incomplete draft destined to be transferred eventually to a final one-tablet version. For copies, see Theo Bauer, "Ein Erstbericht Asarhaddons," *ZA* 40 (1931): 255–259.

37. For the location of Šubria, see I. J. Gelb, *Hurrians and Subarians* (Chicago, 1944), pp. 47 ff. and 82 ff.

38. The first message is introduced by *kīam išpuramma,* "thus he sent me word" (Fragment 2 i 8), and extends from line 8 to line 24. It begins with *umma* "as follows," which is repeated twice to begin sentences in lines 12 and 20, but the content of the message does not follow the style pattern of a contemporary letter, rather it seems to render the wording of a spoken message. The answer of Esarhaddon begins with *kīam aqbīšuma umma* "thus I said to him," and was therefore not given in writing. The second message of the king of Šubria is conveyed by his two sons (*kīam iqbûnim [ma umma],* col. ii 24); the answer of Esarhaddon is introduced by *kīam ašpuršu [umma]* (ibid. 1. 28), and most likely represents a spoken message. It would best fit the style of the episode and its situational logic if all these messages were pronounced by the messengers of the two adversaries in the presence of both armies.

39. As an outsider I will content myself with referring the reader to the most recent books dealing with these events, although I have taken ⁓ognizance of much of the earlier literature on the topics: B. S. Childs, *Isaiah and the Assyrian Crisis* (Naperville, Ill., 1967); K. von Fritz, *Die griechische Geschichtsschreibung Band I; Von den Anfängen bis Thukydides* (Berlin, 1967), pp. 715–723; and A. G. Woodhead, *Thucydides on the Nature of Power* (Martin Classical Lectures, vol. 24: Cambridge, Mass., 1970).

# 5

## EGYPTIAN CIVILIZATION

John A. Wilson

Few would quarrel with the generalizations that the ancient Egyptian saw his wider universe in terms of his own immediate environment and experience and that the state had been entrusted to the divine pharaoh so that he might control and nurture it as a herdsman tends his cattle. Now, however, we are to search for the values which the ancient Egyptian attached to life. If our thesis is valid, that man was an essential part of a consubstantial universe and that man therefore applied the norm of the human to the non-human, we shall need to know what norm he applied to himself. Here we come to the real problem of speculative thought: What am I here for? Here it is not possible to compound out one nice generalization to cover two thousand years of history. And such generalizations as may be made will not find as wide an acceptance among other scholars, because we inevitably use our own personal philosophies to evaluate the philosophies of others. Our conclusions may be fairly accurate on the nature of the evidence, but on the value of the evidence we shall hang our personal estimates.

What were the purposes of life? In order to secure a visible picture of the possible answers, we might make a visit to Egypt and go down into two structures which should be comparable.[1] Each is the tomb of an Egyptian vizier, that highest official of the land, the first deputy under the king. Near the Step

Pyramid at Saqqara we enter the tomb of a vizier of the Old Kingdom, a man who lived about 2400 B.C. The rooms are crammed and packed with vigorous scenes of life and the lust for more life. The vizier is shown spearing fish, while his servants bring a bellowing hippopotamus to bay. The vizier supervises the roping and butchering of cattle, the ploughing and harvesting of the fields, the carpenters and metal-workers in their shops, and the building of boats for his funeral services. He presides over the vigorous punishment of tax delinquents, and he watches the games of children. Even when he is in repose, as when he listens to his wife playing the harp, he gives the impression of high potential, of being ready to spring into action. Non-spiritual and active life is the full account of this tomb. This is his monument for eternity; this is how he wants to be remembered; this is the good life which he wishes to extend into eternity.

We leave this tomb and walk a few hundred yards to the tomb of a vizier of the Late Period, a man who lived about 600 B.C. Eighteen hundred years have brought a quietude, a pious calm. Here we see no exuberant noble, no bellowing hippopotamus, no tumbling children. The walls are covered with ritual and magical texts. There are a few posed and dull pictures of the vizier frozen in hieratic attitude before the god of the dead. There are a few vignettes to illustrate the texts with scenes of the underworld and the genii who live there. The life of this world is completely lacking; the funeral services and the world of the dead are the only concerns of this man. His monument for eternity concentrates on the next world instead of this life. His good consists in magic, ritual, and the favor of his god.

That is our problem. At one pole there is an emphasis on life, on action, and on the material world; at the other pole, an emphasis on death, on repose, and on religion. Clearly our discussion must bridge the gap and must be historical in order to give the change from one stage to the other. We shall see two major periods of Egyptian thought, the aggressive and optimistic earlier times and the submissive and hopeful later times, with a long period of transition between. It was like a hurricane, with strong winds blowing to the east, then a dead center of uncertain balance, and then the winds blowing just as strongly to the

west. The earlier winds to the east were radical and individualistic; the later winds to the west were conservative and
communal. But, as we said before, it depends upon who
analyses the trends; another man has seen the earlier trend as a
compliance to group forms and the later as an interest in personal well-being. Inevitably the discussion involves the religious, political, and social prejudices of the analyst.

## THE OLD AND MIDDLE KINGDOMS

The emergence of Egypt into the light of history seems to be a
very sudden phenomenon, symbolized in the abrupt appearance of stone architecture of highest technical perfection.
Dr. Breasted once dramatized this brilliant flowering in these
words:

> In the Cairo Museum you may stand in the presence of the
> massive granite sarcophagus which once contained the body of
> Khufu-onekh, the architect who built the Great Pyramid of
> Gizeh. . . . Let us in imagination follow this early architect to the
> desert plateau behind the village of Gizeh. It was then bare desert
> surface, dotted only with the ruins of a few small tombs of remote
> ancestors. The oldest stone masonry construction at that time had
> been erected by Khufu-onekh's great-grandfather. Only three
> generations of architects in stone preceded him. . . . There prob-
> ably were not many stone masons, nor many men who understood
> the technique of building in stone as Khufu-onekh took his first
> walk on the bare Gizeh Plateau, and staked out the ground plan of
> the Great Pyramid. Conceive, then, the dauntless courage of the
> man who told his surveyors to lay out the square base 755 feet on
> each side! . . . [He knew that it would] take nearly two and a half
> million blocks each weighing two and one-half tons to cover this
> square of thirteen acres with a mountain of masonry 481 feet
> high. . . . The Great Pyramid of Gizeh is thus a document in the
> history of the human mind. It clearly discloses man's sense of
> sovereign power in his triumph over material forces. For himself
> and for his sovereign the pharaoh's engineer was achieving the con-
> quest of immortality by sheer command of material forces.[2]

This vivid picture illustrates the sudden surge of vigor and the
zest for action and accomplishment which characterized the Old

Kingdom of Egypt. From the same general period come some of Egypt's highest intellectual achievements, such as the philosophy of the Memphite Theology and the scientific attitude expressed in the Edwin Smith Surgical Papyrus. This raises questions about the antecedents of these daring and forceful people. They hardly seem visible in the modest products of pre-dynastic Egypt. And yet we cannot see that this is a reason for assuming that these achievements must therefore have been introduced by conquering invaders. That simply takes an unknown and thrusts it out into unknown realms. Sometimes the spirit of man soars in dizzy flight beyond the plodding pace which cultural evolution would see as normal, and there is good reason to believe that this whole surge of power was quite local, enjoying only the stimulus of similar wonderful developments known from Mesopotamia. The reasons for this sudden spurt of power are not clear. It was a revolution, the abrupt flowering of a slow development under the influence of some stimulation which remains obscure. One may argue that the stability of state and society which permitted the beginnings of the Egyptian dynasties laid new demands on individual men. They were organized more effectively through the specification of function. One man was charged to be an architect, another to be a seal-cutter, another to be a record clerk. These functions had previously been avocations in a more simple society. Now they were important enough to be vocations and called forth the accumulation of abilities which had been latent but growing in the earlier periods. For centuries the Egyptians had been gathering slow strength within the Nile Valley until their day arrived, and they sprang upward with a suddenness which is miraculous to us. The Egyptians also had a sense of something very wonderful. They found themselves capable of great accomplishment. Material success was their first goal of the good life.

We can feel the relish with which a noble of the Old Kingdom relates his advances in station: "(The King) made me Count and Overseer of Upper Egypt. . . . Never before had this office been conferred upon any servant, but I acted for him as Overseer of Upper Egypt to satisfaction. . . . I filled an office which made my reputation in this Upper Egypt. Never before had the like been done in this Upper Egypt."[3] The attitude was a frontier spirit of visible accomplishments, of the first success in a new line. This was a youthful and self-reliant arrogance, because there had been no setbacks. Man was enough in himself. The gods? Yes, they were off there somewhere, and they had made this good world, to be sure; but the world was good because man was himself master, without need for the constant support of the gods.

Man's world was not completely devoid of god, because the rules under which the world operated had been laid down by god, or the gods, and any man who transgressed those rules was accountable to god. Even in this early time, the word "god" is used in the singular in referring to his system, his desires for man, or his judging violations of the system. It is not quite clear in the Old Kingdom what god is involved in this singular use. Sometimes it is certainly the king, sometimes it is certainly the creator or supreme god, who had laid down the broad, general rules for the game of life. But sometimes there appear to be unification and personification of correct and efficient behavior summed up in the will of "the god" who is not as august or as distant as the king or the creator-god. If the hypothesis of consubstantiality is valid, this unification and universality of deity is a problem which we have already faced. It was not monotheism; it was monophysitism applied to deity.

Where the principles of proper behavior concern table etiquette or administrative procedure, it is likely to be "the *ka*" that has a governing interest as "the god."[4] The *ka* was the detached part of the human personality which protected and sustained the individual. As such it could well be the divine force within man which governed his proper and successful activity. The frequency of Old Kingdom names like "Rē-is-my-*ka*" and "Ptah-is-my-*ka*" suggests that, through the principles of consubstantiality and free substitution, the *ka* was thought to be a man's god, sometimes godship in general, and sometimes a specific god, like a name saint or a patron saint.

We are here referring to the Old Kingdom, when the gods of the pantheon were more remote from common man, although not necessarily from his intermediating *ka*. That situation changed later. In the latter part of the Empire an Egyptian expressed a close personal relation to a specifically name god, who was his protector and controller. That direct relation to a personal god may be visible before the Empire in the "town god," the equivalent of the local saint. In the early Eighteenth Dynasty, for example, a wish for a noble runs: "Mayest thou spend eternity in gladness of heart and in the favor of the god who is in thee,"[5] for which a variant runs: "in the favor of thy town god."[6] However, *(a)* these concepts are rarely clear cut or firmly identifiable; and *(b)* in certain contexts "the god" is the king or a specific god of universal control, like the creator-god.

The independent self-reliance of the Egyptian of the Pyramid Age is indicated by the physical decentralization of the tombs of the nobles of the period. At first the high officials were buried in close juxtaposition to the god-king whom they had served; through his certainty of eternity their hopes for continued existence would be realized. Very soon, however, they exhibited sufficient self-confidence to move away from the king and seek their own eternity in their own home districts. Within the general framework of divine rule they were independently successful in this life; they had assurance that this success was applicable to the future. Under their own momentum they could carry on into future life, join their *ka*'s over there, and become *akh*'s, "effective beings," for a vigorous eternal life. Their own accumulation of worldly success guaranteed, by legal contract and by precedent, a conquest over death. In that sense there was a decided democratic—or, more precisely, individualistic—trend throughout the Old Kingdom.

"Individualism" is a better term than "democracy" for this spirit, because it applied chiefly to personal rule of conduct and not to political government. A sense of personal adequacy may lead to decentralization of government and thus bring a limited sense of democratic ambition. But we do not see in ancient Egypt that political democracy which we would indicate for Mesopotamia. The dogma of the divinity of the Egyptian pharaoh was a cohesive force too strong to be fractured by individualistic forces.

No servile dependency upon a god was necessary in this early period for the greatest goods of life: success in this world and continued life in the next. Man was generally accountable to the king, to the creator-god, and to his own *ka*, but he was not humbly suppliant to a named god of the pantheon, and he was not formally responsible to Osiris, the later ruler of the dead. His wealth and position in this life gave him confidence that he was fully effective now and later, and—as the lively tomb scenes show—he wanted a next world just as gay and exciting and successful as this world.

We want to emphasize just as strongly as we can that the Egyptians of these times were a gay and lusty people. They relished life to the full, and they loved life too fully to surrender its hearty savor. That is why they denied the fact of death and carried over into the next world the same vigorous and merry life which they enjoyed here.

We possess for this early period a book of etiquette for an official, "the utterances of beautiful speech . . . as the instruction of the ignorant in knowledge and in the rules of good speech, which are of advantage to him who will listen and of disadvantage to him who may abuse them."[7] This contains the gospel of the "go-getter," the bald rules for a young man who is on the make. It has been summarized as follows:

> The ideal picture is that of a correct man, who wisely avoids impulse and fits himself by word and deed into the administrative and social systems. An assured career as an official awaits him. No moral concepts like good and bad come into discussion here; rather the standard lies in the characteristics of the knowing man and the ignorant man, perhaps best given in the words "smart" and "stupid." Smartness can be learned. . . . So rules are provided for a man's career. If he pays attention, he will be smart; he will find the right way in all life's situations through this smartness; and through his correct attitude he will bring his career to success.[8]

This book contains precepts for getting on with superiors, equals, and inferiors. Thus one who comes into competition with a speaker who is better at argument is advised to "cut down on bad talk by not opposing him"; one who meets an equal is to show his superiority by silence so that the attending officials may be impressed; and an inferior opponent is to be treated with indulgent disregard, for thus "thou shalt smite him with the punishment of the (truly) great."[9] He who sits at the table of a superior is urged to maintain a sedate countenance, to take only what he is offered, and to laugh only when his host laughs; thus the great one will be pleased and will accept whatever one may do.[10] An official who must listen to the pleas of clients should listen patiently and without rancor, because "a petitioner wants attention to what he says (even) more than the accomplishing of that for which he came."[11] It is seemly to found a household, to love and cherish a wife, because "she is a field of advantage to her master"; and one must be careful to hold her from gaining mastery in the household.[12] There is a practical, materialistic wisdom in the injunction: "The wise man rises early in the morning to establish himself,"[13] or in the advice to be generous to one's hangers-on, because no one can foresee the exigencies of the future, and it is wise to build up the insurance of a body of grateful supporters.[14]

It would be unfair to leave the impression that the entire text is opportunistic and materialistic. There is one passage which urges on the official that honesty is the best policy, but even this arises out of experience rather than principle. "If thou art a leader who directs the affairs of a multitude, seek for thyself every benevolent opportunity until thy conduct shall be without fault. Justice is of advantage, and its utility lasts. It has not been disturbed since the time of its maker, whereas there is punishment for him who passes by its laws. . . . It is (true that) evil may gain wealth, but the (real) strength of justice is that it lasts, for a man can say: 'It was the property of my father (before me).' "[15] Here lay the values of that age: a transmittable property and the experience that a man "got on" in the world if he was smart enough to follow certain common-sense principles. A success visible to all men was the great good. These were the supreme values of the Old Kingdom, and they continued in value throughout Egyptian history.

It was easy to worship success as long as success conferred its benefits on all men, as long as well-tended pyramids and tombs were the visible symbols of the lasting power of worldly success. But that happy state did not last. The Old Kingdom of Egypt collapsed into turmoil heels over head. The old values in position and property were swept away in an anarchy of force and seizure. The Egyptians ascribed their woes in part to a dissolution of their own character, but also to the violent presence of Asiatics in the Egyptian Delta. However, it is doubtful whether the Asiatics came in as an invading and suppressing horde; it is much more likely that an inner breakdown of rule in Egypt permitted small groups of Asiatics to come in and settle but that these insignificant penetrations were result rather than cause of the breakdown.

The real source of the collapse was a progressive decentralization. Rulers other than the dynastic pharaohs felt their individual capacity for independence and set up competitive government until the strain fractured Egypt into a lot of warring factions. This was part of the individualistic, self-seeking trend which had been gaining momentum throughout the Old Kingdom. Now, with the single, central control dissipated, there was anarchy in the competing grabs for power, which went right down to the lowest strata of society. Egypt had been moving away from autarchy in the direction of separatism based on individual capacity to act, but the nation was unprepared to take advantage of the breakdown of autarchy by the immediate institution of a system of rule on a broader basis. In the confusion there was no rule.

We have many expressions of the bewilderment of the Egyptian at the overturn of his old world. Instead of the prized stability and security, the land whirled around dizzily like a potter's wheel. The former rich and powerful were now in rags and hunger, whereas the former poor had property and power. We of the present day read with a wry amusement the protests that there was a thoroughgoing cheapening of the high court of justice and a disregard for the statutes of the law, that poor men were now able to wear fine linen, that servant girls were insolent to their mistresses, and the laundryman arbitrarily refused to carry his bundle. The visible continuity of life through the care and preservation of the tombs of the great was abruptly fractured; tombs were plundered, including the pyramids of the pharaohs, and the treasured dead lay exposed upon the desert plateau. The crisp frontier lines which had given geometric order to Egypt were erased; the red desert pushed its way into the fertile black soil, the provincial states were "hacked to pieces," and foreigners from abroad had entered Egypt. When the provinces refused to pay taxes, the central control of agriculture broke down, and no one would plough even when the Nile was in beneficial flood. The old profitable commerce with Phoenicia and Nubia had disappeared, so that the appearance of a few miserable traders from the desert offering herbs and birds was now a remarkable phenomenon.[16]

Egypt may have been moving steadily toward individualism and decentralized power, but it had still had the single keystone of the kingship. When this had been removed, the whole arch had fallen. "Behold, it has come to a point where the land is robbed of the kingship by a few irresponsible men. . . . Behold, the secret of the land, unknowable in its extent, has been exposed, and the (royal) residence has been overthrown within an hour."[17] We have seen in the earlier wisdom literature that the norm for the good life had been the successful official. Now the officials were in hunger and want. "Behold, no office at all is in its (proper) place, like a stampeded herd without its herdsman."[18] "Changes have taken place, so that it is no (longer) like last year, but one year is more burdensome than another."[19] The old values of a successful individual career, which showed to the world property, administrative position, and a tomb provisioned unto eternity had been swept away. What values could be found to replace them?

In the upset, some found only the negative answers of despair or scepticism. Some turned to suicide, and we read that the crocodiles of the river were sated because men went to them of their own accord.[20] One of the finest documents of Egyptian literature records the debate of a would-be suicide with his own *ka,* or soul. Life was too much for him, and he proposed to seek his death by fire. It was symptomatic of the times that the soul, which should have exhibited the consistent and directing attitude toward death, was the wavering member to the debate and could find no satisfactory answer to the man's melancholy. It first was inclined to accompany him no matter what his end might be; then it shifted and tried to hold him back from violence. Still it had no constructive arguments for realizing a good life on this earth and could only urge the man to forget his cares and seek sensual enjoyment. Finally, after the man had contrasted the miseries of this life with the sober pleasures of the next world, the soul agreed to make a home with him no matter what his fate might be. There was no answer except that this world was so bad that the next must be a release.

This document carries a philosophy of pessimism worth our study. The man presented his argument to his soul in four poems of uniform tristichs contrasting life with the release of death. The first poem urged that the man's name would be in bad odor if he followed the advice of his soul to give himself up to pleasure. He had his own standards still, and he would not permit his good name to be damaged.

Behold, my name will reek through thee
　More than the stench of fishermen,
　More than the stagnant swamps where they have fished.

Behold, my name will reek through thee
　More than the stench of bird-droppings,
　On summer days when the sky is hot.[21]

In six more stanzas the man presented the evil odor of his reputation if he followed the cowardly advice of his soul. Then in a second poem he turned to a lament over the breakdown of standards in the society of his day. Three of the stanzas in this poem run as follows:

To whom can I speak today?
　(One's) fellows are evil;
　The friends of today do not love.

(To whom can I speak today?)
　The gentle man has perished,
　But the violent man has access to everybody.

To whom can I speak today?
　No one remembers (the lessons of) the past;
　No one at this time does (good in return) for doing (good).[22]

From these evils of life the man turned to contemplate death as a blessed release.

Death (stands) before me today
　(Like) the recovery of a sick man,
　Like going out-doors (again) after being confined.

Death (stands) before me today
  Like the fragrance of myrrh,
  Like sitting under a shade on a breezy day.

Death (stands) before me today
  As a man longs to see his house,
  After he has spent many years held in captivity.[23]

Finally, the man urged the high privileges of the dead, who had the power to oppose evil and who had free access to the gods.

Nay, but he who is yonder
  Shall be a living god,
  Inflicting punishment upon the doer of evil.

Nay, but he who is yonder
  Shall be a man of wisdom,
  Not stopped from appealing to Rē when he speaks.[24]

This man was ahead of his day in rejecting the active values of this life in favor of the passive values of future blessedness. As we shall see, such submissiveness characterized a period a thousand years later. This was a tentative move in the pessimism of the period—that one should seek death as a release instead of emphasizing the continuance of the life as known here.

In this debate the man's soul at one point urged upon him the futility of taking life seriously and cried out: "Pursue a holiday (mood) and forget care!"[25] This theme of non-moral hedonism occurs again in another text of the period, where the argument is: The old standards of property and position have broken down; we have no certainty about future happiness, so let us grasp what happiness we can in this world. The past shows only that this life is brief and transitory—but transitory to an unknowable future.

"Generations pass away and others go on since the time of the ancestors. . . . They that build buildings, their places are no more. What has been done with them?

"I have heard the words of (the past sages) Imhotep and Hardedef, with whose sayings men speak so much—(but) what are their places (now)? Their walls are crumbled, their places are non-existent, as if they had never been.

"No one returns from (over) there, so that he might tell us their disposition, that he might tell us how they are, that he might still our hearts until we (too) shall go to the place where they have gone."[26]

Since that wisdom which was so highly prized in the earlier age had not guaranteed for the wise a visible survival in well-kept tombs, and since it was impossible to tell how the dead fared in the other world, what was left for us here? Nothing, except to snatch at the sensual pleasures of the day.

"Make holiday and weary not therein! Behold, it is not given to a man to take his property with him. Behold, no one who goes (over there) can come back again!"[27]

Thus the first two reactions to the defeat of a successful and optimistic world were despair and cynicism. But they were not the only reactions. Egypt had still a spiritual and mental vigor which refused to deny the essential worth of individual man. He was still an object of value to himself. If his old standards of value in physical and social success had proved to be of ephemeral nature, he began to grope for other standards which might have a more lasting nature. Dimly and uncertainly he became aware of the great truth that the things which are seen are temporal but that the things which are unseen may be of the very stuff of eternity. And eternal life was still his great goal.

Now the words which we have just used and the words which we are going to use prejudice the discussion in terms of modern ethical judgments. That is deliberate. We consider the Egyptian Middle Kingdom to have reached moral heights in its search for the good life. This is a personal prejudice, in which we follow Professor Breasted, although our own analysis of the factors differs slightly from his. A counterview has been urged by others. They point out that the Egyptians of the earliest fully visible period, the Old Kingdom, reached heights which were never surpassed later—in technical ability (as in the Great Pyramid and in sculpture), in science (as in a remarkable surgical papyrus and in the institution of a calendar), and in philosophy (as in the Memphite Theology). This view would deny any assumption of progress beyond those points. Indeed, it would protest at the claim of progress at all and would insist that we see change only and that this change is within the limits of a culture very largely static from the beginnings. The more it changes, the more it exhibits itself to be the same. There is undoubted truth to this. The materialism which we stressed as characterizing the Old Kingdom was still an important factor in this new period. The social-moral advances which we shall claim for this new period were already indicated in the Old Kingdom (increasing democratization, concept of justice, etc.). This view would also protest at the imposing of our consciously self-righteous standards of moral judgment upon the ancient Egyptians. Have we the right to translate *ma'at* as "justice," "truth," or "righteousness," instead of "order," "regularity," or "conformity"? Have we the right to hail increasing democracy of viewpoint in ancient Egypt as "an advance," which was "good"?

We insist that one has the right to make moral judgments and to talk in terms of progress or decline. These are subjective matters, not strictly scientific. But any generation has the right—nay, even the duty—of presenting the evidence objectively and then of giving a subjective valuation to the evidence. We know that objectivity cannot be completely divorced from subjectivity, but a scholar can attempt to show just what the evidence is and just where his personal criticism comes in. In the period which we are going to examine now, we would agree that a hard practical materialism still continued strong, that the anti-ethical force of magic played a large role, and that the moral impulses which we shall stress had been present earlier and continued later. But we are satisfied that there were changes of emphasis in this period and that these shifts of emphasis look like advances to a modern Westerner.

The two great changes which we can see are a decline in the emphasis on position and material property as being the good of this life, with a corresponding shift of emphasis to proper social action as being the good, and a continuation of the individualistic trend of the Old Kingdom to the point where all good things were potentially open to all men. These two trends are ultimately the same: if the good in life is within the quest of any man, rich or poor, then power and wealth are not ultimates, but right relations to other men are strongly recommended.

Three quotations will give us the new emphasis. A struggle of the previous period had been to build and maintain a tomb, an imposing funerary monument lasting to eternity. The Middle Kingdom continued the physical establishment but introduced a new note: "Do not be evil, (for) kindliness is good. Make thy monument to be lasting through the love of thee. . . . (Then) the god will be praised by way of rewarding (thee)."[28] Here the monument which lasted came through other men's grateful reaction to benevolence. A second passage gives clearly the statement that the god delighted more in good character than in elaborate offerings; the poor man could thus have as good a title to god's interest as the rich. "More acceptable is the character of a man just of heart than the ox of the evildoer."[29]

The most remarkable passage of the period is one which occurs only here and—as far as we know—was not repeated later. It stands isolated, and yet it was not foreign to the highest aspiration of the times; it is a reason for prizing the spirit of this age beyond those which preceded or followed. It stated simply that all men were created equal in opportunity. In these words the supreme god gave the purposes of creation.

> I relate to you the four good deeds which my own heart
>    did for me . . . in order to silence evil. I did four good
>    deeds within the portal of the horizon.
>
> I made the four winds that every man might breathe
>    thereof like his fellow in his time. That is (the first)
>    of the deeds.
>
> I made the great flood waters that the poor man might
>    have rights in them like the great man. That is (the
>    second) of the deeds.
>
> I made every man like his fellow. I did not command
>    that they might do evil, (but) it was their hearts that
>    violated what I had said. That is (the third) of the
>    deeds.
>
> I made that their hearts should cease from forgetting the
>    west, in order that divine offerings might be made to
>    the gods of the provinces. That is (the fourth) of the
>    deeds.[30]

The first two passages of this text state that wind and water are equally available to all men of any degree. In a land where prosperity depended upon securing a proper share in the inundation waters and where water control must have been a powerful factor in setting one man in domination over another, an assurance of equal access to water meant basic equality of opportunity. The statement, "I made every man like his fellow," that is, "all men are created equal," was coupled with the god's insistence that he had not intended that they do evil, but that their own hearts had devised wrong. This juxtaposition of equality and wrongdoing says that social inequality is no part of god's plan, but man must bear that responsibility alone. This is a clear assertion that the ideal society would be fully equalitarian. Certainly, ancient Egypt never came near that ideal, except as we moderns do in the pious postponement of full equality to the future life. But it was still a valid sublimation of the highest aspirations of the time. Wistfully it says: "All men should be equal; the creator-god did not make them different."

The final good deed of the supreme god was to call men's attention to the west, the region of eternal life, and to urge upon them pious service of their local gods in order to attain the west. These were important changes of this period, the democratization of the next world and closer attachment to the gods. All men might now enjoy eternity in the same terms as had the king alone in the previous period. We do not know just what kind of continued existence the ordinary man of the Old Kingdom had been conceded. He was to continue with his *ka,* and he was to become an *akh,* an "effective" personality. The pharaoh of the Old Kingdom, however, was to become a god in the realm of the gods. Now that future of the pharaoh was open also to commoners. They were to become gods as he had become a god. Whereas only the dead king had become Osiris in the earlier period, now every deceased Egyptian became the god Osiris. Further, his becoming an Osiris and attaining eternal blessedness was put in relation to an afterlife judgment in which his character was assessed by a tribunal of gods.

Pictorially, this judgment of character was already a weighing of justice. In the future this was to become a judgment before

Osiris as the god of the dead, with the man's heart placed in the scales against the symbol for justice. Those elements were already present in the Middle Kingdom, Osiris as god of the dead and a judgment of the deceased in terms of justice, but they were not yet put together into a single consistent scene. Instead there was still a carry-over of the older order in which the supreme god, the sun-god, was the judge. There was democratization of the next world and Osirianization, but the entry to the eternal life was not wholly within the control of Osiris. We have reference to "that balance of Rē, in which he weighs justice";[31] and the deceased was assured that "thy fault will be expelled and thy guilt will be wiped out by the weighings of the scales on the day of reckoning characters and it will be permitted that thou join with those who are in the (sun)-barque,"[32] and that "there is not a god who will contest a case with thee, and there is not a goddess who will contest a case with thee, on the day of reckoning characters."[33] It was a tribunal of the gods, presumably under the presidency of the supreme god, to whom the deceased must make his report. "He shall reach the council of the gods, the place where the gods are, his *ka* being with him and his offerings being in front of him, and his voice shall be justified in the reckoning up of the surplus: though he may tell his faults, they will be expelled for him by all that he may say."[34] All this shows that there was a judging of the dead in terms of weighing the excess or deficiency of his good against his bad and that a favorable outcome of the weighing was a prerequisite to eternal blessedness. This weighing was a calculation of *maᶜat*, justice.

We have met *maᶜat* before. Basically, it is probably a physical term, "levelness, evenness, straightness, correctness," in a sense of regularity or order. From that it can be used in the metaphorical sense of "uprightness, righteousness, truth, justice." There was a real emphasis on this *maᶜat* in the Middle Kingdom in the sense of social justice, righteous dealing with one's fellow-men. That was the main theme of the story of the eloquent peasant, which comes from this period. Throughout his pleadings the peasant demanded from the high official simple justice as a moral right. Just dealing had its minimum in the conscientious carrying-out of responsibilities. "Cheating diminishes justice, (but) filling (to) good (measure)—neither too low nor overflowing—is justice.''[35] But justice was not simply legal commerce but was the seeking-out of good in relation to need: ferrying across the river the poor man who could not pay and doing good in advance of any known return. And a theme of the Middle Kingdom was social responsibility: the king was a herdsman who cherished his herds; the official had a positive duty toward the widow and the orphan; in short, every man had rights which imposed responsibilities upon other men. Even the sculptures of the time sought to bring out this emphasis on conscientious character and moved from a delineation of majesty and force to a portrayal of concern for obligations. Such careworn portraits of the pharaohs of the Middle Kingdom are well known.

All this has been eloquently urged by Breasted, and we need not document it in further detail. If one seeks to state his argument differently, it would simply be in a difference of definition of ''conscience'' or of ''character'' and a failure to give the story the simple and straightforward emphasis which he achieves. In the previous period there had been a demand for justice in this world and for the next,[36] and there had certainly been character in the forceful personalities who had built a great state. But here in the Middle Kingdom greater emphasis in some lines and lesser emphasis in others permitted an age of real social conscientiousness, in which the psychological and moral basis was the belief that every man is the care-worthy creation of god.

Up to this time, the Middle Kingdom, the trend in ancient Egypt had been centrifugal and atomistic: individual man had been the valued unit. First his individual abilities had been marked out for value, then his individual rights had been recognized. Egypt had been moving somewhat blindly along the road from theocratic autarchy toward democracy of a kind. The spirit was still an encouragement to fill this life with activity, and each man was given an opportunity to realize the bustling, practical, important life here. Consequently, they continued to love this life and defy death. The definition of success may have shifted slightly, but it was still true that a successful life carried over and repeated itself happily in the next world.

Consequently, the tombs, which were the bridges between two existences, continued to stress the abundance of life. The scenes of hunting, shipbuilding, and merrymaking were as vigorous as ever. Only an increased attention to scenes of the burial and a few representations of religious feasts suggest to us a new sobriety. It was still the case that the greatest good lay in the good life here and not an escape from this life to a different future life or a resigned submission to the gods. Individual man still enjoyed himself.

## THE EMPIRE AND LATER

We come now to the cause of the great transition in the Egyptian ethos. We come to the second political revolution, the Second Intermediate Period, lying between the Middle Kingdom and the Empire, between the eighteenth and sixteenth centuries B.C. Again the central government broke down; again there was competition for the rule by a number of small princelings. Probably a weakening of personal force and character in the central government unleashed the self-seeking individualism of local princes. But the great difference this time was the forceful and conquering incursion of foreigners. Asiatic princes, whom we call the Hyksos, established themselves in armed camps within Egypt and dominated the land with a firmness which was repressive to the still flowering Egyptian spirit. For the first time Egypt as a whole suffered a setback in that philosophy which said: We are the center and summit of the world; we are free to permit expansion of spirit to the individuals of our community. Now, for the first time, that community was aware of a serious threat from the outside world. Now, for the first time, that community had to draw together into a unity in order to meet and avert that threat.

Egypt did unite and throw out the "vagabonds," who had dared to rule the land "in ignorance of Rē."[37] But the threat was not met by driving them out of Egypt; it was necessary to pursue them into Asia and to keep on pounding them so that they might never again threaten the land of the Nile. There was built up a psychosis for security, a neuropathic awareness of danger similar to that which has characterized Europe in modern times. That common sentiment for security welded the

Egyptians into a self-conscious nation. It has been pointed out
that only in this period of liberation do the Egyptians speak of
their troops as "our army," instead of crediting the forces to the
king.[38] There was a patriotic fevor which put the country's interests before the interests of the individual.

Such a unified spirit was born of the sense of common peril.
The common desire for security need not have survived after the
Egyptian Empire extended the military frontier of Egypt well
into Asia and thus removed the peril from the immediate frontier. That should have given the external security which would
relieve the need for communal solidarity. However, it was a rest-
less age, and there were perils on the distant horizon which
could be invoked to hold the community together, since unity
was to the advantage of certain central powers. When the threat
of the Hyksos had subsided, the threat of the Hittites appeared
and endangered the Asiatic Empire of Egypt. Thereafter came
the Sea Peoples, the Libyans, and the Assyrians. A fear
psychosis, once engendered, remained present. And there were
forces in Egypt which kept alive this fear psychosis in order to
maintain the unified purpose of Egypt.

The course of empire is justified in terms of a crusade, the acceptance of a "manifest destiny" to extend one culture in
domination over another. Whether empire is basically economic or political, it must have a religious, spiritual and intellectual
vindication. In Egypt that sanction came through the god-king
who stood for the state, and it came through the other national
gods who participated in the removal of a threat to Egypt by
supporting the extension of the frontiers of the land. The national gods commissioned the pharaoh to march forth and
widen the land; indeed, they marched with him at the head of
the divisions of his army. The extension of the nation was their
own extension.

In how far the gods invested in Egyptian victory in a strictly
economic sense is uncertain. We do not know whether the temples acted as bankers to finance foreign conquest and empire.
They probably did so when they became wealthy and had extensive assets, because empire constantly increased their wealth. At
any rate, they did invest in Egyptian victory in a spiritual-
propagandistic sense, in giving a divine blessing and a divine

guarantee to empire. For this they received an economic return. This is rather explicitly stated in the monuments; the pharaoh erected buildings, established and endowed feasts, and presented land and serfs to the god who had given the victory. The previously modest temples in Egypt grew in physical size, in personnel, in land, and in total property, until they became the dominating factor in Egyptian political, social, and economic life. It has been estimated that, after the Empire had had three hundred years of active life, the Egyptian temples owned one out of every five inhabitants of the nation and owned almost one-third of the cultivable land.[39] Naturally the temples were interested in perpetuating and tightening a system which was so greatly to their advantage. In order to secure their advantage, they had to insist on the group solidarity of the people for the national interest which had made the temples rich and strong. Ultimately they swallowed up not only the people but also the pharaoh.

Now look at the implications of this history in terms of the individual human. The previous tendency from the Old Kingdom up to the Empire had been centrifugal, atomistic, individualistic: the good life was to be found in the fullest expression of each person. Now the tendency was centripetal, nationalistic, communal: the good life was to be found in the group interest, and the individual was called upon to conform to the asserted needs of the group. Any wavering and tentative approach to an individualistic expression was cancelled out; any sense that the Egyptian community was a thing of value in itself was a cardinal doctrine.

A revolution of this spiritual and intellectual kind is not established by a congress which draws up a manifesto of change; it takes place so gradually as to be perceptible only over the centuries. Even a rebellion against the change, such as characterized the Amarna Revolution, was perhaps as much an unsystematized protest against the power mechanics of the change as a protest against the principles of the change. For centuries the Egyptian texts went on reiterating the older formulas, while the Egyptian tombs repeated the older lusty enjoyment of the manifold opportunities of this life. It is just as if Americans should turn gradually to a socialistic government and a rationalistic ethics while repeating the slogans of democracy and Calvinistic Protestantism; they would be unaware of the change for a long time after it had been effective.

Thus there were centuries of empire before the force of the change became visible in Egyptian literature and art. Only gradually were the old stereotypes replaced by new formulas. When the revolution was complete, we find that the goals of life had shifted from a vigorous, individualistic existence in this world, which would be rewarded by repetition in the next world, to a conforming and formalistic life in this world. As far as the individual Egyptian was concerned, his horizon of opportunity had become circumscribed; he was advised to submit because he was presented with an escape from this world's limitations by a promise of better things in the next world. Those better things were now less of his own agency and more the gift of the gods. There was thus not only a shift from the individual to the group but also a shift from an enjoyment of this world to the promise of the next world. That will explain the contrast between those two tombs which we outlined previously, where the earlier monument presented gay and vigorous depictions of field, shop, and market place, whereas the later monument concentrated on the ritual approach to afterlife.

Let us try to document this thesis from the literature and particularly from the wisdom literature. One's first impression is that the late instructions in correct behavior are just like the earlier instructions; in much the same Polonius language they tell the young official how to get on in his profession. Effective practical etiquette—at table, in the street, or in the law court—is the continuing theme. But gradually one is aware of differences. The reasons given for the injunctions have changed. Back in the older days a man had been advised to take good care of his wife, because "she is a field of advantage to her master." Now the man was told to remember the patience and devotion of his own mother and to treat his wife in accordance with his loving gratitude to his mother.[40] Whereas the older texts had enjoined patience and impartiality upon the official when dealing with poor clients, now he was to take positive action on behalf of the poor. "If thou findest a large debt against a poor man, make it into three parts, throw out two, and let one remain.'' Why should one take such an uneconomical action? The answer is that he cannot live with his own conscience unless he does. ''Thou wilt find it like the ways of life. Thou wilt lie and sleep (soundly). In the morning thou wilt find it (again) like good news. It is better to be praised as one whom people love than (to have) riches in the storehouse. Better is bread when the heart is happy than riches under (the weight of) troubles.''[41] This was a change from the older texts; position and property were not so important now as the sense of right relations with other men. A man belonged to society, not to himself alone.

The key word for the developed spirit of this period was ''silence,'' which we may render also with ''calm, passivity, tranquillity, submission, humility, meekness.'' This ''silence'' is linked with weakness or poverty in such contexts as ''Thou art Amon, the lord of the silent, who comes at the voice of the poor,''[42] and ''Amon, the protector of the silent, the rescuer of the poor.''[43] Because of that equation these characteristic expressions of humility have been designated as a religion of the poor.[44] It is true that meekness has always been a virtue recommended to the dispossessed, but our essential point is that every Egyptian of this period was dispossessed in terms of a right to self-expression; he had been cut off from the encouragement to voluntary self-development and was now constrained to a deterministic submission to the needs of the group. In proof of this assertion that the spirit of humility was not confined to the poverty-stricken, we would point out that a very high-placed official was at pains to describe himself as ''truly silent''[45] and that even the high priest of Amon might insist that he was ''properly and truly silent.''[46] In the spirit of the times the active and successful official found it necessary to emphasize his conformance to the national pattern of obedience.

As the objectionable contrast to the silent man, the texts offered the ''heated'' or ''passionate'' man, who was ''loud of voice.'' In terms reminiscent of the First Psalm, the contrast is drawn (also Jer. 27, 5–8):

> As for the passionate man in the temple, he is like a tree growing in the open. Suddenly (comes) its loss of foliage, and its end is

reached in the shipyards; (or) it is floated far from its place, and a flame is its burial shroud.

(But) the truly silent man holds himself apart. He is like a tree growing in a garden. It flourishes; it doubles its fruit; it (stands) before its lord. Its fruit is sweet; its shade is pleasant; and its end is reached in the garden.[47]

Now silence had often been enjoined in the earlier period, but it had been a topical silence: do not speak or resist unless you are smart enough.[48] Indeed, it had been emphasized that eloquence might be found in the lowest grades of society and that it should be encouraged there when found.[49] Now, in this changed spirit, the continuing injunction was silence alone. In dealings with superiors or in the government offices, it was submissive silence which would give you ultimate success.[50] This was related to the designs of the god, "who loves the silent man more than him who is loud of voice,"[51] and whose protection would confound one's opponents.[52] "The dwelling of god, its abomination is clamor. Pray thou with a loving heart, all words of which are hidden. Then he will supply all thy needs; he will hear what thou sayest and will accept thy offering."[53] The well of wisdom is not free for all who wish to drink therefrom; "it is sealed to him who can discover his mouth, (but) it is open to him who is silent."[54]

The new deterministic philosophy was rather definitely stated in terms of the will of god, placed over against man's helplessness. "The god is (always) in his success, (whereas) man is (always) in his failure." This statement of man's essential need of god was continued in an early expression of *Homo proposuit sed Deus disponit:* "One thing are the words which men say, (but) another thing is what the god does."[55] Gone was the earlier reliance upon man himself within the general pattern of the world order; now he specifically and always failed unless he conformed to that which the god directed.

Thus this period came to have a strong sense of fate or external determining force. One may say that this had not been entirely absent in earlier times in some magical force or other. The *ka* had been a semi-detached part of personality which had affected a man's career. But now the god Fate and the goddess

Fortune stood outside the personality in remote but firm control. One could not pursue one's own interest without regard to these regulators on behalf of the gods. "Cast not thy heart in pursuit of riches, (for) there is no ignoring Fate and Fortune. Place not thy heart upon externals, (for) every man belongs to his (appointed) hour."[56] Man was charged not to search too deeply into the affairs of the gods, because the deities of destiny were his controlling limitation. "Do not (try to) find for thyself the powers of the god himself, (as if) there were no Fate and Fortune."[57]

It is possible to emphasize the role of fate exclusively in this period. There was still some voluntarism within the determined scheme of things. The young man was warned against a fatalism which prevents his searching for wisdom: "Beware lest thou say: 'Every man is according to his (own) nature. Ignorant and wise are of one piece (only). Fate and Fortune are carved on the nature (of a man) in the writings of the god himself. Every man passes his lifetime in an hour.' (Nay), teaching is good, and there is no wearying in it, and a son should answer with the utterances of his father. I cause thee to know what is right in thy (own) heart, so that thou do what is correct in thy sight."[58]

If success lay only with god and man was doomed to failure, we should expect to find expressions of the sense of personal shortcoming, ultimately stated as a consciousness of sin. Such expressions do appear at this time. To be sure, the nature of sin is not always clear, and it may involve only ritual irregularity rather than ethical wrongdoing. But we can insist upon an acknowledgment of error when a man says: "Though the servant is normally (disposed) to do evil, yet the Lord is normally (disposed) to be merciful."[59] In another case it was the specific crime of perjury that led a man to say of his god: "He caused men and gods to look on me as if I were a man that does abominations against his Lord. Righteous was Ptah, Lord of Truth, toward me, when he disciplined me."[60]

What is left for men when they are denied voluntary self-expression and are put into a rigid framework of conformance? Well, there was an escape from the limitations of this world in the promise of the next world, and it is possible to see an intensification of the desire for escape in Egypt, leading ultimately to monasticism and apocalyptic promise. But the promise of something distant is an uncertain thing in the day-by-day activity of a person; he wants something warmer right now. Thus the sense of personal wrongdoing called forth its antidote in a sense of divine nearness and mercy. The individual was swallowed up in a great impersonal system and felt lost. Very well, there was a god who was interested in him, who punished his transgressions, and who then healed him with mercy. Again and again the texts call upon a god or goddess to come in compassion to suffering man. "I cried out to my Mistress; (then) I found that she came to me with sweet airs. She showed mercy to me, (after) she had made me behold her hand. She turned about again to me in mercy; she caused me to forget the sickness that had been [upon] me. Yea, the peak of the West is merciful if one cries out to her."[61]

Thus, in compensation for the loss of individual voluntarism and the imposition of group determinism, there emerged a warmer personal relation between an Egyptian and his own god, and the period of the late Empire has been characterized by Breasted as the "age of personal piety." There was love and trust on the part of the worshipper; there was justice and mercy on the part of the god. In the revolution of Egyptian feeling, the good life lay no longer in cultivation of personality but in the surrender of personality to some greater force, with the recompense for surrender a security offered by that greater force.

It would take too long to argue the full development of this changed psychology of a people. The substitution of god's mercy for the encouragement of the individual spirit did not prove satisfactory. The joy went out of life. The Egyptian was called upon to rest content in humility and faith. Humility he did show. But faith is "assurance of things hoped for, a conviction of things not seen." He might and did still hope for better things in the world to come, but his conviction of things not seen was limited by the experience of things seen. He saw that his own personal god, who showed him mercy in his weakness, was also little and weak like himself. He saw that the great gods of Egypt, the national gods, were rich, distant, powerful and demanding. The priesthood of Egypt was still growing in power and control and demanded blind conformance to the system that gave the temples power and control. Individual man was caught in a straitjacket of rites and obligations, and his only comfort lay in soothing words and distant promises. He turned from a lusty appreciation of this life to means of escape from this life.

In the desire for escape from the present, the Egyptian turned not only to the afterworld future but also to the happy past. The Egyptians had always had a strong sense of the achievement, power, and dignity of earlier times. Constantly they invoked the good models of their past, whether the mythological times of the rule of the gods or the hazily historical times of the earliest kings.

Earlier we quoted an old bit of agnosticism, in which the writer said in effect: The former sages Imhotep and Hardedef are much quoted, but they were unable to protect their tombs or their physical property; what did their wisdom avail them, after all? In later times the expression about these ancestors was different: Their wisdom did avail them, for they had left a memorial worthy of reverence. "As for those learned scribes since the times which came after the gods . . . their names have come to be lasting forever, although they (themselves) have gone . . . They did not make for themselves pyramids of metal, with tombstones of iron. They were not able to leave heirs in children . . . But they made heirs for themselves in writings and in the wisdom literature which they left . . . Books of wisdom were their pyramids, and the pen was their child . . . Is there (anyone) here like Hardedef? Is there another like Imhotep? . . . They are gone and forgotten, but their names through (their) writings cause them to be remembered."[62]

This strong sense of a rich and proud past comforted an age which felt uncertainty in its present. Ultimately this nostalgia for earlier times grew into archaism, with a rather blind and ignorant copying of the forms of a distant past. Personal piety was not able to make the concept of a single fatherly god adequate. The search for the spiritual support of religion went instead over to a recourse to oracles and over to strict ritualistic observance, until religion became as empty as Herodotus saw it. Within the confinement of a system of national conformance even the god-king became a mere puppet of the laws, as Diodorus saw him. Egypt had not had the opportunity or the capacity to work out the inter-relation of man and god in terms satisfactory to both. To put it in a different context, Egypt had not had the opportunity or the capacity to work out the inter-relation of the individual and the community in terms of benefit to both. There the Hebrews went further, but there we are still struggling at the present day.

## THE INTELLECTUAL ROLE OF EGYPT

Did ancient Egypt contribute any significant element to the continuing philosophy, ethics, or world-consciousness of later times? No, not directly in fields which one may specify, as in the case of Babylonian science, Hebrew theology, or Greek or Chinese rationalism. One might critically say that the weight of ancient Egypt was not consonant with her size, that her intellectual and spiritual contributions were not up to her length of years and her physical memorial, and that she herself was unable to realize on her promising beginnings in many fields.

But the very size of Egypt left its mark on her neighbors. The Hebrews and the Greeks were deeply conscious of a past power and a past stability of this colossal neighbor and had a vague and uncritical appreciation of "all the wisdom of the Egyptians." This high appreciation gave them two factors for the stimulation of their own thinking: a sense of high value outside their own times and places, so that their philosophies had the benefit of some historical setting, and a curiosity about the more obvious Egyptian achievements: accomplishments in art and architecture, governmental organization, and a sense of geometric order. If in gratifying that curiosity about Egypt they came across intellectual or ethical advances made by Egypt, these could only be valid to them in terms of their own experiences, because they were already ancient history in Egypt. The Hebrews or Greeks had to rediscover for themselves any elements which had already lost persuasive force in Egypt. That culture had reached her intellectual and spiritual heights too early to develop any philosophy which could be transmitted in cultural heritage to the ages. Like Moses, she had had a distant glimpse of the Promised Land, but it was left to others to cross the Jordan and begin the Conquest.

NOTES

1. The two tombs are those of Mereruka, a vizier of the Sixth Dynasty, and of Bekenrenef, a vizier of the Twenty-sixth Dynasty. References in Porter and Moss, *Topographical Bibliography,* vol. 3: *Memphis,* pp. 140 ff., 171 ff.

2. "Dedication Address," 5 December 1931.

3. Urk. I, 105–106.

4. Ptahhotep, passim.

5. Urk. IV, 117.

6. Ibid., 499.

7. Ptahhotep, 42–50.

8. Anthes, *Lebensregeln und Lebensweisheit der alten Ägypter,* pp. 12–13.

9. Ptahhotep, 60–83.

10. Ibid., 119–133.

11. Ibid., 264–269.

12. Ibid., 325–332.

13. Ibid., 573.

14. Ibid., 339–349.

15. Ibid., 84–98.

16. Admon., passim.

17. Ibid., 7:2–4.

18. Ibid., 9:2.

19. Khekheperresonbu, 10.

20. Admon., 2:12.

21. Leb., 93–95; 86–88.

22. Ibid., 103–116.

23. Ibid., 130–142.

24. Ibid., 142–147.

25. Ibid., 68.

26. Harris 500, 6:2–9.

27. Ibid., 7:2–3.

28. Merikarē, 36–37.

29. Ibid., 128–129.

30. Coffin Texts, B3C, ll. 570–576; B6C, ll. 503–511; B1BO, ll. 618–622; see Breasted, *Dawn of Conscience,* p. 221.

31. TR 37; Rec., 30:189.

32. Coffin Texts, I, 181.

33. Bersheh, II, xix, 8:8–9.

34. BIFAO, 30:425 ff.; "thou" changed to "he" in last clause.

35. Peasant, B, 250–252.

36. E.g., Pyr. Spr. 260; cf. Sethe, *Kommentar,* I, 394: "Der rote Faden in dem Texte ist: Gerechtigkeit, in dem was dem Toten im Leben zuteil wurde und in dem, was er selbst nach seinem Tode thut."

37. Urk. IV, 390.

38. Breasted, *Ancient Records,* vol. 2, 39, n.d.

39. Schädel, *Die Listen des grossen Papryus Harris,* p. 67.

40. Anii, 7:17–8:3.

41. Amenemope, 16:5–14.

42. Berlin 20377; Erman, *Denksteine,* pp. 1086 ff.

43. Berlin 6910, Äg. Inschr., II, 70.

44. JEA, 3:83 ff.

45. Urk. IV, 993; cf. ibid., 66; BIFAO, 30:504—all Eighteenth Dynasty.

46. *Bibl. Eg.,* IV, 279, 281; Cairo 42155; both Bekenkhonsu of Nineteenth Dynasty.

47. Amenemope, 6:1–12.

48. Prisse, 1:1–3; 8:11–12; 11:8–11; Peasant, B, 298–299; B, 313–316; Khekheperresonbu, Verso, 4; Sall. II, 9:9–10:1.

49. Ptahhotep, 58–59; Peasant, B, 74–80.

50. Anii, 3:17–4:1; 9:10; Amenemope, 22:1–18; 22:20–23:11.

51. Beatty IV, Recto, 5:8; cf. Beatty IV, Verso, 5:1–2.

52. Amenemope, 23:10–11.

53. Anii. 4:1–4.

54. Sall. I, 8:5–6.

55. Amenemope, 19:14–17.

56. Ibid., 9:10–13.

57. Ibid., 21:15–16.

58. Beatty IV, Verso, 6:5–9.

59. Berlin 20377.

60. British Museum 589.

61. Turin 102.

62. Beatty IV, Verso, 2:5–3:11.

# 6

## INDIAN CIVILIZATION

R. S. SHARMA

### ORAL COMMUNICATION

In ancient India the forms and media for communication were very limited. Originally, oral communication was far more important than any other mode, and in Vedic times public debates were important to the society. We come across references to several Vedic tribal assemblies that performed deliberative functions. The earliest assembly of this type was the *vidatha,* to which people aspired so that they might talk big. Valiant men are described as raising their voices in this gathering. The householder prayed for warding off death so that while he was alive he could speak to the *vidatha.* In the deliberations of this body, advanced age was given some weight, which is a characteristic of primitive assemblies.

Debates were carried on also by the two other Vedic assemblies, called the *sabhā* and *samiti,* although they are not to be found in the early popular assemblies of the other Indo-European peoples. We cannot definitely say that the *vidatha* was a political body, but the *sabhā* seems to have possessed political character. The Vedic king considered its advice to be of supreme importance and could not possibly do without the support of its members, who hotly discussed submitted proposals.

In a passage from the *Atharva Veda,* the *sabhā* is called "interchange of talk." The king prayed for the support of the *sabhā,* and prayer was made there for avoiding discord and securing cooperation. The *sabhā* also discussed pastoral affairs. Because cattle rearing was a great source of livelihood for the people, members of the *sabhā* delighted in dwelling on the virtues of the kine as well as expressing their anxieties about the fattening of the lean cattle.

The *samiti* performed military, religious, and political functions. Its political functions were far more prominent, and it seems that at one stage it even elected the Vedic king. Both the *Rg Veda* and *Atharva Veda* stress the need for achieving harmony in the *samiti.* The poet says that the counsel *(mantra)* be common, the assembly *(samiti)* be common, heart *(manas)* be common, and their thoughts *(chitta)* be united. The *samiti* therefore was a great deliberative body, and it carried on active discussions for achieving concord. Apparently the king-president was expected to conduct the deliberations in such a manner as to bring about a consensus. The insistence on unanimity is in accord with the practice obtaining in primitive societies. All the prayers and ceremonies, charms and counter-charms were directed to one end alone, namely, to get the better of one's rival in the debate, to induce the members present to accept one's viewpoint, to make one's speech pleasant to members, and to bend the minds of those who held different views.

In post-Vedic times we come across the *pariṣad* or the *gaṇa sabhā,* which carried on debate on various questions. The post-Vedic *pariṣad* consisted of mainly the *brāhmaṇas,* who tried to interpret the laws laid down in the *Dharmaśāstras.* The *gaṇa sabhā* was characteristic of the republics and was composed of the *kṣatriya* nobles, who discussed things of common interest affecting the republic.

In addition to these, numerous religious assemblies were held to resolve theological differences between members of the same sect. Such assemblies were held especially by Buddhists. Their councils were successively convened at Vaisalī, Pāṭaliputra, and Puruṣapura, and in all the meetings members of the Buddhist church tried to establish by means of discussion what it considered to be the original teachings of the Buddha. If we rely on the procedure that was followed in the meeting of the Buddhist *sangha* according to the *Vinaya Pitaka,* it will appear that the democratic method of introducing a resolution and inviting opinions on it was followed. A resolution was considered to have been passed only if there was no dissenting voice. If members kept silent it was considered to be a sign of agreement. The views of the members were ascertained through voting, and apparently the majority of votes decided the issue.

In the seventh century A.D. two important religious assemblies were held by Harṣa, one at Prayaga and the other at Kanauj, but for different purposes. They were summoned to preach the virtues of Buddhism, and during them the Chinese pilgrim Hsüan Tsang gave religious discourses to the people.

We have no idea about the rules and details of debate conducted in the various assemblies mentioned above. The mode and the quality of debate may have developed as a result of the growth of *tarka, nyāya,* and *mimāṃsā,* which represented the different branches of ancient Indian logic. It is also not clear how the decisions made by the councils and assemblies of various types were taken to the common people. Obviously they were transmitted orally. The decisions of the religious councils were recorded and written down, but these could be explained only to those who were sufficiently familiar with the idiom of a particular religion. Disputations and argumentation between followers of rival sects were carried on in public, and each tried to establish the superiority of its own religion or viewpoint. The tradition of *śāstrārtha* still continues, and the pandits engage in it in public.

Oral examination played an important part in admission to the great university of Nālandā. The university maintained a *dvārapaṇḍita,* who interviewed the candidates seeking entrance. Only those who gave satisfactory answers were admitted.

### WRITTEN COMMUNICATION

Although the Indians knew the art of writing as early as 2500 B.C., their earliest decipherable records do not go beyond the third century B.C., and between the end of the Harappa period and the reign of Aśoka inscriptions have been so far conspicuous by their absence. Therefore written communication on a large scale started in India only from the third century B.C., when royal orders of Aśoka were inscribed on rocks and pillars and scattered all over the country (except the deep south) and even in Afghanistan. Originally, education in ancient India may have been mainly oral, and so the Indian tradition attached the greatest importance to memory. Although on the basis of the form and content, the Vedic literature is considered to be as old as 1500 B.C., the earliest available manuscripts are not older than the tenth century A.D. Because of the prime importance of memory the Vedic texts are called *Śrutis,* which literally means something that has been heard. Devout Hindus do not consider the Vedic literature to be the creation of any human being, but something revealed by God. The Vedic texts therefore are regarded as so sacrosanct that every word has to be correctly pronounced. Many Vedic hymns *(mantras)* are used in different Hindu rituals, and it is believed that if they are not recited with proper accent they nullify all the merits and the virtues that a sacrificer can otherwise acquire.

The Vedic *mantras,* which belong to different schools of compilers, were passed on from generation to generation of pupils, who retained and recited them faithfully without altering them. Inasmuch as great store was set by memory in disseminating knowledge and information among the literate people, most religious literature of the Hindus was written in verse. As it is difficult to memorize matter composed in prose, the major part of the ancient Indian literature, especially of Vedic times, was written in verse. The verses were easy to reproduce because of rhyming.

Although a good deal of the later Vedic literature comprising the *Brāhmaṇas* and *Upaniṣads* was compiled in prose, it was only in about the fifth century B.C. that there developed the *sūtra* style of prose. The idea was to convey the maximum meaning through the minimum number of words. Pāṇini's *Aṣṭādhyāyi,* a work on grammar, is a model of terse, precise, and condensed work. Several other works in prose following the *sūtra* style were compiled from the fifth century B.C. onward. The *Dharmasūtras* deal with laws regulating state and society; the *Gṛhyasūtras* lay down domestic rituals for householders; and the *Śrautasūtras* treat and elaborate Vedic rituals. Many of these *sūtras* are not intelligible to the modern Sanskritists without the aid of the commentaries. This also may have been the case with the literate and educated people in ancient times. That is why several commentaries were written to explain these *sūtras*. The commentaries served another purpose also: they interpreted the *sūtras* in the light of the changing conditions in subsequent centuries. Thus the scholiasts played a significant part in perpetuating but at the same time marginally modifying the classical laws and traditions. This happened in all the branches of Sanskrit literature such as grammar, literary texts, *Dharmaśāstras*, and so forth. We notice a hierarchical series of commentaries, which appear successively as *bhāṣya, vivṛti, vyākhyā, ṭikā, ṭippaṇi, kaumudī*, and others. Several commentaries appeared in the twelfth century, and one on the grammar of Pāṇini was written in the eighteenth century.

Similarly the Pāli commentaries, called the *aṭṭhakathās*, were written to explain the earlier Pāli canons. The Prākrit texts were elaborated and explained in the *curṇis, niryuktis*, and so on. All these commentaries served more or less the same objective, namely, to maintain the essentials of the old system and at the same time to explain them in such a manner as to meet the requirements of the changing situations.

Despite the prevalence of the *sūtra* style from the fifth century B.C., the use of the verse continued to be popular with the compilers of the ancient Indian law books, epics, and *Purāṇas*. The later law books, compiled in the early centuries of the Christian era, were called *Smṛtis*, which literally means something that can be remembered, in contrast to the *Śrutis*, which means something heard or revealed. To facilitate memorization all the *Smṛtis* were written in the form of *ślokas* or verses. So also were the *Rāmāyaṇa, Mahābhārata*, and *Purāṇas*. In all these texts the most popular verse, called the *anuṣṭupa chanda*, which was the easiest to learn by heart, was used.

### INTERPOLATION AND INFLATION

The various genres of religious literature were meant for the edification of the people, but most ancient authors preferred to remain anonymous. We cannot ascertain the name, date, place, ancestry, and antecedents of most authors from Vedic times to the beginning of the Christian era. Apparently, in the Indian scheme of things individuals did not enjoy much importance; it was the school to which the author or the compiler belonged that really mattered. Thus the compilation of the Vedic literature and the *Mahābhārata* is assigned to Vyāsa, but it is difficult to demonstrate his historicity. Similar is the case of Vālmīki the author of the *Rāmāyaṇa*.

Despite the great importance attached to memory and correct recitation of Vedic and other religious texts, these works continued to be inflated by subsequent writers through interpolations. Because it was not easy to insert matter in the middle of the book, most additions were made at beginning and end. In the case of the *Ṛg Veda*, the earliest specimen of Indo-European literature, Books I–X were added to the main body later. The *Mahābhārata*, which has been a great instrument of propagating Hindu ideas and values, was subjected to a similar process. Originally it consisted of twenty-four thousand *ślokas*, but by Gupta times this number swelled to one hundred thousand. However, its critical edition, compiled through the labors of various scholars working on it for the last fifty years, consists of nearly eighty-two thousand *ślokas*. Its *Ādi Parva*, which literally means the chapter at the beginning, is a later addition, and this also seems to be the case with the *Anuśāsana Parva* and *Śānti Parva*, which lay down the royal duties *(rāja-dharma)*. The younger epic *Rāmāyaṇa*, which continues to play a great part in popularizing typical Hindu values regarding the patriarchal family, consisted of twelve thousand verses in the beginning but came to comprise twenty-four thousand verses by the fifth century A.D. This can be said also of the *Arthaśāstra* of Kauṭilya, intended for the political education of the prince in ancient times. Only Books II and III of this text, which altogether consists of fifteen books, were compiled earlier; all the other chapters were inserted later, possibly at the beginning of the Christian era.

The ancient texts were inflated not because of the authors' penchant for self-glorification; in every case authors opted for anonymity. The commentaries on the ancient texts served the same purpose as their inflation, namely, to adjust the old texts to later ideas, institutions, customs, and the like. The contents of the *Dharmaśāstras* belonging to the pre-Christian era were versified and amplified to suit the developments that had taken place in the first five centuries after Christ. In the process many ancient texts became full of internal inconsistencies and contradictions, but these were ignored and only such portions were highlighted as met the exigencies of time, place, and circumstances.

## PROPAGANDA REGARDING DIVINITY OF KINGSHIP

Propaganda played an important role in upholding political authority in ancient India. An important device to emphasize royal power and to make it acceptable to the common people was to associate divine elements with royalty. The process started in the Vedic period. The later Vedic coronation formulas prescribe prayers to the various gods for conferring their respective qualities on the king. Of course they clearly mention the human parents of the king, but at the same time try to create the impression that the king possesses some divine attributes. At least one Vedic text, the *Śatapatha Brāhmaṇa*, represents the king as the manifestation of Prajāpati, who was the god of creation. In the later portion of the *Atharva Veda* a king is described as the god who is above mortals. The idea of the divinity of the king did not prevail, however, on a large scale in Vedic times. The Maurya King Aśoka displayed divine support in his inscriptions. Although a Buddhist ruler, Aśoka repeatedly called himself *devānāṃpriya,* which literally means dear to god. The title was continued by his grandson Daśaratha.

The concept of the divinity of the king gained wide currency in post-Maurya times. Curiously, it was widely propagated by the Kuṣāṇas, who, though foreigners, had finally settled down as kings of the greater part of northern India in the first and second centuries. The Kuṣāṇa kings called themselves *devaputra,* which literally means the son of the god. This title was as much popularized by the Kuṣāṇa kings as the term *devānāṃpriya* by Aśoka.

The use of the appellation *devaputra* was theoretically justified by the *Suvarṇabhāsottamasūtra,* a Buddhist text of the

*Mahāyāna* school. In this text the question is asked, why the king born as man is called god and son of god. The answer is given that before being born as man he lived among the gods, and because each of the thirty-three gods contributed to the making of his substance he came to be called *devaputra*. A similar explanation of divine origin of the king is given in the *Manu Smṛti,* which was compiled in the second century A.D., and which commanded wide sanction and authority among the Hindus. Manu (chapter 7:8) does not use the term *devaputra* for *king,* but he clearly states that the king is invested with the respective qualities of eight gods. He asserts that even if the king were a child he should not be disregarded, because he functions as a great divinity in the form of a human being. The divinity of the king is strongly represented also in the *Śānti Parva,* which has many verses in common with the law book of Manu.

In the *Śānti Parva* the elder statesman Bhīṣma is asked why the king, who has two hands, two legs, and all the other organs that an ordinary human being has, should be allowed to rule over all the other human beings. Bhīṣma gives a lengthy justification for this phenomenon. He points out that in ancient days anarchy was rampant, and so people made an agreement among themselves. They undertook to shun a person who speaks too much, encroaches on other's property, and violates women's chastity. Fortified by this social agreement they approached Brahmā for a lord whom together they would worship and who therefore would protect them. Brahmā asked Manu to undertake the work of governing these people, but Manu refused because it would be an enormous task to control people who were wicked and untruthful. The people finally overcame the reluctance of Manu by promising to pay one-fiftieth of their gold and one-tenth of their grain to increase his treasury. They further promised that those who would become the foremost in the use of weapons would follow Manu in the same manner as the other gods followed Indra. In return they sought the protection of the king. The king was assured that one-fourth of the spiritual merit that the subjects, protected by the king, would earn would accrue to the king. At another place in the *Śānti Parva* it is stated that Viṣṇu created a son born out of his mind to shoulder the responsibility of administration. Thus at two places the *Śānti Parva* ascribes the origin of kingship to divine agencies such as Viṣṇu and Brahmā. Because the *Mahābhārata* was recited and read at all places, obviously its compilers popularized the divinity of the king to strengthen royal power.

As the law books of Manu and the *Śānti Parva* were compiled in the time of the Kuṣāṇas, they tended to strengthen the royal power of the Kuṣāṇas and their contemporaries. The Kuṣāṇas also adopted a few other means of propaganda to stress their divinity. They erected *devakulas*, or deity-houses, and installed therein the statues of dead rulers, and these structures served as temples. It is suggested that the Kuṣāṇas adopted this practice from the Romans, who had borrowed it from Egypt, where funerary temples were erected in honor of dead pharaohs. The Kuṣāṇa kings were deified also by the representation of the divine aura around their busts on coins. (On the gold coins the shoulders of the Kuṣāṇa kings are surrounded by the shining rays of flames.) The nimbus *(prabhāmaṇḍala)* also appears on some gold coins, especially on those of Huviṣka, who is ornamented with the nimbus, flames, and clouds. The Kuṣāṇa kings therefore used art as an important medium of propaganda.

The Kuṣāṇa adoption of art and writing to demonstrate their celestial origins has some indigenous parallels. The Sātavāhana ruler Gautamīputra Śātakarṇi, who flourished in the second century A.D., is compared to different gods such as Yama, Varuṇa, Indra, and Kubera. This practice was followed also by the Gupta kings, who are compared to Viṣṇu in that they preserve and protect people. Lakṣmī, wife of Viṣṇu and goddess of prosperity, is represented on many Gupta coins. Therefore the Vaiṣṇavite affiliations of the Gupta kings may have served some political purpose. A striking thing about the Gupta kings is that they are called *devas*, which clearly represents them as gods, thus they are unlike the Kuṣāṇa kings, who were called the sons of the gods.

From the sixth to seventh centuries onward the kings began to be given solar and lunar family trees. By that time Surya and Candra had come to be regarded as gods. To the solar dynasty belonged Rāmacandra, who was regarded in the *Rāmāyaṇa* as an incarnation of Viṣṇu, and to the lunar dynasty belonged the famous Pāṇḍavas, or the five heroes of the *Mahābhārata*. Although Aśoka issued numerous inscriptions containing measures to regulate society, religion, and administration, he never mentioned his family tree in them. It is for the first time from the sixth or the seventh century A.D. onward that tribal chiefs who rose to be kings and generously rewarded *brāhmaṇas* were given high and ancient family pedigrees as a mark of gratitude.

Sometimes the horoscope of ancient heroes was ascribed to later kings by the astrologers. The horoscope of the moment when Pṛthvīrāja was conceived by his mother is described after the horoscope of Rāma as given in the *Rāmāyaṇa*. But actually the planetary positions were different in the two cases, and it can easily be seen that the horoscope of Pṛthvīrāj was fictitious. The astrologers tried to represent the occasions of the births of kings as highly auspicious. The births of Harṣa and the Cāḷukya king Vikramāditya VI were described as great propitious events, on the basis of which astrologers foretold their glorious futures. All this was done to emphasize that they were destined to be great rulers. The practice of connecting royal families with old gods and heroes spread throughout the country. In the Jaina literature the Vidyādharas were regarded as important gods in the period between 600 and 1200. Because of their strong influence in western India, the royal families of Śilāhāras ruling at Goa, Kolhapur, and Thana called themselves the descendants of the Vidyādharas.[1]

The priests and other composers told the people of the exploits and achievements of the king. The practice of eulogizing the services of the king started from Vedic times. The earliest example is found in the *dānastutis,* in which the priests highly commend the charities given by the king and point out the meritorious consequences flowing from this activity. This went on, increasing day by day. Whatever little narratives we have relating to kings in the post-Vedic period invariably speak of their success and achievements. Obviously this was meant for propaganda. Thus although Alexander's invasion of India is regarded as a great event in the history of the ancient world, his conquests find no mention in any ancient Indian writing.

The custom of praising the achievements of the king continued throughout ancient times. The earliest instance is furnished by the inscriptions that were issued by Aśoka. They contain a number of royal orders in Prākrit, which was the popular language in those days, and represent Aśoka as a model of virtue and a benevolent father to his subjects. He gave up war and violence when he found that in the Kaliṅga war as many as one hundred thousand people were slaughtered, and many more persons died. Obviously the carnage would seem to be a great boast. The claim of Aśoka that he succeeded in establishing *dharma* in all parts of the country also is boastful; at any rate, after his death his achievements did not prove to be lasting.

Several examples of boastful propaganda in favor of the king are found in Gupta and post-Gupta times. A remarkable example is the Allahabad inscription composed by the poet Hari-ṣeṇa, who recounts the all-round exploits of Samudra Gupta. It tells us that Samudra Gupta conquered numerous peoples and principalities, and even rulers of distant lands sent tributes to him. A similar claim is made about a king called Candra, who is identified with Candra Gupta II. He is said to have extended his victorious arms as far as Bactria, which is identical to north Afghanistan. Again, in the sixth century A.D. a king called Yaśodharman of Malwa is credited by his panegyrist with the victory over the Hūṇas and with conquests wider than those of the Guptas. All these panegyrics, composed to boost the morale of the kings and their soldiers, have to be taken with a grain of salt.

The best example of large-scale eulogy is the *Harṣacarita* composed by Bāṇabhaṭṭa in the seventh century. Bāṇa speaks eloquently of the achievements of his patron Harṣavardhana. From then on began the *carita* or semibiographical literature relating to the princes. It highly exaggerates the attributes and achievements of the patrons. The court chroniclers of the early medieval age catalogued the conquests of their kings after the conventional *digvijayas* of ancient *cakravartin,* and the poet lent his hero the halo of a traditional all-conquering king.[2] Long inscriptions were composed to commemorate the victories. In an inscription the Pāla prince Dharmapāla, who ruled over Bengal and Bihar in the eighth century A.D., claims to have conquered the whole country including the northwestern part of India, although there is not a shred of evidence to establish that his army went that far. However, the eulogist literature contained such metaphors and symbols as could be intelligible only to the prince and his small elitist circle. But all the same, from the early centuries of the Christian era the kings employed and patronized a large number of poet-eulogists who saw only the virtues and victories of their patrons and never noticed any defeats or failures. It will therefore appear that ancient India produced a good deal of literature that was intended to impress the people with the invincible power of the princes.

### SUPERSTITION AND POLITICAL PROPAGANDA

If we believe Kauṭilya, the credulity of the people was cleverly exploited to promote the interests of the state, internal as well as external. To augment the royal treasury, the *Arthaśāstra* suggests several devices that play upon the superstitions of the people. On some nights the king may set up a god or a sacred shrine, or may point out an evil omen. Once the people are made aware of it and start making offerings, either to worship the god or to avert the calamity, the king may appropriate the collections raised in this manner. The king may declare the arrival of a god in the temple garden. A spy in the guise of a *Rākṣasa* (demon) demanding a daily tribute of human beings may appear in a tree, and a false panic may be raised among the people that an evil spirit has appeared. Accordingly, the people of the capital and countryside may be asked to contribute in order to ward off evil spirits. At least some measures laid down by Kauṭilya were put into effect. Patañjali, who wrote a commentary on Pāṇini's grammar, around 150 B.C., states that the images set up by the Maurya kings brought them income by their sale and provided livelihood *(jīvikā)* through the offerings made to them.[3]

A serpent with several heads may be held up before the people, apparently to overawe them with a supernatural phenomenon, and fees in cash *(hiraṇya)* may be collected from the spectators. Or a cobra may be rendered unconscious by diet, and credulous spectators may be asked to witness the sight on payment of a fee. The sceptics may be served some poisonous drink or may be sprinkled over with poisonous water to render them senseless, and then the royal spies may attribute their loss of senses to the curse of gods. Similarly, the spies may cause the condemner of the god to be bitten by a cobra and may spread the rumor that this was the result of the curse of the god. Furthermore, people may be advised to take remedial measures against this ominous phenomenon, and accordingly collections may be raised to fill the treasury. Thus the people, rational or otherwise, are to be subjected to all kinds of rumors and propaganda to cause them to believe in the superstitious practices and to pay money to the government. All the devices mentioned above occur under the section "replenishment of the treasury," which, according to Kauṭilya (*Arthaśāstra*, V.2), is an important organ of the seven-element state.

Kauṭilya makes very clear that religious formalities should not obstruct the acquisition of wealth. According to him, desire for the other world *(paralokāpekṣā)*, adherence to virtuous life *(dhārmikatvam)*, and faith in the auspiciousness of days and stars *(maṅgalatithinakṣatreṣṭitvam)* hamper profit *(lābhavighna)*. In other words, a person looking for wealth should not worry about these religious considerations. Kauṭilya clearly states that wealth will pass away from the childish man who enquires most after the stars. As he puts it (*Arthaśāstra*, IX.4), "wealth is the star for wealth; what will the stars do?" Kauṭilya therefore is ready to dispense with religious customs whenever they stand in the way of the prince. He apparently wants to tell his ruler that religious practices are so many superstitions, which can be used so long as they serve royal interests.

Advantage of this policy is to be taken in dealing with the internal enemies of the state. It is provided that when a seditious person *(dūṣya)* is busy with sacrifice in a forest, spies may murder him and carry away the corpse as if it were that of an outcast. Moreover, a seditious person may be given hopes of acquiring a vast treasure by the spies and on this pretext may be lured into purchasing rich offerings for the god. When he brings out his newly acquired wealth for the purpose, he may be caught red-handed in the very act of the purchase and his whole property confiscated. Hence Kauṭilya does not believe in the performance of sacrifice by the opponents of the state, whom he regards as condemnable and irreligious (*Arthaśāstra*, V.2). On the contrary, religious engagements of a seditious person are to be used to punish him.

Kauṭilya recommends that the enemy may be maneuvered

into the performance of certain sacrifices by the spies of the king, who should kill the enemy when he is busy with the sacrifice. All this would require much persuasion and remonstration on the part of the spies. The king himself may perform expiatory rites to stay the imaginary calamity. His enemy may be asked to follow suit (*Arthaśāstra*, XIII.2). All these religious measures to destroy the enemy apparently involve skilful propaganda and persuasion.

For the success of invasion, the invaded have to be convinced of the omniscience and divinity of the invader. The aggressor is asked to enthuse his subjects and to overawe the enemy by publicizing his omniscience and close association with the gods. Several artifices are to be contrived by spies. Acting on the information fished out by the spies about the activities of the chief officers and seditious people, the king should announce that he knows everything because of his supernatural power. He should attribute his knowledge of foreign affairs to his power of reading omens, although in fact he gets it through a domestic pigeon.[4]

The methods for demonstrating the divine associations of the king are more numerous. The spies may suddenly appear as fire-gods in the midst of fire through an underground tunnel, and the king may talk to them. He can worship such spies when they rise up from water in the form of Nāgas. He may arrange to exhibit the miraculous phenomenon of the spontaneous outbreak of fire in water. He may sit on a raft in the water, which is secretly but securely fastened by a rope to a rock. Lastly, he might perform some magic in the water to demonstrate his superhuman powers before the people (*Arthaśāstra*, XIII.1).

All these measures recommended by Kauṭilya involve a great deal of propaganda. He provides a host of publicity agents to disseminate belief in the divinity of the king. As many as seven classes of officials, astrologers, soothsayers, horologists, *Paurā-ṇikas* (storytellers), *īkṣaṇikas* (a type of astrologer), spies, and *sācivyakaras* (companions of ministers) are to be pressed into the service of the state for the purpose. The first four are regarded by Kauṭilya as priests (*Arthaśāstra*, V.3), which shows their important role in molding public opinion. The priests are called upon to give wide publicity to the superhuman powers of the king throughout his territory. In foreign countries they are to spread the news of gods appearing before the king and of his having received from heaven the powers of the sword *(daṇḍa)* and purse *(kośa)*. The subjects of the enemy are to be told that the invading king can interpret dreams and follow the language of beasts and birds, and hence his victory is assured. Moreover, by means of a firebrand and the noise of drums from the sky the subjects of the enemy are to be convinced of the impending defeat of their ruler *(Arthaśāstra,* XIII.1). Finally, the images of gods may be damaged and blood may be caused to issue in floods; spies may then designate this as an indication of the impending defeat of the enemy *(Arthaśāstra,* XIII.2).

These ingenious measures for propagating the supernatural powers of the aggressive ruler occur in the thirteenth book of the *Arthaśāstra,* which deals with the methods of capturing the capital *(durgalambhopāya).* Because they involve several magical stratagems, they reveal that Kauṭilya himself does not believe in the genuineness and omniscience of the royal divinity and that he does not want the ruler to subscribe to this nonsense. Nevertheless, by means of skillful propaganda carried on by well-organized machinery, he wants to convince the masses of the all-knowing and divine character of the conqueror, so that his subjects could wholeheartedly support his aggressive designs and the enemy might transfer their allegiance to him. These magical tricks, practices, and pieces of propaganda are considered foreign to the *Arthaśāstra,*[5] which is supposed to represent the state of affairs in the Maurya period. But even if these measures are ascribed to the early centuries of the Christian era, they certainly represent a school that relied on propagating all kinds of superstition for the sake of the state.

## COMMUNICATION BETWEEN THE KING AND HIS SUBJECTS

We have some idea of how the ancient Indian princes communicated with their subjects. The earliest examples are the inscriptions of Aśoka in which royal orders are conveyed to subjects. The subjects are told of the duties of administrative and judicial officers, employed to work among the subjects in different capacities. The royal rescripts issued by Aśoka not only lay down administrative duties but also govern society and religion. Through them Aśoka asks his subjects to pay respect to parents, Brahmans *(brāhmaṇas)*, *śramaqs* (monks), and so on, and advises them to show mercy toward slaves and serfs. Apparently these instructions are intended to eliminate social tensions and to keep society functioning.

From the beginning of the Christian era the orders of the kings were communicated to the subjects through land charters engraved mostly on copper plates and occasionally on stone. The charters transferred plots of land and villages with all their taxes to priests and other beneficiaries. Because the transfer was considered to be a very important matter, the charter was addressed to all possible parties who had even the remotest connection with the land or the village. A whole hierarchy of officials ranging from ministers to royal retainers was informed of the grant. All village elders as well as all the castes from the *brāhmaṇas* to the *cāṇḍālas* were informed of these land transactions. The list of the addressees ended with the use of the term *ādi*, or "etc.," which covered those people who not specified in the list of addressees. This was apparently done to avoid disputes and litigations relating to lands and villages in the future. We can visualize that the charters written in Sanskrit could not be intelligible to most people living in the villages. It is likely that their contents were announced, accompanied by beat of drums, by the agents of the king. In the early medieval charters, the operative part was composed in the regional language and the conventional preliminaries in Sanskrit.

In what ways the subjects communicated with the king and brought their grievances to his notice is not known to us. The ordinary people would not have the means to get their statements recorded on stone and copper as the princes did. However, many votive inscriptions commemorate the big and small donations made by merchants and artisans in favor of some religious cause. The demands or the grievances of the people living in the towns and villages may have been brought to the attention of the king through a hierarchy of officials. If administrative oppression proved to be intolerable, the people could revolt and protest, and they attracted royal notice as happened in Taxila whose governor was recalled by the Maurya king on the representation of the local people. But such cases may have been rare. The *Harṣacarita* states that in the course of the military march of Harṣa, villagers lodged false complaints against the oppressions of the *bhogapatis*,[6] who were in the nature of powerful overlords enjoying the revenues of the villages granted to them or placed under their charge by the king. Although these complaints were dismissed as false in this case, it is likely that the subjects took advantage of the royal marches to air their grievances before the king in public.

### PRESERVING THE SOCIAL STRUCTURE

The ancient Indian social order was based on a system in which the Brahmans *(brāhmaṇas)* prayed, the Kshatriyas *(kṣatriyas)* fought, the Vaisyas *(vaiśyas)* produced, and the Sudras *(śūdras)* served the other three. The justification for the social order first appears in an interpolated portion of the *Ṛg Veda,* which states that the Brahmans issued out of the head of the god, the Kshatriyas out of his shoulders, the Vaisyas out of his thighs, and the Sudras out of his feet. This myth is repeated in all the important subsequent texts that deal with the functions of the four *varṇas.* So deeply has it been entrenched in the Hindu mind that even now, illiterate Brahmans insist that the Sudras occupy the lowest position in society because they are born of the feet of the god.

The fourfold varna system being the bedrock of the whole social order, all the ancient law books stress that the chief function of the head of the state is its maintenance. The *Śānti Parva* declares that people can perform the duties pertaining to their castes and social orders only if the state power backs them. The lawgiver Manu proclaims that the kingdom can prosper so long as the purity of caste is maintained. If the bastard people of the mixed castes sully the state, it shall perish together with its inhabitants. Manu can hardly think of the royal functions separate from the caste system. As Hopkins puts it: "Incidental mention of the king standing without particular relation to the other castes can only be sparingly quoted." According to Brahmanical authorities, if anyone defects from his caste functions it leads to calamity. Nārada, a lawgiver of the fifth–sixth century A.D., states that if the king does not punish any caste when they have left the path, the created beings of the world shall perish.

The need to uphold the social order by the royal authority is corroborated by epigraphic evidence. A Sātavāhana Brahman ruler in the middle of the second century is represented as hostile to the Kshatriyas but a preventer of confusion in the fourfold varna system. Similar statements appear in inscriptions of the Gupta age. Several rulers of central India are represented as devoted to the establishment of the *varṇāśrama dharma.* Many Gupta kings and their successors are represented in their inscriptions as busy with settling the systems of varnas and *āśramas* and in keeping the castes confined to their respective spheres of duty. Harṣa's father is described as a regulator of the system of orders and stages. Thus in both books and inscriptions the preservation of the varna-divided society was repeatedly emphasized as the main function of the king.

The duties pertaining to the varna are widely propagated by the celebrated Indian work *Bhagavad Gītā.* Arjuna wavers in taking up arms against his kinsmen. Kṛṣṇa, who is considered to be the incarnation of a god, advises Arjuna to carry out the functions of a Kshatriya, namely, to fight. It is typical of this text that it advises members of all the four orders to perform their duties without any hope for rewards in this world. In other words, it asks the people to resign themselves to the existing situation. The weaker sections of society such as the Vaisyas, Sudras, and women are told to repose their faith in Kṛṣṇa so that they may attain heaven in the next world. Evidently, in the name of the god the *Gītā* tries to defend and perpetuate the existing social order, which is based on disparities and inequalities.

Because all the texts that emphasize the importance of the varna system were written by the Brahmans, it is natural that they give the highest position to the Brahmans. In particular, the law books of Manu and Nārada accord a number of privileges to that caste. Crimes committed by the Brahmans were to be ignored, but those committed against them by members of the lower castes were to be severely punished. The Brahmans extolled the virtues of visiting the places of pilgrimage because the offerings made by the pilgrims brought them great income. The Brahmans further highlighted the spiritual merits accruing from making charities, especially in making land grants. Most of the land grants recorded on copper plates were made to the

Brahmans. For this reason the sections called *bhūmidāna-praśaṃsā* or virtues of land grants occur in various texts. Similarly, the Brahmans also underlined the religious merits of regularly listening to the epics and the *Purāṇas,* whose recitation brought them rich gifts *(dakṣiṇās)* at the end of this function. The Brahmans also propagated the religious merits of the Gaṅgā bath and various other day-to-day rituals. All these acts were accompanied by payment of gifts to the priests, who stood ritually at the head of the social order.

Theoretically the system of the four varnas continued to serve as a model, but there appeared numerous mixed castes. They number sixty in Manu, become one hundred in post-Gupta times, and as many as two thousand subcastes of Brahmans alone are mentioned in the census of 1901. Stagnant social economy, lack of mobility, and the process of absorbing numerous tribal peoples and foreign immigrants and invaders into the pale of the Hindu society account for the caste proliferation. But according to the old theory propounded in the *Ṛg Veda,* there were only four original varnas. Therefore, to justify the absorption and creation of numerous castes in subsequent times, the Brahmans cleverly invented the theory of the mixed castes. They pointed out that the intermingling of these four varnas with one another produced numerous mixed castes. Different law books attribute the origin of the same caste to different interminglings. Such inconsistencies did not worry the compilers so long as they appeared to fit in with their original theory of the origin of the four varnas. Undoubtedly, explanations for the origins of the so-called mixed castes were figments of imagination meant for propaganda. The advent of the Śakas, Pallavas, Bactrian Greeks (or Yavanas), or other peoples in India in post-Maurya times was explained by a legend given in the *Rāmāyaṇa.* According to it, because Viśvāmitra coveted the cow of Vasiṣṭha, these peoples originated from that wonder-working cow to destroy Viśvāmitra and his soldiers. So the process of systematizing the varnas that started in post-Vedic times is found in several legends recorded in the law books, Purāṇas, inscriptions, and historical novels of the medieval age.

Buddhism, Jainism, and several Brahman sects emphasized the sanctity of family and property. Numerous Sanskrit verses place wife and property in the same category and prescribe their protection at every cost. They demand unfailing chastity and fidelity on the part of wife, and they repeatedly stress the preservation of the patriarchal family and private property. This is prescribed as one of the chief duties of the king in the Buddhist and Brahmanical sources. The king is asked to punish thieves and adulterers. He is even asked to restore the stolen wealth to the subject, at any cost. Popular notion identified royal duty with the protection and probably even with the distribution of wealth. This can be inferred from a passage of the *Pañcatantra*, which contains stories that were widely read in ancient India and later translated into most of the important languages of the world. Furthermore, the king is asked always to honor his rich subjects because in every kingdom the wealthy constitute an estate. Manu enumerates eighteen offences out of which ten are connected with property and two with family. Similarly, Kātyāyana lists ten wrongs deserving attention by the king; out of them five relate to property and two to family. Many texts state that poverty lies at the root of all the evils and the poor are full of vices. According to Kāmandaka, men are inherently subject to passion and covet one another's wealth and wife. Therefore, many ancient texts underline the need of protecting family and property. The dominant ideal propagated for the king in ancient India was the attainment of *dharma, artha,* and *kāma. Artha* means the enjoyment of property, *kāma* the enjoyment of family life, and *dharma* the maintenance of the legal system. The *trivarga* ideal therefore was dominated by the concepts of property, family, and caste. The written word was therefore cleverly propagated and manipulated by the educated priestly class not only to maintain their own ritual primacy in society but to preserve the social structure based on the varnas, and the patriarchal family and property.

Floating folk tales, fables, and traditions passing by word of mouth from generation to generation provided wisdom and entertainment and promoted social stability. They constituted a kind of community literature, which was gradually written down and preserved for posterity. This seems to have been the case with the Buddhist birth stories called the Jātakas, and other varieties of stories embodied in the *Pañcatantra* and the

*Bṛhatkathā* of *Guṇāḍhya,* which was later elaborated into the *Kathāsaritasāgara* by Somadeva. Many stories clearly carry the moral at the end. They applaud truthfulness, obedience to parents, observance of the *varṇa-dharma,* and similar other virtues consistent with the maintenance of the Hindu society. In other stories the moral is implicit, and can be drawn by an intelligent reader or listener.

In a society with very limited literacy the number of readers would be too small and that of listeners vast. To entertain the masses of the people and to instill social values in them, the folk tale tradition was developed into the *kathā* system. Certain Purāṇas, especially the Vaiṣṇavite *Bhāgavata Purāṇa,* which is supposed to confer great religious merit on those who organize its recitation and listen to it, were regularly recited. So strong has been the tradition that the recitation of the *Bhāgavata Purāṇa* by priests continues even to this day in India. Women devotees especially listen to it devoutly, and reciters are generously rewarded at the end of the function, which lasts several days.

## COMMUNICATION AND THE FUNCTIONING OF SOCIETY

We have some indication of how members of the various social orders communicated with one another. The early Pāli texts show how the Buddha took his message to the various classes of the people. The forms of address and greetings used in them by persons of different groups[7] suggest that in the social sphere the Brahmans successfully maintained their hostile equality with the Buddha and that they were ritually superior although politically subservient to the ruling Kshatriyas. The modes of address and greetings reveal that the Buddha and his monks cultivated close social intercourse, mostly with the Brahmans, at least in the beginning. But the lay followers who communicated with the Buddha were mostly artisans and merchants. Princely patrons of Buddhism made the order richer and more influential, but artisans and merchants provided him with the mass following.

In the early Brahmanical texts, the Sudras are not addressed on a footing of equality, because they occupy a low position.

The ancient dramas indicate the type of language and communication used by ancient Indians. The higher class people
spoke Sanskrit while women and lower classes invariably spoke
Prākrit. This would suggest lack of sufficient communication
between the weaker and the stronger sections of society.

The dialogue form, which first appears in the Vedic texts, was
adopted in the epics, the Purāṇas and the *Gītā*. But the role of
the question master was not so important as in the works of
Plato. The questions were very short and did not pursue the
arguments further. The answers came in the form of a long narrative, as we find in the *Mahābhārata* at many places, and once
they were given, the questioner felt satisfied.

The epics and Purāṇas seem to have been floating traditions
that were recited in the courts of princes by the panegyrists
called *cāraṇas, māgadhas, sūtas, bandīs, bhāṭas*. The *sūtas* and
others played an important part in the dialogue, and orally
reproduced both questions and answers. In the course of time
these versified accounts were written down and transmitted
from generation to generation with continual additions and interpolations. In Pargiter's view the traditions compiled in the
Purāṇas represent the Kshatriya version of things, in contrast to
the Vedic literature and the *Dharmaśāstras* that represent the
priestly version. But this does not seem to be very sound. Whatever may have been the character of the original Purāṇic traditions, they were certainly Brahmanized in time and were used
by the priests to elevate the position of the Kshatriya patrons, in
return for which the priests received handsome rewards. The
epics and Purāṇas contributed much to the normal functioning
of society. Women and Sudras were entitled to listen to them
but not to the Vedas. The verse in which the epics and the
Purāṇas were written was very popular, and their style easy.
These texts were generally compiled under the Śaivite and Vaiṣṇavite influences. While the Śaivite Purāṇas glorify the religious merits flowing from the worship of Śiva, the Vaiṣṇavite
Purāṇas do the same in regard to the worship of Viṣṇu. Replete
with contradictory customs and statements, the epics and the
Purāṇas really teach the virtues of patriarchal family life and the
functions of the four social orders and life stages. The *Rāmāyaṇa* idealizes the family life, in which, regardless of consequences, the son obeys his father, the younger brother the elder

brother, and the wife her husband. Several stories of *sati* in the epics and the Purāṇas dwell upon the virtues of faithfully following the husband in all situations.

Astrology and divination played an important part in communication between the priests and the common people. To convince the people of their power in forecasting the future of the ruling dynasties, the priests recorded the events in the Purāṇas in the future tense. The original Purāṇas do not go beyond the Gupta period, but their tradition has been kept alive until recent times. The *Bhaviṣyat Purāṇa* states that Queen Victoria would rule in the future.

Chapters on astrology are found in many Purāṇas. The epics and the Purāṇas popularized astrological ideas and practices that touched the lives of the common people. The *Mahābhārata* taught that hating and opposing Brahmans, seizing their wealth, wishing to kill or harm them, taking delight in their condemnation, disliking their praise, ignoring them in rituals, getting angry with them, and committing mistakes are the eight indications of a man's approaching fall. By predicting bad days for those who dare to defy the Brahmans, this astrological formulation tries to ensure the supremacy of the priestly order.

Many astrological practices were borrowed from the primitive peoples right from Vedic times. They were refined and elaborated to serve the cause of the Brahmanical order. The fact that all segments of society, from the prince to the peasant and from the Brahman to the Sudra, believed in these superstitions provided an ideological cementing bond. Because it was preached that everyone would be rewarded according to his fate there was no cause to grumble. Astrological superstition served as an effective device to contain class conflicts and social tensions. The success of mediocrity and the failure of merit did not bother the people because this was all ordained by god. Hence propaganda through astrology was a strong device to keep the whole society together.

Astrologers extended solid support to political authority. They proclaimed the divinity of the king in battles and held out prospects of sure victory to his soldiers. For the start of his conquests Harṣa's astrologers fixed such an auspicious day and *lagna* as would ensure his victory in all the four quarters. They could prevent political upheavals and popular commotions by predicting evil consequences for their sponsors. They also checked thefts by their occult ability to track culprits. Astrologers, because of their preachings and predictions, could prove to be as effective and serviceable as police and soldiers.

Allied to astrological devices was the belief in the idea of rebirth and in the concepts of hell and heaven propagated by the Brahmanical writers. The Buddhists taught that by following their doctrines a person could attain *nirvāṇa,* or liberation from the chain of birth and death. But the Brahmanical texts spoke of rebirth in higher orders and affluent families if a person faithfully observed the various kinds of *dharma* (assigned functions) such as *raja-dharma* (royal duties), *varṇa-dharma* (order duties), *jāti-dharma* (caste duties), *pitā-dharma* (father's duties), *putra-dharma* (son's duties), *strī-dharma* (wife's duties), *pati-dharma* (husband's duties), *dāsa-dharma* (slave or servant's duties), and similar other *dharmas.* This point repeatedly occurs in the epics, Purāṇas, law books and other texts, and it was successfully driven home to the Hindus through constant propaganda, oral and written. Even now there are people who ascribe all their miseries to their actions in the previous life.

Not less effective seems to have been the propaganda regarding belief in hell and heaven. The imprecations given at the end of all land charters granted to priests and temples warn the royal successors, officials, and others that if they violate these grants, seize or disturb them, they are sure to be visited with all kinds of sins and hellish troubles. The picture of hell drawn in literary texts and inscriptions is an extension of the usual miseries that people suffer in this world, but by giving free vent to imagination it is made more and more lurid and horrifying. In sharp contrast to this, heaven appears as a place of perpetual bliss and comfort. Those who perform the duties assigned to them within the framework of the Brahmanical social order are assured of admission to heaven on their death. Hence the Hindu belief in heaven and hell keeps people attached to the functions of the order in which they are born.

### PROPAGANDA FOR MORAL AND SOCIAL CHANGES

Although much that we have seen in the form of communication and propaganda was directed toward preserving the social order, occasionally propaganda also was made an instrument of social change. Some social and religious movements produced considerable literature, which was aimed at transforming the values and the attitudes of their followers. This can be said especially of Jainism and Buddhism, which did not recognize the existing varna system and attached much weight to the preservation of cattle wealth. In order to take their doctrines to the common people, teachers of these religions adopted the language of the masses. Although Sanskrit had been in use in India from Vedic times, the religious sects that arose in the post-Vedic period did not use this language, in which various kinds of *sūtras* were being compiled from the fifth century B.C. On the other hand, the Jains and Buddhists preferred to adopt the popular languages spoken and understood by the people. The Buddhists adopted Pāli, which was understood in north-eastern India, and compiled all their canons and teachings in it. Similarly, the Jains adopted Prākrit, which was widely used by Aśoka.

The Buddhists composed a good deal of popular literature to propagate their social, moral, and religious values. An important genre of this literature comprises the Jatakas, or the Buddhist birth stories, which number about five hundred fifty. Every Buddhist birth story consists of three parts: the present story, the past story, and the moral. In the first part some complaint involving moral or social lapses on the part of a particular individual is made to the Buddha; in the second the Master narrates some past story relating to his own previous birth and that of the individual concerned, in which the individual is said to have behaved in the same manner; and finally from the past story some kind of moral consistent with the Buddhist teachings is drawn. In the nineteenth century when the Hindu reformers wanted to abolish *sati* and child marriage and introduce widow marriage they quoted many Sanskrit texts to prove that the first two practices were not prevalent in ancient times but the third practice did prevail. Centuries earlier the same method had been adopted by the Buddhists to propagate their moral and social ideas by quoting ancient precedents. The past stories were evidently meant to illumine and illustrate the Buddhist moral maxims.

In the early centuries of the Christian era the Buddhists compiled a large body of the *avadāna* literature of the Mahāyāna
form to advertise the miraculous activities of the Buddha in
various roles. Obviously, this was done to prove the superiority
of the Buddha over the other religious teachers. Further, the
*avadāna* literature was composed to prepare the ground for an
important change in Buddhism. It encouraged the worship of
the Buddha, which was not the wish of Gautama Buddha. It
asserted that Gautama Buddha can be born only in a Brahman
or Kshatriya family, which naturally gave weight to the first two
orders in comparison with the two lower orders. Buddhism was
now gradually falling in line with the Brahmanical social order,
which stressed the joint supremacy of the first two orders from
post-Maurya times. Early Buddhism denounced the existing
varna system, which won it the support of artisans and merchants. The early Pāli texts refer to many disputations of the
Buddha with Ambaṣṭha and other Brahmans in which he tried
to expose the hollowness of their claims to superiority based on
high birth and hereditary status. The Buddha tried to convince
them that caste status depended not on the birth of a person
but on his worth.

The early Buddhist texts preached against injury to animals,
because the use of the iron ploughshare in northeastern India
from the sixth century B.C. rendered the needs of agriculture
pressing. Cattle wealth was being destroyed senselessly by the
Brahmans in numerous Vedic sacrifices and also by the
aboriginal tribal people, who domesticated cattle not for the
sake of dairy products but to provide beef for themselves.
Without doubt the preservation of cattle was of the utmost importance to agriculture. Therefore the earliest Buddhist text,
called the *Suttanipāta,* describes the cattle as givers of food,
beauty, and happiness, and hence recommends their preservation under all conditions. The accent on not injuring animals
first laid by the Buddhists was gradually written into the
Brahmanical texts, and from the beginning of the early centuries of the Christian era the Brahmans made the protection of
the cow an article of faith. In the course of time this idea took
such deep roots among the Hindus that now even uneconomic
cattle have to be fed. Along with this there also developed the

creed of vegetarianism, which was particularly propagated by the Vaiṣṇavites in their texts. Most Vaiṣṇavites continue to be vegetarians even in modern times although those in Bengal eat fish.

When Buddhism and other sects tried to preach new ideas they came into conflict with the teachers of the rival sects, who stoutly resisted the onslaughts to their positions. So, in the religious texts composed by the Buddhists and orthodox Brahmanical people we find strong vilification of the opposing sects. The rival sects are represented in a very bad light and associated with all possible vices and evil practices. No text compiled by the Ājīvikas themselves has been known or recovered so far, but we get many references to their denunciation by their rivals. So considerable is the literature of vilification that all uncomplimentary remarks have been carefully collected, sifted, and utilized to prepare a connected history of the Ājīvikas.[8]

The practice of maligning and denouncing rival sects seems to have been widely prevalent in the time of Aśoka. That is why in one of his inscriptions the Maurya emperor teaches the followers of different religions the value of tolerance and synthesis, and advises them not to vilify or condemn one another. He asks them not to glorify one's own faith at the cost of another's faith. This may have succeeded in his lifetime, but a few centuries after his death the whole career of Aśoka is dismissed in a single verse in the Purāṇas, which call him a foolish *(mohātmā)* king.

## CRAFTS, COMMERCE, AND COMMUNICATION

Social changes can be promoted by religious preachings, but in many cases they are brought about by technological developments. Although the same craft may originate independently and fortuitously at different places, generally technological devices spread from some epicenter. Crafts having their origin at one place travel to another as a result of military conquests or peaceful, mostly commercial, contacts between peoples. The ancient Indians practiced numerous crafts, especially iron working and the manufacture of steel. By the fifth century B.C., iron technology reached a high peak of excellence, and it gradually spread to different parts of the country. We cannot say whether propaganda played any part in it. Preserved are polished Maurya pillars, glossy North Black Polished Ware, many objects of beautiful craftmanship in glass and ivory, and the Mehrauli iron pillar, which has not gathered rust even during the last fifteen centuries; but how these articles were made is nowhere indicated in the texts. The section on metallurgy in the *Arthaśāstra* of Kauṭilya is not detailed. As many as sixty-four types of arts and crafts are enumerated in the literary texts, but the processes involved in their practice are nowhere described.

Obviously, crafts were transmitted orally from father to son or from the master craftsman to his apprentices. Where craft is hereditary, in many ways it comes naturally to family members. Imitation in the handling and making of tools and weapons may have been supplemented by oral instructions. Much of the craft skill may have been diffused and transmitted from one region to another through sheer imitation. No conscious propaganda seems to have been made in favor of adopting new types of technology. Most written texts on technology relate to the *Śilpaśāstras* in early medieval times, and deal mainly with architecture, sculpture, and iconography. By and large we notice a divorce between technology and literacy. We get rich theological and priestly literature taught and transmitted by different schools, but very little technological literature. As a literate and educated class the priests wrote down the rituals and religious formulas they followed. Artisans and craftsmen, who generally belonged to Sudra and Vaisya castes, lacked literacy and hence could not record the methods they followed in pursuing their crafts.[9]

Although in some texts different parts of the country are called famous for various products and commodities, apparently there was nothing like modern advertising. We do not come across any promotional propaganda for the sale of goods. However, language was not a barrier in India's foreign trade. South India carried on thriving trade with the Romans, who came in fine ships protected by archers against pirates. Impressed by the discipline of the archers, the Tamil kings employed Roman soldiers as their bodyguards. These Romans are described as dumb, for they could speak to the people of the Tamil land only by gestures. But inasmuch as the Romans had stationed two regiments in the Cera country to protect their in-

terests and had also settled down at Arikamedu and Kaveripat-
tanam, which had a quarter for foreign merchants, evidently
they had learned the local Indian language, particularly Tamil.

Commercial intercourse introduced many Tamil words into
Greek and Latin. The Hebrew word for peacock is a Tamil
word, and the English word *pea* can be traced through Latin
and Greek to the same source. In Greek we find Tamil words for
rice, ginger, cinnamon, and several other items that were exported from India. The Hellenistic Greeks of Egypt learned
Tamil to such an extent that a few Tamil passages are found in a
Greek papyrus record in Egypt. When Egypt became a Roman
province, and the monsoons were discovered about the end of
the first century B.C., the commercial and consequent linguistic
intercourse became frequent. About the beginning of the
Christian era a Pandyan king sent embassies to the Roman Emperor Augustus, which shows that the Romans and Indians
could converse with one another. The presence of colonies of
Roman merchants on the seacoasts of south India suggests that
their position was regulated by diplomatic agreements written
in the language understood by both parties.

The Indians also carried on trade with Southeast Asia from
the early centuries of the Christian era, and Sanskrit influenced
the languages of Southeast Asia. The *bahasa* Indonesia contains
numerous Sanskrit words. On the other hand, people from
south India seem to have acquainted themselves with the indigenous languages of Southeast Asia. The languages of south
India contain several words that can be derived neither from the
Dravidian nor from the Indo-Aryan stock. They are of Southeast
Asian origin and stand for articles and products that were obtained by the Indians from that origin.

## CONCLUSION

Because of the paucity of material it is not possible to present a
fully coherent account of propaganda and communication in
ancient India. But what has been stated above is sufficient to
show that these elements played an important part not only in
preserving the social order but also in upholding political
authority. Despite anonymity, written texts carried great
authority, and the priests who purveyed them enjoyed enormous social prestige and influence. A good deal of literature

was in defense of the four social orders, private property, and the patriarchal family. The original texts were inflated, conveniently interpreted, and subjected to interpolations to suit the exigencies of time, place, and circumstances. Maintenance of the social institutions was regarded as the chief function of the king, whose power was buttressed by the deliberate adoption of superstitious practices and the propagation of the divinity of kingship. The folk tales were manufactured to preserve the existing social order and to preach moral values.

Some literature, however, also was composed to make the moral and social changes acceptable to people. This was done especially by the Jains and Buddhists, and to some extent by the Śaivas and Vaiṣṇavas. In any case propaganda and communication were never used widely to bring about fundamental changes in the ancient social order. Communication was particularly weak in transmitting and diffusing craft skill and knowledge. Because artisans were generally illiterate, it was not possible either to develop technology or to preserve the whole of it for posterity. But language did not stand in the way of India's diplomatic and commercial contacts, although it may not have promoted them.

NOTES

1. For details, see V. S. Pathak, *Ancient Historians of India* (Delhi: Asia Press, 1963), pp. 131–144.

2. Pathak, *Ancient Historians,* pp. 78–79.

3. For details, see Kauṭilya's *Arthaśāstra,* V. 2.

4. For the whole paragraph, please see *Arthaśāstra,* XIII. 1.

5. H. C. Seth, "The Spurious in Kautilya's *AS,*" in *A Volume of Eastern and Indian Studies presented to Professor F. W. Thomas,* p. 25.

6. *Harṣacarita,* edited by K. B. Parab (Bombay, 1937), p. 212.

7. N. K. Wagle, *Society at the Time of the Buddha* (Bombay, 1966), p. 156.

8. A. L. Basham, *History and Doctrines of the Ājīvikas* (London, 1951).

9. This also seems to have been true regarding the knowledge of herbs and drugs that were known to illiterate village priests and physicians. Out of their anxiety to retain monopoly over this knowledge they maintained secrecy. This knowledge was neither recorded nor imparted orally to people outside the family, and thus much of it perished.

# 7

## ON THE SPREAD OF BUDDHISM
## TO CHINA

ARTHUR F. WRIGHT

Among all the encounters between great civilizations, that between China and India is unique. The two civilizations were
remarkably isolated one from another; historically, there were
few military or diplomatic relations between them; rather, their
communications one with another were filtered through middlemen and intermediate cultures; their encounter was pacific
—the movement of ideas, words, books, things—rather than invasion, infiltration or conquest; the flow was mainly one way,
from India to China; the encounter had effects that were
negligible on India and revolutionary on the civilization of
China, which was transformed by the universal religion of Buddhism.[1]

The first characteristic of their relations—relative isolation—is
readily seen on the map of Asia. The areas of the two civilizations, both subcontinental in extent, were separated by the
most formidable land barriers on earth: the Himalayas, the
Hindu Kush, and the Pamirs. For long centuries, each was occupied with the settlement of its vast and diverse territories;
neither was driven by land hunger or deficiencies in its natural
resources to push through the mountain barriers toward the
other, and neither ventured far along the hazardous sea routes

between them. India, of course, was open to influences from
the West—from Persia and the Greco-Roman world. But in early times its isolation from China was almost complete.

A second feature of this unique relationship is characteristic
of the period before the Buddhist penetration of China. This is
the pattern of diffused and indirect contact in the areas between
the two civilizations—contact often through middlemen of one
sort or another. There were no formal exchanges of embassies
between the centers of power in China and in India. Rather,
peoples of the two civilizations began moving into contiguous
areas of Central Asia and Southeast Asia. Traders, adventurers,
military expeditions, colonists moved slowly from both sides into these areas and began to transform the cultures they found
there. Nomadic groups moved back and forth across Central
Asia, assimilating and passing on fragments of the cultures of
the two civilizations. In both areas of contact, encounters between the two civilizations were diffused and diluted by the indigenous cultures and, in Central Asia, by the influence of Iranian civilization.

When problems developed on India's northwestern frontier
and China's western frontier, expeditions were sent out to deal
with the threat in the intervening lands, but until much later no
Chinese army got as far as India, and no Indian army ever came
within thousands of miles of the Chinese frontier. As armies
withdrew, often followed by invasions from the steppelands,
bits of information, a few plants, and artifacts drifted from one
civilization to another. There were wanderers' tales, told and
retold in the caravanserais—typical tales of distant lands—
eldorados, lands of giants, monsters, and other wonders. Thus,
what Chinese or Indians learned about one another was learned
through middlemen from the polyglot cultures of the Southeast
Asian littoral or the trade routes of Central Asia. In China and
India alike the educated elites were absorbed in their own
thought worlds and power interests. On neither side was there a
stimulus to explore and to get systematic knowledge of the
other civilization.

A third feature of the historic relations between China and
India is that the Chinese kept records of what little they learned
of their distant neighbor, not in any special or prominent place

in the dynastic histories but in the biographies of great frontier generals such as Chang Ch'ien and Pan Ch'ao and in the sections of the histories or minor works that dealt with "barbarian" lands. In contrast to this, the Indian historical tradition was relatively weak, much of the record has disappeared, and substantial accounts of China are nonexistent. This difference qualifies all that we can say about the relations between the two civilizations.

A fourth characteristic of the encounter was that influences of all kinds were predominantly in one direction—from India to China. Shadowy traces of Chinese influences are found in the texts of some minor Indian religions; archaeologists have identified a few objects possibly derived from Chinese prototypes; and some Indian plants appear to be of Chinese origin. But India, though often invaded and subject to a variety of alien influences, absorbed little from China. There is a massive record of what the late Dr. Hu Shih called "The Indianization of China," but there is nothing to suggest that this has any counterpart in the history of India.[2] What was the force that drove elements of Indian civilization into China, there to transform a culture which seems historically to have been as self-sufficient as any in the annals of mankind?

Buddhism, which was to become in time a great universal religion, began as one among many revolts against Brahmanism in the Gangetic plain. It was a movement of protest against the religious beliefs prevalent in the fifth century B.C., specifically, against the automatic efficacy of sacrifice as a way to salvation, against the Brahmans as monopolists of the means of salvation, against inherited social status as the sole index of worth and sanctity. Buddhism, like its rivals, attracted followers among those who suffered from the Brahman's monopoly of power and sanctity: poor peasants, merchants, shopkeepers, traders, individualist philosophers and ascetics, the occasional prince who chafed at the power of the priests. Yet the doctrines of early "protestant" Buddhism, like our Protestantism, included many of the ideas of the inherited system against which it made its protest. It accepted the idea of successive incarnations, the notion of life-as-illusion-and-evil, the belief in some kind of self-disciplined life apart from society as necessary for salvation.

Despite its spiritual egalitarianism, it was so closely tied to Indian traditions—local and particular traditions—that it might
well have become one of the thousands of half-forgotten reformist sects in the religious history of India. What made it, instead, a world religion?

In the four centuries after the Buddha's death, a series of
developments effected this transformation. Buddhism, in its
clerical and lay communities developed its own ethic and way of
life. It was adopted and propagated in their realms by powerful
rulers, among whom Aśoka and Kaniśka are the best known.
The founder's sayings were elaborated into a vast and impressive corpus of doctrine, which in time became so varied as to
satisfy a wide range of spiritual yearnings and intellectual interests. More important still, Buddhism developed a great pantheon of saints and saviors, ways of salvation for the many
through devotion and prayer. And along with these a rich iconography evolved, drawn from the sacred motifs and symbols of
several cultures. The salvationist Buddhism of the first century
A.D. had as its center the Bodhisattva—the perfect saint who did
not withdraw into the timeless purity of Nirvana but chose to be
reborn again and again so as to work for the salvation of all sen-
tient beings. It was this saviour who became the inspiration and
model for those who carried Buddhism into distant lands.

There are pious stories of missionaries starting out from
northwest India to carry their message to distant China, which
they called Cīnasthāna. But the spread of Buddhism to China
seems rather to have followed the pattern of slow diffusion via
intermediate cultures, which we have seen as characteristic of
the relations between China and India. The oasis kingdoms and
trading centers of Inner Asia, colonized and developed from India and Persia, gradually became centers of Indo-Iranian culture
and of the Buddhist faith, which, in these cultures was
modified as it was "translated" into Indo-Iranian languages
and adapted to local traditions. From these centers the first missionaries made their way along the trade routes through the
Jade Gate (Yü-men) and on to important centers in far northwestern China; the spectacular archaeological discoveries at
Tun-huang testify to its role as a cosmopolitan trading center
and a point of "transshipment" of diverse cultural elements.

From there, in turn, Buddhism spread gradually along China's internal trade routes. At first, indeed for perhaps two centuries, it was little noticed, or was mistaken for a new variety of Taoism. Many of the early propagators of Buddhism in China were members of trading families who came from Central Asia via the land routes or, later, by sea to southern ports. The former, as we know from their distinctive Chinese surnames, were immigrants from one or another of the Indo-Iranian oasis kingdoms of Central Asia. A lesser number, especially those who came later by sea to Chinese ports were of Indian origin.[3]

The scattered Buddhist enclaves of the second century A.D. had little impact on their communities, much less on the civilization of the Han Empire. What happened, then, to transform Buddhism into a major force in Chinese thought and society? Here we can offer only the barest outline of the momentous events of the period A.D. 180–600 that explain this transformation. The first great united Chinese empire—the Han—began to disintegrate in the second century A.D. Its institutions failed to accommodate to new forces in society, and the disaffected—elite and peasantry alike—withdrew their support or joined movements of dissidence and revolt.

The first great mass rising in Chinese history, the Revolt of the Yellow Turbans, which began in A.D. 184, brought the final dissolution of Han institutions and a violent rending of the social fabric. A war of all against all ensued, punctuated occasionally by moments of uneasy peace enforced by powerful warlords. Characteristic of this period are the mass migrations of the peasantry driven from one area to another by unchecked banditry and by plagues and famines that no one had the power or the will to alleviate. Early in the fourth century, non-Chinese peoples of the borderlands seized control of the whole of north China—the heartland of Chinese civilization, and set up a series of harsh military governments that warred among themselves and occasionally threatened the weak Chinese dynasties set up in the lower Yangtze by émigrés from the north.[4]

This, then, was a period of violent upheavals, of the destruction of older ways of life, of insecurity for all. And, inevitably, it was also a period of doubt, questioning, and experiment in the realm of ideas; it was China's second great age of intellectual ferment (the first being the period of the Warring States, 481–221 B.C.). Among the masses, popular religious movements offering some security and hope of salvation attracted large and fanatical followings; among the elite, there was first a searching and destructive critique of Confucianism, the state orthodoxy of the fallen Han, and then a search for ideas that might explain their plight and point the way to the restoration of a viable society. Taoism ultimately became the main focus of intellectual interest, and its early texts were studied and debated with brilliance and fervor. In this environment and this intellectual climate Buddhism emerged with its new ideas and new formulas for salvation.[5]

It was in this period that Buddhism, and with it, elements of Indian civilization, found their way into Chinese thought and society. If we were to describe this process in the most general terms, we would say that Indian civilization, through Buddhism, made itself felt in China when China's indigenous order was weakened, and that it had its greatest impact precisely at those points where the indigenous order was weakest. This hypothesis is forcefully confirmed by a great eleventh-century Confucian who, in the course of a long polemic against Buddhism, said, ". . . some two hundred years after the Three Dynasties (Hsia, Shang, and Chou) had fallen into decay, when kingly rule ceased and the proper social norms and the standard of righteousness were neglected, Buddhism came into China. It is clear then that Buddhism took advantage of this time of decay and neglect to come and plague us. . . ."[6]

In the balance of this chapter we shall consider a few of these points where Buddhism did penetrate and transform the fabric of Chinese civilization. But first, a brief word on missionary strategy. Since Buddhism had no single center to plan or direct missionary enterprises, the Buddhist penetration of each civilization it encountered tended to be ad hoc, adapted to the specific character of that civilization. Its broad tendency was to adjust, to adapt to seeming needs and vulnerabilities, and to graft itself on to existing values and cults. As it did this wherever it penetrated, there developed as many subvarieties of Buddhism as there were subcultures in the far-flung lands of Eurasia that it reached. We have just noted that it penetrated

China at the weak points and the fissures in its indigenous traditions, and this appears to have been true in its other theaters of
penetration. In missionary enterprise generally there are two
broad strategies: to attempt conversion from the top layer of
society downward, or to begin with the lower social levels and
work upward. In the case we are considering, the former
strategy was dominant. One of the earliest propagators of the
faith remarked to his disciples: "Now we are experiencing a year
of misfortunes. Without rulers of states to rely on it is difficult
to get our religious activities established."[7] In the different
societies of the barbarian-dominated north and the Chinese successor states of the Yangtze valley, the Buddhist appeal was
always first to the ruler and the elite; later, newly converted
monks would move—with the rulers' explicit or tacit
consent—to spread the faith among the peasantry.

Buddhism, as it had evolved over the centuries following
Gautama's death, and in its long passage through diverse cultures and societies en route to China, had absorbed or developed appeals for all manner of men in almost every human situation. To the jaded intellectuals of the Chinese successor states
in the south it offered (at first in familiar terms) fresh ideas to
replace the neo-Taoist notions that had by now led to ennui and
fatalism. To the crude warlords of the north, it offered ways to
calm the haunts and dreads that resulted from lives spent in
murder and rapine. And it offered magical performances to attract the attention and win the faith of all the credulous in an
age of credulity. It drew on traditions of Indian medicine to effect cures, and thereby, conversions. To the wretched peasants
of north and south alike it presented approachable deities
whose help would avail in all the crises of life and formulas that
would take them, in death, to paradises of endless bliss.

Most pervasively, Buddhism offered an easy explanation for
the gross inequities of the Chinese world of the time: each person's lot in life was determined by the karma that had accumulated in previous incarnations, and each person's lot in the next
life would be determined by whether he added or diminished
the store through evil deeds. Thus, the tyrannical and the arro-
gant would be brought low, and the lot of the humble and
compassionate would rise in the lives to come. Once this belief

was accepted, the formulas presented for the improvement of one's karma-store were of almost infinite variety. To name but a few: charitable gifts—from the peasant's mite to the landed magnate's donation of his estate and his mansion to serve as a monastery, acts of worship—from simple invocation of one of the savior divinities to great masses and scripture readings for the multitudes; dedication of the self—leaving lay life for a monastery or nunnery, there to chose one or more of the varied modes of the religious life: translation of the scriptures, preaching, exegesis, meditation, charitable works, or some other; giving oneself as a temple slave or, in a perversion of Buddhist idealism, immolating oneself for the benefit of all living creatures. The list could be extended almost indefinitely.

All this things were new in China, and, as we have noted, they became subtly changed as they were adapted to Chinese culture and changed in ways that would meet specific contemporary needs, add to, modify, or enrich strands of Chinese traditions. We might look briefly at a sampling of the cultural realms in which this occurred; this, let us emphasize, represents but a tiny fragment of the whole, but it may serve to illustrate *how* Buddhism, Indian in origin, transformed the civilization of China.

### SOCIAL VALUES

The imperial Confucianism developed in the Han Dynasty had prescribed standards of behavior for elite and masses; it had insisted on familial values such as the submission of youth to age, of female to male; it placed particular emphasis on the continuity, the sanctity, of the blood line; it exalted the codified traditional norms *(li)* so that they seemed to have cosmic as well as human application; it insisted on the analogy between the son's absolute submission to his father and the official's absolute obedience to his ruler; it exalted the Confucian Classics as *the* source of wisdom, *the* guide to acceptable behavior.[8]

Regarding imperial Confucianism, there were sceptics even in Han times, and the effectiveness of its ideals and values were severely undermined in the chaos that followed the Han breakup in the second century A.D. The family was clung to desperately as an element of order, but men sought new ideas that could explain the chaotic state of society and bring some degree of order and humanity to the body social. The Bodhisattva ideal—with its spiritual attractiveness, and the social values associated with it, went a long way toward meeting this need. It inspired renunciation of self and encouraged compassion and charity, for even the humblest Buddhist partook of the Bodhisattva's qualities when he made a donation for the feeding of the poor, or for the maintenance of dispensaries, hospitals, or homes for the aged.

The Bodhisattva ideal was something new in China's ethical universe. It enlarged the sphere of an individual's ethical obligations far beyond the older limits of duties to the family and loyalty to the ruler. And much that had seemed central to Chinese social thinkers was dismissed by the Buddhists as so many epiphenomena. These things are merely suggestive of the revolutionary value change that Buddhism brought to China.

### STATE IDEOLOGY

The Han empire had elaborated the theory of the emperor as son of heaven and cosmic pivot. But the crises of the declining Han saw puppet, often infant, emperors being manipulated by palace women, eunuchs, and warlords. In the states that morsellized China after the Han collapse, one warlord or local satrap after another proclaimed himself Son of Heaven and Lord of Men and went through the traditional ritual forms of legitimation. Yet these wore thin and unconvincing with repeated and abortive use. And as peasantry and elites alike more and more adopted the new religion, it was natural that those who aspired to rule would invoke Buddhist sanctions, Buddhist legitimation.

In North China, Turco-Mongol rulers, initially under the influence of wonder-working monks, embraced the new religion with enthusiasm, and, in the course of time, used Buddhist ideas to legitimize their rule. The rulers of the Northern Wei (386–534) accepted with enthusiasm the idea that the reigning emperor *is* a Buddha and thus worthy to receive the submission of his subjects on both secular and religious grounds.[9] Rulers in the south also sought the loyalty of their subjects on both grounds. They not only continued the pomp and circumstance of Chinese emperors, they also posed as great benefactors and patrons of the faith *(mahādānapati);* they accepted for themselves such hybrid titles as P'u-sa T'ien-tzu, "Bodhisattva Son of Heaven" and Huang-ti pu-sa, "Sovereign Emperor Bodhisattva." Several monarchs were attracted to the model of the great Emperor Aśoka of the Mauryas (fourth century B.C.) as he was presented in the Buddhist scriptures: a powerful and successful unifier on a subcontinental scale, a Buddhist convert doing penance for his bloody campaigns, a propagator of the faith, a veritable avatar of the holy and effective ruler of the Indian tradition—a Cakravartin-rāja. Aśoka inspired his Chinese emulators to spectacular public acts of penitence, to massive public support of Buddhist charities, to imperially sponsored temple building, translation projects, and much more.[10] Thus for many centuries, Chinese modes of legitimizing political power were elaborated and enriched by Indian Buddhist elements, and the monarchs found personal reassurance in Buddhist definitions of their role.

### WAR

The period of Buddhism's great initial influence in China was a period of the disintegration of the social and political order and of incessant war. Yet, death or disfigurement in battle was particularly abhorrent to those indoctrined with the Chinese cult of filial submissiveness, for one of the imperatives of that cult was that the son should return his body intact to his grave, just as he had received it from his parents. And it was of the greatest importance to be buried near the graves of one's ancestors so that the blood descendants might serve one's shade with appropriate sacrifices and prevent its becoming a homeless and untended ghost *(kuei).*

It is ironical that the Buddhist religion of compassion should be used to lessen men's reluctance to go into murderous battles far from home, but so it was. For the devout, the horror of death in battle was assuaged by the thought of rebirth in one of the blissful heavens over which Buddhas and Bodhisattvas presided. Rulers early introduced the institution of the battlefield temple, permanently endowed, where masses would be said for the souls of those who had died in battle, and the spiritual felicity of their after-lives would be constantly attended to.[11]

Some rulers urged their subjects into battle with the claim that they fought for a righteous cause for nothing less than the transformation of China into an ideal state, a veritable "Buddha-land."

## THE ECONOMY

The monastery as an institution was entirely new in China, and celibate life in a monastery was utterly at odds with familism and the cult of ancestors. Yet, as we have noted, after the fall of the Han and in the ensuing chaos, no values were sacrosanct, and monasticism as an alternative way of life—one dedicated to the high ideal of the salvation of all living creatures—proved attractive to many Chinese. Monastic institutions, as they developed, introduced new elements into China's economic as well as spiritual life. Gifts by the pious added to the positive karma-store of the donor, and donations of land, money, precious metals, and slaves provided the great monasteries with vast amounts of capital. The investment of these gifts of capital so as to yield a return meant that the donor's gift was repeated over time, and the felicitous original purpose was served again and again. Jacques Gernet shows that monastic investments introduced into China the notion and the techniques of the productive use of capital.[12]

The great monasteries developed business offices under the headship of the monastic manager which carried on ramifying enterprises. For example, they invested in mortgages, and often foreclosed—thus adding to the monastery's lands; they built and operated at a profit oil presses and water-driven mills; they sponsored local fairs and rented the stalls or collected a percentage on the merchandise sold; they set up pawn shops and operated ateliers to manufacture holy images to sell to pilgrims, and they established other enterprises.[13]

The monasteries had the capital to embark on large-scale land reclamation and irrigation projects and thus transformed poor tracts of land into productive ones. Since no monk could possess land individually, all lands were held in common and exploited for the maximum benefit of the monastery. As unexpectedly as in reference to warfare, Buddhism had far-reaching economic effects, and Gernet attributes many of the changing configurations of the Chinese economy between the fifth and the tenth centuries to the influence of Buddhism.[14]

## POPULAR RELIGION

In the centuries before Buddhism the cults and observances of popular religion varied enormously from subculture to subculture in the vast land area of China. But we can speak of certain elements that were common to all. One was the belief—common to many primitive societies—in a universe filled with unseen forces that might have effects, for good or evil, on the affairs of men. This underlying belief led to sacrifices, propitiatory rituals, and seasonal observances of all kinds designed to ward off evil and bring into play the forces for good. The objectives of all such observances—led by the elders of the villages—were the fertility of the land and abundant yields. Ancestor veneration was initially in part a supplement to other fertility rites, for the dead were believed to have potency in the affairs of the living and thus could affect the crops as well as the fortunes of their particular families. The dead required appropriate ritual homage and seasonal sacrifices. In addition, there was a variety of spirits, good and evil, that had an interest in the human community and had to be specially dealt with in the best interests of all. These were such spirits as those that presided over wells or springs, the tutelary divinities—often mountain spirits—of a village or an area, and spirits and malevolent ghosts which needed special measures to neutralize the potential harm they might do. Shamans and mediums were thought to command the necessary skills, and they existed in all communities.

The propagators of Buddhism, as they made their way into rural communities, did not require that the peasants renounce ancestral ways. Rather, they gradually gave a Buddhist coloration to existing observances; for example, they would convert a seasonal festival involving blood sacrifices into one that was accompanied by a vegetarian banquet for the Buddhist faithful. As the rudiments of a simple, salvationist Buddhism were spread among the peasantry, new cult figures, Buddhist divinities, were introduced; sometimes these figures replaced in function an older native divinity; sometimes their attributes were subtly merged with the attributes of a local god of long-standing popularity. The spells and incantations of Buddhism were introduced as novel, more potent than the indigenous varieties, and Buddhist ceremonies of all kinds were more colorful, far richer in symbolism than the older rituals.

New institutions of Buddhist origin also came into the peasant villages. Among them were cooperative societies—for mutual aid for burials, for particular seasonal observances, for pilgrimages to holy places. And, as we have noted in connection with the economy, the network of Buddhist monasteries and nunneries, as this expanded, had profound effects in the rural communities. Buddhism also had strong millennialist and apocalyptic traditions, and these were soon put to use to inspire and propel popular revolts against the existing order. It is no accident that for a thousand years after the penetration of Buddhism, Chinese rebel soldiers wore white—the color associated with Maitreya, the Buddha that would bring about the end of the old and usher in a new heaven and a new earth.[15]

After the reintegration of the Chinese empire about 620, strong governments sought to control local Buddhist practices, to eliminate, for example, the unauthorized monks who had taken over many of the functions of the local shamans and exorcists. But in the long period from the arrival of Buddhism to the reunification of empire, ephemeral governments lacked the power to police the beliefs of their peasant populations. And the local elites, which in the Han system were to provide moral guidance and example to the peasantry, had first been scattered and decimated, and then replaced in large part by rapacious local satraps who cared for little but their own enrichment. Thus, Buddhism made its way among a peasant population that was without its traditional guardians and mentors, a peasant population that was in desperate need of help and reassurance in a hostile world. The Buddhist invasion of the peasant communities is one more striking validation of the eleventh-century philosopher's judgment that " . . . when kingly rule ceased and the proper social norms and the standard of righteousness were neglected, Buddhism . . . took advantage of this time of decay and neglect to come and plague us. . . ."

These few pages have been meant to suggest how a protestant religion of the Indo-Gangetic plain became a universal religion, and how it moved slowly across the most formidable geographic barriers on earth, passing to interact with the various cultures along the routes of trade until it finally entered the Chinese world. There, we have argued, it spread in a time that was propitious for a foreign religion, a time when the indigenous community of institutions and values was in crisis, and a combination of internal decay and barbarian invasion had weakened the resistance of Chinese culture to imported ideas and practices.

But, as in all such cases, the native culture did not weaken in every strand, and Buddhism made its greatest inroads where a strand had become attenuated or broken. The subsequent history of Buddhism in China sees the reassertion of indigenous traditions and the creation of Chinese ideas and practices that competed with those of Buddhism and sought to wrest from it those cultural realms where it had had the most success. But it is fair to say that in these reassertions of native traditions there was extensive borrowing from Buddhism—the creation of Chinese analogues to Buddhist ideas and practices, the recasting of existing traditions with the help of Buddhist borrowings, the fusion of deities of similar attributes, and so forth. Thus, in the long run, elements of Buddhism, whether acknowledged or not, became part of the evolving fabric of Chinese civilization.

NOTES

1. Portions of this chapter were adapted from "India and China," which appeared, in 1963, in a special issue of *Cambridge Opinion* (No. 36) devoted to the transmission of culture.

2. Hu Shih, "The Indianization of China" in *Independence, Convergence and Borrowing in Institutions, Thought and Art* (Cambridge, Mass.: Harvard University Press, 1937).

3. For the early history of Buddhist penetration, see Arthur F. Wright, *Buddhism in Chinese History* (Stanford: Stanford University Press, 1959), pp. 21–41.

4. For a vivid account of this age of disintegration see Etienne Balazs, "Political Philosophy and Social Crisis at the End of the Han Dynasty" in his *Chinese Civilization and Bureaucracy: Variations on a Theme* (New Haven: Yale University Press, 1964), pp. 187–225.

5. For a depiction of the intellectual life of this period and its deep discontents, see Balazs, "Nihilistic Revolt or Mystical Escapism: Currents of

Thought in China During the Third Century A.D." in *Chinese Civilization and Bureaucracy*, pp. 226–254.

6. Ou-Yang Hsiu (1007–1070), "Essay on Fundamentals" *[Pen-lun]* translated in W. T. deBary, ed., *Sources of Chinese Tradition* (New York: Columbia University Press, 1960), p. 442.

7. The first great Chinese propagator of the faith, Tao-an, is addressing his disciples, ca. 365. Cf. Arthur E. Link, "Biography of Shih Tao-an" (as translated from the *Kao Seng Chuan* [Lives of Eminent Monks]) *T'oung Pao* 46–1/2 (1958):14.

8. For a brief account of late Han thought and society, see Wright, *Buddhism in Chinese History*, pp. 3–20.

9. The *Wei-shu* [History of the Wei Dynasty by Wei Shou], chap. 114 as translated by Tsukamoto Zenryū and Leon Hurvitz, published as a supplement to volume 16 of Mizuno and Nagahiro, *Unko Sekkutsu no Kenkyū* (Kyoto, 1956), p. 53. The authorship of this convenient theological principle is usually credited to the monk Fa-kuo who was active at the end of the fourth and the beginning of the fifth centuries A.D.

10. The most spectacular reenactment of Aśoka's acts of piety was that of Sui Wen-ti (reign, 581–605). Cf. Wright, "The Formation of Sui Ideology" in J. K. Fairbank, ed., *Chinese Thought and Institutions* (Chicago, 1957), pp. 93–104.

11. A magisterial account of this phenomenon is Paul Demiéville, "Le Bouddhisme et la guerre" in *Mélanges publiés par l'Institut des Hautes Études Chinoises*, vol. 1 (Paris, 1957), pp. 347–385.

12. Jacques Gernet, *Les aspects économiques du Bouddhisme dans la société chinoise du Ve au Xe siècle* (Saïgon, 1956).

13. L. S. Yang, "Buddhist Monasteries and Four Money-raising Institutions in Chinese History." Reprinted in his *Studies in Chinese Institutional History* (Cambridge, 1961), pp. 198–215.

14. Gernet, *Les aspects économiques du Bouddhisme*, p. 90.

15. Cf. Yuji Muramatsu, "Some Themes in Chinese Rebel Ideologies" in A. F. Wright, ed., *The Confucian Persuasion* (Stanford: Stanford University Press, 1960), pp. 241–267.

# 8

## CHINESE CIVILIZATION

### Arthur F. Wright

> Though force remains the ultimate basis of any
> state, control of the people in China is more nearly
> psychological than by physical coercion. Its extent
> would be hard to overstate.
>
> Ross Terrill, journalist-traveller, 1971

Imperial China—the political and social system that prevailed
over half a continent from 221 B.C. to February of 1912—is an
awesome subject of contemplation. It survived almost incredible vicissitudes: years of foreign invasion and domination, long
sequences of natural disasters and destructive rebellions. At the
end of each of these seemingly catastrophic reverses, the system
was somehow pieced together, refurbished, updated, and made
to function once more. Although the active forces that drove
out the invaders or put down the rebellions and thus brought a
semblance of peace to the land were military, it was not military
force alone that assured the restoration of the system, the return
to functional effectiveness of social institutions or the institutions of central and local government. Rather it was the literate
elite reasserting its ancient values and drawing on its formidable
arsenal of techniques for winning consent, cooperation, conformity. Thus imperial China offers in almost unimaginable
richness what Lasswell calls "the techniques of influencing
human action by the manipulation of representations . . .
spoken, written, pictorial or musical . . . ."[1]

There are historical determinants that made this so, and we
should discuss some of these before turning to typical situations
and content studies that will make up the bulk of this chapter.

We might begin by noting the geographical fact that the Chinese empire (expanding continually in the period we are considering) was simply too large and too populous to be governed by the direct use of force in the absence of consent. The oft-quoted remark of a Confucian to the founder of the Han Dynasty, "You may have conquered the empire on horseback, but can you indeed rule it on horseback?"[2] is a proverbial way of making this obvious point. Second, it was a cardinal principle of all Confucianisms that man could, by the persuasion and example of his moral superiors, be changed for the better and that, once this was done, it would be possible to assure harmony among individuals, justice and stability in the political and social orders. This principle became a prime ingredient of the eclectic ideology that we call imperial Confucianism. Belief in the efficacy of persuasion (including example) was a basic article of faith in imperial Confucianism, and it endured through all the doctrinal reformulations that were made over the centuries.

A second historical determinant lies in the genesis of the imperial system itself. In essence the system was based on an alliance for mutual benefit between an emperor who gained his power by the superior use of force and a landed literate elite who could help him and his house maintain power, first by manipulating the symbols of legitimation, second by cajoling and eliciting the consent of the governed, and third by assuming the functions of civil government at the capital and local levels. The literate elite were always antipathetic toward imperial force, splendor, and extravagance, but they could not do without a figure at the top of their hierarchical social and political orders; nor could they—despite their preferences—do without a force to call upon when indoctrination and persuasion failed and domestic rebellion erupted or invaders descended on the land. The imperial system is thus an amalgam of two sets of elements: the sinews and the symbols of the emperor system with its origins in primitive kingship, its developed form in the short-lived empire of Ch'in (221–206 B.C.); the values and the political skills of the literate elite with their origins in the period of the Warring States and the age of the first great Chinese thinkers. The imperial ideology formulated in the Han to rationalize and justify this uneasy but—as it turned out—

enduring alliance was a strange amalgam. For our purposes we call this ideology imperial Confucianism. Let us first note its highly eclectic character. The "Confucians" who commended themselves to the Han rulers and developed this ideology felt obliged to compromise in two ways. First of all, they had to graft the emperor system and its mystique on to the teachings of Confucius and justify it by Classics he allegedly wrote or edited. Second, they were determined that the new ideology should be all-inclusive and that it should put all its rivals out of competition; this led to extensive borrowings from rival schools and the absorption into Confucianism of quite alien strains such as Five Element symbolism, *yin-yang* theory, and much more. It is this amalgam, with many accretions over time, that provides most of the representations invoked—down the centuries—by those who practiced either persuasion or propaganda.

A third determining factor is more subtle. I assume there is no way of assigning different specific gravities to words— especially written words—as these figure in different cultures. But if there were, I believe that the weight of the written word —its assumed efficacy in affecting events—would be greater in Chinese civilization than in others. The obvious explanations are briefly stated. A single symbol system was in continuous use for more than thirty-five hundred years. Those symbols were, in early times, manipulated with great solemnity by a small class of scribes. The written symbols were viewed with awe—as indeed they were in many early societies—because they were thought to evoke the potency of whatever they denominated. Some of this attitude carried over into the culture of imperial China where the mass of illiterates looked up to a small elite above them—an elite differentiated by its mastery of the written word. Further, the individual symbols did not change; they— and particularly those with value connotations—accumulated with the passage of time a tremendous weight of contextual reference and allusive meaning. To this was added what we can only call aesthetic weight, that is, regard for the well-written word as an aesthetic object. It is a striking contrast that, in the West, it was not until the Renaissance that words engraved on durable materials became visually important aesthetic objects.[3]

Words being thus freighted with potency tend, as Granet

argued so eloquently, to acquire an emblematic force, and the conferment of auspicious and appropriate nomenclature was one of the solemn duties of the ruler of men advised by his literate elite. The "Record of Rites" *(Li-chi)*, a highly esteemed and eclectic Classic of imperial Confucianism, asserts that this duty was assumed by the rulers of remote antiquity. Speaking of the Yellow Emperor, sometimes held to be the founder of the Chinese order, it says: "Huang-ti gave correct names to the myriad things and thereby enlightened the people as to the sharing of resources."[4]

In addition to its cumulative store of efficacious words, imperial China inherited and developed a vast and complex range of public enactments intended to propitiate unseen powers and to produce in those who witnessed them quasi-religious awe and submission to established authority. At the very beginning of recorded history the kings are said to have performed three hundred and sixty sacrifices per year. And many of the potencies the early kings evoked or placated, many features of the performances—timing, gesture, music, impedimenta—remained constants in the ceremonies of imperial China; here, as in the case of words, the cumulative weight of reenactment century after century added to the awesomeness of the performances. One underlying assumption of great importance also remained constant: chiefs, kings, emperors were the most potent mediators between the world of men and unseen forces within a single organic universe. It was their responsibility to sense dislocations in the world of nature or of men and to take remedial action (as recommended by official ritualists) of a ceremonial or symbolic kind; the histories have voluminous and detailed records of such performances. For example, as late as 1370, we find an emperor performing in person the act of ritual exposure resorted to since the dawn of time by chiefs and kings to end a period of drought.[5] And, in 1770, on his eightieth birthday, the Ch'ienlung emperor presented two invocations to the gods of T'aishan, the sacred mountain of the eastern quarter; after listing the various offerings presented for the pleasure of the gods, he ends the second invocation with this sentiment: "All this signifies that I have performed an impeccable sacrifice and have offered irreproachable prayers. The mulberry tree of Fu (whence the sun rises) shining at dawn annouces an increased prosperity; the magical *T'ai* amulet which I hold in my hand promises a universal spring for all creatures . . . ."⁶ By Ch'ien-lung's time, the solemn rites at T'ai-shan had been performed by emperors of China for two millennia.

Another feature of the civilization of imperial China was the seriousness and intensity of record keeping and the preservation into our time of the most detailed continuous record of a human society. This is not the place for a disquisition on this impressive heritage, but one of its characteristics is particularly relevant for this chapter. It is that the records were kept by the literate elite and reflect their values and interests, for example, their belief in the moral dynamic in history, their obsessive concern for social stability, orthodoxy, and political legitimacy. It follows from this that the record is blank or incomplete on mass movements that were always knit together by heterodox ideologies and invariably presented a threat to the social order. The record is therefore as thin on the uses and effects of propaganda among dissidents as it is rich on the use of representations by the established powers.

In breaking down our subject into units of analysis, three variables are crucial: (1) the origin of the representation, whether drawn from elite or popular tradition; (2) the intended target of the words, symbols, or ritual enactments; and (3) who (in general, what social class) drew upon the available store of representations to propagandize or persuade. These three variables in different combinations offer a ready-made structure for this chapter. But as in all things human, symmetry and uniformity are not to be expected. As we have noted, the character of the sources provides rich coverage of some combinations, scanty detail on others. The incredible volume of documentation makes it impossible for any scholar to exploit more than a tiny fraction of it. Further, Chinese historians and scholars of the imperial age used no relatively neutral terms that might be equivalent to ''propaganda'' or ''persuasion,'' so one must seek material under a great variety of other rubrics.

### THE USE OF FORMAL REPRESENTATIONS
We begin with the best documented and possibly the most frequent combination: when, in a struggle to gain, consolidate, or

hold on to power, one segment of the elite allied with the emperor manipulates representations so as to win over the rest of the elite. This usually occurs at crisis points in the struggle for power: the attempt to found a new dynasty, the effort to legitimize a usurpation or restore a ruling house that has suffered disastrous reverses. In dynastic foundings, efforts of this kind are usually made when substantial territorial power has been won and a capital captured or established. These are the moments, it would seem, when occupation of the land by force must begin to give way to civil rule. The number and variety of steps meant to win over the various regional elites are staggering. Let us run through a few of them. First the victorious warrior must, in consultation with his specialists, decide upon an auspicious day, month, and year for him to hold his first audience, proclaim a new dynasty, and begin to reign. This is often the culmination of a long series of highly formalized steps divesting the previous power holders of their legitimacy. The name of the dynasty, carefully chosen, must now be proclaimed in an imperial edict (down to the thirteenth century such names reflected the geographic origins of the new ruling house; thereafter dynastic names were chosen for their symbolic resonance). Along with the dynastic name an era-name is proclaimed and all documents begin to be dated accordingly; era-names used for longer or shorter sequences of years are rich in symbols —particularly of the age-long desiderata of the Chinese people: "peace," "tranquillity," "harmony," "prosperity," "good fortune," and the like.

Sometime during the first months, the new ruler must take a great number of other steps, and we give a sampling of them. Advised by his specialists, he establishes an imperial ancestral hall on a correctly located site and gives posthumous names and titles to his ancestors for several generations back. Again, after discussion among the experts, the new emperor will designate a color and a musical note for his dynasty and specify the colors of court robes to be worn by various ranks of officials for different kinds of court functions. Renaming things (whether there is substantive change or not) proceeds apace: street names, palace names, and gate names in the capital; the names of some counties, prefectures, and often provinces; the titles of officials of various ranks and the names of governmental bureaus. All these actions, we should note, involve the conferment of appropriate nomenclature, and the act of conferment itself stakes one's claim to be Son of Heaven, while the grandiloquent style of the edicts is well suited to hide any real shortcomings of the new house and to adduce historical precedent and moral rightness on the side of the new dynasty.

Two key questions immediately arise. How are all these portentuous actions communicated to the target group, and, second, how seriously are they taken by this group? Edicts of great importance may first be read out from a palace gate tower by an imperial herald, so that some at least of the capital population might hear them. Then they are ordered sent by messenger to prefectural capitals already under the control of the new dynasty. At these local centers they may again be read out, or, alternatively, the text posted prominently in the town. The ninth-century Japanese traveller Ennin gives a particularly vivid account of how an imperial rescript was dealt with in a prefectural capital. This event is not in a period of dynastic consolidation, but the procedures designed to give great weight to such communications were probably used under many different circumstances:

> An Imperial Rescript by the new Emperor has arrived from the capital. Two carpets were spread in the courtyard in front of the gate of the official residence inside the city walls, and above the steps on the north side of the great gate was placed a stand, on which was spread a purple cloth, and on this was placed the Imperial Rescript, written on yellow paper. The Administrative Officers and Secretaries of the prefecture . . . the military officials, the common people, and the monks, nuns, and Taoist priests stood in ranks according to their posts on the east side of the court facing west. The Magistrate emerged from his residence, preceded by twenty military officers, ten each leading the way on the left and the right. When the Secretaries, the subprefectural officials, and the others saw the Magistrate come out, they bowed their heads almost to the ground.
>
> The Magistrate called out, "The common people," and they chanted a response all together. The Magistrate stood on one of the carpets and an Administrative Officer stood on the other, both of them facing west (the direction of the T'ang capital). Then a

military officer called out the titles of the various officials, and the row of Secretaries and subprefectural officials chanted their response in unison. Next he called out to the row of Military Guard Officers, Generals, and Commissioners of Troops, and the row of military men chanted their response in unison. He also said, "The various guests," and the official guests and clients chanted their response. Next he said, "The common people," and the common people, both old and young, chanted their response together. Then he said, "The monks and Taoist priests," and the monks, nuns, and Taoist priests chanted their response all together.

Next, two military officers brought the stand with the Imperial Rescript and placed it in front of the Magistrate, who bowed once and then picked up the Imperial Rescript in his hand and lowered his head, touching it to his forehead. A military officer knelt and received the Imperial Rescript on his sleeve and, holding it up, went into the courtyard and, standing facing north, chanted, "An Imperial order has arrived." The Magistrate, Administrative Officers, Secretaries, and the military, all together bowed again. A military officer called out, "Let the common people bow," and the people bowed again, but the monks, nuns, and Taoist priests did not bow. . . . Two . . . Assistant Judges read the Rescript alternating with each other. Their voices were loud, as when government decisions are announced in our country. The Imperial Rescript was some four or five sheets of paper long, and it took quite a long time to read, while no one sat down. . . . [Finally] a military officer called out, "You may leave," and they all chanted their response in unison. The officials, the military, the monks and Taoist priests, and the common people thereupon dispersed.[7]

Note in this description, the numerical, directional, and color symbolism: ten each on the left and on the right; the principal participants on the east (preferred) quarter, the formal gesture of receiving the document facing the north—the direction of the pole star, the center of the universe, the ideal locus of the Son of Heaven. The purple of the cloth on which the rescript was placed was symbolic of the fifteen circumpolar stars and of the emperor's palace; the yellow of the paper was traditionally the imperial color. Note also the elements of liturgy, of "audience participation" in the whole performance.

We asked a second question regarding the probable effects of such communications: how seriously were they taken? It is clear that the people observed by Ennin took the reading of an imperial rescript with deadly seriousness despite the fact—which we know in retrospect—that, by this time, the power of the great dynasty of T'ang had long been on the wane. In cases of a new dynasty, such efforts at suasion had to overcome two sorts of reserve on the part of the elite: the feeling that the new holders of power were usurpers, lacking the legitimacy that would give credibility to such communication. And, second, a reserve—born of historical knowledge and an instinct for self-preservation—regarding the ultimate success of the challengers. In periods of protracted strife, a man might have seen, in his lifetime, several aspirants going through similar performances only to fail in the end. What convinced were sustained success, the reappearance of civil officials, the repair of governmental installations, and so forth. Symbolic manipulations, however deeply rooted in history and culture, are effective only when signs have begun to appear that the new power holders are likely to succeed.

Wang Mang (reign, A.D. 6–23), who usurped the power of the great Han and founded his own dynasty, appears to us in the record as a man obsessed with the manipulation of representations. The sources, which may be suspected of some measure of caricature, depict him as spending a disproportionate amount of time on matters of nomenclature and ceremonial enactments to the neglect of practical affairs. "Wang Mang's notion was that once institutions were fixed, the empire would pacify itself. Hence he thought in detail about symmetrical, geographical dispositions, about instituting proper rituals, about the composition of appropriate music. To discuss how to harmonize the theories of the Six Classics in regard to these things, the ministers entered the palace at dawn and left at dusk. The discussions went on for years on end without coming to any decisions. . . ."[8] The text goes on to say that as a result Wang Mang did not have the time to review law cases, to deal with crises among the people, or to appoint qualified officials or supervise their performances.

Some seven centuries later (at the high tide of Buddhist influence in China) another usurper showed the same anxious concern for the use of all representations that would persuade people of her legitimacy. This was the Empress Wu, who—after three decades of de facto rule—in 690 established her own dynasty of Chou and went so far as to have herself proclaimed "emperor." She found malleable Buddhist monks who tampered with a sacred text so that it showed her to be an incarnation of the Buddha Maitreya sent by Yama, king of the netherworld, to rule the earth; special temples were established in each prefecture where this text would be expounded. She decreed that her capital was to be called the "divine capital" *(shen-tu)*—the center of a state cult supporting her claims to legitimacy. She, like Wang Mang, engaged in large-scale conferment of new nomenclature, and like him she expended great resources in building a *ming-t'ang,* or cosmic house—a building that was traditionally constructed as a microcosm of the universe in which the Son of Heaven could perform the various seasonal enactments meant to assure harmony in the cosmos. She built her *ming-t'ang* on a grand scale, and it was dramatic testimony that she indeed presided, in her "divine capital," over all the forces of the universe. To press the symbolism home, she had erected a great metal column 105 feet high, which she called *T'ien-shu,* or pivot of the sky—the name given to the all-important pole star in Chinese astronomy and, following Confucius, used metaphorically for the capital, the center of virtuous and effective government on earth. On the pillar the empress (emperor) wrote the chief inscription, which read "The celestial pivot commemorating the ten thousand virtues of the Great Chou Dynasty."[9]

These brief remarks on two usurpers show them as obsessively concerned with acts and symbols that would shore up a dubious legitimacy. The histories record—certainly in the case of Empress Wu—the protests of scholars and imperial censors against the extravagance, the pretensions of many of her acts. But, of course, her dynasty did not last, and the historians' records favor the T'ang, which was restored in 705. So we can never know—any more than we can in the case of Wang Mang whose rule is recorded by Han legitimists—what the contemporary reaction to all these actions really was. In the case of the Empress Wu, a guess would be that by the closing years of her reign, her symbolic extravaganzas probably impressed very few.

Let us turn to another case in which a newly enthroned

emperor was bidding for the allegiance of many who deplored his rise to power and the means by which he had seized it. This is T'ang T'ai-tsung (reign 626–649), who has come down in history and in myth as the paragon of princely virtue, but whose accession followed on his murder of two of his brothers—one of them the crown prince—and the forced retirement of his father. In 626 the T'ang dynasty was eight years and one reign old; parts of the country were newly conquered, the full consolidation of power was yet to be accomplished, and the young T'ai-tsung had need of all available means to strengthen his position. One of those means was the manipulation of words and symbols. And one of the traditional forms was the edict of amnesty—a standard enactment by emperors on such occasions as the proclamation of a new era-name, a victory in war, a notable harvest, the recovery of an imperial family member from an illness, an imperial progress of importance. T'ai-tsung's edict of amnesty and others issued in situations following a coup had the practical purpose of allaying the fears of those who, in a power struggle, had sided with other parties than the victor's, thus reducing the danger of rebellions born of desperation. Let us look at the document, which we may break down into five sections.[10]

The first part opens with a cosmological fanfare, meant to cast an air of solemnity on what is to come: "Heaven alone is great, and the seven heavenly bodies (sun, moon, and the five principal stars) are the means of conferring the timely seasons. Only the sovereign receives Heaven's charge, and then the three spheres (of heaven, earth, and man) can harmoniously nurture the myriad creatures . . . ." The section continues with rhetoric that evokes images of celestial and terrestial harmony, and the whole of this part is filled with allusions to the archaic phrases of the venerable *Book of History* and to the metaphysical portions of the *Book of Changes*. All is appropriately resonant of cosmic forces and grand, if vague, concepts.

The second section is a grandiloquent account of how the great dynasty of T'ang, by a fortunate concatenation of cosmic forces, "grandly received the dragon plan and first initiated the phoenix annals." The dragon is of course an allusion to the yang force, while the phoenix symbolizes the yin. The "dragon plan'' is another term for the "river plan" *(ho-t'u)* one of the primordial portents of emperorship supposedly brought up out of the Yellow River on the back of a dragonlike horse and presented to the mythological Emperor Fu-hsi. The T'ang founder, referred to as "the retired emperor," is praised in extravagant terms: he took the throne and acted as a sage; he was both clever and respectful, and he "grandly took possession of the whole country" [after some seven years of bitter civil war!]. It goes on to praise his tirelessness, his punctilious performance of ritual. "He was deeply respectful of the ancestral hall and the altars of the land and grain; righteously he preserved the sacrifical offerings." It need hardly be added that this section, too, is full of allusions; embedded among the encomiums derived from imperial Confucianism are two that refer to the *Lao-tzu* and to the ideal mode of governing by nonstriving, noninterference. This is apt because, of course, the T'ang ruling house regarded itself as descended from Lao-tzu.

Section three, in which T'ai-tsung uses the imperial "We," makes the usual formal declaration of unworthiness and speaks of his having declined, unsuccessfully, this preeminent place. Thus, "Our spiritual destiny having matured, we ascended to this exalted position. A prince, presiding over all people, follows in the footsteps of the myriad rulers of old. It is like crossing a great river, not knowing who will help one [from the "Great Announcement"—*Ta kao*—chapter of the *Book of History*] . . . . Now, continuing our dynasty's fortunate beginnings and responsive to the blessings of Heaven . . . we declare a great amnesty to the empire."

Section four deals with the indulgences and rewards of the amnesty edict. It provides that the amnesty cover certain types of crimes committed before dawn of the fourth day of September, 626 (the day of T'ai-tsung's formal accession and first audience, a *chia-tzu* day, the first day of a sexagenary cycle). Those who were sentenced to banishment any time after the establishment of the T'ang in 618 were declared free to return to their homes. Then the edict goes on to confer more exalted feudal titles upon certain of the nobility, rewards for officials above a specified rank, remission of taxes in different regions—one or two years according to the prefecture. Then the edict specifies the material rewards in silk, grain, and the like for certain meritorious groups; here we have one way of seeing what values the T'ang, and particularly T'ai-tsung, wished to single out for public notice. Respect for age comes first, and exalting age over youth provides the basis for a stable social hierarchy. Those eighty and older are especially rewarded, those a hundred or more are lavishly rewarded and are also given special patents as tangible testimony to their great age. Gifts are to be made to widows and orphans. Those who are known for their filial behavior (submission to their elders) in their community are to be conducted to an imperial pavillion and generously given fine clothes as a mark of recognition. Men of unusual probity and women who are notably obedient are to have a flag flying to make this known to their villages. Those who are of great age or notable learning, those who are direct in speech and upright in remonstrance are to be recommended by local officials for governmental posts.

Section five specifies some of those excluded from the measure (certain crimes usually excluded from amnesties, such as patricide or the murder of a master by a slave, are not mentioned). Those who are hiding out in the mountains or swamps or are unlawfully sequestering arms have a hundred days to come forward. If they do not, they will be subject to the usual punishment. Anyone who falsely reports a crime as falling before the effective date of the amnesty (and is found out) shall suffer the same punishment as would be meted out for that crime.

We have considered the way representations were manipulated by dynastic founders, usurpers, and successors whose hold on power was initially tenuous. Let us consider briefly a somewhat different situation, that of Sui Wen-ti (reign, 581–604), and focus attention on his final drive to reunify China after more than two and a half centuries of division. He had gained control of the extensive and populous North China plain as well as of the western area of Szechwan; he had a large war machine with multiple forces well prepared for a coordinated attack by land and water. His object was the Ch'en dynasty with its capital at Nanking on the Yangtse. It claimed to be the legitimate heir of the long-vanished Han dynasty and of Han cultural traditions, but by the 580s, the Ch'en was greatly enfeebled by military disasters, internal discord, and the successive loss of strategically important territories. With such advantages as the Sui had, men of other cultures might well have not paused to engage in psychological warfare and the manipulation of representations targeted at the southerners. But the Sui founder was shrewd enough to know that it was necessary to lay the groundwork for his postconquest task of winning consent to his rule. Furthermore, Sui Wen-ti and his cohorts were men of mixed blood and mixed culture, northerners living at the end of three centuries of invasion and the interpenetration of cultures in the north; inasmuch as there was no alternative model for a political *oekumené*, this led them to be particularly punctilious in laying the ideological groundwork for reunifying China along traditional Chinese lines.

While going meticulously through the complex ritual steps of establishing the Sui, Wen-ti maintained formally correct relations with the legitimate dynasty at Nanking for seven years (meanwhile preparing to crush it when he was ready). Wen-ti in 588 issued an edict referring to the sourthern emperor as Ch'en Shu-pao. By using Ch'en's surname and personal name, Wen-ti meant to deprive him of all the exalted nomenclature appropriate to a ruler. The edict goes on to accuse him of the classic crimes of an oppressive ruler—the crimes that in Confucian theory justify a ruler's replacement by another and make of that other not a rebel but a righteous savior fit to receive heaven's appointment. The crimes include bad faith, wastefulness, licentiousness, oppression of the people, execution of honest remonstrators, the extermination of blameless families, and so on. He then sent to the wretched Ch'en Shu-pao an "imperial letter" listing the twenty crimes of an oppressive prince. More interestingly, Sui Wen-ti took a further step, which— to my knowledge—is unprecedented in China before the invention of printing. He ordered the edict denouncing the Ch'en ruler copied in three hundred thousand broadsheets, which he had distributed south of the Yangtse. We have no way of estimating the effect of this propaganda; the next year the Sui armies conquered the south with ease.[11] But, as Wen-ti had anticipated, this was only the beginning of a long effort to integrate the southerners and their long-diverging culture into a truly reunited empire. That effort was a many-faceted operation in *Kulturpropaganda* including adroit use, particularly by Wen-ti's successor, of patronage of southern scholarship and of southern Buddhist and Taoist communities, deference to southerners' pride in their preservation of ancient traditions, and so forth. But to examine this would take us away from propaganda and deeply into the realms of policy formation and cultural strategy. Let us rather turn for a moment to a form of propaganda closely akin to Wen-ti's use of three hundred thousand broadsheets; this is the manifesto.

### MANIFESTOS

This type of communication (called *hsi*) is much less high-flown in its language and much less allusive than the formal edict. It is usually issued in the name of an emperor or of a challenger. It presents an appeal for support to the population generally of a region, it does so in relatively straightforward terms, and it often calls on local officials or local members of the elite to present the case. The first and most famous of these manifestoes— dating from 131 B.C.—is that of Ssu-ma Hsiang-ju, the noted poet, who was charged by Emperor Wu of the Han to pacify the populations of Pa and Shu (in modern Szechwan), which had been outraged by the heavy requisitioning and draconian penalties inflicted on them by T'ang Meng, a military commander sent initially to use these areas as a base for the penetration of aboriginal areas farther south.

Ssu-ma's manifesto is a political document of great interest. It is formally addressed to the governors of Pa and Shu. It begins by recounting the emperor's tireless efforts to control the barbarians and assure peace to China, and his many successes. It then presents a bland account of T'ang Meng's purpose and veiled references to the efforts of the people of Pa and Shu to profiteer off the expedition. He goes on to say that exactions on the people of these regions was never in the emperor's mind, and the misconduct of his commander far from his intent. Ssu-ma then praises the brave men of the other frontier provinces, their readiness for action and for death in battle. He depicts the satisfactions, the glory and rewards that have come to such men. What then is the matter with the people of Pa and Shu? Their young men (who joined T'ang Meng's expedition) have killed, robbed, or run away, thus showing that their elders have failed to instruct them. So, his majesty has sent Ssu-ma both to apologize for T'ang Meng's excesses and to rebuke "the elders and mentors of the people for failing to give them proper instruction." Ssu-ma closes by saying that, because it is the planting season, he has not wanted to call the people together to address them and he fears that those living in remote valleys and mountain regions might not hear his message. "I have therefore issued this proclamation to be delivered with all speed to the districts and marches, so that everyone may be informed of His Majesty's will. Pay heed to what it says!"[12]

The same type of communication can be traced down the centuries, and in each case the manifesto was issued in the name of someone with real, residual, or potential authority seeking the support or acquiescence of the population in a given region. In cases when official channels of distributing messages were available, they were used. When Li Yüan, who was later in the same year (618) to found the T'ang dynasty, first openly challenged the reigning dynasty that he had long served, he did so with great caution. He had assembled an army of one hundred and thirty thousand men supplemented by Turkish forces and ample logistic support. Further, his cousin the reigning emperor had by this time given up and was waiting for the end at this sourthern capital, Yangchow. Li Yüan, before marching on the imperial capital, harangued his troops in the traditional way and sent a manifesto to the various prefectures and counties telling of his intention to give the reigning emperor the title of T'ai-shang huang, "retired emperor," and enthrone one of his youthful grandsons. This manifesto may have eased the consciences of a few loyalists, but it was in fact a transparent announcement—for anyone who knew historical precedent—that Li Yüan intended to found a new dynasty.[13]

The manifesto to the people of the North China plain issued by Chu Yüan-chang, the Ming founder some seven centuries later, is more interesting. He was a native of the Huai valley, and his first successes were in the south; he was to become the first southerner to be emperor of all China, but when he issued his manifesto in 1368, he had yet to take the north. In it he appeals to the people of the rich and populous plain of the Yellow

River, and, because China had been under oppressive Mongol rule for nearly a century, Chu Yüan-chang appeals to Chinese pride. The manifesto opens: "From ancient times ever since rulers presided over the world, the Central Kingdom [that is, China] was in the inner area in order to govern the barbarians. The barbarians were in the outer area in order to serve China. I have not heard of using barbarians to govern the world [that is, it is unthinkable]." He goes on to say that from Sung times on, the northern barbarians come to lord over the Central Kingdom, and then he turns to the Mongol Yüan dynasty, to its manifold exactions and oppressions, its subversion of the proper moral relationships, and so on. Then he says: "The ancient saying that the cycle of rule by barbarians is less than a hundred years has been proved true. On this very day do you not believe this is so?"

He goes on to dismiss the rival claimants to the throne who had set themselves up as satraps in the north. Then he reviews his own story of the taking of Nanking and his long and successful struggle to consolidate power in the south and west. He outlines his formidable military preparations, specifies his orders to his troops to avoid harming anyone unnecessarily. Then he comes to the peroration: "Those who adhere to me will help bring eternal peace to China [literally, the central cultural florescence]. Those who turn their backs on me are exiling themselves beyond the frontiers. Now, my Chinese fellow countrymen, Heaven has surely ordained that the Chinese shall bring peace to the land! How can barbarians succeed in governing it? My people, take this to heart!" This is the end of the manifesto, but provisions are added that Mongols and Central Asians *(se-mu)* who show themselves capable of understanding the Chinese principles of propriety and righteousness and pledge themselves to be loyal subjects are to be looked after in the same way as Chinese.[14] A legend of some antiquity has it that Chu Yüan-chang sent a manifesto to the people of the North China plain setting a day for a simultaneous rising against their alien masters. The message, it is said, was circulated inside the "moon cakes" *(yüeh-ping)* traditionally eaten at the mid-autumn festival.

The manifesto of 1368 is very much in the style of earlier and later propaganda documents of this type. To recapitulate, all of them we know about are couched in far plainer language than the formal acts of governments or would-be governments; they generally present the most favorable case possible for whoever issued them and contain a section devoted to the crimes and shortcomings of their adversaries; they make quite usual promises of moral satisfaction and political rewards for those who heed them. And, because they were intended in the centuries before printing to be read aloud and intended thereafter to be read by large numbers of ordinary people, the layered allusions and the hyperbole of official pronunciamentos are notably absent.

## ENFORCED MEMORIZATION OF VALUE STATEMENTS

The immediate historical background of the example we shall consider first is briefly stated. The northern dynasty whose power the Sui usurped in A.D. 581 had been founded by Yü-wen T'ai, a non-Chinese warrior who, shortly after seizing power, sought to pattern his regime on the best Chinese models. To aid him in this he called upon the services of a Chinese scholar named Su Ch'o (498–546) who, among other things, drew up a concise text in six articles covering the principles of Confucian government. Yü-wen T'ai was greatly impressed with this statement, and "He ordered his court officials to practice reciting it and decreed that none of his local officials—governors, prefects, magistrates, or village headmen could remain in office unless they mastered the six articles. . . ."[15] This was an effort to give a new set of values to the rude and uneducated men who served Yü-wen T'ai.

Su Ch'o's son Su Wei subsequently became a high official under Sui Wen-ti, and, after the south was conquered, Su wrote a short text on morals called the "five teachings" (one suspects, on the model of his father's six articles), and the Sui officials taking over in the south ordered everyone to memorize this, no doubt with a view to ensuring uniform adherence to the values the Sui wanted to prevail. This, added to ominous rumors then circulating, triggered a violent southern revolt against their conquerors; Sui officials were killed, and one history tells us that when the southerners disemboweled Sui officials, they said: "This will make you better able to recite the five teachings!"[16]

The revolt was crushed, and a far more subtle and gradual series of measures were taken that eventually accomplished the Sui's purpose.

What we have just described are two instances in the use of enforced memorization of value-laden texts intended to produce uniform submissiveness and conformity among the target group. All Confucians of all times held to the view that the patriarchal family was the ideal model or microcosm of the state, and of course, from very early times, the standard way of shaping children to desired patterns of behavior was to enforce the daily memorization and recitation of value-laden texts. Su Wei, just mentioned, quoted the dictum of his father Su Ch'o that the "Classic of Filial Submissiveness" *(Hsiao-ching)* was sufficient both for the formation of individual character and for governing a state.[17] That "Classic"—attributed to a disciple of Confucius, but of Han date—was a staple of home and school education for two thousand years, and the "Twenty-four filial sons" (exemplars of filial virtue) were portrayed in vernacular stories and in pictures to drive home the lessons to the uneducated.

It is therefore not surprising that the use of the memorization device was extended to the political arena by those wishing to control whole populations. (As we shall see, it was used as much by rebel groups as by established governments.) Thus what underlies the use of memorized texts in the political arena is the seemingly unshakable and universal belief in the power of certain reiterated words—written or spoken—to induce desirable patterns of behavior. The only subculture I know of that holds to the same article of faith is, of course, Madison Avenue.

Turning back to Wang Mang at the beginning of the first century A.D., we find that when he still held only de facto control of the empire, he composed a set of eight admonitions for his descendants. One of his political protégés suggested that it would be appropriate to distribute the text throughout the empire and order the educational officials to teach it. The proposal was referred to the highest ministers (all Wang's men), who asked that an order be issued that all officials in the empire who could recite Wang Mang's text should be given a merit rating on the official roles equal to those who could recite the "Classic of Filial Submissiveness." From scanty evidence it is clear that for an aspiring usurper to have his admonitions taught in the schools on a par with the ''Classic of Filial Submissiveness''—that cornerstone of Han morality—was to give him the status of a sage, equal, by implication, to a disciple of Confucius.

The Empress Wu, already mentioned, composed a *Ch'en-kuei*, ''Rules for Subjects,'' under ten headings and rhymed. Memorization by all aspiring officials was required.

For yet another variety of the memorization device, we jump some fourteen centuries to 1368 and the founding of the Ming dynasty. The founder, whose manifesto to the people of the North China plain has been discussed, was of humble origin and fought for long years against innumerable rivals to end a century of Mongol rule to reestablish a Chinese dynasty. As the first emperor of that dynasty, he was harsh, despotic, pathologically suspicious, and he instituted draconian measures of social control. Even before he had completed his military conquest he ordered the codification of a body of laws.[18] Throughout his reign he used legal sanctions of ever greater complexity to consolidate his hold on power. But he remarked sadly toward the end of his reign (in 1397) that although the laws and ordinances had long been promulgated, the number of criminals was still enormous. Therefore, he goes on to say, ''We have written a *Ta-kao* to be made known to the people, to enable them to know the way of pursuing good fortune and avoiding calamity.''

The term *''Ta-kao''* itself has enormous historical resonance. It is the title of one of the most revered documents in the *Book of History*, one that is supposed to have been written by the great Duke of Chou in the founding years of the Chou dynasty (circa 1122–247 B.C.). Yü-wen T'ai, in his effort in the mid-sixth century to found a Chinese-style dynasty, adopted the suggestion of his minister Su Ch'o that the documents of the dynasty should follow the style of the *Ta-kao,* and Su Ch'o himself wrote such a document for his master. Now the peasant founder of the Ming used the same ancient and prestigious term, but the content and purpose are quite different. So is the style, which is believed to be that of the self-educated emperor himself.

T'ai-tsu's *Ta-kao* was meant to acquaint people—not just officials—throughout his vast empire with the harsh laws that were to guide their lives. It was written with an effort at simplicity and was circulated among officials and commoners alike; special masters were appointed to teach it in village schools. Article 74 of the recently reconstituted text of the *Ta-kao* reads: "We have issued this announcement *[kao]* to make perfectly clear the roots of fortune and misfortune. Among all the officials and the people and among all sorts of men, if their households have a copy of this book, and if their crime is one which calls for the bastinado or banishment, they may have their sentences reduced one degree of punishment per crime. If they do not have a copy, their sentence is to be raised one degree per crime. Let officials and people, wherever they are, earnestly read this book as a set of rules and warnings."[19] Here T'ai-tsu's model for controlling his people was close to that of the first unifying empire of Ch'in and to its legalist measures aimed at coercing the people—made aware of the laws—to police themselves and each other.

But in the intervening fifteen hundred years sweeping changes had occurred: the vast geographical expansion of the Chinese empire, its great population growth, and—most important in the present context—the invention of printing and the spread of literacy. These developments made it possible for a ruler such as T'ai-tsu to demand that his people actually possess and in some cases be able to read and memorize his book of rules. The Chinese Communist party's recent mass distribution of the "Sayings" of Mao Tse-tung enabled them to be read, studied, memorized, recited, and physically owned by nearly all Chinese, who used the "Sayings" as Bible, catechism, and amulet.[20] It is worth noting that the title of the "Sayings," *Yü-lu*, was the same as the "sayings" of Chu Hsi, the twelfth-century reformulator of Confucian orthodoxy, which in turn was an echo of the title of the "Analects" *(Lun-yü)* of Confucius, memorized by millions upon millions of youth for more than two millennia.

### LATE IMPERIAL INSTRUMENTS FOR POPULAR INDOCTRINATION

Although we have not attempted in this chapter to deal with the whole ramifying question of education in imperial China, we have noted in passing instances of the use of schools for specific propaganda purposes. One of these was the order to the schools to teach the moral exhortations of Wang Mang; another was the much more elaborate measures of Ming T'ai-tsu to assure that special instruction in his *Ta-kao* was given in every locality. As a result of this, the *Ming History* tells us, "Teachers and students versed in the *Ta-kao* who came to pay homage at the court numbered 190,000; they were all given money and sent back to their homes."[21] And it is massive efforts of this kind, characteristic of the later empires, that are our concern in this section. Why only the later empires—actually, the Ming and the Ch'ing, spanning the years 1369–1912? Because this period saw a vast increase in population, which in turn brought steadily growing state budgets and made possible measures on a scale inconceivable in earlier times. Literacy was spread far more widely than in earlier times. The motives of those who devised these measures are much the same as those that inspired the other modes of propaganda we have discussed: to win approval or consent from the general populace, to assure social conformity and thus social tranquillity, to discourage crime and dissent of all kinds.

The Manchus, who, as a tiny minority, ruled China from 1644 to 1912, were extremely sensitive to the need for measures of popular indoctrination. Here they made common cause with the literati class, which was soon won over to their service. The Manchu Emperor Shun-chih drew on the ideology of that class and on standard imperial Confucianism to offer the "Six Maxims" *(Liu-yü)* for the guidance of his subjects, first promulgated in 1652.[22] He ordered the appointment in every locality of a lecturer (of appropriate age and dignity) and an assistant charged with expounding the maxims on the first and fifteenth day of every month. The lecturer was also to record all good and evil deeds of the neighborhood where he spoke!

In 1670 the K'ang-hsi emperor promulgated the "Sacred Edict" *(Sheng-yü)*—a considerably more elaborate set of maxims with more emphasis on the prevention of antisocial acts. It was also decreed at this time that the lecturer was now to be assisted by three or four "honest and prudent persons," that fixed places were to be selected for the semimonthly lectures, and that all those in the empire attending school were to memorize the edict and attend the lectures. No one, no matter what his other qualifications, could sit for a state examination unless he could write the text of the "Sacred Edict" from memory.[23]

An ingenious further device for assuring docility among the people appeared early in the dynasty. This was the "Exposition Pavillion" *(shen-ming t'ing)*, where imperial edicts were posted and where the names of persons guilty of antisocial behavior were to be posted and only removed when the wayward ones had reformed. As Hsiao remarks, "It was a spiritual pillory with which the authorities hoped to shame villagers and townsfolk into better behavior or at least to deter them from straying from the prescribed path of duty."[24]

Apparently, this elaborate system often worked imperfectly, for—as times goes on—there are more and more frequent exhortations to the officials to see that the lecturers are well chosen and that the lectures are given regularly. In the wake of the T'ai-p'ing Rebellion, one noted governor of Kiangsu made the most strenuous effort to put the system back into working order. In 1868 he ordered all the magistrates in the province to send him monthly reports on the lectures; he also ordered local educational officials to go into the countryside and supervise the lectures there.

A great many ingenious ways were devised by officials to communicate these maxims of an approved morality to the people: local dialects were ordered used by the lecturers to ensure understanding by the people; exposition of the maxims was made, as it were, the opening ceremony for rural markets, and roadside lectures were attempted in some areas. With the help of local gentry, meeting halls were built where the "Sacred Edict" would be kept and lectures regularly held; local gentry attached lectures on the "Sacred Edict" to their organized charities. Despite passages in the sources that tell of lives changed for the better, of men turned from ill-doing, the estimate of the effectiveness of these elaborate efforts is generally negative. And here we have both Chinese and Western testimony. Let us quote an early eighteenth-century Chinese appraisal:

> On the morning of the first and fifteenth day of the month . . . the local official goes to the temple of the god of the city walls and

moats. He wears his official robes and sits gravely still, uttering not a single word—hardly distinguishable from a wooden image. The master of ceremonies, joined by the gentry and scholars, requests him to read the Sacred Edict once. The lecturer then talks without making clear the meaning of the text; the audience listens without comprehending what is said. At the end, officials and people disperse in a noisy jumble.[25]

Despite a negative consensus on the effectiveness of the system of lecturers, belief in the efficacy of moral exhortation clearly survived every setback. As we have noted, many efforts to revitalize the system date from the late nineteenth century, and the T'ung-chih Emperor (reign, 1862–1874) expressed his conviction that "the deterioration of the people's hearts and customs" during the mid-century was because of local officials' allowing the system to fall into desuetude.

Local officials in the long twilight of the imperial system carried a heavy load of administration and responsibility in steadily deteriorating conditions. In the face of all their problems of local control, they used all the instruments available to them, including unofficial belief systems. Here is a county magistrate, writing in 1823, commemorating his repair of a popular temple:

When the people are at peace, they are governed and live according to the Confucian rules of proper conduct *(li)*, but when troubles arise, punishments must be used. When these penalties are not sufficient to control the people, the sanction of religion must be employed, for men are frightened by spiritual forces which they cannot see or hear. We know that Buddha lived in ancient times, and we may employ his teaching, with that of Lao Tzu—even though we do not mention their names, to reinforce the doctrines of Confucius. . . .Although the doctrines of the wheel of lives (karma receiving appropriate recompense) and of suffering and blessedness were introduced to deceive the people, yet they proved useful in frightening men, in aweing them to the necessity of right behavior, and in checking their sinful desires. . . . I have rebuilt this temple beside the county magistrate's headquarters in order to inspire good people, and to frighten those inclined to evil. Even when punishments cannot change them they may still be affected by the gods, and by the thought of a future judgment. . . .[26]

The average county magistrate of late imperial times may not have written so bluntly, for all of them, as surrogates of the emperor, were officially involved in observances associated with local cults or popular folk religion. They said the appropriate prayers or performed the appropriate rituals not out of personal faith but out of the belief that these were conducive to social peace and good order—the perennial goals of imperial government.

### THE USE OF RITUAL ENACTMENTS

When we turn from words to ritual enactments, these fall into three groups: those centered in the capital, whose direct effect was upon the capital population; those which, by elaborate arrangements, were almost simultaneously effective in the many prefectural capitals of the empire; and ritual progresses of the emperor to show himself to his people and to perform some ritual act associated with the imperial ideology. Let us consider some examples of each type and speculate on their effectiveness.

In an agricultural empire, crop yields were all-important. Ceremonies carried out by the Son of Heaven were meant to persuade the people, year after year, of his solicitude for their agricultural concerns and of his power to influence cosmic forces in their favor. The emperor's conferment of an annual calendar-almanac was a matter of great seriousness, and these were distributed not only throughout the empire but to the satellite states beyond—a tangible symbol of the superior science at the disposal of the Chinese emperor and a reminder of his unique relation to cosmic forces.

One of the most solemn rituals connected with agriculture was that of plowing the first furrow in the spring. Let us consider it in its T'ang form. An auspicious day was chosen in the first lunar month, and elaborate preparations were made. Long before dawn on the appointed day the emperor—having prepared himself by several days of abstinence—left his palace in a special six-horse chariot on which was mounted a ceremonial plough. Accompanied by guards (according to Ennin, two hundred thousand of them!), officials, and a numerous retinue, he moved in stately procession to a ceremonial area outside the east or south wall of the capital. There, assisted by ranking nobles, officials from the board of agriculture, by musicians, ritualists, and other functionaries, he solemnly took the plough in his hands and proceeded to make a furrow that signalled the beginning of the planting season. He was followed, in order of rank, by other dignitaries who took their turn at the plough.[27] The political elite thus solemnized their collective concern for agriculture. The conclusion of the ceremony was often followed by further steps to assure harmonious concord between nature and the emperor's subjects: an empirewide amnesty, a change of the era-name to begin a new and auspicious time period, and others.

Regarding the ceremony itself and countless similar ceremonies carried out in the capital, the question is: Who observed them and what effect did they have on the observers? In the T'ang example just given, the population of the capital, shut up in walled wards from dusk to dawn, may have seen little of the procession as it passed; they may well have seen it in all its splendor on its return through the residential wards of the city. Ennin, who witnessed such an event in 841, writes, "The many wonders of the occasion were quite beyond count." My guess is that the ceremony had its primary effect on the elite, by reindoctrinating them with ideas of the organic unity of the cosmos, of the role of the Son of Heaven in maintaining cosmic harmony, and of the primacy of agriculture in the empire. For commoners, we may surmise, what they knew of it perhaps impressed them with the grandeur and affluence of their monarch and secondarily with the fact that he was performing his seasonal duties and perhaps assuring a good harvest. In Southern Sung Hangchow (capital, 1138–1279), townspeople were allowed to witness for themselves the spectacular ceremonies in which the emperor paid homage to Heaven at the great altar in the southern suburbs.[28]

The second group of ritual enactments, those designed to impress, persuade, and propagandize the people of the provinces on behalf of the central power, is best understood as part of the complex of systems knitting the provinces to the capital: the multilevel system of local administration, state roads and canals, the imperial post service, the network of central governmental granaries and garrisons, and so forth. In the preimperial system of the Chou dynasty (circa 1122–247 B.C.), the feudal lords in the various states served as ritual surrogates of the Son of Heaven who in the royal domain performed the grand sacrifices to Heaven and to the ancestors of the royal line. The feudal lords worshipped the earth mound ("altars of the land and grain") of their states, they invoked the potency of *their* ancestors, and they sacrificed to the Chou ancestors to whom they were bound by blood or pseudo-kinship ties. With the coming of a centralized system of government, various systems were developed to impress and indoctrinate those in the provinces with the legitimacy and sanctity of the imperial line and with the imperial ideology. The Han dynasty used local schools and the local magistrates' bureaus for this purpose. We have few details on how this worked, but we may recall that Wang Mang's admonitions were ordered "distributed in the commanderies and the princedoms" and the school officials were ordered to teach the book.

For later periods we have more detailed documentation, yet there are strong echoes of old themes as well as innovations. In the age of Buddhist dominance the newly centralized empires of Sui and T'ang established networks of Buddhist temples throughout the provinces. They generally bore the same name in each place, for example K'ai-yüan-ssu was derived from the era-name for the first twenty-nine years of Hsüan-tsung's reign (712–741), while the Ta-yün-ssu was named for the scripture in which Empress Wu's rule was divinely foretold. These temples, as we know from Ennin's diary, were sometimes of impressive size and splendor, and they served as forcible reminders that the emperor was a pious Buddhist and a munificent patron of the faith, that he deserved the Buddho-Chinese title of "Boddhisattva Son of Heaven" and was thus eminently fitted by spiritual endowments to rule over them.

These official temples also provided a locus in each prefecture for a variety of activities: state-supervised ordinations of monks, distribution of relief to the poor, and masses on countless occasions that served to knit together prefecture and capital, for example, masses on the death anniversary of an imperial personage, masses for the relief of plague or drought, masses for the imperial ancestors. Here we have a blending of the cult of

imperial ancestors and the Buddhist faith. The tamed Buddhism of the official temples was a useful means of linking the
capital and the provinces and of adding solemnity to the cult of
imperial ancestors in a Buddhist age.

Only once were there empirewide enactments designed to establish the legitimacy *and* the Buddhist sanctity of a Chinese
monarch. In 601 Sui Wen-ti began a series of spectacular enactments designed to celebrate his completion of sixty years of life,
to accumulate karma for his lives to come and, most of all, to
impress the capital and provincial populations with the fact that
their ruler was a pious Buddhist and a munificent patron of the
faith (Sanskrit: *dānāpati*). The beginning of his edict announc-
ing these events set the tone: "We contemplate with awe the
perfect wisdom, the great mercy, the great compassion of the
Buddha that would save and protect all creatures, that would
carry all classes of living beings across to deliverance. We give
our adherence to the Three Treasures (the Buddha, his
teaching, his order) and bring to new prosperity the holy
teachings. It is our thought and concern that all people within
the four seas may, without exception, develop enlightenment
[Sanskrit: *Bodhi*] and together cultivate fortunate karma. . . ."[29] The edict then ordered the dispatch of commissions to enshrine holy relics (sealed in costly jars by the emperor
himself) in thirty prefectural capitals throughout the country;
eminent monks (of the sixty-nine identified, *all* had suffered
from the previous dynasty's anti-Buddhist measures), heading
each commission, were to be both specialists in the interpretation of supernatural signs (thus able to recognize and make
known portents favorable to the dynasty) and experienced
preachers. En route they were to be accompanied by a secular
official, by two servants, and five horses, and they were to carry
a large quantity of frankincense. On reaching their destinations
the missions were instructed to select a suitable and important
site and build a reliquary pagoda. An hour was selected for the
simultaneous enshrining of the holy relics throughout the empire; for this occasion the monks and nuns were enjoined to
practice strict abstinence, and all governmental bureaus except
the military offices were to suspend business for seven days, so
that the officials could participate in religious observances.

While this was the order of the day in the provinces, the capital was the scene of a magnificent celebration. Three hundred and sixty-seven monks from the great metropolitan temple of Buddhism moved in solemn procession to the imperial palace. After the emperor had burned incense and worshipped, he led the civil and military officials to partake of a sumptuous vegetarian feast.

The following year a similar distribution was made to fifty-one additional prefectural capitals where special reliquaries had been built and ceremonies were conducted along the same lines; in 604 a third was authorized. From a map showing the geographical distribution of these reliquaries, it is clear that they were placed in the principal population centers from modern Peking in the north to Canton in the south, from Hangchow bay on the coast to Liang-chou in the far northwest. Then, if one visualizes the long routes travelled by the reliquary missions—which were no doubt identified by banners—and the spell-binding monks who paused many times for services at places along the route, the whole series of operations appears about as near to a "saturation" effort in propaganda as one can find in any polity of premodern times.

In China from the bronze age onward, the royal progress was a standard political device for manifesting the power of the central places in the outlying areas. The earliest progresses—some of whose itineraries have been reconstructed—were those of the kings of Shang (circa 1500 to 1122 B.C.). In those remote times the progresses had functions that were later dropped: seizure of grain supplies, capture of slaves for labor in the capital, and so on. In imperial China the emperors' progresses had certain principal aims that we can specify: (1) the political and propagandistic purpose of showing the imperial person, amid the opulent splendor of his vast entourage, to the people of different regions; (2) the lesser but still important purpose of enabling the emperor to "see for himself," to talk with local people, and thus to correct the reports he received from commissions of inspection, from the censorate, and from local officials; and (3) religious and semireligious functions that let people in different regions of the empire see that he was their moral and spiritual leader; such were the ceremonial visits to

Confucius' birthplace and by some emperors to the tomb of Lao-tzu, by others to the holy places of Chinese Buddhism, by all emperors or their surrogates to the tombs of their ancestors. In many ways the progresses to the sacred mountains of China combined all three of the purposes we have specified, and we shall discuss one such progress.

The mountain was in early societies a locus of supernatural potency, an object of religious awe; long before a unified empire was founded, various regions of China had mountains where the tutelary divinities of the area were believed to reside and where sacrifices of propitiation and supplication were performed. When the Han dynasty ideologues wove together their system out of the diverse strands of thought and custom that had come down to them, the sacred mountains of China were incorporated in the imperial cosmology. Thus there were five sacred mountains whither the Son of Heaven might proceed not only to pay homage to local gods but also to act out his role as intermediary between cosmic forces and his subjects; in the Han ideology there was a mountain for each of the four directions and one for the center. By far the most important of these was the mountain that presided over the eastern quarter, Mount T'ai in Shantung province. East was the direction associated with the rising of the sun, the *yang* force, with fertility and growth. And in Han times, a special moral-political significance was given to the T'ai-shan observances; they became the occasion on which the Son of Heaven reported (from the top of the mountain) to Sovereign Heaven itself on his performance as holder of the mandate. The rites at T'ai-shan were given an ancient pedigree, and the ritual scholiasts debated over every detail of timing, procedure, impedimenta. The first performance of this elaborated ceremony was that of 110 B.C., and the example I have chosen is that of A.D. 725. The Emperor Hsüan-tsung of the T'ang had, for thirteen years, ruled vigorously, and his reign had brought the empire to a high level of prosperity; it was thus an auspicious time for him to sacrifice to heaven, give it thanks for his successes and call for its blessings upon his descendants and his subjects.[30]

In the tenth moon of 725 the emperor and his entourage departed from the T'ang's eastern capital, Loyang, and proceeded first eastward and then northward across the alluvial plains of the Huai and Yellow rivers. The emperor was accompanied by the imperial relatives, by hosts of officials, by the leaders of subject and tributary states, and by a large number of imperial guards. A standard account tells us that "Every time they made camp, men and animals covered the fields for several tens of leagues *(li)*. . . . The official carts carrying the impedimenta for the ceremony stretched a hundred leagues along the road without a break."[31] This vast company, moving through some of the richest and most populous areas of the China of that day, took twenty-six days to reach its destination. The sheer size and the magnificence of the imperial train, as well as its solemn purpose, no doubt had a powerful effect on the people along the route; so, in a different way, did the requisitioning of supplies that were usually exacted from the populace. Following many progresses, restitution was made to the affected areas by a decree remitting taxes for a period of years. Having reached the vicinity of the mountain, the imperial party encamped. The next day, the emperor put on the special robes and the cap appropriate for the ceremony and went through ritual purification. Leaving most of his entourage to sacrifices to lesser divinities at the foot of the mountain, the emperor—accompanied only by his highest ministers and ritual specialists—mounted his horse and rode up the mountain. There he presented his report to heaven written on jade tablets and performed three solemn sacrifices. When this was finished, a great fire that had been prepared was lit. When they saw the fire, the accompanying officials, the whole imperial entourage at the foot of the mountain, and the guards ranked around its base broke into cries of *Wan sui* (Vivat!). Five days later, after a second ritual purification, the emperor sacrificed to sovereign earth. The next day he held a grand audience in a huge tent that had been prepared. He received officials of all grades, worthies recommended by local officials, literary men who had presented appropriate compositions, descendants of the ruling houses of the two ancient dynasties of Shang and Chou (covering the years circa 1750–247 B.C.), the officially designated descendant of Confucius, representatives of a large number of foreign tribal groups and states from Malaysia in the south to

Japan in the northeast, and from the aborigines of southeast China to the western Turks whose domains stretched to the borders of Persia. To this huge company, the emperor presented an address that ended with the proclamation of a general amnesty. As the giver of all nomenclature and all titles, he conferred on Mount T'ai the title of "Prince equal to Heaven" and at the same time raised the ranks and titles of the other sacred mountains. His orders also forbade the gathering of firewood within a zone ten leagues from the foot of the mountain, made provisions for the upkeep of cult buildings and for the erection of a stela commemorating his worship (this still exists).[32]

The political and religious impact of this elaborate ceremony was—we may suppose—felt differently by two social groups. Upon commoners along the route and among the guards, local people, and the missions from satellite tribes and states, the spectacle of the Son of Heaven proceeding to ceremonial communion with Heaven must have left a strong impression: of the opulence and might of the great T'ang, of the established legitimacy and success of its rule, of the powers of the Son of Heaven to mediate with the unseen forces that presided over the universe. Upon the literati the effect was more subtle. They were no doubt deeply impressed by the total effect, by the assemblage of tributary representatives, perhaps by the presence of the descendant of Confucius (and by the emperor's stopping later to worship at his nearby birthplace), by the ritual perfection that so many of them had helped to achieve, by the emotional effect of participating in a solemn ceremony that (as an imperial sacrifice) went back to the Han and (as a mountain cult) to the dawn of time, and, finally, by the symbolism and the rhetoric of the official pronouncements that echoed and reechoed the key values on which the system operated. In this way, like the sacrifice at the beginning of the agricultural year, the ceremony served to reindoctrinate the elite.

On his way back to the capital, the emperor stopped over in one important prefectural town and entertained the officials in his train and the prefects from nearby areas. He took the occasion to check the accuracy of reports on their performances that had reached him through official channels. He found that the reports had in many respects been misleading, and he proceed-

ed to promote several of the local officials. This checking and
intelligence gathering at the local level was much elaborated in
later imperial progresses. Even in the T'ai-shan progress, where
the element of dramatic and solemn display was of overriding
importance, the intelligence function was not wholly neglected.

### THE USE OF REPRESENTATIONS BY DISSIDENTS

In the history of imperial China there is naturally a high in-
cidence of the use of devices of propaganda and mass persuasion
in periods of the transition of power. And, inasmuch as there is
a continuum from local rebel, to regional rebel, to those who
found a new dynasty, rebel movements have resorted to many
of the devices we have so far discussed. For example, when their
power is apparently waxing (or, out of desperation when it is
waning), rebels will often proclaim a new dynasty, decree a new
era-name, a new official system, and all the rest. In short, a
rebel movement as a subgovernment begins to act as if it had already succeeded, and the target group of its propaganda will be
the literate elite or a regional segment thereof. Once the rebel
had drawn ritualists to his side, ritual enactments often were
performed. Manifestos often were used, and that of the Ming
founder (then a rebel against the Yüan dynasty) is a good example; in these cases the target group is either the literati class or,
in some cases, a broad cross section of the populace.

Yet there is a range of propaganda devices and of propaganda
themes peculiar to rebels and to dissident groups that have not
yet risen in open rebellion. We can deal here with only a sampling. For example, the Yellow Turbans, which became the first
mass rebellion in Chinese history, began as a religious brotherhood, gradually transformed itself into a subgovernment, and
eventually, in A.D. 184, rose against the dying Han. Both branches of the Yellow Turbans, in the east and in the southwest, attracted an early following from among the peasantry by techniques of faith healing. As they drew followers, and a hierarchy
of Yellow Turban adept officials began to emerge, one of the
requirements for a high position was complete mastery (no
doubt memorization) of the old Taoist Classic, the *Tao-te
ching*. I suspect that they drew from this text certain passages
that became a liturgy, perhaps phrases thought to have magical

efficacy. As the moment of their rising approached they passed by word of mouth the slogan ''The yellow heaven will succeed the azure heaven,'' and here at the peasant level the high-flown symbolism of Han ideology was put to use. For it was part of the Five Element system that there was a sequence of colors matched to the sequence of elements. The Han ruled by the element wood, whose color was azure, while yellow (which, they maintained, succeeded azure in the sequence) was the Yellow Turban color. This slogan was no doubt written on many walls, but a more condensed message was purveyed in the same manner by the characters ''chia-tzu,'' those used for the beginning of a sexagenary cycle—thus suggesting a new political beginning, a new dynasty, and, in this particular case, the year A.D. 184 when the Later Han had completed three sexagenary cycles of life and when in fact the Yellow Turban armies finally rose to challenge it.

It is hardly surprising that the slogans and symbols of millennialism were as pervasive in rebel propaganda as they were absent in that of the elite. The T'ai-p'ing tao, ''Path to the Great Peace,'' was their own name for the Yellow Turban movement, and the last great mass upheaval under the imperial order was known as T'ai-p'ing t'ien-kuo or ''Heavenly Kingdom of the Great Peace'' (1850–1864). The propaganda of all other rebel movements promised, vaguely or in programmatic form, a new order—one where the corruption, the inequities of the old would be eliminated and a new beginning made.

Closely related to millennial themes are messianic claims. Buddhism, in the five centuries of its dominance, added to the native store of both millennial and messianic symbolism. For example, countless rebels appeared from obscurity and proclaimed themselves to be incarnations of Maitreya—the Buddha of the new age. They would proclaim Buddhist era-names for their regimes, and claim to control supernatural forces that would confer invulnerability upon their followers and bring success to their movement. Some rebel ideologies were shot through with apocalyptic ideas, particularly that the end of an age (Sanskrit: *kalpa*) was at hand and that Maitreya would descend to preside over a new age and that meanwhile all state laws, tax assessments, debts, and so forth, were invalid. One can imagine the tremors that ran through the property-owning elite when such a movement began to thrive. In the later dynasties— as the pressure of population upon land increased—rebel slogans tended to stress socioeconomic appeals: promises to abolish the hated land tax or to distribute the land equitably.[33]

Perhaps enough has been said, under the six headings of this chapter, to validate the proposition encapsulated in the opening quotation. The author is conscious of the almost unlimited materials stretching away to the horizon in all directions. He can only hope that this chapter will stimulate more detailed studies of the uses of propaganda in particular cases and refinements of the preliminary generalizations advanced here.

## NOTES

1. Harold Lasswell, "Propaganda," *Encyclopedia of the Social Sciences,* vol. 12 (New York, 1934), pp. 521–528.

2. *Tzu-chih t'ung-chien* by Ssu-ma Kuang—an eleventh-century synoptic history (Peking, 1956 ed.), chap. 12, p. 396. The Confucian is Lu Chia, *Shih-chi,* chap. 97, Burton Watson, trans., *Records of the Grand Historian,* vol. 1 (New York: Columbia University Press, 1961), pp. 277–278.

3. John Sparrow, *Visible Words* (Cambridge, 1969).

4. *Li Chi [Record of Rites],* chap. 46. Legge translation, vol. 2, p. 208.

5. Edward H. Schafer, "Ritual Exposure in Ancient China," *Harvard Journal of Asiatic Studies* 14 (1951): 137.

6. Edouard Chavannes, *Le T'ai Chan: Essai de Monographie d'un Culte Chinois* (Paris, 1910), p. 397.

7. Edwin O. Reischauer, trans., *Ennin's Diary* (New York, 1955), pp. 180–182. Some minor verbal alterations.

8. *Han-shu,* chap. 99b. H. H. Dubs, trans., *History of the Former Han Dynasty,* vol. 3 (Baltimore, 1955), pp. 353–354. Some modifications.

9. *Tzu-chih t'ung-chien,* chap. 205, p. 6496; C. P. Fitzgerald, *The Empress Wu* (London, 1956), p. 136. The Confucian reference is to *Analects,* 2.1: "He who governs by moral force may be compared to the pole-star, which keeps its place while the other stars turn around it."

10. Sung Min-ch'iu, *T'ang ta chao-ling chi* [Collection of edicts and ordinances of the T'ang] (Peking: Commerical Press, 1958), p. 6.

11. This use of psychological warfare is discussed in somewhat greater detail in A. F. Wright, "The Formation of Sui Ideology," in *Chinese Thought and Institutions,* ed. J. K. Fairbank (Chicago, 1957), pp. 92–93.

12. The translation, quoted in part, is from Burton Watson, in Fairbank, ed., *Chinese Thought,* vol. 2, pp. 322–324. A complete historical analysis is to be found in Yves Hevouet, *Sseu-ma Siang-ju* (Paris, 1964), pp. 81–95.

13. *Tzu-chih t'ung-chien,* chap. 184, p. 5741.

14. *Huang Ming wen-heng* [Documents of the Imperial Ming] compiled by Ch'eng Min-cheng during the Ming dynasty. Ssu-pu ts'ung kan edition (Shanghai, 1936), chap. 1, pp. 1–2. The author of the manifesto was Wang Lien. A manifesto, specifically directed at the southern gentry, was issued by the notorious collaborator Ch'ien Ch'ien-i in 1645. It urged that they abandon the Ming cause and rally to the Manchu conquerors. Cf. Hsü Tzu, *Hsiao-t'ien chi-nien* 10/467 (T'ai-wan Wen-hsien ts'ung-k'an no. 134).

15. *Chou-shu* [*History of the Northern Chou,* T'ung-wen edition of 1884—used throughout], chap. 23, pp. 10a–10b. See Chauncey S. Goodrich, *The Biography of Su Ch'o* (Berkeley, 1953).

16. *Pei-shih* [*History of the Northern Dynasties*], chap. 63, p. 19a.

17. *Han-shu,* chap. 99b. Dubs, *History of the Han,* vol. 3, p. 183.

18. *Ming-shih* [*History of the Ming Dynasty*], chap. 93 (the monograph on criminal law), p. 6a.

19. *Ta-kao,* Article 72. Cf. newly assembled edition of all three parts of the original in *Ming-ch'ao k'ai-kuo wen-hsien* [Documents on the founding of the Ming dynasty] (Taipei, 1966), p. 82.

20. A statistic gotten in Sian according to the Australian journalist Ross Terrill in "The 800,000,000," *Atlantic* (November 1971), p. 101, is that at the height of the Cultural Revolution in the province of Shensi 100 million copies of works of Mao were distributed among a population of 25 million!

21. *Ming-shih,* chap. 93, p. 6b.

22. Hsiao Kung-chuan, *Rural China: Imperial Control in the Nineteenth Century* (Seattle: University of Washington Press, 1967), p. 186.

23. Hsiao, *Rural China,* pp. 185, 241.

24. Ibid., p. 186.

25. Ibid., p. 196.

26. J. K. Shryock, *The Temples of Anking and Their Cults* (Paris, 1931), pp. 132–133, translating from the *Huai-ning Hsien-chih* edition of the T'ung-chih period. Minor verbal changes.

27. Details are from the *T'ang Hui-yao* (Peking ed., 1955), chap. 10b. The Japanese pilgrim Ennin noted the ceremony in passing. Cf. Reischauer, *Ennin's Diary,* p. 298 for Ennin's observations.

28. For details on this complex of rituals, cf. Jacques Gernet, *Daily Life in China on the Eve of the Mongol Invasion* (London, 1959), pp. 200–202.

29. The quotation is from the *Kuang-hung-ming chi,* chap. 17, compiled by the monk Tao-hsüan in the mid-seventh century. *Taishō Daizōkyō,* vol. 50, p. 213b. I have dealt in more detail with this whole sequence in "The Formation of Sui Ideology," note 11 above. The second enactment of this kind was carried out by a regional satrap in the tenth century.

30. The classic monograph on the T'ai-shan cult that I have used is Chavannes's *Le T'ai Chan.*

31. *Tzu-chih t'ung-chien*, chap. 212, p. 6766. The description of the train of carts is formulaic language for "a long line of carts."

32. Full details on the ceremonial sequence and the full list of those present are to be found in Chavannes, *Le T'ai Chan*, pp. 222–235. His account is based on chap. 23 of the *Old T'ang History*.

33. Yuji Muramatsu, "On Some Themes in Chinese Rebel Ideology," in *The Confucian Persuasion*, ed. A. F. Wright (Stanford, 1960), pp. 241–267.

# 9

## CLASSICAL CIVILIZATION

JOHN FERGUSON

Communication was familiar enough. The most obvious word
for it in Greek *(anakoinoun)* had to do with holding something
in common; the most obvious Latin word *(impertire)* connotes
giving a part to someone else; there is a real difference of emphasis. Other Latin words also are revealing. *Commercium,* a
general word for communication, applicable for example to
speech or writing, has its origins in trade. There was interest in
the origin of language. Was it a gift of the gods, Hermes or
Athene? Or did it, as the Epicureans supposed, arise from
natural animal noises?

*Propaganda* is, on the face of it, a Latin word. It is not, as
many think, a neuter plural, "things to be propagated," but an
abbreviation of the Roman Catholic *societas de propaganda fide*
of 1622 (fellowship for the propagation of the faith). There is
no classical Greek or Latin word for "propaganda" in the
modern sense. If it was yours you called it truth; if it was not
yours you called it lies. The thing existed, nameless though it
might be, and is fascinating to trace.

### BUILDINGS

The most obvious area for public propaganda is one that is
sometimes forgotten—buildings. When Horace wanted an im-

age for his poetic achievement he claimed to have built a monument loftier than the pyramids (*Od.* 3,30); which shows that to
him the pyramids were memorials of their sponsors. *Si
monumentum requiris, circumspice* was peculiarly appropriate
to Wren and St. Paul's, but the principle behind it was neither
unique nor rare. Building schemes might redound to the glory
of an individual; Mausolus of Halicarnassus added a word to the
language in the building he left behind him; Justinian on the
completion of S. Sophia cried "Solomon, I have outdone you!"
They might also redound to the glory of a community or city.
They appear on coins or medallions. Sometimes they seem
almost emblematic of a city. The so-called Seven Wonders of
the World included, along with the Tomb of Mausolus, the
Pyramids of Egypt, the Hanging Gardens of Babylon, the Temple of Artemis at Ephesus, the Colossus of Rhodes, the Pharos
of Alexandria; only Phidias's statue of Zeus is not instantly
associated with a place, and we need only Dio Chrysostom to re-
mind us of the luster that statue shed even on Olympia. The
Artemisium appears on coins; and an architectural feature, not
known from other sources, a door opening onto the pediment,
has been revealed in this way. So does the Pharos, which is also
depicted on a wonderful glass vase.

Sometimes buildings, monuments, or sculptural complexes
are memorials of particular events. There is an excellent example in the great monument erected by Attalus I of Pergamum to
celebrate his victory over the Gauls. The pieces today are scattered and we cannot see them as a whole. Evidently the central
point was the standing group of the Gaul who has killed his
wife and holds a sword poised above his own breast: around this
at the corners of the square plinth were four figures collapsed on
the ground including the statue once famed as "The Dying
Gladiator." What is so impressive about the Pergamene monument is the portrayal of the vanquished. They are characteristically non-Hellenic; the Greeks would have turned up their
noses at them as wild and barbaric. But they are unquestionably
noble. Plainly such a picture adds to the triumph of the victor;
he has conquered worthy adversaries. But propaganda and
humanity have come together.

Rome was not lacking in monuments of this kind. After all,

this is the significance of the triumphal arch *pur sang,* and the Arch of Titus in the forum area is an excellent example, portraying as it does the details of the loot from Jerusalem carried in the triumphal procession. The claims of the Flavian dynasty had initially to be established by a resounding victory, and they had to be reinforced by a publicly visible reminder of that victory. Trajan's Column similarly celebrates his Dacian victory. Here the memorial is everything, for the details of the superb sculpture cannot have been perceptible to the passerby. Propaganda tends to escalate: Trajan's Column was followed by the Column of Marcus Aurelius, the Arch of Titus, *longo intervallo* by those of Severus and Constantine.

The part played by buildings in expressing the glory of a city is nowhere better shown than in classical Athens. We owe the details to Plutarch in his *Life of Pericles,* and the interplay between national and personal ambition is peculiarly fascinating. In 454 B.C. the treasury of the anti-Persian Confederacy was removed from Delos to Athens, and in the years that followed Pericles devoted the funds subscribed for defence to public works on the Acropolis. The allies complained; it was an intolerable insult, it was open dictatorship, and Athens was decking herself out like some whore. Pericles answered that provided Athens guaranteed the security of the allies she was not accountable for her detailed expenditure, that the works fostered employment, *and would afford the Athenians eternal honor* (Plut. *Per.* 12). When his political enemies at home challenged him he offered, according to the story, to pay for the works himself, provided that his name appeared on them. Pericle's calculations were right. His great building scheme did indeed come to symbolize the glory of Athens. Demosthenes (22,13) speaks of the Propylaea and of the Parthenon as emblems of honor achieved at the expense of the Persians. Epaminondas of Thebes used the Propylaea as a symbol of the fame of Athens; for the Thebans to be victorious they must transport the Propylaea to Thebes (Aeschin. 2,105). There is a delightful fragment of the comic dramatist Phoenicides (Ath. 14,652 D):

A: They're for ever singing the praises of their myrtle
    and their honey,

their Propylaea, and, last but not least, their figs.
The moment I landed I tasted the lot—
B: Propylaea and all?

In Rome too the public buildings were a source of pride: the attacks by the satirists on gimcrack tenements are partly influenced by a sense of contrast. Here building was governed at least in part by the desire of individuals to leave a visible reminder behind them. The ambition spread back into republican times. We may recall the Basilica Aemilia of 179 B.C., named after the censor Aemilius, which must have been a dominant structure when first erected, or the Pons Fabricius of 62 B.C., named after the *curator viarum* of that year, or Pompey's Theatre of 52 B.C., or Julius Caesar's restoration of the other old basilica to become the Basilica Julia, or (because it belongs to the same pattern of thought) the Pantheon, which even in its Hadrianic form still bears Agrippa's name (cf. Suet. *Aug.* 29). With the secure establishment of Augustus, building became a matter of imperial pride. In his *Res Gestae* Augustus proudly and in detail records his achievements in this field, his restorations and original foundations (19–21); some of his foundations he used to commemorate others, Gaius and Lucius, Livia and Octavia, or Marcellus (Suet. *Aug.* 29). Suetonius sums up the purpose of this: ''The capital was subject to fire and flood and unworthy of the dignity of empire. He developed it to such an extent that he was justified in boasting that he 'found it brick and left it marble' '' (ibid. 28).

Where Augustus led others followed. Tiberius promoted building on the Palatine; Claudius developed the water supply and made the Porta Praenestina a combination of the functional (carrying two aqueducts) and the glorious; Nero had his megalomaniac plans for the Domus Aurea, turning, said the satirists, the whole city into a single house. The Flavians, with the need to establish their prestige, began to build in a big way. Vespasian started with a great forum, a hundred meters and more square, containing a Temple of Peace. His most enduring monument was the Flavian Amphitheater, which since the Venerable Bede has been known as the Colosseum. Bede quotes a Saxon pilgrim's proverb, which shows something of the symbolic importance of such a building: *quandiu stabit Coliseus, stabit et Roma; quando cadet Coliseus, cadet et Roma; quando cadet Roma, cadet et mundus,* or as Byron has it in *Childe Harold:*

> While stands the Coliseum, Rome shall stand;
> When falls the Coliseum, Rome shall fall:
> And when Rome falls—the world.

It would be needless to touch on each emperor in turn. It is enough to mention Domitian, using an able architect Rabirius, and sustaining his gigantic palace on concrete vaults; Trajan, whose brilliant architect Apollodorus opened up a new area for forum and shopping-precinct and imparted in so doing a unified design to the whole center of the capital; or, later and inevitably farther out, the great baths inaugurated by Caracalla and Diocletian.

If Augustus and his successors made Rome a worthy capital, Rome left her mark all over the Mediterranean world. The presence of Rome was open to the eye. In many parts of the empire the traveller from outside would meet a visible *limes*. Sometimes it might be merely a series of disconnected fortifications, but in some places it was a continuous boundary, like the palisade in Germany, or the Hadrianic and Antonine walls in Britain. Once within the *limes* two reminders of Roman power could be seen striding across the countryside—the raised ramparts of the roads and the arches of the aqueducts. The first was a reminder of military dominion and the swift movement of armies. Both spoke of civilization, of the water essential to life and to cleanliness, of easy travel and the consequent unification of empire. Frontinus is worth quoting on aqueducts: "Look at those indispensable structures for all these waters, and compare, if you will, the idle pyramids, and the famous but useless works of the Greeks." The towns, too, are reminders. There is a sense in which they were miniatures of Rome with their paved streets, forum, porticoes, temples, stone-built shopping centers, theaters, baths. Think of Sallust's account of the simple *mapalia* of the African village (Sall. *J.* 18,8) and then contrast the great amphitheater of El Djem to sense something of the visible impact of the Roman presence. Or, again from Africa, think of the dozen or more public baths, some of colossal dimensions, in the not very large settlement of Timgad, or the gigantic baths of Antoninus in Carthage, rivaling those of Caracalla in Rome. Or, in Britain, the astonishing palace at Fishbourne, one of the three largest of the Roman world, the hallmark of a ruler who allied himself to Rome. And there were emperors who put their peculiar stamp on the colonies. The temple of divine Claudius at Colchester was the visible sign of Roman dominion; as such it was the especial object of Boudicca's destructive revenge. Of Hadrian, his biographer wrote, "In almost every city he left some building and sponsored a celebration of the Games" (SHA *Hadr.* 19). The Severan dynasty were particularly generous to their native Africa: witness, among much else, the great Severan forum at Leptis Magna, or the Arch of Caracalla at Volubilis.

## SCULPTURE

Already we have seen how monumental sculpture might play an important role in propaganda, and how Attalus used it to honor his victory over the Gauls. A few years later Eumenes II celebrated a similar victory in monumental sculpture, using this time symbolism rather than direct representation. On the great Altar of Zeus the gods are depicted victorious over the giants. Civilization has conquered barbarism: this is the message. The giants are monsters, powers of destruction. There is nothing of the keen observation of human nature in an unfamiliar culture that characterized the earlier monument. Humanity is found in the Altar in the subsidiary frieze to the local hero Telephus; this too is in its own way propaganda for Pergamum.

The protectress of Pergamum was Athene, and she was prominent in the main frieze. The Pergamenes saw themselves as the successors of the great days of Athens: this too was a propaganda touch. The Athenians knew the value of sculpture to express the city's glory, and of Athene as the symbol of the city, and they employed Phidias, the greatest sculptor of the fifth century B.C., for that end. He portrayed the goddess standing at the side of Miltiades in a dedication made by Cimon at Delphi. He cast the great Athene Promachos, still in honor of the victory over the Persians; from far out at sea (even if not, as Pausanias wrongly proposed, from Sunium) the sun caught the crest of her helmet and tip of her spear, and spoke of the glory of Athens. In his maturity he shaped the chryselephantine statue of the goddess for the Parthenon, and directed the wonderful frieze of the Panathenaic procession to the honor of Athene and her city.

Another very obvious example of propaganda in sculpture is to be found in the numerous representations of Nike, or Victory. Two of these stand head and shoulders above the rest as works of art and must have been peculiarly impressive memorials. The first dates from the fifth century and in all probability celebrates the victory of the Messenians and Naupactians (as allies of Athens) over Sparta at Sphacteria in 424 B.C. The goddess is depicted as sweeping through the air, and it has been suggested that the pedestal was painted blue to help the illusion; the drapery of her clothes clings closely to her body or swirls past. Equally fine is the Victory of Samothrace some two and a half centuries later, now in the Louvre. She is landing on the prow of a ship, and stood originally in a pool of water, which must have made possible some exquisite reflections.

The reign of Augustus saw the Altar of Peace, the Ara Pacis Augustae, at Rome. This is beyond doubt the masterwork of the Augustan age. It was designed to celebrate the emperor's safe return from France and Spain, but its interest is wider, for it sums up symbolically his achievement as he wished it to appear. The frieze depicts a religious procession. Augustus himself has stopped to offer a libation. Behind him are the Vestals, the priests, and the pontifex maximus; they are followed by the imperial family, the senators, and the people, men, women, and children. It is hard not to think that the emperor scripted this personally: it speaks so clearly of so much that he professed and proclaimed. No one knew better the political value of religion; he was careful to foster it; and here is an eloquent tribute to priestly office and liturgical ritual. Politically he appears as *princeps, primus inter pares.* He is no oriental divine monarch receiving homage: Julius had been killed for no more. Augustus did not aspire to divinity in his lifetime. But he surrounded himself with a religious aura; witness the title Augustus. The frieze depicts, in the strict sense, a political hierarchy, the emperor, his family, the senate, the people. The imperial household, not least in the children, are an indication of Augustus' determination for dynastic continuity: poor Tiberius suffered in that cause. The senate comes next, and occupies a disproportionate amount of the remaining space. Augustus had purged the senate more than once, and was eager to encourage the illusion, and, within limits, the actuality of continuing senatorial responsibility: the empire has often been called a dyarchy. Socially it was Augustus' policy to foster family life, fertility and parenthood, and racial purity; and it is this that the final procession of citizens with their wives and children proclaims.

Besides the procession four panels speak in myth and symbol of Pax Augusta. On one we see Aeneas arriving in Latium and sacrificing to the Penates, a cult that Augustus restored. A second depicts Romulus and Remus suckled by the wolf; unfortunately it is very fragmentary and we cannot comment on details. A third, also fragmentary, shows the goddess Rome seated in peace with her armor laid aside: this is subtle propaganda, for it speaks both of military power and of peace. Finally there is the depiction of the blessing of peace, Mother Earth in all her fertility.

The influence of this propaganda spread even to Africa. The Altar of the Gens Augusta at Carthage is a kind of epitome of the Ara Pacis. It too has four panels. One depicts Augustus himself sacrificing. A second shows Apollo, the presiding deity of Actium, and symbol of the light and culture of the new age. A third shows Aeneas, here escaping from Troy rather than landing in Latium, but the essential point is the same. Finally we see the goddess Rome holding a pillar bearing a figure of Victory, and gazing at an altar on which stand the cornucopiae and the orb of authority: so the representations of Rome and Mother Earth in the Ara Pacis are here fused in a single scene.

Another good example of imperial propaganda may be seen in the arch of Trajan at Benevento, dating from A.D. 115. Here Jupiter, with the Capitoline goddesses Juno and Minerva flanking him, and the other Olympian gods in attendance, is shown handing over the thunderbolt of power to Trajan. Nothing could be clearer: the emperor is the gods' vice-regent upon earth.

A different, less obvious use of propaganda in sculpture may be seen in portrait busts. A few examples will have to suffice. There is a well-known bust of Pericles by Cresilas, known to us in a number of later copies. He appears helmeted, bearded, benign, aloof. Was this what he looked like? No doubt it was recognizable. But Pericles was nicknamed "the Olympian" (Plut. *Per.* 8); Cratinus called him "our squill-headed Zeus" (fr. 71); Aristophanes (*Ach.* 530) describes the Olympian Pericles as thundering and lightning. This portrait by Cresilas is surely the more flattering aspect of the nickname; in it Pericles is assimilated to Zeus.

A second example, which is particularly interesting because politics are not in issue, is found in the portraits of Socrates. Three different types have been identified. The first can be traced back to a portrait executed either in his life or shortly after his death, when his memory was still green. It shows him ugly, balding, snub-nosed, with eyes *à fleur de tête*, and corresponds well enough with written descriptions: this is, near enough, what Socrates looked like. The second is a type attributable to Lysippus. It bears the same relation to Socrates that Cresila's portrait does to Pericles—it is recognizable but idealized. The uglinesses are softened. This, so to say, is what Socrates ought to have looked like. The third, which dates from later in the Hellenistic Age, is the most interesting. It bears only a remote likeness to the original. It is assimilated to the portraits of Chrysippus. It is the Hellenistic Age's concept of *The Philosopher*. It is a means of establishing visually the authenticity of succession from Socrates to the Stoics.

As a third example we may take the famous Cleopatra, as she exemplifies well a common fact of the ancient world, that portrait-busts in marble or bronze are more flattering than images on coins. In her larger portraits she appears quite beautiful, but the coins show a rather scrawny neck, severe features, formidable brows, and a nose too prominent. It seems reasonable to suppose, here and elsewhere, that the larger, more monumental representations have a strong element of propaganda about them.

Another example may be taken from the Julio-Claudians. Suetonius gives us a description of Augustus (*Aug.* 79). He says that his general looks were striking and attractive; he had piercing eyes; but he was unduly short, with sandy hair and bad teeth, aquiline nose and fairly swarthy complexion, and was careless about his personal appearance. I doubt whether the description could be taken as matching the noble representation from Prima Porta. More, the type of Augustus once established, the other Julio-Claudians are assimilated to it. Tiberius was quite different in looks. According to Suetonius (*Tib.* 68) he was much taller and broad-shouldered, his complexion was lighter, he wore his hair rather long at the back, held his neck stiffly, and was subject to pimples (although we could hardly expect the imperial sculptor to depict him "warts and all"); and when we can detect a difference in the portraits, we can see a different hair-style, a broader face and stronger jaw, a tight-lipped mouth. But we cannot always detect a difference, and the Vienna cameo is only one example that has been variously identified. The grotesque, slobbering Claudius with his quavering head and weak knees is another case in point, although Suetonius grants him a certain dignity in repose (*Claud.* 30). This recluse, though he proved to be a sane and wise ruler, had little obvious qualification for the task except his membership of the *domus divina*; it is natural that he should be portrayed in such a way as to recall the prestigious Augustus. Even with lesser members of the family the same is true. A portrait in the Lateran now identified as Nero Drusus was formerly thought to be Augustus.

As a last example—and these are examples only—of propaganda in portraiture, we may take the colossal head of Constantine from a statue that once stood in the Basilica of Constantine in Rome. There is now scarcely any pretense of naturalistic portraiture. The sculpture is on a superhuman scale. The mood is hieratic, awesome, numinous; the large, staring eyes speak of the emperor's unresting watchfulness over his people. We are in fact well on the way to Byzantine religious art. And when Constantine in his city of Constantinople put up his statue with the rayed crown of the sun-god, made as he believed from the nails of the true Cross, was he not claiming that the sun-god who had protected his own family and Aurelian's Rome, and the Christ whose religion had spread so widely and mysteriously, had come together to crown him as the representative of God in the government of the world?

## ACTIONS

Actions, says the old proverb, speak louder than words, and there are various ways, some direct and some dramatic, in which actions can be made to serve some public purpose by suggesting or encouraging a particular view of a situation.

Two episodes in the career of the Athenian dictator Pisistratus will form an illustration. For his first attempt at power he appeared in the center of Athens seemingly wounded; he displayed his wounds and declared them to have been inflicted by enemies of the people. This demonstrative act persuaded the Assembly first that he was a friend of the people and second that he stood in need of protection. They granted him a bodyguard, which he used to secure the acropolis. His success was only temporary. After a year or two he was driven out by a coalition. He planned his return carefully. In one of the villages, he found a woman named Phye, whose height was unusual and carriage imposing. He induced her to play the part of Athene bringing back the hero, and this little drama encouraged the sense that he was under Athene's especial protection.

Alexander's life is full of the use of such dramatic touches to establish or to reinforce some aspect of policy. We may take, for instance, the way at Tyre he took command of the Phoenician squadrons, which was the prerogative of the Great King. Issus was past, but Darius was still alive; it was an assertion that Alexander himself now held the power. Again, the firing of Persepolis was clearly a political demonstration, seeming to Babylon that Xerxes' destruction of their temple was avenged and that Alexander was thus their champion and liberator. Again, the whole policy of fusion between Macedonians and Persians needed careful and tactful handling, which Alexander did not always provide. But he did his best to use dramatic propaganda to this end. There was the attempt at Bactra to introduce *proskynesis,* which Callisthenes and the Greeks refused. There was his heroic standing as a founder of cities, west and east. There was his demand for deification, clearly primarily as a political act. There was the ceremonious act of intermarriage at

Susa, where Alexander married Darius's daughter Barsine, eighty of his officers married Persian noblewomen, and ten thousand of his troops married their Asiatic concubines. There was the banquet at Opis to celebrate the conclusion of peace. We do not need to follow Tarn's more extravagant theories about this. It remains, at the very least for Macedonians and Persians, seated at the same table, a great symbolic occasion, with the libation offered by Greek seers and Persian magi; and Alexander's prayer for partnership in empire between the two peoples.

An interesting example of a propaganda pageant that did not come off is found in a story of Mithradates of Pontus. In 87 B.C. he staged an elaborate scene in the theater at Pergamum. He used the stage-machinery to lower from the heights a life-size figure of Victory with a crown that would thus descend from the heavens gently and accurately upon his head. Unfortunately the figure of Victory disintegrated in mid-air, and the crown fell aimlessly to the ground.

The Romans, despite Cicero, were men of action rather than of words and were adept at producing the dramatic expression of their purpose, authority, or achievement. A simple example is the bundle of rods and axes carried by the lictors, representing vividly for all to see the powers of corporal and capital punishment; or the eagle on the standard, a symbol of predatory power, which has become a propaganda emblem of those who fancied themselves the heirs of Rome whether in Europe or America. A more elaborate example is to be seen in the great triumphal processions. A particularly dramatic example may be found in a story of C. Popillius Laenas. He was sent with a despatch to the king of Syria. Popillius drew a circle in the sand round the king as he read the letter and forbade him to break the circle before he had given a decisive answer. It was a symbolic demonstration of the power of Rome.

Consider next an episode in the life of Julius Caesar. It is the more interesting because, although it was clearly stage-managed by Caesar himself for propaganda purposes, ancient and modern historians alike are divided in their interpretation of it. The issue was the title of *rex,* king, which had belonged to the ancient autocrats of Rome and was the contemporary prerogative of the oriental divine monarchs. The episode began with the anonymous placing of the fillet of royalty on Caesar's statue. The tribunes, C. Epidius Marullus and L. Caesitius Flavius, ordered its immediate removal, in defense, they said, of Caesar's political reputation. Then on 26 January, 44 B.C., Caesar attended the Latin Festival on the Alban Mount. As he rode back into Rome, the crowd cheered, and the word *rex* was heard. Caesar turned it with a joke, calling *non sum rex sed Caesar* "I am Caesar, not *rex*"; his mother belonged to the Marcii Reges. The tribunes acted again, and arrested the man whom they accused of starting the antirepublican demonstration. There was a clash between the dictator and the tribunes; each claimed that the other was interfering with his prerogative. Helvius Cinna, Caesar's man and another tribune, attacked his colleagues; the senate condemned them to death; Caesar intervened for clemency and the sentence was commuted to deposition. Now came the Lupercalia on 15 February. Antony, the consul and another Caesarian, three times offered Caesar the royal crown and three times he ostentatiously refused it. The last scene in this drama came when a phrase in the Sibylline Books was discovered and alleged to mean that the Parthians would be conquered only by a king. It was this that intensified the rumors that on 15 March the proclamation would be made, this that fed the conspirators' determination to strike.

What was happening? We do not know. Interpretations unfavorable to Caesar, as that of Gerard Walter, claim that he organized the whole thing. He was ambitious to be king; each episode was a piece of propaganda and a test of public opinion. Antony's act at the Lupercalia received a negative response from all except claqueurs; Caesar to his chagrin was forced to reject the crown. A more favorable interpretation, as that of F. E. Adcock, suggests that the earlier pressures were engineered not by Caesar but by overenthusiastic supporters or even by enemies seeking to discredit him, and that Caesar staged the Lupercalia incident as a counterblast. It certainly does not seem likely that the Lupercalia was a coup d'état that fell flat, but it is possible that it was an instance of *reculer pour mieux sauter*. Whatever the explanation, there is little doubt that the scene at the Lupercalia was a contrived drama with Caesar as author.

As an example of propaganda action from Augustus' reign we may take the Ludi Saeculares of 17 B.C. It happens that we possess, in addition to the odd notes in the *Res Gestae* (22) and the historians, the text of the Sibylline oracle prescribing the ritual and an account of the ritual itself in Zosimus (2,5), some more general observations in Censorinus (*DN* 17), an inscription of major importance, now in the Museo delle Terme, giving the official record of the proceedings, and Horace's hymn. There are dim traces of earlier celebrations in 463, 363, and 263 B.C. A new cycle was inaugurated in 249 B.C. and there was a further celebration in 146. Only a forcing of evidence could contrive 17 as an appropriate year, and clearly no one could remember the last celebration. But the whole ritual was entirely appropriate to Augustan propaganda; he ordained it and took a close personal interest in it.

The basic idea of the Ludi Saeculares was renewal, and ideas of renewal had been for some time in the air; witness Vergil's fourth eclogue or the Sibylline oracles that Cleopatra made her own (3, 46–54, 75–92, 350–361, 367–380). The ceremonies began with three days on which the means of purification (torches, bitumen, and the like) were distributed by the priests to all free people: so the pollution of the past was burned or seared away. Then all was ready for the ritual by the Tiber. Here stood a subterranean altar to the deities of the underworld, and here, in the traditional ritual black, victims were offered to them on three successive nights. On this occasion the ritual was carried out by Augustus and Agrippa, and carefully adapted to the new situation. The sacrifices were not to Dis and Proserpina but to the Moirae, who bore Rome's destiny in their care, to Eilithyia, goddess of childbirth, and to Mother Earth. A greater innovation still was the introduction of ritual by day. The Moirae and Eilithyia were Greek divinities. The ritual by day offered the appropriate sacrifices to the two great Capitoline deities Jupiter and Juno. Then on the third day they turned to the deity of the new reign and the new age, Apollo, and his sister Diana, and Horace's hymn was sung on the Capitol and on the Palatine, for the old gods and the new. The hymn is carefully scripted. It begins and ends with Apollo, and recurs to him in the middle, but takes account of the deities honored in the nightly ritual and the ultimate power of the Capitoline gods. It plays on the three themes of religion, morality, and fertility, links all with the traditions of Rome, and has a delicately veiled reference to Augustus. The whole ritual is one of renewal. The past is purified; its evils are buried. The future is filled with light, fertility of human and field, prosperity. And the whole pivots on Augustus.

The emperors knew how to use demonstrative action to provide a psychological basis for their power. The most obvious example is the continuing prevalence of donatives, whether of corn or of money and whether to troops or to the people at large, and public displays, Juvenal's "bread and circuses." Successive emperors vied with one another in the elaboration and extravagance of their displays. It had already begun under the Republic; Scaurus in 58 B.C., Pompey in 55, Milo in 53 gave massive spectacles. Under Augustus regular shows, without special occasions, took 66 days of the year; under Marcus Aurelius 135; and by the middle of the fourth century as many as 175 days. Titus inaugurated the Flavian Amphitheater with 100 days of spectacle; Trajan's similar celebration of his second Dacian triumph in A.D. 106 lasted 123 days. These extravagances lasted into the great days of Byzantium, and Justinian claimed a record expenditure of 288,000 *solidi* to celebrate his consulship of A.D. 521.

We may notice how an emperor whose claims to the throne might seem insecure required a demonstrative military victory, not for its own sake but to establish his prestige: for its propaganda value, in other words. Claudius' motives in undertaking the invasion of Britain were no doubt various; there was the hope of economic gain, and the elimination of a piratical base and refuge for the disaffected; there was the need to maintain the honor of Rome by fulfilling Caligula's expressed intention; but there was also his own need to demonstrate resoundingly that he stood in the practical and military traditions of Roman imperialism. Similarly, Vespasian gave Titus orders to storm Jerusalem instead of awaiting the inevitable but leisurely consequence of a siege; he had no genetical claims to the throne and needed the immediate practical demonstration of his authority.

Or we may think of Caracalla's attempt to establish himself as a second Alexander, talking of Alexander in season and out of season in order to keep the idea of Alexander before his people, ordering statues of Alexander to be erected in every camp, recruiting a special regiment to be armed exactly as Alexander's troops had been, negotiating a marriage with a Parthian princess so as to become heir to Alexander's empire, drinking from a cup reputed to be Alexander's, using weapons reputed to be Alexander's, scowling like Alexander, powdering down his complexion to the pallor of Alexander, spending hours in front of a mirror imitating the way Alexander held his head askance.

An interesting example of dramatic support for an aspect of the imperial regime is given in Herodian's account of the apotheosis of an emperor in the third century A.D. It is important to realize that the apotheosis of the previous incumbent might be an important ingredient in the position of his successor, who thus became *divi filius,* son of the divinity, with a religious aura and the possibility, like Heracles and Asclepius, of future apotheosis for services to mankind. According to Herodian's account, a wax image of the dead emperor, pallid as in sickness, lay in state for seven days, with noble attendants in vigil, the men in black, the women in white. At the end of seven days the court doctors declared life to be extinct. The body was carried first to the forum, where hymns were sung, then to the Campus Martius where it was placed on an elaborately decorated pyre, with chambers one on top of another. In one of these were placed spices and aromatics from all over the empire. Then followed a procession of chariots around the pyre with masked figures representing heroes from the past. After this the pyre was fired, and as the flames rose from the topmost story an eagle was released to carry the emperor's soul from earth to heaven.

As a last example—and once again these are examples only—we may consider the impact of the procedure at the Byzantine court on a petitioner from one of the remoter parts of the empire. Norman Baynes in his brief but admirable *The Byzantine Empire* (London: Oxford Univ. Press, 1952, pp. 72–73) has evoked the scene:

> He has been royally entertained, under the vigilant care of imperial officials he has seen the wonders of the capital, and to-day he is to

have audience with the Emperor. Through a dazzling maze of marble corridors, through chambers rich with mosaic and cloth of gold, through long lines of palace guards in white uniforms, amidst patricians, bishops, generals and senators, to the music of organs and church choirs he passes, supported by eunuchs, until at last oppressed with interminable splendour he falls prostrate in the presence of the silent, motionless, hieratic figure of the Lord of New Rome, the heir of Constantine, seated on the throne of the Caesars: before he can rise, Emperor and throne have been caught aloft, and with vestments changed since last he gazed the Sovereign looks down on him, surely as God regarding mortal men. Who is he, as he hears the roar of the golden lions that surround the throne or the song of the birds on the trees, who is he that he should decline the Emperor's behests? He stays not to think of the mechanism which causes the lions to roar or the birds to sing: he can scarce answer the questions of the Logothete speaking for his imperial master: his allegiance is won: he will fight for the Roman Christ and his Empire.

Such is the propaganda of pageantry.

### ORACLES AND MYTHS

Martin Nilsson in his contribution to the monumental *Studies Presented to David Moore Robinson* (vol. 2, p. 743) discussed the part played by oracles and myths in political propaganda in sixth-century Athens. Pisistratus was nicknamed Bakis (the name of a famous mythical prophet), and this suggests that he was adept at manufacturing oracles for his own ends. Two stories relating to the dynasty illustrate the importance of this element in the propaganda of the period; both are told by Herodotus. One tells how Hipparchus banished Onomacritus for inserting an oracle into the oracles of Musaeus. This oracle prophesied the disappearance of the islands in the vicinity of Lemnos. The foreign policy of the Pisistratids was based on control of these islands and with them the corn-route through the Hellespont. The proposed insertion was a piece of political propaganda. The exiled Onomacritus went to the Persian court, and recited to the Great King oracles favorable to Persia, suppressing others. The islands of Lemnos and Imbros did indeed disappear; the Persian general Otanes occupied them (*Hdt.* 7,6). Again, when Cleomenes took possession of the Acropolis he found oracles of the Pisistratids prophesying assaults by the Spartans on Athens, evidently politically calculated to strengthen Athenian resistance (5, 90).

Oracles were similarly used in the Peloponnesian War. Aristophanes, as a parodist, is only exaggerating what actually happened when he depicts Cleon controlling Demos by favorable oracles, and being outbid by the sausage-seller (*Kn.* 997 ff.). We remember also the descent of the oracle-monger on Cloudcuckoocity (*B.* 961). In more sober history Plutarch (*Nicias* 13) records the way in which the rival parties used oracles to support their policy over Sicily.

The Roman aristocrats used the Sibylline Books to sustain their policies. Religious innovation had a political basis. A good example dates from 399 B.C. during the Siege of Veii (*Liv.* 5,13). A bad winter was followed by a torrid, pestilent summer. A week-long *lectisternium* (a ceremonial banquet of the gods) was decreed—the six deities concerned were Greek—and alongside it open house, the end of quarrels, and goodwill and general holidays. Fifty years later in time of pestilence, theatrical performances were decreed, presumably to distract the people (*Liv.* 7,2). The disasters of the Punic Wars saw frequent recourse to the Books. The results of the consultation after the battle of Trebia are particularly interesting, mingling religion and politics as they do: a purification of the whole city, a *lectisternium* for Juventas, the deity of the young recruits; an act of adoration to Hercules; five special victims for the Genius, the spirit of fertility in the male, perhaps looking ahead to a long war and the need to increase the birth-rate of male children; and a special vow if the state survived for ten years (*Liv.* 21,62 ff.). In general the senate seem to have relied on distracting the people by festivals, directing propaganda to national unity, and replacing the failure of old procedures by innovation. Occasionally their policies recoiled; they introduced the Great Mother from Pessinus with inadequate staff-work, were shocked at the ritual, and promptly banned the Romans from participation.

Cleopatra, as we have seen, used Sibylline Oracles to support her claims. She was destined to throw Rome down from heaven to earth and then to raise her from earth to heaven, inaugurate a golden age for Asia and Europe alike:

> Tranquil peace shall journey to the land of Asia.
> Europe shall then be blessed, the atmosphere be fruitful,
> lasting, sturdy, free from rain or hail,
> bearing all creatures of the world, winged and earthbound.
> Blessed above all the man or woman who shall see that day. . . .
> For from the starry sky, in its fullness the rule of law
> and righteousness will descend upon man, and with it
> the saving grace of concord, cherished beyond all else by
>     mortals,
> love, trust, friendship with the stranger. Far from men
> poverty will flee, compulsion will flee,
> and lawlessness, carping, envy, anger, folly,
> murder and deadly strife and bitter conflict,
> robbery by night and every evil—in those days.
>
> (*Or. Sib.* 3,367 ff.)

There are few more illuminating glimpses of ancient propaganda.

Myth might be similarly employed. Pisistratus developed the myths of Theseus, which came into new prominence at this time, for political purposes. He subdued bandits and made possible the peaceful agriculture fostered by Triptolemus. There is here a claim on Eleusis, as well as propaganda for the *pax Pisistrata*. Another series of myths was invented to buttress Athenian claims in the northern Aegean. The dance of deliverance from the Minotaur was transferred from Crete to Delos, a sign of Pisistratid interest in that area. Another myth told how Pandion, king of Athens, married a Megarian princess by whom he had a son Nisus; this was a support for Pisistratus' occupation of the Megarian port Nisaea.

The Romans invented or developed myth for their own purposes. Michael Grant has written of "the quest for a Roman past." The Homeric Aeneas has no association with Italy, but he alone of the Trojan princes has a future. Hellanicus first landed him in Latium, but it was only after the Roman conflict with Greece that the idea was taken up in a big way to give to the Romans a background in that Greek culture that they had come to admire, but from among the enemies of the Greeks. Similarly Romulus and Remus (or Romus) are back-formations from the name of Rome, and have acquired a deal of folklore in the process. Their story cannot be traced back beyond Fabius Pictor in the third century B.C., as there is no reason to suppose that the Capitoline Wolf, which is older, had any babies originally attached to it. It was a remarkable piece of patriotic mythography to contrive two seemingly conflicting foundation-stories and maintain them both.

### COINS

The principal propaganda instrument of the ancient world in general, and the Roman Empire in particular, was the coin. At first blush this is unexpected. Yet, once the potentiality is realized it is obvious enough. A single coin may pass through hundreds of hands; a particular coin-type through millions. A word or two can carry a message for the literate; a suitable image or emblem will speak to literate and illiterate alike.

Coinage began, it seems, in Lydia in the seventh century B.C., and was swiftly adopted by the Greek settlements on the Asia Minor coast, and so spread over the Greek world. In its simplest form the coin meant that the seal of the state was set upon a small lump of gold or silver as a guarantee of its reliability. This was most obviously done through an emblem. The lion was the emblem of the Lydian king, and the lion guaranteed the new coin, although one king, Alyattes, began to put his own name alongside the lion, and the daric and shekel of the Persian Empire carried the image of the Great King himself.

Plainly there is already something prestigious about the emblem on the coin, and the states did not take it lightly. Greek coins are among the masterpieces of Greek art, finely executed in high relief; those responsible for commissioning them were no protagonists of art for art's sake, and would not have gone to the trouble had it not been politically worthwhile. Athens, the first city to produce coins with emblems on both sides, used the goddess Athene on one side and the owl, the symbol of wisdom, on the other; the latter emblem was so popular and prestigious that the coins were nicknamed "owls." Her

rival Aegina used a sea turtle. The creature was a natural emblem for a mercantile power, with its easy movement through
the water and its armor-plated defense; it was also sacred to
Aphrodite, protectress of the island, as Athene was of Athens.
It is significant that when Athens conquered Aegina, ousted her
commercially and controlled her politically, the emblem was
changed to a tortoise. Some of the states advertised their commercial prosperity. Cyrene showed the silphium plant, Naxos a
bunch of grapes and the god Dionysus, Metapontum an ear of
corn, Selinus the wild parsley from which it took its name.
Sometimes the emblem is a punning allusion to the name itself.
Acragas began by depicting the sea creatures that helped its
fishing industry to prosper, but changed to an eagle in reference
to the "fierce" of the city's name. Himera, which is akin to the
Greek word for "day," chose a cock, the bird of morning. Zan-
cle was a Sicel word for "sickle" and put a dolphin in a sickle-
shaped harbor on its coins. Some of the finest of all coins came
from Syracuse. There the protecting goddess, Artemis Arethu-
sa, appeared, surrounded by swimming dolphins; on the other
side a four-horse chariot conveys the power and wealth and
abiding passion of the rulers, amply reflected in Pindar's odes.

Alexander changed the world. On his coins appeared Apollo,
the god of the Hellenic culture which the Macedonians professed and spread; Athene, deity of war and wisdom, daughter
of Zeus as Alexander was acclaimed son of Zeus, and goddess of
that Athens which had defied Philip and yet which epitomized
the Greek world that he yearned to lead; Nike, goddess of victory; Heracles, son of Zeus, and legendary ancestor of the royal
house; and Zeus, king of the gods, Alexander's reputed divine
father, and already identified with the Egyptian Ammon. But it
was Alexander who mattered more than the gods. Already in his
lifetime the mint of Alexandria was producing coins in which
the type was Heracles but the face Alexander, and before the
end of the century Lysimachus was putting Alexander's head on
his coins, and in this way claiming for himself the prestige of
Alexander.

In the classical period prestige attached to the city and to its
emblem. In the Hellenistic world prestige attached to the
monarch. The Seleucid dynasty in particular has given us in its

coins a wonderful series of individualized portraits. Furthermore, this spread over much of the territory to which Alexander
had penetrated. From Bactria or Pontus the rulers leap up at us
from their coins as flesh and blood. "This is your ruler," they
seem to say; "acknowledge him."

The great difference between Roman imperial coinage and
anything that had gone before lay in its deliberate use for immediate propaganda. The symbolism of the Greek coins remained unchanging for long periods. The precise presentation
might vary with changing fashions, but the symbolism is
remarkably consistent. Syracuse is a case in point. We can look
at a series of coins, say from 510 to 399 B.C. All show on one
side the goddess with the dolphins swimming around, and one
could almost write a treatise on women's fashions by examining
them in succession. On the other side the four horses begin by
standing soberly in close parallel in front of their chariot; by the
end of the century they are in a vigorous but disciplined gallop,
or plunging triumphantly; this is an advance in artistic technique—but the symbolism is unchanged. The Roman emperors
changed their designs each year and might indeed introduce
several new designs in a single year.

Alföldi in his contribution to *Essays in Roman Coinage
Presented to Harold Mattingly* (R. A. G. Carson and C. H.
Sutherland, eds., London: Oxford Univ. Press, 1956) offered a
notable analysis of political propaganda in Roman Republican
coinage. In the third century the symbolism is public. It speaks
of the Roman state as a whole, and is directed to the central Italian heirs of the Etruscans (hence the prominence given to Ilia)
and to the Greeks of the south (hence Greek deities and Greek
symbols such as the wreath, palm, and fillet). At the same time
the coins assert Rome: they use Roman lettering and show the
wolf and the twins. In the second century the individual families of the optimates begin to take over. Rome remains on the
obverse, but the state gods are replaced by the special protecting
deities of the individual families or with allusions to their earthly achievements. Sextus Pompeius Fostlus claimed descent from
the sheperd Faustulus, and shows the wolf and the twins in
families as well as patriotic pride; C. Augurinus shows the corn
market, because one of his ancestors had served the corn supply

well. By the first century even Rome disappears. The protecting deities take over. Abstract personifications refer to an immediate political situation. Thus Libertas is appropriate to the policies of the Gracchi or the assassination of Caesar, Salus to the danger of the Social War, Concordia as a general counterblast to civil disturbances, Victoria to military victory. Some of these personifications acquire immediately recognizable characteristics, the olive-branch of Pax, the rudder of Fortuna, the sacrificial dish of Pietas. The appeal to the commons is incarnate in the figure of the Genius populi Romani. Toward the end of the period there is an appeal to the soldiers, either in the form of military standards or in the plough, which refers to new settlements. And individuals often quite obscure put on the coins references to their own achievements, and even their own likenesses.

The coinage of the early empire has been the subject of a brilliantly readable study by C. H. Sutherland (*Coinage in Roman Imperial Policy 31* B.C.–A.D. *68,* London, 1951). The Roman emperors were heirs to Alexander and to the Hellenistic Age as well as to the Republic. As with the Hellenistic monarchs their images on coins were of primary importance both (it should not be forgotten) for authenticating the coin and for spreading an impression of the emperor. Sometimes the portraits are idealized; Augustus tends to be assimilated to his patron Apollo. Sometimes they are political; the artists under Tiberius and Gaius are thinking first of imperial power and only second of the individual emperor. Sometimes the character of the individual emperor comes through very clearly *as he wished it to appear;* this may be seen in the anxious concern in the face of Claudius or the baroque aestheticism of Nero. In the centuries that followed we can trace a fluctuation between idealism and realism, which is only partly a matter of artistic fashion and which, more importantly, reveals something of the values of the emperors themselves and the way they wished their subjects to think of them, as the leisured purveyors of peace and culture or as tough military realists.

Equally interesting are the inscriptions, and the scenes that appear on the other side. Consider, for example, the coinage of Augustus, with, in early days, its careful record of his legal

titles, Caesar (the name, said Antony, to which he owed everything), IIIVIR, Imperator (the *imperium* was one of the two
props of his power), *tribunicia potestate* (the other prop), Consul (his election was backed by the sword, but the coin seems to
record a legal republican office), Pontifex and Augur (both
stressing his concern for religious tradition and adding to the
religious aura that surrounded him), and above all Divi Filius,
son of the divine Julius portrayed on the other side of the coin.
Or consider the way the coins show him with the beard he had
vowed not to shave until he was avenged on Caesar's murderers,
and the temple of Mars Ultor, Mars the Avenger, which appears
after the vengeance is accomplished. Or consider how he, no
great soldier himself, stresses the theme of victory, how he
shows a crocodile with the text AEGYPTO CAPTA, and how he
portrays on his coins the Roman standards recovered from Parthia by negotiation and accompanies them with the misleading
slogan ARMENIA RECEPTA, "the recapture of Armenia."
Note how his victory in a civil war with Antony is concealed by a
conflict between Rome and Egypt or Rome and Parthia. As his
power becomes more secure he stresses the blessings of peace.
Pax, Peace herself, appears on his coins; an issue from Chios
shows the rich beauty of the corn harvest. He makes much of
the *clipeus virtutis,* the "shield of virtue" voted him for his
valor, piety, justice, and clemency. Traditional republican
forms, SPQR, SC, and the like abound. Augustus is the
liberator, the savior. He receives oak wreaths and laurels for his
life-giving work. He carefully conceals the fact that his power
depends on the legions. He appears as Pontifex Maximus, or as
Pater Patriae, Father of the Fatherland. This is propaganda from
a master hand.

Tiberius was less politic, less subtle, more honest than
Augustus. He had been a fine soldier, and this is stressed in his
early coinage, which celebrates his victories in Germany toward
the end of Augustus' reign. It is wholly characteristic of
Tiberius not to introduce changes. He knew that he was abler
than Augustus in any obvious sense; he knew that Augustus
had a political flair that he himself lacked; and he tended to
play it safe. But the main propaganda stress of the reign is on
the emperor's *providentia,* his forethoughtful care of the whole

empire: a good example is to be found in his active benefactions to the cities of Asia Minor when they were devastated by a disastrous earthquake. We see him on a fine coin seated, upright, and imperial. The inscription is CIVITATIBVS ASIAE RESTITVTIS, "the restoration of the cities of Asia." It is curious that LIBERALITAS does not appear on the coins. Other qualities do, notably CLEMENTIA and MODERATIO, and it looks very much as if the senate voted him shields for these qualities. No other emperor includes moderation in his coin propaganda.

Claudius came to the throne after the tyranny of Caligula. His propaganda needed from the outset to declare a change of policy. So his early coins stress LIBERTAS AVGVSTA and PACI AVGVSTAE. *Pax* here is more than peace; it is the imperial goodwill, the human equivalent of the *pax deorum*. The dative of dedication is noteworthy. So is the image of Pax, with the wings of Victory, the staff of Prosperity (Felicitas), the snake of security (Salus), the gesture of Modesty (Pudor). Claudius also stresses his constitutional position and the authority of the senate. Such claims are commonplace after a period of more naked autocracy. At the same time he did not forget the praetorian guard to whom he owed his position. For many years his coins show the camp, or his reception there. Claudius, as we have seen, needed a resounding military victory to establish his power, and found it in Britain. He gave publicity to this by a coin with a triumphal arch on it. But in general his genius was constructive. He did important work on the harbor at Ostia. We know it better from a coin of Nero, who brought it to completion, but Claudius proudly proclaimed CERES AVGVSTA, which might be roughly paraphrased as "the corn supply secured by the emperor," although the original, with its religious overtones, is subtler. A new imperial virtue appears for the first time in this reign. This is CONSTANTIA, Pertinacity, and she is accompanied sometimes by civic, sometimes by military emblems.

Nero's coinage is particularly interesting. He, or his advisers, begin by stressing the continuity represented by the new reign. Nero is shown with his mother Agrippina; on the other side Augustus is escorting Claudius to his place among the gods,

and the inscription EX S C is a reminder that Nero began under
the guidance of Seneca and Burrus as a constitutional monarch
paying due attention to the senate. By A.D. 56 he appears as
Pater Patriae; his portrait is bare-headed and unassertive; the
wreath of civil virtue is prominent. The coins of A.D. 61 introduce three new types, Ceres, Virtus, armed and helmeted,
and a military representation of the goddess Rome. There is
nothing sinister here. The emperor wished to appear in control
of domestic and foreign policy, and Boudicca's rebellion called
out the new emphasis on military might. The last four years of
his reign, from 64, saw more radical changes. The emperor now
appears with a laurel wreath, his titles are richer and less formally controlled. We can trace a tension between the emperor's
ambitions and the conservatism of his advisers. He won a
chariot-race in Greece; the coin commemorating this bears the
inscription DECVRSIO ("military exercises"). He sang in
public; and a coin shows Apollo with the lyre; yet the traditionalists have contrived to make it a reference to Apollo's
patronage of Augustus, although they could not prevent him
portraying himself with Apollo's radiant crown. And the coins
allude to more substantial achievements, the opening of a new
provision market, the completion of Claudius' harbor at Ostia
(with ships at anchor among the warehouses under the protection of the river god Tiber), the rebuilding of the Temple of
Vesta, the closing of the Temple of Janus made plausible by the
Armenian settlements and agreement with Parthia.

Nero fell, and "the Year of the Four Emperors" saw a succession of pretenders. Their short-lived coinages form an interesting study in propaganda. C. Vindex, who raised a rebellion in
Gaul, seems to have issued a coin showing the Genius of the
Roman People, as an old man with the scepter of authority, and
on the reverse Mars Ultor, the god of war, but with a half-
punning allusion to Vindex's own name. L. Clodius Macer was
less modest: he used his own likeness, but claimed to be mint-
ing as propraetor by authority of the senate. He pictured a
galley on the reverse. This was one of Antony's emblems, a
counter to the Augustan pretensions of Nero, and a declaration
of his own intention to control the sea routes and the corn supply. Galba came from Spain to the throne. He showed the god-

dess of Spain presenting him with the Palladium, the symbol of eternal Rome. He also honored Livia; she had indeed advanced him in his youth, and formed a link with Augustus; he showed her with scepter and sacrificial dish. Other coins portray liberty and victory. Otho, who ousted Galba, optimistically proclaimed World Peace and portrayed Pax with the olive branch. Vitellius, his successor, proclaimed CLEMENTIA IMPeratoris GERMANici. This is in its way masterly. Clementia was one of the imperial virtues, laid upon Nero by Seneca at the outset of his reign. *Imperatoris* reminds us that Vitellius' power depended upon his legions. *Germanici* states which legions; at the same time it forms a link with the Germanicus of the *domus divina.* Vitellius also stressed his sacrosanctity and priestly office, and showed the raven, dolphin, and tripod of Apollo; there is here a counter to Nero's Apollo; aesthetics must yield to religious destiny. Vespasian, as we have seen, consolidated his power with victory in Judaea. He publicized this in a superb coin showing Judaea mourning under a palm tree; the inscription proclaims IVDAEA CAPTA.

Nerva came in briefly after the Flavian dynasty had sunk into tyranny. He tried to achieve a reputation for generous dealing. One coin proclaimed the remission of the cost of the postal service; the scene shows an empty cart and a grazing mule. Another announced the removal of the false charges that were the basis of taxation in Judaea; the tax, however, stayed. Nerva's subsidy for the education of orphans was popular enough to be celebrated on coins by Trajan some years later. Nerva and Trajan both portray scenes of the distribution of largesse by an imperial officer under the emperor's supervision. The figure holding a tally may be Liberalitas. Trajan also showed his constructive measures for the water supply in a coin showing a river god pouring water bountifully from a jar. He naturally gave publicity to military victories; another river god appearing on his coins is the Danube. A notable design from 116 or 117 shows the emperor leaning on a spear. At his feet are the river gods of the Tigris and Euphrates; between them the weeping figure of Mesopotamia, to whom the conqueror is haughtily indifferent. A different mood altogether is shown in Hadrian's celebration of the defeat of the revolt in Judaea. Here the emperor is seen raising Judaea (who is accompanied by three children with palm branches) to her feet. The propaganda element is clear; the emperor is the restorer of the years that have been destroyed. Similarly Hadrian protrayed Britannia in British costume and with British armor. Later emperors honor their own country of origin, Severus Africa, Decius Pannonia.

To take one last theme, the old gods gradually appear less frequently, and the coins become a vehicle for religious propaganda. We can see the patron god of Elagabalus in the black betyl of Emesa, or the sun god in whom Aurelian hoped to find a unifying factor for the empire, and finally the victory of the Christians can be traced in the symbolism of the coins.

### ORAL COMMUNICATION

It may seem strange to have written so much about propaganda and communication without making more than incidental reference to words. But we, as McLuhan has sufficiently reminded us, are grandchildren of an age of printing, and children of an age of radio, and members of an age of television. Before there were these possibilities of mass communication the word had to take its place alongside the work; the act was more important than the *acta*. Furthermore, the primary means of verbal communication were oral. It should never be forgotten that a speech delivered in the Assembly at Athens would be heard by far more people than would read it if it were issued as a pamphlet, at least in that generation.

The spread of news was oral. In Athens the barber's shop was the great center of dissemination. Plutarch in his *Life of Nicias* (30) tells how a foreigner arrived in Piraeus and discussed the Athenian debacle in Sicily as if the Athenians knew all about it. The barber dashed from the shop and ran the not inconsiderable distance to the other main area of oral contact, the agora or city-center of Athens itself. So in Aristophanes' *Wealth* (338) it is in the barber's shop that the news of Chremylus' surprising enrichment is heard. Aristophanes is forever accusing the "student generation" of hanging around the city-center talking politics instead of taking exercise or hunting (*Kn.* 1373 ff.; *Eccl.* 62 ff.; *Fr.* 1015). The Forum Romanum served the same function at Rome.

All ancient literature is in some sense oral. Obviously there is a considerable difference between the production of traditional epic by the formulaic methods of the bards and the later productions, whether in poetry or prose, that were composed in writing. But all ancient literature was meant to be heard. Herodotus no doubt retailed his wares in the marketplace; Gilbert Ryle even suggested that Plato wrote for performance in public competitions. An ancient reader, even on his own, read aloud; Philip *heard* the eunuch reading Isaiah (*Acts* 8,30), and Ambrose was exceptional in reading silently to himself (Aug. *Conf.* 6,3). Ancient literature is for this reason a much more rhetorical means of communication than is modern literature.

Two things follow that have some political importance. First, as in traditional West African society, the gathered wisdom of the "tribe" was expressed in readily memorable gnomic aphorisms. *The Sayings of the Seven Wise Men* in Greece are a good example of this; so is the Hebrew *Book of Proverbs*. Such habits die hard. The aphoristic attitude can be seen in Hesiod, or Theognis; it also can be seen very strongly in Democritus. At Rome it is there in the ancient traditionalists of the Republic; it also can be seen in a Stoic like Seneca.

A second consequence with political implications is the development of the institution that at Rome was called the *recitatio,* but that also was to be found in the Hellenistic courts. This was the "publication" of works through public reading in the presence of a patron and a select audience. It could have positive virtues: a discerning patron could encourage a young writer, and the *recitatio* might be the occasion of constructive critical comment. Equally the values might be those of a closed coterie. Many of the qualities and defects of Silver Latin, the overstylized rhetoric, the flashing epigrams, the parade of learning, the tendency to hyperbole, the taste for horrors, the moralizing and apostrophizing, the attempts to startle, the titillation of the ear, arose from the *recitatio*. But it also gave the rulers the chance to exercise a relatively tactful censorship.

## INSCRIPTIONS

A record carved in stone and set in a public place had one advantage over the spoken word. The spoken word was a means of communication only to those present on a given occasion. The inscription declared its message to any who might pass that spot. Plainly, to carve letters in stone is an expensive and laborious business. It was therefore mainly used for those who wished their message to be conveyed to posterity. Epitaphs are an obvious example, and to those with little hope of "something after death" it was of special importance to leave a name behind them. Hence the proud record of offices held and honors received.

We may here pick out two examples of major inscriptions used for the communication of what one might in the broad sense term propaganda. The first is the *Monumentum Ancyranum,* otherwise the *Res Gestae Divi Augusti,* the great inscription set up in different parts of the empire (of which an example survives from Ankara in Turkey, as well as fragments from Apollonia and Antioch in Pisidia) in which Augustus laid down the view of his rule that he wished to disseminate for his contemporaries and for posterity. It is an extended and elaborate *elogium,* primarily directed to the people of Rome. It is not overwritten, although the first person singular dominates it. Care has been taken to avoid statements that could be refuted. It is a list that balances honors and services. Failures are omitted; the reign might seem to have been one of unremitting glory. Opponents are dismissed; they are not even named; Antony is "a faction," Brutus and Cassius enemies of the state, and there is no indication that Augustus ever faced later opposition. Augustus stresses several times that he held only legal republican offices. True; but he does not say that in his case they were accumulated and permanent in a thoroughly nonrepublican way. The climax is his pride in the shield of virtue and the title *pater patriae.*

The second inscription is of a quite different kind. Around the town-center of Oenoanda in Asia Minor, a wealthy Epicurean named Diogenes set up an exposition of Epicurean philosophy; it is long and detailed. What is of particular interest is his account of his motive (fr. 2):

Unaccustomed as I am to public speaking, I am using the inscription to say these things as if I were present, in the endeavor to show that what is naturally best, peace of mind, is the same for one and all. I have now given the second reason for the inscription, our concern. I proceed to add its nature and character. I have now reached the sunset of life through old age. I am all but ready to weigh anchor from the shores of life with a noble paean upon the fulfilment of pleasure. I have now resolved to help those of sound judgement, in case I am taken away too soon. So, if only one or two or three or four or five or six, or, friend, as many more such as you wish, and yet not too many, were lying sick of soul, then calling on them all individually I would do everything in my power for the best advice. But since, as I have already said, the majority are smitten alike and together as if in a plague by the disease of false judgement about the world, and their numbers are still growing—for like a flock of sheep one catches the disease from another through mutual imitation—and it is right furthermore to help those who will come after us—for they too are our kin though yet unborn—and, besides, love of our fellows is assuredly shown in aiding even foreigners who fall in with us: so since the assistance provided by the inscription reaches a greater number, I have decided to use this colonnade to proclaim in public the prescription of salvation.

## GRAFFITI

The inscription, formally conceived, was an expensive business. But walls could be scrawled on in the ancient world, as in the modern. At Pompeii literally hundreds of graffiti were found relating to municipal elections. Aemilius Celer recommends the election of L. Statius Receptus—and curses anyone who deletes his "poster" (Dess. 6409). Popidius Natalis joins with a company of Isis devotees to commend Cuspius Pansa (Dess. 6419f). Some of the slogans are simple, but one "agent" even tries his hand at verse (Dess. 6422b). Sometimes the endorsement came from a guild, the dyers or bakers or cartwrights, rather than an individual, and this led to a certain amount of parody; at least it is hard to take very seriously the commendation of the drinkers-late or the sleepers, and one which professes to come from a teacher contains a grammatical howler.

Not all the graffiti relate to politics. Some are advertisements. One of the most interesting (*CIL* 4,1595) is not a trade-advertisement but a commendation of a member of the

*Iuventus* named Septumius or Septimius for his skill in riding
his horse along the "snake-course." The two elegiac couplets
are strung out in the form of a snake. Some of the graffiti are by
girls who have fallen for gladiators. Celadus is described as "the
girls' dream and idol," Crescens as their "master and night-
doctor."

In this connection we must mention some of the early Christian graffiti, painted in vermilion, written with charcoal, or
scratched in mortar. Mostly these survive from the catacombs
and relate to the dead; they consist of a name and the simplest
of formulas. Sometimes a symbol is used, the fish (i-ch-th-u-s is
an acronym for "Jesus Christ, God's Son, Savior" in Greek) or
the anchor. One suspects that such symbols were used as a kind
of secret password in days of persecution. A particularly interesting symbol, which has been found in a number of places
(Pompeii, Dura-Europos, Aquincum on the Danube, and
scratched on wall plaster at Cirencester), is the palindromic
word square ROTAS OPERA TENET AREPO SATOR. It is not
at first sight a Christian formulation, although the language
bears some relation to Ezekiel. But in its present form it has the
cross (T) at four key points flanked by A and O, and can be rearranged to give PATERNOSTER twice intersecting on a common
N, with the A-O formula twice.

Graffiti of course are usually concerned with more trivial purposes; yet they too may be communication and propaganda of a
sort, whether they are from the forum at Timgad (a phallus, for
example, or the sentiment, expressed with a fine disregard for
grammar "Hunting, Bathing, Fun, Laughter—that's life") or
from a tile factory in Britain ("Austalis has been going off on
his own every day for a fortnight"). But on the whole graffiti
are for letting off steam rather than for communication. He was
a wise Pompeian who wrote "The man who wrote this did so
because he wanted to."

## PUBLIC RECORDS

From the Greek world, for obvious reasons, we know most
about the preservation of records at Athens. If the record was
clearly only of temporary use it was preserved on whitened
boards called *leucomata*. The bulk of the records were inscribed

on papyrus and kept in the Metroon. These would be regarded in their day as durable, but across the centuries they have naturally proved evanescent. Only the more important decrees and records were carved in stone, but they were numerous enough. Turning over the pages of a standard publication we may note a sixth-century decree relating to Salamis; a memorial to those who died fighting in 459; tribute lists; a decree about relations with Chalcis; a decree relating to the colony at Brea; an expedition to Corcyra; a treaty with Leontini; an alliance (in 420) between Athens, Argos, Mantinea, and Elis; a decree for the Samians; honors for the returning democrats after the recognition of the representatives of other cities in Athens; and so on and so forth. Athenian foreign policy was more complex than that of many cities, and their records consequently more elaborate. Further, their resources were fuller, and their records consequently more permanent. But other cities followed their example.

At Rome the public records were known as *acta;* the *acta forensia* were legal records compiled by clerks, the *acta militaria* were legionary records, probably preserved in the military treasury, the *acta senatus* recorded the motions, views of the principal speakers and decisions of the senate. The *acta diurna* was a daily gazette published officially in Rome and the provinces from the time of Julius Caesar. It included extracts from the *acta forensia* and *acta senatus;* an official version of domestic and foreign politics; births and deaths; finance; the corn supply; a court circular; prodigies and news of religious significance; and a certain amount of diverting material. It corresponded to a government-controlled newspaper under a totalitarian regime, except that it had no competitors at all. It was obviously an instrument of major importance for the control of news and the manipulation of public opinions.

### THE WRITTEN WORD

Despite the absence of printing, the written word had certain advantages as a means of communication. First, and most obviously, it was a means of communicating at a distance. Hence the emphasis on the letter. It is a curious fact, so familiar that we forget its oddity, that one-third of the sacred book of the

Christians consists of letters. Second, and not so obvious, it made possible anonymous and pseudonymous publications. Everyone can see who is delivering a speech; no one can tell at a glance who has composed a writing. This is important for propaganda purposes. Words whose genuine source might be obviously tainted could circulate freely. Views would seem to be more authoritative appearing under the name of some famed figure of the past. This last practice was well enough known in antiquity. *The Book of Daniel* is a good example, purporting to be a series of narratives and visions of the sixth century B.C. but patently written in the second century as an encouragement to the Jews under the persecution of Antiochus Epiphanes. Or, to take a relatively noncontroversial example from the New Testament, the second letter of Peter hardly can be by the apostle, or by the author of the first letter, and must be dated to about A.D. 150. There are plenty of examples from the Graeco-Roman world, from the extraordinary miscellany of poetry going under the name of Homer, through work by later Platonists foisted upon the master, to the Appendix Vergiliana (some of which may be, but all of which cannot be, authentic Vergil) and beyond. The work that goes under the name of Dionysius the Areopagite blends the two traditions.

Third, the written word made possible the consultation of a work as a permanent record. This (although the matter is controversial) seems to be what Thucydides means when he makes his famous claim (1,22): "I shall be content to have the seal of utility stamped on my work by those who in the future want a clear view of past events, events that will recur in closely similar pattern, human nature being what it is. I have composed it not as an ephemeral entertainment, but as a permanent possession." Polybius takes a similar pragmatical view; the great value of historical writing lies in the advance of scientific understanding that makes possible the methodical handling of current situations (9,2,5). To this view historical writing is a kind of reference book for statesmen. Or again, much of the work of the Lyceum lay in the methodical recording of data and generalizing from those records; witness the collection of constitutional histories inaugurated by Aristotle, or his own records of biological observations.

Fourth, the written word made easier the development of prose style. Despite M. Jourdain, we do not normally speak prose. Prose is a highly artificial and sophisticated medium, and J. D. Denniston claimed that in Greece it existed somewhat embryonically in the Ionian philosophers but only came to any real position in the fifth and fourth centuries, after which it degenerated. Finally, the written word made possible a permanence of poetic fame for both poets and their subjects. *Exegi monumentum aere perennius* has as its counterpart

> So long as men can breathe, or eye can see,
> So long lives this, and this gives life to thee.

A few examples follow of propaganda in literature. Solon, (5,5–6), justifying his policies in verse, starting with lines that rebut accusations of a lack of patriotism, and establish a religious dimension for social policy, going on to criticize the excesses of the rich in the light of an ethical theory that Satiety breeds Excess *(hybris)* and is punished by justice, and ending with a justification of his own policy of Good Order and impartiality.

> I flung my stout shield in defence of both sides and stood firm,
> I did not allow injustice to triumph either way.

Pindar (8,95), immortalizing his petty patrons (in proportion to the fee they could afford) by setting their trivial athleticism in the context of mighty myth.

> We are creatures of a day. What is a human? What is he not?
> A man
> is a dream of a shadow. Yet when a ray comes sent from heaven,
> there rests on men a radiant light, and life is kind.

The champions celebrated were no doubt amply content with the oral celebration, the pageantry, the choir, and the dance. It was Pindar's genius to spread their fame outside their own city and generation.

Examples abound of the political content of Athenian drama. Phrynichus is fined for a tactless treatment of political disaster in *The Capture of Miletus*. The political dimension of *The Oresteia* is clear in the resolution of the last play. There is the stress on dictatorship in Sophocles's *Oedipus* ("Dictators are the children of Excess"—872). There is the consistent witness of Euripides across twenty-five years against the Peloponnesian War, from *Heracles's Children,* where the violence of Alcmene in the end triumphs over the sacrificial spirit of Macaria, through the mighty power of *The Women of Troy,* to the final degradation of violence in *Orestes.* Aristophanes attacks the demagogy of Cleon and appeals for peace and sanity.

There is the beginning of the political pamphlet in the hands of the right-wing propagandists of the fifth century: Stesimbrotus uses biographical studies to flay Themistocles and Pericles and exalt Cimon; the "Old Oligarch" with his antidemocratic bias upholds "the decent citizens" against "the rabble."

Consider, further, the war of pamphlets, again political, over Socrates in the 390s. The key figure here was a radical democrat named Polycrates, who appears in the pages of Xenophon as "the Accuser," and who charged Socrates, with his influence on Critias and on Alcibiades, with encouraging indifference to social and political responsibilities, with teaching a critical attitude to democratic institutions, with selecting subversive passages from literature, and with fostering a revolt of the young. It is probable that Polycrates was countering the writings of Socrate's followers that upheld his integrity and protested that he was unjustly executed. His work in turn called out answers from Lysias, Xenophon, and a host of other followers of Socrates.

Isocrates used the pamphlet. Here was a man with fertile and constructive ideas, marked out from his youth for distinction yet prevented by a weak voice and personal diffidence from making his impact through oratory. So it had to be through teaching and writing, and his works are an eloquent defense of his political and educational ideals.

Consider also Polybius' position in the "Scipionic circle," the literary and intellectual coterie gathered together by Scipio Aemilianus. To Polybius, history was universal history, and the climax of history was the gathering of the known world under the dominion of Rome (1,1; 3,1). We need not doubt that he was sincere in this—but would he have received the encouragement of patronage if his theme had been different?

Julius Caesar, wrote his *Commentaries* (virtually a new form of literature) to maintain the view of his personality, career, and actions that he wished to hold before the eyes of the aristocracy in Rome during his absence. T. E. Page once said "Caesar's *Gallic War* indeed—a subtle political pamphlet beginning with the words 'All Gaul is divided into three parts.'" The propaganda is in fact very subtle; it is not overdone. Part of the effect is achieved by omission: there are judicious silences in the narrative of the invasion of Britain. Part is achieved by the stress on military achievement rather than on policy. In general we are left with the picture of an honorable patriot who fought only when forced to by the barbarism of others.

The war of propaganda between Antony and Octavian (the future Augustus) appeared in diplomatic correspondence for official publication and in charge and countercharge. Each was accused by the other of aping divinity, each attacked the other's morals at vulnerable points (Octavian's cowardice and Antony's drunkenness), each assailed the other's associates and relatives. Antony wrote ("vomited up" said the elder Pliny: *NH* 14,28,148) a volume in defense of his drinking habits. We must not forget that Octavian won, and it is his propaganda that survives; we can trace some of the charges leveled by Antony in the pages of Suetonius.

The fostering of literature was accomplished by Augustus through Maecenas and others. Augustus was far too subtle to impose the more obvious forms of censorship and imposition. He preferred to guide rather than to direct: he might offer Horace a dependent position, but he did not insist that he take it. This tactful guidance has its effect. Vergil and Horace both moved away from the Epicureanism of their upbringing (distasteful to Augustus partly because of its association with Cassius, partly because it stood for political withdrawal rather than for responsible involvement, and partly because it opposed the sort of religion that Augustus thought politically necessary) to a greater sympathy for Stoic and traditional Roman values. *The Georgics* may not have had much effect on the rehabilitation of Italian agriculture, but there is no reason to doubt that

Vergil was encouraged to write the poem with this end in view.And *The Aeneid* is patently not about Aeneas but about Rome, and the climactic passage of the sixth book (6,851–853) proclaims Rome's imperial destiny:

> Roman, do not forget, rule the nations with authority
> (here lies your gift), and make a habit of peace,
> spare the humbled, and war down the haughty.

Horace too came to the solemnities (despite certain ambiguities) of the so-called Roman odes (3,1–6), to accepting a scripted commission to write a hymn for the Ludi Saeculares, and to the unabashed patriotic militarism celebrating the victories of Tiberius and Drusus in Germany (4,4). By contrast Ovid, who, faced with the imperial encouragement of moral and didactic poetry, wrote a didactic poem on *The Science of Making Love,* was pounced upon and severely punished for a political indiscretion. He was clear that his offenses were two, "a poem and a mistake" (*Tr.* 2,207). It was typical of the emperor's combination of tact and ruthlessness that he waited eight years before he saw the opportunity to strike. Sir Ronald Syme, who was under no illusions about autocracy, writing as he was in the 1930s, included a brilliant chapter on Augustus' "organization of opinion" in *The Roman Revolution.*

In this connection Livy's *History* is particularly interesting. Augustus dubbed him in not unfriendly banter as "a Pompeian" (Tac. *Ann.* 4,34). The emperor, once secure, was prepared to tolerate such deviation in face of the historian's massive and uncritical patriotism. Livy's is the counterpart of the "English history written to the tune of *Rule Britannia*"; his is Roman history written to the tune *Roma Aeterna.* One has only to look at the portraits of Hannibal drawn by Polybius and Livy to see the difference between history and propaganda. Confronted with a conflict in source material Livy has no critical standards—or rather he has too many, and never knows which one to use—and once at least he confesses to choosing of different versions "the most glorious."

Two examples from much later: The last fling of paganism. Julian thinking it important to write as well as to act. The propaganda element in the very title *Against the Galileans,* with its suggestion of a petty, local, provincial cult. Libanius subtly using the story of Socrates in defense of paganism, covertly identifying (in *The Silence of Socrates*) Socrates with the pagans and the accusers with the Christians. Symmachus publishing his appeal for the restoration of the Altar of Victory, an appeal contrived with dialectical acumen and rhetorical elaboration.

Finally, the use of the written word in Christian controversy is important because, as the church spread, many of the controversies ceased to be local, and because either side might stand on the authority of a champion, an Athanasius, or an Augustine. The Pelagian controversy will serve to illustrate. It began when in Rome in A.D. 405 a bishop quoted to Pelagius Augustine's famous prayer "Grant what you command, and command what you will"; Pelagius thought that this destroyed moral effort. Already we see the importance of the written word. The Prayer came from *The Confessions* (10,29), written seven years earlier; and Augustine was in Africa. Pelagius wrote a letter to Paulinus, which he claimed was filled with the grace of God, and Augustine, who read it, found a hymn to the glory of man. Pelagius, with his associate Caelestius, four years later moved first to Sicily, then to Carthage. From there Pelagius went to Palestine; Caelestius stayed to teach and train teachers, was accused of heresy and excommunicated, and left for Ephesus. The heretical views remained and spread. Augustine preached against them, wrote books and pamphlets. The Pelagians wrote treatises. Augustine, at the request of the statesman Flavius Marcellinus, wrote three books *On the Due Reward of Sin*. This led to fresh controversy and a fresh treatise, *On the Spirit and the Letter,* and fresh preachments, which were duly published. Next a noblewoman named Demetrias resolved on the vow of Christian virginity. Jerome wrote to her from Palestine to encourage her to fasting and to warn her off theology. Pelagius wrote to her a letter of "sage and sobering" moral exhortation. Augustine thought that this stressed human endeavor at the expense of the grace of God; he wrote a letter to Demetrias' mother, and a treatise speaking to the situation. It is important to note that such letters were also public property.

Hilary now wrote to Augustine from Sicily about the spread of Pelagianism there. Augustine answered with a letter so elaborate that it was almost a theological treatise. There was circulating an attack on Augustine's theology, anonymous (an important point in this pamphlet war) but clearly to be attributed to the excommunicated Caelestius. Augustine answered this in the treatise *On the Perfection of Human Justice*. Pelagius had in the meantime himself written a major work *On Nature*. This was sent to Augustine for reply, which he did in his work *On Nature and Grace*. It is significant that Augustine does not mention Pelagius by name, and treats him personally (although not his views) with friendly respect.

Jerome now entered the fray. He never understood the controversy, as Augustine did; he was chasing the specters of Origen and Jovinian. Pelagius tried to establish personal relations with him. In letters (of course for publication and wide circulation) Jerome threw him off and added a *Dialogue against the Pelagians. Paulus Orosius too, who attacked the Pelagians in synod and, when they stood up to the test, wrote his own Defense.* The news of the acquittal of the Pelagians reached Augustine; he felt it serious enough to demand his intervention and comment, which he provided in *On the Events in Palestine*. Augustine's party started to pressure Rome. The bishops of Carthage wrote officially; so did the bishops of Numidia; so, as individuals, did Augustine, Aurelius, Alypius, Evodius, and Possidius. Augustine wrote also to Paulinus of Nola. Pelagius meanwhile had completed a major exposition of his views in four books *On Free-Will;* Augustine was to examine these in two works, *On the Grace of Christ* and *On Original Sin*. Letters passed to and fro between Rome, Palestine, and Africa. Decisions were made, reversed, and reversed again. Political pressure was used, and, despite more letters and protests from some of the Italian bishops, led by Julian of Eclanum, the Pelagians were condemned.

This is a summary account of a typical church controversy. Personal contacts, letters, sermons, treatises, pressure groups, political authority all play their part.

### THE PUBLICATION OF BOOKS

We have seen that much "publication" in the ancient world was in fact carried out by public readings. There was no process of multiple copying such as was made possible through the invention of printing. Nonetheless, books did circulate in significant numbers and were available for private, and later for public, libraries.

We know comparatively little about the book trade in Greece. It seems to have grown up in Athens in the fifth century, and to have been stimulated by the desire of those who did not have the opportunity of seeing the great tragedies; yet copies of Euripides were not available at Syracuse in 413 because Syracusan enthusiasts went to the prisoners of war for memorized scraps from the plays. Books were in fact rare. Euripides had a library, using his slave Cephisophon to copy texts for him, but Socrates was surprised to find Euthydemus with a complete Homer (Xen. *Mem* 4,2,10). The famous cheap copy of Anaxagoras (Plat. *Apol.* 26D) was secondhand and out of date: that is the point. There was some kind of an export trade (Xen. *Anab.* 7, 5,14), but it was not systematically organized, and a much-quoted jibe charged Hermodorus with "travelling in" Plato's dialogues (Zenob. 5,6). In 330 B.C. Lycurgus carried a motion that the works of the three great tragedians should be preserved in the public archives (Plat. *Mor.* 841F); it was this copy that was used in the library at Alexandria. It was in fact the Ptolemies and Attalids who really developed the public library and this pattern was followed at Rome. The first libraries, those of Aemilius Paullus, Sulla, and Lucullus were pillaged from Greece. Lucullus threw open his library to the public. The first true public library was planned by Julius Caesar, and appropriately Varro was appointed to see it through, but Caesar's assassination prevented its foundation, and Asinius Pollio was the first founder. Libraries spread, and by the fourth century A.D. there were twenty-nine in Rome and many in provincial towns. Timgad, not far from the Sahara, had one of attractive design, capable of holding some twenty-three thousand books.

It was at Rome that the book trade was really systematically organized, and it was Cicero's friend Atticus who turned a private hobby into an industrial concern. The author would take the copy to a bookseller who had a staff of copyists. Mostly they worked by eye, and the majority of manuscript errors are explicable through the visual confusion of letters or groups of letters, skipping of passages between a repeated word and the like, although there must have been some dictation, as some errors arise from confusion of sound rather than of shape. Editions must have been small, and one thousand would be a very large issue indeed. Booksellers listed books available on the pillars of the portico outside the shop.

Publication and distribution were always subject to imperial censorship. Suetonius has an account of the execution of a dramatist and a historian under Tiberius (*Tib.* 61,3) and the destruction of their works, and of Domitian's execution of the historian Hermogenes and the copyists of his history. (*Dom.* 10,1). Augustus suppressed from the libraries some of Julius Caesar's minor works (*Jul.* 56, 7); Caligula had most of the copies of Vergil and Livy removed from the libraries, and thought of doing the same to Homer (*Cal.* 34,2). The issues here were in part literary. It was censorship, whatever the motive, and it is clear that the imperial agents could use their power to encourage approved literature and check the circulation of unapproved sentiments.

### CONCLUSION

We started from nonverbal communication and propaganda and have ended with the written word. There was a Greek myth about Cadmus of Thebes. One of his achievements was to introduce the alphabet; another was to sow the dragon's teeth and to reap a harvest of armed soldiers. Wrote McLuhan: "Like any other myth, this one capsulates a prolonged process into a flashing insight. The alphabet meant power and authority and control of military structures at a distance." Something in that.

# 10

## JUDAISM: THE PSYCHOLOGY OF THE PROPHETS

MAX WEBER

### *POLITICAL ORIENTATIONS OF PRE-EXILIC PROPHECY*

After the lull in the conquest policies of the great states which had facilitated the emergence of the Israelite Confederation, in the ninth century, the great kings of Mesopotamia, like those later of Egypt, once again resumed their expansionist policy. Syria became a theatre of hitherto unprecedented military events. Never before had the world experienced warfare of such frightfulness and magnitude as that practiced by the Assyrian kings. Blood fairly drips from the cuneiform inscriptions. The king, in the tone of dry protocol, reports that he covered the walls of conquered cities with human skins. The Israelite literature preserved from the period, above all, the oracles of classical prophecy, express the mad terror caused by these merciless conquerors. As impending gloom beclouded the political horizon, classical prophecy acquired its characteristic form.

The pre-exilic prophets[1] from Amos to Jeremiah and Ezekiel, viewed through the eyes of the contemporary outsider, appeared to be, above all, political demagogues and, on occasion, pamphleteers. Isaiah, for example, directed a pamphlet against Shebna (22:15f.) with a postscript against Eliakim, who in the

first draft had been mentioned honorably. In the same category
belongs the written curse which Jeremiah placed upon Semachiah. This characterization of the prophets (as demagogues
and pamphleteers) can indeed be misleading, but properly
understood it permits indispensable insight. It means that the
prophets were primarily *speakers*. Prophets as writers appear
only after the Babylonian Exile. The early prophets addressed
their audiences in public.

Except for the world politics of the great powers which
threatened their homeland and constituted the message of their
most impressive oracles, the prophets could not have emerged.
They could not have arisen on the soil of the great powers for
the simple reason that "demagogy" was impossible there. To
be sure, the "great king" of Assyria, Babylonia, and Persia, like
the Israelite king and every ancient overlord, permitted his
oracle to determine his political resolutions, or at least allowed
for the oracular determination of the time and particulars of his
measures. The Babylonian king, for instance, before nominat-
ing a high official, consulted the oracle priests as to the candidate's qualifications.

This, however, was strictly an affair of court. The political
prophet did not speak in the streets nor address the people
directly. The political preconditions for doing so did not exist,
nor would it have been tolerated. There are indications that
public prophecy was expressly forbidden, which prohibition is
consistent with the conditions of the bureaucratic states, particularly in the time of the Jewish Exile when sources indicate
that there were probably sharp repressive measures. Nothing is
known of the existence in the great states of political prophecy
comparable to that of the classical period in the Near East and
in Egypt. Things were different in Israel and especially in the
city-state of Jerusalem.

The old political prophecy of the time of the confederacy had
addressed itself to the collectivity of the confederates. Such
prophecy, however, was sporadic, for the confederacy had no
fixed and common oracular sanctuary like Dodona or Delphi.
The priestly oracle by lot, the only form of consulting the deity
recognized as classical, was technically primitive. Under the rule
of the kings free war-prophecy became obsolete and the con-

federate oracle decreased in significance in proportion as the court prophet's rose.

Free prophecy developed only with the rising external danger to the country and to the royal power. According to the tradition, Elijah had publicly stood up to the king and his prophets, but was forced to flee the country. This held also for Amos under Jeroboam II. Under strong governments or under governments supported by a "great power," as for instance, Judah under Manasseh, prophecy, even after Isaiah's appearance, remained silent—or rather was reduced to silence. With the decreasing prestige of the kings and the growing threat to the country, the significance of prophecy again increased and the scene of the prophet's activities moved closer and closer to Jerusalem.

Among the early prophets Amos made his appearance at the sanctuary of Beth-el, and Hosea in the Northern realm. Even Isaiah identified pasture and wasteland (5:17; 17:2), in the manner of an outright Jerusalemite. Apparently Isaiah preferred the public courtyard of the Temple as a scene for his appearance. Finally Yahwe commanded Jeremiah: "Go thou into the streets of Jerusalem and speak in public."

In a time of distress a king like Zedekiah would secretly send for the prophet requesting a divine word. As a rule, however, the prophet personally confronted also the king and his family in the street, spoke in public, or—though this was unusual —dictated his word to a disciple and had it circularized. This last is illustrated by Isaiah who had his disciples seal one of his oracles (8:16) and by Jeremiah's written oracular curse against Babylon (51:59f.). Occasionally individuals or deputations of elders requested and received oracles from the prophets, Jeremiah included (21:2f.; 37:3; 38:14; 42:1f.).

However, usually the prophet spoke on his own, i.e., under the influence of a spontaneous inspiration, to the public in the market place or to the elders at the city gate. The prophets also interpreted the fates of individuals, though as a rule only those of politically important persons. The predominant concern of the prophet was the destiny of the state and the people. This concern always assumed the form of emotional invectives against the overlords. It is here that the "demagogue" appeared for the first time in the records of history, at about the period when the Homeric songs threw the figure of Thersites into relief.

## HELLENIC AND JUDAIC PROPHECY

In the early Hellenic polis, however, the assembly of notables as found in Ithaca was one in which the people, as a rule, listened and at best participated through acclamation. There was orderly debate; the floor was granted by handing over the staff to the speaker. On the other hand, the demagogue of Periclean times was a secular politician, leading the demos through his personal influence and speaking before the sovereign ecclesia.

In Homeric times the seer was recognized and consulted in the midst of the assembly of knights. Later this practice decayed. Figures such as Tyrtaeus and the demagogic war poetry of Solonic times enjoining the conquest of Salamis come closest to the ancient free political prophecy of the Israelite confederacy. However, the figure of Tyrtaeus was bound up with the development of the Spartan army of disciplined hoplites and Solon, for all his piety, was a secular politician. Solon's mind was lucid and clear and his profoundly "rationalistic" spirit fused the knowledge of man's insecure fate with the firm faith in the value of his people. Temperamentally he was a preacher of genteel and pious custom.

Orphic and Israelite prophecy and religiosity were more closely related. Tyranny, friendly to the plebs, particularly that of the Peisistratids, sought contact with these plebeian theologians. The same was true, at times, for the politics of the Persians, at the time of the attempts at conquest. During the sixth and early part of the fifth century, "chresmologists," itinerant vendors of oracles, and vaticinating mystagogues of all sorts wandered through Greece and gave consultations for a price. They were consulted by private citizens as well as politicians and especially by exiles. On the other hand, nothing of religious demagoguery in the manner of the Israelite prophets is known ever to have intervened in the politics of the Hellenic states.

Pythagoras and his sect gained very considerable political influence, and ministered spiritual guidance to the nobility of the Southern Italian cities, but the Pythagoreans did not constitute prophets of the street. Genteel philosophers of the type of Thales not only predicted solar eclipses and formulated rules for prudent living, but actively engaged in politics in their cities, at times in dominant positions. However, they lacked the quality of ecstatic men. The same holds for Plato and the academy—their political ethic was, in the last analysis, utopian—which were of great influence upon the fateful development (and disintegration) of the realm of Syracuse. Ecstatic political prophecy, however, remained hierocratically organized at the official oracle places which answered the official questions of the citizenries in well-turned verses. The firm military structure of the city was averse to free emotional prophecy.

In Jerusalem, on the other hand, the purely religious demagogue was spokesman and his oracles highlighted obscure fates of the future like lightning out of somber clouds. Such prophecy was authoritarian in character and averse to all orderly procedure. Formally, the prophet was strictly a private citizen. For this very reason, he was, naturally, by no means an indifferent figure in the eyes of political authority. Jeremiah's collected oracles were brought before the council of state and the king by distinguished citizens in the king's service. For each such oracle was an event of public significance. This was so, not merely because the oracle influenced the mood of the masses, but also because as an anathema, a good or evil omen, it could exert magical influence upon the course of events.

## ESTABLISHED AUTHORITY VERSUS THE PROPHETS

The holders of established power faced these powerful demagogues with fear, wrath, or indifference as the situation warranted. Sometimes they sought to draw the prophets into their service. Sometimes they behaved like King Joiakim who, sitting in his winter garret with ostensible composure, listened to the collected oracles of doom and as they were read to him by court officials threw them sheet by sheet into the fireplace. Or, again, the power holders took action against the prophets.

As the lament of Amos indicates, under strong governments, like that of Jeroboam II, prophecy was forbidden. When this prophet (Amos) proclaims God's wrath over Israel because of the attempts to suppress prophecy, his complaint is quite comparable to the demand of the modern demagogue for freedom of the press. Actually, prophetic words were not restricted to oral communication. With Jeremiah they appeared in the form of open letters. At times friends and disciples of the prophets wrote down the spoken word and turned it into a political pamphlet. Later on, at times simultaneously (as was also the case with Jeremiah), these sheets were collected and revised. They constitute the earliest known example of political pamphlet literature directly addressing itself to contemporaneous events.

The form and tenor of pre-exilic prophecy was in accordance with this phenomenon and the entire situation in which it appeared. Everything was calculated to loan word-of-mouth demagoguery a timely influence. Micah introduced the opponents of the prophets as speakers. The prophets were personally attacked and pilloried, and frequently we hear of violent conflicts. All the recklessness and frantic passion of the party struggles, e.g., of Athens or Florence, was equaled and, at times, surpassed in the angry addresses and oracular pamphlets, particularly of Jeremiah. Curses, threats, personal invective, desperation, wrath, and thirst for revenge are to be found in them. In a letter to the Babylonian exiles Jeremiah slandered the counter-prophets for their alleged dishonorable way of life (29:23). Jeremiah's curse brought death to the counter-prophet, Hananiah. When, despite all abomination, Yahwe left unfulfilled the threats against his own people which he had put in the prophet's mouth, Jeremiah fell into a rage and, in view of the derision of his enemies, demanded that God let fall the day of prophesied doom (17:18), that he avenge him on his persecutors (15:15), that he let stand his opponents' sin against him (18:23) without expiation, in order that Yahwe deal with them the more terribly in the time of his anger. Often he appears actually to revel in the representation of the frightful doom of his own people which he prophesied as certain.

However, in contrast to the party demagogues in Athens and Florence, after the disaster at Megiddo and later, after the catastrophe prophesied for decades had befallen Jerusalem, there is no trace of triumph over the fact that the prediction was correct. Also, there is no longer, as previously, sullen despair. But alongside grave mourning there appears hope for God's grace and better times. And in his passionate wrath over the impenitence of the listeners he allows Yahwe's voice to warn him not, through ignoble words, to forfeit the right to be Yahwe's mouthpiece. He is to speak noble words, then Yahwe will turn the hearts of men to him (15:19). Indeed, unconfined by priestly or status conventions and quite untempered by any self-control, be it ascetic or contemplative, the prophet discharges his glowing passion and experiences all the abysses of the human heart. And yet, despite all these human frailties, characteristic of these titans of the holy curse, it is not their private motives but the cause of Yahwe, of the wrathful God, that reigns supreme over the uproar.

The prophet's vehement attack was countered by an equally vehement reaction of the public. Numerous verses, particularly again of Jeremiah, occasionally might suggest monstrous delusions of persecution mania and describe how the fiend now hisses, now laughs, now threatens and mocks. This was actually the case. In the open street the opponents of the prophets engaged them, insulted them, and struck them in the face. King Joiakim caused Egypt to surrender the prophet of doom Uria to him and had him executed. And when Jeremiah, who was repeatedly taken into custody and threatened with death, escaped this fate, it was due to the fear of his magical power.

Always the life and honor of the prophets were in danger and the opposition party lay in wait to destroy them by force, fraud and derision, by counter-magic and especially by counter-prophecy. After Jeremiah went for eight days with a yoke on his shoulders, to illustrate the unavoidable subjection to Nebuchadnezzar, Hananiah opposed him, seized and broke the yoke, to destroy the evil omen before all people. Whereupon Jeremiah, at first quite taken aback, left to return with an iron yoke and scornfully demanded that the opponent try his strength upon it and prophesied his early death. These prophets were torn in the midst of a snarl of party antagonisms and conflicting interests, especially with respect to foreign politics. This could not be otherwise. The question for the national state was to live or be crushed between the Assyrian world power on the one hand, the Egyptian on the other. No one could avoid taking sides and no man active in public could escape the question: whose? As little as Jesus was spared the question whether it be right to pay the Roman tribute!

Whether the prophets wished it or not they actually always worked in the direction of one or the other furiously struggling inner-political cliques, which at the same time promoted definite foreign policies. Hence, the prophets were considered party members. After the second fall of Jerusalem, Nebuchadnezzar, in his relation to Jeremiah, took into account the fact that the prophet had promoted faithful allegiance to the king. When we see the sib of Saphan support the prophets for many generations[2] as well as the Deuteronomic movement, we may well infer that foreign-political party interests played a part. But it would be a grave error to believe that political partisanship of the prophets, for instance, for Assyria by Isaiah or for Babylon in the case of Jeremiah, determined the content of the oracles, by which they advised against alliances with these great powers. Under Sennacherib the same Isaiah[3] who had previously seen Assur as the tool of Yahwe, turned sharply against the "great king" and against capitulation in opposition to the faint-hearted king and his aides. As, in the beginning, he almost welcomed the Assyrians as executors of well-deserved punishment, so he later cursed this godless, overbearing, inhumanly cruel royal sib and people determined only to overpower and destroy others. He prophesied their downfall. When, later, this occurred it was jubilantly hailed by the prophets.

Jeremiah, to be sure, had incessantly preached submission to the power of Nebuchadnezzar to an extent which we would nowadays call high treason; for, what else is it when he (21:9), in the face of the approaching enemy, holds out grace and life to those who will desert and surrender and destruction to the rest? However, the same Jeremiah who still in his last oracle from Egypt occasionally referred to Nebuchadnezzar as the "Servant of God" (43:10) and who, after the capture of Jerusalem, receives gifts from the king's representative and an invitation to come to Babylon gave the travelling marshal of King Zedekiah a sheet with a prophetic curse of Babylon to take along on his journey with the commandment to read it there aloud and then to throw it into the Euphrates (Jer. 51:59ff.) in order, through this magic, to secure the downfall of the hated city.

As all this indicates, according to their manner of functioning, the prophets were objectively political and, above all, world-political demagogues and publicists, however, subjectively they were no political partisans. Primarily they pursued no political interests. Prophecy has never declared anything about a "best state" (disregarding Ezekiels' hierocratic construction in the Exile) nor has it ever sought, like the philosophical *aisymnete* or the academy, to help translate into reality social-ethically oriented political ideals through advice to power holders. The state and its doings were, by themselves, of not interest to them. Moreover, unlike the Hellenes they did not posit the problem: how can man be a good citizen? Their question was absolutely religious, oriented toward the fulfillment of Yahwe's commandments.

Certainly this does not preclude the fact that at least Jeremiah, perhaps consciously, assessed the actual power relations of his time more correctly than did the prophets of grace. Only this was not decisive for his attitude. For these concrete power relations were what they were only through Yahwe's will. Yahwe could change them. Isaiah's admonition to stand fast against Sennacherib's attacks ran counter to all realistic estimate of political probability. To seriously maintain that, even ahead of the king! he had had news concerning the circumstances which caused Sennacherib to move away, is rationalism, indeed, equivalent to those attempts to explain the miracle at the wedding of Cana by means of liqueur which allegedly Jesus secretly brought with him.

Quite unconvincing is one suggestion as to the relationships of the Yahwe prophets to inner-political parties—a "priest and citizen-party"—of the world empires, especially the Mesopotamian, relations which some pan-Babylonians have tracked down with ingenuity. There is no doubt that the respective foreign-political relations, also partisanship, almost always had internal religious ramifications. Egyptian partisans practiced Egyptian cults, those of the Assyrians, Babylonian ones, and Phoenicians also had their special cults and, in the case of a political alliance, worship of the respective gods was an almost indispensable affirmation which a great king, however tolerant otherwise, probably demanded as a sign of political obeisance. Furthermore, there are sufficient records to indicate that, e.g., Nebuchadnezzar was not disinclined after the first as well as the second conquest of Jerusalem and the abduction of the Egyptian partisans to use the influence of the Yahwe believers similarly as a support of his domination as, later, did Cyrus and Darius. Also Necho's policy after the battle of Megiddo, already appears to have pointed in a similar direction[4] without thereby winning the prophets for Egypt. As the beginning of this important maxim, deviating from old Assyrian ways, namely, to rule with the help of native priests, one may well consider the reported way of the Assyrians of meeting the religious needs of Samaria after the destruction (2. Ki. 17:27f.).

With this turn of religious policy of the great states, for the prophets their foreign domination lost much of its religious terror and it may well be that this fact has co-determined Jeremiah's attitude. However, the causal significance of such factors is obviously incomparable with respect to the importance which "church-political" reasons presumably had for the behavior of Hellenic oracles, particularly of the Delphic Apollo opposite the Persians. Also here the attitude of the oracles basically presupposed that fate was with the Persians, since the miraculous rise of Cyrus and Darius. However, the flattering devotion of the king and of Mardonius and the substantial gifts which they proffered combined with the justified expectation that, in case of victory, the Persians would also here manage to tame the disarmed citizenry with the help of the priests. Such were the quite substantial props to the attitude. No such material considerations existed for the prophets. Jeremiah evaded the invitation to come to Babylon, and it seems quite some distance from his correct assessment of the power situation to the assumption of some pan-Babylonians that there existed an international party-following of priests and burghers on the one hand and military nobles on the other. Such assumptions are quite unacceptable and we shall see that the prophets' stand with respect to foreign alliances generally and particularly their constant disinclination against the alliance with Egypt was determined by purely religious motives.

## STATUS ORIENTATIONS AND INNER-POLITICAL ATTITUDES

The attitudes of the prophets toward internal affairs were, however pronounced, just as little primarily based on political or social-political considerations as their views on foreign policy. In status origin the prophets were diverse *(uneinheitlich)*. It is out of the question that they were, for the most part, derived from proletarian or negatively privileged[5] or uneducated strata. Moreover their social-ethical attitude was by no means determined by their personal descent. For they share the same attitude despite their very diverse social origins.

Throughout they argued passionately for the social-ethical charity-commandments of the Levite exhortation for the benefit of the little people and hurled their wrathful curses preferably against the great and the rich. However, Isaiah, who among the older prophets was most vehement in this, was the descendant of a genteel sib, closely befriended by distinguished priests, had intercourse with the king as his councillor and physician and in his time was, without doubt, one of the preeminent men of the city. Zephaniah descended from David and was a great-grandson of Hezekiah; Ezekiel was a distinguished Jerusalemite priest. These prophets were, thus, wealthy Jerusalemites. Micah stemmed from a small town, Jeremiah from a village. Jeremiah came from a landed sib of rural priests, perhaps the old house of Eli's descendants.[6] He bought land from impoverished relatives. Only Amos was a small-stock-breeder: he called himself a shepherd who had lived on sycamore fruit (the food of the poor) and he came from a small town of Judah, but was obviously well educated. It is Amos, for example, who knew the Babylonian Tiamat-myth. However, like Isaiah, with all his grave curses against the great, he yet pronounced the rule of the uneducated, undisciplined demos as the worst of all curses. So, also, Jeremiah despite his more democratic descent and still sharper language against the outrages of the court and the great was just as sharp against the plebeian ministers of Zedekiah. He took it for granted, too, that little people understand nothing of religious duties. Of the great one might expect it and therefore they deserved the curse. A personal factor might have played a part with this prophet in his particularly sharp opposition to the

Jerusalemite priests, if he really were a descendant of the priest
Abiathar, whom Solomon once had exiled to Anathot for the
benefit of Zadok. But even this played, at best, an aggravating
part in comparison to the substantive reasons.

In any case, no prophet was a champion of "democratic"
ideals. In their eyes the people need guidance, hence, everything depends on the qualities of the leaders (Is. 1:26; Jer. 5:5).
Moreover, no prophet pronounced any sort of religious
"natural law," even less a right to revolution or self-help of the
masses suppressed by the mighty. Anything of the sort would
undoubtedly have appeared to them as the very pinnacle of
godlessness. They disavowed their more violent forerunners.
Hosea condemned Jehu's revolution, a work of the school of
Elisha and the Rechabites, with the sharpest curses and he
prophesied Yahwe's revenge. With the characteristic exception
of Ezekiel's theological construction of an ideal state of the
future during the Exile, no prophet proclaimed a social-political
program. The social-ethical demands which they rather presup-
pose than raise, suggest the Levite exhortation, the existence
and knowledge of which all prophets treat as self-evident.
Hence, the prophets were not, for their part, champions of
democratic social ideals. But the political situation, the existence of strong socio-political opposition to the corvée-exacting
kingship and the *gibborim,* these provided the sounding board
for their primarily religiously determined message and also influenced the content of their conceptual universe. This however
was mediated by those strata of intellectuals who were devoted
to the old traditions of pre-Solomon times, and whose social
position was close to that of the prophets.

### *SOCIAL CONTEXT OF THE PROPHETIC MESSAGE*

One important principle united the prophets as a status group:
the gratuitous character of their oracles. This separated them
from the prophets of the king, whom they cursed as destroyers
of the land. And it distinguished the prophets from all groups
that made an industry of prophecy in the manner of the old
seers or dream-interpreters whom they despised and rejected.
The complete inner independence of the prophets was not so
much a result as a most important cause of their practice. In the

main they prophesied disaster and no one could be sure whether on request, like King Zedekiah, he might not receive a prediction of doom and therewith an evil omen. One does not pay for evil omens nor expose oneself to them. Primarily unbidden and spontaneously impelled, rarely on request, the prophets hurled their frequently frightful oracles against their audience.

However, as a status principle this gratuitous practice is, indeed, characteristic of a stratum of genteel intellectuals. The borrowing of this principle, later, by the plebeian intellectual strata of the rabbis and, from them, by the Christian apostles form exceptions of great importance for the sociology of religion. Moreover, the prophets did not by any means find their "community," so far as that term applies either solely or primarily in the demos. On the contrary, if they had any personal support at all, it was from distinguished, individual, pious houses in Jerusalem. Sometimes for several generations such served as their patrons. Jeremiah was supported by the same sib which also took part in the "finding" of Deuteronomy. Most sympathetic supporters were found among the *zekenim,* as the guardians of the pious tradition and, particularly, the traditional respect for prophecy. Such was the case for Jeremiah in his capital trial; it was also true of Ezekiel, whom the elders consulted in Exile.

The prophets never obtained support from the peasants. Indeed, all prophets preached against debt slavery, the pawning of clothes, against all violation of the charity commandments, which benefited the little man. In Jeremiah's last prophecy, peasants and shepherds were the champions of piety. However, this form of prophecy was true only for Jeremiah. The peasants belonged as little to his following as the rural squirearchy; in fact, the *'am ha-aretz* were among the more important opponents of the prophets, especially of Jeremiah who was opposed by his own sib. Because they were strict Yahwists, the prophets declaimed against the rural orgiasticism of the fertility cults and the most tainted rural places of worship. Above all the prophets declaimed against the shrines of Baal, which meant much to the rural population for economic as well as ideal reasons.

The prophets never received support from the king. For the prophets were champions of the Yahwistic tradition opposing

kingship, which was compromised by politically necessary concessions to foreign cults, intemperate drinking, and by the innovations of the Solomonic corvée state. Solomon was not of
the slightest importance for any of the prophets. When a king is
mentioned at all, it is David who is the pious ruler. Hosea
viewed the kings of the Northern realm as illegitimate, because
they had usurped the throne without the will of Yahwe. Amos
mentioned the Nazarites and Nebiim among the institutions of
Yahwe, but not the kings. Indeed, none of the prophets denied
the legitimacy of the Davidians. However, respect even for this
dynasty, such as it was, was only conditional. Isaiah's
Immanuel-prophecy, after all, may well be considered as the
prediction of a God-sent usurper. Yet it was for Isaiah that
David's age represented the climax of national history. Relentless attacks against the conduct of the respective contemporary
kings grew in intensity. Such raging outbursts of wrath and
scorn as those of Jeremiah against Joiakim are rarely to be
found. Joiakim shall go to earth like an ass (22:19) and the
queen mother, who apparently participated in the Astarte-cult,
shall have her skirt pulled over her head that all might see her
shame (13:18ff.). But even Isaiah called his woe down on the
land the king of which "is a child and is led by women," and
he stood up boldly to the grown-up king in a personal encounter.

  With obvious intent the prophetic tradition preserved the account of Elijah's conflicts with Ahab. The kings returned these
antipathies in kind. They tolerated the prophets only in uncertain times, but, whenever they felt sure of themselves, they had
recourse, like Manasseh, to bloody persecution. Beside the
politically conditioned worship of foreign deities or incorrect
cults, the wrath of the prophets against the kings was, above all,
directed at world politics per se, the means and presuppositions
of which were unholy. This applied particularly to the alliance
with Egypt. Although fugitive Yahwe prophets, such as Uria,
sought refuge in Egypt, and although Egyptian rule was lenient
and certainly religiously non-propagandistic, the prophets rebelled with especial bitterness against this alliance. The reason
is made obvious in Isaiah (28:18).

  Dealings with Egypt are an "agreement with Sheol," that is

to say with the chthonian gods of the realm of the dead which they loathed.[7] Obviously in this the prophets rest their political attitudes solidly on the priestly tradition; their political stand is throughout religiously conditioned. As against the king, so the prophets declaimed against the mighty, particularly the *sarim* and *gibborim*. Along with the injustice of their courts, the prophets cursed, above all, their impious way of life and debauchery. But obviously the opposition of the prophets was independent of such single vices. The king and political-military circles could make no use whatever of the purely utopian exhortations and counsels of the prophets.

The Hellenic states of the sixth and fifth centuries regularly consulted oracles but in the end and precisely in the days of decision, as, for example, during the Persian war, they failed to honor the advice of their oracles even though they were politically oriented. As a rule, it was politically impossible for the kings of Judah to heed the advice of the prophets. And the knightly sense of dignity, which here as elsewhere is aloof from prophetic belief, necessarily made them reject as beneath them Jeremiah's advice with respect to Babylon. They disdained these screaming ecstatics of the streets.

On the other side, the popular opposition against the distinguished knights and patricians of the time of the kings which the intellectual strata had nourished played its part in the attitude of the prophets. Avarice is the preeminent vice, that is to say, usurious oppression of the poor. The prophets are not interested in the royal army. Their future kingdom is a kingdom of peace. In this they did not by any means represent something like "Little Judah" pacifists. Amos promised to Judah dominion over Edom and over those people which are called by Yahwe's name (9:12). The old popular hope of world domination recurred repeatedly. Increasingly, however, the idea gained currency that the political aspirations of Israel would only be realized through a miracle of God, as once at the Red Sea, but not through autonomous military power, and, least of all, through political alliances. Ever anew the wrath of the prophets turned against such alliances. The basis of the opposition was again religious. It was not simply because of the danger of strange cults that such antipathy was felt. Rather, Israel stood in the *berith* with Yahwe. Nothing must enter competition with the *berith,* especially not trust in human help, which would bespeak of godless disbelief and evoke Yahwe's wrath. As Jeremiah saw the matter, if Yahwe had ordained the conquest of the people by Nebuchadnezzar, one must accept the fact.

Defensive alliances against the great kings were offenses against God so long as the great kings were executors of his will. If they were not and if He wished to help Israel, He would do so alone, Isaiah taught. Probably he was the first for this reason to preach indefatigably against all and every attempt to work out an alliance. Clearly, the whole attitude toward internal as well as foreign affairs was purely religious in motivation, nothing bespeaks of political expediencies. The relationship to the priests also was religiously conditioned.

No prophet before Ezekiel spoke favorably of the priests. Amos recognized, as noted, only the Nazarites and Nebiim as Yahwe's tools, but he failed to mention the priests. The very existence of their type of free prophecy was, from the time of its appearance, a clear symptom of the weakness of priestly power. Had the place of the priest been like that in Egypt, or even in Babylon, or in Jerusalem after the Exile, free prophecy would doubtlessly have been suppressed as dangerous competition. Since originally, in the confederate time, there was no central shrine and no official sacrifice, this was impossible. Meanwhile the prestige of the old royal prophets and seers and then of Elijah and Elisha-school was firmly established. Powerful sibs of pious laity backed the prophets. Therefore, the priests had to tolerate them despite frequent and sharp antagonisms. But, they were by no means always antagonistic to the priests. Isaiah had close relations with the priests of Jerusalem and Ezekiel was throughout priestly in outlook. On the other hand, we find the sharpest conceivable personal conflicts with the cult priests, first with Amos in Beth-el and last with Jeremiah in Jerusalem. The latter's trial (Jer. 26) suggests almost a prologue to what was to happen in the same place six hundred years later. Tradition of the events possibly exerted some actual influence later.

Jeremiah was charged with a capital crime because he had prophesied for the Temple the fate of the shrine in Shiloh which the Philistines once had destroyed. He was dragged before the court of officials and elders, and the priests and prophets of salvation acted as his accusers. However the difference of the times is evident in the result. Jeremiah was acquitted on advice of the elders, in spite of the complaint of the priests, on the ground that there existed the precedent of Micah's case. Micah, they said, had prophesied under Hezekiah similar events.[8] The occurrence indicates that prophecies against the Temple itself were rare. Above all such oracles in the last analysis implied no doubt in the Temple's legitimacy. Later, to be sure, Jeremiah readily comforted himself and others for the loss of the Ark of Covenant under Nebuchadnezzar. His prophecy, nevertheless, deals with the destruction of the Temple as a grievous misfortune which was only conditionally held out as a punishment for sins in case of failing conversion (26:13).

In fact, no prophet attacked the Temple proper. Amos called the sacrifice in Beth-el and Gilgal transgressions (4:4; 5:5) presumably meaning by this only the cult practices of the peasants. Such cult practices were deeply hated by all representatives of shepherd piety.The people should not frequent these places, but "seek Yahwe" (ibid.). Amos knew Zion as the seat of Yahwe in the same manner as Hosea acknowledged Judah as the one undefiled seat of Yahwe. Isaiah's trust in the invincibility of Jerusalem in his late oracles doubtlessly rested on the presence there of the Temple. It was in a temple vision during his youth that he had seen the heavenly court. For Micah, despite his oracle of doom, Mount Zion remained the future place of the pure Torah and prophecy of Yahwe. The prophets preached only against the impurities of the cult practiced there, particularly against defilement by sacred courtesans. In the case of Hosea almost the whole strength of the prophet was absorbed by the fight against the worship of Baal, a fight which runs through pre-exilic prophecy. But they never preached for the correct priestly cult.

Jeremiah has evidently at first welcomed Deuteronomy and thus the centralization of the cult in the Temple of Jerusalem (2:3), but later (8:8) he terms it the product of the lying "pen of the scribes" because its authors held fast to false worship (8:5) and rejected the prophetic word (8:9). The implications of this are clarified elsewhere (7:4; 11ff.), namely, the Temple in

itself is useless and will suffer the fate of Shiloh unless the decision is made to change conduct. What is particularly stressed
here, alongside single social ethical wrongs, is trust in "unprof-
itable lying words" (of Zion priests) (7:8). This was the one
decisive thing, the failure of the priests to heed those divine imperatives which the prophet announced as directly inspired by
Yahwe. Besides the prophet criticized their personal sinfulness.

Thus, in characteristic fashion, the bearer of personal charisma refused to recognize office charisma as a qualification to
teach if the priestly teacher is personally unworthy. For, the
prophet who did not participate in the cult naturally considered
the teaching of God's word *(dabar)* as he received it as religiously all important, hence also in priestcraft the teaching *(torah)*
not the cult (Jer. 8:6; 18:18). This held also for Jerusalem (Mic.
4:2). Likewise the prophet naturally considered as important for
the people only obedience to the *debarim* and the *torah* and not
the sacrifice nor ritualistic prescriptions like observance of the
Sabbath and circumcision which later in the Exile obtained such
decisive significance. Even with Amos, a shepherd, Yahwe is
impatient of the Sabbath of the disobedient people,[9] and
Jeremiah opposes to external circumcision the "circumcision of
the foreskin of the heart" (9:24ff.) as the only truly important
fact.

This does not necessarily imply a denial but, rather, a strong
devaluation of all ritual. The prophets, here too, have accepted
the intellectual's conceptions which grew out of the *torah*.
Yahwe, at least according to the postulate, was a god of just
ethical compensation and they considered the mundane fortune
of individuals—of which Isaiah speaks (3:10)—just as much as
the direct "fruit of their doings," as that of the people. The
older prophets at least juxtaposed this massive ethical
righteousness of deeds to the equally massive ritualism of the
priests. The opposition to the priestly evaluation of the sacrifice
increased until, with Amos and Jeremiah, it was completely
depreciated. Sacrifice is not commanded by Yahwe and
therefore it is useless (Jer. 6:20, 7:21). Even Amos (5:25) argued
that no sacrifice was offered in the desert. If the people are
rebellious and their hands bloody, then, according to Isaiah
(1:11f.) their sacrifices and fasts are an abomination to Yahwe.

Considering Isaiah's relationship to the priesthood and his esteem for the fortress-Temple, it is safe to assume that such words imply no unconditional rejection of cult and sacrifice. The same may well be true of the other prophets. Nevertheless the attitude toward sacrifice in the oracles is cold to the point of emnity.

Through all prophecy sounded the echoes of the "nomadic ideal" as the tradition of the literati idealized the kingless past. To be sure, the shepherd Amos who promised Judah riches in wine (9:13) was as little a Rechabite as Jeremiah. And Jeremiah was the one prophet who entered into personal relationship with the order and upheld its piety as exemplary for Israel. But in his old age, Jeremiah bought an acre of land. Compared to the luxurious and therefore haughty present which was disobedient to Yahwe, the desert times remained to the prophets the truly pious epoch. In the end, Israel will again be reduced to a desert and the Messiah king as well as the survivors will eat the nourishment of the steppes: honey and cream.

The total attitude of the prophets has often been described as "culture hostility." This should not be understood to mean their personal lack of culture. The prophets are conceivable only on the great sounding board of the world-political stage of their times. Similarly, they are conceivable only in connection with extensive cultural sophistication and a strong cultured stratum, though, for the reasons previously discussed, only in the frame of a small state somewhat similar to Zwingli in a single canton. They were all literate and on the whole obviously well informed as to the peculiarities of Egyptian and Mesopotamian culture, especially, also in astromony. The manner in which the prophets used sacred numbers, for example Jeremiah's use of the number "70" may well permit us to infer that they had more than a hazy knowledge of Babylonian astronomy. In any case, tradition records no trait that would permit the inference of any attempts at flight from the world or the denial of culture in the Indian sense.

In addition to the *torah,* the prophets knew also the *chokma* or *'ezah* (Jer. 18:18) of the teachers of prudent living *(chakamin).* However, the educational level of the prophets may well have been more comparable to that of the Orphics and folk prophets of Hellas than to that of the genteel sages as represented by Thales. Not only all aesthetic and all values of genteel living in general, but, also, all worldly wisdom was viewed by them with quite alien eyes. These attitudes were sustained by the anti-chrematistic tradition of the puritanically pious in their environment who were suspicious of the court, the officials, the *gibborim* and the priests. In its inner structure, however, these attitudes of the prophets were purely religiously conditioned by the manner in which they elaborated their experiences. To these we must now turn.

## PSYCHOLOGICAL PECULIARITIES OF THE PROPHETS

Psychologically viewed most pre-Exile prophets were ecstatic men. At least Hosea, Isaiah, Jeremiah, and Ezekiel professed to be and undoubtedly were. Without gross carelessness, one may safely assume that all were ecstatics, though of various kinds and in different degree.

As far as we know, the way of life of the prophets was that of peculiar men. Jeremiah, upon Yahwe's command, remained solitary, because disaster was anticipated. Hosea, upon Yahwe's command, seems to have married a harlot. Isaiah, upon Yahwe's command (8:3) had intercourse with a prophetess whose child he then named as previously ordained. Strange, symbolic names of children of prophets generally were found. The prophet's ecstasy was accompanied or preceded by a variety of pathological states and acts.

There can be no doubt that these very states, originally, were considered important legitimations of prophetic charisma and, hence, were to be expected in milder forms even when not reported. Some prophets, however, expressly recount such states. Yahwe's hand "fell" upon them. The spirit of the Lord "took" them, Ezekiel (6:11; 21:14) smote with his hands, beat his loins, stamped on the ground. Jeremiah was "like a drunken man," and all his bones shook (23:9).

When the spirit overcame them the prophets experienced facial contortions, their breath failed them, and occasionally they fell to the ground unconscious, for a time deprived of vision and speech, writhing in cramps (Is. 21). After one of his visions, for seven days long Ezekiel (3:15) was paralyzed. The prophets engaged in strange activities thought to be significant as omens. Ezekiel, like a child, built himself out of tile stones and an iron pan a siege play. Jeremiah publicly smashed a jug, buried a belt and dug the putrid belt up again, he went around with a yoke around his neck. Other prophets went around with iron horns, or, like Isaiah for a long time, naked. Still others, like Zachariah, inflicted wounds upon themselves, still others were inspired to consume filth, like Ezekiel. They screamed *(karah)* their prophecies aloud to the world, partly in indistinguishable words, partly in imprecations, threats, and benedictions with saliva running from their mouths (*hittif "geifern"* means to prophesy), now murmuring or stammering. They described visual and auditory hallucinations and abnormal sensations of taste and feeling of diverse sorts (Ezek. 3:2). They felt as if they were floating (Ezek. 8:3 and repeatedly) or borne through the air, they experienced clairvoyant visions of spatially distant events like, allegedly Ezekiel in Babylon at the hour of Jerusalem's fall, or of temporally distant events to come, like Jeremiah (38:22) of Zedekiah's fate. They tasted strange foods.

Above all, they heard sounds (Ezek. 3:12f; Jer. 4:19), voices (Is. 40:3f.) both single ones and dialogues, especially often, however, words and commands addressed to themselves. They saw hallucinatory blinding flashes of light and in it the figures of superhuman beings, the splendor of heaven (Is. 6, also Amos 9:1). Or they saw actually indifferent objects: a fruit basket or a plummet and suddenly to them, most usually through a voice, it was plain that these objects signified fateful decisions of Yahwe (especially Amos). Or they fall, like Ezekiel, into autohypnotic states. One meets with compulsive acts, above all, with compulsive speech. Jeremiah felt split into a dual ego. He implored his God to absolve him from speaking. Though he did not wish to, he had to say what he felt to be inspired words not coming from himself. Indeed, his speech was experienced by him as a horrible fate (Jer. 17:16). Unless he spoke he suffered terrible pains, burning heat seized him and he could not stand up under the heavy pressure without relieving himself by speaking. Jeremiah did not consider a man to be a prophet unless he knew this state and spoke from such compulsion rather than "from his own heart."

Such ecstatic, oracular prophets have not as yet been demonstrated in Egypt and Mesopotamia or pre-Islamic Arabia, but only in the neighborhood of Israel (as kingly prophecy like in Israel), in Phoenicia and, under rigid priestly control and interpretation, in the oracular establishments of the Hellenes. But nowhere is there a tradition of free demagoguery and prophesying ecstatics in the manner of the Israelite prophets. This could hardly be due to the lack of the respective states of mind. Rather it is because in bureaucratic kingdoms, such as the Roman empire, the religious police would have intervened. Moreover, among the Hellenes in historical times such psychic states were no longer viewed as holy, but as sicknesses and undignified and only the traditional priest-regulated oracles were generally acknowledged. In Egypt, ecstatic prophecy made its appearance only under the Ptolemies and in Arabia only in Mohammed's time.

This is not the place to classify and interpret, as far as that is possible, the various physiological, psychological, and possibly pathological states of the prophets. Attempts made thus far, especially with respect to Ezekiel, are not convincing. It affords, furthermore, no decisive interest for us. In Israel, as throughout antiquity, psychopathic states were valued as holy. Contact with madmen was taboo still in rabbinical times. The royal overseers appointed over the prophets (Jer. 29:24f.) were called "overseers of madmen and prophets." And tradition reports that even Jehu's officer, at the sight of the prophet's disciple offering the ointment to the king to have asked "Wherefore came this mad fellow to thee?" But our concern here is with something very different.

Of interest, in the first place, is the emotional character of prophetic ecstasy per se, which differentiates it from all forms of Indian apathetic ecstasy. The preeminently auditive nature of classical prophecy, in contrast to the essentially visual apathetic ecstasy of the ancient "seers," was purely historically conditioned by the contrast between the Southern Yahwistic conception of Yahwe's revelation and the conception of the North. The corporeal "voice" of God appears in place of the old corporeal epiphany, which the North, with its different representation of God, theoretically rejected and which did not agree with the psychic quality of Northern piety, which had sublimated orgiasticism into apathetic ecstasy. With the increasing recognition of the auditive character of the inspiration as the sole badge of authenticity was correlated the intensification of the political excitement of the listeners. This corresponded to the emotional character of prophecy.

A further important characteristic is that the prophets interpreted the meaning of their own extraordinary states, visions, compulsive speeches, and acts. Despite their obviously great pyschological differences their interpretations always took the same direction. The act of interpretation per se, however close it seems to us today, could by no means be taken for granted. A prerequisite was that the ecstatic states were not valued for themselves, as personal and sacred possessions, but an entirely different meaning was ascribed to them, that of a mission. This is still more obvious in the homogeneity of interpretations, a point which deserves more detailed elucidation.

Only at times did the prophets speak out of direct ecstasy (Is. 21:3, 4; Jer. 4:19f.). Usually they speak about their ecstatic experiences. The typical oracle begins with "Yahwe said unto me . . ." There are diverse shades. Ezekiel, on the one hand, squeezes whole treatises out of some of his visions although he was an apparently quite pathological and ecstatic character. On the other hand, there are numerous short verses of pre-Exile prophets which were thrust into the addressee's face in supreme passion and apparently in a state of esctasy. The most ecstatic and timely pronouncements were forthcoming without the prophet being asked[10] but solely inspired and pressured by Yahwe. The prophet was then carried away in the face of an especially dangerous situation of the country or under an especially shattering impression of sin.

In contrast we find among the classical prophets those relatively rare cases in which the prophet had been previously asked to prophesy. He seems but rarely to have answered at once. Like Mohammed he brooded in prayer over the case; Jeremiah once did so for ten days until the ecstatic seizure occurred (Jer. 42). Even then, as a rule, the visionary or auditory experience was not at once broadcast among the tarrying listeners, for such experience was often obscure and ambiguous.

The prophet then pondered in prayer about the meaning; only when he possessed the meaning would he speak out. Some of the prophets used the form of divine speech—Yahwe spoke through them directly in the first person—other prophets used the form of reporting about Yahwe's words. Human speech predominated with Isaiah and Micah, divine speech with Amos, Hosea, Jeremiah, and Ezekiel. Finally, all prophets were given to the interpretation of events including those of their workaday life, as significant manifestations of Yahwe (cf. especially Jer. 32).

Characteristic of the typical dicta of the pre-Exile prophets in general is that they have been spoken or, as is once said of Isaiah (5:1), chanted, in tremendous emotion. To be sure, one may find occasional verses which were perhaps left deliberately ambiguous, as was the well-known *kroisos* oracle of the Delphian Apollo and individual intellectual elaborations such as those of Ezekiel. But this was not the rule. Moreover, it is probably justifiably held that one may discern the conscious adherence to certain stylistic rules of prophetic poetry. For instance, usually the name of the person thought of is not mentioned unless it is to be cursed.

These rules did not alter the timely and emotional nature of prophecy. The conception of deity, though, delimited the content of experience. The corporeality of Yahwe's voice for the prophets meant that the prophet on the one hand felt decidedly "full of God" and on the other that the traditional nature of Yahwe's majesty precluded a true "embodiment" of God in the creature. Therefore, the euphemisms for the corporeally inaccessible were chosen.[11]

All Hellenic oracular dicta known to us were delivered on request. In their tempered and "perfect" form they do not remotely attain the emotional forcefulness of the spontaneous prophetic verses of Amos, Nahum, Isaiah, Zephaniah, and Jeremiah. In the partly fragmentary tradition, the great power of rhythm is yet surpassed by the glow of visionary images which are always concrete, telling, striking, concise, exhaustive, often of unheard of majesty and fecundity; in this regard they belong to the most grandiose productions of world poetry. They only lose in articulateness when the great acts of the invisible God on behalf of Israel had to be fashioned out of a vague vision of fantastic but indeterminate images of the future.

Whence did this emotion come if the truly ecstatic and pathological excitement was already dated and had faded out, as was often the case? The emotion simply did not flow from the pathos of these very psycho-pathological states, but from the vehement certainty of successfully having grasped the meaning of what the prophet had experienced. The prophet, unlike ordinary pathologically ecstatic men, had no vision, dreamed no dreams, and heard no mysterious voices. Rather he attained clarity and assurance through a corporeal divine voice of what Yahwe had meant by these day-dreams, or the vision, or the ecstatic excitement, and what Yahwe had commanded him to say in communicable words.

The tremendous pathos of prophetic speech in many cases was, as it were, a post-ecstatic excitement of in turn semi-ecstatic nature which resulted from the certainty of truly having stood "in Yahwe's council," as the prophets put it—to have said what Yahwe had told them or to have served as a mouth-piece, through which Yahwe literally spoke. The typical prophet apparently found himself in a constant state of tension and of oppressive brooding in which even the most banal things of everyday life could become frightening puzzles, since they might somehow be significant.

Ecstatic visions were not required to place the prophets in this state of tension. When the tension dissolved into a flash of meaningful interpretation, coming about in the hearing of the divine voice, the prophetic word burst forth. Pythia and the interpretive priestly poet were not separated here. The Israelite prophet united both in his person. This explains his tremendous élan.

Two further circumstances are important. First, these psychic states of the prophet were not connected—as, for example, was the ecstasy of Pythia—with the use of traditional ecstasy means of the Nebiim, nor, generally, with any external mass stimulation, hence, an ecstatic community. We find nothing of the kind among the classical prophets of our collection of scriptures. They did not seek ecstasy. It came to them. Besides, not one of them is reported to have been received into a guild of prophets through the laying on of hands or some such ceremony or to have belonged to any sort of specialized community. Always, rather, the prophet's calling came directly from Yahwe, and the classical prophets among them told us of their visionary or auditory "call." None of them used any intoxicants, the use of which they cursed on every occasion, as idolatry. Similarly, we hear nothing of fasting as a means of ecstasy evocation among the pre-Exile prophets, though tradition once recounts of Moses (Ex. 34:28) fasting. Thus, emotional ecstasy does not appear among them in the form of the early Christian community (and its possible antecedents).

In the apostolic age the spirit did not come upon the solitary individual, but upon the faithful assembly or upon one or several of its participants. This, at least, was the rule and the form of experience which the community evaluated as typical. The "spirit was poured out" to the community when the Gospel was preached. Speaking in tongues and other gifts of the spirit including, also, prophecy, emerged in the midst of the assembly and not in a solitary chamber. All these things obviously resulted from mass influence, or better, of mass gathering and were evidently bound up with such, at least, as normal precondition.[12] The culture-historically so extremely important esteem for the religious community as depository of the spirit in early Christendom had, indeed, this basis. The very community, the gathering of the brethren was especially productive of these sacred psychic states.

This was totally different for the ancient prophets. Precisely in solitude did the prophetic spirit come. And often the spirit first drove the prophet into solitude, into the fields or desert, as happened, still, to John and Jesus. But when the prophet was chased by his vision into the street among the multitude, this resulted only from his interpretative construction of his experience. Be it noted that this public appearance of the prophet was not motivated by the fact that the prophet could experience holiness only in public under the influence of mass suggestion like the early Christians. The prophets did not think of themselves as members of a supporting spiritual community. On the contrary. Misunderstood and hated by the mass of their listeners they never felt themselves to be supported and protected by them as like-minded sympathizers as did the apostles of the early Christian community. Hence, the prophets spoke at no time of their listeners or addressees as their "brethren." The Christian apostles always did so.

Indeed, the pathos of solitude overshadows the mood of the prophets. Before the Exile it was preponderantly hard and bitter—or again, as in the case of Hosea, it was soft, melancholy prevailed. Not ecstatic crowds, but one or several faithful disciples (Is. 8:16) shared their solitary ecstasy and their equally solitary torment. Regularly and obviously they were the disciples who recorded the prophet's visions or they had the prophet dictate his interpretations to them as Baruch, the son of Neriah, did for Jeremiah. On occasion they collected the prophecies in order to transmit them to those concerned. Once the pre-exilic prophet stepped forth and raised his voice to speak to the multitude he regularly had the feeling of facing people who were tempted by demons to do evil, to engage in Baal orgiasticism or idolatry, to commit social or ethical sins or the worst political blunder by rebelling against Yahwe's ordainment. In any case, the prophet felt himself to be standing before deadly enemies, or to face men whom his God intended to make suffer terrible misfortunes. His own sib hated him (Jer. 11:19,21; 12:6) and Jeremiah hurled forth an anathema against his native village (11:22, 23). The prophet of doom emerged from his solitude after having experienced his visions and born out his inner conflicts. He returned to the solitude of his home viewed with horror and fear, always unloved, often ridiculed, threatened, spit upon, slapped in the face.

The sacred states of the prophets were in this sense truly personal[13] and were thus experienced by them and their audiences, and not as the product of an emotional mass influence. No sort of external influence, but his personal God-sent condition placed the prophet in his ecstatic state. And during the very epoch of the prophets the tradition and high esteem of ecstasy per se as holy, clearly receded into the background. After all, both prophecy and counter-prophecy confronted one another in the street. Both equally claimed ecstatic legitimation and cursed one another. Where is Yahwe's truth? everbody had to ask. The conclusion was, one cannot know the true prophet by ecstasy alone. Therewith the substantive significance of ecstasy declined, at least with respect to its manner of communication. Only exceptionally and only as a means to an end is it mentioned which emotional states the prophet has experienced in his ecstasy. For, in contrast to Indian counterparts, this did not count. Ecstasy did not guarantee genuineness. Only the hearing of the corporeal voice of Yahwe, the invisible God, assured the prophet that he was Yahwe's tool. Hence, the tremendous emphasis upon this point.

This, the hearing of the voice of Yahwe, is the prophet's self-legitimation, not the nature of his holy states. Hence, the prophet abstained from gathering a community about him which might have engaged in mass ecstasy or mass-conditioned ecstasy or ecstatic revivals as a path to salvation. Nothing whatever is known of this with regard to classical Yahwe-prophecy. The nature of its message contradicted it. Unlike the possession of pneuma in the early Christian sources, the prophet's attainment of a state of ecstasy or his ability to hear Yahwe's voice is nowhere said to be a prerequisite also for his audience. Prophetic charisma rather was a unique burdensome office—often experienced as torment. Unlike early Christian prophets, the Yahwe prophets never aimed at allowing the spirit to come over the audience.

On the contrary, the prophetic charisma is their privilege. It is a free gift of godly grace without any personal qualification. In the accounts of their ecstasy of calling, this first ecstasy, giving the prophet his "call," is never presented as the fruit of asceticism or contemplation or moral attainments, penances, or other merits. On the contrary, it was always in agreement with the endogenous nature of the psychic state, a sudden unmotivated occurrence. Yahwe called Amos away from the flocks. An angel of Yahwe laid a glowing coal upon Isaiah's mouth, Yahwe himself touched with his hand the mouth of Jeremiah and thus consecrated them. At times, the prophet resisted, like Jeremiah, with anxiety, this charisma which was laid on him as a duty; at times he offered himself joyfully to the God in quest of a prophet, like Isaiah.

And, in contrast to Indian as well as Hellenic prophets of the type of Pythagoras and the Orphics and, also, the Rechabite Puritans, no Israelite prophet ever thought of taking to a ritualistic or ascetic path of salvation superior to workaday ethic. Nothing of the sort. This shows the great importance of the *berith*-conception, which unambiguously established what Yahwe demanded of his people in connection with the Levite Torah, which had fixed the divine imperatives as universally binding. Here it came to fruition, that the Torah did not develop out of the personal quest for salvation of literary stratum of genteel thinkers, but out of the cure of souls by practitioners, ministering the confession and atonement of sins. Without regard to this circumstance the entire development remains completely incomprehensible. It found its expression also in the qualification of the prophecy.

We noted that ecstasy as such no longer served as legitimation, but solely the perception of Yahwe's voice served this function. But what assured the audience that the prophet had actually, as he maintained, heard the voice of Yahwe? This question was answered in part historically, in part religiously and ethically. Historical conditions and Yahwe's ominous nature determined Jeremiah (23:29) to present as criterion the traditional opposition to the kingly prophets of good fortune. The explanation is to be found in the social struggle against kingship and its servitudes and the *gibborim*. The true prophet held out no good to the great ones.

Commitment to Yahwe's commandment as known to all (23:22) was ethically conditioned. Only the prophet who morally exhorted the people and sanctioned sins (through threats of doom) was not a lying prophet. Yahwe's commandments, however, were generally known through the Torah. Thus the Torah is always the completely self-evident presupposition of all prophecy. It is seldom explicitly referred to because it went without saying.

The Hellenic teachers of wisdom of the sixth century, too, preached the unconditionally binding character of the moral law. Substantively this law was similar to that of the prophets— as the social ethic of the Hellenic *aisymnete* enactments is intrinsically related to that of the Book of the Covenant. But the difference was that in Hellas as in India the specifically religious saviors and prophets joined salvation to special prerequisites of a ritualistic or ascetic nature, indeed that they were bringers of "salvation" and especially of salvation in the beyond. In the precise reverse, the Israelite prophets annunciated doom, at that, in the here and now and this in retribution for sins of Israelites against the universally binding law of their God. By upholding abiding adherence to this workaday ethic as a special duty of Israel by virtue of the sworn *berith,* the mighty pathos of eschatological threats and promises worked for adherence to these plain commandments which all were able to follow and which, in the view of the prophets, also non-Israelites would abide by at the end of time. The great historical paradox was that the later official workaday ethic of the Christian West, which substantially differed from ancient Hellenic and later Hellenist theory and everyday practice only in sexual matters, here was raised to a special ethical duty of a people chosen by its God, the mightiest of all, and exhorted by utopian promises and punishments. The special promise of salvation held out to Israel made morally correct action and the abidance by everyday ethic all important. However banal and self-evident this may seem, here alone it was made the basis of religious prophecy.

NOTES

1. G. Hölscher's work *Die Propheten* (1914) deserves special mention. It has great merit although various theses are controversial in detail. Hölscher is informed by modern psychology and presents the entire historical background. For single prophets see the modern commentaries.

The ecstatic proclivities of the prophets are discussed with his usual brilliance by H. Gunkel, "Die geheimen Erfahrungen der Propheten," (lecture, *"Suchen der Zeit,"* vol. 1, 1903). The *Schriften des Alten Testaments,* vol. 2, 2, contain excerpts of this besides translations and partially excellent single commentaries by H. Schmidt on Amos and Hosea (vol. 2, 1) and a very useful introductory analysis of the literary peculiarities. Of other literature see Giesebrecht, *Die Berufsbegabung der alttestamentlichen propheten* (Göttingen, 1897); Cornill, *Der israelitische Prophetismus* 6th ed. (Strassburg, 1906); Sellin, *Der alttestamentliche Prophetismus* (Leipzig, 1912). Further literature will be mentioned at the respective places. Ernst Troeltsch makes many correct observations on the "ethos" of the Old Testament prophets in *"Logos,"* vol. 6, p. 17 and justly places greater emphasis than is usual on the utopian nature of their "politics." Here we shall not go into details.

2. See for Jeremiah, 26:24; 29:3; 36:11; 40:6.

3. For Isaiah's political position see especially Küchler, *Die Stellung des Propheten Jesaja zur Politik seiner Zeit* (Tübingen, 1906). Cf. also the observations of Procksch, *Geschichtsbetrachtung und Geschichtsüberlieferung bei den vorexilischen Propheten* (Leipzig, 1902).

4. This is suggested by the fact that the king placed on the throne by him was given a theophoric (Yahwe-) name.

5. This has been maintained especially for Amos (for example by von Winckler). Küchler, *loc. cit.,* disputed this for good reasons.

6. For this obviously unprovable assumption speaks his way of repeatedly mentioning Shiloh as the first place of pure Yahwe worship and the manner in which he compares the destruction of Jerusalem with the undoubtedly half forgotten devastation of Shiloh centuries ago.

7. It is a conjecture of Duhm that, at another place, it is Osiris presumably who is named among the deities whom Yahwe will destroy.

8. The present version of the text, Micah 1:55, is not entirely correct in this.

9. It has been generally assumed, and rightly, that Jeremiah is not the author of Jer. 17:19 f.

10. Ezekiel, however, was once seized by ecstasy in the presence of the elders who consulted him (Ezek. 8:1).

11. Sellin, *loc. cit.* p. 227 rightly observes that the form in which the divine word reaches the prophet as a rule is not stated in detail. What was decisive was that the prophet had given an interpretation of his intentions which was evident and therewith conclusive to him.

12. This holds for all "speaking with tongues" and also for the "prophecy" which then addressed itself to the present. Similarly it reappeared among the Anabaptists and Quakers of the sixteenth and seventeenth centuries; today it occurs most characteristically in the American Negro churches (also of the Negro bourgeoisie, for example, in Washington, where I witnessed it).

13. Consideration must always be given the fact that all contrasts are linked by transitions and that similar phenomena are to be found also with the Christians. Among them, too, individuals are the psychic "centers of infection."

# 11

## CHRISTIAN MISSIONS IN THE ANCIENT WORLD

### CHARLES W. FORMAN

For close to two millennia Christians have been engaged in the effort to communicate their beliefs to other men. There have been times, to be sure, when very little seems to have been done along this line, but there has not been any period when the effort was completely abandoned. Always, in one part of the church or another, communication with non-Christians was being carried on, and at certain times this was done with great intensity and wide participation. One of those times was the ancient period, the first centuries of the church's life. At that time there seems to have been a burst of energetic activity in communication that has served as a model but has never been equaled in subsequent periods of Christian history.

At first sight it is surprising that followers of Jesus the Nazarene should have launched so wide-reaching an effort as they did, because Jesus himself was little interested in a wide-reaching mission. His concern was for his own people, the Jews. His clear statements that he was sent and that he sent his disciples only to "the lost sheep of the house of Israel" (Matthew 15:24; cf. 10:5–6, 23), as they are found in the New Testament, could not but represent the very earliest layer of Christian tradition, because the later church busily engaged in a mission to the gentiles would scarcely have invented such limitations.

But Jesus, even though he was interested in only a limited group, was clearly engaged in a mission. His religion was not a matter of some ineffable experience drawing him into isolation but a matter of relating God to daily life and relationships and involving him in a constant effort at communication through stories, instructions, and actions. His whole ministry, including his final acts, was intended as communication. Furthermore, the content of his message was such as to imply a wider audience than he himself envisaged.

He announced the coming of the Kingdom of God, the messianic kingdom foretold by prophets in the past, and prophets had expected that the time of the establishment of this Kingdom would be the time when all the nations would be gathered together and would acknowledge the God of Israel. Jesus believed that in his lifetime the Kingdom was beginning to be realized, which meant that salvation was being brought within reach of all nations. His teachings about the acceptance of non-Jews into the Kingdom and his readiness to acknowledge the faith of gentile believers (Luke 7:2-10, Mark 7:24-30) followed from this perspective. It is in this light, too, that we may best understand the statements in Matthew's gospel about foreign cities being preferred to Israel's towns and about many people coming from east and west and sitting down at table with Abraham, Isaac, and Jacob in the Kingdom of Heaven, while the sons of the Kingdom are thrown into the outer darkness (Matthew 11:21-24, 8:11-12). These sayings sound strange on the lips of one who did not take any interest in or participate in a mission to the gentiles, but they are completely intelligible in the eschatological perspective. Jesus looked forward to the imminent consummation of the world's history, and although he announced this new Kingdom only to the Jews, within whose tradition it had been expected, the implications of that consummation encompassed all men. The mission to the Jewish community was the sign of the coming of the new age. The call to mission within the Jewish community was the final act before the full sunrise of the eschatological Kingdom that would include all nations. Even the more particularist Jewish group in the early church, although they did not believe in gentile missions, recognized this wider significance of the message to the

Jews. The other groups in the church went further and drew the expectable conclusion that the message also should be shared with the gentiles, who were to be so much involved in the consummation.[1]

The main body of Christians was thus early involved in a mission directed to all mankind. The New Testament books concentrate on the work of one apostle, Paul, with his travels through Asia Minor, Greece, and on to Rome, but there is also passing reference to Peter's work in various parts of Palestine and Asia Minor and his presence in Rome (1 Peter 5:13), as there is to John's preaching in Samaria and to various lesser missionaries who traveled about with Paul or independently. Later traditions ascribing to each of the original apostles a particular part of the world as his field of mission are quite evidently a pious fiction, but there was some sense of division of labor from the beginning (Galations 2:9).

The mission as it was carried out at first was very closely related to the outreach of the Jewish people. All over the Mediterranean world the Jews had carried their message that centered in teachings about the one true God and his moral law. A large number of followers had been secured, chiefly in the urban centers of the eastern part of the empire. Some became full proselytes, observing the Jewish law in its entirety. Others, and they were the great majority, accepted the central beliefs of ethical monotheism but did not take on the observance of the ceremonial law. They were known as God-fearers. It is not hard to understand the appeal to such people of a new religion that kept the ethical monotheism but dispensed with the ceremonial law and preached salvation by faith. The early Christian ambassadors, therefore, moved along the network of these Jewish and Judaized communities of the empire. They found in them a ready-made religious community to which they could relate. The sacred literature they knew was already acknowledged; there was a habit of regular worship and control of private life. Above all, ethnical monotheism was taken for granted and messianic expectations were familiar.

The message of the earliest missionaries was particularly adapted to this kind of audience. An analysis of the examples of apostolic preaching shows a considerable diversity but also a common thread that runs through most of the speeches. They begin with references to the Jewish prophecies, which they claim are now being fulfilled. The messianic age, they announce, has dawned in Jesus, a man born of the lineage of David, who after his death rose again on the third day. This Jesus is now exalted on the right hand of God. The Holy Spirit in the church is the sign of his present power and glory, and the new age he announced will reach its consummation with his imminent return. This outline of beliefs is followed in the preaching by an appeal for repentance and an offer of forgiveness and new life in the new age to those who enter the Christian community.[2] It is striking that many of the basic Christian beliefs were omitted in this preaching. Nothing is said about the one God in whom all things cohere and who gives meaning and purpose to the whole of creation. There is no attack on idolatry or the worship of the work of man's hands nor on polytheism with its fissiparous interpretation of the world. The basic commandments that should govern human behavior are not mentioned. Obviously these omissions arise from the nature of the people being addressed. As those related to the Jewish faith, they presumably were thoroughly familiar with all these things and the preachers felt no need to rehearse the obvious. It was the new and the distinctive that was emphasized, although with enough mention of familiar beliefs—the prophesies, the messianic hope, the divine rule—to enable the listener to see connections between his present position and the new allegiance that was being urged on him.

But after the first generation the audience changed decisively and the content of the message consequently underwent a major transformation. After the first group of converts from Jews and God-fearers had been secured, it became clear that further response was not to be expected from the synagogue and that the future hope of the church lay with the gentiles. Paul had recognized this fact at an early stage. By the end of the first century most Christians recognized it. Judaism itself was undergoing a narrowing tendency consequent upon the destruction of Jerusalem and perhaps in some reaction to the denationalization that Christianity showed to be inherent in any outreaching and Hellenizing movements. As Judaism withdrew from its missionary outreach among the gentiles the church moved almost totally into a gentile mission.

The second and third centuries then showed a new emphasis in Christian communication. It is revealed most fully in the written works, known as apologies, which were produced during that period. We cannot assume that the written apologies were in all ways the same as the oral presentations of the faith to non-Christians. Preaching would normally call for exhortations to believe, which formed the final section of the early preaching we have examined, but these were much less in evidence in the written apologies. Yet it seems reasonable to presume that there was a large degree of similarity in the main line of thought of the two statements. "What is defended is that which has been or is being preached,"[3] and if the audience were such as would be convinced by a certain line of argument in defense of the faith, they presumably would be moved by a similar line in its presentation. The apologies emphasized everything that had been neglected in the earlier preaching and reduced to a secondary place or disregarded most of the things that previously had been stressed. We can see an early example of this in the discourse attributed to Paul in the seventeenth chapter of the book of Acts, a discourse that has been regarded as a forerunner of the apologies.

The new approach concentrated above all on the arguments against polytheism, using polemical traditions derived from both Jewish and pagan sources. Sometimes these were couched in philosophical and positive terms, stressing the greatness of the one God who made everything, the necessity of worshipping him and turning away from the worship of all lesser things, especially from the gods made by men's hands. This was the line followed, for example, by Lactantius and Origen. At other times the approach was more negative, making fun of the idols, of their helplessness as mice gnaw them or spiders spin webs on their faces, and of the foolishness of men who turn to such things for help. The moral character of the gods was also attacked as being below the level of conduct that is expected even of mortal men. The holiness of the true God and the moral law that was his will stood out in contrast to all this. References to Jesus and the messianic age, which dominated the earlier preaching, were reduced to a secondary place in the apologies. There was still much more interest shown in ancient Hebrew texts, which could be stretched to imply prophetic reference to Jesus' life, but this was more to show the antiquity of Christian origins than to empower immediate messianic expectations. The Psalms were the most common quarry for prophetic texts: "I laid me down and slept and rose again" (Psalms 3:5) was said to prefigure the death and resurrection of Jesus. The prophets, especially Isaiah, also were used: "I have spread out my arms to a disobedient and gainsaying people" (Isaiah 65:2) was taken as referring to the crucifixion.

In addition the apologists were full of practical arguments for their faith. They told about their own conversion and the effect it had had upon their lives, a line of argument that has continued in popularity down to the present day. They also spoke of the effects of Christian faith on the lives of their fellow believers, of how they had been involved in all the evils present in the society around them but after their conversion had been raised up to new dignity and responsibility in their conduct. The fact that this argument was made so frequently and with such assurance implies that there was a considerable reality behind it to which the preachers could turn with confidence and that the rumors about Christian immorality that were circulating in those days could not have had a wide acceptance. The close and mutually supportive relationships that existed in the Christian community were referred to in this same connection. The fact that Christians loved each other, gave freely of their goods to help their own poor and to help strangers in need, and called each other brothers and treated each other as kinsmen was used as a strong argument in favor of their faith. A new kind of community was being born in the world, one that did not depend on political, ethnic, or kinship ties and yet encompassed men who lived within a variety of these groupings.

Before long there could be added to these practical arguments the claim of success. These writers had no qualms about boasting. Tertullian's famous hyperbole (*Apology*, 37), coming from the end of the second century, typifies this attitude: "We are but of yesterday, and we have filled every place among you—cities, islands, fortresses, towns, markets, the very camp, tribes, companies, palace, senate, forum—We have left nothing to you but the temples of your gods." The claim was that past successes would lead to future success; one justification for adoption of the new faith was its growing acceptance in the world.

The oral communication of these and similar arguments took place in a number of different ways. The way that might be most naturally expected, public presentation by reasoned discourse in urban gathering places, was one of these. Lactantius (*Divine Institutes,* V. 20) describes this type of communication when he calls upon the polytheists to imitate the Christians in this regard:

> Let them call us together to an assembly; let them exhort us to take part in the worship of the gods, persuade us that the gods are many. . . . And let them confirm all these things not just by their own assertion . . . but by some divine testimonies as we do. There is no occasion for violence or injury since religion cannot be imposed by force. . . . If their system is true, let it be asserted . . . let them imitate us and set forth a reasoned statement of the whole matter. For we do not, as they say, entice. We teach, we prove, we show. We keep no one against his will for he is of no use to God who lacks devotion and faith.

Evidently Christians were trying to persuade men by public speeches. But reasoned public discourse was not the only approach. More popular was attracting attention and showing power through feats of exorcism. This, of course, might well go along with some of the more reasoned preaching that has been mentioned, but it also stood in its own right as a strong argument for the faith. If men could be healed of sickness or demon-possession in the name of Christ, this would provide greater validity than much reasoning for having faith in him. Tertullian (*Apology,* 23) describes the scene vividly:

> Now for a test case. Let a person be brought before your tribunals who is plainly demon-possessed. . . . All the authority and power we have over them is from our naming the name of Christ and recalling to their memory the woes which threaten them from God at the hands of Christ as Judge. . . . So at our touch . . . they

come out of the bodies as we command, unwilling and distressed and before your very eyes put to an open shame.

But probably more effective than these public presentations, whether of reasoned argument or spiritual power, was private communication within the home, or from individual to individual, of the new faith that was spreading. This was probably the major form of communication, especially during the long periods in the second and third centuries when Christianity was officially frowned upon or persecuted and hence debarred from any widespread public presentation. The large proportion of converts in this period who were women, often women of high estate, also suggests the primary importance of personal communication in the home. In the nature of the case, this type of activity was less likely to be reported than was the public missionary work. Our fullest description of it comes in the attack levelled against it by one of the opponents of Christianity, Celsus (Origen, *Contra Celsum,* 3, 55):

We see, indeed, in private houses, workers in wool and leather, washermen and persons of the most uneducated and rustic kind. They would not venture to open their mouths in the presence of their elders or wiser masters. But they get hold of the children privately and certain women who are as ignorant as themselves. Then they pour forth wonderful statements. "You ought not to heed your fathers or your teachers. Obey us. They are foolish and stupid, neither know nor can perform anything that is really good, being busied with empty trifles. We alone know how men ought to live . . . " While they are thus speaking they see one of the school teachers approaching or one of the more educated class or even the father himself . . . so they whisper, "With him here we cannot explain . . . but if you like you can come with the women and your playmates to the women's quarters or to the leather shop or the laundry that you may get all there is." With words like these they win them over.

One need not assume that private communications were always of this anti-intellectual or obscurantist type. Presumably if the people who were the objects of the approach had been of a more intellectual sort, some of the more reasoned presentations that make up the bulk of the apologies would have been put to use. But whatever may have been the level of the discussion, the picture drawn here suggests that private discussions were a constantly used method of communication for the early Christians.

Celsus' words imply much as to who were the primary agents of Christian communication during the second and third centuries, and this is a matter on which we have not touched thusfar. Christianity, through most of the centuries of its existence, has been carried from place to place by missionaries sent specifically for that purpose. It has been the "missionary religion" par excellence. But it is evident that in the period with which we are concerned, if the major line of communication was through private discussion, the major missionary force consisted not of people especially sent for that purpose but of the rank and file of church members and adherents. Each one in his or her daily life used the contacts that he had to spread the knowledge of and make converts to the faith. This happened spontaneously. There is no suggestion in the contemporary writings that the church inculcated any obligation for Christians to be "nonprofessional missionaries." There was no theory of "each one teach one." There was rather a community of believers bound together in an all-encompassing way and acting contagiously on those outsiders whom it touched. The rank and file spoke to others of what they had experienced and out of their own enthusiasm rather than out of any particular doctrine or demand.

In addition, however, the church did have special individuals who were used for missionary activity and who operated in more public ways. There were wandering preachers, called apostles or prophets, who were normally penniless and depended for their livelihood on the hospitality of those among whom they moved. Origen mentions people who "have made it their business to itinerate not only through cities, but even villages and country houses that they might make converts to God" (*Contra Celsum*, 3, 9). The prophets were particularly those who spoke "in tongues" (glossolalia), although apostles might also do this. There is some question as to whether the prophets preached to those outside the church as well as to those inside.[4]

Both types were regarded as receiving their call to service from the Holy Spirit and were outside the ordinary hierarchy of church offices. As time went on they tended to decrease in importance and finally disappeared.

A more enduring service was given by those who were called teachers. At first these appear to have been catechists giving basic instruction to converts, but later on they seem to have been more like the philosophers so well known to the ancient world. References to their activity continue until well into the fourth century. Many of them wore the philosopher's garb and, like the other philosophers, they maintained schools where they could teach youths of various religious beliefs. They taught them not only the Christian faith but also the other subjects necessary for a cultivated mind: logic, geometry, physics, ethics, literature, and philosophy. In this breadth of curriculum they resembled the schools that Christian missions have maintained in Africa and Asia in more recent centuries. The most famous of their schools was the one in Alexandria and its offshoot in Caesarea.

The teachers, like the apostles and prophets, were outside the church structure, people recognized for their ability and inspiration but not given formal appointment by the church. It is a significant fact that the work of communicating the faith to the nonbelievers was done chiefly by those who were not part of the organized church structure. Clearly the structures were developed for the inner unity and discipline of the church rather than for the church's mission. Of the three ecclesiastical offices—bishops, priests, and deacons—only the bishops finally were given responsibility for missionary work, and this role developed for them only gradually as the role of the more charismatic types which we have mentioned declined.

The most famous example of a bishop engaged in missionary work in the days of the Roman Empire was Gregory Thaumaturgos, bishop in Pontus from about 240 to 270. He led something like a mass conversion to Christianity, making the transition easier for the people by substituting festivals in honor of the martyrs for the festivals of the old gods, and opposing pagan miracles with Christian ones. He also disciplined Christians who compromised their faith and so was not simply involved in smoothing the way for an easy transition. However, his steps toward relating Christianity to the old religious practices of the people reveal an important new development in the communication of the Christian faith, one that was to be carried much further in later periods.

We have been examining thus far the communication of the Christian faith to those who were completely outside the community of belief. We should also take at least brief note of the communication to those who were on the threshold of the community, ready to step inside. These were the catechumens, and their instructors were known as catechists. We have remarked already that the first "teachers" of the church were really catechists for these newcomers. The church regarded the communication to this group as even more important than the communication to outsiders; at least this seems to be the implication of the fact that organized church programs gave much more attention to catechetics than to missions.

The process of teaching the catechumens developed slowly. At first anyone who confessed faith in Christ was forthwith baptized and received into the community. But as time went on the church learned, doubtless from sad experience, the need for careful instruction of those who were to join its ranks. In the *Apostolic Tradition* of Hippolytus, early in the third century, we find that the church in Rome kept converts under instruction for three years before they could be baptized. Missionary preaching had given them only the basic beliefs and central event of Christian faith. It was necessary to elaborate for them the story of the event and to explain its significance. Much teaching probably had to be memorized, and some of the elements of Christian worship to which the neophytes were admitted, such as the lectionaries and the repetition of the creed, were well suited to this purpose. The gospel of Matthew is full of devices for being remembered, which suggests that it also was used for such teaching.

The main elements of the instruction as they have come down to us are, however, more directed to training in a certain style of life than to knowledge of certain material. The main points were: prepare to suffer, hope, and love; seek wisdom; love God and your neighbor; put off the old ways and put on the new;

worship; watch and pray; submit yourself to authority; resist the evil one and stand firm. Along with the instruction each person's conscience was examined and every sin was tracked down to its source. The church was obviously determined to express a distinctive kind of life in its corporate existence, and it was as important to communicate this life to the new Christians as it was to communicate the distinctive Christian beliefs.[5]

Having looked at the processes of communication, we must now say something about the different areas where the communication took place and the varying responses it received. The missionary activity of the Christians did not take place uniformly all over the ancient world, nor did the various regions respond uniformly to it.[6] Palestine, with which we may begin because it was the home base for Christianity, was one of the most unresponsive areas. The early churches there were strongly Jewish and therefore made little appeal to the gentiles. Yet the Jews, as we have already noted, early ceased to come into the church and hence Palestinian Christianity remained limited to a small and fairly rigid community. In Phoenicia the Christian group was more numerous, and Antioch of course had one of the oldest and strongest churches of the ancient world. The patriarch of Antioch was one of the five highest dignitaries of the ancient church. The Christians of the region were chiefly Greek-speaking at first and so must have been city people, but later the Syriac-speaking church developed and Antioch became a center of Syriac Christianity. The area where Christianity was adopted most widely was Asia Minor. Perhaps because the native culture had already disintegrated under Greek influence, the people responded readily to the Christian message. The provinces of Asia, Phrygia, and Bithynia showed the earliest Christian strength, and after the time of Gregory Thaumaturgos, Pontus could be added to their number. Greece presented an uncertain picture during the second and third centuries. There were Christians in most parts of the country, but apparently as a very small minority.

South of the Mediterranean, Christianity had two of its strongest areas, Egypt and Africa. The church was introduced into Egypt very early, and by the year 200 it was strong there. The Alexandrian school is an indication of its vitality. Not only the Greek-speaking people but also the old Egyptian stock were found in the church, and translations of the gospel were made into Coptic. The province of Africa was second only to Asia Minor in its number of Christians. It was the first home of Latin Christian literature. But the church does not seem to have become domesticated among the Punic population of the cities or the Berber peasantry. At least there was little Punic literature and few Punic bishops, and none of either from the Berber side. The difference between this and the Coptic situation was marked and may go far to explain the later total disappearance of African Christianity.

Italy, at least in its central and southern parts, had a vigorous church. There were about a hundred Italian bishops by the year 250. In north Italy things moved more slowly and what Christianity there was came from Dalmatia. Rome, as might be expected from its central position, early had a large body of Christians, and it was noted for sending aid to other churches. In Western Europe there were only weak churches in Spain and Britain, but Gaul had a flourishing Christianity, which developed first along the trade routes leading up the Rhone valley. The Christians were primarily from the Greek colonists of the area, if we may judge from the names which have come down to us.

Outside the Roman Empire the church was also making significant progress in the second and third centuries. Constantine had not yet made the identification between Rome and Christianity, which later proved to be such a handicap in the lands beyond Rome's eastern border. The small city-state of Edessa just over the border probably received its first Christians from Antioch, and about the end of the second century it made Christianity its state religion, the first place in the world to do so. It was also the first center for the spread of Syriac Christianity. Further east in the Parthian Empire there were widely scattered churches with a fairly small membership. Mesopotamia had twenty bishops by the year 225. Arabia and India also had small groups of Christians by the time of Constantine.

The greatest achievement of Christian missions outside the Roman Empire was in Armenia. The Armenian kingdom was a border state, like Edessa, and also like Edessa it became officially a Christian land, the first country of any size to adopt this religion. The way in which Christianity was accepted there opened up a new style of communicating the faith, one that proved to be a precedent for many lands during the succeeding centuries. An Armenian noble, known as Gregory the Illuminator, became a Christian while in exile in Caesarea and carried his new faith home with him late in the third century. Prior to that time there had been a few Christians in Armenia, but they had had little influence. Thanks to Gregory's presentation of the faith it was adopted by the king and thereafter it was adopted very quickly by the people following the royal example. The old religious forms of the country were simply transposed into Christian ones. The former shrines often became churches and the former pagan priests or their sons entered the clergy. Gregory was made the bishop and was succeeded in that office by his lineal descendants. The level at which Christianity could be communicated in this way would seem to be very superficial, and yet, because it was identified completely with the national life, the Armenian church showed a continuing strength and commanded a continuing loyalty from its adherents even up to the present time, which many more deeply founded churches could not boast.

The pattern of Armenia was soon transposed to the Roman Empire itself. Christianity, which had been carrying on its missions in the ways we have described, under great handicaps and restrictions, suddenly was elevated at the beginning of the fourth century to a position of official favor by the Emperor Constantine. The powers of the state were not used directly to bring people to accept the faith; Constantine himself was not baptized until he was on his deathbed. But the imperial favor that was showered on the church naturally led to mass conversions, first among the leaders of society and then among the people generally. Gradually, too, restrictions against the old religions were multiplied. In this situation the communication of the faith was a very different process from what it had been in the two previous centuries. The bishops became more important in leading people into the church, following the pattern set by Gregory Thaumaturgos; and the former missionary types, the apostles and prophets and eventually the teachers, disappeared. As in the case of Gregory Thaumaturgos and Gregory the Illuminator, syncretism was not just accepted but promoted. The attacks on polytheism were not so important now as were the provisions that were made for the needs of polytheists through the institution of festivals of the various saints. Christianity was presented to the mass of the population as the imperially sponsored religion of mysteries with its holy persons, holy books, holy doctrine, and sanctifying cult. In this guise it rapidly became the predominant and eventually the only religion of the empire.

This final triumph can be attributed only in part to the long and varied efforts at communication that we have described or to the later imperial favor we have noted. The ancient world in the second, third, and fourth centuries was in several ways particularly receptive to what the Christians were trying to communicate, and this was equally responsible for the success of the communication. Late antiquity was, most significantly, an extremely "religious" age, increasingly other-wordly in its interests. The material world was more and more regarded as evil, and human beings were seen as strangers in this world. "Contempt for the human condition and hatred of the body was a disease endemic in the entire culture of the period," writes E. R. Dodds.[7] Christianity fitted into and accentuated that "disease." Christians went to more extreme lengths than others in mortifying the flesh and in separating themselves from the world. They also treated death as a conquered enemy and looked forward joyously to eternal life. Of course Christianity was to some extent being shaped in this direction by the demand of the times. In our own more materialistic age it has been shaped in other ways, and Archbishop William Temple has described Christianity as the most materialistic of all religions. Yet, even though this may be true, it is still a religion and thus has a point of reference and source of hope that lie beyond the material world. It was this that gave it great appeal, along with other religions, in a day when the material world was suffering from political disintegration, the depredations of contending armies, omnivorous taxes and requisitions, famine, pestilence, and ever new invasions of barbarians.

The despair about events was accompanied by a despair about the understanding of events, which also opened the way for Christianity. Here it was not a matter of Christianity fitting in with the trend of the time but a matter of providing a needed antidote. The ancient world had worked its way through various understandings of the human story. It had early believed that there was an underlying pattern to events, that the conflict of opposites tended to an equilibrium, that immoderate desire would always meet its nemesis, and that what was reasonable would prevail. But increasingly it had become aware of the incalculable forces of irrationality that seemed to have the final disposition of affairs in their hands. They both built up and destroyed men. These irrational forces were identified as "Fortune," and Roman writers explained the rise of Rome and of the Caesars by reference to Fortune. The worship of Fortune and of Fortune's favorites developed as the natural consequence. "With this dismal conclusion the quest for historical intelligibility came to an end."[8] In contrast Christianity asserted that all of human history was under the providence of a good and loving God and that the irrational and incalculable things that happened were somehow being used by him for his good purposes. Man had freedom and evil was strong, but the final outcome was secure in the divine economy. The receptiveness to this assurance in a time of loss of faith and loss of hope is understandable.

The distinctive characteristics of the Christian community also matched a need of the times. Society was becoming more and more cosmopolitan with the mixing together of peoples under the rule of Rome. Urban men no longer felt the close relationships and mutual support of their ethnic communities as they had in the past. They tended to drift as unattached individuals, and when sickness or poverty overwhelmed them they could no longer count on a community to support them. The Christian community was outstanding among the religious communities for its close, supportive relationships. We have noted how the apologists made much of this fact. Christians from the beginning were devoted to the care of the sick and the poor, of orphans and widows, primarily within their own group but also among outsiders. Especially where there was some natural calamity Christian assistance was given regardless of creed. Prisoners were the object of special solicitude, and the humane treatment of slaves was insisted on. This loving community was open to all, without the ethnic limitations of some religions or the demand of others for the expenditure of large sums in initiation ceremonies.

The cosmopolitanism of the times was also leading to a breakdown of traditional morality, and here again Christianity came in with a strong antidote. Not only the apologists spoke of this—even the non-Christians and the enemies of the church recognized that Christianity produced a new life of moral power, of earnestness and holiness, as well as loving concern for all men.[9] Christians were extremely strict about sexual relations. They were honest in their dealings. They refused to countenance the bloodier or more profligate types of entertainment. They believed in loving their enemies. In their writings they often referred to this love but seldom or never expressed hatred or the desire for revenge or imprecatory prayers against those who were persecuting them.[10] Many men who bemoaned the laxity of the times and the decline from the moral standards of the past were ready to turn to Christianity because of these qualities.

The need for religious assurance, for a sense of meaning in history, for a loving community and a vigorous morality was met then by a faith that was possessed of these qualities to a marked degree and that was engaged in a constant and vigorous missionary effort, partly through workers specially selected for the purpose and partly through the rank and file of its believers. These men carried a message of a new age coming, of an ethical monotheism as the coherent structure of existence, of a new community (the "third race" after Jews and Romans-Greeks), and of a holy church sanctifying all things. These emphases in their message, while to some extent successive, were also cumulative. The combination of a highly receptive social situation with constant and eager proclamation of these convictions is what brought about the effective communication of Christianity to the ancient world.

NOTES

1. Ferdinand Hahn, *Mission in the New Testament* (London, 1965), pp. 26–63.

2. C. H. Dodd, *The Apostolic Preaching and Its Developments* (London, 1936), pp. 18, 25–28. For emphasis on the diversity of teaching, see E. Käsemann, "The Canon of the New Testament and the Unity of the Church," in *Essays on New Testament Themes* (London, 1964), pp. 95–107.

3. Abraham J. Malherbe, "The Apologetic Theology of the Preaching of Peter," *Restoration Quarterly* 13 (1970): 205. The analysis of the postapostolic preaching that is given here follows the treatment in John Foster, *After the Apostles. Missionary Preaching of the First Three Centuries* (London, 1951), which assumes that the apologies and the missionary preaching took the same line.

4. Kenneth Scott Latourette, *A History of the Expansion of Christianity*, vol. 1 (New York, 1937), pp. 115–116.

5. Godfrey Phillips, *The Transmission of the Faith* (London, 1946), pp. 50–51, 59–61, 81–88. Adolf Harnack, *The Mission and the Expansion of Christianity in the First Three Centuries*, vol. 1 (New York, 1908), pp. 391–392.

6. The basic work of piecing together all the small references to Christian activity and the response to it in the ancient world has been done by Harnack in *Mission and Expansion of Christianity*, vol. 2, chap. 3.

7. *Pagan and Christian in an Age of Anxiety* (Cambridge, 1965), p. 35.

8. Charles Narris Cochrane, *Christianity and Classical Culture. A Study of Thought and Action from Augustus to Augustine* (Oxford, 1944), pp. 456–516.

9. Harnack, *Mission and Expansion of Christianity*, vol. 1, pp. 160–172, 211.

10. Latourette, *History of the Expansion of Christianity*, vol. 1, p. 167.

# 12

## COMMUNICATION IN CLASSICAL ISLAM

GEORGE KIRK

### THE KERYGMA

A study of communication in Islamic society before the rise of
the Ottoman Empire circa A.D. 1300 has a particular pointed-
ness: for not only was that society derived from the practice of a
particular religion, but also that religion had its origin in the
personal experience and teaching of a particular individual, the
prophet Muhammad (circa A.D. 570–632), who is a historical
personality in his own right. The "quest for the historical
Jesus" undertaken by solemn German Protestant theologians in
the nineteenth century proved to be a will-o'-the-wisp. Whatever the historical facts about the son of Joseph and Mary may
have been, Paul of Tarsus, the oral traditions that lie behind the
four Gospels, and the Greek Fathers of the Church have between them done their work so thoroughly that, at least for the
Anglo-Catholic who writes these lines, the Man of Nazareth has
been subsumed in the Second Person of the Nicene Creed:
"true God . . . of the same Nature as the Father . . . who for
us men and for our salvation . . . was made flesh of Blessed
Mary AND WAS MADE MAN. . . ."

Not so with Muhammad. In comparison with what Paul
called "the unsearchable riches of Christ," Muhammad, when
the accretion of legend has been stripped away, remains a

plausible historic figure receiving his first religious experience in solitary withdrawal from the busy caravan town of Mecca, but by no means in a cultural vacuum. In the pagan Arab tribal society out of which the commercialism of Mecca and the incense traffic had recently crystalized, the main channel of communication seems to have been the tribal poet whose function it was to commemorate the military valor, generosity, and magnanimity of the tribe's chiefs and heroes, and to ridicule and disparage their enemies outside the tribe and their possible detractors within it.[1] The fact that these pre-Islamic poets used a more or less uniform dialect of Arabic suggests some intercommunication between tribes, and we hear of the kaleidoscopic fusion and dissolution of tribal alliances and confederations in the centuries before Muhammad. During the last of these, the appearance in western Arabia of small monotheistic communities, both Jewish and Christian—whether the product of actual immigration or mainly of native conversion—betokens cultural communication from the Fertile Crescent and/or Egypt, the cultural recompense of that trade in incense and spices which was the staple of southern Arabia's commerce with the Mediterranean; and we hear that some Arab contemplatives, outgrowing spiritually the astral and meteoric cults of traditional Arab paganism, had begun to seek a unifying divine principle for themselves.[2]

Although modern psychologists in their various schools and persuasions may disagree as to the objective nature of Muhammad's first religious experience, his own converts had no doubt about what happened. A supernatural person, later identified with the archangel Gabriel, appeared and commanded him:

Recite! in the name of thy Lord who created,
created man from a clot of blood.
Recite! for thy Lord is the most generous,
who taught [the older scriptures] by the pen,
taught man what he did not know. . . . (Sūra 96.)

From this word *recite (iqra')* the sacred Book that was later compiled from the series of divine commands to Muhammad took its name, *al-Qur'ān,* "the recitations." The point was made at the very outset that the God who was commissioning Muham-

mad as his messenger *(rasūl)* was the same God who had in
times past revealed himself to the Jews and Christians through
the patriarchs and prophets culminating in Jesus; who now in
these days was revealing himself to the Arabs in their own
language.

The early messages that Muhammad took from these successive encounters with the Divine to his fellow citizens of Mecca were warnings to acknowledge the oneness of God in place of
their traditional polytheism, and to face the imminence of the
Judgment Day when maligners and scoffers, the purse-proud
and those neglectful of the traditional tribal obligations to the
widow and orphan (Muhammad himself had been orphaned at
an early age) would be called to account. In these passages
Muhammad was sometimes styled "prophet" *(nabī)* like the
biblical prophets, sent by God to preach and warn the heedless.
But there seems to be a more particular role for the "messenger" *(rasūl)*:

A messenger is sent to every nation;
when their messenger comes, justice is done among them. . . .

We have sent you forward as a blessing from your Lord,
to forewarn a nation to whom no messenger has been sent before.
(*Sūras* 10.47; 28.46.)[3]

However, a trading town whose prosperity depended in part
on the annual pilgrimage *(al-hajj)* from the surrounding regions
to its polytheistic shrine *(al-kaʿba),* and in which the superior
business skills of some had been dissolving the older social code
of tribal cooperation, was not readily persuaded by this would-
be social reformer from a modest family background. The
curious matter of the "satanic verses," ostensibly communicated by the archangel to Muhammad but later abrogated by him,
perhaps reflects an early but abortive attempt at compromise on
his part.[4] His support came from his own kin, some younger
men, and some older members of lesser clans;[5] but the leading
merchant clan organized a boycott of those who heeded his call
to "make their peace" *(islām)* with God;[6] and when in A.D.
622 a deputation from the faction-ridden town of Medīna, two
hundred fifty miles to the north, invited him there as an impar-

tial outside arbitrator of their troubles, fewer than a hundred men and their families shared in this Muslim emigration (*al-hijra*, conventionally "hegira") from Mecca.

### FROM "COMMUNE" TO EMPIRE

These Meccan emigrants, however, not being capable of absorption into the tribal structure of Medīna, came logically under Muhammad's direct authority, based upon his continuing to receive messages from the All-Knowing God. He thus became the leader *(imām)* of a social unit *(umma)* based not, like the tribes, on a kinship tradition but on a unifying religious profession *(al-shahāda):* "There is no god but God, and Muhammad is his messenger." They were joined in this primeval Islamic *umma* by an increasing number of converts in Medīna, attracted by Muhammad's evident and growing charisma; and after he had led his young fighting men to harass and plunder the north-bound Meccan caravans, on the whole successfully, deputations from the opportunistic Bedouin tribes of the wastes of western Arabia began to come and pay their respects to this evident man of destiny. Conversely, those citizens of Medīna who were reluctant with their support were ruthlessly chastised; and finally the Meccan commercial aristocrats themselves decided to clamber on his bandwagon and allow him to purge their Kaʿba of its pagan idols. Already, when scoffed at by the influential Jewish minority in Medīna for his evident ignorance of their Torah, Muhammad had disengaged his infant cult from its original observance of Jerusalem, the Sabbath, and Yom Kippur, and reoriented it upon the Meccan Kaʿba, the fasting month of Ramadān, and Friday as the weekly day of public worship. In becoming Arabian, Islam was in the process of creating an Arab nation.

Muhammad died quietly at Medīna in A.D. 632, the unchallenged leader of an important part of Arabia, both town and tribe, but leaving no son or designated successor. Potential anarchy was averted when one of his most vigorous younger supporters, ʿUmar (conventionally, Omar), raised the hand of the older Abu Bakr, who had been appointed to lead the community prayers when the Prophet was indisposed, and proclaimed him as the Successor *(khalīfa*, hence "caliph"), not to those divine revelations that had been completed by Muhammad's death but to his *leadership* of the Islamic community "in the way of God." Many of the tribal shaykhs, however, had paid their homage to Muhammad the charismatic personality; and faced now by a "successor" whom they hardly knew, they sought to reassert their traditional independence. A short war was necessary to impress upon them that their *islām,* their "peace with God," was *not* terminable upon the death of the Prophet but owed equally through the caliph, the "chief executive" of the divine commands. 'Umar, succeeding the aged Abu Bakr in that role, saw the statesmanlike utility of giving the tribal warriors occupation and the chance of material gain by directing them to raid the Fertile Crescent lands to the north of Arabia. Those peoples had been exhausted and alienated by a generation of war between their respective masters, the Byzantine and Iranian (Sasanian) empires. By the time of 'Umar's death, only twelve years after that of the Prophet, Egypt, Palestine, Syria, and Iraq had fallen to the Muslim Arab bands, and the bands were spreading westward along the North African coast and northeastward onto the Iranian plateau.

Compared with the millions of townspeople and peasants of these easily conquered lands, the Muslim Arabs were a small band of nouveaux riches. Contrary to popular Western belief, their leaders could never have contemplated offering their new subjects the alternative of "conversion of the sword": the Arabs lacked most of the skills, both of craft production and of agriculture, necessary to the economic exploitation of the newly won lands. Furthermore, most of the inhabitants were Christians, Jews, or Zoroastrians with scriptures reflecting the will of the One God even if not (according to Muslims) with the purity and inerrancy of this latest and final revelation to Muhammad. The politic 'Umar is thus credited with constraining the non-Muslim majority to accept the temporal "protection" of the Muslims and assume the obligations of a land tax and poll tax in token of that subjection—a fiscal yoke initially lighter than that imposed by their previous Byzantine or Iranian rulers. Conversion to Islam was positively *discouraged,* lest the Islamic community chest suffer from the cessation of this protection money *(kharāj)*—until a later finance minister, noting that conversion to the religion of the dominant minority was taking place anyway, ordered that a landed property that had once been assessed for *kharāj* should continue to pay it, notwithstanding the conversion of its occupant and his descendants.[7]

Meanwhile the third caliph, 'Uthmān, one of the Prophet's early Meccan converts but himself now elderly, had allowed his kinsmen of the Umayyad clan to apply their considerable commercial acumen to the lively trade of the Fertile Crescent lands. The immense personal profits accruing to a few contrasted sharply with the modest status of the tribal warriors whom the stern 'Umar had restricted, when not on campaign, to garrison camps on fixed stipends; and he employed his heavy camel stick to discipline those caught with surreptitious loot. In A.D. 656, protestations made to the caliph against this flagrant breach of the Prophet's rule of equity found him too old or to beholden to his powerful kinsfolk to pay heed. A band of malcontents murdered him in Medīna and proclaimed 'Ali, the Prophet's nearest male relative (cousin and son-in-law) but three times passed over in the choice of caliph, in his place. However, a kinsman of the murdered 'Uthmān had been governor of the wealthy province of Syria since his appointment by 'Umar: when he now called upon Caliph 'Ali to bring the murderers to justice, the latter weakly temporized and was finally murdered in his turn by a small faction of rigorists who, proclaiming that "judgment belongs to God alone," condemned him for not suppressing the Syrian "rebel." Those serious Muslims who were already applying themselves to the study and interpretation of the Qur'ān as a guide to righteous and godly living had initially sided with 'Ali; but alarmed by the evident drift toward anarchy they now (A.D. 661) accepted the authority of the victorious governor of Syria, who made his capital, Damascus, the new seat of a hereditary Umayyad caliphate.

Twenty years later 'Ali's younger son, Husain, was persuaded by a faction of discontented tribal garrison troops in Iraq to lead a forlorn revolt against the Umayyad "usurpers," in the name of the "legitimacy" of 'Ali's and Husain's claims to the caliphate as kinsmen of the Prophet. The revolt was a disastrous failure that ended in their massacre; but it left a memory, among the underprivileged and disaffected, that the Shī'at 'Ali ("partisans of ʿAli'') were the defenders of Right as against Might; and to this day about 10 percent of Islam, especially in Iran where the Shīʿa since about A.D. 1500 has been the state religion revere ʿAli and Husain as martyr saints endowed with even greater charisma than Muhammad himself.

The Arab garrison troops, who had regarded the tax revenues of their respective provinces almost as their own property, were forced to yield some ground to Umayyad caliphs whose model of fiscal and administrative centralization was the Byzantine empire.[8] Centralized rule from Damascus was, however, unattainable over an empire that came to extend for five thousand miles from the Atlantic to Central Asia, and from the Sahara to the Caucasus—but significantly *excluding* the Byzantine Empire west of the Taurus mountain range. The non-Muslim cultivators, a majority of the total population, furnished the bulk of the revenue, and the Muslims, Arabs or converts, were a small, dominant and increasingly exploitative[9] minority. Conquest on the expanding frontiers, as in Turkestan, enabled the Umayyad caliphs to divert thither some of the most unruly of their Arab troops; but this was only buying time, it did not make them more obedient. Administratively the Umayyads enjoyed the skilled services of some of the Syrian Christian families that had hereditarily staffed the internal revenue service of the Byzantine rulers; and Byzantine architects and artists provided the skills and taste that embellished the Great Mosque at Damascus and the Dome of the Rock (miscalled ''Mosque of Omar'') at Jerusalem. Pious verses from the Qur'ān replaced imitations of the Byzantine emperor's portrait on the gold *dīnar,* and Arabic replaced Greek and Middle Persian as the language of administration.

A consecrated building or location has never been necessary for the performance of the ritual daily prayers *(al-ṣalāh)* by a Muslim individual or group, but only some indication of the direction of Mecca that the worshipper has to face. The emphasis placed by the Prophet at Medīna on the community's Friday midday prayers, however, did call for a ''mosque of assembly'' *(masjid jāmiʿ);*[10] and these were among the first buildings to be erected in each city taken over by conquest or surrender (for example, *al-Aqsā*, the real "Mosque of Omar," at Jerusalem) and in each new garrison town. The ban on the representation of living creatures was an obstacle to the development of Islamic art as a form of communication. By way of compensation, however, the high aesthetic possibilities of the Arabic script were developed very early. But whether the decorative repetition of dogmatic phrases from the Qur'ān is to be interpreted as a means of communication between the learned and the simple (see below), or rather as communication between man and God, must be left to an enquiry of greater insight than the present. The community repetition *(al-dhikr)* of divine names and epithets as a part of Sūfi rituals (see below) clearly falls into the second category—comparable with the Sanctus or Trisagion of conservative Christian worship.

In the field of law, the Prophet, especially during his ten years of administering the Muslim community at Medīna, had providentially received revelations conducive to the furthering of social justice, for example, enacting a tax whose proceeds would be devoted to the relief of the needy, regulating the distribution of a dead man's property among his kinsfolk, and defining women's and slaves' rights against exploitation. These pieces of legislation, compiled after the Prophet's death as part of the Qur'ān, had all the sanction of divine command; but because the Prophet's death was held to have placed the final seal on divine revelation, this source of legislation was now closed; and the caliph was, in theory at least, not a legislator but only the chief executive of a divine "constitution." Each Friday midday, at the community prayers instituted by the Prophet for that occasion, the caliph in his capital, or his deputy in each garrison town, mounted the pulpit, and girt with his sword of authority he delivered an address *(khutba)* that combined pious admonitions derived from the Qur'ān with pragmatic ad hoc orders by way of exegesis upon them. "Obey God . . . and the rulers whom He has sent" is a good example of the normative character of such Islamic precept; although it is only fair to add that, as in Judaism and Christianity, the diligent searcher of the scriptures could usually find a text to be interpreted in a diametrically opposite sense—if he could get away with it!

The positive legislation issued through the Prophet at

Medīna and incorporated into the Qur'ān contained, however, only a fraction of what was needed for the administration of this vast and heterogeneous empire. Rooted in the Islamic revelation, it was not applicable at all to the adherents of the Jewish, Christian, and Zoroastrian scriptures who still collectively constituted a large majority of the population of that empire; and provided that these non-Muslim subjects *(dhimmis)* gave no political trouble, they were allowed to continue under their own respective religious laws administered by their local rabbis or bishops.[11] For the Muslims themselves, the legal precepts of the Qur'ān came to be supplemented by the pre-Islamic customary law of whatever Arab tribe provided the majority of each garrison town; Byzantine or Iranian precedent was sometimes invoked in the former provinces of either of those empires; local administrators *(qādi)* sometimes relied on their personal judgment to resolve an ambiguity or fill a lacuna. Toward the end of the Umayyad dynasty, Islamic law had become a hodge-podge that distressed pious seekers after righteousness. They believed that the only legitimate basis of law lay in the divine revelations to the Prophet, and that all else was accretion and innovation, typical of the purse-proud Umayyads, who as a clan had been among the last in Mecca to accept the Prophet's message and later had usurped and retained by force the authority of his first "rightly guided" successors.[12]

Such conscientious objectors would not have sufficed by themselves to overturn the Umayyads; but after the Indian-summer reign of Hishām (724–743) all the pent-up frustrations of those Arab factions that were not the beneficiaries of Umayyad patronage found an outlet and a leadership. They were abetted by those artisan and other adherents of the Shīʿa who continued to identify legitimacy with the descendants or kin of the Prophet; and the conversion to Islam of substantial numbers of educated Iranians, who could now identify the Good Principle of their ancestral Zoroastrianism with Allah and his Messenger Muhammad but were still treated as dependents *(mawāli)*, swelled the revolutionary ranks.

In three short years (747–750) the Umayyads were swept from power and massacred, except for a survivor who escaped to rule in distant Spain. The new ruling clan traced their descent from the Prophet's uncle ʿAbbās; and because they had drawn the bulk of their revolutionary support from the provinces east of the Syrian Desert, they shifted the seat of their government eastward to the Tigris River and established a new capital at Baghdad, not too far from the seats of power in the Babylonian, Seleucid, Parthian, and Sasanian kingdoms of the past thirteen centuries. For some eighty years the ʿAbbāsids provided a succession of strong rulers under whom the agricultural and commercial economy of Iraq and the Persian Gulf made great advances; and they placed their authority on a more positive Islamic basis than the Umayyads had done. Those who sought in Islam a guide to right living had looked to the ʿAbbāsids to provide a government firmly rooted in the Qurʾān and in the verbally transmitted traditions of the Prophet's day-to-day behavior that the pious had begun to collect (or, where necessary, to invent) as precedents for this or that legal principle. The pious merchant, contemplating his Qurʾān and using his surplus of the world's goods for charitable purposes *(zakāh, waqf)* gradually replaced the warrior, except on the frontier, as the ideal Muslim.[13]

This is the milieu that provided the cultural setting for the much later *Thousand and One Nights*. But while that popular collection of tales romanticized the government of the Caliph "Aaron the Just" (Hārūn al-Rashīd, 786–809),

> . . . what was involved in the Abbasid revolution was the continued existence of the caliphate as an effective governing institution; and that in turn depended upon its becoming a truly Muslim institution, standing in a proper relation to all the institutions derived from the principles of the Islamic ideology. History . . . seems to show that the Abbasids failed in this respect as signally as the Umayyads, and in their failure, only a few decades after the reign of Harun, dragged the caliphate down with them. The nemesis of the over-rapid conquests of the Arabs—and the political tragedy of Islam—was that the Islamic ideology never found its proper and articulated expression in the political institutions of the Islamic states.[14]

## WITHIN EMPIRE, FACTION AND SECT

Hārūn's son al-Maʾmūn, born of an Iranian concubine and prevailing over his well-born half-brother, managed in an eventful reign of twenty years (813–833) both to provide an official institution for the translation of scholarly works from Greek, Syriac, and Persian to supplement the slender Arabic cultural heritage, and to adopt as his heir a short-lived descendant of ʿAli as a means, presumably, of reconciling the still dissident Shīʿa with the ʿAbbāsids as being at least kinsfolk of the Prophet *(ahl al-bayt)*. By this time, however, opposition to the Shīʿi assertion that the caliphate legitimately belonged only to ʿAli and his descendants had found expression in a counter-doctrine that legitimacy rested with the majority community that followed the supposed routine *(sunna,* literally "path") of the Prophet that provided no exceptional place for ʿAli. Further to exclude the Shīʿi emphasis on heredity, some of these Sunni theologians had interpreted phrases in the Qur'ān to mean that its verbal text did not merely convey what had been successively dictated to the Prophet by his supernatural mentor, but was the verbatim earthly copy of a Scripture existent in Heaven by God's command before His creation of the world! Al-Ma'mūn, perhaps in his effort to conciliate the Shīʿa, now required his judge-administrators *(qādi)* to make a formal repudiation of this doctrine of an eternal and uncreated Qur'ān; but this test act *(mihna)* imposed by al-Ma'mūn and his two successors served only to consolidate the noncooperation of those individual researchers into Islamic law and theology who now began to take on a corporate existence as the *ʿulamā* ("the learned," plural of *ʿālim* and equivalent to the Jewish rabbinate). Caliphs had perished before this, as we have seen, at the hands of individual assassins or armed revolution; but this was the first time that a caliph (al-Mutawakkil, circa 849) found it necessary to give way to the passive resistance of the scholars of Islam and tacitly to concede that they, and not he, were the proper guardians of Islamic orthodoxy and its transmission to future generations.[15]

This partial surrender of caliphal authority perhaps would not have been necessary if other surrenders had not already been exacted in still more sensitive areas. The eastward shift of the ʿAbbāsids' seat of government had led them to enlist the competent services of the Iranian secretary class *(kuttāb),* whose hereditary skills had come down from the Sasanian administration but whose rivalry with the unlettered Arab garrison troops was thus further emphasized. Although the revelation to the Prophet had minimized the tribal sense of pride based on kinship—"The noblest of you in God's sight is he who fears Him most"—the Old Adam had not been slow to reassert itself. We have already seen how the commercial acumen of the Umayyad clan had taken advantage of their indulgent kinsman, the Caliph ʿUthmān. In the following century the conversion to Islam of wide strata of the Iranian gentry had enabled them to preserve

> . . . their landed property, their social standing, their political influence—all this while keeping within their own traditional class hierarchy. With their inclusion in the leading stratum of the ʿAbbāsid capital two social systems came to coexist at court: the Arab-Muslim, which relegated the non-Arab to the bottom of the ladder, and the Iranian, which classed people according to profession rather than descent.

The competition between these two ethnic groups found expression in literary polemic and "on the whole . . . was conducted in a manner not worthy of the excellent scholarship of a goodly portion of the contestants."[16]

By the tenth century a series of local Iranian dynasties had secured their virtual independence of the Baghdad caliphate and were using a revived Islamic-Persian language as their vehicle of culture. At the same time, however, by a strange irony, the pre-Islamic rivalry between "Irān" and "Turān," between the Indo-European speaking occupants of the Iranian plateau and the speakers of other languages in Central Asia,[17] was being decided in favor of the latter because of their short-term utility as slave-soldiers obedient to their more sophisticated Arab or Iranian masters. Conversion to Islam was meanwhile being effected, both by the induction of these "Turkish" youths into the armed forces and by the individual "missionary" example of Muslim merchants trading beyond the frontiers *in partibus infidelium*.[18] However, the introduction of these semi-barbarous household troops among the turbulent populace of Baghdad, already begun by Hārūn, led to clashes between them and the underemployed xenophobic rabble,[19] until in A.D. 836

the Caliph al-Mu'tasim yielded to the Baghdad populace by withdrawing himself and his household troops to a new capital at Sāmarrā, three days' journey up the Tigris.

This retreat did not purchase any peace for the caliphs, however. Instead, the commanders of the household troops, promoted from the ranks for their toughness and ability to command obedience, soon became veritable king-makers. Caliphs who resisted them were murdered or forced to abdicate, and another helpless scion of the polygamously numerous 'Abbāsid clan substituted as caliph—*appellatio sine corpore ac specie,* as Julius Caesar was reported to have said of the Roman "republic" of his time.[20] The military governors of the outlying provinces, although they continued to pay lip-service to the caliphate, remitted a rapidly diminishing proportion of their revenues to the central treasury: they sought to make their provincial authority hereditary in their own families, and they waged little wars of aggression or revenge against neighboring governors.

By A.D. 900, the unity of the Islamic empire *(dār al-Islām),* which, given its vastness and the slowness of its communications, had always been a figure of speech rather than a political organism, had lost any pretension to reality. However, the breakdown of political centralization resulted in a cultural flowering and healthy diversity. Independent rulers came to have their courts extending in a chain from Bukhāra and Samarqand in the northeast to Palermo, Fez, and Cordova in the west. The example previously set by the 'Abbāsid caliphs in Baghdad caused some of these rulers to extend their patronage to poets, scholars, physicians, artists, and so forth; and for three or four centuries culture flourished in their courts as later in those of the Italian Renaissance.[21]

But the radiation of that high culture did not extend far beyond those courts, and outside the cities it was rarified indeed:

No matter how important the contribution Muslim scholars were able to make to the natural sciences, and no matter how great the interest with which, at certain periods, the leading classes and the government itself followed and supported their researches, those sciences (and their technological application) had no root in the fundamental needs and aspirations of their civilization. Those accomplishments of Islamic mathematical and medical science which continue to compel our admiration were developed in areas and in periods where the elites were willing to go beyond and possibly against the basic strains of orthodox thought and feeling. For the sciences never did shed the suspicion of bordering on the impious. . . . That is why the pursuit of the natural sciences as that of philosophy tended to become located in relatively small and esoteric circles. . . .[22]

A small group calling themselves the "Brethren of Purity" *(Ikhwān al-Safā')* produced at Basra in the tenth century a "massive, though often ill-organized, verbose and repetitious compendium" of the sciences. Its first Western translators overstated its value, and there is no evidence for its diffusion outside the group.[23] The distinction between *al-khāṣṣ* and *al-ʿāmm*, between "gentle" and "simple,"[24] was probably no less sharp then in Islam than in the contemporary West: only the greater numbers, activity, and prestige of the merchant class raised that civilization above that of Europe as the latter began imperceptibly to emerge from its "dark age."

The de facto military rulers in *dār al-Islām*, whatever their ethnic origin, had their ruthless and effective methods of enforcing their wills and stamping out opposition.[25] But it cannot be too much emphasized that for the ordinary Muslim, and still more for the *ʿulamā*, the *amīr*, or *sultān* or whatever his title might be, although a military ruler wielded power of life and death, he lacked the legitimacy that inhered to the caliphate (however impotent in fact) because of its apostolic succession from the Prophet's deathbed and consequent link with the Divine *fiat lux* of Islam. For all but the most uncompromising *ʿulamā*, the *de facto* ruler was to be endured or obeyed, as long as he defended the frontiers of Islam and did not openly outrage its precepts; but unlike the caliph he was not the explicit "commander of the faithful" *(amīr al-mu'minīn)*, and there was no sin in flouting his edicts and evading his commands if this could be done with practical impunity.

The *ʿulamā* asserted that their consensus should be accepted as representative of the whole body of Muslims, but such a role was never institutionalized either by the rulers or the masses;[26] and political speculation among the *ʿulamā* during this "time of troubles" (circa 830–1060) consisted largely in devising the theoretical critera for choosing and maintaining an *ideal* caliph, or in condoning the unedifying present reality by invoking the principles of *ḍarūra* (necessity) and *istiṣlāḥ* ("public interest"), that is, the choice of the lesser evil![27]

Insofar as individuals felt loyalty to any institution beyond their family or clan, it was not (except for the courtier) to the ruler or any ephemeral territorial state, but to *dār al-Islām* as an idealized abstraction. The inculcation of Islamic doctrine and ethics was the self-imposed duty of the *ʿulamā,* not yet however in any organized seminaries or schools but in the one-to-one relation of teacher to pupil, taking the Qur'ān as the basic text and proceeding from rote-learning, through reading and grammar, to exegesis at varying levels of subtlety. The spread of Islam from the towns, where it began, to the peasantry of the countryside is something we cannot measure even approximately. The villagers encountered the town-dwellers essentially as collectors of taxes or rents, or as hard bargainers in commercial transactions; and as in the earlier conversion of the *pagani,* or "heathen," to Christianity, it often must have been a following the line of least resistance, if not yielding to coercion or material inducement, rather than a conversion from the heart.

The study of the urban structure has been complicated until recently by a paradox not unlike one resolved by Sherlock Holmes: the "remarkable behavior of the dog in the night-time,"[28] which consisted in his doing nothing in circumstances that should have provoked a canine challenge. Forty years ago a most distinguished European scholar of Islam advanced a theory postulating the existence of craft "guilds" in the Islamic cities going back to the tenth century A.D., although he admitted that the detailed evidence still had to be brought together. By 1965, on the contrary, the absence of such evidence had been laid bare; and the counterassertion was made that it was the city governor's institution of an official to regulate material and moral standards among the artisans *(al-muḥtasib),* and the latter's appointment of a responsible spokesman within each craft, that gave the first impetus toward the formation of guilds, which took on a more genuinely corporate character under Ottoman rule (and therefore beyond the limits of the present chapter).[29]

In the cities, however, serious men and women (inasmuch as the social seclusion of women was something borrowed gradually from Iranian or Ottoman example, rather than inherent in Islam) had come to contrast the material wealth and ostentation of their well-to-do contemporaries with the traditions of simple living attached to the memories of the Prophet and the first caliphs, especially ʿUmar. Little informal groups of ascetics, most of whom belonged to the artisan classes,[30] received the nickname of *Ṣūfīs* because of their garments of coarse wool *(ṣūf)* worn as a challenge to the silks and brocades around them. Later, some of these reacted further against the scholarship of the *ʿulamā* that sometimes degenerated into logic chopping in defense of ritual, doctrinal, or legalistic minutiae. This, said the *Ṣūfīs,* is a religion of the limbs merely, not the religion of the heart that God sent us through His Messenger. For further edification they looked beyond the conventional limits of Sunni Islam, some to the Shīʿa with its ecstatic passion play in annual commemoration of its martyrs, ʿAli and Husain and his companions. Others ventured outside Islam to imitate rituals practiced by Iranian, or Oriental Christian, or even Hindu sects whereby the individual sought by degrees to divest himself of his encumbering ego and achieve total absorption *(fanāʾ)* in the divine Essence. One itinerant *Ṣūfī* boldly challenged the conventionally pious: "If ye do not recognize God, at least recognize his signs. I am that sign. I am the Creative Truth, because through the Truth I am a truth eternally"—for which "blasphemy" he was tortured and crucified by the civic authorities with the evident approval of the outraged Baghdad rabble.[31]

Again in the cities, the ordinary man's lack of legal recourse against excesses committed by the troops of the local military commander led to a type of spontaneous self-help. Sturdy unmarried young men were organized into groups, banded together by initiation ceremonies and a kind of uniform, that were ready to engage in street fighting with the local soldiery with or without provocation. They were sometimes supported by the storekeepers, *ʿulamā,* and other well-to-do elements and called by such complimentary titles as *al-futuwwa* or *al-aḥdāth,* the "junior league." Some city authorities even gave them temporary official status as a municipal police force; but at other times or places such groups degenerated into operating "protection rackets" at the expense of more substantial citizens, and in such cases hostile writers describe them as *al-ʿayyārūn,* "riff-raff."[32] This, after all, is how the Cuban bourgeoisie regarded Castro, and perhaps how the Cardinal Archbishop of Armagh privately regards the Irish Republican Army.

### SHIʿI SECESSION AND SUNNI REFORM

Besides these manifestations of social diversity within Islam there were militant secessionist movements to harass the self-appointed "delegates" of the Baghdad caliphate. One such group seized control of the Gulf coast and part of central Arabia circa A.D. 900 and, according to their "orthodox" opponents at least, extended their interpretation of the social justice enjoined by Islam to enforce the sharing of property and even wives! Of longer duration and greater significance was the simultaneous seizure of power in Tunisia and Sicily by a group who were an offshoot of the Shīʿa in claiming legitimate caliphal descent from ʿAli and the Prophet's daughter Fātima (whence the term Fātimid for this new dynasty). Onto the Shīʿi trunk, however, their principal ideologue seems to have grafted an esoteric set of doctrines derived from the Gnostic and Neoplatonic theories of the pre-Islamic Near East and stemming ultimately from Iranian dualism. Between the Transcendent God who presides over the universe and the sordid material world of man's senses, there interposed a lengthy hierarchy of "principalities and powers," high among them the Logos or divine Reason that, having taken part in creating the universe, had then voluntarily accepted separation from the Godhead in order to implant some sparks of Light in our "muddy vesture of decay": some men at least might apprehend enough of this Light to retread the laborious ascent back to union with the Eternal.[33]

The indebtedness of some *Ṣūfī* thought to these doctrines will be evident; and both groups saw the conventional scriptures, including that of Islam, as a mere starting point for the common man which the more adept would leave behind in his quest for the divine Gnosis (in Arabic, *ma'rifa,* contrasted with the dead book learning, *'ilm,* of the *'ulamā).* But whereas the *Ṣūfī* brotherhoods were mostly (although not all) peaceful contemplatives, the Fātimids mobilized the soldierly qualities of the Berbers of North Africa (who earlier had provided most of the manpower, under Arab leadership, for the conquest of Spain), and by A.D. 969 had wrested control of the immensely fertile Nile valley from an effete line of Turkish military adventurers.

From their new capital at Cairo the Fātimids proceeded to wage war against the self-appointed "delegates" of the feeble Baghdad caliphate, and this not merely by military means. The first Fātimids, with their elitist conception of man's ascent to divine Truth, could hardly have been further removed from the crude materialist egalitarianism of our latter-day communists; but they shared with Lenin and his disciples a keen awareness of the efficacy of subtle agitation and propaganda in undermining the wills and morale of their opponents. To make converts among the toiling, unimaginative peasantry and craftsmen of their Egyptian power base was no part of their purpose; but their Cairo seminary of *al-Azhar* (founded A.D. 972) was planned to train their missionaries who would go out by ones and twos into the eastern lands and assiduously turn men's minds from the humdrum theology of the Sunni *'ulumā* to their own teaching:

> To the spiritual, they brought a warm, personal, emotional faith, sustained by the example of the suffering of the Imams and the self-sacrifice of their followers—the experience of Passion, and the attainment of the Truth. To the discontented . . . they offered the attraction of a well-organized, widespread and powerful opposition movement, which seemed to provide a real possibility of overthrowing the existing order, and establishing in its place a new and just society, headed by the Imam—the heir of the Prophet, the chosen of God, and the sole rightful leader of mankind.[34]

Believing that the conventional religions were merely the foundation stones of their own spiritual power edifice, the

Fāṭimids showed tolerance and alacrity in admitting Jewish, Greek, and Armenian men with financial, military, or administrative talents to the highest positions of their government, with only perfunctory evidence of their conversion. Although both the Umayyad and the ʿAbbāsid caliphates had traded with the Byzantine Empire in the intervals of warfare, the Fāṭimids went further in supplementing Egypt's import needs (particularly in lumber, other accessories for shipbuilding, and white slaves) by establishing closer trade relations with the rising commercial cities of Italy, especially Amalfi; and the precious documents preserved in the Cairo *genīza* demonstrate in detail how the correspondence of Jewish traders from the western Mediterranean to India converged on the Fāṭimid capital.[35] As Baghdad and Iraq languished under their military exploiters, the Red Sea took the place of the Persian Gulf as the main trade route by which the commodities of India and China were exchanged for those of *dār al-Islām*.

The confrontation in Syria, between the militant Fāṭimid caliphate and the adventurers (some of them men of ability and culture) battening upon the Baghdad caliphate, had two consequences. First, the Byzantine emperors seized the opportunity of Islamic division to annex an important part of coastal Syria, including the Christian patriarchal city of Antioch, and establish relatively peaceful relations with the Fāṭimids in the early eleventh century. More important for the future of Islam, some *ʿulamā* of the cities of Khurāsān (northeast Iran) seem to have instituted a more structured educational system than anything attempted hitherto in Sunni Islam. This was the *madrasa*, in which students received instruction in the sacred law *(al-sharīʿa)* and in juridical theology.[36] By a fortunate coincidence for Sunni Islam this educational innovation coincided with the expansion into northeast Iran from the Oxus region about 1040 of a Turkish tribal confederacy whose leaders, descended from one Seljuq, undertook the military conquest of the Islamic East. As part of Baghdad's resistance, the Friday midday *khutba* was actually given out in the name of the *Fāṭimid* caliph (1059), just before the Seljuq *sultān* established himself as the latest "delegate" of the ʿAbbāsid caliph, even to obtaining eventually the hand in marriage of the latter's daughter—a descendant of God's Messenger yielding to the embraces of a barbarian from the back of beyond![37]

For the next thirty years a consummate Iranian administrator for the Seljuq *sultāns,* Nizām al-Mulk, extended his powerful patronage to a whole series of *madrasa,* whereby the tide of Fātimid "subversion" was stemmed and eventually turned backward whence it came. It does not seem to have been a deliberate item of Seljuq policy to pick a quarrel with the Byzantine Empire; but the Seljuq advance southwestward from the Oxus River had been accompanied by a westward drift of thousands of their tribal followers in search of pasturage for their herds. The diversion of these unruly tribesmen to the north of the Fertile Crescent against the eastern borders of the Byzantine Empire brought disaster (A.D. 1071) upon a Byzantine army enfeebled by two generations of destructive intrigue between its "feudal" commanders and the jealous civil bureaucracy. While the Turkish hordes overran the greater part of Asia Minor, subjecting its nominally Christian peasantry to their overlordship, the Seljuq sultanate itself fell apart. The Seljuqs, after all, were only three generations removed from the nomad pastoral life and, deprived of the worldly wisdom of their Iranian *vezīr* by the assassination of Nizām al-Mulk (1092), they proceeded on the death of Malik Shah, which shortly followed, to parcel out their vast "real estate" among the many scions of their ruling family. Those who were under age were furnished with "guardians" *(atābeg)* of more mature administrative experience, and most of these were not slow to make their provincial or local authority absolute. Amid the headlong collapse of Seljuq unity a Byzantine emperor appealed to the Pope for manpower from the West to recover the lost lands of the East and especially the Holy Places of Christendom.

The First Crusade of 1099 was the response. From the Islamic point of view it meant that what Arab legalists had called *dār-al-ḥarb,* the regions inhabited by unbelievers in which Islam might lawfully wage war and take slaves and other booty as a pious exercise *(jihād fi sabīl Allāh),*[38] had recovered its morale and cohesion and begun a counteroffensive, first in Spain and North Syria, then in Sicily, and now in the eastern Mediterranean itself. More significant than the Frankish counteroffensive itself, however, was the feebleness and tardiness of concerted Muslim resistance. The two main centers of Seljuq power were now Konya in Turkey, bypassed by the Crusader advance from Constantinople, and Isfahān in distant Iran. The caliph in Baghdad was as helpless as ever. Local Turkish commanders in Aleppo and Damascus, inveterately jealous of one another, had to organize their local defenses and sometimes conclude bilateral pacts with a local Crusader prince after the Franks' successful lodgement along the Levant coast and in Jerusalem.

It was forty years before an *atābeg* of Mosul in northern Iraq, taking advantage of the quarrels now endemic among the Crusader leaders themselves, began to expel the latter from their most exposed position in northern Syria. His greater son, Nūr al-Dīn, moving his base of operations to Aleppo, took further advantage of the Crusaders' preoccupation with advancing southward at the expense of the now moribund Fātimid caliphate in Egypt. The young Kurd Salāh al-Dīn (Saladin), despatched with his uncle to Egypt by Nūr al-Dīn to consolidate Muslim resistance there, supplanted the last Fātimid by force in 1171; and the death of Nūr al-Dīn three years later enabled Salāh al-Dīn (not without some jealous Muslim opposition) to complete the encirclement by land of the Crusader kingdom of Jerusalem and inflict on it the shattering defeat of the Horns of Hittīn (1187).

This restoration of Muslim supremacy in the Levant by no means had been purely military, however. As they consolidated their control successively over Aleppo, Damascus, Cairo, and elsewhere, Nūr al-Dīn and Salāh al-Dīn had followed the example of Nizām al-Mulk in establishing in each city a Sunni *madrasa* that would train not merely canon lawyers but administrators for the Islamic state—it was now that *al-Azhar* at Cairo was stripped of its Shī'i origins and became the seminary of Sunni Islam, which it remained without interruption until the present century.

The picture provided by our sources of the influence that Salāh al-Dīn's propaganda had exercised over Damascus, Aleppo, and Mosul, before he annexed those cities [1174, 1183, 1185], is very fragmentary and incoherent. What emerges incontestably from these sources is that, partly before and partly after their annexation, this propaganda effectively won over the men of religion to Salāh al-Dīn's side. It was through them that his regime acquired a popular base. There is no more eloquent proof of this adherence of the men of religion than the fact that they took it upon themselves to disseminate his "holy war" propaganda and actively engaged in that war. At least 17 out of the 23 propagandists whose names we know belonged to that class without adding many others, such as mosque preachers, whom we cannot identify. . . .

The men of religion were of the first importance not only in calling for the "final struggle" against the Crusaders, but also in maintaining the morale of Salāh al-Dīn and his army in the course of the struggle. . . . The part played by both ʿulamā and ṣūfīs in combat was also an example and a stimulus. . . . This apparently reached its peak at the battle of Hittīn where the Muslim army included many "volunteers, men of pious and austere habit and dedication, ṣūfīs, ʿulamā, and scholars."

.    .    .

However, the ideological movement launched by Salāh al-Dīn saw its forces stretched to their limit, and the symptoms of decline and detente were already visible in the last years of his life (1189–93). The limitations of the idea of the *jihād* revealed themselves: the failure to interest distant Islamic countries in the war; the inability to maintain for long the warlike fervor in the countries nearer to the Levant coast; finally the excessive dependence on a single man. His removal threatened the movement with ruin.[39]

For the first time in Islam, however, higher education for government and public service was being given a unified structure:

In the early centuries, the colleges did do much to stimulate intellectual activities, even if the range of humanistic studies was restricted within by the exclusion of philosophy and the natural sciences, with the sole exception of medicine. . . . But in the course of time every institution tends to run down unless rejuvenated by influences from outside; its actions become stereotyped and its range narrows. This was particularly true in the Islamic *madrasas,* where the forms, subjects, methods, and textbooks became so standardized that ultimately . . . it became difficult to distinguish between books produced in Cairo, Delhi, Istanbul, or Timbuktu. The *madrasa* thus led to intellectual sterility, not in the sense that its scholarship was not thorough and refined within its own sphere or that it was not productive or creative . . . , but because it closed the minds of its members to anything outside its established range of religious and philological studies.[40]

In the *madrasa,* as in the medieval European university, communication was essentially confined within that clerisy whose professional education was the purpose of the institution.[41] To the urban craftsman, and still more to the peasantry, that higher education had nothing directly to offer, although the occasional "lad of parts" was never excluded from it, and *ʿulamā* were the source of expertise to whom the common man turned as we go to attorneys with our legal problems. More significantly, however, the "religion of the heart" pursued in the informal *Ṣūfī* brotherhoods had effected some compromise with formal Sunni "orthodoxy." The initiative seems to have come from some individual *ʿulamā* who, conscious that their book learning was spiritually barren and making contact with some *Ṣūfīs,* found (like stalwart John Wesley at the Aldersgate Street meeting) that their hearts were "strangely warmed" by the experience. The turning point came when al-Ghazāli, professor of Sharīʿa law at Nizām al-Mulk's endowed Baghdad *madrasa,* resigned his chair to spend the next ten years as a *Ṣūfī* contemplative. Thereafter, although the two functions remained separate, some *ʿulamā* came to concede that *Ṣūfī* rituals might legitimately reinforce the masses' obedience to Islam; and the endowment by pious and wealthy men of *Ṣūfī* seminaries *(zāwiya, khānaqāh, ribāt)* gave more formal instruction to the *shaykh* or *dervīsh* or *pīr* who went out to preach among the common and largely illiterate people. Through this dual channel of religious propaganda a loose unity of Sunni Islam was retained, despite political vicissitude and economic stagnation, until the impact of secular "modernisms" from the unbelieving West in the last hundred years.[42]

Translation from the Greek, unofficially undertaken already before the end of the Umayyad dynasty, had long introduced some Islamic theologians to Greek philosophy and to the possibility of discussing Islamic dogma in terms of Greek philosophical conceptions. Within this intellectual spectrum, however, there was clearly a very wide range. At one end the *ʿulamā* were primarily Islamic apologists but (with the exception of the rigorist Ḥanbali school) justified the borrowing of systematic logic from Greek scholarship as a weapon for defending their own doctrinal positions and combating those of rival schools. At the other extreme were men who were primarily freethinkers, and often at the same time physicians and scientists like Ibn Sina (Avicenna), who were nevertheless able to adapt a framework of Islamic conceptions to their philosophy. In so doing they illuminated the Islamic revelation for other intellectuals who lacked their own originality of thought;[43] but such independence naturally became suspect to the *ʿulamā* as they gradually closed the "door of *ijtihād* ";[44] and the patronage extended by the Seljuq and later rulers to the *ʿulamā,* in the interest of ideological solidarity against Fātimid "subversion" and the Frankish or Mongul invaders, naturally made the philosophers increasingly isolated: Ibn Sina was specifically refuted *(tahāfut)* by the "Restorer of Islam," al-Ghazāli. In distant Spain the reaction of the North African Almoravid and Almohad dynasties to the Christian conquests of the eleventh century was to insist on the dissemination of religious conservatism among the Islamic masses, while at the same time the freethinking Ibn Rushd (Averroes) was briefly tolerated at the Almohad court. This involved Ibn Rushd (like St. Thomas Aquinas?) in some degree of casuistical double-talk. By the time of his death (1198) the period of court toleration was over as the external political situation worsened; and "the thought of the great Aristotelian penetrated more easily into Christian Europe than into the Islamic heartlands. . . . "[45] The same can be said two centuries later of the thought of the sociologist of Islam, Ibn Khaldūn, whom recent "Arab" scholarship has rediscovered via his European admirers![46]

### THE END OF "CLASSICAL" ISLAM
The dissolution of Seljuq unity had released the ʿAbbāsid caliphs in Baghdad from their subservience, at least in lower Iraq; and shortly after Salāh al-Dīn's death in Damascus an

unusually long-lived caliph, al-Nāsir (reign, 1180–1225) seems
to have attempted to strengthen the newly devised institutions
of Sunni solidarity still further by extending his patronage and
some organization to those young men's groups *(al-futuwwa)* to
whose informal origins and confused purposes we have referred
above.[47] Before such measures could have any effect, however,
eastern Islam was disrupted by an external enemy far more terrible than the compromising later Crusaders, namely, the Mongols. The rich cities of Iran were successively looted of their treasures before the death of Chingiz Khan in 1227. Thirty years
later the ill-judged defiance of a caliph left Baghdad exposed to
pillage and deportation at the hands of Hulāgu. In the following fifty years the great cities of Syria suffered devastation at the
Mongols' predatory hands, and it was only the commanders of a
Turkish slave army (the Mamlūks) based in Egypt that drove the
Mongols back east of the Syrian desert and at the same time dis-
lodged the last despairing Crusaders from their toeholds on the
Levant coast.

In 1243, meanwhile, the Seljuq sultanate of Rum ("Rome"),
that had greatly extended its hold on Turkey after the Venetian
and Crusader rape of Constantinople in 1204, had had to accept
the role of mere tax collectors for the seemingly invincible Mongols. The resultant Seljuq fragmentation left inter alia an obscure family ruling locally in northwest Turkey to confront the
scanty remnant of the Byzantine Empire. From these descendants of Osman there was to spring a dynasty that would establish a new Islamic imperial power over the Near East and a large
part of southeastern Europe; but "classical Islam" had expired
in the sack of Baghdad, and the study of communication in the
Ottoman Empire will be the subject of the next chapters of this
study.

### CONCLUSIONS

From the foregoing there emerges clearly the tardiness and in-
completeness of any attempt to integrate the society of "classical Islam" in any meaningful communication system; but in
this, Islam was no more culpable of neglect than its two elder
sisters among the monotheistic religions. The indifference of
the *ʿulamā* for the peasant masses is paralleled by the rabbinic
disdain for the *ʿam-ha-āretz* in post-exilic Judaism, and by the

communication gap that separated the monasteries of medieval
Christendom from the serfs outside their walls. More serious for
the effectiveness of classical Islam as a political organism was the
relatively early breakdown of executive authority, vested as if by
divine sanction in the caliphate, into the two mutually opposed
groups of soldier-administrators (*ahl al-sayf*, "men of the
sword") and scholar-jurists, the *'ulamā*. The factionalism and
undiscipline of the original Arab tribal warriors had left the
ninth-century caliphs with no real choice except to recruit slave
troops; but the alacrity with which the commanders of the latter
took the caliphs prisoner, and the disdain that the *'ulamā* felt
for these commanders on account of the superficiality of their
Islamic culture and ethic, had the effect of fatally dividing
the ruling class.[48] The military commanders needed the professional skills of the *'ulamā* to fill vital positions as judge-
administrators *(qādi)*; but the more scrupulous of the *'ulamā*
deplored the moral compromises incurred by their more needy
brethren in serving the "Mammon of unrighteousness," and
preferred the independence and irresponsibility of dissent. The
classical Arabic word *mukallaf*, which implied responsibility for
one's religious duties,[49] has been replaced in contemporary
Arabic by *mas'ūl*—not "one who can answer" like the Latin
*responsible*, but "one who is asked" or, more idiomatically, a
"fall guy." It is also pertinent that Arabic, while rich in words
embodying the sense of divine or political unity *(waḥda, taw-
ḥīd, ittiḥād)*, has no word that adequately conveys the Roman
law concepts of "federation" or "confederation." The word
*i'tilāf* that was used by liberal opponents of the Young Turk
"Committee of Union and Progress," 1908–1914, means no
more than "harmony, agreement, coalition" and lacks the
greater precision of our borrowings from the Latin.

Islamic thought, in fact, seems to lack any intermediate concepts between dependence and independence, between free-
man and slave. Man's relation to God in the Qur'ān is that of a
slave to his master;[50] and although that master is generous
*(karīm)* and forgiving *(raḥmān)*, the slave has still at the Judgment Day to cross that bridge "as slender as a hair and as sharp
as the edge of a sword." Moreover, evil is somehow part of
God's creation, and it is never clear whether man's evil acts are
predestined by God's will or part of man's individual responsi-

bility.[51] Muhammad, as we have seen, is merely the "messenger" of God, not an atoning mediator between man and God as Christian doctrine made of Jesus: the modern popular concept of Muhammad "the Friend" is apparently an attempt to borrow from Christian thought to fill this psychological hiatus. In classical Islam there was the more comfortable doctrine that the simple Muslim declaration of faith in the One God and his Messenger would in itself keep a man out of those various hells designed for the various sects of unbelievers; and that acts of piety and charity, especially the dedication of part of his property to religious purposes, would secure him a place in heaven. Once again, the parallelism of classical Islam and some aspects of Latin Christianity is striking.

If the soldiery, despite their internecine factions, extended and for centuries maintained the wide frontiers of Islam, it was the *ʿulamā* who defended its intellectual heritage. Although the period A.D. 800–1250, first in the Persian Gulf area and then in Egypt, was a period of great commercial activity (great, at least, in comparison with the European decline after A.D. 150 and notwithstanding its slow recovery after A.D. 1000), it is striking that biographies of notable men, which constitute an important part of classical Arabic literature, apparently contain no lives of merchants per se.[52] Such biographies were, of course, compiled by the *ʿulamā*, and although they might commemorate a scholar who owed his economic independence to trade (as many did in the early centuries), the career of a "merchant prince" as such would make no more intrinsic appeal to them than, say, the career of a J. Pierpont Morgan to an Arnold J. Toynbee. Medieval Muslim sociologists apparently were not confident how to classify "trade"; and political theorists at the height of the Ottoman Empire circa 1500, attempting to define the ideal society as an equilibrium of four social classes on the analogy of the four natural "elements," relegated merchants and traders to the third class, the "people of the bazaar" *(ahl al-sūq),* only one notch above the lowly peasantry.[53] The analogy with the Hindu caste structure and with the former disdain of the English gentry and professional classes for anything connected with "trade" is striking.

The military commanders of the slave troops (Mamlūks), who between 1250 and 1300 repelled the Mongol invaders of Syria and Palestine and expelled the last of the Crusaders from the Levant ports, established a dynasty that (not without many bloody struggles for the succession) lasted in Egypt and Syria until it was overthrown by the Ottoman advance in 1516–1517. Initially these Mamlūks had been recruited by the short-lived dynasty (1171–1250) founded by Salāh al-Dīn, and in many respects they continued the policies of their patrons by cruder means. The student of ancient history is tempted to make an analogy with those stern military commanders who struggled to restore order to the Roman Empire out of the "great anarchy," A.D. 235 to about 260.

The Mamlūks thus continued to favor the *madrasa* and the Sunni *'ulamā* as instruments of policy, while leaving the common people "between violence and impotence."[54] The abortive attempts at collusion between Crusaders and Mongols, however, made them ruthless toward the former and the hapless oriental Christians; and the Mongol tendency, at the sack of Baghdad and elsewhere, to show greater clemency to the Shī'a made the Mamlūks correspondingly repressive of the Shī'a, which until then had been strongly represented in the Syrian cities.[55] By this time the Coptic-speaking Christians, who had been a strong majority of the inhabitants of Egypt during the early centuries of Islam, but had been gradually yielding to Islamization and Arabization, succumbed to their military masters.[56] The last vestiges of the Christian kingdom of Nubia, in what is now the northern Sudan, were snuffed out;[57] and except where mountain ridges provided a refuge for minority sects (The Druze and the still Aramic-speaking Maronites of Mt. Lebanon), or a warlike frontier made for some fluidity (as for the Shī'a of lower Iraq with their relation to Safavi Iran after A.D. 1500), the process of institutionalization and *Gleichschaltung* had already begun.

When at the end of World War II the Lebanese Republic was recognized as a sovereign state, an embittered French scholar remarked with some justice that Lebanon was not a nation but "no more than an *emulsion* of sectarian communities . . . ."[58] One might retroject his metaphor by suggesting that classical *dār al-Islām* had been an "emulsion" of ethnic, social, and economic groups held in loose association by an "emulsifier," the Islamic faith of their ruling classes. The founders of the Ottoman Empire, shocked by the defection of many of their Muslim-Turkish vassals in 1402 to Timur Leng, their rival for the sultanate in Islam,[59] found it necessary to supplement the Islamic "emulsifier" by a series of institutional "prosthetics." The final failure, in our own century, of the Ottoman Empire to adapt its institutions to a rapidly changing world has left *dār al-Islām* carried about with every wind of (secular) doctrine; and "The Search for an Islamic Democracy" seems even further from its goal today than when Sir Hamilton Gibb propounded the question some twenty years ago.[60] Among his last published words he added:

> When the religious leaders of Islam once again—as in the early centuries—study their disciplines in the immediate environment and in personal contact with the intellectual movements of their own age, and when they can fully understand the challenges of a developing social economic organization to the older and simpler social structures and ideological molds, they may learn how to meet them and at the same time transform Islam in their own thought from an inert to a dynamic principle. And when the secular leaders, administrators, and professionals, in their turn, learn to understand the spiritual values that inhere in Islam, this understanding may in time discipline the pragmatism and control the subjective impulsiveness which, in seeking to restore the strength of Islam as a political concept, destroy its inner spirit and tear the historical Community asunder.[61]

FIDEI HAVD INDIGNAE SYMBOLVM
LVX PERPETVA LVCEAT EIS[62]

NOTES

1. See Irfan Shahīd, in *Cambridge History of Islam,* eds. P. M. Holt et al. (Cambridge University Press, 1970), vol. 1, pp. 22–23 and vol. 2, pp. 658–659.

2. See W. Montgomery Watt, *Muhammad: Prophet and Statesman* (Oxford University Press, 1961), p. 117.

3. See A. J. Wensinck, "Rasūl" in *Shorter Encyclopaedia of Islam,* eds. H. A. R. Gibb and J. H. Kramers (1965), pp. 469–470.

4. Watt, *Muhammad: Prophet and Statesman,* pp. 60–65.

5. Ibid., pp. 36–39.

6. Grammatically, *islām* is the verbal noun of the verb *aslama;* its active participle is *muslim*, to be preferred to the conventional form "Moslem," an example of French pseudophonetics with nothing to recommend it in an English context.

7. See Bernard Lewis, *The Arabs in History* (London, 1964), pp. 77–78.

8. See M. A. Shaban, *Islamic History*, A.D. *600-750* (Cambridge University Press, 1971), pp. 111–117, 166–167.

9. H. Idris Bell criticized "an exaggerated emphasis on the fiscal factor" in the "Umayyad Administration of Egypt," *Byzantinische Zeitschrift* 28 (1928): 285–286.

10. The root *JMᶜ* is semantically related to both "synagogue" and "convent," and from it Arabic formed the verbal noun *ijmāᶜ*, "consensus." This came in practice to be embodied in, or usurped by, the consensus of the scholar-jurists, and led eventually to the closing out of independent judgment (see discussion of *madrasa*, below).

11. In Iran, where the influence of the Zoroastrian clergy had collapsed, this administrative role continued to be filled by the *dihqān*, or village headman. See Ann K. S. Lambton, in *Encyclopaedia of Islam*, vol. 2, 2d ed. (1965), pp. 253–254.

12. For laymen the treatment of this subject by N. J. Coulson, *A History of Islamic Law* (Edinburgh, 1964), chaps. 2 and 3, is recommended, despite the strictures of the distinguished Central European scholar Joseph Schacht published in *Middle Eastern Studies* 1 (1965): 388–400.

13. See Maxime Rodinson, "Le Marchand Musulman," in *Islam and the Trade of Asia*, ed. D. S. Richards (1970), pp. 28–29 and references there cited.

14. Hamilton A. R. Gibb, *Studies on the Civilization of Islam* (1962), p. 45.

15. Al-Ma'mūn had relied too much on the rational views of a minority. See W. Montgomery Watt, *Islamic Philosophy and Theology* (Edinburgh, 1962), pp. 47, 62–63, and *Islamic Political Thought* (Edinburgh, 1986), pp. 87–89. The attempt of the *ᶜulamā* to gain governmental recognition as representing the community never got beyond theorizing; see Malcolm H. Kerr, *Islamic Reform* (Berkeley: University of California Press, 1966), pp. 159–166.

16. Gustave E. von Grunebaum, *Medieval Islam* (University of Chicago Press, 1961), pp. 202–204. This Kulturkampf was called by the Arabic historians *al-shuᶜūbīya*, from the plural of the Arabic *shaᶜb*, "people," "nation."

17. See Richard N. Frye and Aydin M. Sayili, "Turks in the Middle East before the Saljuqs," *Journal of the American Oriental Society* 63 (1943): 194–207.

18. See J. Spencer Trimingham, *A History of Islam in West Africa* (Oxford University Press, 1970), pp. 27–33.

19. See J. M. Rogers, in *The Islamic City*, eds. A. H. Hourani and S. M. Stern (University of Pennsylvania Press, 1970), pp. 128–130. Present-day "confrontations" between self-appointed urban rabble and "the military" will readily occur to the reader.

20. "A mere name without body or substance."

21. On the distinction made between the Islamic and the "foreign" or "useful" arts and sciences, see G. E. von Grunebaum, *Islam: Essays in the Nature and Growth of a Cultural Tradition* (London: Routledge and Kegan Paul, 1961), chap. 6, "Muslim World View and Muslim Science."

22. Ibid., p. 114. For a justification of the Muslim pursuit of "spiritual perfection and deliverance," as against the Western post-Renaissance pursuit of quantification and technology, see Seyyed Hossein Nasr, *Science and Civilization in Islam* (Cambridge, Mass.: Harvard University Press, 1968), Introduction, especially p. 39.

23. Majid Fakhry, *A History of Islamic Philosophy* (New York: Columbia University Press, 1970), p. 203; cf. Watt, *Islamic Philosophy and Theology*, p. 102; S. Pines, in *Cambridge History of Islam*, vol. 2, p. 804.

24. Joseph Schacht, "An aristocratic disdain of the 'common people'," in *Theology and Law in Islam*, ed. G. E. von Grunebaum (1971), pp. 8, 20.

25. See Nizām al-Mulk, *The Book of Government or Rules for Kings*, translated from the Persian by Hubert Drake (1960). For the significance of the author, see discussion in text, which follows.

26. See Hamilton A. R. Gibb, "The Heritage of Islam in the Modern World," pts. 1 and 2, *International Journal of Middle East Studies* 1 (1970): 232–233; Kerr, *Islamic Reform*, pp. 159–166.

27. See Gibb, "Heritage of Islam," pp. 8–13, and E. I. J. Rosenthal, *Political Thought in Medieval Islam* (1962), chap. 2, "The Caliphate, Theory and Function."

28. In invoking this analogy I find myself in the distinguished company of Russel Meiggs, *The Athenian Empire* (Oxford University Press, 1972), p. 137.

29. See two articles in *The Islamic City*, eds. Hourani and Stern: "The Constitution of the Islamic City," by Stern (pp. 25–50), and "Y a-t-il eu des corporations professionelles dans le monde musulman classique?" by Claude Cahen (pp. 51–63).

30. Gibb, "Heritage of Islam," (1970) p. 224.

31. A. J. Arberry, in *Cambridge History of Islam*, vol. 2, pt. 8.6, "Mysticism," especially p. 612.

32. See Claude Cahen, *Mouvements populaires et autonomisme urbain dans l'Asie musulmane du moyen age* (1958–1959).

33. See Hans Jonas, *The Gnostic Religion* (1958, 1963); Bernard Lewis, *The Origins of Ismaᶜilism* (1940).

34. Bernard Lewis, *The Assassins* (1967), chap. 2, "The Ismailis."

35. See S. D. Goitein, *A Mediterranean Society: The Jewish Communities of the Arab World as Portrayed in the Documents of the Cairo Geniza*, vol. 1 (Berkeley: University of California Press, 1968).

36. "Law is Islam's religious science. . . . Theology, in its rationalist expression . . . sought its own identity away from law, and succeeded; but it found no place in the regular curriculum of the institutions of learning" (George Makdisi, "Law and Traditionalism in the Institutions of Learning of Medieval Islam," in von Grunebaum, ed., *Theology and Law in Islam*, p. 75 [hereafter cited as Makdisi, 1971].

37. See George Makdisi, "The Marriage of Tughril Beg," *International Journal of Middle East Studies* 1 (1970): 259–275. The fact that the *sultān* survived the marriage by little more than six months is not in itself sufficient to equate the events with the famous "Ball of Kirriemuir."

38. See Majid Khadduri, *The Islamic Law of Nations* (Baltimore: Johns Hopkins, 1966), pp. 10–22.

39. Emmanuel Sivan, *L'Islam et las Croisade: Ideologie et Propaganda dans les Réactions Musulmanes aux Croisades* (Paris: Librarie d'Amérique et d'Orient Adrien Maisonneuve, 1968), pp. 102–103, 123.

40. Gibb, "Heritage of Islam," pt. 3, *International Journal of Middle East Studies* 2 (1971): p. 142.

41. For the likenesses and differences between *madrasa* and medieval university, see Makdisi, 1971, pp. 76–80.

42. See Gibb, "Heritage of Islam," (1970) pp. 225–226; J. Spencer Trimingham, *The Sufi Orders in Islam* (Oxford University Press, 1971), pp. 7–14.

43. See Watt, *Islamic Philosophy and Theology*, pts. 2 and 3.

44. Cf. Makdisi, 1971, pp. 84–86.

45. W. Montgomery Watt, *A History of Islamic Spain* (Edinburgh, 1965), pp. 137–142, 172. Cf. von Grunebaum, *Classical Islam*, p. 187; "Averroes shows the Janus face of the religious scholar and the a-religious philosopher. . . ."

46. See Franz Rosenthal's introduction to his translation of Ibn Khaldun, *The Muqaddimah*, vol. 1 (Bollingen Foundation series, no. 43, 1958), pp. c–civ; and Gamāl al-Dīn al-Shayyāl, in *Historians of the Middle East*, eds. Bernard Lewis and P. M. Holt (1962), pp. 405, 408.

47. "How far their filiation was politically significant and how far purely a snob game is difficult to say" (von Grunebaum, *Classical Islam*, p. 197).

48. "Fatally," that is, from the point of view of consensus in government. Theoretically the split might have operated to the benefit of the exploited peasants and craftsmen; but in fact both segments of the ruling class competed in later centuries in maximizing their exactions from their social inferiors. The result was magisterially summed up for late eighteenth-century Egypt by Sir Hamilton Gibb: "For centuries before . . . , the peasant had pit-

ted his craft against the exploiters and failed; and failing, the genius of the race, inferior to no other in capacity and depth of feeling, had turned in upon itself in bitterness and sought revenge, as it were, in limiting production to the minimum of its requirements, in a tenacious opposition to all changes, and an almost deliberate harshening of all its conditions of life. The fertility of the soil served only to raise up oppressors on every side, and since, in the *fellāh*'s experience, it seemed that only by oppression could anything be gained, he also, by a natural reaction, became an oppressor of his own kind." (H. A. R. Gibb and Harold Bowen, *Islamic Society and the West,* vol. 1, pt. 1 (1950), p. 264.

49. See Gibb, "Heritage of Islam," (1970) p. 223.

50. See Trimingham, *Sufi Orders in Islam,* p. 2.

51. See W. Montgomery Watt, *Free Will and Predestination in Early Islam* (1948). On the contemporary situation a Christian Arab, Dr. Nabīh Fāris, wrote: "Communism and Islam are alike in their understanding of the nature of evil. There is no conception of original sin in the Muslim religion. If man is evil, it is because of external factors—not because of anything inherent in man himself." "Islam and the Appeals of Communism," *Middle East Forum* (Beirut) 31, no. 8 (Summer 1956): 9.

52. Claude Cahen, in *Cambridge History of Islam,* vol. 2, p. 522.

53. See Rodinson, "Le Marchand Musulman," p. 22; Rosenthal, *Political Thought in Medieval Islam,* pp. 220, 229–230; Gibb, "Heritage of Islam," (1970) p. 221.

54. See Ira Marvin Lapidus, *Muslim Cities in the Later Middle Ages* (1967), Contents, pp. xiii–xiv.

55. Ibid., pp. 13, 164, 243 (chap. 1, n. 4).

56. See Edward Wakin, *A Lonely Minority* (1963), p. 7–8.

57. See A. J. Arkell, *A History of the Sudan to* A.D. *1821,* 2d ed. (1961), pp. 195–197.

58. Robert Montagne, "L'Union arabe," *Politique Etrangère,* (May 1946), p. 182.

59. See Paul Wittek, "De la défaite d'Ankara à la prise de Constantinople," *Revue des Etudes Islamiques* 12 (1938): 1–34.

60. This was the subtitle of an article, "Social Reform: Factor X," reprinted in *The Middle East in Transition,* ed. Walter Z. Laquer (1958), pp. 3–11.

61. Gibb, "Heritage of Islam," (1971) p. 147.

62. Joseph Schacht, died 1969; Hamilton Gibb, 1971; Gustave von Grunebaum, 1972; *ex umbris et imaginibus in ueritatem.*

THE OTTOMAN EMPIRE: A COLLOQUY

# 13

## THE MODERNIZATION OF SOCIAL COMMUNICATION

ŞERIF MARDIN

> The community which permits a common history to
> be experienced as common, is a community of com-
> plementary habits and facilities of communications.
> It requires, so to speak, equipment for a job. This
> job consists in the storage, recall, transmission,
> recombination and reapplication of relatively wide
> ranges of information.
>
> Karl W. Deutsch
> *Nationalism and Social Communication*
>
> All intellectual actions . . . are shaped within a
> context of tradition.
>
> "Intellectuals"
> *International Encyclopaedia of the Social Sciences*

The Ottoman Empire was a polity of the type described as a
"traditional empire," and, to a greater or lesser extent, it
showed the characteristics imputed to such "historical bureaucratic"[1] systems. One way of approaching the changes in social
communication that accompanied the modernization of the
empire is to see them as changes in the system of communication proper to this bureaucratic system. Such antecedents explain some—but not all—of the characteristics of the com-

munication "revolution" in Turkey, for the change may be seen as the consequence of cultural diffusion: the new media and the changes in patterns of communication that mark modernization in the Turkish context appear first during the modernization of communication in Western societies. A description of changes in the Ottoman Empire must thus focus on changes in technology and communication patterns that have been found to be significant in the West and on their diffusion and their adoption as the result of prescriptive reform. These changes may be subsumed under the following headings: (1) new communication media, (2) new educational institutions, (3) a new, autonomous group of communicators, the intelligentsia, (4) new governmental structures—a developed bureaucracy—providing both a net of linkages within government, which was much circumscribed when the process of change set in, and also a gradual widening of this network to take in a larger part of the population, and (5) new values stressing "openness," increased access to knowledge, and broader popular participation in public affairs rather than esotericism and segregation.

Under all of these headings, the direction of change was away from partially differentiated, closed, narrowly elitist and dependent structures to more clearly functionally differentiated, open, socially mobilized, participatory, and partially and increasingly autonomous structures.

The consequences of these developments cannot, however, be spelled out as an unequivocal transformation to a more "modern" society, when "modernization" is considered a systematic change in which many characteristics of an "end state" hang together. A survey of the "modernization" of communication in the Ottoman Empire does not yield a very clear picture of "modernization." Thus the old cultural elitism of Ottoman culture was replaced by a new, albeit more subtle, form of cultural elitism. The "openness" of communications was not necessarily accompanied by the disappearance of traditional values. Often, modern media are new vehicles for carrying old ideas. In four instances, however, the modernization of communication did fit the paradigm of consistent modern characteristics: media escaped overwhelming control by state-embedded literati; intelligentsia replaced these small circles; segregated subcultures were affected by the larger span of a new, national network of communication; formally restricted literary genres gave way to more flexible molds that catered to less restricted audiences and had an expanding, catalytic effect of their own.

Altogether, differences between the traditional Ottoman system of communication and that of modern Turkey can be understood only if Western advances in communication are placed within the context of a complex historical occurrence that, for lack of a more precise concept, may be called the transformation of a system of vertical integration into one of horizontal integration. It is in the commitment of intellectual resources to the economic and political institutions of horizontal integration that the new characteristics of Ottoman communication can be understood.

A society of vertical integration is one in which the localistic influences of tribes, ethnic groups, religious sects, provincial notables, and craft groups still prevail over a system of national integration. It is a society with a centrally powerful but not as yet penetrative state, with undeveloped nationwide economic, educational, and communicational networks.[2]

To understand the problem posed for communication in such a society it is useful to remember a characteristic of symbols. A symbol derives its power not only to its meaning referent—that is, the sultan's seal stands for the sultan—but because of the effective charge carried by this symbol—the sultan's seal inspires unfailing awe. The official communication system was set off from that of the ordinary citizen to enable it to carry this message with force in circumstances in which it was easy for the personal charisma of the sultan to become dissipated because of the great distances, looseness of control, and other characteristics of the Ottoman patrimonial state.

This patrimonial state may be described as follows: the empire was considered the patrimony of the ruler and the latter ruled through a patrimonial sultanic bureaucracy.[3] With time, the ruler withdrew from the scene as the paramount political leader and reemerged with these features only on rare occasions. This occurred twice during the movement of reform initiated at the beginning of the nineteenth century, in the case of Sultan Selim III (1800–1807) and Sultan Mahmud II (1806–1839).[4] One other strong sultan, Abdulhamid II (1876–1909), appeared at the end of the nineteenth century. At other times, the sultan's officials and palace cliques controlled governmental affairs.

Statesmanship was a specialized occupation and much care went into the training of officials. Participation of the ruled in key political decisions was not a tenet of Ottoman politics. Neither did there exist "constituted bodies"[5] of the type well known to Western Europe. In the West, both these and earlier feudal estates set a pattern of reciprocal obligations and balances between the state and bodies outside it or between the sovereign and his vassals. This compromising climate is seen in the Ottoman state only to the extent that subgroups within the governmental class engaged in a struggle for power that usually stopped short of total annihilation of the unwanted individual or group rival. In the absence of "intermediary" structures with corporate legal personalities between the bureaucracy and the lower classes, the exercise of direct legitimate political authority and power was restricted to a relatively small group. This restriction was reinforced by the bureaucracy's control over communication, which was a means of keeping the fragmented and segmented social structure of the empire together.

Such a control was the product of three policies: reliance on special schools for the training of officials and Doctors of Islamic Law; restriction of "higher" knowledge almost exclusively to the program of these schools; and later, elaboration of a mannered, flowery, and allusive literary language, which the uninitiated could not understand. Several specialized official styles of communication and scripts often were less flowery but still hard to decipher and far removed from the language of the common people.[6] All of these were enhanced by a basic activity of central government: namely, the production of legitimating documents such as patents, permissions, grants, decrees and orders, and the system of central state record keeping.[7] Such a focusing of the ruler's rule on recording, on scribal activities and diplomatics, was the consequence of a type of patrimonialism in which the center was highly organized but not penetrative. The importance of scribal activities may be traced far back in Middle East history. The scribal protocol involved in the drafting of these documents reinforced the restriction of communication,[8] but patrimonialism had its effect on communication at a number of levels of which this is only one.

## SPECIAL SCHOOLS

There were two main formal paths to acquiring a "secular" official culture: either through state training institutions or by in-service apprenticeship and training in state offices.

The official schools consisted of a complex of institutions under the supervision of the palace. Capping this edifice was the most prestigious of the lot: the Palace School. Many Ottoman officials not specialized in Islamic law were groomed for their functions in the Palace School of the sultan. Recruitment into this school was based on levies of children of non-Muslim families with a record of service to the state. Recruiting from non-Muslim families, a feature that lasted into the early eighteenth century,[9] isolated the candidate for an official post from ascriptive groups, thereby breaking kinship ties and increasing dependence on the good will of the patrimonial officials or the sultan himself. The bureaucracy thus recruited has been characterized as a "slave" (*kul* in Turkish) bureaucracy, rising largely by merit and occasional good fortune to the most responsible positions.

The subjects taught in the Palace School were the Koran, Arabic and Persian literature, the arts of war, and those of peace such as music and drawing.[10] This complex operated at a number of levels with the purpose of separating out candidates according to ability. At the base of the pyramid, channeled into a military career after a minimum of training, were palace guards and the lower ranks of the janissaries; at the apex were the ablest candidates who received the longest training. Theoretically, they would fill posts in the retinue of the sultan. Persons showing intermediate promise became lesser military commanders or administrators.

Immersed in the atmosphere of the palace, candidates for military and administrative posts became experts in governmental procedure and palace ceremonial and adept at survival in the atmosphere of intrigue that at times suffused the sultan's abode. Profiting from only a restricted form of the "civil rights" of the majority of the population,[11] their group identity stemmed as much from their quality of cognoscenti as it did from their devotion to the ideology of the state *(devlet);* a whim of the sultan or a political machination could endanger their lives.

A second main avenue of training for the patrimonial bureaucracy was that of official bureaus.[12] Here, apprentices were given on-the-job training for years. A successful career meant rising to be a bureau chief. Scribes who went into the finance department learned a special scribal code, the *siyakat.*[13]

The main difference between the two Ottoman streams of staff recruitment was that this scribal class had separate status from the *kul.*[14] This difference continued even after the policy of staffing the state with "slaves" was discontinued. The scribal clan also saw itself as different from the *ulema,* or Doctors of Islamic Law. In the case of Kâtip Çelebi (1608–1656), an Ottoman scribe who became the premier encyclopedist of the empire, we know that the higher *ulema* returned this compliment. They treated him with disdain because of his spotty *medrese* (seminary) record.[15]

Halil Inalcik has characterized the recruitment policies and the authority relations prevalent among the scribal class as guildlike.[16] The net effect of this type of arrangement was the partial co-optation of one generation of clerks by the former generation. In times of economic decline, when state employment was sought especially eagerly, this system tended to fill the ranks with a redundant number of incompetents with official backing.

Power relations within the Ottoman political elite, which largely assumed the role of intellectual elite, also placed restriction on the propagation of knowledge. An example is the case of Şanizâde Ataullah (d. 1826), a Doctor of Islamic Law, who was the first person to prepare a text on medicine that aimed at familiarizing Ottomans with the approach to medicine used in the early nineteenth century in the West. If the sultan had looked over this work and approved it the book would have had state support. Şanizâde might have been appointed imperial physician. His presentation was blocked by jealous officials, however, and it took three years for the first volume of his work to get into print.[17] In short, success as an intellectual was not independent of one's position in the power alignments within the "ruling institution." What is meant by *literati*, in part, is this embeddedness of communicators in the structure of power.

A third type of Ottoman elite training was provided by schools wherein religious personnel were educated *(medrese)*.[18] Graduates of these institutions could become lower-level judges *(kadis)* performing many administrative functions. They also could become higher judges, experts in religious law, teachers in lower or higher institutions of learning or members of the "secular" clergy, prayer leaders and functionaries in mosques, physicians, or astrologers.[19] Religious schools seem to have admitted Muslim boys from a variety of backgrounds,[20] but here, too, the understanding was that a watershed separated the "higher" learning in which religious knowledge blended with "reason of state" from simple religious learning. By the end of the eighteenth century those controlling the religious institutions had managed to transform the "learned profession" into a semihereditary aristocracy.[21]

Because the *ulema* spanned Ottoman society from its highest to its lowest reaches this so called learned institution was an important communication link between the governing and the governed. The higher *ulema* were directly involved in political decisions, some of the middle-level *ulema* were judges who combined with this function those of administration, and the lower *ulema* officiating in mosques were part and parcel of the lives of the masses. Symbols of legitimacy being largely religious, the entire symbolic structure of legitimacy was connected from the official level down to that of subjects by various links in the "learned institution." But side by side with this symbolism was another, only partially overlapping symbolism referring to the majesty and power of the sultan that may be termed "secular."

The widest educational network in the provinces was provided by the *ulema*, and whereas strict equivalent of the modern public secondary education did not exist, provincial *medrese* were important educational centers that graduated students of various levels excluding the highest, the latter being concentrated in the Ottoman capital. It may be argued that the *medrese* thus did provide the closest equivalents to traditional secondary education. The difference from modern education is that this stream, too, cannot be described as "public" instruction in the modern sense; there were too few *medrese* graduates for this sense to apply. Even in the early nineteenth century, foreign observers were to complain that a lack of educational institutions of intermediate status, that is, institutions between the elementary and the elite level, was the great defect of Ottoman education.[22] By that time the functions of the Palace School had dwindled, and what these observers meant was that continuing education beyond primary school would have meant embarking on more than twenty years of study required of a Doctor of Islamic Law who aspired to a career.

In the nineteenth century, modernization caused the religious symbolism associated with politics and administration to decrease gradually. This had a cumulative effect on the decline of *ulema* standards, complaints about which had been voiced long before the nineteenth century.[23]

In the traditional setting, religious training did not emphasize the secular reason of state as strongly as did the Palace School.[24] Nevertheless, religious instruction proper by its very nature and esoteric content created concentric circles of those who knew only its basic tenets and others who were initiated into its more esoteric truths. Training was long. About fifteen years of advanced study were required of the elite men of religion. Such an overt form of restriction was accompanied by an ideology about knowledge that supported the system in a much more subtle way, namely, the idea that "higher" knowledge is the appanage of those who have made their own the ideology of system, the literati. Only they can be trusted.[25] This was not a conception that directly derived from the Islamic religious component of Ottoman culture. A distinguished student of the idea of knowledge in Islam finds that Islamic culture is suffused by a generalized search for knowledge.[26] But even though Islamic sources stressed the cumulative aspect of knowledge,[27] there was an important restriction in their approach to cumulation. This appears clearly in relation to the Islamic categorization of knowledge. According to this conception, knowledge could be knowledge about Islam itself, mystical illumination, philosophical speculation, and finally a rise in the general educational level.[28] This total conception is one that promotes a conservative view of education. It also may be called authoritative because its core is the primacy of authoritative religiously grounded knowledge.

Among some of the later more conservative Ottoman Doctors of Islamic Law one sees a narrower attitude toward knowledge, namely, that knowledge is what already exists as knowledge. This change from an earlier, seemingly less rigid view was associated with a marked intellectual decline among the members of the "learned institution" that coincided with the decline of the empire.[29] Kâtip Çelebi had already commented on the retrograde step of taking out of the *ulema* curriculum philosophy and science.[30] During the nineteenth century the number of learned, sophisticated members of the *ulema* decreased more markedly.

An amusing illustration—in its most baroque form—of the attitude regarding the boundedness of knowledge may be found in an anecdote that is recounted about the behavior of a Doctor of Islamic Law during the reign of Sultan Abdulhamid II (1876–1909). Even though this learned man was living at a time when the whole cultural scene was changing, he was still interested in widening his knowledge by poring over as many traditional sources possible. As the sultan had a large collection of manuscripts, which existed nowhere else, the Doctor of Islamic Law asked permission to see them. The sultan granted him permission, but, suspicious as usual, had a spy observe the behavior of his client. The sultan's informer saw that the man would take notes from a rare manuscript—presumably a thought or an interpretation that was original enough to be recorded—and that he would then stealthily pour drops of ink on the passage he had noted so that no one would use it after him.

The Ottoman educational system derived from the basic assumption about knowledge held by traditional Ottoman society, with the best of knowledge concentrated at the top, a very simple educational fare at the bottom, and, most important of all, no middle-level public education of any extent. With time, the authority of the literati as a group was partly transformed into that of the books produced by them. The idea that knowledge was the latent fund contained in basic religious sources or commentaries on them became more persuasive. Both ideas may be found in the Ottoman Empire. In all these ways, knowledge was a relatively "closed" and limited enterprise in Ottoman society. This characteristic of the traditional system may be pinpointed and a framework for the efforts of educational expansion during the nineteenth century may be set by citing a statistic: in 1927 literacy in Turkey was 10 percent.[31]

In the era preceding the introduction of printing in the Ottoman Empire, even among the scribal class—which was in the ascendant and the representative of the "secular" branch of Ottoman culture—there was a surprising lack of active concern for the wider propagation of knowledge. Thus, the seventeenth-century encyclopedist clerk Kâtip Çelebi[32] and others tried to follow the new Western advances in geography but in other works cautioned that knowledge was not for scattering "into the mouths of dogs."[33] Knowledge is meant here in the sense of the higher realm of Ottoman learning. What the Ottoman elite, of all provenances, thought was most dangerous to spread among the masses was the potential for controversy in the religious "sciences." Popular treatises for self-instruction concerning secular subjects, by contrast, were part of the fare available to the literate.[34] The restrictions placed on knowledge by the political and religious elite continued in the Ottoman realms at a time when in the West it was being eroded by Humanism, by the Renaissance and the multiplicity of centers of power that existed in Western European society, and in particular by the expansion of the commercial and urban integrative network.

An illustration of the way in which, in contrast to the cumulative effect of the political and social structures of the Ottoman Empire, a new economic structure, educational expansion, and increasingly sophisticated knowledge meshed together in the West to produce a more dynamic network for communication may be found in the field of geography. With all the commitment of resources to emulate the navigational achievements of the Portuguese, the Ottomans were never as successful in the development of fundamental navigational science. The Portuguese, whose economic goals were much more clearly outlined behind their policy, were able to achieve training far more sophisticated than that provided in the Ottoman Empire. Political motivation was not sufficient to force the Ottomans to devise their own modern view of geography.[35] To express it with greater clarity, the lack of commitment to a new naval science by the Ottomans seems to be the result of self-satisfaction, whereas the positive achievements of the Portuguese appear to be a function of their economic goals. It has also been stated that the *ulema* lost their opportunities to engage in scientific activity by becoming too closely dependent upon the center of political power, the ruling institution, in the seventeenth century.[36]

## STYLISTIC CHARACTERISTICS OF ELITE CULTURE

A general characteristic of the culture of the elite was the value placed on a cultivated mind, on allusive references to a common heritage of classical lore rather than on originality or innovation. The literati considered that increased ambiguity rather than greater clarity was the sign of sophistication. Part of this was because of the richness and complexity of symbolism in the official culture. While the cultural system as a whole became of less use, the highly charged symbolic system referred to above lagged behind and acquired a life of its own because of its prestigious connotations. Residues of this process still can be found among present-day Turkish intellectuals and is a source of low efficiency in communication.

A related aspect of elite control of communication was the difficult literary style used by both the official set and the Doctors of Islamic Law. This "polite" language could be mastered only by those with a thorough grounding in Arabic and Persian.[37]

Because the Islamic classics were written in Arabic—a language not used in everyday life by Turks—only the brighter, more learned *ulema* could use original sources effortlessly. The study of religion was indeed partially Turkicized, but there was a deep chasm between an upper and a folk variety of Islam. There was a communication barrier between those with a classical Islamic education and those who had not been exposed to it.[38] In the era of the decline of the empire, competent scholars with control over Arabic became scarcer. One often encounters complaints, beginning at the end of the seventeenth century, that scholars are inept. In those years too a higher value than before was placed on manuscripts, leading to an interdiction to export manuscripts from the Ottoman capital.[39]

The complicatedness of the official style did not fit in well with the major characteristic of modernized politics, namely, wider governmental penetration into the social life that slowly emerged as a necessary adjunct of modernization. Charles MacFarlane, who was in the Ottoman capital in 1828, asked a number of persons in the city what their reaction was to a book then recently printed. The work was the official version of the elimination of janissary corps in bloody encounter with the reformist side. The book was written by Esad Efendi, who has been called the first modernizer of the Turkish language.[40] MacFarlane's findings were as follows:

> On having inquiries made among certain Turks who were not exactly of the lowest condition but what we should call of the middling class, I was surprised to learn that there was hardly a man among them who could understand it. Though intended for general circulation it was written in too high a style, or too much in the manner of superior bureaux—a motley *ex-officio* language in which the comparative poor Turkish is so bespattered with Arabic and Persian as to sound a foreign idiom in the ears of a Stambouli.[41]

The esotericism of the language of the literati is a complex occurrence that has not received adequate treatment from historians of culture. The simplest thesis in this respect is that Ottoman Turkish, the polite language, was difficult, convoluted, and heavily encrusted with loan words from Persian and Arabic and thus completely incomprehensible for the masses. Critics of this thesis point out that simple Turkish was used by men of letters and statesmen.[42] A third explanation might be that stylistic involution in official places was an outcome of the decline of the empire. Be this as it may, Ottoman reformers of the nineteenth century were still complaining of the difficulties of communication created by the official style.[43] What interests us more here is the reformist perception of the problem than the problem itself. Part of the difficulty would seem to be that the mobilizing intelligentsia, which appeared in the late 1860s, did not find the existing genres of classical literature adequate for their goals. Literature for pleasure had to be replaced by literature that had a thesis to present regarding the individual's relation to the forces of modernization, and this type of literature had to be created anew. Also, a new vocabulary had to be created to label new aspects of a modernizing society, for example, the term "public opinion."

Turkish modernizers have concentrated an enormous amount of energy on changing Ottoman officialese and on forging a unified language understandable to all. Both the time taken to modify this aspect of Turkish and the repeated association of "simplification" with reformist movements into the twentieth century show in the extent to which cultural cleavage was a central aspect of traditional Ottoman society. Even today, linguistic reform is considered an adjunct of Turkish political radicalism[44] and is used as a banner by the upwardly mobile.

### OTHER SCHOOLS

Ottoman equivalents of primary schools had a restricted view of what today we would call "literacy."[45] This is already clear in the text that was used in primary school, the Koran. The final test in deciding whether one had completed the local elementary school was above all the extent to which one had learned to recite the Koran.[46] Most of the Muslim inhabitants of the empire did not know Arabic, the language of the Koran. This meant that the primary-school student learned only a series of clichés with no verbal but with significant cultural meaning for him. Not only was this true for reading (which, for the duller students and less qualified teachers consisted of identifying the sounds that correspond to signs without understanding the significance of these sounds), but it was also true for writing. Often writing consisted of learning how to give shape to certain standard Arabic letters and phrases and to learn to do so with good calligraphy. This did not mean that the graduate of the Ottoman community primary school could write a letter.

Today, this remains true for part of the rural population that has graduated from primary school in Turkey. Some of them some years after graduation are unable to write a letter. In this light, the older system might even seem to have had more important functions: at least it supported the existing system by teaching the correct type of incantation as a means of cementing social solidarity. But today this semiliteracy is achieved by default, while in the classical system primary education seems to have aimed more clearly at inculculating the common values of Ottoman society. During modernization, increasingly, a type of knowledge was given in primary school that enabled the graduate—if he got the full benefit of instruction—to achieve autonomy. This does not mean that the teaching of values had no part in modern primary education, but the "mix" in the modern curriculum is qualitatively different, with the use of knowledge for national, mobilizing and at the same time autonomous, individualized goals slowly emerging. This was a characteristic of an instruction that in modern industrialized nations is in great part secular and public.

Even in the earliest stages of medieval education in the West, the elementary school curriculum had a relatively secular and practical focus, progressing from "letters" and "song" (reading) to Latin grammar,[47] at least a mixed fare with some vernacular included. The vernacular developed in schools with greater vigor from the fourteenth century onward as a characteristic of the preparation for commercial careers pursued by municipal reading and writing schools.[48]

### EXCEPTIONS TO THE MONOPOLY OF ACCESS TO COMMUNICATION AND LEARNING

Not all communication in the Ottoman Empire flowed through official channels. Side by side with "polite" literature and the official style flourished popular literature. The great majority of the population did not read the ornate poetry of the literati but listened to stories recounting the lives of religious personalities, the adventures of separated lovers, or the exploits of eponymous Turkish heroes. In this category should also be included the literary activities of bards *(aşık)* and even such fleeting messages as graffiti on caravanserai walls.

It is an indication of the extent to which the traditional pattern for works sold among the lower classes persists that in an informal survey of the materials sold by ambulant hawkers carried out in 1967 in the cities of Istanbul and Izmir, the same romances that had been read for centuries emerged on top of the sales list. It is true that this time a few novels with half-naked ladies on their covers and titles about James Bond figure side by side with Battal Gazi, the fighter for the faith; but Battal, at a lower unit price, still outdistanced his modern rivals.[49]

Of the literature that found an audience outside official channels, one genre, the literature of mysticism, had a special importance in Turkish cultural life.[50] One branch of this literature was, by and large, in straightforward Turkish.[51] It found a clientele in both the upper and lower reaches of society and thus provided cultural linkages. As a type it could overcome the pretensions of official esotericism by its own allusiveness, which in its more disfigured form could verge on the cabalistic. This provided a means for the lower classes to be one-up on, or at least on a par with, officialdom insofar as access to a secret world veiled from common mortals was concerned. To the extent that some of the religious orders, where religious literature found a haven, opened their doors to the lower classes, there existed a means of countering official pretensions by one's own brand of secretiveness and by one's ersatz status provided by membership in a dervish order. One of the processes by which the Doctors of Islamic Law kept in touch with lower classes, and conversely the means by which educational and social mobility was provided for the young with such origins, may be followed in the life-pattern of a well-known Doctor of Islamic Law, Şem'i Efendi, who devoted his spare time to the education of children from lower classes and the sons of servants of the upper classes.[52]

Religious structures provided one further means of creating audiences with mixed class backgrounds. Sermons of able preachers—just as in Christianity—were much appreciated and had their dedicated listeners, as in modern times secular authors have a devoted group of readers.[53] In the nineteenth century this tradition became useful for more clearly political purposes and, in particular, rabble rousing. The increasing alienation of a part of the Westernized elite from Islamic culture at that time,

and conversely the feeling of the masses that Westernized intellectuals were now adopting a culture that not only towered
about them but was also alien, is one aspect of this form of protest against modernization.

Even though much of the literature of mysticism is superbly
lyrical and moves us even today, there is no doubt that here too
the allusive and the esoteric were considered part of the higher
realm of culture. The symbolic system, regardless of its locus,
was not "open" in the Ottoman Empire.[54]

### OTHER CHARACTERISTICS OF THE OTTOMAN EMPIRE

Because numerous feedbacks through the existing structures are
part of the total communication picture, there were Ottoman
institutions that cannot be neglected in a survey of the traditional situation in the empire. These are the so-called *millet*
system and the structure of the Ottoman economy.[55] In both
cases, boundaries were set that were important for communication and that were part of what was described as the "segmenta-
tion" of the Ottoman Empire.

Ottoman social life was partially compartmentalized by the
institution of the *millet*. This system divided the Ottoman Empire into communities gathered around their religious leaders.
Apart from the dominant Muslim *millet*, there was the Orthodox *millet*, the Jewish *millet*, and later other denominations
administered by their religious heads. Such a compartmen-
talization did not preclude a common life of the various *millet*s
with the Muslim *millet*. It provided the framework for a complicated system in which each social group had its place. Nevertheless, social exchange with Muslims was across the boundaries
of the *millet* system. Thus, the Jews, Armenians, and Greeks
could, for a long time, operate a system of printing in the Ottoman Empire without it affecting the Ottoman Muslims.[56] The
cultural products of one *millet* had the tendency to be restricted
by *millet* boundaries, even though in the area of music there
was partial cultural interpretation. This was the consequence
not only of language differences but of the separateness of
cultural worlds that increased with time. It has been stated that
"between 1453 and the end of the 17th century, the *millet*

replaced the *devlet* [state] as the local center of life of the non-Moslem population."[57] These boundaries thus have to be taken into account in relation to the process of the modernization of communication. During the nineteenth century, the very reform policies set by Ottoman statesmen for the non-Muslim Ottoman *millet*s caused rivalries that seem to have resulted in a reaffirmation of the particularism of each unit. Nationalism also found fertile ground here. Muslims turned inward, and it is probable that toward the end of the nineteenth century there was a lowering of the level of social exchange between Muslim and non-Muslim communities that affected the entire picture of social communication and mobilization.

## THE ECONOMY

The most important aspect of the economy of the Ottoman Empire was that it was precapitalistic. What is meant by this is that the Ottoman Empire missed both the social and the economic transformations of structure that may be followed in the West. There was no unification of internal markets as had occurred during the age of mercantilism in Western Europe. Neither was there the tearing of the traditional social fabric that accompanied enclosure or the industrial revolution.[58] True, there were important structures that disintegrated in the empire, but the specific type of social transformation that accompanied the evolution of a market economy, a "corporative" society of capitalism, did not come about. The latter, however, had had important consequences for communication in Western Europe. The interaction potential of the proletariat that was created as the result of the industrial revolution is a feature that Marx pinpointed in his characterization of what was new in European history.[59] It was part of his hopes that the latter would form a new collectivity that would bring about the revolution. This collectivity was so defined by Marx partly because of the communication network it formed. Another consequence for communication of the rending of traditional structures and of the industrial revolution in the West was that the bourgeoisie collectivity, which operated within the new horizontal system of integration, was now ready to form an audience or a public for printed works, which had not existed before.

In England as in the Ottoman Empire, the lower classes, up to the time of the industrial revolution, also had been reading or listening to "ballads" and "abbreviated chivalric romances." Ian Watt states that this pattern changed with the general transformation of society in Britain after 1750.[60] One of the results was the appearance of the novel. There were several modifications regarding both communicators and the messages that underlay the transition to the novel as a genre. First, "irregulars" appeared among writers. Dr. Johnson, faced by these new authors, complained that "the province of writing was formerly left to those who, by study or appearance of study, were supposed to have gained knowledge unattainable by the busy part of mankind."[61] This was not so any more. Second, the novel as a genre introduced a serious concern with the daily lives of ordinary people. Finally, the successful novelists Defoe and Richardson "were able to express the needs for their audiences from the inside much more freely than would previously have been possible," because they "themselves were wholly representative of the new center of gravity of that public," that is, "middle class London tradesmen."[62]

These developments in social communication that followed upon the industrial revolution in England came about a century later in the Ottoman Empire and then not primarily as the result of economic development. In Turkey, they were the consequences of a reform policy marked by the modernization of education, the reshaping of the Ottoman bureaucracy, and the creation of a new audience within its extended ranks.

## CHARACTERISTICS OF MODERN COMMUNICATION SYSTEMS

A large literature exists in our time that attempts to show that patterns of socialization among the lower classes restrict them in availing themselves of higher education.[63] If these classes were to take advantage of these institutions, goes the theory, the equilibrium of the system would be upset, and a type of mobility, which the elite appears to support but which in fact it subtly undermines, would have a chance to emerge. Thus there are still many modern attitudes that even at present bolster cultural elitism, obstruct educational mobility, and keep the "system" in equilibrium.[64] No doubt four centuries ago these features were more salient in Europe. But if this ideologically produced, cultural constriction is true for Western Europe, it was much truer for the Ottoman Empire. The traditional political structure of the Ottoman Empire played an important role in this connection; the absence of "intermediate classes" as corporate bodies with a legally defined personality and a political power, recognized in law as well as in fact, is another significant aspect of Ottoman political structure.[65] Privileges and freedoms, charters, and estate immunities built into Western law provided the boundaries behind which each group could try to establish its own variants of educational institutions geared to the legitimized purpose of the group as such. This appears most strikingly in the Western European competition between church schools and secular, town schools. The latter, a product of the autonomy of Western towns, may be traced to the thirteenth century.[66] The lack of legitimization and the absence of firm guarantees given to groups outside the state made similar processes difficult in the Ottoman Empire. Culture was the culture of the literati, and even the rival centers of dervish culture were suspect because they provided an alternative to it. In the West, on the other hand, cross-fertilization (as well as rivalry) between church and secular schools and between elite and popular culture made the social dissemination of knowledge a much different type of undertaking. In the Ottoman Empire we have to wait for a realization among the literati, the officials, that everything did not proceed as it should for a new impetus to be given to communication.

### MODERNIZATION

The problem of modernization of communication appeared first as an adjunct to the main worry of post–sixteenth-century Ottoman statesmen, namely, streamlining the Ottoman tax structure and the military machine dependent on it. Ottoman statesmen showed an early awareness of the difficulties that beset the empire, and they seem to have been open to suggestions as to how to change its basic military structure. This meant in fact the separation of civilian from military administration, as the founder of printing in Turkey, Müteferrika, was to point out.[67]

Another important problem was that of Ottoman finances

and administration in a wider sense. Changes in the system of communication were involved in the attempt to modernize both. If the Ottoman Empire wanted to regain its superiority on the military field, it had to learn modern tactics and strategy from the West.[68] It also had to establish schools in which new subjects such as mathematics and algebra would be taught to the military. The modernization of administration meant taking up practices of enlightened despotism and establishing the bureaucratic structures that this policy had fostered.

At their broadest, these attempts at the modernization of communication in the sense described above were opposed by persons with interests in the maintenance of the ancien régime as a whole. In its narrowest form, the protest was one by the specialists in communication, who thought that they would be adversely affected by the change.[69]

The explorations by responsible statesmen into the means offered by the West for the military regeneration of the Ottoman Empire had a wide scope and resulted in measures of general cultural renovation of which the most important was the establishment of the first Ottoman printing press in 1729.[70] When one analyzes the obstacles encountered by the officials who established this state press, it is difficult to separate the opposition of the copyists who were part of the religious establishment from the oft-invoked fanaticism of this establishment. Selim Nuzhet [Gerçek] has suggested an interesting explanation for the lack of interest felt toward printed works at a time when the invention of printing and printed books became known to the Ottomans.[71] According to him, this negative response resulted from the inability of printed works to meet aesthetic standards set by manuscripts. But it is still possible to ask whether among the opponents of printing there not also was a group who saw the problem in the much wider perspective of an undermining of the cultural premises of Ottoman politics. Culture was becoming more ''open,'' and this was not welcome. Later, a Turkish envoy to Revolutionary France could find no worse accusation to damn the revolutionaries than to say they used ''easily understandable phrases,'' to influence the masses.[72]

Systematic Ottoman reform had been initiated by a special

group of Ottoman officials, the so-called men of the pen, earlier described here as the "scribal class."[73] This central bureaucratic staff had increased its control over governmental policy in the eighteenth century, possibly because of the increasing complexity of administration. As it became important to reform the existing structure, the demand for persons who could investigate the available financial resources and draft new projects of financial administration gave these bureaucrats a premium.[74] It was this new importance of *civilian* over *military* administration that might have given the clerks their new power. At the same time, the religious establishment stagnated as it turned into a semihereditary upper class. Thus an alternative solution to staffing chanceries lost its value.

The heads of chancery supported the modernization of communication to the extent that this step contributed to the elimination of the bottleneck described; namely, the death of qualified scribes. The constriction was felt because of the increased complexity of governmental work but also as regards diplomatic relations. The development of the latter underscored the importance of a new type of document: the diplomatic note. But the bottleneck can be understood only in the light of another practice that eroded the governmental process in the empire: patronage and nepotism, an important mechanism in appointment to official positions. This meant that one could not assume that an official would have the training appropriate to the position he filled. The "men of the pen," from whose ranks grand viziers were increasingly drawn, were interested in fostering methods that would enable them to "fix" knowledge in manuals when both the supply of competent clerks and the teachers of clerical skills were declining.[75] This meant official willingness to support media innovation such as printing (the existence of which they had known for a long time) and later journalism. It also meant explorations into the field of modern education. Attempts to introduce new centers for modern military education, for example, were fostered by this central bureaucratic staff.

Three important milestones in the history of reform in the Ottoman Empire are the era of Ahmed III (1703–1730), when the first reforming cultural contacts with Europe were sought;

1826–1839, the time at which internal reform was adopted as a policy for the empire (called the *Tanzimat* after 1839); and 1878, when Sultan Abdulhamid II prorogued the first Ottoman parliament and introduced his own brand of tutelary modernization for the empire. The expansion of mass media, of Western-modeled education, and of the bureaucracy itself may be fitted into this chronological frame. The change in values can also be seen in this perspective.

### MEDIA

The explorations by responsible Ottoman statesmen of the means offered by the West for the regeneration of the Ottoman Empire had a wide scope. A now famous voyage to the France of Louis XV by an envoy of Sultan Ahmed III resulted, eventually, in the establishment of the printing press in the Ottoman Empire.[76] The sponsorship of the state gave the undertaking the authority that was necessary for it to succeed. The first works to come off this press showed quite clearly the purpose of these publications: they included a dictionary, a biographical register of Ottoman naval commanders, historical texts, a text on the means of reforming the Ottoman Empire, a geographical treatise, and a historical chronology. All of these aimed at providing a basic reference library for bureaucrats.[77]

The press continued to publish books of the same type up to the end of the eighteenth century with two interruptions, 1744–1750 and 1759–1781.[78] Around 1794–1798, its type began to wear out and the effect is visible in books printed at that time.[79] It thereafter stopped operating and part of its type was transferred to a new press.[80] A total of roughly four hundred titles were published between 1729 and 1839.[81] A cursory look at some of the titles published during the first half of the eighteenth century is instructive.[82]

Attempts to introduce Western science, clearly for military-educational purposes, are underscored. Thus we see the printing of a text on geometry in 1802 and about the same date tables of logarithms, a translation of Bonnycastle's geometry, and a text on surveying. In 1804 appears the Turkish translation of Faden's atlas. These works bear the mark of an era of reform that was violently interrupted in 1807. In the following years science retreated, and religion and literature came into the forefront. Nevertheless, in the 1820s we have the first work on anatomy. In the 1830s a treatise of advanced mathematics (1831–1832) and another on geography (1831). The translation of Pinelle's text on pathology appears in 1836.

The frequency of legal codes increases as we approach 1839. The early 1840s are again marked by mostly religious publications. Nevertheless, in 1843, we have another medical publication and a treatise on fortifications; in 1848, a text on chemistry, another on physics, and another on astronomy. A number of the works printed in Turkish were published at Bulak in Egypt, and a wider selection of works to be used for modernization seems to have been the mark of these series.

In Istanbul, the 1850s are the first years during which we can see a relatively steady stream of publications geared to modernization such as J. B. Say's *Political Economy* (1852), texts on geography, zoology, geology, navigation, and the telegraph. It is only in the 1860s and the 1870s, however, that the proportion of such works begins to rise markedly. In the 1860s begin to appear translations in book form of Fenelon and Voltaire, but other literary currents and fashions arise that soon cut off the production of translations from the philosophies.

The influence of media sometimes gave more vigor (or scope) to some old beliefs and attitudes. The printing, and thus potential propagation to a wider audience of old Ottoman authors on religion and law such as Kadi Birgevi and Molla Husrev[83] provide an illustration. The first has been described as a "fanatic," and the second's strictures concerning treatment to be meted to non-Muslims were acidly commented upon by von Hammer.[84] It is also interesting that Birgevi's *Tarikat-i Muhammediye* was being retranslated. According to the new translator this was so that the book would be understood by as wide an audience as possible.

The extent to which intellectual activity picked up with the reform movement is evident from yearly publication figures of new titles: during the first 110 years of the history of printing in Turkey, close to four new titles per year appeared, in the next nineteen years about forty new titles a year were published on the average, and in the following seventeen years ninety-five titles a year appeared.[85] The number increased in the first years of Sultan Abdulhamid's reign (r. 1876–1909) but seems to have decreased markedly at the turn of the century.[86]

The most interesting aspect of this cursory survey is that the few texts on science and military organization or law translated from the West constitute a small fraction of works published. The greatest bulk up to 1875 consists of two main categories: dictionaries, grammars, and work on syntax on the one hand and classics of Islam and of Ottoman lay or religious literature on the other. One surmises that these had up to that time been buried in inaccessible manuscripts. Thus, printing provided access to classical Ottoman culture for a larger number of persons. Exactly what effect this had cannot be ascertained. One would think that a new circle of readers formed around the already active literati. It was presumably partly through such processes that an audience for printed matter was formed.

We have one source that enables us to follow these printing activities into the reign of Sultan Abdulhamid II, and that is a bibliography of the works published between 1876 and 1890.[87] The classification of these works is as follows: two hundred on religion; five hundred on language, grammar and alphabets; one thousand on literature; one thousand on what may broadly be described as the social and physical science, and twelve hundred on law and administration. Two trends are visible: first, the steep rise during Abdulhamid's reign in the number of titles published, and, second, the increasing number of books that come under the rubric of "science." This was an important development, the intellectual consequences of which will be taken up below.

By 1883, there were fifty-four printing houses in Istanbul for a population of nearly a million; of these, nineteen were owned by Muslims, twenty-eight by non-Muslim Ottomans, four by foreigners, and one by the State.[88] The ownership of two of these plants could not be traced. Our information also points out another important aspect of the development of communication in the empire: the extent to which non-Muslims and foreigners filled the positions of communicators even in communications addressed to Turks. Thus, one of the newspapers to survive the reign of Abdulhamid, the *Sabah,* was owned by an Armenian, Mihran. By 1908 the number of presses had increased to ninety-nine.[89]

### NEWSPAPERS

The first Ottoman newspaper, the *Takvim-i Vekayi*, was a government publication aiming to enlighten the reading public about the goals of the reform, to spread knowledge about education, science, industry and commerce, to and inform officials of the latest edicts passed by the government. Distribution was, in fact, limited to officials.

An unexpected interpretation of the purpose of this publication, however, was that it continued to serve the function that Ottoman historiographers had performed at an earlier time. In the words of the first leading article: "To know the events of the past serves to keep up the laws and the character of the Empire and the solidarity of the nation. It is for this purpose that the government has always employed historiographers and published historical works."[90]

If sincere (but most probably not) this justification was to meet with overwhelming unanticipated consequences as the century proceeded. But the slip is not accidental, underlining the strong link between the production of knowledge and the stabilizing of the system that prevailed in the traditional order. It should not be forgotten that printing books in Turkish (although not the sponsorship of works to be printed) was a state monopoly in the Ottoman Empire up to the era of reformers, and that it was only in 1842 that the government decided to free the sale of books to provinces from internal customs dues as a measure for the spread of public instruction.[91]

The official gazette was published in a Turkish (1832) and a French (1831) edition.[92] According to the law of Administration of Turkish provinces (1864) an official printing press was to be established in all Ottoman provincial centers.[93] By 1874, twenty-four provincial centers boasted a newspaper.[94] Most of these were no doubt officially sponsored publications. At the time there was a total of thirty provincial units in the empire.[95] It was an enterprising Englishman by the name of Churchill who published the first privately owned newspaper in Turkish, the *Ceride-i Havadis* (1840).[96] Churchill kept this monopoly for twenty years, until the appearance of the *Tercuman-i Ahval,* (1860), the first private venture into journalism by two Turks.[97]

The years between 1865 and 1876 were a boon to Turkish journalism before its progress was checked by Sultan Abdulhamid II in whose reign newspapers were cut back to include only those that praised official policy. The following is a count of the new newspapers—most of them short lived—that appeared in these years.[98]

| 1863 | 1 | 1869 | 9 | 1875 | 11 |
| 1864 | 1 | 1870 | 10 | 1876 | 6 |
| 1865 | 1 | 1871 | 4 | 1877 | 1 |
| 1866 | 4 | 1872 | 4 | 1878 | 6 |
| 1867 | 7 | 1873 | 4 | 1879 | 4 |
| 1868 | 1 | 1874 | 11 | 1880 | 1 |

In 1872 there were published in the Ottoman capital, in Turkish: three dailies, two papers appearing three times a week, one semiweekly humorous publication, one weekly humorous publication, one weekly police gazette, one weekly commercial journal, one weekly military gazette; in French: six dailies, one weekly; in Armenian: three dailies, two semiweeklies, six weeklies; in Greek: one daily, two appearing three times a week, three semiweekly, one fortnightly; in Bulgarian: three weeklies, one monthly; in Hebrew: one weekly.[99]

By 1876, the number of Turkish dailies had more than doubled, rising to seven, but there were approximately the same number of newspapers in languages other than Turkish.

By the 1890s, four to six dailies had been able to weather the storm of Abdulhamid's reign, and two important weeklies— journals of opinion—existed.[100] To this we have to add five new gazettes of government departments, such as the military gazette, three reviews (medical, commercial, and law), and an illustrated fortnightly. In the 1890s two of the three most important dailies in the capital had a circulation of, respectively, 15,000 (*Ikdam,* established 1894) and 12,000 (*Sabah,* established 1876). The third (*Tercuman-i Hakikat,* established 1878) had a circulation of 2,000 at the beginning of the twentieth century.[101] Thus we get a daily readership of Turkish newspapers of 30,000 for a population of close to a million but with a very sizeable non-Muslim proportion (approximately 400,000).[102] It is probable that some of these papers were read by more than one person.

Although newspapers were constantly in danger during Abdulhamid's reign, the first ten years of his era were marked by a recrudescence of literary and scientific reviews. A first and preliminary count of a sample shows that the following numbers of new periodicals appeared at the time:[103]

| | | | |
|---|---|---|---|
| 1876–1880 | 10 | 1891–1895 | 12 |
| 1881–1885 | 37 | 1901–1905 | None |
| 1886–1890 | 30 | | |

A true assessment of this intellectual activity should take into account the fact that many of these publications disappeared after a few issues.

Newspapers in the provinces were, almost in all cases, published by the administrative authorities to provide news about developments in the province itself such as announcements of auctions. An exception was Izmir, where the important newspaper *Hizmet* started appearing in 1886.[104] Three important literary reviews appeared in Bursa, Salonika, and Izmir toward the end of the century.[105]

Despite the varied fortunes of Turkish journalism, it had an undeniable influence. Churchill's paper had an encyclopedic content that set the tone for its most stable immediate successor, the *Tasvir-i Efkar*. The latter started publication in 1862. To the aim to inform, it added a political dimension, which made it the center of repeated controversies with the government. These and other similar disturbances were the reasons the Ottoman government brought out the first comprehensive censorship law.[106] With respect to overall cultural influence, in 1868 an informed observer was already stating that the *Ceride-i Havadis,* the *Tasvir-i Efkar,* and the *Tercuman-i Ahval* had created through their publication a taste for reading inexpensive—which did not mean inconsequential—books.[107] In the 1870s, daily newspapers with their coverage of European news and their treatment of internal political matters were trying to imitate European journalism. Reading the daily newspaper was an established habit, and the price of newspapers was lowered between the 1870s and the 1890s, but this did not raise the circulation figures.[108]

The events of the year 1876, which resulted in the deposition of one sultan and the adoption of the first Ottoman constitution, show clearly that a "public opinion" partly mobilized by the media did exist in the Ottoman capital at that time. Only later, however, after 1900, was it to become completely clear that this "public opinion" had become mobilized around two differing frames of values, one more clearly Islamic, the other the modernist-secularist. Already in these years, however, the Islamist *Basiret* showed how traditional views could be expressed through new media with ease.

During the reign of Sultan Abdulhamid II, discussion of foreign affairs was still possible if the publisher could evade references to internal politics. Thus a paradoxical situation developed in which many Ottoman readers were better informed about the intracacies of Franco-German relations than about developments on their own doorstep. Three newspapers may be said to have had a sufficiently long existence and influence to mark this era; first there was *Tercuman-i Hakikat,* published by Ahmet Midhat Efendi and devoted to the task of pulling the Turks up by their own bootstraps to economic prosperity. Second, came the *Sabah.* Finally in 1894 began to appear the *Ikdam,* which, although cautious in its political utterances, became the center for a cultural revival.[109] Between 1886 and 1890 appeared the *Mizan,* a weekly, which readily accepted the Orientalist Vanbery's view that it was a Turkish equivalent of the British *Saturday Review.* The *Mizan* was somewhat less inhibited in its discussion of national matters and was suppressed for this reason.

### THE WIDER CONTEXT OF COMMUNICATION

Roads and postal communications also are aspects of the modernization of communication that we cannot ignore. Roads had long been neglected in the empire,[110] and this was considered a great impediment to commerce by foreigners. There was not much improvement of the road system during Abdulhamid II's reign, even though a system of compulsory work on roads was instituted. Said Pasa, who enforced this obligation after 1879, states that 5,000 kilometers of roads were constructed under his administration, but this figure seems exaggerated.[111] On the other hand, railroad construction was energetically pursued and 5,000 kilometers of railroads existed in Europe and Asia by 1900.[112]

The first telegraph lines were strung in the empire during the Crimean War. The first telegraph message was received in 1855. By 1864, there were 76 telegraph stations with 267 "leagues" of line.[113] In 1900, the Ottoman Empire had 755 stations and 36,640 kilometers of telegraphic lines over which were laid 56,220 kilometers of wire. A total of approximately 3 million telegraphic dispatches a year were sent; of those, 2.3 to 2.4 million had a destination within the empire, 440,000 to 450,000 were international dispatches, 60,000 were in transit, and 200,000 were "service" messages. At that date the Ottoman post had 1,700 postal stations with the traffic letters shown in table 1.[114]

TABLE 1.　Mail Traffic in the Ottoman Empire in 1900

|  | Letters | Postcards | Printed Matter and Samples |
|---|---|---|---|
| Domestic | 8,300,000 | 49,000 | 2,300,000 |
| Foreign | 2,500,000 | 81,000 | 1,140,000 |
| Transit | 2,100,000 | 50,000 | 1,210,000 |

## THE EDUCATIONAL CONTEXT OF THE MODERNIZATION OF COMMUNICATION

The first steps in the modernization of education in the Ottoman Empire had been toward better training for military personnel. In 1732 a renegade Frenchman, the Marquis de Bonneval, was entrusted with the formation of an artillery corps, and in 1734 a school of mathematics was established in the capital to train military engineers.

A number of other military schools followed:[115] the joint military-engineering Military Academy (1796), and the Naval Engineering School (1776–1796). The Faculty of the Military Medicine was founded in 1827 (modernized anew in 1839). The

Military Academy was established in 1834 and the statue of military preparatory school in 1845. The reform of civilian education followed military institutions with the regularization of teaching in primary schools in 1846–1847, the establishment of five- to six-year "secondary" schools, *rusdiye* (1848), the Normal School (1848), The Faculty of Civil Medicine (1867), the School of Civil Engineering (1868), and the Trades School (1868). In 1869, the general law on education came into force. This was the first time elementary education was made obligatory. The training of civil servants at the higher level was attempted with the establishment of the School of Political Science (1859), but it was only in the 1880s that the latter began to acquire importance. Fully constituted (intermediate—junior high) schools began to spread throughout the empire in the years 1882–1890. A school of civil engineering was established on a permanent basis (1887) during the reign of Abdulhamid, the School of Fine Arts was inaugurated (1882), and an attempt was made to develop girls' trade schools. A school of commerce was founded (1884). In 1900, an Ottoman University, which had had two earlier unsuccessful beginnings (in 1866 and in 1870), became a going concern. Nevertheless, Ottoman primary education suffered losses during this time: the sultan ordered Ottoman history and geography withdrawn from the program of instruction in 1904.

Sultan Abdulhamid was also interested in the training of the middle-rank bureaucrats. During his reign professional schools were established that prepared one for the middle-grade positions in the Court of Account and the Ministry of Finance. In 1891, a school of agriculture at the college level was created. The practical interests of the sultan and his concern with education to serve economic life are visible here. By 1900, one report has 896,932 students in all schools under the Ministry of Public Instruction serving a population of 23 million: an impressive figure, which, however, depends on the definition of "school."[116] Server Iskit states that an investigation he carried out for the *vilayet* (province) of Konya in 1903 showed that for nearly 2,000 students studying in modern schools there were 12,000 studying in *medreses*.[117]

Many important residues of Ottoman culture were to clash

head on with Western-based, modern education during the modernization government.

Two general observations are in order here. The era of reforms, the *Tanzimat,* revised the standards of elite education. There is nothing qualitatively new here. But the *Tanzimat* also institutionalized public education, and this is of the utmost importance. Public education meant giving attention to the education of the nonelite, extending the range of knowledge. It also meant providing the individual with greater uncontrolled possibilities for changing his own prospects in life and changing his physical and social environment. Compared to the earlier system, which at the lower level was meant to produce a common core of values more than to give a store of knowledge that then was to be urbanized with other knowledge, this was a very great change. By making education available to the nonelite, an element of contingency that only existed to a very small degree in the traditional system was introduced into society. Education in this sense constitutes a watershed in which the indeterminant effect of modern media is underscored.

Modern secondary education, which spanned the range between the Koran and elite education, was of necessity truncated in the first years of the *Tanzimat.* It appeared first in the *rusdiye,* an institution that was half primary school, half secondary. Because of this lack of differentiation it is difficult to determine precisely where the new element of *publicness* stops and what elements of elite education are still present. Nevertheless, the watershed was real.

Second, we have to underline the strategic role that elite education played even in this era. There are four types of institutions that are important in this respect: the Lycée of Galatasaray, founded in 1868; the Military Preparatory Schools established as a going concern in the 1870s; the Military Academy and the Military Medical School, which had been in operation since the beginning of the nineteenth century; and the School of Political Science.

The Lycée of Galatasaray was the product of a type of reform that had been fostered by reformist Ottoman statesmen since the 1840s.[118] It was patterned on the French lycées of the Second Empire. The majority of the courses in the school were taught in French. In the late 1870s, higher education was integrated on its premises and for a while it was the place in which the first Ottoman law school functioned. The statesmen who had been instrumental in its establishment had hoped that French culture would provide a neutral ground where Ottomans of different religious denominations could meet. Non-Turkish Ottomans did flock to the lycée but not with the results expected. Non-Muslim graduates of Galatasaray had not become close friends of the Muslims; the lycée fostered separatist currents.[119] From the beginning also, the fact that it produced persons who had a tendency to cut themselves off from the roots of Ottoman culture and look at it with some disdain alienated some of the social mobilizers who wanted to bridge the cultural gap in the Ottoman Empire. Galatasaray produced a sufficient number of young fops to cause much criticism. There were notable exceptions, such as the poet Tevfik Fikret, but the general understanding was that the Galatasaray graduate could converse well in French but was relatively uninvolved in national affairs.

The complex of military preparatory schools closely integrated with the Military Academy in 1876 by the director of Ottoman military schools, Süleyman Pasa, had exactly the opposite purpose.[120] His goal in establishing their program was to raise a generation of officers completely devoted to their country and conscious of its past glory. The importance given to the course on the history of the Ottoman Empire was the Pasa's contribution. In addition, the preparatory schools were supposed to provide technical proficiency. Süleyman Pasa's declared goal was to replace patronage with professional competence. Many of the students of the military academy came from these schools. When they arrived at the Military Academy or the Medical School, a relative unity of ideology had been obtained and Ottoman patriotism already was instilled in them. It is to this early experience as well as to their later training that we may trace the unity of outlook of the new young generation of officers and probably even the origin in military schools of the Young Turk movement.

The School of Political Science established in 1859 was fully activated only after the accession of Sultan Abdulhamid.[121] The sultan's own understanding of progress being greater administrative control, he had no objections to administrative streamlining.[122] Thus during the first years of his reign the quality of teaching at the school was high, while the subjects taught in the school followed a pattern found in similar institutions in Western Europe.[123] It was only beginning with the late 1880s that the school became suspect because of what were interpreted as political activities on the part of its students.

## CULTURAL POLICIES

We have seen that an attempt to facilitate literacy was associated with Ottoman modernization policies. The prominence of this feature continued during the *Tanzimat* era. One of the difficulties of Ottoman Turkish had been its reliance on the Arabic script. Vowels could not be unambiguously recorded with this script, and words often had to be identified by their context. In addition, in the traditional system, placing words in alphabetical order meant to place them in the order of their so-called radicals, the basic skeleton of the word; alphabetizing by placing words in the order of their letters was thus an important nineteenth-century innovation.[124] In the mid-nineteenth century, persons associated with the reform movement such as the historian Cevdet Pasa and the grand vizier Fuad Pasa had first attempted to introduce new rules for reading certain letters, when the letters were used as vowels. They had adopted this system in transcribing foreign names in the Ottoman State Annual.[125]

Europeans had long commented on the difficulties of the Arabic script. In 1862, Munif Pasa was already taking up the question of reforming the Arabic alphabet in the *Ottoman Scientific Society*.[126] Throughout the 1860s these questions—including the possibility of adopting the European alphabet—were debated by Ottoman intellectuals. Together with the facilitation of literacy through the simplification of the alphabet came the simplification of the language. Early in the nineteenth century, Sultan Mahmud II had already complained that the cumbersome Ottoman phraseology resulted in the garbling of battlefield dispatches.[127] In 1860, on the occasion of the opening of the short-lived Imperial Academy of Arts and

Sciences, we get the first glimpse of the difficulties involved in filling the cultural gap, a task that the reformist bureaucracy had taken so much to heart. The statutes of the academy declared in part, that in the past:

> . . . most writers limited their amibition to making a show of eloquence and vying with each other for the palm of success; they lived only to overembellish their style with ornamentation and did not go beyond various types of poetry and rhetoric. Consequently, the pearls which had been previously retrieved from the ocean of science remained hidden in the shell of abstract terminology, and ideas were enveloped in the veil of subtleties. Similar to the virginal betrothed they could not make their face seen to the gaze of all. Such writings, as may well be imagined, were accessible only to the intelligence of cultivated minds, the lower classes eliciting no profit from them. Yet it is well known that the salutary goal of general civilization can only be reached by the prior diffusion of diverse kinds of knowledge. Consequently, while encouraging the production of purely literary works aiming to entertain men of discrimination, insistence is [hereby] placed on the drafting of scientific and technological books written in a single style and fitted to the needs of the popular intelligence so as to provide the means of widening and completing its instruction.[128]

The banner of linguistic simplication was to be taken up later by liberal intelligentsia associated with journalism. The best remembered of the pieces written in this vein is Ziya Pasa's article entitled "Poetry and Prose" (1868), in which the accusation was leveled against the classical style for being an instrument for the perpetuation of elite rule.[129]

## THE INTELLIGENTSIA: PARTIAL DIFFERENTIATION

The Ottoman literati functioned at two levels: one was that of official preservers of the symbols of legitimacy, and second, in the privacy of their homes, they met as communicators, but this time for pleasure. The two groups had much overlap: persons drafting a document in the morning met at night to recite poetry to one another. Thus there existed in traditional Ottoman society the equivalent of the French salons, although its performing personnel were less marginal and more established. This practice continued into the nineteenth century. But at that time, some of the salons became specialized in the study of Western thought. The first of these, at the beginning of the nineteenth century, was the so-called Besiktas Circle where mathematics, astronomy, and medicine were discussed. Later, in the 1850s and 1860s, the mansions of Sami Pasa and Suphi Pasa became centers where the works of the "enlightenment" were taken up. Here we are still dealing with literati,[130] with persons who have close ties to officialdom; but some of the participants in these discussions, such as the poet Namik Kemal, had already acquired the characteristics of an intelligentsia. The first steps in the formation of this intelligentsia occurred in journalistic circles.[131]

When the Ottoman government decided to establish a journal it had to staff the offices of its *Official Gazette* (strictly translated, *"The Calendar of Events"*) with persons who had some understanding of the modern West; one of the versions of the paper was to appear in French. Churchill's newspaper, on the other hand, was produced by a number of disgruntled minor officials who had turned to journalism as an alternative to an official career, or as an additional source of livelihood. This characteristic of persons recruited into journalism continued into the 1860s. Thus the first private newspaper was a natural gathering place for opponents to the government. But, with their new skill, the latter could undertake their own ventures in journalism: the first step in the direction of "free floating" was thus taken. In the brief period between 1860 and 1865 newspapers began to criticize official policy. It was in their columns that constitutionalist ideas were elaborated.

The complete transition from literati to intelligentsia had not occurred and would not come about for a long time. This may be seen in a use of journalism that was often associated with political criticism, namely, actual or threatened political blackmail.[132] Many of the members of this incipient intelligentsia were still casting covetous glances toward well-remunerated offices and entered into negotiations in which they offered to desist from publication in exchange for reinstatement to political life. It was only in the case of the papers published by exiles that this could be done overtly, but the same theme appears in muffled form in the history of Ottoman journalism.

The uses of such latent or covert blackmail did not exclude sincere concern for the fate of the Ottoman Empire and a tendency to see oneself as responsible for its social mobilization. It was in the pages of these newspapers that information about science and humanities took the liveliest form. The services rendered by them, indeed, surpassed those of the short-lived Ottoman Academy of Sciences. More important than the official efforts, too, was the continuing support by litterateurs and journalists of the simplification of language.[133] A battle began to emerge, which, in somewhat modified form, continues today. This conflict took on the dimensions of a heated public controversy only later in the 1880s, when the cultural context of the issue—whether to go back to the Islamic "ancients" or to find new sources of inspiration—surfaced more clearly. But it was as much by the elaboration of a new journalistic language— as it was to be called by a member of the intelligentsia who soon defected for government service and later became Grand Vizier Said Pasa[134]—as through the discussion of the issue that the journalists made their contribution.

Toward the end of the nineteenth century, a "Fleet Street" appeared in Istanbul—*bab-ı Âli,* the Sublime Porte, so-called because of the proximity of the journalists' and publishers' quarters to governmental headquarters. This was no longer a salon type of gathering. It was part of a functional differentiation of cultural activities and a new step toward the formation of an intelligentsia. The new journalists were no longer "men of the pen" products of bureaus, increasingly they were graduates of the schools established during the *Tanzimat.* However, a characteristic of journalism that still leaves its imprint on Turkish journalism today was also prominent then, that is, the relative absence of news and the importance given to more "weighty" problems of foreign policy, economics, and education, often reported in quasi-editorial fashion. Among the intellectual leaders an attitude may be found that still exists: that of Platonic guardians bearing a special responsibility for the fate of the Ottoman Empire. This attitude was, no doubt, reinforced by the bureaucratic locus of much of Western influence. Proposals of interested Westerners concerning the modernization of the empire went through official channels. Officials and intellectuals, with their remaining official connections, had an advantage in this respect.

A mechanism was involved here that made for cumulation: the new educational institutions often were staffed by bureaucrats whose houses had libraries in which books from the West figured; and the litterateurs who produced the new literature, in great part, also filled positions in the Ottoman administration in addition to their literary journalistic functions.

Thus, when he was a boy, Ahmed Ihsan, later the publisher of the outstanding literary periodical *Servet-i Funun,* saw in Damascus, in the library of Süleyman Sudi Efendi, an official, the *Journal des Voyages* and was fascinated by it.[135] When Ihsan's father, another official, was appointed to Istanbul, Süleyman Sudi Efendi made the boy a present of fifty volumes from his library among which figured Western works on science and history. Even before the gift, little Ihsan's enthusiasm had been aroused. His father had not had modern and Western books in his house because he objected to illustrations. Ahmed Ihsan, however, prevailed upon his father to buy him such books. When Ahmed Ihsan went to the School of Political Science in the early 1880s, among his teachers were such men as the imperial physician (Hekimbasi) Salih Efendi, whose lectures on botany gave Ihsan a completely new understanding of life processes.[136]

In this way, then, any intellectual advances scored by one generation of bureaucrats were shared and recirculated in bureaucratic channels. On the other hand, in the Ottoman Empire during the nineteenth and even in the first years of the twentieth century there was no development comparable to that which in Russia made the university an autonomous locus for the creation of an alienated intelligentsia. In Turkey the French tactic of establishing *grandes écoles* was much more important.

### A NEW UNDERTAKING

The task that the modernist intellectuals set for themselves in the Ottoman Empire during the nineteenth century was an undertaking quite different from that in which the literati had been engaged in preceding centuries. The difference centered in the social-mobilizing goal of the intelligentsia. As such the latter had to incorporate new values into their products, to address them to a new (and often fictitious) audience, and to use genres that would suit these purposes.

This was done primarily through the introduction of Western-type theater and the novel. The first Ottoman writers who worked in these genres often used them for exemplary purposes and even more to change traditional society. The contrast here was between the measured, timeless stance of classical Ottoman literature and the new view of writers and their audience as targets for mobilization. Thus a well-known play of the poet Ibrahim Sinasi poked fun at prearranged marriages, and the historical novels of the Turkish poet Namik Kemal attempted to recapture what he considered the core Ottoman values of bravery associated with devotion to one's nation.[137] Namik Kemal's friend and collaborator Ebuzziya Tevfik has underlined a more subtle dimension of the change in values that came with the abandonment of classical Ottoman models. He states that Ottoman literati counted among their central values a disenchantment derived from the classical attitude of a search for an answer to worldly problems in mysticism. This created another mannerism: that of "coolness," of meeting events with equanimity. According to him, even the initiates of the modernization movement had been unable to shake this "fatalism." He implies that this value changed together with the introduction of a literature that was concerned with the events of daily life rather than with patterned romantic themes and the world beyond.[138] What seems quite certain is that the great emphasis of Western scientific rational thought on transforming man's environment was now pervading the Ottoman Empire.

Here again is a different type of involvement, this time of the reader in the sense of the proximity to the scenes presented in the new literature.[139] In addition, Ebuzziya Tevfik's implied comment on how much more pleasant and appealing the new genres were underlines a new dimension of the influence that they exerted: that of pleasurableness. For the new, Westernized upper class, classical literature stopped being a pleasant diversion and became a bore. It is only in the fourth quarter of the nineteenth century, however, that novels began to have a readership of more than a few hundred. In 1877, a French observer of Ottoman cultural developments probably had in mind a new rash of penny-novels when he voiced his alarm at the spread of "light literature."[140]

Somewhat different from this invasion by the penny-novel were efforts to popularize the intellectual fare that was offered in the West. This was the achievement of the encyclopedist and popular novelist Ahmed Midhat Efendi (1844–1913).[141] Although he had the same social-mobilizing goals as Sinasi and Kemal, Midhat was much more dedicated to attracting a readership of people who would not otherwise have come into contact with Western values in the course of their lives. It seems he was thus able to win over new middle-level bureaucracy that had been created by the reform movement. This he did primarily through his literary production, both in his daily, the *Tercuman-i Hakikat,* and in books. His contribution was to bring to his audiences a world of action centered on what were supposed to be modern real-life problems, themes, and situations—even though many of his stories were full of wildly romantic actions and convenient coincidences that, he insisted, the novel should avoid.

Kenan Akyuz has called this protorealism of Midhat's productions "an attention turned not toward oneself but toward the outside."[142] Here again, and more subtly than in the theater, the scenes and action from everyday life that had long figured in folk stories but had occurred within stereotyped genres broke these rigid molds and rose to become legitimate characters of the polite literature, which was being read by the expanded elite. The stories told in the novel were freer in form and less stereotyped although, as many commentators on Turkish literature have emphasized, their origins still showed. This innovation was one of the structural changes that presented a breakdown of the closed traditional world of divan literature.

By placing institutions such as the family within the context of a historical era—that of the fin de siècle Ottoman Empire—this new type of novel added a new element to the stimuli that had led the Ottoman intelligentsia to become aware of historical and social change.

It is an exaggeration to say that Ahmed Midhat's works displaced the materials traditionally read by the "people," the lower classes.[143] Here, again, the picture given by the Turkish journalist and man of letters Hüseyin Cahit (Yalçın) of his family, gathered after dinner listening to one of them reading a novel by Ahmed Midhat, would seem closer to what his influence must have amounted to. It was among middle-level employees such as Yalçın's father that Ahmed Midhat probably gained his most devoted audience.

Midhat's "populism," his interest in the life of the "honest poor,"[144] and his ethos of hard work and thrift were partly derived from his own lower-class background. But his interest in self-help was also partly influenced by Western values. Regardless of its origins, his emphasis on "real life" situations was welcome to a middle-level bureaucracy with increasingly Westernized orientations. Thus, Ahmed Midhat, rather than induce the lower classes to pull themselves up by their bootstraps, found support in the "embourgeoisement" of the middle-level bureaucrats. It is in this group that the audiences for the novel, which in English had been produced by the industrial revolution, developed.

## CUTTING OFF CULTURAL MOORINGS

In the sense that they were educated in the new, Westernized schools, the modernizing elite had alredy cut themselves off from traditional society. There is another aspect of this severing of ties that is not usually underlined but which would seem to be equally important. At an earlier time, values of the masses centering around bravery and warlike qualities had also been incorporated into the fund of values of the upper classes. Members of the upper classes indeed give us repeated indications that they first acquired a taste for reading in their youth by poring over the same tales of valor that were the staple nourishment of the masses. H. Cahit Yalçın in his memoirs gives a good description of how these values became functional: "The feats of courage of the Prophet [Caliph] Ali, the stories of Battal Gazi [a muslim fighter for the faith], the epopees of Kara Davut, the lofty conduct of the poet Nesimi . . . the soaring feelings that all these supernatural, great, beautiful things inspired were well in accord with the unfettered life I led in Rumelia reminiscent as it was of the Middle Ages."[145]

In Cahit's case as well as in that of many other Turkish modernists such folk themes encountered during childhood were vividly remembered as a significant part of the process of socialization. Cahit also states how alien to him as a young man had become the style of the more abstruse treatises on religion, even though religion played an important role in his adolescence. If this is true, Cahit's generation as a whole was still familiar with values acquired through this channel. This situation might well have lasted into the first two decades of the twentieth century. With time, increasingly few school-educated Turks retained the link with folk literature. Although later, after the turn of the century, a special effort was made among the more Westernized, the tie was almost completely severed. This severance together with the modern educational background of the intelligentsia made for a new type of cultural elitism, which worked counter to all the trends towards involvement that we have examined here. The effort of the intelligentsia to create neologisms that would express the concerns, emphases and nuances of feeling, which one found in Western literature, was attacked as a revival of the worst features of the old language. What the communication data tell us are that the boundaries of the official class were gradually widened. The number of participants in government, which now included the middle bureaucracy, increased in the 1880s, but the new upper bureaucracy (and especially its two subgroups of dandies and members of the Westernist intellectual avant-garde) was even more cut-off from sources of popular culture than the old. This was especially true at the beginning of the twentieth century. It is in this connection that some old networks of communication such as mosque sermons began to operate with increased vigor as the medium of the lower classes. But this was not acknowledged by the new ruling elite.

## A NEW WORLD VIEW

Even though the great majority of Turkish journalists saw themselves as social mobilizers, this goal could take at least two distinct forms. One of these was that of political criticism. The fortunes of this approach fluctuated. Curbs on free expression were introduced as early as 1864 and were increased in the second part of the reign of Sultan Abdulhamid II from 1886 onward.[146] A second, less controversial, form of emphasizing that Turks had to pull themselves up by their own bootstraps was the thesis that the Ottomans should work hard and apply themselves to economic tasks. This was never banned and provided a platform for the continuation of social-mobilizing themes in the Turkish press throughout the last half of the nineteenth century. Thus, despite the ban on libertarian ideas during the reign of Sultan Abdulhamid, the encouragement of social activism could go on. Even discussions concerning cultural identity could be assimilated in this theme.

Although censorship limited the number of works produced, the modernizing litterateurs found ways of maintaining and expanding the interest of their readers. In newspapers and journals the recurrent issues discussed were culture, national identity, language, and education;[147] in short, problems of the modernization of the empire. The ground covered here was much wider and the contribution much more important than is usually realized. At a time when censorship began to hit harder, science and the scientific advances of the Western world became themes around which some outstanding members of the intelligentsia rallied.[148]

Other writers kept the attention of their audience by elaborating new poetic genres and forging a language fitted to these innovations. They introduced new psychological analyses in their prose writing under the influence of Paul Bourget. In both cases, the influence of European models was paramount.[149] On each occasion, even these incursions into modernism at the purely formal level were correctly characterized by conservatives as subversive to the static cultural order that the sultan found congenial for the preservation of the empire.

Although interested in art for art's sake, the Turkish fin de siècle writers of the *Servet-i Funun* school built some realism into their prose work. This was true to the extent that their short stories and novels looked at their contemporaries and described in detail family scenes or journalistic circles of the time.[150] The disenchantment pervading the younger generation of more idealistic litterateurs could—as in Halit Ziya's *Mai ve Siyah* (Blue and Black)—emerge as a necessary portion of the novel. In addition, the end-of-the-century Ottoman vogue for realism and naturalism had patent aspects of social criticism. Science, realism, psychological probings, all of these had the net effect of introducing a new image of man: man as part of an inter-related system of nature, society, and personality. Hüseyin Cahit Yalçın relates his own estrangement from traditional culture resulting from this intellectual climate. He recounts how a book by Muhiddin-i Arabi that his father "never let out of his sight"[151] became meaningless to him. Yalçın also tells us how despite and maybe because of, his access to Western literature, he felt hemmed in by a cultural "Wall of China" separating the Ottoman Empire from Europe.[152] A further ex-tension of the same feeling was the severing of links with Arab culture. At the time of Abdulhamid both the sultan and cultural conservatives stressed the Arab root of Ottoman cul-ture. They thus hoped to keep under control libertarian ideas on one hand and Western cultural influences on the other. For the sultan this was also an attempt to give a new unity to what was left of the Ottoman Empire. Hüseyin Cahit took him to task for this attitude. "What is it to us," he asked, "even if the Arabs had a developed civilization?" Science was the most im-portant contemporary current, and that current was found in the West, not in Arabia.[153]

Literary production was altogether a more sensitive area of society than the activity itself would warrant. By the end of the reign of Sultan Abdulhamid, orientation toward Western-influenced literature was a sort of free-masonry, which provided the Turkish intelligentsia with communication links that were diffuse but nevertheless operated both as a catalyst and as a ce-ment, as a modernist worldview in the broadest sense. Those educated in the new schools also managed to keep in touch with Western European and also with émigré Turkish journalism.

Because the Ottoman Empire did not progress economically at a very significant rate in the second half of the nineteenth century, these advances in communication had an impact primarily limited to official circles. The type of linkages that result in a society "learning to work together" were not well es-tablished.[154] Changes in communication had their most visible impact on differentiation within the ruling groups and new subgroups, such as the intelligentsia. One further way in which this differentiation occurred was by the progressive establishment of some of the Weberian characteristics of rationality in the Ottoman bureaucracy. Karal has provided the details of this growth and thus I shall not dwell on it here;[155] but I wish to emphasize some communication consequences of this growth.

### ADMINISTRATION

Traditional Ottoman administration was analogous to a truncated pyramid with a base and an apex but hardly any middle. Another way of saying the same thing is that the state had virtually no instrumentality for providing services such as health, education, and welfare on an empire-wide basis. These services were very limited in Ottoman Turkey. During the era preceding the administrative reforms of the nineteenth century, the government had been primarily involved in the collection of taxes and the regulations of the military machine. Late in the eighteenth century, even these functions had been substantially lost to competition of local notables. A function of the central authority of the state in Western Europe that became crucially important during the rise of the modern state, that is, collaboration with local authorities for the development of the economy —and eventually interference in local affairs for these purposes —had been essentially absent before modernization in the Ottoman state. The building of new roads, the establishment of postal systems, or the elimination of internal tolls had not been policies that the state supported. On the contrary, in many instances, it was the state which legitimized barriers to internal trade (tolls) because it used them as a source of revenue. To the extent that the penetrative activities of the modern state were absent in Turkey up to the nineteenth century, a staff, which of necessity had to be created in Europe to bring about these changes, did not come into being.

The *Tanzimat* meant to change this structure.[156] Government now existed on the one hand for the collection of taxes, as always, but on the other for the dynamic improvement of the life of its citizens rather than the older, static, patrimonial protection of public order and justice. This new type of administration acquired regularized institutional bases only after the 1870s.

In Europe, the creation of the bureaucratic apparatus had brought its own communication channels. The growth of the number of bureaucratic positions eventually resulting in a diamond shape had also fostered the growth of red tape and of a new standardized intrabureaucratic style of communication.[157] This has not as yet been made the subject of detailed historical studies, but the general development is well known. We can surmise that interbureaucratic communication through memoranda, governmental directives, and reports also probably changed the entire climate of bureaucratic work in the Ottoman Empire.

The *Tanzimat* governor was an official responsible to the center and in communication with it. This new type of governor, whose educational standard was rising very gradually, was now encumbered by a flow of red tape. His time was taken up in correspondence with the center and directives to his own bureaus, which were in the process of greater differentiation.[158] He had to work with a local council that occupied an important and growing part in local administration. All of these developments created new channels of communication. The governor and his staff had to circulate directives, fill statistical tally sheets, and keep dossiers. At an earlier time, it is true, the clerks had kept records, but the new type of record keeping was not related so much to the will of the sultan, it was increasingly self-justifying and legitimizing. In these circumstances, official correspondence could be used both to avoid making decisions and to have the directives of the center implemented. On the other hand, the inconsistencies in the policy of the central authorities had more of an opportunity to emerge. Bureaucracy as a going concern became the subject of discussions among upper- and lower-rank employees. The governor had less power, but government was more visible. It is true, of course, that this visibility was relative and in some places almost nil.

In these circumstances, the fact that administration is a whole and that administrators are part of a total structure impresses itself more forcefully. Conversely, procedural exceptions, favoritism, or the treatment of individuals on an ascriptive basis are underlined. They become more flagrant to the extent that they violate standard procedure. Rule making emerges. All in all, then, changes in the structure of the administration also had consequences for the structure of communications within the administration.

In the more developed parts of Turkey the new visibility of government also had striking effects. In the Balkans, the policy of reform was interpreted as being one that would curb the power of local landowners and initiate a land reform. When land was not redistributed promptly, bloody revolts ensued in the 1840s and the Ottoman government had a hard time convincing the population that landowners retained their property rights.[159] Thus for persons with grievances in the more developed Ottoman provinces the establishment of improved administrative links itself had a communication effect. The capacity "to disseminate messages [of] the central political authority" increased even before the mass media took up this task.[160] The bureaucracy itself was more closely linked within its own ranks, however, by new media such as administrative messages on the one hand and the new fund of modern media such as newspapers and books on the other.

A final dimension of change under the rubric "administration" was the erosion of the complex linkage structure for symbols of legitimacy. Through Islam as a cultural system and the learned institution as a structure for spanning the distance between officialdom and the lower classes this linkage had been achieved. The officials of the *Tanzimat* were now building up a new system of legitimacy, that of a different type of state, as an end in itself. Here "different type" is as important as "end in itself." For in the traditional system the state, in a way described above, had been an end in itself. Conceptions of the state as a secular entity had also been adumbrated in earlier Ottoman state practices. It is the newness of the entire enterprise of building a nation-state that has to be kept in mind here to underline the changes in legitimacy symbols; the de-emphasis on *millets* and localities, the larger state apparatus, the attempts at establishing empire-wide codes of administration and structures of education.

The rulers of the *Tanzimat* had difficulties in carrying out their intention. To create governmental and administrative structure was difficult enough. To build a new frame of reference for the intelligentsia, an ideology was devised and launched by intellectuals in the 1870s and received sympathetic consideration by Sultan Abdulhamid. It was only partly successful as a section of the intelligentsia was not yet satisfied that Ottomanism included the libertarian guarantees they thought were essential. To link the lower classes to a new symbolic system of legitimacy or to integrate the old and the new was where the modernizers were least successful. Thus with time the masses began to be alienated from the entire enterprise of officially sponsored Westernization.

## COMMUNICATION AND THE PARTIAL GROWTH OF THE ECONOMY

One of the consequences of the Crimean War was the growth of interest in the Ottoman Empire as a center for economic development and foreign investment. Just as in the case of the Stuart and the Tudor bureaucracies, which tried to preserve selectively some socially beneficial aspects of the old order, there are indications that Ottoman statesmen were wary of involving the empire in accelerated economic change. They vaguely perceived that economic concessions granted too liberally would place the Ottomans at the mercy of foreign interests.[161] The example of the undermining of local Ottoman handicrafts in the early nineteenth century was before their eyes. Others, however, were more willing to spark development by a policy of disastrous financial loans from Europe. Here they were brought to the point that they had tried to avoid in the first place. Finance capital, aided and abetted by capitulatory privileges, supported by the Great Powers and helped by local minority groups got a tight grip over the economy of the empire. Nevertheless, it is very doubtful that this hold was as tight as is sometimes woefully described, because the Ottoman statesmen's aims had succeeded in one respect: the Ottoman Empire was so little developed as a whole that large infrastructural investments had to be undertaken before a profit could be made even by foreign investors. In a limited coastal region, however, trade was brisk and profits easy. Istanbul, Izmir, and Salonika were the three leading centers. The growth of trade meant the growth of communication for these centers. Thus, a calculation based on the figures provided by Rougon shows that telegraphic communications per person in the town of Izmir were ten times what they were for the empire as a whole.[162]

All of the changes described earlier led the new bureaucratic middle group to disassociate itself from the central administration in the last years of the century. The latter was still staffed by many more parasite favorites than might be gathered from the declared policy of the Sultan Abdulhamid II and his real efforts to improve the situation.[163] In addition, the higher reaches of the administrative pyramid were less subject to financial worries, while the middle and lower strata were left to fend for themselves on inadequate salaries often in arrears. A great number of administrators from the provinces lost by the empire were resettled in such unattractive posts. To compound their difficulties, many new posts were created for them and the limited resources were spread thinner and failed to satisfy the expectations of the swelling newer bureaucracy.[164]

A much larger proportion of the middle stratum of the bureaucracy had now graduated from the new schools established since 1839. The stratum may thus be described as both absolutely and relatively deprived. Development had meant the rise of this discontented middle stratum. What existed of the framework of a rational bureaucracy made this group desire to close the circle, to establish a civil service with real guarantees of security and hopes of professional advancement. Indeed, the exposure of the group to the universalistic achievement values of schools, to rationality in administration, and to the beginning of bureaucratic rule making created dissatisfaction in its ranks in addition to resistance to the older, large residue of "oriental" administration and procedure. "Science," which had been reported to rule over societal action in Western countries, was the ideological capstone of this discontent.

There ensued what may be described as a "complementarity of communication"[165] in the bureaucracy that functioned with most effect among the discontented. Although the bureaucrats were united by a common reliance on ideas concerning "contemporary civilization," their unity of outlook was not the old unity of outlook of the servant of the *porte* trained in the

Palace School. The new view had a universalistic context. It was formed around such concepts as humanity, science, liberty, and progress. It was dependent not so much on internally anchored feelings of subservience and superiority, as on external cues, on the mobilization dynamic of the newly developed media. The media depended on participation on the part of an audience, and as such they acted as the shapers of a new consensus. There was much greater room in this new outlook for identifying oneself with the lower classes, especially as more extensive social mobilization was a goal of many of the more forward-looking bureaucrats. Modern media, then, had strongly influenced the new, active groups that appeared within the bureaucracy; ideology emerged. The mindless turmoil of palace camarillas was thus replaced by the action of ideological groups. By this I mean groups using a type of intellectual framework that has as a necessary corollary appeal to and dependence upon increasingly wider circles, culminating in the conception of "the people." This is very different from—although not necessarily better than—the closed ideology of traditional Ottoman bureaucracy. It should not be forgotten that some of the characteristics of the new communicators—and, in particular, the increasing concentration of modernist intellectuative pursuits in a new caste cut off from the large mass of the public—went counter to the trend toward openness, and that part of the press rallied around traditional values. A total assessment of the modernization of communication in Turkey should take both tendencies into account.[166]

## CONCLUSION

Taken as a whole, the modernization of communication is an immensely complex process. It is complex because so many processes are subsumed under communication, and because, in the case of Ottoman Turkey, information concerning these processes is limited and diffuse.

The materials gathered here are tentative to the extent that they are based on areas that have been scantily researched. In this chapter, the modernization of communication was placed within the framework of the modernization of the Turkish bureaucracy. A hypothesis advanced was that this process is illuminated when one keeps in mind that within Ottoman society Ottoman bureaucracy was a numerically relatively small sultanic-patrimonial machine. This top of the iceberg was possibly responsive to the needs of the lower classes but it did not provide what we understand today by "public" service. In addition, the "secular" branch of government was geared to elite education. The modern nation based on the social mobilization and horizontal integration had to develop a much different system of communication.

The preceding has aimed at underlining how much the study of communication is system-specific. In the case of the Ottoman Empire we have to understand the political system to understand the modernization of communication. One point that arises in this respect is whether in the theory of power we have neglected "information" as a third fundamental dimension of power that should be placed side by side with "domination" and economically derived power.

In the Ottoman Empire domination and information were closely linked. In the absence of strong autonomous economic institutions the dissociation of information from domination had the same contingency potential that the growth of an autonomous economic system brought about under different circumstances in Western Europe. Thus during the transformation of Ottoman institutions both the attempts of the economic sector to acquire autonomy and the concept of an autonomous communication system encountered opposition from various groups in the establishment. At the same time, some of the old features for the control of communication were refurbished. New elite educational institutions continued the tradition of the guardian caste. Control features also appeared later in the educational theories of Emrullah Efendi, minister of public instruction. The core of this theory was that modernization could best be obtained by educating a class of Turkish modernist leaders. This aspect was one that also was the core of the system enforced in Republican Turkey. A recent reflection of the state's concern with elite education has been the 1971 decision of the Turkish Constitutional Court that private schools in higher education are unconstitutional.

The modern Turkish state's shadow over education has been

one aspect of the perpetuation of the Ottoman constriction of knowledge. A second development working in the same direction has been the "esotericization" of knowledge, as knowledge has increasingly become an enterprise with a Western European foundation. Because socialization in the lower-class families remained an exclusively Islamic process, a barrier was set to the transition from this background into the Westernized educational establishment. Cultural and educational boundaries became class boundaries. The cultural boundary between a lower-class Islamic culture and an upper-class Western culture caused alienation on both sides.

Nevertheless, a third aspect of the modernization of communication has worked in the opposite direction. Subsumed under this rubric are generalized public education and the autonomy potential of modern media. To the extent that this liberalizing potential of media is vitiated by political or economic control, the potential is often not realized. Nevertheless, the dissent possibilities opened up even by privately held mimeographing machines are clear.

Public instruction, on the other hand, has the widest contingency possibilities. As the system of public instruction becomes more successful in turning out persons with skills for combining and using information individually, we are increasingly faced with a communication "mix" different from that which existed in the traditional system and one the outcome of which is increasingly difficult to predict.

## NOTES

I am grateful to Professors Fahir İz and Howard Reed for their comments on the first draft of this chapter.

First issues of newspapers: *Sabah*, 1876, 25 February; *Tercüman-i Hakikat* 1878, 26 June; *Tasvir-i Efkâr* 1862, 30 Zilhicre; *Mizan* 1886, 22 Muharrem; *İkdam* 1894, 23 June; *Servet-i Fünun* 1891, 5 March.

1. See S. N. Eisenstadt, *The Political Systems of Empires* (New York: Collier Macmillan, 1969).

2. See Max Gluckman, *Politics, Law and Ritual in Tribal Society* (New York and Toronto: Mentor Books, 1965), pp. 155–201.

3. Max Weber, *Economy and Society*, 3 vols., (New York, 1968), 3:1006–1069.

4. On Selim, see Stanford J. Shaw, *Between Old and New: The Ottoman Empire under Sultan Selim III, 1789-1807* (Cambridge, Mass., 1971). On Mahmud II, see *Islâm Ansiklopedisi* (hereinafter cited as *IA*), 7:165-170; H. A. Reed, "The Destruction of the Janissaries by Sultan Mahmud II in 1826," Ph.D. dissertation, Princeton University, 1951.

5. On this expression, see R. R. Palmer, *The Age of Democratic Revolution* (Princeton, 1959), vol. 1, p. 23. For earlier "estates," see C. J. Friedrich, *The Age of the Baroque 1610-1660* (New York, 1952), pp.14 ff.

6. See Fahir İz, *Eski Türk Edebiyatında Nesir* (Istanbul, 1964), vol. 5. On the control of the so-called divan literature by an educated elite, see Walther Bjorkman, "Die Klassisch Osmanische Literatur," in *Philogiae Turcicae Fundamenta* (Wiesbaden, 1964), vol. 2, p. 427. See also Agâh Sırrı Levend, *Divan Edebiyatı* (Istanbul, 1941), pp. 8ff.

7. "Reis ül-Küttab," *İA*, 9:671-683.

8. See "Inshâ," *Encyclopaedia of Islam* (hereinafter cited as *EI*) 3:1241-1244; "Dıwān," *EI*, 2:323. On the growth of such tradition in the office of Nişancı, see "Nişancı," *IA*, 9:299-302.

9. See "Devshirme," *EI*, 2:210-213.

10. See Faik Reşit Unat, *Türkiye Eğitim Sisteminin Gelişmesine Tarihî bir Bakış* (Ankara, 1964), pp. 10 ff., and Barnette Miller, *The Palace School of Muhammed the Conqueror* (Cambridge, Mass., 1941).

11. See "Askari," *EI*, 1:712; "Musadere," *IA*, fasc. 87 (1959), pp. 669-673; and, for a general description, Ahmet Mumcu, *Osmanlı Devletinde Siyaseten Katl* (Ankara, 1963), p. 71.

12. "Reis ül-Küttab," *IA*, 9:676-677.

13. See L. Fekete, *Die Siyaqat Schrift*, 2 vols. (Budapest, 1955).

14. For the feeling of being different from the *ulema*, see "Reis ül- Küttab," *IA*, 9:676-677.

15. For Kâtip Çelebi, see Abdülhak Adnan Adıvar, *Osmanlı Türklerinde İlim*, 2nd ed. (Istanbul, 1943), p.118.

16. "Reis ül-Küttab," *IA*, 9:679.

17. Ibnülemin Mahmut Kemal [İnal], *Son Asır Türk Şairleri* (Istanbul, 1930) vol. 1, p. 113, quoting Cevdet Paşa, *Tarih*, vol. 11, p. 13.

18. For the training of religious personnel, see "Softa," *IA*, 11:735-736. For a biography that enables us to follow the career of an intellectually inclined Doctor of Islamic Law, see I. H. Uzunçarşılı, "Değerli Türk Âlimi ve Güzel Sanatlar Üstadı Abdülbaki Aziz Efendi," *Belleten* 22 (1958):101-115.

19. H. A. R. Gibb and Harold Bowen, *Islamic Society and the West* (London, New York, Toronto, 1957) vol.1, pt.2, p. 95.

20. Bernard Lewis, *Istanbul and the Civilization of the Ottoman Empire* (Norman, 1963), p. 151.

21. See G. B. Toderini, *De la Litérature des Turcs*, 3 vols. (Paris, 1789), 2:29.

22. James Porter, *Turkey, Its History and Progress* (London, 1854), vol. 2, p. 144.

23. See Ünat, *Türkiye Eğitim*, pp. 3–6; and Çağatay Uluçay, *Manisa Ünlüleri* (Manisa).

24. On the difficulties encountered by Doctors of Islamic Law in grasping the system of executive regulations by the imperial power, see "Kanun-nâme," *IA*, 6:191; also "Örf," *IA*, 9:480.

25. For a statement on the dangers of disseminating lay or religious knowledge indiscriminately, described, in this instance, as "throwing pearls into the mouths of dogs," see Orhan Şaik Gökyay, *Kâtip Çelebiden Seçmeler* (Istanbul, 1968), p. 222. N. R. Keddie has commented on some of the subtler effects of the permeation of culture by religious and elitist views: "Modern scholars have sometimes noted that attitudes towards the nature of truth and the extent to which truth is to be disseminated among society at large were very different in Medieval Islamic society from what they are in the modern West. Medieval Muslim thinkers of various schools both orthodox and heterodox tended to think that society was inevitably divided into an elite which was capable of understanding the full truth and a majority of persons who were not capable of such understanding and for whom education in the ways of truth might be more harmful than helpful. Intellectuals or religious sectarians with such assumptions did not show any compunction about representing themselves in public as believing something other than what they truly believed." ("Symbol and Sincerity in Islam," *Studia Islamica*, 19 (1963):27.)

26. Franz Rosenthal, *Knowledge Triumphant: The Concept of Knowledge in Medieval Islam* (Leiden, 1970). But compare G. E. von Grunebaum, *Islam* (1961) p. 112: ". . . to be fully relevant and fully justifiable science will have to inquire into the data of revelation."

27. Rosenthal, *Knowledge Triumphant*, p. 309.

28. Ibid., pp. 71 ff., 155 ff., 194 ff., 240 ff., 309–310, 334 ff. Rosenthal does not reach unequivocal conclusions concerning knowledge in Islam.

29. For an analysis of this type of decline in an earlier Islamic context, see Willy Hartner, "Quand et Comment s'est Arrêté l'Essor de la Culture Scientifique de l'Islam," in *Classicisme et Déclin Culturel dans l'Histoire de l'Islam* (Paris, 1957), pp. 319–334. Hartner attributes the decline in Islamic science to a tendency for freezing into dogmatic molds. For the concept of "open" as opposed to "closed" communications systems, see John T. Dorsey, Jr., "An Information Energy Model," in *Papers in Comparative Public Administration*, ed. Ferrel Heady and Sybil L. Stokes, (University of Michigan: Institute of Public Administration, 1962), pp. 44 ff.

30. For a discussion of the evidence of decline with regard to the highest religious officials, see Sabra F. Meservey, "Feyzullah Efendi: An Ottoman Şeyhülislâm," Ph.D. dissertation, Princeton University, 1965, pp. 17 ff. For

Kâtip Çelebi's remarks, see Adıvar, *Osmanlı Türklerinde İlim*, p.119; for an exception, see "Kâtip Çelebi," *IA*, 6:432, on Kadızâde.

31. Howard E. Wilson, İlhan Başgöz, *Türkiye Cumhuriyetinde Milli Eğitim ve Atatürk* (Ankara, 1968), p. 246.

32. See "Kâtip Çelebi," *IA*, 6:434–435; also "Hadjji Khalifa," *EI*, 2:204–206.

33. See Gökyay, *Kâtip Çelebiden Seçmeler*, p. 222.

34. Communication from Professor Fahir İz.

35. See Aydın Sayılı, "Üçüncü Muradin İstanbul Rasathânesindeki Mücessem Yer Küresi ve Avrupa ile Kültürel Temaslar," *Belleten* 25 (1961): 406–426; and compare Andrew C. Hess, "The Evolution of the Ottoman Seaborne Empire in the Age of the Oceanic Discoveries, 1453–1525," *American Historical Review* 75 (1970):1892–1919, in which Ottoman hubris is well analyzed; see particularly, p. 1899, note 26.

36. See Abdülhak Adnan Adıvar, *Osmanlı Türklerinde İlim*, p. 55.

37. See Agâh Sırrı Levend, *Türk Dilinde Gelişme ve Sadeleşme Evreleri* 2nd ed. (Ankara, 1960), pp. 8–13. Also İsmail Habib, *Edebiyat Bilgileri* (Istanbul, 1943) pp. 289–291.

38. See Unat, *Türkiye Eğitim*, p. 3. Meservey, "Feyzullah Efendi," p. 158, states that the library of a late seventeenth-century Doctor of Islamic Law consisted of 2,270 books: twenty-four in Persian, twelve in Turkish, and all the rest in Arabic.

39. For the scarcity of certain books see, "Ahmed III," *IA*, 1:167. See also *IA*, 1:329. The poet Nedim was grateful to have been promoted to a librarianship because he owned only "a few books." See "Nedim," *IA*, 9:170. The printing activities of the press do not seem to have eased the difficulty of obtaining books. On the expensiveness of texts, see Toderini, *Littérature*, 2:31. For one work he states that a decree of the reigning Sultan Abdulhamid (end of the eighteenth century) mentioned a price that enabled him to calculate that the manuscript cost sixty times as much as the same volume printed would have cost in Italy, Ibid., p. 32. Thus we gather that the communication crisis had not been solved by the introduction of printing.

40. Fuad Köprülü, "Milli Edebiyat Cereyanının Ilk Mübeşşirleri," in *Edebiyat Araştırmaları* (Ankara, 1966), p. 297.

41. Charles MacFarlane, *Constantinople in 1828*, 2nd ed. (London, 1829), vol. 2, p. 23.

42. Compare İz, *Eski Türk Edebiyatında Nesir*, vol.5, who does not hold this view to be correct, with Walther Bjorkman, "Die Klassisch-Osmanische Literatur," in *Philologiae Turcicae Fundamenta*, (Wiesbaden, 1964) vol. 2, 442, and with Levend, *Türk Dilinde*, p. 21. Köprülü, "Milli Edebiyat Cereyanının," p. 296, states that beginning with the late seventeenth century there was a reaction in literary circles against widespread use of Persian and Arabic.

43. See Said Paşa, *Hâtırat*, vol. 1, p. 27.

44. For the history of language reform see U. Heyd, "Language Reform in Modern Turkey," *Middle Eastern Affairs*, 2 (1953):402–409; for new words, see Levend, *Türk Dilinde*, p. 88.

45. "Mekteb" *IA*, 7:656. Calligraphy was still in the process of being introduced at the end of the eighteenth century. Reading and writing in Turkish were part of the program after 1838. Ünat, in *Türkiye Eğitim*, p. 9, criticizes Osman Ergin's view that Arabic was the languge of elementary instruction, but evidence to this effect may be found in İhsan Sungu "Tevhid-i Tedrisat," *Belleten* 2 (1938):397–431. But as Ünat says, *explanations* to students had, of necessity, to be in Turkish in addition to which songs and the fundamental operations of arithmetic *(Karacümle)* were taught in Turkish. See also Mehmet Zeki Pakalın, *Osmanlı Tarih Deyimleri ve Terimleri Sözlüğü* (Istanbul, 1956), vol. 3, p. 202. Ünat, *Türkiyede Eğitim*, p. 9, mentions "middle schools" outside the *medrese* system, but these were exceptions to the rule.

46. This reliance on abstruse classics seems to have have been true of traditional China, but there the greater sophistication of the primary school program is clear. It is probable that those who succeeded in completing the arduous course in Chinese elementary education had a more substantial culture than did the graduates of traditional Ottoman elementary schools. See Martin C. Yang, *A Chinese Village* (New York and London, 1965), pp. 146–147.

47. Robert Holmes Beck, *A Social History of Education* (Englewood Cliffs, New Jersey, 1965), pp. 25–26.

48. Ibid., p. 33. Even though higher education in the West for centuries bore the imprint of Latin, the situation was not the same as with Arabic in the Ottoman Empire. Latin seems to have been much more widely used as an international language. In addition, with the decline of the empire, it became increasingly difficult to get good teachers of Arabic. (The new Faculty of Divinity at Ankara has also faced this problem since its inception in 1949). In Europe, on the other hand, the teaching of Latin was constantly perfected. See Howard A. Reed, "The Faculty of Divinity at Ankara II," *The Muslim World*, 47 (January 1957):22–35.

49. During a survey of worker religiosity sponsored by the Turkish Social Science Association. For a typology of folk literature see İlhan Başgöz, *İzahlı Türk Halk Edebiyatı Antolojisi* (Istanbul, 1968), pp. 9–13 and footnote 47.

50. Agâh Sırrı Levend, "Halk ve Tasavvufi Halk Edebiyatı," *Türk Dili* 19 (December 1968):171–185. Also Ahmed Kabaklı, *Türk Edebiyatı*, 1st ed. (Istanbul, 1966), vol. 2, pp. 108–109; and İsmail Habib, *Eski Nesirde Saf Türkçe*, p. 35.

51. Because it was directed to the "common people," as described by Kabaklı in *Türk Edebiyati*, vol. 2, p. 109. Another branch was somewhat closer to divan literature, see Pakalın, *Osmanli Tarih Deyimleri*, vol. 3, p. 446, citing Yücel, *Türk Edebiyatına Toplu bir Bakış* (Istanbul, 1932), p. 49.

52. Danışman, ed., *Tarih-i Nâima* (1965), vol. 1, p. 112. Also for contemporary Turkey, Aziz Nesin, *Böyle Gelmiş Böyle Gitmez* (Istanbul, 1966), pp. 36 ff.

53. Lessons in Koranic exegesis were one of the types of public lectures that were appreciated. See "Nedim," *IA*, 9:170.

54. For the concept of "openness" in communication, see above note 29.

55. For the millet system, see Alfred Carleton's Hartford Seminary Foundation Ph.D. dissertation, "The Millet System for the Government of Minorities in the Ottoman Empire," 1937; also Gibb and Bowen, *Islamic Society*, vol. 1, pt. 2, pp. 207–261.

56. Franz Babinger, *Stambuler Buchwesen im 18. Jahrhundert* (Leipzig, 1919); Adıvar, *Osmanlı Türklerinde İlim*, p. 146.

57. Alfred Carleton, "The Millet System," p. 112.

58. For Europe, see Karl Polanyi, *The Great Transformation*, (Boston, 1968; first published, 1944).

59. Reinhard Bendix and Seymour Martin Lipset, "Karl Marx's Theory of Social Classes," in *Class, Status and Power*, ed. Reinhard Bendix and Seymour Martin Lipset, 2nd ed. (New York, 1966), pp. 8–9.

60. Ian Watt, *The Rise of the Novel* (London, 1960), p. 42.

61. Ibid., p. 58.

62. Ibid., p. 59.

63. See in particular the selections in A. H. Halsey, Jean Floud, and C. Arnold Anderson, eds., *Education, Economy and Society* (New York, 1961), pp. 37, 74, 88, 274, 291.

64. For political implications regarding "consensus," see Michael Mann, "The Social Cohesion of Liberal Democracy," *American Sociological Review*, 35 (1970):423–439.

65. Şerif Mardin, *Comparative Studies in Society and History*, 11 (1969):264–270.

66. See Harry G. Good and James D. Teller, *A History of Western Education*, 3rd ed. (London, 1969), pp. 94–95. The purely academic undertakings of the guilds described here also have no exact counterpart in the Ottoman Empire, pp. 93–94.

67. On the separation of the civilian from the military, see N. Berkes, "İlk Türk Matbaası Kurucusunun dini ve fikri kimliği," *Belleten* 26 (1962):718.

68. A typical comment of a Western observer that must have been effectively channeled to the rulers goes as follows: "As to their want of skill in military matters it is evident to all the world. How should this be transmitted amongst a people who, strangers both to the Manual Exercise and the Press are reduced to oral tradition. Must it not inevitably decrease amongst them every day . . . ." Tott, *Memoirs* (London, 1785), vol. 2, Appendix, p. 43.

69. Ruffin, a French expert on Ottoman affairs, made the following

perceptive remarks concerning the introduction of printing: "The writings of the Turks being liable to double meanings, to enigmas, to a play on words, naturally gives them that taste; and they annex little value to anything which does not fatigue the understanding. This was precisely the case in Europe before the invention of Printing, which would operate in Turkey the same miracle it has wroght with us; it would fix the Turkish idiom, multiply their books, facilitate their literature and completely refine and polish it. But to produce this effect, this useful art must be sincerely patronized by the Ulemat's [Doctors of Islamic Law]; and it cannot be denied that these literati jealous of that pre-eminence which their Science, such as it is, secures them over the people will, with great difficulty, be prevailed upon to make this sacrifice." (Tott, *Memoirs,* vol. 1, p. 9.)

70. Preparations were started in 1726, but the first book came off the press in 1729. See Server İskit, *Türkiyede Neşriyat Hareketleri Tarihine bir Bakış* (Istanbul, 1939), pp. 6–7. Compare "İbrahim Müteferrika," *EI,* 3:996–998, which gives the date as 1727.

71. Selim Nüzhet [Gerçek], *Türk Matbacılığı* (Istanbul, 1928), p. 24; Jâle Baysal, in her *Müteferrikadan Birinci Meşrutiyete Kadar Osmanlı Türklerinin Bastıkları Kitaplar* (Istanbul, 1968), p. 13, strongly supports the "fanaticism" thesis. Berkes, "İbrahim Müteferrika," *EI,* 3:997, states that the innovation saw no opposition from religious interests. This seems to have been a result of the restriction of printable matters to "secular" sciences and other screening devices. See Ahmet Refik, *Hicrî On İkinci Asırda Istanbul Hayatı* (A.D. 1100–A.D. 1200) (Istanbul, 1930), pp. 90–91. İskit, *Türkiyede Neşriyat Hareketleri,* p. 7, indicates that religious interests opposed printing on the grounds that "too many" religious books circulating created a danger for "public order" and "religious practices." See also Babinger, *Stambuler Buchwesen,* p. 7.

72. See Şerif Mardin, *The Genesis of Young Ottoman Thought* (Princeton, 1962), p. 227.

73. "Reis ül-Küttab," *IA,* 9:671–683.

74. See İnalcık's description of the rise of the bureau of *Âmedi,* which might either have been a sign of the increasing concentration of power into the hands of the scribal elite and the Reis ül-Küttab or of increased state business in the amedi's office; "Reis ülüttab," *IA,* 9:675.

75. During the reforms of Selim III (1789–1807) the scribal posts in bureaux of the Grand Vizier were strictly limited so that only competent scribes would be appointed. But these positions had been so overstaffed at the onset of reforms that it is difficult to judge what their reduction from 200 in 1789 to 110 in 1798 achieved in terms of rationalization. See Shaw, *Between Old and New,* pp. 171–174.

76. See "İbrahim Müteferrika," *EI* 3:997.

77. İskit, *Türkiyede Neşriyat*, pp. 12–13 ff. The aim of the publications to serve as guides for bureaucrats is only part of the picture. More wide-ranging intentions such as to open the eyes of the Ottoman statesmen to the general situation of Western Europe, to underline the importance of geography as a science, to induce tolerance to the advice of experts also appear. See Berkes, "İlk Türk Matbaası," p. 718. At the same time Müteferrika seems to have thought that the main benefit of printing would be to spread literacy to all classes of society. See Osman Ersoy, *Türkiyeye Matbaanın Girişi ve İlk Basılan Eserler* (Ankara, 1959), p. 32. Only at the time of Selim III (1789–1807) do the more specialized military aims come out in a sustained series of publications concerning military science and mathematics as compared to earlier scattered efforts.

78. Baysal, *Müteferrikadan*, pp. 31, 33.

79. Ersoy, *Türkiyeye Matbaanın Girişi*, p. 25.

80. Baysal, *Müteferrikadan*, pp. 61–62.

81. İskit, *Türkiyede Neşriyat*, speaks of 500 titles. Baysal, *Müteferrikadan* pp. 56–62 has 436. Similar to the effect of printing must have been the gradual introduction in offices of human figures and photographs proscribed in the traditional order. For portraits of the Sultan, see Horatio Southgate, *Narrative of a Tour . . .*, (New York, 1840), vol. 1, p. 679.

82. Fehmi Ethem Karatay, *İstanbul Üniversitesi Kütüphanesi Türkçe Basmalar Alfabe Kataloğu 1729-1728*, 2 vols. paged consecutively (Istanbul, 1956), p. 67. Numerals, which in the text follow the works mentioned, refer, if they consist only of a numeral, to the page in von Hammer, *Histoire de l'Empire Ottoman* (1839), vol. 14, pp. 492–507; when preceeded by a "D" they refer to the same author's *Gerscichte der Osmanischen Dichtkumst* (Pest, 1838), vol. 4, pp. 598–603, and when preceded by "K" to Karatay.

83. "Birgewi" *EI*, 1:1235; "Husrev," *IA*, 5, pt. I; 605–606.

84. *Journal Asiatique*, series 4, vol. 3 (March 1844), p. 217.

85. These figures are based on Baysal, *Müteferrikadan*, pp. 56–71, and include the Bulaq press (Egypt) publications.

86. İskit, *Türkiyede Neşriyat*, pp. 126–127.

87. İskit, *Türkiyede Neşriyat*, p. 102, commenting upon Mizancı Murad, *Devr-i Hamıdı Âsarı*.

88. These figures are approximate, as the number of non-Ottoman citizens and non-Muslim Ottomans has been ascertained from their names. The list is given in İskit, *Türkiyede Neşriyat*, pp. 98–99.

89. Ibid., pp. 113 f.

90. Ahmed Emin [Yalman], *The Development of Modern Turkey as Measured by Its Press* (New York, 1914), p. 30.

91. İskit, *Türkiyede Neşriyat*, p. 32.

92. See "Djarida," *EI*, 2:464. For a general history of the press in Turkey, see "Matbuat," *IA*, 7:367–380.

93. For the activity of all provincial papers, see the relevant article of the law, Art 9; see also George Young, *Corps de Droit Ottoman* (Oxford, 1905), vol. 1, p. 38; cf. [Yalman] *Development,* p. 42, and İsmail Eren, "Tuna Vilayeti Matbaası ve Neşriyatı 1864–1877," *Türk Kültürü,* 3 (January 1965):311–318.

94. Selim Nüzhet Gerçek, *Türk Gazeticiliği 1831–1931* (Istanbul, 1931), p. 64.

95. Karal, *Osmanlı Tarihi,* vol. 8, pp. 337–341.

96. See "Djarida," *EI* 2:465.

97. Server İskit, "İlk Müstakil Gazetemiz Tarihini Açan Agâh Efendi ve Gazetesi Tercüman-ı Ahval," *Resimli Tarih Mecmuası* (February 1952), pp. 1272–1275.

98. Gerçek, *Türk Gazeticiliği,* pp. 84–89.

99. [Yalman], *Development,* pp. 40–41.

100. Compare Ahmed İhsan, *Matbuat Hatıralarım,* vol. 1, p. 58, with [Yalman], *Development,* p. 75. Emin's figures based on the official annual seem more reliable.

101. For circulation figures see [Yalman], *Development,* p. 78, and Kushner, "Expressions of Turkish National Sentiment," p. 24.

102. Edwin A. Grosvenor, *Constantinople* (Boston, 1895), vol. 6, p. 8, gives a total of 500,000 minoritarian and foreigners for 450,000 Muslims. The minoritarian element here seems exaggerated, but is is interesting that about the same figures occur in a report that embodies statistics compiled in June 1924. See Ernest Mamboury, *Constantinople* (Istanbul, 1925), p. 19. Other accounts for the 1870s may be found in A. Ubicini and Pavet de Courteille, *Etat Present de l'Empire Ottoman* (Paris, 1876), p. 19: Muslims 620,000 non-Muslims 580,000.

103. Based on a count of the periodicals listed in the mimeographed catalogue of holdings of the National Library, Ankara. Gerçek, *Türk Gazeticiliği,* pp. 91–92 has more than twice as many periodicals listed for the period 1876–1880 (inclusive) than are listed here; the statistics presented are thus very tentative. İhsan, *Matbuat Hatıralarım,* vol. 1, pp. 48–49, dates the blow dealt to new periodicals as 1888. This did not prevent him from establishing his own new periodical in 1890. For the gradual tightening of censorship between 1885 and 1894 see Server İskit, *Türkiyede Matbuat İdareleri ve Politkaları* (Istanbul, 1943), pp. 80–86.

104. See Ziya Somer, *Bir Şehrin ve bir Adamın Tarihi, Tevfik Nevzat: İzmirin İlk Fikir ve Hürriyet Kurbanı* (Izmir, 1948).

105. [Yalman], *Development,* p. 76.

106. Karal, *Osmanlı Tarihi,* vol. 8, pp. 263–264, 412–414.

107. Belin, "Bibliographie Ottoman," *Journal Asiatique,* ser. 6, 11 (April-May 1868):490.

108. [Yalman], *Development,* p. 79.

109. See "Matbuat," *IA*, 7:370, 371.

110. J. Lewis Farley, *Modern Turkey* (London, 1872), p. 274. Cf. Hakkı Tarık Us, *Meclis-i Mebusan 1293-1877: Zabıt Ceridesi* (Istanbul, 1939), vol. 1, p. 110. The earlier situation in the Ottoman Empire is discussed in Cengiz Orhonlu, *Osmanlı İmparatorluğunda Derbent Teşkilâtı* (Istanbul, 1967), pp. 65-66, 119, 149. Orhonlu gives a good illustration of what was involved in the separation of civilian from military administration. Roads, which were entrusted to members of the military class and also to villages (p. 32), became, in the nineteenth century, the responsibility of the Ministry of Works and the police (p. 149).

111. Karal, *Osmanlı Tarihi*, vol. 8, p. 462.

112. Ibid., pp. 465-471. Charles Hequard, *La Turquie Sous Abdulhamid II*, (Brussels, 1901), p. 385, has the figure 4,800 as a total but credits Abdulhamid with 2,900 km.

113. Bernard Lewis, *The Emergence of Modern Turkey*, 2nd. ed. (London, Oxford, New York), pp. 185, 186.

114. Hecquard, *La Turquie Sous Abdulhamid II*, pp. 414, 416.

115. This information on the evolution of Turkish education in the nineteenth century is based on Unat, *Türkiyede Eğitim*.

116. Hecquard, *La Turquie*, p.300. Population figures are from *Meyer's Reisebucher: Turkei und Greichenland*, 4th ed. (Leipzig, Wien, 1892), vol. 1, p. 129. Ubicini and de Courteille, *Etat Present de l'Empire Ottoman*, give for the 1870s and a wider territory the population figure 28 million.

117. İskit, *Türkiyede Neşriyat*, p. 113.

118. İhsan Sungu, "Galatasaray Lisesinin Kuruluşu," *Belleten*, 8 (1944): 315-347.

119. Niyazi Berkes, *The Development of Secularism in Turkey* (Montreal, 1964), p. 192.

120. Süleyman Paşa, *Hiss-i İnkılâb* (Istanbul, 1910), pp. 3-4. See also Unat, *Türkiyede Eğitim*, pp. 44, 67; Ahmed Emin Yalman, *Yakın Tarihte Gördüklerim ve Geçirdiklerim*, vol. 1, 1888-1918, (Istanbul, 1970), pp. 24-25; Halid Ziya Uşaklıgil, *Kırk Yıl* (Istanbul,1969), p. 19. The first middle schools ever established in the empire (1845) were military schools. They seem to have been operating already at a relatively high level in the late 1860s. See M. Orhan Okay, *Beşir Fuad* (Istanbul, 1969), p. 41, and, for the early inculating of nationalism, p. 58.

121. See Unat, *Türkiyede Eğitim*, p. 70.

122. Karal, *Osmanlı Tarihi*, vol. 8, p. 395.

123. İhsan, *Matbuat Hatıralarım*, vol. 1, pp. 21-22, 28-30.

124. Karatay, *Basmalar*, p. 459.

125. X. Bianchi, "Bibliographie Ottomane," *Journal Asiatique*, 4, no.16 (October, November 1860):335.

126. F. A. Tansel, "Arap Harflerinin Islahı ve Değiştirilmesi Hakkında İlk Teşebbusler ve Neticeleri," *Belleten* 17 (April 1953): 223–249, especially pp. 224–225. In the early twentieth century Pears was still attributing the greater literacy of Greeks and Armenians to "the greater simplicity of their written characters." See Edwin Pears, *Life of Abdülhamid,* (New York, 1917) p. 30.

127. Habib, *Edebiyat Bilgileri,* p. 291.

128. E. d'Eschavannes, "Academie des Sciences de Constantinople," *Revue de l'Orient de l'Algerie et des Colonies,* 12 (1852):363–364.

129. Ziya Paşa, "Şiir ve İnşa," *Hürriyet,* 7 September 1868, pp. 4–7.

130. For the concept of literati, see R. Redfield and M. Singer, "The Cultural Role of Cities," *Economic Development and Cultural Change,* vol. 3 (1954); "Intellectuals," *International Encyclopaedia of the Social Sciences,* vol. 7, pp. 339–415. For biographies of Ottoman literati see İ. H. Uzunçarşılı, "Tosyalı Celâl Zâde Mustafa ve Salih Çelebiler," *Belleten* 22 (1958):391–441; and for the early nineteenth-century "salon" described by İsmail Hakkı Uzunçarşılı, "Nizam-i Cedid Ricalinden valide Sultan Kethüdası Meşhur Yusuf Ağa ve Kethüdazâde Arif Efendi," *Belleten* 20 (1956): 485–525.

131. For details, see Ş. Mardin, *Genesis,* pp. 125–127.

132. See Ş. Mardin, *Genesis,* pp. 51 ff; and the same author's *Jön Türklerinin Siyasi Fikirleri* (Ankara, 1965).

133. Ahmed Hamdi Tanpınar, *XIX ncu Asır Türk Edebiyatı Tarihi,* 2nd ed. (Istanbul, 1956), p. 329.

134. Said Paşa, *Gazeteci Lisanı* (Istanbul, 1909). He complained that in his own time the official language was still too cumbersome: Said Paşa, *Hâtırat* (1910), vol. 1, p. 217. "Simple" Turkish was made the subject of decree in Abdulhamid's reign (1894); see Kushner, "Expressions," p. 141. On Turkish becoming the official language in the first Ottoman constitution, see Karal, *Osmanlı Tarihi,* vol. 8, p. 556.

135. Süleyman Sudi was a writer on the financial history of the Ottoman Empire. See *Türk Meşhurları* (Istanbul, 1946), p. 360.

136. İhsan, *Matbuat Hatıralarım,* vol. 1, pp. 10–11, 28–30. For a positivism as the ideal of the Servet-i Fünûn School, see Hilmi Ziya Ülken, "Türkiyede Pozitivizm Temayülü," *İnsan,* 2 (April 1939):350.

137. For Şinasi, see Kenan Akyüz, "La Littérature moderne de Turquie," *Fundamenta,* 2:474; for Kemal, Ibid., pp. 477, 489, 500.

138. Ebuzziya Tevfik, "Rical-i Mensiye," *Mecmua-i Ebuzziya* 19:439 ff. The lack of involvement was supposed to be an adjunct of the mystical attitude—one looking for deeper truths than daily occurrences. This might well have been emphasized during the period of Ottoman decline.

139. This corresponds to Ian Watt's concern with the daily lives of ordinary people; see *Rise of the Novel,* p. 60.

140. See Belin, "Bibliographie Ottomane," *IA*, 7th ser., 9 (1877): 122–123. Paul de Cocq and Xavier de Montepin were two favorites.

141. For Ahmed Midhat, see Kâmil Yazgıç, *Ahmed Midhat Efendi: Hayatı ve Hatıraları* (Istanbul, 1940); also Akyüz, "Littérature Moderne," p. 497.

142. Akyüz, "Littérature Moderne," 2:495, 497.

143. For this thesis, see "Ahmed Mihat Efendi," *IA*, 1:186–187; for Yalçın's description, see Hüseyin Cahit Yalçın, *Edebı Hatıralar* (Istanbul, 1935), p. 6.

144. Ahmed Hamdi Tanpınar, *XIX ncu Asır Türk Edebiyatı Tarihi*, 2nd ed. (Istanbul, 1956), pp. 445–448.

145. Yalçın, *Edebi Hatıralar*, pp. 9–10.

146. See İhsan, *Matbuat Hatıralarım*, vol. 1, pp. 48–49, and İskit *Türkiyede Matbuat İdareleri ve Politikaları* (Ankara, 1943), pp. 79–81.

147. Kushner, "Expressions."

148. See M. Orhan Okay, *Beşir Fuat* (Istanbul, 1969), pp. 201–215.

149. Akyüz, "Littérature Moderne," p. 531; on Paul Bourget, see Yalçın *Edebi Hatıralar*, pp. 31–32.

150. Akyüz, "Littérature Moderne," pp. 530–531, 535.

151. Yalçın, *Edebi Hatıralar*, pp. 7, 62, on his revulsion from classical literature, and on the "lack of thought" pervading Turkish literature to the end of the nineteenth century.

152. Ibid., p. 86.

153. Ibid., p. 51.

154. See *Culture and Behaviour: Collected Essays of Clyde Kluckholm* (Free Press, 1962), p. 21; and Karl W. Deutsch, *Nationalism and Social Communication*, 2nd ed. (Cambridge, Mass., 1966), p. 87, citing Ralph Linton, ed., *The Science of Man in the World Crisis* (New York, 1965), p. 79.

155. Karal, *Osmanlı Tarihi*, vol. 8, pp. 191 ff.

156. For a description that still holds see Engelhardt, ed., *La Turquie et le Tanzimat*, 2 vols. (Paris, 1880–1882), and R. H. Davison, *Reform in the Ottoman Empire, 1856–1870*.

157. "Little as the Turks like railway, they are great patrons of the telegraph, because it is a most powerful instrument for a despot who wishes to control his own officials. It is no longer necessary to leave a province to the direction of a governor and trust that he will come home to be beheaded when that operation seems desirable. With the telegraph one can order him about, find what he is doing, reprimand him and recall him, instruct his subordinates to report against him and generally deprive him of all real power. As the officials of the capital seek little of the public convenience, they frequently summon a governor to the telegraph office, and monopolize the wire for as

long as they choose in communication with him." Sir Charles Elliot, *Turkey in Europe* (London, 1900, 1908, 1965), p.149.

158. See Karal, *Osmanlı Tarihi,* vol. 8.

159. Halil İnalcık, *Tanzimat ve Bulgar Meselesi* (Ankara, 1943).

160. "Communication," *IESS,* vol. 3, p. 48.

161. Karal, *Osmanlı Tarihi,* vol. 8, p. 470; see F. S. Rodkey, "Ottoman Concern about Western Economic Penetration in the Levant," *Journal of Modern History* 30 (1958):348–353, for early reactions.

162. Rougon, *Smyrne* (Paris, 1892).

163. Karal, *Osmanlı Tarihi,* vol. 8, pp. 254 ff.

164. Ibid., pp. 332 f.

165. An idea systematically developed by Deutsch in *Nationalism.*

166. Even the language of the new litterateurs was attacked as bringing back the preciosity of Old Ottomans, but this time drawing its inspiration from modern French literature. See Kushner, "Expressions," p. 124.

# 14

## OTTOMAN POLITICAL COMMUNICATION

BRUCE McGOWAN

### *INTRODUCTION*
#### *An Approach to the Subject*

Any attempt to characterize Ottoman political communication must be concerned with Ottoman political structure as such. A conception of communication based upon modern *means* of communication would be likely to miss the crux of the matter by concentrating upon such means, which offer the most striking and obvious features of communication in the modern world. We are accustomed nowadays, as an example, to seeing political communication take place through the manipulation of mass media and the organization of political campaigns, both under the supervision of professional communicators. The face-to-face communication that still animates the heart zone of political life remains hidden from view. But in dealing with an earlier era when functions were far less differentiated and the technical apparatus for mass communication was lacking, these concrete face-to-face situations, and the political arrangements they imply, must take the center of the stage. The following discussion will treat political communication not as an adjunct to political life in the modern style, but as an aspect of political life and imbedded in it.

An examination of the Ottoman political system at the

height of its expression in the sixteenth century yields several principles that seem to be at work, each with a strong communication aspect. These principles are for convenience's sake labeled as follows: (1) incorporation, (2) demonstration, (3) integration, (4) agency, and (5) record keeping. Because the meanings of these labels may not be self-evident an expansion of them is in order.

The *incorporation* principle, indispensable to the operation of the Ottoman system, can be seen in the fact that the social classes created and sponsored by the Ottoman regime, as well as the guilds and the religious communities of the empire, were organized into recognizable corporations along with the to-be-expected military and governmental functioning groups. Communication to and from these groups passed through their leaders. The increment of control and the increase in communication efficiency resulting from such a reduction and clarification of communication channels goes far to explain how important matters were handled before the era of mass communication.

Public comprehension, imitation, and compliance were gained through public *demonstrations* whose function it was to clarify basic power relations and behavioral norms that were cultivated by or shared by the regime. Much of this comprehended and imitated behavior was nonverbal and falls outside the most conventional conception of communication, an exclusion that a moment's reflection will show to be erroneous. All the rich ceremonial of Ottoman times can be related to the operation of this principle.

An extraordinary amount of care and attention was devoted in the classic era (that is, the sixteenth century) to *integration* of the values and behavior of elite groups through education and cooperative efforts. This was particularly true of all those state servants who passed through the schools maintained by the palace. The almost Platonic amount of attention that was devoted to the socialization and training of candidates for the elite was justified by the results: results that included an efficiency of communication that is possible only in a body whose members know each other intimately and who are utterly confident about their own shared values.

The *agency* principle employed by the Ottomans is a corollary to the integration principle. Where feasible, the Ottoman state of the classic era employed members of the integrated elite to fill key posts in the provinces. Bearing within them those values and norms that were shared by the Istanbul elite, these agents of the regime represented the capital and exported its viewpoint with a degree of conviction that could scarcely be expected from provincial nominees.

The impressive amount of *record keeping* done by the Ottomans served both a memory function and an evidential function. Without the legal, fiscal, cadastral, and administrative record keeping, which were habitual in the classic era, continuity with past decision making and control of behavior through written evidence would have been impossible.

In the following discussion these principles should be kept in mind even where they are not explicitly stated. Without them it would be difficult to explain the peculiar power and capacity to endure that were inherent in this remarkable system.

### The Uniqueness of the Ottoman System

The Ottoman problem with distances can be grasped with one glance at a map. This was an empire of Alexandrine proportions, a fact that affected its techniques of communication and its techniques of political management.

A second peculiarity lay in the fact that the Ottoman problem with ethnic and linguistic variety started right at home in the capital city of Istanbul, the very center of the empire. Typically, historic empires have had at their center a capital city surrounded by a heartland of considerable size that was populated by a more or less compact ethnic constituency from which the imperial coterie mostly was drawn and upon which the imperial ruler could count in moments of danger for that esprit de corps that flows naturally from possession of a common language and a shared body of custom (unless the crisis was internal and arose within the heartland itself). The Ottoman case was different when, after 1453, the occupation of Constantinople placed the seat of Ottoman power squarely inside what had been until then the center of the Byzantine state. That coveted city has remained a polyglot collection of peoples from that day to this, and it has been only in the period since the demise of the Ottomans that the Turkish Moslem portion of the Istanbul populace has become an absolute majority.

A third factor of importance during the development of the classic Ottoman political system was the fact that the Turkish-speaking population of Anatolia was still predominantly pastoral and to a degree nomadic, or at least transhumanic, until well into the sixteenth century. Pastoralists always represent a problem in governance because of their mobility, their affinity for arms, and because they are organized in kinship groups large enough to be worrisome, even for a government that has its own roots in a pastoral past. They do not provide ideal support for the apparatus of stable government.

Was it in spite of these difficulties or because of them that the Ottomans succeeded in working out so successful a system of government, a system remarkable not only for its endurance but—regarded at the height of its development during the sixteenth century—remarkable in every other way as well? In answering this question one must bear in mind that the imperial techniques employed by the Ottoman statesmen were mostly reshaped by them out of materials handed down by other empires not long dead—the Seljuks, the Ilkhamids, and the Byzantines, to name those that lay in the more recent past. Each of these contributing imperial cultures had in turn inherited or exchanged techniques of government or occasionally invented something of its own. To trace the origins of a single isolated technique of government is invariably a complicated business, unsatisfying and full of pitfalls. Here we shall limit our curiosity about origins and be satisfied with the general statement that there is very little in the vocabulary of Ottoman governmental technique for which no parallel could be found in one or more of the prior empires—parent empires they can be called, because without this inherited vocabulary of technique it would have been impossible to hold together for long the vast Ottoman domains.

That which *was* Ottoman was the way in which inherited techniques were selected, emphasized, made to fit together, and made to work. It is the whole melange of borrowings and the way in which they are reworked that give an imperial culture its peculiar character. Two examples will suffice. The role of the Moslem judge, the executor of the law of Islam, had, long before the Ottomans, been discussed, defined, and in theory understood. What the Ottomans did was to give these judges more work, more power, and more general administrative responsibility than can be shown in any preceding Moslem state. Likewise the device represented by the fiscal survey had occurred in one form or another in many preceding states. But it remained for the Ottomans to bring this instrument to an unparalleled peak of scope and precision. But for the moment, discussion of these secondary features will be postponed in order to draw attention to two primary features that pervaded the Ottoman world during its middle period, features that gave it its fundamental structure and that today provide the framework for a discussion of Ottoman political communication. These are: (1) the basic two-class system and (2) the state slave system.

### The Two Great Classes

The division of the whole population into a smaller "military" class distributed among a much larger "subject" class was a fact first and only subsequently a conscious social and legal convention. The military class included all those who worked for or fought for the state and who drew their living from the state (roughly speaking all those who consumed state revenues). Thus this class included all those to whom the sultan had delegated religious or executive power through an imperial diploma, namely, officers of the court and the army, civil servants, and *ulema* (clergy),[1] as well as the great armies of cavalry that were posted on their "livings" throughout Anatolia and on the European side. The more numerous subject class included all villagers and townsmen who (regardless of religion) provided the revenues that sustained the government in its operations. It is true that there were anomalous groups, such as Moslem townsmen or tax-exempt auxiliaries, which do not fully fit into this system. But there remains the rough truth that two great classes did exist, each with its characteristic designation and a status that went with that designation. The military class, the smaller of the two, was far too large to be described as a nobility,[2] and the idea of nobility *by birth* was not in any case a part of the Ottoman outlook, aside from the dynasty. But the "military" designation was at the very least a kind of first-class citizenship. It bore with it its own dangers and responsibilities and for that reason may not have been universally coveted. Besides that, it pertained almost wholly to Moslems and Moslem families (the wives and other dependents of "military" men were also "military," a fact that sharpens the status aspect of the designation). It should be emphasized that to be a Moslem and to be a member of the military class were entirely separate matters; most Moslems belonged to the subject class along with almost all non-Moslem subjects.

The division of the populace into two great classes had important consequences from the point of view of political communication. It is true that the territorial cavalry, which comprised the greater part of the military class, lived in dispersed places, in provincial towns and sometimes even in the villages that had been assigned to them by the government as their "livings," and it could be argued that this dispersion brought them close to the land and close to the villagers from whom they drew their sustenance. But theirs was a different universe of experience from that of the ordinary villager. This was the class whose men went to war, who often died fighting, who competed for booty, and perhaps even more important usually themselves collected, or arranged for the collection, of the taxes that sustained them. This was a class that had its own interests to defend and its own lore with which to defend them. The different universe of experience shared by this smaller class separated them in a very real way from the state's ordinary subjects.

It is not difficult to see one way in which the difference between the two groups must have manifested itself. The communications of the military class with the center, channeled through its leaders, were incomparably swifter and better than the communications of the more numerous class. In the provinces, the clique that surrounded the local governor and the local judge, the few who were trusted by them and with whom they conversed most freely, were invariably both Moslems and members of the military class. Each member of the inner clique would have his own ring of confidants or at least his own ring of subordinates—cavalry, clerical officials, or garrison. What the subject class learned of governmental policies, instructions, or intentions was from the mouths of the military class. Without a doubt, the emanations of the Istanbul government were reinterpreted, distorted, or even withheld from members of the subject class in such a way as to serve the interests of the military class of that locale. Conversely, the advantageous position of members of the military class must have been regularly exploited to mask, distort, or *prevent* complaints of the subject class from being heard in places where it mattered. This would be particulary noticeable at the provincial level, because such complaints were hardly likely to be channeled to the central government even when given audience by provincial authorities.

Seen from the governmental point of view, it was a distinct advantage to be able to communicate swiftly news of general importance—a call to arms, for instance, or news of a distant victory—through the nerve system provided by these dispersed and structured forces, especially in Anatolia and in the European provinces where the military class was more numerous. Seen from the point of view of either of the two symbiotic classes—the producers and the defenders—the better communication position of the defender must have been an important aspect of status. It could not be a mistake to imagine that members of each class used a different tone of voice and a different way of speaking when communicating with members of the other class. And it is just as easy to see why there were matters on either side that would be withheld from the other or distorted in communication.

### The "State Slaves"

Included within the military class, and comprising perhaps a third of its numerical strength, was an inner core of military and administrative personnel who were known as "slaves of the state." This class within a class had unique features of its own, properties that made it invaluable as an instrument of Ottoman government in the era of its greatest success.

This state slave system may be regarded as the most brilliant of the Ottoman innovations. As usual, this institution had its roots in Moslem empires that had gone before, for the use of slaves as soldiers was nothing new. Yet the Ottomans gave to this usage such a a breathtaking, unexpected emphasis that it deserves to be thought of as sui generis. Agents of the state used a periodic dragnet to recruit a harvest of boys and adolescent males from among certain of their subject populations, particularly the Albanians and the Bosnians. Moslem families were never subjected to the levy. As the effect of this exclusion, the Moslem portions of the Ottoman populace—and prominently among these the Turks—were systematically cut off from participation in the mechanism by which the government replenished the ranks of its salaried military forces and from the best posts in its administrative services.

According to normal procedure, the young male recruits thus levied were supplemented according to circumstance by captives, taken on campaigns, who likewise were young and fit and were put through a course of training, at Istanbul and nearby centers, that was designed to render them an obedient, skilled, and more or less Ottomanized candidate corps. Some were selected at an early stage for special training of a more intellectual nature, especially in the Islamic sciences. These were destined to enter the palace service, there to provide candidates for further promotion to posts of power and influence, both in the capital and in the provinces. The greater part of these young recruits were destined to a future in one of the corps of paid soldiery, either the renowned infantry known in the West as the janissaries or else the more prestigious corps of paid cavalry (not to be confused with the vastly more numerous cavalry forces who were dispersed throughout the "original" provinces and who drew their sustenance directly from villagers). Another possible assignment would be to one of the other smaller special corps found in and around the capital city. All of these recruits, regardless of their destiny, were skilled in military arts—appropriately in a state whose avowed business was conquest. Virtually all of them were converts to Islam, no doubt possessed in some degree of that zeal that is commonly attributed to proselytes. And all of them, most important, knew themselves to be the creatures of the sultan, unable to leave his service, responsive to his wishes, and likely to lose their property and their heads if detected in a serious malfeasance. The fact that no social stigma was felt by members of this powerful class does not detract from their very real and special vulnerability, and it accounts for the aptness of their designation by both themselves and others as slaves of the Ottoman state.

The consequences of this system, in terms of communication, were profound. First and foremost, the system cut off, from almost all prospects of penetrating the inner core of government, the very Moslem Turks who had been the fount of Ottoman strength during the earlier phases of the dynasty's history.[3] Their communications with the center were thus pinched and restricted. Native Moslems had little say, or much less than they would have liked, in the operations of the state, even though they might acquire as individuals modest reserves of comfort and security as members of the far-flung military class or as functionaries within Moslem establishments connected with worship, education, and charity.

There may have been several reasons behind this key policy of the Ottomans, but one of them is obvious: it protected that state from the family and its claims. The family everywhere has some claim on the loyalty of its members, and in the Middle East this claim is relatively large, both then and now. Any other loyalty having economic aspects competes with loyalty to the state; this was part of the tacit lore of the Ottomans. Hence the dynasty attempted to protect itself from the ambitions, and the intrigues, and the recriminations of families of co-religionists by cutting off these families from involvement in the inner affairs of the state. This policy also must have had the effect of weakening the power of provinces as compared with that of the center, because it forestalled the projection of family influence from the provinces into the center arena.

From the point of view of the individuals who were netted into the system and formed by it, the consequences were just as striking. Profound differences separated them from meaningful communication with their own families and the peoples from whose midst they were taken—a different religion, a different way of subsistence, a different loyalty, and a different universe of experience. To this it must be added that the janissaries, precisely because they had a great potential for mischief in their role as praetorians, were denied the privilege of marrying, at least until their retirement, so long as the classic Ottoman system was maintained (that is, until the last quarter of the sixteenth century). Their loyalties to their fellows in the ranks and to their sultan were undiluted by family worries or family ambitions.

To these preventive effects of the policy there should be added an important positive effect. It is an accepted tenet of communication theory that the more intimate and tightly woven a group, the more efficient the communication among its members. This principle applies to the elite of the Ottoman state as well as to the state slaves from whose ranks they were raised. Drawn from diverse beginnings at an early age, these men were shaped by shared experience into a well-knit brotherhood. Whether he rose or did not rise, each state slave was surrounded by fellows with whom he had learned to speak the one tongue common to them all, with whom he had prayed, eaten, slept, and drawn the bow. So it was that this class within a class came to possess a matrix of shared understandings that made communication among them swift and sure.

Naturally, in view of the sacrifices and temptations involved, the system described here was difficult to maintain in its classic form. There was always within it a tension produced by pressure from both without and within. The fortunes of the Ottoman state and its slave system declined together; the extent to which the decline of each contributed to the decline of the other will probably always be a matter for speculation.

## THE COORDINATION OF THE ELITE
### The Prestige of the Dynasty

The Islamic world has outlived numerous dynasties. Most of these did not last long, a fact that caught the attention of the great Tunisian historian Ibn Khaldun. The six-century rule of the Ottoman dynasty was a brilliant exception to the long-established tendency. Its rise to great power was almost as gradual as its subsequent decline, a gradualness that allowed for the gestation and testing of governing techniques suited to the Ottoman situation.

By capitalizing on a good position and by displaying a talent for decisiveness and, above all, for organization, Osman and his successors built up a war machine and a territorial base so formidable and so renowned that the defects that lay within them went long unnoticed both by foreign observers and by the Ottomans themselves. By the middle period of Ottoman history, the so-called classic period of this survey, the dynasty had accumulated a very useful reputation for success. Especially after the addition of the Arab provinces and most of Hungary to the Ottoman domains during the sixteenth century, comparisons with the empire of Alexander became more and more apt— conquests less speedy perhaps, but almost as vast and far more enduring.

The men of the Ottoman elite (including here not only the state slaves and the military proper but also the religious officials who were in theory part of the military class) identified themselves with the terrific military success of the dynasty. That success was so impressive to these inheritors that it gave rise to convictions of legitimacy that were a constant protection to the dynasty in its weakest moments both before and after the period considered here. Widespread identification with the dynasty was made easier by the fact that the rulers of that dynasty had gradually eased themselves into a truly imperial position, free of dependence on any single ethnic element. All could share in their identification as Ottomans who could find it in their hearts to do so, a process natural enough for all those whose livelihood and whose outlook were linked to the success of the state.

The prestige and legitimacy of the dynasty thus became through a process of identification a part of the self-esteem of all the people connected with it. The maintenance of the dynasty in all its glory was a controlling value shared by them all. It is scarcely necessary to emphasize that this controlling value, which formed so large a part of the identity of these imperial men, had its part to play in securing the acceptability and authoritativeness of communications between them, in making these communications more economical in moments of stress, and in reducing the petty ethnic rivalries that must have made themselves felt even in palace circles despite the unifying forces enumerated here.

### The Sword of Islam

To win the willing cooperation of the Islamic establishment, the Ottoman sultans succeeded in attracting to their line a great fund of credit in their role not merely as conquerors but as defenders of the Islamic faith. During the first half of Ottoman history this role was primarily aggressive, a confirmation of the zealous enmity that was believed to the proper stance of the Moslem toward the miscreants beyond the pale. Thus in their period of waxing, every Ottoman war was a holy war; beyond the mundane motive of each war there was supposed to be a sacred purpose. Through this habit of making war in the name of Islam the Ottomans moved on to a rationale of war for war's sake. Later on, as Ottoman power waned, these holy wars became more and more truly defensive and the impulse to war became less automatic.

What matters for the purposes at hand is that the all but ceaseless warring of the earlier reigns had a galvanizing effect on all participants not only by reason of the successes that customarily crowned these efforts but because they dramatized again and again the ostensible role of the state (focused in the person of the sultan) and its identification with the enormous prestige borrowed from Islam. Especially after the conquest of the Arab provinces, the Ottoman sultans could claim hegemony in the Islamic world. Of course this hegemony had its price—respect for the laws of Islam, for its learned men, and for its ideas of charity and public welfare. But all this came naturally to the Ottoman sultans, who seem to have been perfectly sincere in their role as defenders of the faith and upholders of the ideal community that had always been a part of the Islamic vision.

The identity of the ruler with Islam meant by extension the identification of all his supporters with the same cause. In the discussion of the state slave system it has already been shown that ethnic unity was deliberately avoided. But unity of values, as embodied in a shared religion, was indispensable. It would be possible to speak of the Ottoman system as having fostered a nationality based on Islam and war. The subject class, particularly the non-Moslem subjects, could not be expected to share these values fully or to support them with much enthusiasm, a fact that at a much later date was to contribute to the breakup of the empire. And to the extent that they did not share them they were not Ottoman. For the nationality meant here was a nationality of shared values, and of interests that were inseparable from the cause of empire.

Here, too, the shared commitment to a family of values, in this case the values of Islam, was of the greatest importance in securing the coordination of the Ottoman elite and efficient communication among themselves. Every overt communication among the elite was fully understood and fully understandable only by other Ottomans. Indeed, each such act of communication, whatever its form, was by accretion a reassertion of their common identity and their common destiny.

### The Process of Becoming an Ottoman

The process by which a soldier becomes a soldier is only partly a matter of overt instruction. The larger part of the transformation happens through imitation and acquiescence to example. This might be said of members of any disciplined organization that must function in close cooperation, and it was certainly true of the Ottoman elite, all the more so as an individual drew nearer to the inner circles of power.

For those youths who were moved up in the Ottoman system as candidates for the palace services and after that for posts in the administration, there were a number of hurdles to overcome. The values of Islam, a rudimentary knowledge of its laws, and a conception of the mission of the Ottoman state—these things could be conveyed through formal teaching. But to become Ottoman and to communicate with governmental servants at a high level there were other, more subtle matters that could not be conveyed by teaching alone. The young candidate had, for instance, to become proficient in the Ottoman language, which, although basically Turkish, had with time become increasingly a language of artifice and complicated conventions, larded with Persian and Arabic vocabulary, but all used in a peculiarly Ottoman way. For those who hoped to reach the pinnacle there were still more difficult and subtle desiderata—mastery of Arabic and Persian, knowledge of a body of literature, a capacity for style, a good pen-hand, and possibly the mastery of special scripts used in different departments of government. To these must be added a thousand rules of etiquette and the various "don'ts" of Ottoman life, much of which had to be learned through observation. The Istanbul elite had its special pleasures, its own tastes—kinds of music peculiar to the culture of the capital; a cuisine that developed into one of the world's greatest; a taste for riding, archery, poetry, flowers, and miniatures; its own great architecture; its own code of dress—in short, a cluster of refinements learned through observation, and acquiescence to the inhering values. The mastery of this body of lore separated the Ottoman of the palace circles from the common cavalryman, like him a member of the military class, just as surely as it separated him from peasant life and the ethnic group from which he had been extracted. Refinement *in the Ottoman style* and a sense of decorum *in the Ottoman way* were indispensable to men who would rise within the system and who might be chosen to exercise great power.

Once he had mastered the greater part of this special lore that was a part of the Ottoman identity, once, in other words, he was on his way to becoming an Ottoman, a candidate might hope for a rapid rise and a career approaching the spectacular. Rapid upward mobility was the reward in the game in which the palace recruits were involved. Can history offer a more striking example of a system that deliberately raised men from obscurity to power?

To look down the pyramid of state servants from above is instructive. To have become a grand vizier after beginning, let us say, as a maker of sweetmeats in the palace kitchens, obviously set a stamp on an individual's outlook. To become top dog in this sealed-off system required ambition, talent, and friends. This was no aristocracy. A man might fall far faster than he rose. Although biographical details on the great men of the empire are characteristically lacking in intimate detail, one catches glimpses in the histories and accounts of contemporaries of what they were like. Insecurity was a fact of life, and the higher one rose the more this was so. Thus it should not be a surprise that the arrivistes of this system were often intensely envious of one another and eager to have themselves seen in a good light. Many were intriguers. Some were noted for sternness, some for uprightness, or piety, or a special talent. And to move upward all of them had to have friends.

In looking for an analogy for the Ottoman inner ring, the best that comes to mind is the Kremlin in our own day. Although outsiders are not intended to see clearly, they draw their conclusions nonetheless about the way in which the system operates. Powerful men gather unto themselves numerous protégés whom they place as well as they can, both in the capital and elsewhere. These protégés in time gain clients of their own within the system. Each such pyramidal combination forms an information-sharing unit, providing its members in both directions with special knowledge, often critically useful knowledge. In the Ottoman case these microsystems within the elite were increasingly used (or abused) as the system aged to provide well-placed individuals and favorites with special opportunities and advantages outside the capital city. This tendency to allow individuals to enrich themselves far beyond their official remuneration was heightened whenever appointments to provincial posts linked men within the palace service to friends in the provinces.

Alliance and realignment between powerful men produced factions that then took sides on current issues. Here it is not so much special knowledge but interpretation of information and, often enough, personal enmities, that are the chief factors. Men linked to each other in mutual interdependence will tend to agree on political issues. Thus the same pyramids of influence that were formed for mutual protection and information end by investing one or another competing view on policy with political energy. But any view, in order to succeed, had to win the ear and the favor of the sultan, and also his chief executive officer, the grand vizier.

### The Sultan's Harem

To reach the ear of the sultan it was necessary to find him. More and more, as the system aged and especially after the death of Süleyman the Magnificent, the place to reach the sultan was in the harem, and the way of reaching him was through its inmates.

The earlier sultans had maintained numerous women; this was one of the attributes of kingship in the Middle Eastern style. But this did not prevent the sultans from taking a vigorous role in government, generally the leading role. And it did not prevent them from maintaining direct contact with their subjects in audiences concerned with the administration of justice or from personally escorting their armies on campaign. Süleyman, whose death marks the beginning of the end of the classic period, died on campaign. Moreover, Ottoman princes before Süleyman's time had customarily been given a province to govern while still young. The dauphinage away from the capital was the best possible preparation for the greater responsibility of the sultanate. Thus the vigorous participation of the sultan was the hallmark of the first half of Ottoman history.

But it must be cited against the same Süleyman that in his long, and admittedly exhausting, reign the student detects a waning of the sultan's interest in the hard work of governing, as evidenced by his failure to attend regularly the meetings of the imperial council, or divan. Power was germinating within the harem,[4] the domain of the sultan's women and the eunuchs who guarded them. Witness the efforts of Süleyman's favorite, Roxelana, in winning the throne for her son. Of course, power and influence is always a potentiality with royal women. What makes this potentiality sinister is its coupling with isolation from the facts of common life, not only of such women but of the monarch upon whom they depend.

Viewed at the end of the classic period, the harem must already be seen with an eye to the pernicious role that it was thereafter to play and to some extent already did play. The wall around the harem was a communication factor of the greatest importance in Ottoman affairs. The wall had two chief effects. To the extent that a sultan preferred to remain in the salons of his harem, as was increasingly the case, that wall acted to block his direct knowledge of the world. Later sultans did occasionally leave the palace according to their inclinations and upon the advice of their ministers. But the flattering comforts of the harem pulled them steadily inward to the extent that they were likely to lose contact with the outside world and to prefer the hothouse atmosphere of the harem to the outer reality.

A second effect of that wall was to create an inner system of communication in which the sultans became enmeshed. Thus it was possible for relatively unqualified persons to usurp a key role in policy matters because some harem assignment kept them in the immediate vicinity of the sultan. Of course these inner advisors were as habituated to harem life as the sultan himself and were, even more than he, in danger of ignorance of the real facts and forces at work outside the palace. With such an arrangement malicious inventions were easy to manage. Even an astute monarch would have found it next to impossible to discriminate among rumors, verifying some and rejecting others, unless he had constant recourse to the outer circles of his government and unless he deliberately cultivated wider communication than the network provided by the harem services.

The members of the state slave system naturally had to deal with the system as they found it. This meant finding allies within the harem or in a second zone within the palace where the sultans bathed, dressed, and relaxed. One curious feature of the harem is that it could be visited by women from the outside—not any women, but women themselves who had formerly been inmates. This peculiarity was the precondition for a machine of influence. Partly because of this entrée into the harem, former inmates were sought as wives by ambitious men.[5] Their visits to the harem (whose inmates could not themselves leave) provided a back door by which a route could be found to the sultan in order to animate a special interest or to plant biased information in his ear. Women thus took an active part in politics.

The sinister result of this increase in harem influence over the thinking of the sultan (as distinct from the influence of his chosen ministers of state) was to allow the divorce of power from competence. Sultans after Süleyman retained the power to remove the head of any servant of the state, however powerful, but they increasingly did not have the competence for and interest in governmental affairs that alone could have assured a prudent use of that power.

The importance of the harem during the period when the Ottoman system was at its zenith should not be overstated. Yet, that the potentiality for influence and mischief was already felt within this inner communication system cannot be ignored. According to a Turkish proverb, fish start to decay at the head.

### The Imperial Council

By the end of the classic period, the flow of paper emanating from the various secretariats of the capital city had reached quite a respectable volume. The vast majority of this paper, of which a sizable sampling still survives, was concerned with routine administrative processes.[6] Appointments to office, transfers, collections, disbursements, and a variety of diplomas account for a large part of this flow of paper. In addition, the Ottoman penchant for systemization found its expression in the numerous logs, account books, inspection records, and surveys that were used in recording and controlling the operation of these various secretariats and their correspondents in the provinces. Each such log, each such certificate was evidence of some administrative act. It can easily be seen how this routine administrative paper performed an indispensable function, increasing the orderliness of the normal processes of government.

In contrast to routine processes that worked themselves out in the secretariats were those nonroutine situations that seemed to require special action. One is tempted to call them situations that required political decisions, but in fact many of these situations were fairly petty and did not involve any perceptible shift in power relations. These problematic situations were distinguished by the fact that they contained some element of novelty or, alternatively, had been reported by some correspondent (a provincial official, for instance) who required a decision on whatever he perceived to be a special situation. Correspondence bearing on situations containing such novel elements thus bypassed the secretariats and was funneled to the one central body competent to deal with novelty—the Imperial Council, led by the grand vizier.

Because of the increasing complexity of imperial affairs resulting from repeated annexations of territory, it had become customary for the sultans to delegate the responsibility for most of the work of governing to a paramount council. This council, or divan, met four times a week in times of peace. Some of its members were ex officio, carrying responsibilities apart from their membership in the council. A second group of council members were ministers of general competence whose chief responsibility was to deliberate in the council.[7] These viziers, as they were called, were men whose distinguished service in military, administrative, or (occasionally) financial affairs had caused them to be singled out and promoted to the council to help with the day-to-day problems of governing. The prestige of the viziers was therefore great. Whereas correspondence to other officers of the empire was addressed to the office in question and did not bear a personal name, correspondence directed to a vizier who was charged with some mission away from Istanbul—to serve, for instance, as the governor of Budapest—was invariably addressed to the vizier personally, mentioning him by name, as though official recognition as a person were a privilege of the vizierial rank.

Presiding over the council was the grand vizier, a man usually chosen from among the viziers to act as the final arbiter within the council. It is difficult to generalize about the degree of his preeminence. Although theoretically he personified the full delegation of all the sultan's powers, his sway over the council of course varied according to his personality.[8] His responsibility, in any case, was undeniable. And being, like all the rest, a creature of the sultan, it was the grand vizier who was most likely to pay with his office and possibly with his life if policy went awry.

Contact between the Imperial Council and the sultan was maintained both formally and through surveillance. It was the custom for the chief officers of the council to have an audience with the sultan twice a week, at which time a verbal report of matters of import was given by at least two of their number, normally the grand vizier and the chief treasurer. In addition to verbal reports, written proposals were submitted to the sultan for his examination and disposal. These were supplemented by formal reports with characteristic designations. From the grand vizier, the sultan received an occasional summary, or white paper, called a *telhis*. From the chief treasurer, the sultan received a regular account of the state of imperial finances (as distinct from his own, because sultans had their own personal treasury as well). In addition to these formal audiences, the sultan might at his discretion resort to a device first hit upon by Mehmet II in the mid-fifteenth century—that of observing the council's deliberations through a small grilled window while himself remaining unseen. Active sultans until Süleyman's time saw much more of the world than is suggested by these arrangements, inasmuch as they frequently campaigned in faraway places and hunted with hawks in the environs of the capital city.

Within the Imperial Council were exercised all those delegated powers that nowadays would be rationally subdivided into legislative, executive, and judicial. The council was at one and the same time a supreme headquarters, a legislative chamber, and, when it chose, an inquisitorial court. Problems that could not be handled through regular administrative and judicial processes tended to come to rest in the council. Such problems might be petty or they might be grave, because it was their novelty rather than their importance that brought them to the attention of the council. Although occasionally the council reached decisions on problems that they spontaneously recognized as such (with prompting), the more typical case would be for the council to deliberate upon and then reply to a letter or petition from the provinces or from the capital city outside the walls of the palace wherein their meetings took place. For cases involving situations nearby, the petitioner himself was frequently present.

From the Imperial Council orders and regulations flowed to the secretariats and directly or indirectly to the provinces. These diverse issuances went by varying names that overlapped but expressed in some degree the imagined importance of problems being dealt with. A letter, an order, or a regulation might be addressed to a relatively insignificant official in a relatively remote place, or might be addressed to one of the mighty servants of the empire. Occasionally it might be addressed to whole classes of officials as, for instance, to "all the judges of Anatolia" or to "all the judges and governors on the road to the Holy Cities of Mecca and Medina." Fortunately, because copies of these orders and regulations were maintained for reference and copies of correspondence containing them survive from as far back as the mid-sixteenth century, it is possible to obtain a clear impression about the general character of the orders and regulations that the council then issued.[9] Among the matters that were deliberated by the Imperial Council and were subjects of its directives, one finds the following recurrent themes:

Protection of merchants, officials and ambassadors while on the road or during the performance of their duties;

Control and recall of contractors who undertook revenue farming throughout the imperial domains;

Forwarding, transfer, retention, or assignment of revenues due to provincial treasuries;

Measures for the provisioning of the army or navy;

Provisioning of the capital city of Istanbul;

Prevention of smuggling, particularly the illegal exportation of goods deemed of strategic value;

Judgments on officials accused of malfeasance or preparations for such judgments as well as judgments on unlucky guarantors (for tax-farming contracts and other franchises);

Calls for the preparation of record books bearing on special administrative problems, as, for example, the payment of garrisons;

Suppression of brigandage, rebelliousness, and other grave crimes;

Restraint or encouragement of military commanders on the frontiers;

Mobilization, quartering, and demobilization of military contingents;

Relations with foreign powers;

Relations with rulers under Ottoman suzerainty and requests for their cooperation;

Adjustment of tax rates and the collection of special taxes;

Disciplining of merchants and others violating the fixed prices and other regulations in the four wards of Istanbul;

Establishment of garrisons or the construction of fortifications, bridges, or other facilities;

Regulation of the prerequisites and duties of the military class or relations between the military class and the subject populations, especially where abuses were involved; and

Special acts of justice involving return of individuals unlawfully enslaved or goods unjustly confiscated, or provisions unnecessarily levied.

Even though this list is incomplete, it will afford the reader an idea of the range of subjects that fell within the jurisdiction of this supreme body of Ottoman statesmen. Their handling of these problems reflected the strength of the system by which the Ottomans recruited governmental servants. The viziers and the other high functionaries of state epitomized the virtues of the state slave system. Their common education, their common experience of conversion to Islam, their long mutual acquaintance, and their common dependence upon the sultan's favor—these plus a widespread love of glory and fear of failure as well as the spur of jealousy contributed to their esprit de corps. In the lives of these men nothing could compete with their involvement with the system. And if their formal schooling was scientifically inferior, judged in relation to the inquisitiveness of contemporary Europe, this did not prevent these distinguished veterans from entering the council richly clothed with experience in the arts of governing, specific and relevant experience that immediately could be put to work. To match its omnibus responsibilities for every sort of consequential novelty, this highest Ottoman council drew upon every branch of governmental service—soldiers, judges, administrators, and accountants—to form a pool of experience that could meet the challenge.

### The Moslem Establishment

As a partner to the governing establishment there existed a religious establishment made up of educated Moslems who were born into their religion. This establishment was responsible for Moslem public worship, administration of Moslem pious foundations, the education of Moslems, and the interpretation and application of the law—both the body of Holy Law inherited from the Islamic past and also an ever-evolving code of Ottoman secular law. Regarded from the outside, this Moslem establishment gave the appearance of being a second pyramidally organized bureaucracy with its own head—the *sheyhulislam,* chief jurisconsult of the capital city. This was the conventional view of the Ottomans themselves, who used a single traditional term to designate the entire establishment, calling them the *ulema,* or "learned men."[10] But there was something deceptive in this outward appearance, as we shall see.

Technically the Moslem establishment was part of the "military," or governing, class and as such its members shared the privilege of exemption from taxation. But in addition to this critical distinction they also enjoyed a relative security of property and person unknown to the slave establishment. Whereas summary execution was a real possibility and posthumous confiscation of goods a standard procedure for the grandees of the first establishment, the higher officials of the Moslem establishment were in a much better position to improve upon temporary advantages of office and income and pass them on to their inheritors. The story of how this was actually accomplished, thereby creating a native aristocracy that had not been there before, belongs to the period following the sixteenth century. But even in the sixteenth century the respect with which they were treated and which was their traditional due was consequential enough to justify their being characterized as a class within a class and a counterpart to the slave bureaucracy within the larger framework of the military class, quite aside from their different functional responsibilities within the Ottoman system.

As the living repository for the traditions and values of Islam, this learned establishment naturally had its part to play in upholding the legitimacy of the regime and in reviewing laws shaped by the ruler and his advisers upon their request. One conscious part of the raison d'être of the state was to protect and advance the interests of Islam. Therefore the Ottoman dynasts, like all Moslem rulers, desired the perennial approval of the leading men of Islam to confirm them in their role as champions of the faith. To secure the cooperation of the *ulema* the sultans took great pains. In addition to the privileges that the sultans allowed them as a class (that is, freedom from taxation and security of property and person), the learned establishment was also bound to the interests of the state by financial means, both direct and indirect.

Appointments to judgeships in the provinces and to the staffs of mosques and schools everywhere were made by the state, that is to say, by the first bureaucracy, operating through two chiefs of military justice who had seats in the Imperial Council. The salaries of the judiciary were drawn directly from state revenues.

School and mosque officials, by contrast, were typically provided for from pious foundations established for the purpose by the grandees of the realm, led by the sultans themselves. In either case, supervision and control by the governing establishment was involved, thus vastly reducing the chance that the "learned men" as a class might develop a climate of opinion unfriendly to the state.

The binding of one establishment to the other was given ceremonial expression in a number of ways. The most obvious of these ceremonies centered upon the *sheyhulislam,* the titular head of all religious learned men throughout the empire. This Moslem patriarch received investiture at the hands of the sultan himself. And if he did not sit on the Imperial Council (doubtless for the reason that his theoretical independence would be thereby prejudiced), he nonetheless received visits and other gestures of great respect from the sultan personally. Following a traditional pattern of behavior by which Moslems reconcile their acts with the requirements of the Holy Law through consultation with a legal scholar, sultans resorted to visits and consultations with the *sheyh* whenever a new piece of legislation or an important act was envisaged. The *sheyh* on his part confirmed the envisaged executive or legislative act by issuing an opinion pronouncing it to be in conformity with the Holy Law. Should the *sheyh* refuse to confirm, a more compliant successor could easily be found. Refusal was a rarity.

Here, then, was an anomalous bureaucracy. Except for certain higher offices, most of the patronage was only partially under the control of the putative chief of the establishment. Nor did that personage himself draw upon a treasury nourished from below; control of revenues devoted to pious purposes was retained within the governing bureaucracy. Like any petty mosque official, the *sheyhulislam* was himself dependent upon the government for his sustenance. Even his religious authority was limited. According to theory, the legal opinion of any recognized legal scholar of the empire was conceivably as valid as that of the *sheyhulislam.* It was custom and his proximity to the sultan and not his primacy as a scholar that made him head of the learned bureaucracy. Nor was there any conciliar tradition in Islam that would have allowed the learned men of the empire to gather, to confer, and to put forth authoritative views. Taking these facts into consideration, it cannot surprise us that the second bureaucracy of the Ottoman state, the religious establishment, was fully a captive of the first during the period under scrutiny.[11]

The paramount communication feature of this part of the classic Ottoman system was the practice by which the putative chief of the *ulema* repeatedly sanctioned policies of state through the issuance of written opinions. Through this ritual trickle of paper, the two great establishments were symbolically locked together.

A second aspect of the learned establishment worth noting was the communication position of the real chiefs of patronage, the two chiefs of military justice who sat on the Imperial Council. Themselves responsible for legal problems involving the military class, they were in a direct line to hear intelligence coming in from provincial judicial officials dealing with disputes and grievances within the military class and between the military class and the subject populations. Hence they were bound to be particularly well informed about abuses of privilege in the provinces and about the just grievances of the governed.

## THE COORDINATION OF THE NONELITE

The inner system of the Ottoman Empire—the military groups, the palace circles, and the twin establishments—was characterized by hierarchical organization, by fairly dense intercommunication between but especially within these hierarchies, and by a matrix of shared values. Given the limitations of that era and its technology we can describe this inner system as communication-rich.

Ranged around the inner hierarchies were the far more numerous subject populations, people who did not enjoy the usufruct of the revenues taken in by the state, but to the contrary helped to provide revenues. Whether near the capital or far from it, these (revenue-producing) subject populations can be said to belong to the outer system of the Ottoman Empire, the nonelite, or, to use the Ottoman term, the nonmilitary. The subject groups that belonged to this so-called outer system were generally less hierarchical, less interactive, and less tied to the state's views either by economic interests or by shared values. This outer system can be characterized as relatively communication-poor. The Ottoman government did not expect to exercise the same degree of control over this outer system, at least from the point of view of communication with the center. Nonetheless, for dealing with the problem of political control and communication among the nonelite the government did have a variety of techniques, which will be taken up here one by one.

### The Village

Isolation was the almost invariable concomitancy of village life throughout the Middle East down to very recent times. In Ottoman times this isolation was scarcely an unwelcome thing. Contact between village and government was almost always for the government's reasons and almost always these had to do with taxation or with the levying of men or goods to meet some emergency. If the levy were illegal, such contacts would be even more unfavorable to the villager, amounting to some form of extortion. A position near a road or near a commercial center could be advantageous for a village only from a marketing point of view, presuming that there was surplus to market. A more remote village might be unable to market anything whatever, but otherwise was better off. Of course, if the village were located on the "living" of a military man or an offficial it could not hope to escape his visitations or those of his agents. These would, of course, know how to find the villagers.

Aside from involuntary contacts with representatives of the government, which brought the villager little benefit, the most frequent contact between the villager and the outside world took place when he found reason to leave the village, generally to travel to a nearby market or seasonal fair. There he would find a degree of stimulation in the course of bargaining, and perhaps even something like entertainment in contacts with healers, holy men, musicians, and magicians, and even in hand-puppet plays (in which an expression of protest and mockery was ever near the surface). Such contacts with men in the market and access to the rumors passed between them must al-

ways have been highly valued by the villager. Even today the
social prestige of an individual Anatolian villager partly depends upon the number of contacts he has outside the village.

Aside from occasional visits to such markets or the experiences provided by corvée or military servitude, the villagers'
lore, their meagre notions of the broader world, their bitter
proverbs and worn jokes, can only have passed between them in
chance encounters on rural paths, at springs and waterholes,
and at lonely shrines where one might perchance find an
itinerant, a dervish, or perhaps strangers from a nearby village.

Given such poorly developed contacts with the village the
government's claim to the willing cooperation of the village,
could never have amounted to much. But the voluntary participation of the governed was not really necessary. What the Ottoman state required from the villager, Moslem and non-Moslem
alike, was unquestioning acquiescence to the activities and demands of the wielders of authority.

### Pastoral Groups

In certain zones, especially near the Taurus Mountains and in
desert zones to the south, a form of pastoral nomadism persisted well beyond the period under scrutiny. In fact it was only
during the sixteenth century that the balance shifted in
Anatolia away from the pastoral life toward sedentary agriculture. But the nomadism of Anatolia was of the limited kind,
more technically known as transhumance: a yearly cycle of
movement, varying little, in which animal raisers might move
no more than fifty miles in order to shift from winter to summer
pastures and back again, making of them little more than tran-
sient villagers. Nonetheless, this increment of movement and
experience is significant from the point of view of communication. Contact with many villages along their route of travel
meant that nomads often were bearers of news, although
generally news of a limited sort.

The more truly nomadic groups, such as Bedouin and
Saharan tribes, were more closely associated with camel trading
and with interregional trade, hence in a better position to communicate news over longer distances. But these groups, lying on
the outer fringes of the empire, were treated by Ottoman

statesmen more as a potential annoyance on the periphery of the civilized world than as a part of the system itself. Their communications with the center were indirect and erratic.

### Communication Centers

Markets, fairs, ports, bridges, passes, commercial inns, and places of pilgrimage provided most of the peaceful opportunities for contacts between townsmen from different towns and between townsmen and villagers. Among these communication centers, the markets, which were either weekly or continuous (distinct from fairs, which were seasonal events), offer the most interesting example. In the market there prevailed some kind of balance between governmental and nongovernmental aspects, whereas in the other kinds of nexus mentioned, either one aspect or the other predominated. Put another way, in the market one could find both a communication system linked to the government and its exigencies and other communication systems existing among and for the benefit of ruled groups.

The governmental aspect of communication in the marketplace is easy to perceive. Seats of governmental authority at all levels naturally existed in the vicinity of markets. In fact these markets sometimes owed their origins to the establishment of a governmental center, a fortress, or the like. The governor, the judge (who was also an administrative official), and the police commandant all needed the market in order to function. To announce proclamations of interest to the district, to gather information relating to conditions in surrounding localities or concerning abuses and crimes and fugitives, to control the commercial life of a district through its merchants and vendors, and to reach quickly all men of influence living near the market for whatever reason—for all these purposes the market was an indispensable center of communication from the governmental point of view. Besides the officials mentioned above, who were almost always found near markets, there existed in some markets a special official in charge of the market whose role as market controller was of ancient origin, dating back at least to the early years of Islam. This official was especially concerned with maintaining the government's list of fixed prices and other commercial ordinances, and in this function he served not only to communicate but to enforce the government's fiat. Naturally a market was socially linked also to communication subcenters in the vicinity—an inn, for example, or the courtyard of a mosque or some other place of worship.

The nongovernmental aspects of communication in the market are less obvious yet equally real. Each ethnic subgroup participating in a market had its own patterns of communicating, enhanced of course by links within and between the extended families belonging to that group. A second pattern of communication within the market was offered by groups held together by a common economic interest—craftsmen practicing the same craft, or merchants dealing in the same goods. Often there was congruence in a larger cosmopolitan market between an ethnic group and an economic interest group, because one activity or another tended to be "cornered" by a single ethnic group. A third contribution to the market structure was made by traders, drovers, rivermen, and seamen who were operating over distances: men like these brought news from other markets and communication centers and carried away news in exchange. As a matter of course, these long-distance men would have their own connections within the market, often one or more merchants of the same ethnic group or from the same place of origin. Within the market, information (or rumors) flowed between groups, but selectively. Information of general interest (news of important political events or interesting gossip) moved fastest. Other information of specific economic significance or of specific intraethnic significance, or information concerning some faraway interest or locale, moved more slowly or was hoarded. Aside from these general features, allowances must be made for a great deal of local variation in every respect. Doubtless some markets were excellent listening posts, with a reputation as such, whereas others were not so blessed.

Other types of communication centers were dominated either by a governmental or by a nongovernmental aspect. Fortresses, ports, bridges, and passes were places under the charge of military men, or police, or internal customs agents. On the other hand, seasonal fairs (whose locations responded to economic and geographic factors rather than to governmental convenience) were primarily taken up with the needs of villagers; the governmental presence there might be very small or nil. Places of pilgrimage, especially in the home provinces of the empire (that is, the non-Arab provinces), also were points at which people gathered naturally with relatively little governmental interference. For historical reasons, many shrines and holy places in Anatolia and in the Balkans were frequented both by Moslems and by Christians; perhaps the communication barrier represented by a difference in faiths should not be overemphasized.

Lastly there were the caravanserai, or commercial inns, fortress-like resting places found along much-traveled routes that offered to the traveller shelter, security, and provisions. These must always have been buzzing with news, because they were used predominantly by itinerant merchants and by travelling officials and their retinues (officials who did not, it must be noted, have an administrative responsibility for the milieu in which they found themselves that night). Often arriving by convergent routes or from opposite directions, these travellers must have generated many lively controversies, filling the air with rumors—true or false, or perhaps both true and false.

### The Town

Wherever people live in groups, their communication can be described by external aspects (communication between dispersed collectivities) and by internal aspects (communication within these collectivities). In the preceding brief discussion of rural life, an attempt was made to characterize the typical village collectivity as being poorly connected externally, or at most connected haphazardly with the outside world through occasional visits to markets or fairs. Distance, poor understanding of the world resulting from want of education, and lack of organizing experience all contributed to keep the villager in a relatively disconnected and therefore politically helpless state. The internal communication of the typical village was of course a different matter altogether. However, inasmuch as this was mostly between individuals and families, it does not form a part of the discussion of political communication as intended by our definition.

Ottoman towns, on the other hand, are interesting for their external and their internal communication, both of which concern relations between groups that can be politically defined. Even while granting latitude for considerable local variation, the subject offers a field for certain generalizations. Certain communication centers already mentioned, especially marketplaces and mosques, are part of the definition of township in this era. From the Moslem point of view the mosque was an indispensable attribute without which a town was not a town. But the mosque primarily was a nexus of internal communication, especially with the Moslem portion of that town's populace, whatever number that might be (and this proportion varied greatly from one region to another). This important intracommunication center was invariably associated with a marketplace, which was, by contrast with the mosque, more immediately connected with the world outside the town and therefore more noteworthy for its external aspects. The strength of the external communication of a town was determined also in part by the additional presence of representatives of the central government. The governmental presence might be made known through a court of law, resident members of the military class (who were of necessity better informed of governmental intentions than the average man even when their responsibilities lay outside the town, as in the case of the typical cavalryman), a fortress, port facilities, or a customs station. Each of these features offered to the state an obvious increment of information among the elite of that place, regardless of its distance from the center.

Ottoman towns also had other internal aspects that are of interest from a communication standpoint, features that made them different from villages in other ways than size and also different from purely governmental conglomerates such as fortresses, military encampments, or other subcenters of governmental power. The most important of these internal aspects was the organization of towns into wards, each defined not only spatially but often with a special socioeconomic character as well. The number of such wards might be large or small depending upon the size and ethnic complexity of the town. What is more important than the number of such wards is the fact that they tended to have a distinct identity that might stem from religious, or ethnic, or vocational differences as well as differences based on income or other sources of status. Towns thus organized can be imagined as collections of differently colored cells, each cell having its own way of shaping the news according to its own interests. Whether speed of diffusion was greater or less than in the more centroid towns of Roman times, or than in modern towns with their newspapers and telephones, can only be guessed at. What seems obvious, however, is that the news, such as it was, was selected, preshaped by the representatives of each ward even before reaching the ward, then shaped again within the ward in keeping with its special interests and its identity. Thus did a rumor first heard in the marketplace, or in the townhouse of the governor, or at dockside, flow outward via the courtyards of mosques and churches, or the ever-wending vendors, into the various wards.

A second important aspect of communication within towns, really an aspect of Ottoman government generally but one that takes its most concrete and observable form in the towns, is the role of intermediaries standing between the government and the various interest groups that made up the populace. The use of such intermediaries was very advantageous under premodern conditions. When a bureaucracy is relatively small, the populace is mostly illiterate, and modern means are missing, it is to be expected that a government should deal with its subjects, so far as possible, in groups and through intermediaries. Under such conditions, operating through intermediaries yields maximal efficiency—more reliable political control as well as greater speed and reliability of communication. Within the context of Ottoman town life three kinds of (nongovernmental) groups offered scope for some kind of intermediary control: guilds, non-Moslem religious communities, and unorthodox Moslem sects that existed outside the formal Moslem establishment.

### The Guilds

The organization and discipline of town populations was understandably a matter of importance for Ottoman policy makers. Townsmen, although they might not be members of the military governing class or of the learned class, were nonetheless still one cut above villagers and distinct from them in status, despite the fact that they too were numbered among the governed.

The Ottoman word for "subject" *(reaya)* was not used for the town dwellers, to whom a special term *(sehirli)* was applied. The government could not afford to treat townsmen with quite the same brusque one-sided arbitrariness that was customary in the countryside, first because their concentration near governmental centers gave them a leverage that was a potential source of trouble, second because they were largely connected in one way or another with market processes and thus in a position to affect directly both the economics of governmental operations and the style of life of the governing class, and finally because in any emergency townsmen represented the most immediate source of assistance aside from governmental personnel. Their sympathy was a distinct advantage for the state.

Guilds and guild-like organizations were the chief instrument employed by the Ottoman government for two-way communication and effective political control within the towns. By the end of the classic period, the Ottoman guild system had reached a degree of articulation that went far beyond the less differentiated associations of earlier times.[12] All economic groups within the towns (and even some groups that were nonproductive economically, such as students) were organized into guilds with a recognized head, an internal hierarchy, and internal customs and regulations. Each such guild therefore represented not only a shared economic and professional concern but also a structured societal unit. Guild members subscribed to the rules and understandings that gave the guild its integrity and invested their energies in fraternal relationships upon which they drew for their identity and solidarity. This organization into well-defined (and, in larger towns, quite numerous) groups is quite unlike the organization of modern towns and cities, and it gave to the Ottoman townsman an advantage not shared by the villager or the tribalist; he had the security of a relatively small and cohesive social group but without the isolation of rural life.

Whether the Ottoman guild system owed its fullest development to encouragement by the government, or whether the system evolved spontaneously by a process that political scientists describe as "interest articulation," is not yet clear. But it is clear that the system offered strong advantages both to the government and to the guildsmen. Viewed from either side the communication aspects are almost inseparable from questions of economic and political influence and control.

The existence of guilds and of guild heads (or of middlemen appointed to communicate with them) gave an obvious boost to the efficiency of Ottoman government in all matters related to the market. Whether the question was one of requisitions, of price or quality control, or of taxation, it could be quickly communicated to all those directly concerned by taking advantage of the guild system. The route had few links: the will of the Imperial Council was communicated to the governor or judge or market inspector of one or more localities (unless the decision originated with the local authority himself) and through these to the heads of the guilds concerned. The last in turn informed their members. An instruction thus addressed was communicated not only with relative speed but with relative specificity, as there was almost invariably a logical correspondence between the content of the communication and the nature of the guild or guilds thus addressed. As an example, a question regarding the price of footwear might concern both the tanners and the shoemakers of a given locality but no one else; by employing the avenues offered by the guild system the regulation on this matter might be addressed to those two groups and to them alone. Completeness of dissemination could be assumed by the government once the guild head had been contacted. Even if dissemination within the guild was not in fact complete, the social authority of the guild head within the guild, and his undoubted responsibility for the actions of the guild, served as effective guarantees. Another great advantage of the system from the government's point of view was that it minimized the amount of governing to be done by leaving many quasi-governmental matters in the hands of the guildsmen themselves, particularly the administration of justice, the enforcement of economic regulations, and individual distribution of the tax burden. Clearly, by delegating both authority and responsibility to the heads of the guilds, the Ottoman government was able to obtain maximum effect with a minimum of effort.

From the guildsmen's point of view there were corresponding advantages. They received disciplining at the hands of those

who knew them personally and who could be expected to behave with paternal moderation. Because avenues of communication with political and judicial authorities were clear and
operative, grievances would receive a hearing; likewise through
the guild heads it was often possible to negotiate with the
authorities on questions of economic consequence, both to
discuss and to object. Most important were the advantages offered by solidarity. No man need stand alone. And on issues affecting all tradesmen or all merchants, or both, it was possible
to present to the authorities a massive and unified front expressed through the very men whom the government wished to
use as its intermediaries.

### The Non-Moslem Communities

Many of the advantages of the guild system can be read also into
the system by which the Ottoman authorities dealt with the
non-Moslem religious communities. Here, too, the individual
was submerged and insulated from direct dealing with governmental authorities as a result of his membership in a group that
was recognized as a legitimate entity by those authorities. The
precedent for such an arrangement was even more ancient in the
case of the religious minorities than in the case of the guilds,
because the relations between the religious community of the
Prophet, on the one hand, and the Jewish and Christian communities, on the other, had been discussed in the Koran itself.

The working principle nonetheless was the same as with the
guilds. The Ottoman government dealt with the heads of the
non-Moslem religious communities, located at Istanbul. Insofar
as it was possible the government left to them the settlement of
problems that rose within these communities, providing they
were not consequential outside of those communities. Here,
too, one is impressed by the relative efficiency of an arrangement that, by delegating authority, resulted in the necessary
control without great effort on the part of the government. The
government was assured of a point at which to apply pressure, a
personage both responsive and responsible. The members of
these communities were on their part assured an avenue for major grievances and the advantage of group advocacy in their
dealings with the political authorities.

Some differences existed between the functioning of the guild system and that of the minorities system, however, and these are worth mentioning. Whereas the guilds were in all very numerous, the non-Moslem religious minorities were in practice only three: the Orthodox Christians (by far the largest minority, especially west of the Bosphorus), the Armenian Christians, and the Jews. It is instructive of the Ottoman mentality that these religious distinctions meant much more than differences in language. Inside the Islamic pale it was confessional differences rather than ethnic differences that counted. Thus the fact that the Ottomans were dealing politically with one gigantic community encompassing Greeks, Bulgarians, Serbs, Albanians, Bosnians, and Romanians, all through the ecumenical patriarch located in Istanbul, disturbs us far more than it did them. Although these peoples had in the past been aware of their identities as nations and would be again, the general effect of the functioning of the Ottoman system in its classic period was to mask and smother those differences. (North of the Danube, traders from all of these language groups were lumped together as "Greeks," that is, members of the Greek Church.)

Another difference was that whereas the guilds were all local in their orientation, and had to be dealt with through local political authorities, the religious minorities were organized on an empire-wide basis. Although making allowances for some degree of local autonomy and for local political arrangements that might weaken this generalization, the generalization stands nonetheless: the heads of the three religious minorities exercised some authority over their co-religionists wherever they were located within the Ottoman domains. And inasmuch as most Orthodox Christians and most Armenians lived in villages rather than in towns, patriarchal authority was very widespread.[13] The Istanbul Greeks, who reserved the ecumenical patriarchate for themselves, and for whom the minorities system was even more convenient than for the Ottomans, guarded their own interests by stressing the use of Greek in all churchly affairs, including such education as there was, and by working to preserve the supremacy of the patriarch against the claims of other ethnic groups within the ecumenical community.

Lastly, whereas communications to and through guild heads

were relatively frequent and concerned mostly with economic
matters (and therefore vitally connected with the exigencies of
the period), communications to and through the heads of the
religious minorities were relatively infrequent and tended to be
more political in nature, except when taxation was the subject.

### The Dervish Orders

Ottoman towns and villages in Anatolia and in Europe were
connected to one another by at least three distinct systems, each
with different properties. Two of these have already been mentioned: first, the military forces garrisoned throughout the
zone; second, the scattered markets and fairs that, if they did
not integrate the whole zone described, at least tended to knit
together regions within it. One of these systems was wholly controlled by the government, the other partially, and both had a
communication potential.

A third system whose presence was felt wherever there were
Moslems can be seen in the orders of Moslem dervishes represented by member lodges both in towns and in the countryside.[14]

The dervish brand of religion was different from the book-
ish and somewhat intellectual religion associated with the
mosques, being much closer in spirit to the illiterate masses and
their needs. Some dervishes were mystics, some only wished to
be mystics. Some clung to convents close to home while others
wandered (although in this respect, and in many others, there
were great differences between the orders). All were respected
by the common people, who regarded them as the elect. From a
distance it can be seen that they presided over the religion of the
Moslem nonelite, a syncretistic body of beliefs and practices in
which pilgrimage to holy places, miracle working, esoteric doctrines, and the worship of saints living and dead all had a place.
In later centuries more and more members of the Ottoman elite
were to find it natural or expedient to maintain a connection
with one of the orders.

The political potential of the dervishes as rebels, or as
chaplains to rebels, was demonstrated several times during the
course of Ottoman history. As an example, early in the sixteenth century during the reign of Selim I (the Grim), dervish

convents in eastern Anatolia helped spread political propaganda favoring the new Persian dynasty, a dynasty that had itself sprung from dervish beginnings. This threat was taken very seriously by the Ottoman government, and the outcome was a punitive campaign and new conquests in the east. Thus even though dervishes had played a cooperative role in the early years of the dynasty when the Ottomans ruled a frontier state, their loyalty to the regime in subsequent centuries was not to be taken for granted. The danger represented by the influence they exercised over common people was compounded by the association of the dervishes with other social organizations, such as guilds. The most famous of these associations was the one-to-one relationship between the janissaries and the Bektashi order.[15] Given these political potentialities it may be asked what the Ottoman government did to exercise control over the dervish orders.

One way of exercising indirect influence over the orders was by means of charitable endowments, established by individuals, even though those endowments were not on the scale of those associated with the formal Islamic establishment. The relationship between the dervish orders and the elite groups was still evolving during the sixteenth century. That there existed an unresolved tension between them during this period seems certain. Not until the subsequent period of Ottoman decline does one witness a confederation of the orders and the mosques and of the different ideals that animated these two modes of Islam. At some point, confirmation of the appointment of sheikhs by the *sheikhulislam* became customary,[16] but this in all probability took place after the sixteenth century.

Lack of knowledge of governmental affairs and a basic lack of interest in the everyday world may have combined to inhibit political activity by the orders and to prevent their acting in unison under ordinary circumstances.

Moreover, the centripetal forces that held the orders together as entities were offset by centrifugal tendencies, particularly their natural tendency to splinter and reorganize around the personalities of individual leaders, a tendency that had the effect of enhancing personal power at the price of organizational power. Finally, although there is little doubt that dervishes and dervish orders exercised local influence both in the towns and outside them, this is not the same as to say that they bound together townsmen and peasants. Both had grievances against political authority; but they were not the same grievances nor did they occur at the same time. Only with a unified and politically alert effort could the two worlds have been made to pull together. The dervish orders apparently had neither the unity, the political skills, nor perhaps the desire, to mobilize such an effort by themselves.

## COPING WITH DISTANCE

Superimposed upon problems of communication and control arising from the kaleidoscopic social structure of the Ottoman Empire were other problems that arose from the formidable distances involved. To handle the problems of distance, Ottoman policy makers drew upon an assortment of techniques that formed a sort of invisible inheritance from the past. Whether a particular technique was actually a remembrance of the way things had been done by the Seljuks or the Ilkhamids or any other government of the near past, or whether it represented a device reinvented by the Ottomans in response to their own situation, often can be argued. Certainly parallels for most of these techniques can be found not only among the defunct states of the Mediterranean basin but wherever premodern governments have striven to operate effectively over great distances.

### Provincial Organization

To explain why the Ottomans were as successful as they were in holding together such a collection of territories over such a stretch of centuries would require an examination of many factors. A historical approach to the subject would show how the Ottomans had endeavored to suppress or to manage local forms of power, both incipient feudal power and residual power exercised by the leaders of conquered populations. Such an approach would show the development and subsequent decline of the controls exercised over the cavalry army and its auxiliaries settled upon the land in the home territories of Anatolia and Ottoman Europe as well as over garrisons located all the way to the periphery of Ottoman influence—along the North African shore, in the Crimea, or at the extremity of Yemen. However, for the limited purpose of sketching an outline of the Ottoman system of political communication at the height of Ottoman power it would be superfluous to dwell upon the development of the system or upon its decline. Our concern is to describe the solutions worked out to handle communication with provincial governments during the period when the system did work well.

An abstraction of the Ottoman system of managing provincial governments yields the following four principles: (1) replication of form, (2) alternative lines of communication, (3) rotation in office, and (4) a toleration for anomalous arrangements in correlation with distance from the center. Each of these principles has significance both from a political point of view and from a communication point of view.

Replication of form means here the reproduction in provincial capitals (and even in the governmental centers of the districts into which provinces were typically divided) of the same basic intragovernmental relationships that prevailed at Istanbul. Of course these arrangements were greatly scaled down in the provincial capitals, and in the district centers they were merely skeletal—but the principle remains. In place of the Imperial Council, the grand vizier and his secretariat, the treasurers and their secretariats, the judicial secretariats, and the janissary and cavalry regiments, all found in Istanbul, one encounters in the typical provincial center a governor and his retinue, a provincial council, two or more treasurers, a chief of garrison, and a judicial officer. The possibility that the reader may find this an unremarkable situation should not prevent us from considering the distinct advantages that this replication offered. It meant a division of power (and to some extent a sharing of power) among functionaries who had become accustomed to their roles during their separate apprenticeships in Istanbul. They had each one become accustomed to a standardized way of doing things, literally an "army way," before any of them reached the provinces. As governmental agents they carried with them to the provinces a host of understandings about working together that bore the stamp of the capital city; any one of them, if transferred, would be replaced by a functionary who, although he might arrive from a great distance, would know how to behave when he got there and would know what his own role in sharing power would be. Moreover, because a full array of governmental functions was represented at provincial level, the great majority of provincial difficulties could be managed on the spot, thus creating foreshortened communication arcs and diminishing vastly the necessary flow of communications to and from the capital city—a consideration of some importance, given the difficulties involved in the traffic of messages between Istanbul and the provinces.

The fact that the Imperial Council at Istanbul in addressing itself to problems in the provinces was able to use alternative lines of communication can be seen at a glance from the destinations of letters drafted by the secretariat of the council. Any of the provincial officials mentioned above might receive a *direct* communication from the center. This meant that no one man in a province, not even the governor, could control fully the communication of that province with the center. The same can be said for the districts, or subprovincial centers, where missives could likewise be received *directly* from Istanbul rather than via the capital of the province. This arrangement obviously made it difficult for a provincial governor *(beylerbey)* to monopolize power in his province. Although his power could at times be very great, even viceregal, the provincial governor had always to keep in mind the fact that others around him could communicate with Istanbul without his permission. This was particularly important in the case of the putative judicial officer, who both at the provincial and at the subprovincial level exercised considerable power as an inspector and as an executive in various administrative matters and could, if uncorrupted, offer a countervailing power to that of the governor.

Another practice that, like the last mentioned, was partially intended to make it more difficult for officials to become too settled and too powerful in any locality, was the practice of rotating men in office with reasonable frequency. This practice, still incipient during the classic period, became more marked during the period of decline when frequent rotations were deliberately induced to increase the fees that flowed upward as a result of making new appointments. But even though this practice was less marked during the classic period, its rationality in a system that strove to prevent delegation from turning into usurpation is quite clear. In this situation, where the separate fates of whole classes of itinerant officials were determined in a distant capital, there arose a corresponding counterpractice that likewise became more highly developed during the subsequent period of decline. To protect their interests at the center and to maneuver for preferred posts, officials in the provinces maintained agents in Istanbul who cultivated others on their behalf. This resulted in a tangled skein of influence peddling, which lay beneath the visible official structure. How interesting it would be to be able to sample some of the *un*official correspondence that found its way between the capital and the provinces!

The fourth principle, that of toleration for greater variety in distant places, follows naturally from the difficulty of controlling men who are serving at great distances from the capital. It also follows from the greater likelihood that areas on the periphery were more vulnerable to foreign influence and sometimes in a better position to assert their claims to special treatment, or even to switch loyalties—an ever-present potentiality along the border with Persia. Finally, this principle derives from an even broader principle of Ottoman government, already discussed, that of dealing with corporations that minimize the need for controls by conceding numerous petty powers to subject communities, to other interest groups or (in this case) to peripheral peoples. As a consequence of this policy of economy of effort, a number of anomalous regimes existed within but especially at the periphery of the Ottoman domains: in the north—Transylvania, the Romanian principalities, and the Crimea (all of which did duty as buffer states); in the east, the Kurdish sheikdoms; in the south, Egypt, the Holy Cities, and the pirate ports of North Africa. In allowing greater play and greater autonomy to distant provinces and to tributary regimes, the Ottomans were applying a Machiavellian axiom: nothing is more dangerous than to change the laws of a place. The deliberateness with which this policy was developed can be seen in the histories of provinces that once had been peripheral but later lay well within the periphery: in such provinces laws had been changed somewhat gradually, being bent rather than broken, toward a standard that prevailed throughout the central provinces of the empire.[17]

### The Ottomans on Campaign

During the sixteenth century, Ottoman military prowess was superior to that of any neighboring state. Mostly this was the result of the extraordinary degree of order with which the Ottomans invested their warring. They had made a habit of war and, being very frequently on campaign, were easily able to keep their war machine in good working trim even while their readiness to adjust to changes in military technology was slowing down.

It was during the same period, and particularly during the last third of the sixteenth century, that the Ottomans were slowly being forced to recognize the practical limits of their capacity to carry war to the limits of their own frontiers. The accumulations of their past successes had put these frontiers so far from the center that inordinate efforts were now needed, both east and west, to go farther. In Europe the rather ponderous Ottoman forces arrived at the periphery too late in the campaigning season to be able to persevere for long. On the Persian border the enemy was not so much distance itself, nor the Persians, as it was the terrible sparseness and difficulty of the terrain in which the army and its animals were obliged to find sustenance. Ottoman methods of mobilization, transport, and supply had reached natural limits.

Yet another constraining factor was the perennial possibility of having to fight on two distant fronts. Although the Ottomans were successful in avoiding this dilemma, the effort of throwing the bulk of their forces first in one direction, then far in the opposite direction, put a considerable strain on the system they had worked out.

One important easement that was incorporated into the Ottoman campaign system is of interest from the communication point of view. When on campaign, the warring sultans of the sixteenth century (Selim I and Süleyman I) brought their governments with them. Treasurers and their record books and the like actually made the journey to the frontiers along with these marching monarchs, who personally led their forces and left only a skeleton government behind them in Istanbul.

Although this seems strange from a modern point of view, it was natural enough for the Ottomans, who at that time regarded war as the chief business of state. The camp where the sultan and his council reposed was also a temporary capital. The result was a speedy handling of the exigencies of war and an avoidance of friction between the government in the field and the skeleton government left behind in the capital.

Campaigns were also educative. They brought the ruling elite into contact with realities and local problems that otherwise would have been remote and beyond their ken. Even under the best conditions it must have been a catastrophe for the peasantry to lie in the path of the Ottoman army, with its vast grazing appetite. But some compensation, however small, must have arisen from the opportunity these excursions gave to the sultan and his advisers to observe the geographic and ethnic realities of the outer domains that it was their duty to govern. Also, at lower levels in the armies raised by the sultans, the campaigns were vastly educative, bringing together, as they did, masses of men from localities remote from one another and intensifying their firsthand experience with governmental operations and with the viewpoints of their most distant peers.

### Communication with the Provinces

The normal course of events, even in the quietest of times, required that couriers regularly ply their ways between Istanbul and the provinces as well as between neighboring provinces. These couriers were organized into a regular service branch clothed with the authority necessary for the fulfillment of their missions. Too liberal a use of these couriers naturally put a strain upon villages lying along their routes; hence, occasional attempts were made to restrict this traffic.

A host of auxiliary services sped the Ottoman courier on his way. By using tax exemptions as an incentive, the Ottoman government was able to maintain a variety of specialized villages in key places along the courier routes. Some of these villages maintained hostels where couriers or other travelling officials might rest or eat or change horses. Others were charged with guarding passes or doing service on the docks, or maintaining bridges or ferryboats. In Europe a special police corps endeavored to hunt down brigands and keep order both in the forests and along the

more important riverine routes. Water routes as well as land
routes were employed, the importance of water routes being
very great in the case of several of the more remote provinces
and dependencies—the Crimea, Egypt, and the North African
littoral. The Danube, although closed in winter, offered an
alternative and generally safer route between Istanbul and
Hungary. Safety was of course a more important consideration
than speed when the shipment of money metals was called for.

Occasionally the central government had need of an agent
who could do more than could a common messenger. Thus for a
variety of special tasks involving the gathering of intelligence or
a trustworthy handling of money matters or the execution or
recall of some official, the government had recourse either to
especially trusted couriers or to other dependable men who were
maintained for such purposes and who constituted a select corps
with a special name.

Some attention has already been given to the dynastic legend
and to the way in which sentiments of legitimacy helped to
bind Moslem subjects near and far into a more or less obedient
and coherent polity. Along with this positive image of an
esteemed and all-powerful sultan there existed a darker, more
fearful image that likewise functioned to guarantee, or at least
to encourage, probity and discipline in distant posts and garrisons. Terror, the ever-present possibility of recall, execution,
dishonor, perhaps even execution without the formality of
recall, worked upon the imagination of higher state servants.
The higher a man's position, the greater the likelihood of his
being singled out for such unwelcome attention. The more distant the post, the more desirable from the point of view of
governmental efficiency to be able to count upon terrifying
sanctions to strengthen the desire of officials to perform their
duties with probity. Seen from this point of view, the communication aspect of a reasoned use of terror seems quite apparent.

### Communication with the Outside World

In their understanding of the world outside the Islamic world,
the Ottomans were handicapped by attitudes that belittled or
ignored things unfamiliar to them. The classic period, im-

pressive though it was in other respects, was also a time of waning interest in foreign things. Even military innovations, which formerly had attracted avid interest, now were adopted only after an increasing lag in time. In keeping with their growing arrogance, the Ottomans (with one exception to be mentioned) made almost no effort to keep abreast of technical or scientific development in the outer world. Indeed the notion of progress, of technical development, was not part of their outlook at all. In an era when Europe was well launched upon a career of accelerating technical change, it was difficult even for literate Ottomans to realize that the rules of the game were changing.

In the field of diplomacy those negligent attitudes show up quite clearly. Whereas the incipient European state system was in this era cultivating the art of intelligence gathering and representation through permanent diplomatic agents, and practicing these skills upon the Ottomans, the latter made no attempt to do likewise. Their exchanges with the agents of foreign powers took place almost wholly on their own ground. They thought this situation flattering to themselves and neglected to see the dangers inherent in this one-sided arrangement. Likewise they made little attempt to learn foreign languages and, while consenting to the occasional use of European languages for diplomatic communication, seemed scarcely to have grasped the possibility of employing such languages for the purpose of learning useful things. The drastic price that would one day be exacted for this neglect could not have been foreseen.

An exception to this image of the Ottoman world as a closed world is offered by all that relates to maritime affairs. The half-pirate Ottoman navy was far from allowing itself the luxury of dismissing foreign innovations out of hand. The best example of this relative alertness can be seen in a still extant map, drawn by an Ottoman admiral and dated 1514. This famous map demonstrates clearly that the Ottoman naval command had impressive information regarding the coastlines of the New World, within two decades of Columbus's first voyage. Ottoman fleets, although they dominated the eastern Mediterranean during the sixteenth century, were obliged to share the sea with Spanish, Italian, and French squadrons. The influence of the Venetians was especially marked in the period, because of the special place they occupied in the markets of Egypt. Thus it is that Turkish maritime jargon remains to this day larded with Italian words.

Smugglers, who were otherwise a nuisance to the government, contributed along with legitimate merchants to keeping some Ottoman ports in a better state of information than prevailed in the Ottoman domains as a whole. Likewise, certain provincial centers, such as Baghdad, were advantageously located to hear foreign news travelling along routes of trade. But the extent to which such intelligence was a help to the center depended upon a number of factors, starting with the alertness and vigilance of the officials resident in those places, their cooperativeness, and the esteem and credibility they enjoyed in Istanbul.

One other source through which the Ottomans might have been able to supplement their insufficient understanding of the world outside was the constant supply of slaves that their warring produced. Especially numerous during the sixteenth century were the Hungarians drained off from the northern frontier. Less numerous but still significant were the Italians and others who were victims of Mediterranean raiding expeditions. But like the non-Moslem minorities, these slaves were burdened by a social stigma that prevented their being consulted in any systematic way.

NOTES

1. H. Inalcik, "Turkey," in *Political Modernization in Japan and Turkey,* Robert E. Ward and Dankwort Rustow, eds., (Princeton, 1964), p. 44. The most important description of this two-class system and the fiscal principle on which it was based appears in Turkish in H. Inalcik, "Osmanlilar'da Raiyyet Rüsûmu," *Belletin* 23 (1959): 594–598.

2. The ratio of one class to the other obviously fluctuated over time, but in the middle of the sixteenth century it was on the order of one to fifteen. The closest analogy for the military class may be the lesser nobility of Poland and Hungary in the same period.

3. It should be emphasized that this discussion deals with the system at its height. By the eighteenth century, recruitment had reverted to a more natural pattern favoring native-born Moslems, while promotion within the system had become geared to specialization so that transfers between the executive,

clerical, and financial hierarchies were increasingly rare. For the later Ottoman pattern, see N. Itzkowitz, "Eighteenth Century Ottoman Realities," *Studia Islamica* 16 (1962): 73–94.

4. The harem was placed close by the chancelleries only in Süleyman's reign.

5. Harem women who had not been advanced into the circle surrounding the sultan were commonly married to governmental officers; thus they left the harem, yet without breaking all connection with it. See F. Davis, *The Palace of Topkapi in Istanbul* (N., 1970), p. 206.

6. By systematic study of surviving documents it should be possible to uncover processes that involved a shift in power relations, that is, truly political processes. The historian sometimes is in a position to see more clearly than did the subjects of his investigation what was politically significant and what was not. Perhaps it would be better to qualify the expression "routine administrative processes" to mean processes that were treated as routine by the Ottomans even though sometimes they contained a significance whose gravity the Ottomans did not realize.

7. Inseparable from the responsibility of deliberating imperial affairs was the privileged communication position that went with it. Part of the power of those who sat in the council lay in their being better informed than anyone else, an advantage that was naturally open to abuse.

8. An interesting and seemly authentic account of the operation of the council was left behind by Ottavio Bon, Venetian envoy of Istanbul from 1606 to 1609. An English version of his account is available in Bernard Lewis, *Istanbul and the Civilization of the Ottoman Empire* (Norman, Oklahoma, 1963), pp. 82–86. Especially noteworthy is what Bon has to say about the grand vizier's own methods of classifying cases and delegating decisions among other members of the council.

9. These are contained in the so-called Registers of Important Affairs *(Mühimme Defterleri)* now stored at the Prime Minister's Archives in Istanbul.

10. Discussing town life in Syria and Egypt in the period preceding the Ottoman conquest, Ira Lapidus has characterized the *ulema* as a largely avocational grouping, which included many merchants and even craftsmen: *Muslim Cities in the Later Middle Ages* (Cambridge, Mass., 1967), p. 108. There is an obvious need to take a close look at the *ulema* of the chief Ottoman towns to discover whether this characterization applies to them also. If so, the prevailing idea of a professional Ottoman Moslem establishment will have to be enlarged.

11. The political and social power of the *ulema* in the seventeenth and eighteenth centuries is quite another story, involving one of the fundamental shifts of power that took place after the close of the classic period.

12. On the development of guilds, and their differentiation from the earlier associations of tradesmen, see G. Baer, "The Administrative Economic and Social Functions of Turkish Guilds," *International Journal of Middle East Studies* 1 (1970): 28–50.

13. Regarding the elevation of the Greek Orthodox patriarch, his place in the Ottoman system, and his methods of controlling his far-flung community, see T. H. Papadopoullos, *Studies and Documents Relating to the History of the Greek Church and People Under Turkish Domination* (Brussels, 1952), pp. 11, 32, passim. It was not always an easy matter for the patriarch to control his flock, but the Ottoman authorities as a rule backed his authority to the hilt and even assisted him in making his collections: J. Kabrda, "Les Documents Turcs Relatif au Droits Fiscaux des Métropolites Orthodoxes en Bulgarie an XVIIIᵉ Siècle," *Archiv Orientalni*, (Prague) 26 (1958): 59–80, especially pp. 69 and 72.

14. A nineteenth-century account of dervish life can be found in J. Brown, *The Dervishes, or Oriental Spiritualism* (London, 1868, 1968), especially pp. 286–291. The fact that the membership of the orders, including the sheikhs who headed the member lodges, were hierarchically organized, that the lodges assisted one another in their public services, and that the sheikhs of the lodges of an order might take counsel together to elect a general for the order—all these suggest that the dervish orders represented some kind of communication system, doubtless functioning more effectively along internal lines but also to some extent as a whole. For a portrayal of the role of dervish sheikhs in integrating town life, see Lapidus, *Muslim Cities*, pp. 111, 113, 135.

15. Bektashi stories, which have been handed down to our times, are typically ironic and bitterly antiauthoritarian.

16. Lapidus, *Muslim Cities*, p. 291.

17. See H. Inalcik, "Ottoman Methods of Conquest," *Studia Islamica* 2 (1954): 103–129.

# 15

## PROPAGANDA FUNCTIONS OF POETRY

TALAT SAIT HALMAN

We have lost the Yen-chi-san mountain
The beauty of our women was wrested from us
We have abandoned the valleys of Chi-li-yen
Nowadays our cattle find no pastureland[1]

This stanza, preserved in Chinese translation, is presumably from a Turkish song dating back to the second century B.C.: lyrics lamenting military defeat and its aftermath of humiliation and deprivation.

How about it, let's join our hands.
You hit twice, and I'll belt two.
Has he stolen
Or sucked the nation's blood and sweat?
You belt four, and I'll strike four more.

Twenty sent abroad to buy ships, thirty to select tea . . .
Did the Foreign Minister get a cut,
While our hairless children starve in mudbaked villages,
And our baby dolls sell their pure flesh night after night?
You hit seven times, and I'll belt seven more.[2]

This virulent attack on malfeasance and corruption in the 1960s is by Fazil Hüsnü Daglarca, a prominent modern poet.

Between the dirge for Turkish women's beauty ravaged by the foe and the protest against iniquity stretches a poetic tradition of twenty-two centuries. From its emergence until the present time, poetry has been an abiding force in Turkish culture and perhaps its best achievement. There can be no true understanding of Turkish social and intellectual history without a basic grasp of the themes embodied and the functions performed by Turkish verse. Among these functions, "communication" and "propaganda" have always figured prominently—and still do to a considerable extent.

The survey of the interaction between poetry and society within the framework of the Turkish experience clearly demonstrates that this experience is probably more significant in Turkish history than it may have been in many other cultures, because poetry traditionally formed the vital center of Turkish literature that served as the core of the pre-Islamic and the Islamic Ottoman civilization of the Turks.

Long before the emergence of the Ottoman state, Turkic nomadic and settled communities had channeled their creative energies into epic literature and lyric poetry. The most enduring legacies of the antiquity are usually pottery and poetry. Virtually no pottery, however, has come down to us from the early Turkic civilizations. Long peripatetic adventures and the ravages of time have denied access to palpable works but poetry has survived. It gives us, as no other single medium can, insights into the history, collective life, language, social organization, and the ethos and mythos of the Turkish antiquity.

Perhaps the crowning achievement of Ottoman culture, too, was poetry. Finding favor at the court and at the coffeehouse, it satisfied the aesthetic needs of the elite and the man in the street. Significantly, two-thirds of the Ottoman sultans were poets themselves—some of them first-rate, for example, Mehmed the Conqueror and Süleiman the Magnificent.[3] For the Ottoman intellectual, who usually spurned prose as being too easy, poetry was a sine qua non of self-expression. E. J. W. Gibb, writing in 1900, opened the preface of his six-volume study entitled *A History of Ottoman Poetry* with the following words: "The History of Ottoman Literature has yet to be written. . . . Such books as have appeared up till now deal, like the present, with one side only, namely, Poetry. The reason why Ottoman prose has been thus neglected lies probably in the fact that until within the last half-century nearly all Turkish writing that was wholly or mainly literary or artistic in intention took the form of verse. Prose was as a rule reserved for practical and utilitarian purposes.''[4] In addition to the massive output of lyric and mystic poetry, a great many didactic, theological, narrative, historical, and scholarly works also were written in verse.

In the rural areas of the Ottoman state and among the lower classes in general, poetry was a major province of entertainment and enlightenment. Troubadours, minstrels, resident bards would read or improvise poems, often with musical accompaniment, and the *meddah*s (story tellers) would recite epics and narratives, often with verses interspersed.

Poetry was the vital ingredient of Ottoman high culture as well as popular culture. Of crucial importance is the fact that it preempted the functions of prose, even arresting the development of prose as a vehicle for artistic or intellectual expression. Consequently, we must turn to verse for many areas of Ottoman studies with more frequency—and usually with greater profit—than would be true in the case of other states and cultures of the past. Of the two longest chapters in a prospective intellectual history of the Ottoman Empire one probably would be entitled "Islam" and the other "Poetry."

Beginning with the *Tanzimat* period, when legal and governmental reforms were introduced following the issuance of the Gülhane Rescript in 1839, new genres and prose writing—mainly fiction, drama, and journalism—curtailed the supremacy of verse. But poetry was to retain much of its hold over Turkish intellectual life. Particularly at times of social upheaval, it often has played a considerably wider and more effective role than many other media.

In the nineteenth and early twentieth centuries, poets were the principal champions of fundamental rights and freedoms—the conveyors of the concepts of nationalism, modernization, social and political reforms. In the 1920s and 1930s, many poets served as propagandists for the élan of the burgeoning Republic of Turkey and its ideology, Atatürkism (also known as Kemalism). Left-wing movements, too, have been allied with poetry from the outset. It is significant, for instance, that the most famous—also the most effective—Turkish communist in the first fifty years of modern Turkey was the poet Nazim Hikmet (d. 1963).[5] Today poetry remains a more potent force in Turkey than it is in most modern nations. An estimable group of poets is serving at present as social critics, agitators, stewards of political conscience, and ideologues.

Turkish society has traditionally taken its poetry very seriously, and continues to do so. In the Ottoman Empire poetry could be a matter of life and death. Because of their unorthodox (or allegedly "heretical") ideas expressed in widely read poems, Nesimi (d. 1404) was skinned alive, and Pir Sultan Abdal was hanged (sometime in the sixteenth century). For satire directed against high-ranking officials—perhaps even at the sultan himself by implication—Nef'i was condemned to death, and was either strangulated or drowned in 1635. Because of poems of protest or criticism, many poets, for example, Izzet Molla (d. 1829) and Namik Kemal (d. 1888) were penalized and sent into exile. In modern Turkey, Nazim Hikmet spent seventeen years of his adult life in prison and died an expatriate in Moscow after a self-exile of twelve years. Few professions, in fact, have been as rewarding or as risky in the course of Turkish history as has the practice of the poetic arts.

It is safe to assume, then, that poetry—on the strength of its huge volume, the nature of its substance, and the dynamics of its functions—has figured prominently in all periods of Turkish cultural history and on all levels of society.

The present chapter deals with the communication and propaganda aspects of poetry and society within the context of the Turkish experience and confines itself to functional relationships. The quantity of verse produced throughout Turkish history is a statistical truism that need not be documented. Insofar as the manner in which a society reveals itself in its poetry is concerned, this phenomenon remains outside of our survey although of course it would make a fascinating study in itself. For our present purposes, we shall take it for granted that, as in all literatures, Turkish poetry is a direct product of its social and cultural context, and embodies and reflects the values and the norms of the society of its time. This stands in relation to the

Aristotelian concept of *mimesis* (imitation of life) as the essence of literary expression, which includes the prerogatives of the creative artist as *zoon politicon.*

Hippolyte Taine's dictum that literature is the product of "the race, the milieu, and the moment" also will be taken as a self-evident truth, but perhaps as a partial truth in the Turkish frame of reference, because Turkish poetry sometimes has been a forerunner or anticipator of social action.

As for the Marxist view that art is limited to its time, voicing the values typical of the dominating class, we shall consider this observation as outmoded in general terms, and as only partially or superficially valid for the Turkish experience, because Turkish poetry, both in the past and in the modern age, has indeed performed the functions of protest, opposition, and resistance to the powers that be. Innumerable poems in Turkish contain outright attacks on the values of the dominating class, in cogent contrast to the Marxist interpretation of art.

The aesthetic debate on poetry in terms of subjective versus objective reality is germane on a theoretical plane. But Laura Riding's generalization about the function of poetry is, in my view, a grievous error: "The ultimate effect of poetry is to clarify nothing, to change nothing." The author essentially agrees with Paul Ramsey's observation that "the society in poetry is always, in a sense, invented rather than actual," but does not subscribe to Susanne Langer's simplistic statement that "poetry is never *about* society, since it is always pure invention." Obviously the poet is not a scientist or a historian, and takes personal liberties with external reality, internalizing it, and placing on it his subjective interpretation. Pasternak has referred to this process in the following terms: "Poetry dislocates reality." But certainly poetry also serves the function of direct commentary that is free of excessive transformation—to avoid the use of a term of opprobrium like "distortion"—of objective truth or external reality. Similarly, Alain Bosquet's statement "Le poème l'écrit" (The poem writes itself), which posits the poet as a mere intermediary devoid of rational choice or command over what he writes, is untenable.

The premises of this chapter are that, in the Turkish experience, poetry has served both as a cohesive force and as a factor of social innovation. Having kept the vernacular alive, it has helped to preserve the ethnic, cultural, and theological identity. Often functioning as a myth maker (in a broad anthropological sense), it has come to perpetuate, as well as criticize, the patterns of communal life and values. Poetry both affirms and dislocates faith, political power, and ideology. It communicates prevalent concepts and also may undermine them. It serves the ends of propaganda and protest. It embodies the conflict between the real and the ideal, and usually offers the contrast between the crass aspects and the best potential of life. It converts, contraverts, and subverts.

Turkish poetry, taken in its entirety, offers us, inter alia, a rational system of intentional and indirect social functions. The present treatise will show how poetry exerts influences and contributes to society through communication and propaganda—both pro and con. In the Turkish experience, the norms and the impact of this poetry-society relationship can be established in three major categories: continuity and cohesion, commentary and criticism, and impetus to change.

## *CONTINUITY AND COHESION*

Throughout their history, Turks went through numerous major changes, including some cataclysmic transformations, in terms of locale, cultural orientation, faith, system of government, allegiance, and so forth. Particularly the pre-Ottoman stage of Turkish history is a saga of exodus, dispersion, major wars and small skirmishes, conversion to various religions, assimilation of elements from diverse cultures. In spite of such changes, the Turks maintained a strong sense of solidarity and perpetuated their identity. Flute songs of shepherds, which are among the earliest Turkish lyrics, dating from the fourth to sixth centuries A.D., include aphoristic references to the theme of "strength in unity":

> One branch can never make a tree
> Nor could one tree make a forest

These lyrics of love and war are typical of tribes threatened by hostile communities or natural disasters. The pre-Islamic Turkish lore is replete with poetic accounts of the ceaseless fight for survival, of exile, of unjust rule, of brave deeds and communal predicaments. The recurrent themes are heroism and endurance. The protagonists of the epics are courageous men, aided by superhuman powers, who lead their tribes into safety after struggling against extinction. The cruelty of time is depicted as the death of the hero, of the saviour:

Is Alp Er Tunga dead and gone
While the evil world lives on?
Has time's vengeance begun
Now hearts are torn to shreds.

Poetry held an important place in pre-Islamic Turkish life—from birth to death. It was customary to chant poems at prehunt rituals *(Sigir)* and at the festivities *(Sölen)* after the hunt. At funerals and memorial services *(Yug)*, elegies *(Sagu)* were recited. In many communities poetry had a thaumaturgical function. Resident and wandering *ozans* and *bahsis* who read poems, usually accompanying themselves on the string instrument *kopuz,* not only responded to the aesthetic needs of the communities but also served to keep alive the Turkish epopee and the Turkish language. The tradition of poetry as *the* lively art continued through the centuries, contributing massively to the perpetuation of a Turkic sense, to a Turkish identification. In the survival of the Turkish language—even at a time when the Turks of the Ottoman Empire preferred to regard themselves Moslems or Ottomans rather than Turks or actually sneered at any Turkish identity—a strong collective consciousness (in the Jungian sense) remained alive, and this consciousness was successfully revived in modern times for the cause of Turkish nationalism.

Language, in fact, became the major determinant of being a Turk. Over the centuries it has proved so resilient, so stable in structure and so firm and resourceful in its integrity and tenacity despite changes of orthography and massive borrowings of vocabulary that it is easy to understand how a certain mystique of the Turkish language evolved over the centuries.

In the eleventh century, Yusuf Has Hacib devoted a long section of his monumental treatise in verse, *Kutadgu Bilig* (The Knowledge of Blissful Government), to the focal significance of language: "Man's legacy to man is words. . . . Whoever is born must die, but his words live on. Language is the interpreter of thought and science. It gives man dignity. Human beings attain happiness through language. But it can also demean man and cause heads to roll. It is on words that man can rise and acquire power and prestige."[6]

When Turks, during and after their conversion to Islam, fell under the pervasive influence of Persian and Arabic cultures, they increasingly regarded Turkish as an inferior and inadequate language. In the thirteenth century, Mawlana Djalal al-Din Rumi, the great mystic poet-philosopher, produced his vast output in Persian, bypassing the Turkish language that was the vernacular of the Anatolian Seldjuk heartland where he lived. His son Sultan Veled, also a poet in his own right, found it essential to compose poems in Turkish in order to spread the faith of the Mawlawi sect in Anatolia, but stated in the Turkish section of his *Rebabname* (The Book of the Lyre) that his command of the Turkish language was not strong enough.

In the early part of the fourteenth century, Asik Pasha delineated the language crisis among the educated classes in the following lines:

> Nobody holds Turkish in esteem
> No heart goes out to the Turks
> Turks themselves don't know their own tongue.

Turkish identification was also shaken by the Ottoman elite's preference for allegiance to Islam and to the Ottoman state. This attitude stood in sharp contrast to the sense of linguistic pride and superiority that had marked *Divan ü Lugat-it Türk,* the eleventh-century compendium of Turkish words, sayings, and verses compiled by Mahmud of Kashgar: "God Almighty said: 'I have an army to which I gave the name *Turk.* I had the Turks settle in the East. When a nation displeases me, I send the Turks against that nation.' "[7] Later centuries were to witness self-disparagement among Ottoman Turks whereby "Turk" became synonymous with "coarse, crude, cruel." One of the greatest of classical poets, Nef'i, wrote in the early part of the seventeenth century:

> God forbad the fountain of learning to the Turk.

A century later, Vahid Mahdumi reeled against being a Turk:

I am ignorant, an ass of a Turk, ill-bred,
A thick-headed donkey, fodder is what I'm fed.

It is a remarkable phenomenon that, in the face of such vituperative abuse, both a sense of Turkishness and the Turkish language itself could survive. The explanation lies in the fact that, while the educated classes bore primary allegiance to being Ottoman, professing an admiration for Persian literature, and opening the floodgates of Persian and Arabic vocabulary, rural communities and the urban lower classes kept the Turkish language viable if not intact. Thus the oral literature of the common people, in contrast to the elite, withstood the intrusions of hybrid vocabulary, and continued the epic and lyric traditions of the pre-Islamic and pre-Ottoman period in forms and norms that owed virtually nothing to Persian aesthetics or Arabic concepts. In terms of language, most folk poets retained and revitalized the pristine elements of their own language.

It is regrettable that no study of Turkish poetry has been undertaken from the standpoint of linguistics or philological continuity nor is there an anthropological study of how pre-Islamic features of Turkish culture manifested themselves during the Islamic period or how archetypal patterns persisted. Even a cursory glance at the earlier lore of the Turks points to many aspects of thematic and linguistic continuity, for example, *Divan ü Lugat-it Türk* (1072) by Mahmud of Kashgar includes the proverb "Birds will not fly without a guide" and, more than two centuries later, the folk-mystic poet Yunus Emre (d. circa 1320) incorporates the proverb into one of his lines: "Birds will not fly without a guide through all these mountains and meadows."

Significantly, it is not difficult for a Turk living in the twentieth century to understand many of the major poems of Yunus Emre while he may find it well-nigh impossible to make sense of the verses of the great classicist Seyh Galib, who died at the end of the eighteenth century. From beginning to end, Turkish folk poetry is easily intelligible to a contemporary Turk whereas Ottoman classical verse is not only an acquired taste but also a matter of rigorous specialized study. Taken in its entirety, Turkish folk poetry charts the continuity of the language—and language, as intensified and purified in poetry, has been a major element of communication and cohesion in Turkish culture.

Language reforms have been sweeping and remarkably successful in modern Turkey. In 1928, by governmental decree, the Arabic script, in use for nearly ten centuries, was abandoned, and the Latin alphabet was adopted. In 1932, the semi-official Turkish Language Society was formed and assigned the task of "re-Turkifying" the language. Hundreds of words were revived or revised from folklore and scores of new words coined to replace the borrowings from Arabic and Persian. The educational system, the press, and a large majority of the writers contributed immensely to the popularization of revivified Turkish. The success of this reform movement is unparalleled by any country in modern times. For example, the ratio of Turkish words in the 1924 Constitution of the Turkish Republic is only 25 percent, whereas the ratio has gone up to 70 percent in the 1961 Constitution.[8] Journalistic language used less than 25 percent Turkish vocabulary in 1920 but about 80 percent by 1970. This rapid and far-reaching reversal can be traced to the fact that the Turkish language retained its integrity in folk speech and literature, which served as a repository of living words, and that, consequently, the reforms introduced were not synthetic but derived strength from and struck a responsive chord in the patterns of continuity.

The "re-Turkification" process received further impetus from literary precedents. In the first half of the sixteenth century, for instance, a movement called "Türki-i basit" (Simple Turkish), led by Nizami of Edirne (d. after 1554) and Mahremi of Tatavla (d. circa 1536), advocated the use of colloquial Turkish, free of Arabic and Persian borrowings and of all Persian *izafet* formulations, in the classical stanzaic forms utilizing the Arabic-Persian prosody ("aruz") and showed, on the strength of their large and impressive output, that success could be achieved along these lines, pointing to the emergence of an original body of "national literature."[9]

In many stages of Turkish history, poetry also served as a principal propaganda device in the service of the dynasty or of the governmental leadership. It often propagated a faith or ideology, be it Islam or Turkish nationalism. Its myth-making function was in full use at the epic stage of Turkish literature in the pre-Islamic era. Poetry as *propaganda fide* was in the forefront of the adoption of Islam and its cultural context, and once Islam became the official religion of the Turks and formed the vital center of Ottoman civilization, poets were called upon to consolidate and disseminate its themes and values. Consequently, from the end of the eleventh century until the middle of the nineteenth century, a principal preoccupation of the poets close to the theocratic establishment was the production of a vast body of literature that consisted of books of ethics, Islamic narratives, translations of religious texts, lives of the Prophet and his successors, gnomic and hortatory works, and more.

Throughout the history of the Ottoman state, poets laureate and versifiers loyal to the court produced a massive amount of panegyrics. Divan (classical) poetry, in general, as practiced by generations of conformists, gleefully perpetuated its own aesthetic principles for more than six centuries—and served to keep alive and communicate most of the prevailing values of Ottoman high society. The outcome was a rigid, static, self-serving system of values—socially and culturally. The dominant patterns of the Ottoman elite culture were essentially parallel to the characteristic of the traditional society as observed by Daniel Lerner: "In the traditional society, inertia was the modal principle of personality for most people. . . . What sustained traditional society was the routinization of life patterns in a self-sealing system that required no ingenuity and rewarded no initiative from its population." Ottoman high classes and high literature accepted their own norms with unquestioning dedication and used all available resources for the purpose of reinforcing their own beliefs and values.

Very often, folk poetry, which was essentially divorced from the Ottoman establishment and urban culture, served the function of disseminating themes of loyalty to authority, of the value of bravery in the service of the sultan, of the great deeds of heroes and commanders, of the supreme significance of conquest—all of which were vitally important to the causes of Ottoman expansion and dynastic continuity.

Modern panegyrics and elegies in the past five decades were focused on Mustafa Kemal Atatürk, founder of the Turkish Republic, who is perhaps the most extensively celebrated political figure in poetry in any country, with no less than five thousand rhapsodical poems written about him during and after his life. Turkish nationalism under the aegis of Atatürk as well as before and after him utilized—and continues to utilize—verse as a cogent, if not the most effective, vehicle of propaganda and proselytizing.

Period after period in Turkish history, poetry gave Turkish society the aesthetics of unity and continuity and served the function of communication as well as social cohesion.

## COMMENTARY AND CRITICISM

A central function of Turkish poetry has been at work in the domain of comment on and critique of political norms and social values at all stages of Turkish history. A majority of the poets, even those who are strictly lyrical or essentially apolitical, seem to have performed their social functions along the lines of Archibald MacLeish's dictum: "Poetry should deal with public issues and the human heart. And the human heart is a social organ, not just a private one."

For a vast portion of theological argument and ideological debate, the student of Turkish history must turn to verse. From the earliest times to our day, poetry has reflected the themes and values of Turkish life in greater depth and breadth than has any other single medium. Similarly, it has been the repository of nonconformist views, even of heresy, of criticism and protest, of defiance and rebellion.

The pre-Islamic epic, particularly the Oguz Epic, voices the ancient preoccupation with the questions of justice, leadership, and honest rule. Likewise, Yusuf Has Hacib's monumental treatise, *Kutadgu Bilig,* composed in sixty-five hundred couplets, devoted much space to concepts of just and efficient government. It postulates, for instance, three requisites for a ruler: "Sword in your right hand, benefaction in your left hand, sweet words in your mouth." Many of the themes explored by the Ottoman poets in later centuries, such as the transitory character of the kingdom on earth, the ethical aspects of the exercise of power versus ideal virtues, and others, were posited by Yusuf Has Hacib in the eleventh century. And the abiding question of government depicted in terms of glory and of public welfare is focal in *Kutadgu Bilig,* where the word *kut* connotes both bliss or well-being and the state. The same concurrence of state and well-being was to continue in the double entendre of the term *devlet* (Arabic: *dawlat*) in Ottoman poetry. From the outset, Turkish men of letters established the principle of good government in terms of just and equitable rule in the service of the people and placed a high premium on the physical prowess, administrative efficiency, and moral scruples of reigning monarchs and of persons in positions of leadership. The comments and criticism levelled at the powers that be usually passed judgment on competence and performance in terms of these generally accepted norms.

The Ottoman dynasty was intensely dedicated, particularly in its earlier centuries, to official support of the poets as the vanguard of high achievement in culture and art. Also motivated by considerations of public support, the sultans endeavored to utilize the persuasive powers of encomia composed by the leading poets. Consequently, the Ottoman state, virtually from its inception, maintained a system of patronage and favoritism to which many poets ambitious for status or anxious for financial security responded with enthusiasm and loyalty. Laureates, palace hacks, verse chroniclers, poetasters turned out huge quantities of *poèmes d'occasions* and panegyrics. The hallmarks of this brand of poetry were stylistic refinement, erudition, abstract conceits, and Arabo-Persian forms and vocabulary. Poets close to the court became entangled in the web of rewards, and their work, in an attempt to be perfectly attuned to the values of the elite, missed the opportunity of internal change and cross-fertilization.

By and large, divan poetry, as the Turkish "elite poetry" influenced by Arabic and Persian literature is often called, conformed, almost subserviently, to the empire. An empire can seldom afford to be empirical and its literature runs the risk of becoming empyrean. So the conformist poets, century after century, perpetuating the same norms and values, offering variations on unchanging themes, and looking to virtuosity as the highest literary virtue, wrote celebrations of the triad of the Ottoman system: dynasty, faith, and conquest. When no

special occasion was being committed to verse, these "establishment poets" turned out lyrics of private joy and agony sufficiently safe as comments on life and couched in abstractions.
That is why divan poetry is often characterized as having been
"hermetically sealed" from life.

In my opinion, however, this "house organ" aspect of Ottoman poetry has been oversimplified and overemphasized. The
empire also produced a large body of nonconformist, subversive, protest poetry. This corpus of literature consists of the
following categories: mystic poetry, folk verse, *tekke* or sectarian poetry, and poetry of direct criticism.

Taken in its entirety and in anagogic terms, mystic poetry
may be regarded as a continuing opposition to, and an undermining of, the theocratic establishment—a quiet, undeclared
war against central authority. By refusing to serve as the amanu-
ensis of imperial glory, but, far more significantly, by insisting
on the supremacy of love over "cardinal virtues," by passing
over the sultan for absolute allegiance to God, by ascribing the
highest value to the afterlife and denouncing mundane involve-
ments, by rallying against the orthodox views and institutions
of Islam, the mystics not only maintained a stand as "independent" spirits, which in itself was detrimental to a literature and
culture seeking to be monolithic, but also eroded the entrenched institutions and endeavored to explode some of the
myths of the empire. So, while the palace poets subserved, most
of those outside of the cultural hierarchy subverted. The
mystics, over the centuries, maintained a vision of apocalypse
not only in the metaphysical but also in a political sense. Ottoman mystic poetry must be scrutinized, in my opinion, with
an eye to its covert secular commentary and social criticism. Its
depictions of human misery are not atrabilious souls stripped
naked, but more plausibly, carefully guided and guarded stabs
at the perversity or at least the unworthiness of the powers that
be. For the mystic poet, the Kingdom of God was probably a
utopia standing in cogent contrast to the sultan's kingdom,
which represented life on earth, with all the agony it perpetrates
and the travesty it stands for.

The mystic strain seems to have embodied the sense of alienation experienced by the Ottoman intellectual. A famous couplet by Nesati (d. 1674) epitomizes this feeling:

We have so removed our physical existence
We are now hidden in the gleaming mirror.

The same sense of dissociation from reality in its worldly or external aspects, the anguish of exile, the sorrow of spiritual banishment, that run through Ottoman mystic poetry are not simply the stock sentiments of Islamic mysticism, but also statements of discontent about the structure and the functioning of society. The tone is almost always pessimistic, and often nihilistic, albeit in anticipation of ultimate happiness. A sullen craft and art, the poetry of the mystics nurtured a special branch of literature, as it were, of complaint, chronic dissatisfaction, and disenchantment with the times. The great classical poet Fuzuli (d. 1556) voiced this gloomy attitude in many well-known lines:

Friends are heartless, the world ruthless, time without peace,
Trouble abounds, no one befriends you, the foe is strong, fortune is
   weak.

The state is topsy-turvy like a cypress reflected on the water.

Rifts are rampant, the community of peace is rent with fear,
I am at a loss, for I can find no true pathfinder.

Within the theocratic framework, the sultan was seen and shown by the poets as sacrosanct. Ottoman panegyrics charted a progression of love—from an ordinary sweetheart to the sultan and ultimately to God. In fact, in many Ottoman poems, written by the court poets as well as by the independents and mystics, a three-level interpretation of the "beloved" is possible: darling, king, and divine being.

This progression—or perhaps deliberate obfuscation—growing in concentric circles was reinforced by the attribution of absolute beauty *(cemal-i mutlak)* and absolute perfection *(kemal-i mutlak)* to God. The element of *celal* (implying might, greatness, and awesome presence) also figured prominently. So the composite picture of the "loved one," of the sultan, and of God in divan literature is one of inaccessibility, beauty, glory, and cruelty. In a much subtler conception than mere masochism, the divan metaphor equates beauty with pain and strives to arrive at *pathei mathos,* that is, wisdom through suffering. In a sense, establishment poets seemed to present the sultan or any person in power as having the divine right—like God—to inflict pain and misery. The mystics, in their insistence on the human predicament whereby separation from God is woeful, intensified the myth—particularly when they offered the ideals of love's torture and self-sacrifice. Lines from Fuzuli's poetry illustrate the point:

> I wish I had a thousand lives in this broken heart of mine
> So I could sacrifice myself to thee once with each one.

> A lover is he who sacrifices his life to his loved one.

The metaphorical progression from the "beloved" to the sultan and further on to God had its concomitant of complaint. Prostration became, in effect, a form of protest:

> Fuzuli is a beggar imploring your grace's favor
> Alive he is your dog, dead he is dust at your feet
> Make him live or die, the judgment and the power are yours,
> My vision my life my master my loved one my royal Sultan.

Because the poets frequently bemoaned their suffering in the hands of the loved one, the complaint was thereby about the sultan and about God, whose will the sultan represented on earth.

Those sultans who were themselves poets also contributed to the view of their reign being less valuable than love, particularly love of God. Mehmed the Conqueror (d. 1481) expressed this concept in a pithy line:

> I am the slave of a Sultan whose slave is the world's sultan.

Kanuni Süleiman (along with many other sultan-poets, including Selim I, Ahmet I, Mustafa III, Selim III) denigrated worldly power, choosing to glorify the supremacy of love:

> What they call reigning is nothing but worldly quarrel
> There is no greater throne on the earth than the love of God.

So it devolved on the fifteenth-century poet Ali Sir Nevai to indicate the focal significance of the monarchy in mystical as well as political terms:

The heart apart from the loved one is a land without a sultan
And a land without a sultan is a body without soul.

A thorough study of the ramifications of the darling–king–
divine being triad, which is offered here more in speculation
than in substantiation, would give us a new understanding of
divan poetry—particularly mystic poetry—as a massive subversive literature, a strong protest about ruthless rule by the sultan
who dispenses cruelty although his subjects profess their love
for him.

Seen in this light, the sultan, metaphorically depicted, is a
ruthless tyrant who symbolizes cruel love, a supreme being, like
God, who has no feelings for his suppliants. Mystic poetry eventually lost its nonconformist function when it veered away from
its original concept of man as an extension of God and insisted
on the bondage of the lover to God the beloved, thereby becoming almost identical with the orthodox view of "submission," and suffered a weakening of its valuation of man as
possessing Godly attributes. But Ottoman mystic poetry in general validates Péguy's observation: "Tout commence en mystique et finit en politique."

Popular culture in the Ottoman state, keeping alive the
Turkic rather than the Islamic patterns of thought and values,
also constituted a sub rosa system of deviation from the Ottoman norms. Folk poetry came to typify and embody the gulf
between the urban elite and the common people of the rural
areas. It retained, in archetypal form, and regenerated the
pre-Islamic and nomadic values of the Turks. Written (or composed) by ill-educated and often illiterate minstrels and troubadours, it had little susceptibility or proclivity for the characteristics of divan poetry, which boasted of erudition. The folk poet
probably had no sense of participation in the Arabo-Persian
flavor of Ottoman culture; his concern was local autochthones,
and for purposes of direct communication he used a simple vernacular immediately intelligible to his uneducated audiences.
So, the substratum of indigenous culture resisted the tempta-
tion to borrow from the elite poets who, in turn, were imitating
their Persian and (occasionally) Arabic counterparts. In this
sense, one could conceivably regard the corpus of folk poetry as

a massive resistance to or a constant subversion of the values adopted by the Ottoman ruling class. It also gave voice at times to the spirit of rebellion against central authority and local feudal lords. The sixteenth-century poet Köroglu, for instance, wrote poems of defiance and became a legendary hero who rebelled against oppression and exploitation.

*Tekke* poetry, which served as the main repository of theological sectarianism, was in itself a poetry of dissent and discord. In form and manner, it availed itself of both divan and folk genres, and in substance it ran the gamut from devotional passion to denominational dialogue. It embodies the schism between the Sunni and Shiite segments of the Moslem-Turkish population and embraces a whole spate of unorthodox doctrines *(tarikat)*, from *tasavvuf*, libertarian mysticism, to anarchical Bektashiism and the Hurufi, Yesevi, Mevlevi, Bayrami, Alevi, Kaadiri, Halveti, Melami sects, and so on, that were often hotbeds of political opposition within the theocratic system and contributed to unrest and strife in Anatolia.

In contrast to the overall subversive nature of mystic, folk, and *tekke* poetry in the Ottoman state, the critical function throughout the history of Turkish poetry was often operative against specific targets and made its statements in explicit terms. Yunus Emre (d. circa 1320), probably the greatest Turkish poet of all time, said in the early days of the Ottoman state:

Kindness of the lords ran its course
Now each one goes straddling a horse,
They eat the flesh of the paupers,
What they drink is the poor men's blood.

The first humanist in Turkish culture, Yunus Emre, postulated the value of man in poems that lashed out against the zealot and the pharisee:

Better than a hundred pilgrimages
Is a single visit into the heart.

Yunus Emre says to the pharisee
Make the holy pilgrimage if need be
A thousand times, but if you ask me
The visit to a heart is best of all.

If you don't see man as God
All your learning is useless.

Yunus Emre struck hard at the calloused rich people, the aristocrats, and the rulers who remained deaf to the pleas of poverty-stricken people:

The lords are wild with wealth and might
They ignore the poor people's plight
Immersed in selfhood which is blight
Their hearts are shorn of charity.

His social consciousness had its roots in previous ages when, as far back as the fourth century A.D., a Turkish poet reprimanded high officials in the following words:

The governor and the generals go into the tavern
They have no money but they sit down and drink anyway
They scribble the list of their debts on clay.

Similarly, in the eleventh century, Yusuf Has Hacib's *Kutadgu Bilig,* the first Turkish work that represents the confrontation of the poet-philosopher and the king, had admonished the ruler in the following words:

This palace is but a guesthouse;
Others stayed here before you and passed on.

Many Ottoman poets reminded the sultan that he is only human and shall perish. Hoca Ahmet Fakih, as early as the thirteenth century, had referred to death as the great equalizer:

Death is a door through which together
The Sultan and the shepherds shall enter.

Among the mystics who remained outside the mainstream of Ottoman life it was a common occurrence to disparage the sultan's authority by swearing allegiance to a "higher authority." In the early part of the sixteenth century, Hayreti wrote the following defiant words:

We are neither slave to Süleiman nor vassals to Selim,
Nobody knows us: we are in bondage to a mighty Sultan.

Fuzuli, perhaps the greatest of the classical poets, who once wrote a letter of complaint in prose, which includes a proverbial line about corrupt officials, often lashed out against exploitation and malfeasance:

I greeted, they did not respond because it was not a bribe.

The tyrant grabs coins by cruelty.

Many divan poets protested against the chasm between the rich and the poor. In the sixteenth century, Yahya of Taslica wrote:

The poor must survive on one slice of bread,
The lord devours the world and isn't fed.

He who gives a poor man's heart sorrow,
May his breast be pierced by God's arrow.

A janissary commander and poet, Gazi Giray, at the end of the sixteenth century, sent the following report in verse to the sultan about impending defeat and disaster:

Infidels routed the lands which belong to true Moslems,
You have no fear of God, you take bribes and just sit there.

If no action is taken, this country is as good as lost,
If you don't believe what I say, ask anyone in the world.

There were animadversions against tyranny. Pir Mahmut wrote in the latter part of the fourteenth century:

The oppressed who stay awake and moan from torment
Will bring on their oppressors' dismemberment.

Baki, Süleiman the Magnificent's laureate, who was close to the throne for most of his life, could denigrate earthly kingdom:

We don't rely on the golden sceptre of state
We rely on the grace of God's perfection.

Thank God, the worldly state comes to an end.

In the seventeenth century, Ruhi of Baghdad, a vehement critic of the establishment, railed against the peddlers of status:

What good is a lofty place if it has its price,
Boo to the base fellow who sells it, boo to the buyer.

Also in the sixteenth century, Usuli defied the sultan in the following words:

We never bow our heads to this land's crown and throne,
On our own thrones we are sultans in our own right.

There were a large number of poems of protest and complaint directed against, not the central government, but local authorities and religious judges. In the fifteenth century, Andelibi denounced a judge for taking bribes:

Go empty-handed, his Honor is asleep, they say;
Go with gold, they say: "Sir please come this way."

Less than a century later, Pir Sultan Abdal lambasted another judge:

You talk of faith which you don't heed,
You shun God's truth, command and creed,
A judge will always feed his own greed,
Could Satan be worse than this devil?

Pir Sultan Abdal defied his persecutor Hizir Pasha, who was to have him captured and hanged:

Come on, man! There, Hizir Pasha!
Your wheel is bound to break in two;
You put your faith in your sultan:
Some day, though, he will tumble too.

Critical views of Ottoman life and manners were offered by some poets in *kasidah*s (long odes) and *mesnevi*s (narrative poems). Among these, the detailed commentaries by Osmanzade Taib (d. 1724) on commodity shortages, black market operations and profiteering, the plight of the poor people, the indifference of the officials and judges are particularly noteworthy.

A dominant mode of critique was satire. In Ottoman culture no "tragedy" evolved, and "comedy" was confined to the shadow plays *(Karagöz)* and the commedia dell'arte *(Orta*

*Oyunu)*. Tragedy places the human predicament in an identifiable setting and usually depicts personal or social rifts by
dint of the vicissitudes of heroes, and comedy pokes fun at
society in explicit terms. Conceivably, the Ottoman society,
particularly the theocratic establishment, had little sympathy
for such representations by live actors. Or perhaps poetry was so
pervasive and satisfying that authors did not consider it
necessary or useful to experiment with other genres. In the
vacuum, satire flourished. It performed (in the manner of the
Provençal *sirvente*) the function of exposing folly, challenging
the prevailing values, unmasking hypocrisy, and denouncing
injustice. In more recent times, the focal targets of satire have
been morals and manners, cant, political norms, and politicians
themselves.

In the fifteenth century, a physician-poet named Seyhi wrote
a blistering satire of socioeconomic inequity. In his verse
allegory entitled *Harname* (The Donkey Story), he contrasted a
starving donkey with well-fed oxen:

> Once there was a feeble donkey, pining away,
> Bent under the weight of his load, he used to bray.
>
> Carrying wood here and water there was his plight.
> He felt miserable, and languished day and night.
>
> So heavy were the burdens he was forced to bear
> The sore spots on his skin left him without hair.
>
> His flesh and skin, too, nearly, fell off his body;
> Under his loads, from top to toe, he was bloody.
>
> Whoever saw his appearance remarked, in fact,
> "Surprising that this bag of bones can walk intact!"
>
> His lips dangled, and his jaws had begun to droop;
> He got tired if a fly rested on his croup.
>
> Goose pimples covered his body whenever he saw,
> With those starving eyes, just a handful of straw.
>
> On his ears there was an assembly of the crows;
> Over the slime of his eyes the flies marched in rows.

Whenever the saddle was taken off his rumps,
What remained looked altogether like a dog's dumps.

One day, his master decided to show pity,
And for once he treated the beast with charity:

He took the saddle and let him loose on the grass;
As he walked on, while grazing, suddenly the ass

Saw some robust oxen pacing the pastureland:
Their eyes were fiery and their buttocks grand,

With all the grass they gobbled up, they were so stout
If one hair were plucked, all that fat would seep out.

Jauntily they walked, carefree, their hearts filled with zest;
Summer sheds, winter barns, and nice places to rest.

No halter's pain for them nor the saddle's anguish,
No heavy loads causing them to wail or languish.

Struck with wonder and full of envy, he stood there,
Brooding over his own plight which was beyond compare:

We were meant to be the equals of these creatures,
We have the same hands and feet, same forms and features.

Why then is the head of each ox graced by a crown
And why must poverty and dire need weigh us down?

This depiction of oxen graced by crowns was certainly courageous as satire, because the target in the allegory could well be
the sultan and his entourage.

In the sixteenth century, Ruhi distilled the same theme of inequity into one couplet:

Hungry for the world, some people work nonstop
While some sit down and joyfully eat the world up.

The nineteenth-century satirist Izzet Molla wrote many verses
in which he denounced prominent public servants by name. In
the following quatrain built on satiric puns, his victims are
Yasinizade and Halet, whose names could be roughly translated
as ''Prayer'' and ''State'':

Mr. Prayer and Mr. State joined hands
To inflict all this on the populace:
One brought it into a state of coma,
The other gave his prayers for solace.

Even God was not spared from badinage. Kaygusuz Abdal,
who lived in the fifteenth century, wrote several poems that
have barbs against God:

You produced rebel slaves and cast them aside,
You just left them there and made your exit my God

You built a hair-thin bridge for your slaves to walk on,
Let's see if you're brave enought to cross it my God.

The great debate through the course of divan poetry was between the mystic and the orthodox, the independent spirit and
the fanatic, the nonconformist and the dogmatist, the latitudi-
narian and the zealot *(rind* versus *zahid)*, who hurled insults at
each other. Nef'i (d. 1635), for instance, put down a conventional theologian with the following invective:

The wily pharisee is bound by beads of fraud;
The rosary he spins becomes the web of cant.

As if deploring the ''publish or perish'' dictum two hundred
fifty years ahead of time, Nedim wrote:

Forgive me philistine, your volume is a bit weighty,
Your vulgarity may be found in the size of your book.

In 1404, Nesimi was being skinned alive for heresy. The
religious dignitary who had decreed his death was on hand
watching the proceedings. Shaking his finger, the Mufti said:
''This creature's blood is filthy. If it spills on anyone, that limb
must be cut off at once.'' Right then, a drop of blood squirted,
smearing the Mufti's finger. Someone said: ''Sir, there is a drop
of blood on your finger. According to your pronouncement,
your finger should be chopped off.'' Scared, the Mufti protested: ''That won't be necessary, because just a little bit of
water will wash this off.'' Hearing this, Nesimi came out with
the following couplet in extempore and in flawless prosody
while being skinned alive:

Cut his finger and the pharisee will flee from God's truth,
They strip this poor believer naked, yet he doesn't even cry.

In a famous quatrain, Nef'i gave the following retort to Sheikh-ul Islam Yahya, the empire's chief religious dignitary and himself a prominent poet:

So the Mufti has branded me an infidel:
In turn I shall call him a Moslem, let us say.
The day will come for both of us to face judgment
And we shall both emerge as liars that day.

Nef'i once devastated the orthodox theologian Hoca Tahir Efendi in four lines utilizing a word-play on Tahir, which means "clean":

Mr. Clean, they say, called me a dog;
This word displays his compliment indeed,
For I belong to the Maliki sect,
And dog is clean according to my creed.

*Tanzimat,* the reforms in the mid-nineteenth century, brought into Turkish poetry a brave new substance—a systematically formulated political content. Patriotic poets, particularly Namik Kemal (d. 1888), lashed out against the sultan and his oppressive regime. Namik Kemal's poems were richly rhetorical pleas for freedom and justice.

Esref, the most biting and exciting satirist of Turkey in the past one hundred years, struck hard at the sultan and his entourage:

O my Sultan, this country nowadays is a tree
Its branches get the axe sooner or later.
What do you care if our homeland is lost,
But at this rate you may have no people left to torture.

In a different poem, Esref stated in no uncertain terms:

You are the most vicious of the world's sultans.

Elsewhere he satirized the Sublime Porte, the seat of Ottoman power:

Everyone's honor and honesty belong to you, my Sultan,
So there is no need for either one in your Court.

Ziya Pasha (d. 1880) produced a long satiric poem, many parts of which were committed to memory by his contemporaries and are still widely quoted among the Turks:

Those who embezzle millions are ensconced in glory
Those who filch pennies are condemned to hard labor.

How could a uniform make a base fellow noble?
Put a gold-lined saddle on him, the ass is still an ass.

Pardon is the privilege of the holders of high office;
Is the penal code used only against the meek?

Anatolian poets, too, bemoaned the social and economic conditions and levelled strong criticisms at the government. In the nineteenth century, Serdari wrote:

The tax collector rips through the village,
His whip in his hand, he tramples on the poor.

His contemporary Ruhsati complained:

There is no justice left, cruelty is all.

Seyrani raised his voice against the exploitation of the poor people by the merchants:

Alas, poor people's backs are bent,
We are left to the mercy of commerce.

During the first two decades of the Turkish Republic, very few poets turned out works critical of the government. The major exception was Nazim Hikmet (d. 1963), whose ideological poems were condoned when Turkey's relations with the Soviet Union were amiable, and banned—and the poet penalized —when relations deteriorated. But among the other leading poets, Yahya Kemal Beyatli (d. 1958) turned out neoclassical poems of love, Ottoman glory, and natural beauties of the city of Istanbul; Ahmet Hasim (d. 1933) produced nonpolitical symbolist poems; Mehmet Akif Ersoy (d. 1936), the author of the National Anthem, left Turkey because of his opposition to Atatürk's religious reforms.

When Mehmet Akif wrote the words of the national anthem in 1921, his numerous religious references were acceptable, but they proved curiously antirevolutionary at the time of the abolition of religious education and institutions in the second half of the 1920s. What became a sort of "national anthem syndrome" resulted from such pious references as follows:

Let it howl, fear not! How can it strangle such a faith as ours
That monster with one tooth left which you call civilization?

The days promised to you by God are about to dawn.

Those calls to prayer must resound forever in my land
Those affirmations are the foundation of faith.

From the early 1940s onward, Turkey witnessed a splurge of criticism via poetry. At a time when freedom of speech was virtually nonexistent during World War II and during Ismet Inönü's presidency, the utmost that the socially engaged poets could do was to launch what might be called "poetic realism," which they defined in a brief manifesto:

The literary taste on which our new poetry will base itself is no longer the taste of a minority class. People in the world today acquire their rights to life after a sustained struggle. Like everything else, poetry is one of their rights and must be attuned to their tastes. This does not signify that an attempt should be made to express the aspirations of the masses by means of the literary conventions of the past. . . . We can arrive at a new appreciation by new ways and means. . . . We must alter the whole structure from the foundation up. In order to rescue ourselves from the stifling effects of the literatures which have dictated and shaped our tastes and judgments for too many years, we must dump overboard everything that those literatures have taught us. We wish it were possible even to dump language itself, because it threatens our creative efforts by forcing its vocabulary on us when we write poetry.

The author of the manifesto, Orhan Veli Kanik, and his two coauthors, Melih Cevdet Anday and Oktay Rifat, proceeded to challenge the conventional values of Turkish society and poetry. In an age that placed great value on patriotism, Orhan Veli Kanik (d. 1950) was able to say:

All the things we did for our country.
Some of us died,
Some of us gave speeches.[10]

Since the 1940s, social criticism has been a recurring theme in Turkish poetry. The criticism finds its expression in stark depictions, as in a poem entitled ''A Small Place in the Provinces'' by Necati Cumali (b. 1921):

The people I used to know there
Gazed at the sky with fear
Gazed at the sea with fear
And trembled at the sight of the landlord
Scared of God scared of death
Scared of the gendarmerie
Scared of all government officials.

Halim Yagcioglu (b. 1918) delineated the tragic life of southern Anatolia in an angry poem entitled ''Anzelha'':

This land unawakened and unstirred
Still lives in the fifth century, Anzelha
And you live in the twentieth century
Is this how you absorbed civilization?
Shame.

Shame on you, Anzelha
In endless thoughts
Nights torture the sleep
Is this where the East starts, Anzelha
Is this Islam
Steeped in filth so deep?

In the 1960s, there was virtually no socioeconomic problem or political upheaval that did not find its way into Turkish poetry. In the foreground of socially committed poetry was the work of Fazil Hüsnü Daglarca, who, after the death of Nazim Hikmet in 1963, became the most significant poet living in Turkey. Some of the political poems written by Daglarca in the 1960s (published in widely circulated books and periodicals, and some posted on the window of the bookshop he owns and operates in Istanbul) gave voice to public indignation over

problems plaguing the lower classes. His "Jobless" is one of the
best specimens of lyric protest against injustice:

> He called fate
> His foundering in the street.
> For three years he had no job, no fear, no respect.
> In dreams a multitude of mouths craved bread.
> > So hungry were his hands and feet
> > He ate his fist.

> The wind was good; it fondled him at least
> As it fondles bird and beast.
> Its cool air, which sets no one apart,
> Brought no food, but a little solace.
> > So hungry was he as he grew in the quiet
> > He ate his lips.

> Now darkness shivered with blood.
> When passersby could not see
> Neither the stars
> Nor even God,
> > So hungry was he for life
> > He ate his breath.[11]

When charges were brought against Daglarca, he defied the
public prosecutor by invoking the poet's superiority over a functionary who remains impervious to the suffering of deprived
people:

To The Public Prosecutor

> Prosecutor, did you ever think
> What gives the hills their crowned height?
> Day or night, they never hush but shout from the peak.
> A jobless man from the hills stands barefoot at your door.
> Even you pity his plight.

> Prosecutor, did you ever think
> What gives the knives their bite?
> A right never claimed, bloodshed never questioned . . .
> The toil and sweat of this man or that
> Crowns the head and makes it bright.

Prosecutor, did you ever think
What you find in writings to indict?
Huge with mind and soul, days against the night . . .
But, down the ages, over you
What gives me all my might?[12]

## IMPETUS TO CHANGE

Impetus to social change and intellectual reorientation has been
the third major function of poetry in Turkish culture. Most of
the leading practitioners of the poetic arts seem to have believed, like Samuel Taylor Coleridge, in "the close connection
of poetic genius with the love of liberty and genuine reformation."

In ancient and classical Turkish culture, as in ancient Greece,
poetry was a forerunner of philosophical, political, and social
thought, and served a catalytic function not only for linguistic
and literary innovation but also in terms of anticipating and
promoting social change. The significance of poetry in disseminating Islam among the higher as well as the lower classes of the
Turkish communities, although never systematically studied,
must have been enormous. Judging by the available works, it
would be safe to assume that poetry was probably a principal
propaganda tool for the Islamization of the Turks. A graphic illustration of the transformation of faith, literature, and
language in Turkish life may be charted through four major
works written within a period of one hundred years from *Kutadgu Bilig* and *Divan ü Lugat-it Türk* in the 1070s to *Divan-i
Hikmet* by Ahmet Yesevi and *Atebet-ül Hakayik* by Edib
Ahmet in the second half of the twelfth century. The former,
although influenced by Islam and Arabo-Persian culture, had a
very strong enchorial Turkish substance and flavor while the latter were notable for Islamic content and Arabo-Persian forms
and styles. The thirteenth and fourteenth centuries witnessed
an effusion of original Islamic works by Turks as well as Koran
translations and commentaries, religious epics, *mawlid*s (poems
dedicated to the birth and life of the Prophet), narratives about
Islamic themes, Persian legends, and so forth. Moreover, the indigenous Turkish epics, principally the Oguz epic, were Islam-
icized and the Dede Korkut tales, which antedate the Turks'
conversion to Islam, acquired an Islamic flavor.

The majority of the works produced after the fourteenth century, with the notable exception of folk verse and the *Türki-i basit* (Simple Turkish) movement, had none of the nationalistic purpose or the linguistic pride that had marked the *Divan ü Lugat-it Türk,* with its mission "to prove that the Turkish language could compete against Arabic like a thorough-bred race horse." The absorption by the Turkish authors of the pervasive influence of Islam and its Arabo-Persian cultural context was to become the single major aspect of Turkish literature until the mid-nineteenth century. But literature was not only a recipient or a repository of the Islamic aspect. It placed, in turn, its propaganda powers in the service of Islam, and without the capacity of Turkish poetry to popularize ideas and sentiments the conversion of the Turks to Islam probably would have been a considerably slower process.

After completing its function of heralding change, and once established in its genre and confident in its intellectual orientation, divan poetry remained recalcitrant to internal change. It was only after several centuries of sclerotic continuity that, suffering from tired blood, divan verse introduced various formal and substantive changes. A significant innovation was undertaken by Nedim (d. 1730), the poet of the so-called Tulip Age, who lived *dolce vita* and wrote of Sardanapalian pleasures. He dropped the abstractions and some of the hackneyed clichés of his predecessors in favor of depictions of physical beauty (aesthetic, human, and topographical), made an attempt to "democratize" conventional verse by increasing its appeal through greater intelligibility, and dispensed with the masochistic and misogynistic implications of the divan poetry of the previous centuries, replacing them with the joys of love and living. Seyh Galib (d. 1799), the last of the great romantic mystics, also made an important renovation by getting away from the clichés and the frozen conceits and making original metaphors a new vehicle of artistic expression.

The poetry of the *Tanzimat* period, from 1839 onward, had the imperative of revamping its forms, style, and content. It also assumed the task of giving voice to civil disobedience. The *Tanzimat* poets often acted as provocateurs and agitators for reform and social innovation. A major literary change was the introduction of the various genres of European literatures, including the novel, the drama, and the journalistic essay. This exerted a confining impact on verse, but the cogency of poetic propaganda was to continue for many decades, particularly in rebellion against tyranny.

In the second half of the nineteenth century, most poets were in the forefront of the Westernization movement. The ideas and shibboleths borrowed from the West found their most effective champions in Sinasi (d. 1871), Namik Kemal (d. 1888), and Ziya Pasha (d. 1880). Poetry became a standard-bearer for such concepts as justice, nation, reform, sovereignty, modernization, freedom, progress, and rights. The fiction, drama, and journalistic writing of these literary figures were less a substitute for poetry than an extension of it. Their articles and novels were read with greater interest and their plays made a stronger impact because they were, first and foremost, famous poets.

The socially engaged poets of the *Tanzimat* era launched a consciously utilitarian view of poetry. In their verse, they fulminated against the entrenched Oriental traditions and the repressive Ottoman society. In the past, too, there had been occasional philippics against oppressors, for example, the rousing words of the folk poet Pir Sultan Abdal in the sixteenth century:

> Come, soul brothers, let's band together,
> Brandish our swords against the Godless
> And restore the poor people's rights.

Folk poet Dadaloglu (d. about 1868) is famous for the following lines, which were meant, in Pir Sultan Abdal's tradition, to fire the blood of the masses:

> The state has issued an edict against us
> The edict is the Sultan's but the mountains are ours.

But, occasional outbursts of the rebellious spirit in folk poetry aside, it was during the *Tanzimat* period that, for the first time, dissent and outright criticism in poetry for the sake of social and political change became systematic. Unlike in the pre-mid-nineteenth-century eras, the *Tanzimat* poets did not only lament social conditions but also advocated revolutionary or evolutionary change to remove them. It is small wonder that the leading poet rebels of the period who asked for nationhood, constitutional government, basic freedoms, fundamental rights, and populism were persecuted or banished.

The idea of sacrifice, valued highly by the divan poets when done for the loved one, assumed the form of sacrifice *pro patria* in the *Tanzimat* patriotic poetry:

> Let fate heap upon me all its torture and pain
> I'm a coward if ever I flinch from serving my nation.

This couplet by Namik Kemal, whose voice was perhaps the strongest in the nineteenth-century Ottoman Turkey for freedom and the rule of law, is typical of the new sense of mission that emerged at the time:

> Let the cannons burst forth and fire and brimstone spread
> May Heaven's gates fling open to each dying comrade
> What is there in life that we should shun falling dead
>
> Our greatest joy is to become martyrs in strife
> Ottomans find glory in sacrificing life.

In another poem, Namik Kemal reiterates the themes:

> A soldier's proudest medal is his wound
> And death the highest rank a man can find
> It's all the same beneath or on the ground
> March heroes march and fight to save this land.

Namik Kemal, having established his fearlessness, also gave vent to his fury against the oppressors:

> Who cares if the despot holds an exalted place
> We shall still root out cruelty and injustice.

Like Adam Myckiewicz or Sandor Petofi, he could stir the people into action. And the great debate in Turkish poetry from the middle of the nineteenth century to our day centered around the poet's freedom to follow the dictates of his heart and art, as contrasted with his duty to serve his society.

Tevfik Fikret (d. 1915) combined in his poetry both the concept of art for art's sake and the function of spokesman for protest and civil disobedience. He propagated a novel view of man and society. Standing squarely against the traditional orthodox and mystic conception of man as a vassal to God, he regarded man as having an existence independent of God. Tevfik Fikret placed his faith in reason over dogma, in inquiry over unquestioning acquiescence, in science and technology.

Tevfik Fikret defended the proposition that right is far stronger than might and that the people's rights will ultimately prevail:

> If tyranny has artillery, cannonballs and fortresses
> Right has an unyielding arm and an unflinching face.

In poems that were often memorized and circulated clandestinely, Tevfik Fikret railed against the oppressors:

> One day they will chop off the heads which do injustice.

> We have seen all sorts of injustice . . . Is this the law?
> We founder in the worst misery . . . Is this the state?
> The state or the law, we have had more than enough,
> Enough of this diabolical oppression and ignorance.

His assaults on malfeasance and profiteering were equally vehement:

> Eat, gentlemen, eat, this feast of greed is yours,
> Eat, till you are fed and stuffed and burst inside out.

At the end of the nineteenth century, when an assassination attempt at the life of Sultan Abdülhamid failed because the sultan's carriage arrived on the spot a minute or two after the planted bomb exploded, Tevfik Fikret in his poem entitled ''A Moment's Delay'' referred to the would-be assassin as ''the glorious hunter'' and bemoaned the brief delay:

> The villain who takes pleasure in trampling a nation
> Owes to a moment of delay all his jubilation.

Fikret was a foe not only of the sultan and his henchmen but also of religious faith, senseless combat and strife:

> Faith craves martyrs, heaven wants victims
> Blood, blood everywhere, all the time.

In vociferous opposition to Tevfik Fikret, a pious poet, Mehmet Akif (d. 1936) advocated the revival of Islam and had the vision of uniting all Moslems in an Islamic superstate. His nationalism was based on religious identification and he considered Islamic *summum bonum* as the substance and the mission of his poetry.

It is interesting to note that in the first two decades of the twentieth century—a critical phase of the Ottoman state—three rival and occasionally embattled ideologies were publicized by and publicly fought among poets. Tevfik Fikret championed social and governmental reforms, including secularism and Westernization; Mehmet Akif propagated the Islamic faith as a panacea for the decline of the Ottoman Empire; Ziya Gökalp and Mehmet Emin Yurdakul called for national unity based on the mystique of Turkism and nationalism.

After the establishment of the Turkish Republic, the Kemalist reforms found enthusiastic supporters and propagandists among poets. Several major poets, however, either chose silence on the reforms launched by the government (Yahya Kemal Beyatli, Ahmet Hasim, Abdülhak Hamit Tarhan) or left the country (Mehmet Akif).

The strongest voice for change, even for revolution, was that of Nazim Hikmet, an avowed communist, who once wrote in a burst of youthful enthusiasm:

> I am a poet
> I know what poetry is
> and the lyric I love best
>     is Engels' Anti-Dühring.

Like Lenin he believed that "literature must become a part of the proletarian cause as a whole," and he wrote lilting poems in which he voiced the hopes and frustrations of the lumpen proletariat:

> They are teeming
>     like ants in the ground
>     or fish in the sea
>     or birds in the air
>
> They are timid or brave
>     ignorant and wise
>     and childish

They are the ones
>       who destroy and create:
In my songs there are only their adventures.

He brought to Turkish verse the concept of materialism: "Those who oppose us," he stated, "really oppose / the eternal laws / of the dynamics of matter." And in the 1930s he proclaimed, like Stalin: "I conceive of art as an active institution in society. To me the artist is the engineer of the human soul." "The poet is a citizen who stands in the midst of life and organizes life." As a young man, Nazim Hikmet boasted:

We
>   keep in step with the march of history
>       and strike at the roots of imperialism
>           we are the ones
>               who build the future.

His "Advice to Our Children" was

Scratch the pages of the Koran.

Nazim Hikmet's idealistic and combative spirit is manifest in the following defiant lines he wrote in 1931:

I will shout my prison song
>       like a battle cry

We shall meet again
>           dear friends
>               we shall meet again

Together we shall flout the sun
>           together we shall fight on.

In the vein of the Russian *samizdat* literature, he wrote in 1951 a poem called "Sad Freedom."

You squander the gleam of your eyes
and the sparkling toil of your hands
to knead dough for countless loaves of bread
>           which they won't even let you taste.
All this great freedom is yours to slave for others,
to turn into Croesus those who suck your blood:
>               You are free.

The minute you are born, they swarm around you
and build mills of lies which grind till the day you die.
All this great freedom is yours to bury your head in your hands
and rack your brains about freedom of conscience:
You are free.

Your head is bent as if they cut it at the nape,
your arms weigh down at your sides.
All this great freedom is yours to drift here and there,
out of work, jobless,
You are free.

You love your country with all your heart,
but some day they might sell it, maybe to America.
All this great freedom is yours so you may be sold
or become an air base:
You are free.

Wall Street grabs you by the neck with its cursed hands:
You might be shipped out to Korea some day.
All this great freedom is yours to fill a grave
or to take the name of the unknown soldier:
You are free.

You say man must live not as a tool or number or cog,
but like a human being.
All this great freedom is yours for them to handcuff you,
yours to be jostled, jailed or even hanged:
You are free.

No iron curtain, no bamboo curtain, no lace curtain in your life
No need for you to choose freedom:
You are free.
This freedom is a sad thing under the stars.

Nazim Hikmet died an exile in Moscow in 1963. One of his last poems, entitled "Last Will and Testament," entrusts Turkey to his son in the following words:

Our nation has suffered and is suffering
But it will have a happy end.
You, together with our people,
Shall establish Communism, Mehmet.

The tradition started by Nazim Hikmet in calling for revolution or at least vast social change is firmly entrenched now, and many poets—almost too numerous to mention—encouraged by the wider freedom of speech secured by the Constitution of 1961 are criticizing the established order in vehement, and even vitriolic and vituperative terms, and calling for sweeping changes.

In 1963, in a revolutionary poem, which brought charges but no conviction against him, Talip Apaydin (b. 1926), a poet born and raised in Anatolia, vowed to eradicate the old order and to build in its place a wholly new social structure:

Old Order

We strike our pickaxe into its depth
Shallow sounds echo down below—
This building rotted for countless years
We'll rebuild it from the base up.

Go ahead, try a bit more—go on
Already it's trembling all over
The bugs and the lice in its burrows
Are in a hue and cry as in doomsday.

We'll demolish it—there's no other choice
We'll raze it and from foundation to roof
We'll build a new and decent house
In which we shall live like human beings.

Minatory statements also come from Asik Ihsani (b. 1930), a village poet who has become a common sight in the major cities of Turkey, where he sings his poems. In one poem cautioning "the gentlemen and the noblemen," Ihsani says:

You heap misery upon us
But don't think we'll stay like this
One day we shall rise
Then you will know who we are.

In present-day Turkey, "engaged" poetry often has such a tenor and thrust. Many poets subscribe to the spirit of Yev-tushenko's observation about the role of the poet in Russia where "the poet is more than a poet . . . in whom a proud civic spirit dwells and for whom there is no comfort, no peace. The poet is the image of his own age and the phantom herald of the future."

The prominent poet Fazil Hüsnü Daglarca (b. 1914) envisaged and encouraged vast change in Turkey's social order in a poem that led to legal proceedings against him (he was eventually acquitted):

The Cock

The cock that crows before the time has come,
Crow, crow again in the night that clings on,
Resounding through the stillness,
Breathe fear into the hearts of thieves in the dark.
     Crow and make the black hills turn red
     So the onward march of my braves will be sped.

To wake up, like a flashing dagger drawn to the future,
To set off a brave new awareness, truth and struggle,
To awaken the horses and the sheep, the axes and the shovels,
In offering emancipation along the sun.
     Crow and make the black hills turn red
     So heaven and earth shall tremble in dread.

They chop off the head of a cock that crows too early,
They will cut yours again and again, yet it shall not fall:
But in each age, in every century, each day,
Your golden voice shall usher in our light.
     Crow and make the black hills turn red
     So starving hands may clutch the fields of the well-fed.

Progressive Turkish poets strive to be both attuned to and ahead of their time culturally and politically. In the vanguard of intellectual development, they concern themselves with the vital questions not only of social ethics and just rule but also of the artist's obligation and prerogative to stir his countrymen to action. Many Turkish poets equate this responsibility with the primary task of the creative artist and hope for, in John Mansfield's words, "the best rewards the poet needs / To know his words result in worthy deeds." On the strength of this conviction, Turkish poetry has frequently served as a fulcrum that helped lift ideas poised against stagnation and satrapy.

### CONCLUSION

Having surveyed the panorama of poetry in Turkish society in terms of the patterns of continuity, critique, and change, we must grapple with two essential questions.

One is the age-old question of the artistic merits of socially committed poetry. Inasmuch as subjective responses and private sentiments are among the fundamental features of the poetic art, particularly "political poetry" carries in itself the aesthetic problem of internalizing to the point where sentimental romanticism holds sway or externalizing to such an extent that it creates the impression of detachment or disengagement or at least loses its immediacy.

The role of the poet in his society has been commented upon by ancient and modern poets and literary authorities from a variety of vantage points. According to Mallarmé, the artist —particularly the poet—is "on strike against society." Quasimodo offered the following on the poet as a moral agent: "The true poet is no dilettante. His role is moral. Not that he determines the morality of his people. His morality . . . is in finding the forms that will express anew for his generation the reality of human dignity. That is why the poet does not deal in the worn-out forms of past ages. The image of man is no eternal thing. We must remake it generation by generation. . . . The poet's morality is to recognize the eternal worth of humanity through every change."

Camus has observed that "the urge to rebel is, in reality, an aesthetic urge." But does this urge, this *esprit d'opposition* necessarily provide for success in poetic terms? It is a truism that protest literature usually suffers from banality. It often violates a rule eloquently posited by Samuel Johnson: "The end of writing is to instruct; the end of poetry is to instruct by pleasing." Rhetorical devices are usually antithetical to aesthetic enjoyment.

While engaged poetry serves as a constant obtrusion into government, in a broader sense, it creates the obstructions of its own aesthetic performance. Political verse, like pornography, is often a reductio ad absurdum. At least, it shares the problems of programmatic music. Frequently, a poem that addresses itself to an immediate social situation loses its cogency, and remains devoid of universal or transcendent validity, when the situation itself no longer exists. Lack of aesthetic autonomy usually becomes the bane of poetic worth in the long run.

The lyric transformations of social urges and commitments confront the poet with far too many pitfalls. In Turkish poetry, too, sheer invective and ideological polemics, on the whole, have been devoid of literary merit. The strength of the poetry of social criticism or action lies in the widest popular appeal, which in itself is a dislocation of the central concern of poetry. While attempting to popularize orthodoxies or heresies, the poet frequently runs the risk of vulgarizing. Furthermore, the dissidences of yesteryear have a way of becoming the self-evident truths or conformities of the present. Battle cries against the old order often crumble into the battle hymns of a newly emerging order. In this sense, Turkish poetry has had its share of vulgarity. In fact, it has occasionally served as "the great vulgarizer." But among the classical, folk, and mystic poets of the past as well as in the modernistic poetry of the last one hundred years, there also have been many specimens that stand as superb combinations of social criticism and artistic merit.

The second question: How effective is poetry as a means of communication, criticism, and propaganda? Is the pen mightier than the sword? Does a poet's frontal attack on society or his assault on any specific folly or social injustice as his target produce any results or contribute to betterment? Isn't there impotence where a poet claims he is giving impetus to change? Does bombast shake more than a bomb? After all, the Persian poet Abu Shukur Balkhi had proclaimed: "Speech overthrows the pulpit and the palace." But a greater Persian poet, Firdausi, cautioned: "No country has yet been freed from tyranny by talk alone." How can a poet, no matter how successful in terms of his *vita contemplativa,* succeed in *vita activa,* particularly when he is pitted against entrenched social forces?

As a matter of fact, how essential is poetry? How justified is Nekrassov's statement: "I prefer a piece of cheese to all of Pushkin." Or Pisarev's pronouncement: "I would rather be a

Russian cobbler than a Russian Raphael." Isn't the protesting poet quixotic? Isn't his attitude "Let them eat poetry." Perhaps what Gandhi once said to Tagore epitomizes the quandary of the poet as a social commentator: "The hungry millions ask for one poem—invigorating food."

These questions and their implications are focal in Turkish poetry, because throughout Turkish history there has been a correlation between the nature of society and the impact of poetry. In a sense, poetry has been—at least partially—"equipment for living" along the lines of Kenneth Burke's concept, not only creating symbols but also providing symbolic strategies to cope with life and its crass realities. Standing *media vitae,* the Turkish poet has served as a spiritual guide as well as a courageous reformer. But this role is caught in a process of unmistakable—and perhaps irreversible—change. As a society becomes pluralistic, industrialized, fragmented, and as it experiences the expansion of mass media, the power of poetry dwindles. Turkey is presently witnessing such a phenomenon. But, in terms of the functions actually performed by poetry in Turkey in the past, the impact has been impressive, and continues to be strong.

In verse the vista of many eras and intellectual developments have been preserved for us, charting the course of Turkish culture. Turkish poetry, through the centuries, has been noteworthy for *semination* in both senses of the word: sowing seeds of dissent and protest as well as spreading, or disseminating, antagonistic or opposing ideas. It might be naive to expect aesthetic pleasure from the poetry of social commentary and criticism—although pleasure arts and public arts are by no means mutually exclusive. Nevertheless, more often than not, reading some rhetorical poems is like embracing a porcupine.

It is unrealistic to expect poetry to launch a revolution. But the significance of protest poems can be found not in their stimulus to outright action, but in their cumulative effect—like Chinese torture, drop by drop, on the head of the ruling class. As in the past, Turkish poets today continue to act as spokesmen for social justice or at least as the monitors of the political process, and poetry in Turkish culture remains a most faithful index of transformation.

As far as the Turkish experience goes, poetry has been—and continues to be—a converting and subverting force. Art, politics, and poetry still coalesce in Turkish life. Communication, continuity, critique, and change—these are among the time-honored traditions of the dynamic intercourse between poetry and society within the framework of the Turkish experience.

## NOTES

*All the translations of the poems and excerpts in this chapter are by Talat Sait Halman.*

1. Muhaddere N. Özerdim, "Cin'in Simalinde Hanedan Kuran Türklerin Siirleri," *Ankara Universitesi Dil ve Tarih-Cografya Fakültesi Dergisi* (1943).

2. Fazil Hüsnü Daglarca, *Selected Poems,* translated by Talat Sait Halman, Introduction by Yasar Nabi Nayir (Pittsburgh: University of Pittsburgh Press, 1969), p. 155.

3. For extensive information on the sultan-poets, see Astour Navarian, *Les sultan poètes* (Paris: Librairie orientaliste Paul Guenther, 1936), and Hilmi Yücebas, *Sair Padisahlar* (Istanbul: Ahmet Halit Yasaroglu Kitabevi, 1960).

4. E. J. W. Gibb, *A History of Ottoman Poetry* (London: Luzac and Co., 1958), p. v.

5. Talat Sait Halman, "Nazim Hikmet: Lyricist as Iconoclast," *Books Abroad* 43, no. 1 (Winter 1969): 59–64.

6. Yusuf Has Hacib, *Kutadgu Bilig,* 2 vols., ed. Resit Rahmeti Arat (Ankara, 1947 and 1959).

7. Kasgarli Mahmud, *Divan ü Lugat-it Türk,* 5 vols., ed. Besim Atalay (Ankara: Türk Dil Kurumu, 1939–1943).

8. Ömer Asim Aksoy, *Özlesen Dilimiz* (Ankara: Türk Dil Kurumu, 1967), pp. 12–13.

9. Köprülüzade Mehmed Fuad, *Milli Edebiyat Cereyaninin Mübessirleri ve Divan-i Türki-i Basit* (Istanbul, 1918).

10. Orhan Veli Kanik, in *I am Listening to Istanbul: Selected Poems,* translated with an introduction by Talat Sait Halman (New York: Corinth Books, 1971).

11. Daglarca, in *Listening to Istanbul,* p. 151.

12. Ibid., p. 157.

# 16

## COMMUNICATION PATTERNS IN CENTRALIZED EMPIRES

S. N. EISENSTADT

The patterns of communication that developed in traditional bureaucratic centralized empires[1] exhibit in a most articulate way some basic characteristics that were inherent in the more differentiated—"archaic" and "historical"—traditional societies.[2] In fact, the problems and tensions generated by these communications were rooted in the continuously growing differentiation of the structural and symbolic spheres of these societies. Difficulties were especially evident insofar as there developed within societies:

1. A growing structural differentiation of the broader social units of the society, and especially between the periphery and the center;
2. A growing socioeconomic differentiation within center and periphery alike and a concomitant development of some wider strata or classes;
3. A growing differentiation in the symbolic definition of relations between extant units and the symbolic expression of the various centers;
4. A general disembodiment of symbolic spheres from their anchorage in primordial symbols; a growing development

of varied autonomous symbolic systems; and a growing development of systems of religious philosophy; and,

5.  A growing differentiation and specialization *between* societies.

Insofar as there developed in these societies some combination of structural and symbolic pluralism, the autonomy and importance of symbolic spheres in general and of communication in particular tended to increase and to pose several crucial problems, especially for the elites.

All traditional societies have experienced continuous—albeit in different degrees—development, increase, and accumulation of the different types of specialized knowledge of technology (including social technology) and science and of various types of "symbolic" knowledge. This symbolic knowledge is formed around the central attributes of cultural identity and enjoys its major manifestations in various religious, mystical, and philosophical schools.

There existed in all these societies some concept of the applicability of systematic "technical" knowledge to the running of an efficient society or polity. The many "Mirrors of Princes" and similar treatises, as well as the many special arrangements for the accumulation of information—in census, intelligence, or similar forms—fully attest to the importance of such knowledge in the more developed traditional societies. Their rulers (elites, and counterelites alike) recognized also the significance of the various symbolic types of knowledge for the elaboration, maintenance, and possibly modernization of existing traditions.

Both the elites and the broader groups in these societies were cognizant of the potential power of technical as well as symbolic knowledge in achieving far-reaching societal changes. The elites were especially sensitive to the need to control the development of technical knowledge. Of primary concern to the rulers was the control of simple accumulation of technical and scientific knowledge as well as of intellectual criticism. Also important to them was control of possible impingement of such knowledge on institutions, which expressed the basic premises of their regimes (the cultural and social orders and the distribution of power).

The rulers were keenly aware that unlimited development of technical and scientific knowledge—and of some types of symbolic knowledge—could easily touch on the basic sociocultural premises of these societies. Also, they were aware that the merging of technical with symbolic types of knowledge related to the major value premises of their tradition—particularly those that were subject to rational exploration—and that could undermine the basic premises of their cultural orders. Free public access to such knowledge could undermine as well control of resources and their distribution between (and within) center and periphery.

Accordingly, within the societies themselves, the rulers tended to develop several kinds of restrictions on the accumulation and diffusion of the different types of knowledge and communication. The most important of these efforts were attempts:

1. To segregate the major types of communication available to different groups in society, and to minimize the access of broader groups to more "central" ones;
2. To segregate the symbols of identity of local and kinship communities from those of the more central political and religious ones;
3. To monopolize the more central symbolic ("hierarchical-normative") types of communication[3] as well as the linkages between central and local symbols—those in the hands of specialists subservient to them;
4. To restrict access to central symbols to specified groups formed by special channels of socialization and education;
5. To minimize the development of specialized communicators and, insofar as such specialists did develop, to assure the rulers' control over them.

The center also attempted to restrict intellectual criticism that could be seen as dangerous to the maintenance of its basic premises. Here, significantly enough, traditions based on ritual or on direct mystic experience could much more easily cope with the growth of specialized types of knowledge by segregating them from the elite's central symbolic premises. Those civilizations—like the Grecian, Judean, and Christian—with traditions whose basic premises were couched in terms of learning and knowledge were more susceptible to challenges to the validity of their basic premises.

Restrictions on the extension of the critical attitude were upheld not only by those opposed to rational premises but also, significantly enough, by those whose orientations comprised the symbols of rationality—learning, contemplation, intellectual construction of a meaningful environment. Attempts at segregating the flow of knowledge and channels of communication sought to avoid impingement on the distribution of power and values among different sections of the society. Hence, in most such societies a series of policies developed that aimed at segregating technical information from the more symbolic knowledge and beliefs that were "allocated," as it were, to different parts of the society.

These communication policies also were connected with attempts to maintain certain patterns of communicative behavior within the social groups of the periphery. Perhaps the most important of these were efforts to maintain within these groups a large degree of differentiation and separation among the various types of normative communication (that is, between simple "normative" and central "hierarchical").[4] At the same time there was relatively little differentiation between normative, technical, and cognitive ("gossipy") communications.[5]

Many attempts were made to separate the "simple" from the "hierarchical" types of normative communications. They were rarely transmitted together, in the same situation, and by the same opinion leaders or communicators. The simple norms were applied almost exclusively to daily situations; many technical communications, however, were interwoven with these simple normative orientations. For example, technical arrangements concerning work, handicrafts, house building, and so forth, carried definite moral connotations such as the duty to perform well in one's work. At the same time, attempts were made by the elites to maintain close control over all the linkages *between* the different types of communications.

These tendencies to control information through such segregative policies can be seen best in the structure of the educational institutions. In most traditional societies the process of education usually was divided into several rather compartmentalized aspects. The central educational institutions were oriented primarily to the education of the elite and the upper strata—the persons responsible for development and maintenance of the central cultural tradition in all its varied manifestations.

The local educational institutions in villages and towns, usually connected only loosely with the central institutions, were oriented mainly to the diffuse and rather passive identification of the broader strata of peasants, artisans, and merchants with the overall symbols of society. The control system, however, did not permit these peripheral classes any close participation in central political or cultural activities. The local institutions also provided technical know-how in the realms of agriculture, handicrafts, and rituals that was appropriate to their position in society. Between the two types were several educational institutions that served either as channels of restricted "sponsored" mobility into the central spheres of society—as for instance the Confucian schools in China—or as channels of specific, specialized vocational preparation, as in a school attached to a guild.

On the whole, the educational system was geared to the maintenance and perpetuation of a "given" and relatively unchanging cultural tradition. It did not serve as a channel of widespread occupational and social mobility or of overall active participation in the broader cultural and political order. The type of education given to different classes was mostly, although not entirely, determined by their existing socioeconomic position.

Thus, education did indeed maintain, within all the varieties of traditional societies, a close relationship between control of information, levels of participation, and the elaboration of "meaning" in different spheres of human existence. Hence, these systems also attempted to ensure that the diffusion of knowledge and information—whether the technical instrumental type or the more symbolic parameters of tradition—would be segregated among the existing social strata. This minimized the possibilities of their impingement on the central symbols of tradition and of the distribution of power within its institutions.

But, however strong were the controls used to maintain the balance between different types of knowledge and to regulate the access to institutional participation, they were never fully successful. Indeed, they could not be—because of the process of invention and innovation, both in technology as well as in cultural symbolism, has been a continuing factor even in traditional societies. The impact of innovation was, of course, greatest in situations of accelerated social change, especially of rapid structural differentiation, of far-reaching economic changes, and of changes in fundamental situations—war, migration, invasions, and the like.

In situations of deep structural change, the processes of innovation were often connected with changes in the patterns of communication, notably with the development of:

1. Less marked differentiation between simple and hierarchical-normative communication and between symbols of local and central communication;
2. Greater differentiation between the bearers of various types of information, the scope of their activities, and the degree to which informal "opinion" leaders develop;
3. Less formalization of communicative relations and the development of impersonal mass media;
4. In general, growing differentiation of patterns of communication. These patterns are characterized by: (a) special emphasis on professional or semiprofessional communications; (b) the development of communications specifically oriented toward collective values and symbols of identification; and (c) growing differentiation between local and countrywide leaders of opinion and communication.

These processes of change often tended to undermine the actual patterns of communication controlling the existing elites. Indeed, it was especially in such situations that tendencies toward heterodoxy and change—attempts to reformulate different symbolic parameters and institutional aspects of the "given" traditions—were to become most prominent. These tendencies could manifest themselves either by extension of the critical orientation and substantive rationality or by restrictive antirational orientations.

The latter are a reflexive and defensive process: the greater the potential for criticism in any society, the greater also may be the attempts by the carriers of tradition (the holders of power) to narrow the range of such criticisms. Also, there may arise among intellectuals or others what may be called "irrational"— magical, demoniac, constrictive, and "alienated"—ways of responding to the new problems of change. These responses— often given in terms of antirational antinomianism—may become connected, in a great variety of ways, with movements of social protest which tend to arise in such situations of accelerated change.

Accordingly, rapid social change posed serious problems for the elites of society—the general problem of reconstructing the social and political system, and also the specific problems of finding new symbols of cultural identity, of developing new communicative techniques, and of relating the new communications to the prevailing cultural and social organization.

All these problems of relatively developed traditional societies appear in their most articulated form within the centralized empires,[6] to wit:

1. The ancient empires—especially the Egyptian and Babylonian (1900–641 B.C.)—and possibly the Incan and Aztec (A.D. 1100–1521) empires as well.
2. The Chinese empire—from the Han period to the Ching (200 B.C.–A.D. 1912).
3. The various Iranian empires—especially the Sassanid (A.D. 226–650) and, to a lesser extent, the Parthian (600–330 B.C.) and Achaemenid (sixth to fourth centuries B.C.).
4. The Roman Empire (31 B.C.–A.D. 527) and the various Hellenistic empires.
5. The Byzantine Empire (A.D. 330–1453).
6. Several ancient Hindu states—especially the Maurya (327–174 B.C.) and Gupta (A.D. 320–495)—and the Mogul empires (A.D. 1526–1705).
7. The Arab Caliphate (especially from the reign of the Abbasides [A.D. 750–940] and Fatimides), the Arab Moslem states in the Mediterranean, Iran, and the Ottoman Empire (A.D. 1451–1789).
8. European states during the Age of Absolutism and to some

extent their initial colonial empires, especially insofar as they were assembled with the idea of the direct extension of the patrimony and its central authority rather than as merchant colonies or colonization settlements of small groups. Of these, the Spanish-American empire (early sixteenth century to eighteenth century) is probably the nearest to the "ideal type" of historical bureaucratic empire.

The systems of the centralized bureaucratic empires, which are among the major historical premodern systems—along with the various types of tribal federations, feudal systems, city-states, patrimonial regimes, or mixtures thereof—have constituted the most compact, continuous, and enduring entities.[7] The majority of these empires developed from one or another of the other types of premodern political systems mentioned above. Their diverse origins greatly influenced the differential course of their history—their political symbolism, their international setting, their "longevity" and "continuity"—as well as the directions of their subsequent transformations.

But despite their great variety of historical origins, the empires shared some common basic characteristics. The most general of these, which distinguished them from other premodern societies, was that they encompassed widely dispersed and yet highly centralized territories. The center, as embodied both in the person of the emperor and in the political institutions, constituted an autonomous entity. Usually these characteristics were forged in the first stages of establishment of an empire.

The initiative for the establishment came from emperors, kings, or the ruling elite, such as the more dynamic element of patricians in Republican Rome. In some instances, the initiative was launched by usurpers coming from lower-class families, who attempted to establish new dynasties or to conquer new territories. In other cases, the initiators were conquerors who attempted to establish their rule over various new territories.

In most cases, such rulers arose in periods of unrest, turmoil, acute strife, or dismemberment of the existing political system. Usually their proclaimed aim was the reestablishment of peace and order. They did not attempt to restore the old order in its entirety, although for propagandistic and opportunistic reasons they sometimes upheld such restoration as a political ideology or slogan. They always had some vision of the distinctive goals of a unified polity. They aimed to establish a more centralized system in which they could monopolize political decision making and the setting of political goals without being bound by traditional leaders or mores.

The aims of the rulers often were oriented against, and encountered the opposition of, existing social and political groups. These hostile elements usually felt themselves menaced by the aims and procedures of the new rulers. Accordingly, they often attempted to deny them resources and support, plotting and working against them either by open political warfare or by infiltration and intrigue.

Out of such ferment grew some of the basic structural characteristics of these empires, especially the fullest differentiation, specification, and crystallization of societal centers in general, and of political centers in particular, as autonomous, structurally and symbolically distinct entities. This could be seen throughout these empires in many ''external'' manifestations, such as temples and palaces in which the basic conception of cosmic or cultural centrality could be found. But such monuments of centrality probably could be found also within many patrimonial regimes. The distinctiveness and autonomy of the imperial centers was manifest mainly in the specific nature of their crystallization of the symbolic and institutional aspects.

In structural terms, the autonomy and distinctiveness of the center was evident in its separation from all social units of the periphery, in its ability to develop and to maintain its own specific criteria of recruitment and organization, and in the consequent development of a relatively distinct ruling class. Some of the characteristics of this class we have already mentioned above. Even more distinct was the symbolic articulation of the political center in particular. In all these empires the political centers—and, as we shall see, the cultural-religious centers as well—were conceived as autonomous, self-contained foci of the sociopolitical order, and often also of the cosmic cultural order. The political center often became the major embodiment of the charismatic qualities of the cosmic order as reflected in the social order.[8]

The symbolic and structural autonomy of the centers was based on a prevailing conception of the distinctiveness of the different orders of human and social existence—the cosmic, religious, cultural, and sociopolitical orders—and on the ideological (theological) rationalization and symbolic articulation of these separate spheres. Thus, it necessarily gave rise not only to a growing distinction between center and periphery but also to a multiplicity of different centers. It was not by chance that these empires were also the seats of the great universal religions—Christianity, Islam, Buddhism, Confucianism, and Hinduism—and of the more "secular" ideological systems derived from the traditions of the Greek and Roman city-states. The multiplicity of centers within these empires was based on the same symbolic and structural autonomy as the political center, each such other center tending to serve as the major focus of its respective societal sphere.

In all these empires, with the very partial exception of India, a total distinction between these orders and centers never developed. Rather, there arose a competition between the representatives of these orders about their particular nature, about their relative place in the overall scheme of the world, and about the right of representation by the various centers.

The development of the distinction between center and periphery on the one hand, and the multiplicity of such autonomous centers on the other, was connected with the emergence both of a special ruling class and of a relatively independent, autonomous religious (or sometimes secular) intelligentsia. The extent of autonomy of the different centers and of the intelligentsia differed greatly among the various empires. These differences could be explained mainly in terms of the relative strength of their basic constituent elements.

The full-fledged development of such an intelligentsia took place only in the West. But important comparative indications could be found also in other societies. India constitutes a somewhat special case, because its religious caste was organized as distinct from the political one, and yet superior to it in terms of status. There it was the religious caste that constituted the main bearer of "great," that is, countrywide, traditions.

The autonomy of different cultural centers in various imperial systems could be seen best in their capacity for survival beyond the life of the imperial systems. In many cases—for example, those of most Christian, Islamic, and Buddhist organizations—the cultural centers outlasted the political systems of the empires within which they developed.

These centers—political, religious, and cultural—constituted the foci and loci of the several Great Traditions that developed in their societies. It was within these centers that the autonomous symbolic and institutional development of Great Traditions—as distinct from local traditions not only in content but also in the very symbolic and organizational structural characteristics—tended to develop. In this respect, they differed greatly from other premodern political systems.

Thus, although many tribal federations and city-states often did develop the symbolic aspects of Great Traditions within such centers, their structural basis was very weak. Most of the patrimonial systems made little basic distinction between central and local traditions. Some cases, such as Egypt, bordered on the imperial systems, but in these, differences of degree became differences of kind.[9] Among the premodern political systems, it was mainly within the empires that the specific characteristics of Great Traditions could become both institutionally and symbolically organized, and thereby become centers of the social, political, and cultural orders.

The multiplicity of centers exhibiting structural and symbolic autonomy explains the special relation between center and periphery and other specific characteristics of their social structure. Two such characteristics are of crucial importance here. First is the relatively great—and yet limited—permeation of the periphery by the center and the concomitant impingement of the periphery on the center. Second is the coexistence, within the same institutional framework, of different levels of structural differentiation.

Unlike patrimonial systems, imperial systems developed the assumptions that the periphery indeed could have some access, at least symbolic, to the new center. Such access was largely contingent on some weakening of the sociocultural self-sufficiency of the periphery and on its active orientation to the sociocultural order represented by the center. This permeation of the center into the periphery could be seen in the development by the centers of very widespread channels of communication and in their attempts to break through (even if in limited degree) the ascriptive ties of the groups on the periphery. The uniqueness of the center was its role as sole guardian of the tradition and its legitimacy in these societies. Hence, the impingement of the periphery on the center had to be much weaker than the permeation of the periphery by the center.

These basic characteristics of the empires greatly influenced the structure of communication within them, the ways in which various channels of communication functioned, and the problems of continuity that they posed for the rulers of these systems. Given that these empires developed a new conception of centers, the central elite (the emperor and his immediate entourage) tended to develop new symbols of its centrality—symbols that contained relatively strong universalistic elements that were disassociated from the more ascriptive territorial or kinship units.

Among such universalistic symbols were the role of the emperor (or of the empire) as such and of the ideals or structures they upheld. There were also symbols that glorified imperial activities—mandatory, legal, and the like. A great variety of new technical means was used to transmit such symbols—temples, monuments, coins. Emperors instituted new festivals and special festive days that often competed with the old ones.

These symbols contained potentially broader and more pluralistic definitions of the political and cultural communities, all of which became important elements in the definition of the new central, symbolic, and hierarchical communication systems. Unlike other types of traditional societies, the empires permeated the periphery with these symbols, connecting the new symbols of collective identity with the earlier local identities. By integrating these new central symbols with the existing identity symbols of the local communities, the centers restructured and expanded the relationships of symbolic and hierarchical communication.

These new symbols also were communicated through a variety of new channels. Of special importance were the new monuments of centrality: the various new channels in the bureaucracies, central armies, special royal emissaries, pictures in coinage and postal systems. These new channels were activated mostly by new central specialists in communication drawn from the intellectual, professional, and bureaucratic groups. These specialists interacted with both old and new organizations, with the old aristocracy and the various centers of local traditions.

These specialists also were fully anchored in the new centers of learning and of professional life. Strong tendencies developed for the accumulation and organization of knowledge. Dissemination of these new and multiple symbols through the new channels created several important "fronts" for the rulers and elites of the empires to face. First, there were the various local symbols, whether local-temporal or kinship, that bespoke preexisting "Small Traditions." Second, as most such imperial systems tended to develop together with broader universalistic religious and cultural symbols, they had to compete in the communication of these symbols. The third front that any imperial system had to face was a broader international system that involved important political, religious, cultural, and economic elements.

On all these fronts, the empires faced the problem of how to make their own new symbols more encompassing and, at the same time, how to keep them relevant to the symbols of the local communities, the universal religions, and the various international settings. Of crucial importance were the ways in which these new types of communication specialists and the messages they tried to transmit became interwoven into the older local patterns of opinion. This had significant bearing on the degree to which communicators developed an autonomy of their own and became centers of activity independent of their rulers.

It should be remembered that given the basically "traditional" orientations of the imperial systems, their conceptions of the center could not go beyond certain symbolic and structural limits. This created an additional level of tension—namely, that between the "traditional" and the broader components of the imperial symbols that cut across the different fronts mentioned above.

With regard to all these problems of communication, rulers faced problems with regard to other social forces: on the one hand, how to develop and maintain relatively differentiated symbols, disassociated from more local ascriptive units; on the other hand, how to control these forces so that they would not develop beyond the basic ideological premises of the regimes. Different imperial systems were able to deal with these problems with varying degrees of success, which can be measured only in the relative longevity of their regimes.

The study of conditions that made for such differences in longevity is beyond the scope of this chapter.[10] But it is important to point out that the centers of communication, in close conjunction with other cultural forces, played a very important role both in generating the forces of change in these systems as well as in influencing the direction of the changes. As generators of change, they served as independent foci of cultural identification. They could create and disseminate various cultural products—such as religious beliefs and systems, philosophies, and technologies—which were not tied to the boundaries of the existing political systems.

Whether such products were of the more "traditional" or more differentiated types, an outstanding characteristic was that they could create relatively independent sociocultural systems cutting across political boundaries. Often they survived the demise of such polities—as for instance in the case of the Eastern Church. Thus, they enhanced both internal differentiation within and differentiation between societies or systems.

The new communicators could generate the differentiated forces that would undermine the *traditional* premises of their empires; or they could, through an emphasis on more traditional orientations and activities, deplete the "free" resources needed for the survival of these empires. Depending on which orientations and forces they promoted, they also could greatly influence the concrete direction of changes in these political systems.

The internal transformation of the imperial societies was greatly facilitated by the autonomy of strong social, cultural, and political institutions, as in the cases of Europe, Japan, and, to some extent, India. In the cultural order, such autonomy facilitated the development of new symbols legitimizing central institution building. Autonomy in the sphere of social organization facilitated the crystallization of viable new organizational nuclei without disrupting the whole preexisting order. Thus, the new order was enabled to use, at least to some extent, the forces of the old one.

In all these processes the symbols, carriers, and networks of communication—being one of the relatively more autonomous cultural forces—played a very significant role. This role, although not identical in its force to that fulfilled by the communication system in modern societies, does come very close to it.

### NOTES

1. On these empires, see: S. N. Eisenstadt, *Political Systems of Empires* (New York: Free Press, 1963), where a full bibliography is given; and S. N. Eisenstadt, ed., *Political Sociology,* Introduction to chap. 8 (New York: Basic Books, 1971), pp. 263 and 264.

2. These types of traditional societies are discussed in detail in the various sections and introductions to Eisenstadt, ed., *Political Sociology.*

3. The nature of these different types of communication is discussed in S. N. Eisenstadt, "Conditions of Communicative Receptivity," *Public Opinion Quarterly* 17, no. 3 (1953): 363–374; "Communication Systems and Social Structure," *Public Opinion Quarterly* 19, no. 2 (1955): 153–167; "Communication and Transformation of Symbolic Systems: Some Problems of Communication in Developing Societies," in Lee Thayer, ed., *Communication Theory & Research: Proceedings of the First International Symposium* (Springfield, Ill.: Charles C. Thomas, 1967), pp. 482–509; and "Some Problems of Communication Research in Israel," *UNESCO International Social Science Journal* 14, no. 2 (1962): 337–348.

4. This analysis follows that in Eisenstadt, *Political Systems of Empires.*

5. In these researches we have distinguished among the following types of communications. First there are what may be called "technical" communications, whose main aim is to transmit various methodical information appropriate to given settings.

The second type is what may be called general "cognitive," which are seemingly without direct reference to concrete social situations. Gossiping about international personalities and, to some extent, general, inarticulate, diffuse interest in political events may be included in this category.

The third category includes what may be called "normative" communications. By this we mean oriented to the transmittal and maintenance of various social standards and to the definition of the proper behavior of the various roles in social situations. This category may be further subdivided into the types of norms that are to be prescribed, such as:

(1) general guidelines—for example, good/bad behavior;

(2) appropriate behavior for all members of a group;

(3) appropriate behavior for particular broad categories of social roles and subgroups (age, sex, etc.);

(4) hierarchy of values and preferences for ambiguous situations;

(5) possible role choices.

6. See in greater detail Eisenstadt, ed., *Political Sociology,* Introduction to chap. 8.

7. For the various types of these systems, see Eisenstadt, *Political Systems of Empires.*

8. Eisenstadt, *Political Systems of Empires.*

9. The differences between various types of traditional systems are more fully elaborated in Eisenstadt, ed., *Political Sociology,* especially chaps. 2, 4, 5, and 6.

10. For greater detail, see Eisenstadt, *Political Systems of Empires,* chap. 12.

# 17

## WESTERN CIVILIZATION: THE MIDDLE AGES

ROBERT BRENTANO

Propaganda was the characteristic gesture of Western medieval societies. It was a box, or a stage, in which Western medieval peoples lived. A great painted, carved, scrolled, furnished, incensed church, in which a king was being crowned, or a sermon preached, or even a mass said (and God's body eaten), disseminated or rather concentrated on all the senses of its communicants, and perhaps particularly the children, those intricate patterns of propaganda that had evolved through many centuries. Although this propaganda could be particular and locally political, it spoke most frequently in support of a prevailing but adjustable set of commonplaces and beliefs. It was used, although not always consciously, as an agent of cohesion, to give unity and malleability and thus shape to society, to ward off recurring fears of an often ill-defined "old chaos." It suggested reassuring answers (and thus made the askers better able to function socially) to the sort of terrifying questions suggested by Bede's royal counselor in his story of the conversion of the Northumbrians, for whom the life of man was like the flight of a sparrow through a warm and lighted mead-hall—from, and to, the dark, mysterious cold of winter.[1]

Even when its purpose was very general, the channels for communicating medieval propaganda are sometimes obvious.

A delivered sermon went from the mouth of its speaker to the ears of its hearers. A procession revealed itself to those who stood along its path. The magnificent seated figure of Charles of Anjou in the Capitol at Rome proclaims that king's power directly. But sometimes there was a queer disjuncture. Medieval chroniclers for instance repeatedly wrote highly shaped, distorted narratives and analyses to establish and presumably to project a specific point of view without suggesting in their writing that they had any specific notion of the audience, of any audience, whom they were trying to persuade. Potentates and particularly prelates mouthed high-sounding harangues, rhetorically shaped to the purposes of strong and pointed propaganda, when, in fact, their own purposes seem to have been very uncertain even to themselves. Symbols and images were produced with all the theatrical shading that should suggest a clear, compelling message when sometimes there seems to have been no message at all, only an obscure and general memory. That is to say, external posture that suggests propaganda was such a characteristic medieval gesture, such a facile creature of rhetoric, that is seems not infrequently to have been employed almost mechanically, because it was characteristic, the accustomed way of proceeding, not because it had something specific to say.

The effect is disconcerting to later readers and viewers, something like the "huge and hideous" mask, "large and misshapen, and so white that there was no possibility that it could be human," that Blakeley wears in David Storey's novel, *Radcliffe,* "motionless and inexpressive," reflecting "nothing of the feelings which lay behind it."[2] The immediate effect upon the reader or viewer of a surviving piece of medieval propaganda is often that of an ornate but inadequately articulate, isolated exaggeration. Among the reasons that shaped medieval statement to this effect, two are immediately apparent: the heavy tradition of learned and absorbed patterns of rhetoric and thought; and the inadequacy, the physical difficulty of transportation and communication, of conveying a specifically pointed persuasion to a wide and pertinent audience.

The whole problem of medieval propaganda is closely connected with medieval mobility and immobility, with the nature of medieval transportation and communication. Over a long period of time, a succession of Western medieval societies generally cared less about perfecting roads and (early on, at least) establishing sea routes, than did their predecessors and successors—although certainly in the later Middle Ages they made efforts to improve matters. This is, moreover, certainly not to say that medieval men were all stable and stayed at home. Very many Viking victims would have wished that were so, and so, too, would most of the residents of the Holy Land. Pilgrimage and crusade are, like propaganda itself, characteristic medieval gestures. The city of Rome in the Jubilee Year, 1300, for example, burst with crowds of people who had come from the whole western world, who trampled each other and tested beyond capability the ability of contemporary observers to count, and who provoked to amazing capacity the provisioners of the city (and who absorbed the specific propaganda of the see and city of Rome). But for very many people, the overwhelming majority in most places at most times, the neighborhood was enclosing, as it was for the thirteenth-century peasant in the diocese of Worcester who probably would never have travelled farther than twenty or thirty miles from the place where he was born.[3] This cloistering neighborhood demanded peculiar powers of penetration of propaganda in order to pierce its walls.

The difficulty of transportation is constantly underlined in medieval literary sources, from carefully planned itineraries to the saints' lives in which the protagonists show their sanctity by overcoming natural impediments to travel: "Many a strange object served in the capacity of a boat. . . . Hia used a branch. . . ." It is sung in poems: "Our pilgrims have no wish to eat."[4] It is underlined, too, in the actual time it took, for instance, to get from Canterbury to Rome (sometimes six weeks), in the tremendous fuss that accompanied Ceolfrith's final departure from Wearmouth toward Rome, in the deaths of archbishops of Canterbury in the cold of the Alps (and one sometimes wonders how many uncatalogued ones still lie frozen there), in an abbot of Bury's avoiding capture by shouting nonsense and pretending to be a Scot.[5] Nothing could be more obvious or apparent. But this evidence would seem to be contradicted by evidence in quite another direction when, for example, by 1159 John of Salisbury had crossed the Alps ten times, or when in the middle of the thirteenth century we find friar missionaries discoursing with Mongols in the middle of Asia after long if not easy journeys, or in the early fifteenth century we find Margery Kempe, an ecstatic townswoman from Lynn, in Assisi, Rome, Compostella, Venice, Danzig, Aachen, by the river Jordan, and on the coast of Norway—and within the century Christopher Columbus was in the Indies. (The "miraculous" spread of news, in March 1172, of the murder of Charles the Good, from Bruges to both London and Laon in two days, as Bruges students in Laon and Bruges merchants in London witnessed, argues both ways.)[6] In the fifteenth century, particularly after the establishment of royal posts relays, news, true or false, could travel very fast indeed. News of the battle of Barnet in 1471 travelled the 130 miles to Cerne Abbas in one day, and the landing of Queen Margaret at Bamborough in 1462 had travelled the 325 miles to London in five days. Edward IV could in 1482 expect a series of riders to carry news over a distance of 200 miles in two days.[7]

Less startling but more overwhelming is the evidence of the late sixth-century historian Gregory of Tours. Gregory's seems at first a still, dull but violent world increasingly cut off from the Mediterranean and civilization. But in its stillness there is much motion. Gregory and his characters appear in one place and then another distant one with very little sense of movement between; a merchant's trip (he by land and his goods by water) is mentioned only in order that an incident that occurred during it may be spoken of.[8] And in Gregory both stillness and motion occur in a place in which tribes and nations are changing or have recently changed their places of habitation. The point is not that medieval people were stable and motionless, but that their travel and that of their products was irregular and erratic, or channeled along very specific routes with specific purposes such as the quest for spices and relics, or for their buyers. The Middle Ages was, throughout its great central period, essentially without maps (although not without illustrated itineraries) and so without clearly understood, spatial relationships, except for the grand general intellectualized, spiritualized map of the round world with (in part, because of Psalm 74) Jerusalem at its center.[9] The world map is itself a splendid emblem of the mental shape of the medieval world.

At the heart of the medieval world was Jerusalem, and at the heart of the medieval propaganda, in its broadest sense, as one would expect, was the Bible. Life as a whole was made to look as if it conformed to biblical experience. To this effect, the "Frisians, comparing themselves to the chosen people, inverted the order of events in their history."[10] The Frisians were extreme in their distortion; but constantly the event was shaped, the echo was pressed by quotation (as it had been in the New Testament itself): the Arnulfings were made to act and to look like the House of David; Matthew Paris grumbled against his enemies with biblical imprecations; Francis said life is the New Testament. The Bible itself was also the subject of propaganda. The fathers (like Ambrose) and their successors (sometimes, as Cassian did with categorical precision, sometimes, as Bede did, more casually) had to make Christian readers read the spirit, not the letter, of the Old Testament; readers had to be so conditioned that they would see it as spirit.[11] Their success, which was based on the intellectual convenience of their "students," was one of the reasons that Francis and his successors, much later, had to fight the other way with the New Testament, to teach their contemporaries to read (their versions of) the literal text.

Much can be clarified through an example of the sort of persuasive didactic literature that could be seen as propaganda of the more general Christian sort. The "Life of Saint Guthlac," which was written by the monk Felix, probably in the 730s, about twenty years after the death of its Mercian anchorite protagonist, is, like many saint's lives, a richly resonant document, humming with echoes, not only of the tradition of lives stemming particularly from those of Saint Anthony and Saint Martin but also of an instructive corpus of biblical, classical, and Christian literature, echoes of phrase, of image, of concept, and of morality. But the particular richness of "The Life of Saint Guthlac" as propaganda is that it not only attempts to persuade its reader to venerate and emulate Guthlac and venerate and visit the pilgrimage and later monastic place, Crowland, in which he died, but also does this through a narrative in which earlier persuasions, earlier successful operations of propaganda, are central. This propaganda-within-propaganda style, in which the style itself, in this sense, becomes an additional persuader, the use of a model who followed models, is not unusual (witness Augustine) nor is it confined to verbal-literary pieces. Nice visual examples occur, for example, in the thirteenth-century frescoes of the legend of Pope Silvester and Constantine at the Quattro Coronati in Rome, where the viewer is not only himself overwhelmed by this crucial story of the power of the apostles Peter and Paul in their successor pope, but he sees the emperor equally overwhelmed by the great propaganda portraits of the two saints with which, in his debility, he is successfully confronted.

Guthlac, a good child, the son of a royally connected family, when he grew to be a youth "remembered" with, no doubt, the memory of heroic songs,"the valiant deeds of heroes of old." "As though waking from sleep" he changed himself and his way of life, gathered a war band, and became a marauder. After he had led, for about nine years, the warrior-leaders's life, his breast was pierced by "a spiritual flame." Guthlac remembered, with the memory of oral history, the history of past kings, their "wretched deaths" and "shameful ends," and he imagined his own similar death. On the morrow he told his followers to choose another leader, and he, at twenty-four, took himself to a monastery. He learned his letters, became a cleric, and in the monastery he read, in "lives" that were a model for his own, "about the solitary life of monks of former days," the men of the desert. At the end of two years, moved by these lives, Guthlac decided to find his own desert but in an English translation (unlike the hermit in the south of Gregory of Tours' Gaul, in Nice, who imported Egyptian herbs). Guthlac took himself to a haunted barrow in the darkest parts of the foggy, trackless fens, to Crowland. There, in the pattern of his predecessors, including his greatest Predecessor, he worked miracles, gave examples of having "sight," advised pilgrims, fought devils, died, remained uncorrupt, and was translated. During his life, his place, seat, locus as a seer, model, and center of men's attention was so great and so clear that his attendant, Beccel, planned to kill him and to assume the position and oc-

558 Western Civilization: The Middle Ages

cupy the place himself. As propaganda the "life" tries to persuade its reader to specific acts, beliefs, patterns of behavior,
but probably more important, it reassures him of the existence
of a world in which God rules and in which virtue triumphs in
the end, in its way. Its message was preserved and propagated
not only through the multiplication of its own manuscripts and
their translations and adaptations but also through its being
available as a source to teachers and preachers in search of *ex-
emplum*, and through its forming part of that continuing chain
of repeating and reinforcing lives of Christian saints.[12]

But, although "The Life of Saint Guthlac" is a nice example
of one of the most prevalent, powerful, and central categories of
medieval propaganda, its category is not one of those closest to
the modern conception of propaganda. For such examples one
may turn first to the Crusades, obviously a fertile field for propaganda study, and to that direct, effective, and widespread
means of broadcasting propaganda, the sermon. The two sermons, first to be considered here, come from contemporary,
eyewitness accounts, but almost surely neither of them is a verbatim account. They move at least slightly away from what a
sermon actually was toward what it was remembered as having
been, or what it was thought it should have been, so that the examples may seem to hover somewhere between Donne and Pericles. This is less a qualification of the direct importance of the
evidence than it may at first seem. These are at the very least examples of the way in which acutely observant contemporary
eyewitnesses thought they could convincingly describe to their
contemporaries very effective and successful, and presumably
very famous, examples of propaganda.

In 1095 at Clermont, Urban II preached Crusade. He
preached to a society already inclined to crusade, as eleventh-
century movements to Iberia, England, and Sicily show, and as
the *Song of Roland* (in its earliest now preserved version, probably slightly later than Clermont), with its striking similarities
to Clermont, shows even more clearly. Thus, the speech that
Robert the Monk remembered having heard Urban speak was
one that its audience was prepared to hear because they, like Urban, must have been previously disturbed by disquieting news
from the East. Still it was Urban who with his 1095 performance

shaped the Crusade movement, formed its direction, and incited its action. He was effective, and his effects were important for his own time and for the future. (And more than eighty manuscripts bear witness to the popularity of Robert's version of how the Crusade began.)

"Oh, race of Franks, race from across the mountains, race chosen and beloved by God"—he addressed "Franks," who were not necessarily in any genetic way Franks at all, but who were men who could feel that they were the descendants of men who had fought with Charlemagne, and Roland and the peers, for the fair France of the distant heroic Christendom-defending past. Urban told the Franks, the favored of God as their works showed, that they, to whom he brought the news of disaster and the plea for help, were distinguished by their country's situation, their faith, and the honor of the church. The bad news that Urban brought, spreading a tale from Jerusalem and Constantinople, was that a race "utterly alienated from God," from the kingdom of the Persians, had come forth for pillage with fire and sword. It had captured and tortured men, destroyed or appropriated churches. Altars had been defiled and destroyed, Christians circumcised, and the blood from the circumcisions smeared on altars or poured into baptismal fonts. Men's navels had been perforated, and their entrails dragged out as the men were driven away from their intestines' ends, which had been tied to stakes. Arrows were shot at men bound to stakes, extended necks chopped. And the rapes! And the land of the Greeks dismembered! Who could avenge all this? "You," to whom God has given victory, valor, vigor, and renown.

Urban then pleaded specifically that the Franks be moved by the memory of their ancestors' deeds (of Charles and Louis and other kings) and the terrible thought of the polluted Sepulchre of Christ "possessed by unclean nations." He begged the Franks not to be degenerate, but again to recall their ancestors' valor.

Then Urban turned to the Franks' possible concern about leaving their families and countered that with the admonition of Scripture. Then he turned to worry about property. He said that the land of the Franks was narrow, enclosed by sea and mountain, too stiflingly small for its population, and insufficiently wealthy, hardly able to sustain the men who farmed it, as was obvious because its poverty had driven the Franks repeatedly to internecine war. He said that they should take themselves away from this self-destructive war to the advantages of the land of "milk and honey," to Jerusalem "the navel of the world," to "another paradise." Jerusalem and her riches begged the Franks to liberate them. Their coming would free them of their sins' punishment and offer them, when they died, the kingdom of heaven.

To all of which the Franks called out repeatedly and in unison, "It is the will of God." It seemed to them, as it must seem to any reader, to its purpose a perfectly effective speech, elegantly balanced to combine the sensational provocation of pride, memory, horror, salacious delight, greed, stoicism, demographic anxiety, piety, confusion, and finally action.[13]

And its incident is a perfect propaganda model. The representative of the moving institution-agency was its highest dignitary, his position enhanced by all the moral, historical, ceremonial, and representative (of God) splendor of his unique office. Although the pope's see was across the mountains in Rome, he himself, the man Urban II rather than the pope-figure, was derived from the "Frank's" own caste of leaders, a man of the sort they were accustomed to listen to and to follow as they went forth to war. He was directly present as preacher before the men he chose to incite. They were pressed together to form an excitable, reacting crowd; he, before them, was in a position to use visual symbol and the rhetoric of tone and gesture; he did not need to rely on the effect of words alone. That to which he incited them, although horrifyingly complex in its ramifications, was in its way a simple, positive act of group aggression. The pope offered his listeners the belief that they could indulge their bellicosity, greed, and morally reprehensible impulses in a way that would be not merely morally neutral but morally as well as physically heroic. In acts that themselves had the savor of sin men could gain remission for sin. They were offered two worlds, the space and wealth (the milk and honey) of the Holy Land, the "other Paradise" and, should they die, the happiness of the first Paradise (where they could join the fierce Archangel Michael, their own prototype).

But the pope's offer was not mere blunt paradox; it offered a variety of incitements. The Crusaders were lured by ambitious self-sacrifice, by the abandonment, for a while, of domestic ties, an act fortified by Scripture, following, in the lure, descriptions of sadistic acts that suggest, in their subliminal sexual imagery, the provocation of lust as well as anger—descriptions enhanced by the smoky, intoxicating figures of blood-smeared altar and polluted font. The evil of heathen filth was an incitement as well as a further repression of moral scruple. The imagery provoked the reaction of sword to the action of sword. Urban called to the continuing medieval social and personal need for revenge, for appropriate, just, savage rebalance. The pope also built on the romance of a history that the "Franks" wanted to believe was their own; their justification of that history in acts of new valor would be a testimony to its really having happened as well as its honorable continuation. And at the same time, the pope played on that love of the idealized group-place, fair France, the contemporary potency of which is underlined in the *Song of Roland*. To each man the pope offered danger, suffering, and the perfect heroic climax of Roland's death on the hill before God, not only glory for the nation and victory for the church of God but individual heroism for each knight who, in the end, might offer his glove to God and be accompanied by angels into Paradise. Urban's speech played on a whole preexisting and shared, trembling web of human and temporal preconceptions—"memories," desires, fears, and inclinations—seen in the phantasy of the *Song of Roland*.

At a slight angle from Urban's sermon, and at the distance of half a century, but also representing this obvious and direct propaganda of rationalization and action, pungently preached by an ecclesiastical leader to a listening crowd of warriors, is the sermon of Peter, bishop of Oporto, before the siege of Lisbon in 1147. Like Urban, Peter built a verbal structure that made it possible for his listeners to define and realize what they wanted to do and, at the same time, allowed them to believe that what they wanted to do was not only allowable but in fact what ideally they should do. Also, he convinced them that what they wanted to do and should do were both in fact identical to what he wanted them to do. It was Peter's job to deflect to his own purposes the action of a band of northern European Crusaders, in the course of their voyage around the Iberian peninsula on their way to the Holy Land, without dampening their ardor or lessening their greedy, bellicose hatred for the infidels. Peter and the king of Portugal wanted the Crusaders to stop and take Lisbon from its Moors, to fight in their local, close crusade, south of Compostella, rather than the far one by the Holy Sepulchre. In many ways this course was, in fact, to everyone's (except the local Moors') mutual advantage. It was Peter's job, again, to make that advantage apparent, and to make it seem morally positive, and at the same time to fan any partial spirits that might have begun to flag after the navigation of the Bay of Biscay.

Peter's sermon, like Urban's, is preserved in a "literary" source, a chronicle history. Its readers do not hear the spoken words, or read the sermon's notes; they read its memory in "eyewitness" literary surroundings. Because it is not, as Robert the Monk's Urban speech is, one of a competing group of equally familiar accounts, it does not have about it the dubious air that Robert's Urban does for many readers. But there is no reason to believe that this very literary speech, filled as it is with learned citation, was not polished by its recorder. If it was, like Urban's speech it shows us at least what a contemporary thought the propaganda that he was recording should have sounded like. But, to move in the opposite direction, the literary learning of Peter's recorded speech does not at all establish the fact that it was not given exactly as it is recorded. Much surviving evidence makes it clear that even very unlearned audiences were accustomed to hearing very learned sermons, and for them the learning provided part of the aura that gave the sermon its effective dignity and connected it with a continuing strand of revealed and reasoned truth.

With the crowd from the Crusaders' ships around him, early in the morning on the hilltop before the cathedral church, because they could not fit inside the church, the bishop of Oporto preached on the spiritual Jerusalem and the virtue of vengeance. He spoke of the rich young man in the Gospel and, unlike him, the Crusaders who had given up even wives and children for their pilgrimage and had shown in their act, again, the power of the cross. He showed them the desolation of Spain and its ruined church begging vengeance for its dead sons. He argued against the seduction of the physical Jerusalem and paraphrased Jerome on the importance not of having been to Jerusalem but of having lived well on the way. He preached Ambrose on the duty of warding off injury to others, and he preached of a courage full of righteousness, so that Matthew's "who lives by the sword shall die by the sword" might be rightly interpreted to support the arms of righteousness used in Isidore's just war. He made Augustine and Chrysostom join Jerome in the cry for battle and in the drowning of the subversive interpretation of Matthew; and he recalled to the minds of his hearers the belief that a watching God gives to the righteous the victory in battle. Finally, he promised them money.[14]

The sermons of Urban and Peter moved their hearers and then were copied into works that could move future readers and inspire the sermons of future oral propagandists. The sermon was a mighty instrument. It had been recognized as one early in Christian history; it had been an instrument of Christ's. Martin of Braga in the later sixth century sent a sermon to a fellow bishop, a sermon that would twist the perception of the rustics he would castigate, so that they could see the world and its history through Christian eyes in a Christian mold.[15] It was a manufactured piece of propaganda sent abroad, and one used again in later centuries. Sermons were still potent at the end of the Middle Ages, still preached and sometimes kept when they had not actually been preached, and still copied.[16] Sermons opened councils and synods, large and small, and persuaded their participants to a proper understanding of their business. In late medieval England, they preached political and constitutional propaganda at the opening of parliaments: "It behoves us to ordain for the kingdom" (I Maccabees, 6:57); the newly and increasingly formal parliamentary institution seems to grow out of ancient verbal gesture of persuasion.[17] In late medieval England, sermons preached religious along with political propaganda and a mixture of both, as at Paul's Cross (where books were also propagandistically burned), and bound their civilization to that which had listened to Christianizing sermons around the ancient crosses of Northumbria.[18] Between these distant eras orders of friars had formed themselves to preach around the world, and King Robert the Wise of Naples, for example, preached to his subjects on many matters, including the saintliness of his dead bishop brother, Louis of Toulouse, both Angevin prince and Franciscan friar.[19] Through centuries of change (and of retention) the sermon remained a central means of persuasion.

The specifically Christian world-view, the instilling or confirmation of which was the primary object of sermons like Martin of Braga's, was also instilled or confirmed by nonverbal propaganda particularly effective, no doubt, in its persistence, in its confronting the peasant in his church every time he entered it from youth through old age, in directly proclaiming a set of spiritual values and explanations at the same time that it, subliminally, continually strengthened a way of looking at a variety of objects and acts. So the Bonanno Pisano doors at Pisa told the life of Christ, as did the paschal candle at Gaeta and (with particular nice reference to and involvement of contemporary figure and dress) the paschal candle at St. Paul's outside the Walls of Rome. Henry III of England could look at his walls and be reminded of Lazarus and Dives, and the monks of Ferentillo had the creation of the world explained to them by theirs. With fine elaboration the sculptural programs of Chartres (and many other great churches) exposed a compelling view not only of the world order and its proper interpretation but also of specific points of belief and opposition to specific heresy—as in the proper interpretation of the Eucharist.[20] At Tre Fontane near Rome, viewers were taught by painting of the psychology of the senses.[21] Windows, capitals, rood screens, roof bosses, chasubles, panels, galleries, mosaiced apses, doors, archivolts, ceilings, and walls bore messages, whispered insistently the meaning of the world.

Visual messages could also be political or partly political, as Edward II's tomb sculpture at Gloucester or Henry VI's rood figure at York make clear (and as the Yorkist removal of Henry VI makes even clearer). Italian communes used painted walls as instruments "of municipal justice" and then as weapons "of party struggle."[22] The Wilton diptych, one of the most famous but also one of the most puzzling of all medieval paintings, proclaims the cult of Richard II, with the kneeling king in remembered youth, surrounded by his relatives disguised as his saints (or the other way around), adoring a Christ in the Virgin's arms and surrounded by angels wearing the badge of Richard's white hart (not unlike the little metal badges of horsed rider or shell pilgrims wore to advertise Canterbury or Compostella and their own visits there). The white hart speaks the propaganda of livery, a late growth of chivalry, which itself not only made recognizable men's identities or their allegiances but also called men to certain values, secular but semireligious, too, like the values of the Garter or, finally, the Golden Fleece.

Nor was visual propaganda always static. It was a game of chess that played its royal hierarchy into its players' minds. And Edward IV's sister, as she knelt and then danced her homage before Edward's dubious queen, Salome-like but in a very distant translation, proclaimed a message from and about Edward's court to the foreign visitors there and also to Englishmen.[23] Three-dimensional mobile propaganda was characteristic of Edward's century, in which those religious plays that had been developing for five centuries moved with particular effectiveness and articulateness through the streets of provincial towns. And this sort of propaganda had a peculiarly homely and yet spectacular quality in its attendance upon royal entries into cities, like Henry VII's reception in York. For that reception, mayor, aldermen, and council of the city planned, in the hope of conciliating the king, a ceremony, with a duly organized profusion of act, symbol, and verse, with many layers of citizens and officials in scarlet, violet, and murrey, at eight stations (the last being that of the Virgin) with figures (acting out pointed little masques and playlets) and devices (raising figures and dispensing elements like mock-hail and comfits). At the third station, at an entrance to the city—after the place where the king should have passed children gathered together around Saint James chapel, "calling joyfully, 'King Henry,' after the manner of children"—the king would come upon a scene "craftily conceived," after the manner of heaven. Under it would be found a world empty except for trees and flowers, into which should then spring up a "royal, rich, red rose" conveyed by a device and after it and to it "another rich, white rose." To them together should bow down all the flowers, and a crown should descend from a cloud to cover them, and a city (called "Ebrauk" or York) full of citizens should appear before them. And thus mechanically York should advertise its submission to the successfully crowned, Tudor union of the two roses of Lancaster and York.[24]

The crown was itself a symbol of propaganda, and with it the tiara, and all the furniture, scents, and liquids of coronation and kingship, like the oil which from the time of the Arnulfings (short-haired kings) and Offa's son could not be washed (nor its memory of David) away, or the special miraculous oil of Becket with which Lancastrians bolstered their lean royalty. The postures and symbols of kingship (and nonroyal rule) changed, but slowly, and at any time a figure of proper rule could be conveyed. Odo of Deuil and Jean of Joinville in brilliant but stylized strokes are able to convey the concepts of kingship represented by their two kings, Louis VII and Louis IX, as for instance one visits a hospital for lepers and the other dispenses justice under a tree.[25] Galbert of Bruges, perhaps even more strikingly, produced the pantomime of the virtuous ruler, rich in ruler attributes, in his Charles the Good at the moment of his death. In a work particularly full of the armorials of propaganda, of symbols to guide the reader's reaction (although in fact to an ultimate confusion because Galbert started to write before he knew his own conclusion), this first placing of the position of the readers' or hearers' reaction is particularly telling.[26]

The royal (and papal) coronation, and its echoes through the crowned's reign, are the ultimate pageant of propaganda, and in secular terms surely the most serious, in the Middle Ages. These ceremonies, particularly in terms of their use of a specific sort of royal praise, the *laudes regiae,* have been studied in a work that is, probably incidentally, the most effective existing examination of medieval propaganda in its larger sense, Ernst Kantorowicz's *Laudes Regiae.* The *laudes—Christus vincit, Christus regnat, Christus imperat—*in an ambience of litany, liturgy, sequence, and the gathering of all Christian society around its royal vicars or vicar are seen to become in the later Middle Ages almost the property of the kings of France, to be placed with the miracle of healing, the vial of balm, the oriflamme, and the lilies. Louis IX put the phrases on his coins. And Louis IX was that embodiment of the long process of royal propaganda who, in Kantorowicz's words, "bestowed the thin and light air of the angelic kingdoms upon his country and assimilated, for the last time, the French chivalry to the militant celestial hosts." Miracles, God's propaganda, were tied to the king's.[27]

Miracles were more obviously God's propaganda for his converting saints. These saints and the church that launched them, or permitted their launching, into unconverted or half-converted territories, had, moreover, a battery of instruments or paraphernalia more aggressively effective than the royal crown, orb, sceptre, and oil. They, of course, had relics, which could not only support martyrs but come to replace them when blood was no longer being spilled. As Victricius preached at the end of the fourth century to the city of Rouen, festive in receipt of relics: "No torturer has stretched us on the rack yet we bear the Martyrs' trophies."[28] And, a century later, Clovis enhanced by the propagandistic splendor of Remigius' very public baptism had also the relic and cult place of Martin of Tours, who once alive, as a Christian, refused to fight, but who now dead fought for Christianity and Clovis together. The dead earth, or what would at first seem the dead earth, of Jerusalem was a relic, too, and was moved, as a recent historian has said, in a sort of "topographical transfusion," and in part for reasons of propaganda, from Jerusalem to the new Jerusalem of Rome.[29]

Peculiarly interesting as a Christian instrument in illiterate and semiliterate societies was the book. The book was used often enough, obviously, directly for its message. The Bible and its commentaries told people how to shape their minds. It was the source of sermons. Or it could be cracked open, in Egypt, in Milan, in Tours, to give instructions or predict the future as the searcher's hand and eye found the passage that fortune exposed to him. But the book was also an object. In the 730s the great missionary Boniface wrote back from Germany to an English abbess asking for a copy of the epistles of Peter written in gold to gain for them "honor and reverence . . . from the eyes of the heathen."[30] In the 1250s the friar William of Rubruck and his companions were carrying the message of Christianity through the lands of the Mongols. William of Rubruck, dressed in precious vestments, entered the dwelling of Sartach singing the *Salve Regina* and carrying on a cushion the Bible that Louis IX had given him and the beautifully illuminated psalter that he had been given by the queen. The books were oddly effective; when William was leaving Sartach's encampment he was afraid to take the queen's psalter because the gold illuminations had attracted too much notice.[31]

If relic and miracle were the coin of the missionaries, coins were the relics and miracles of kings. They came with messages, verbal and visual, attached to their clear power to propagandize their issuer and the concept of his kingship. They were seals to the transactions of ordinary life, recalling ordered governance, Rome, the king's name, ideas of security, power, and tradition. And a familiar passage from scripture reminded men to be aware of the face on the coin. So Offa, a king of the Mercians (757–796) who was enlarging the fact and notion of English kingship, produced his fine, durable silver pennies, and set a pattern for centuries to come.

Offa, like his predecessor Aethelbald, also experimented with the title he had used for himself in his official documents, which in turn broadcast his definition of his own position to his subjects. The "king of the Mercians" *(rex Merciorum)* became the "king of the English" *(rex Anglorum),* and even the "king of the whole land of the English" *(rex totius Anglorum patriae).*[32] Thus Offa used, as did a long and complex line of medieval royal and nonroyal rulers, important documents, which left his secretarial office to be treasured by those on whom they conferred or to whom they confirmed benefits, to carry a concept of his notion of his rule. So medieval popes, among many other often obliquely related propagandistic messages, confirmed their continuing position as the *servi servorum Dei.* Beyond title, rulers' documents carried the formal message of harangues that talked of the nature of existence and of politics, and, through the importance of the documents to which they were prefixed, insured the propagation and preservation of their ideas—although the message itself might, because of its conventionality, only subliminally penetrate the minds of its readers.[33]

The kings of Anglo-Saxon England, particularly from the time of the ascendancy of the West Saxons after 825, provide a series of stimulating examples, a developing, echoing pattern, of the royal use of multimedia propaganda. These men, like many other kings, had to describe, project the image of, and win support for an evolving structure of kingship. Of them, deservedly, the most famous is Alfred (871–899). He, in defiance of, and at the same time with the help of, harshly destructive Danish invaders, constructed and won acceptance for the strengthened concept of the English nation. Alfred's efforts were in many directions. He fought wars and often and visibly won battles. He issued laws and carefully pretended, at least, not only to be following the pattern of Biblical law but also to be collecting old laws (selecting from among them) from the three old, strong southern kingdoms, Kent, Mercia, and his own Wessex; and his laws advertised the position of a controlling kingship strong enough to strengthen the bonds between lord and man. In connection with him was created the Anglo-Saxon Chronicle, the multicopied vernacular version of the newly realized nation's history, which emphasized the role of Wessex and obscured the role of Mercia in the composite nation's past. Alfred also caused to be translated, or himself translated, into English some of those great Latin classics that he knew sat unread in clerical libraries, and he had them (impregnated with his own ideas and images) sent to central places about the kingdom for men to read, so that those men might "dwell" within the extensions of the written thoughts of Augustine, Gregory, Boethius, Orosius, and Bede, live in a world of thought and understanding formed for them by their teaching king, who in teaching exposed to them the nature of the kingship he wished them to accept: "Consider now, if your lord's letter and his seal comes to you. . . . "[34]

Alfred taught them, too, that they were divided into estates of workers, fighters, and prayers, taught them to see themselves functioning within a total community.[35] And, practically and publicly, he reduced the hysteria of their fear of the Danes by showing them not only was victory still possible but also that practical, reassuring, visible efforts could be made to encourage it: ships could go out to meet the Danes; armies could be divided so that some men were always at home; little fortress *burhs* could be built through the kingdom so that security could always be near at hand and visible. And when Guthrum, the Dane, could be and was brought to treaty, his men could be established on the land with Christian-like wergelds (those bold advertisements of relative worth) and knowable laws, and Guthrum himself could be baptized, reduced to human or raised to Christian stature, be called Athelstan and Alfred's godson. Through visible act and word Alfred led his people to a desirable way of life presided over by himself, a powerful king. His was an elaborate piece of propaganda with many facets, complex but not necessarily less effective than the harsh, sharp, bloody propaganda of battle, of, for example, Ottar the Black's "Knutsdrápa": "you made corselets red in Norwich"—rather appropriate instead for another sort of society, leader, and action.[36]

Alfred's godson Athelstan (924–939) extended himself more baroquely. He brought foreigners to his court, and, as a very Christian king, collected elaborate relics. His scribes sent out documents filled with flamboyant Hesperic prose. He moved and, more, he gathered important subjects to him. His laws, presumably, proceeded to local courts. And every Friday, at every minster, he ordered fifty psalms sung for him and "for all who desire what he desires. . . ."[37] Athelstan's grandson Edgar (957/9–975) proclaimed his kingship to the nation at a famous late and ceremonial and oath-signing coronation at Bath in 973. His fame and devotion to his kingship were broadcast through the reformed monasteries of his realm; he and the monastic reformers formed an inseparable team and publicized each other in prayer and book, in picture and ritual act. The story was also later told that he exposed his power over the eight other minor kings of Britain by having them row him on the River Dee in a boat of which he held the rudder—a later elaboration of a simpler act of subjection, probably, but an interesting example of the way in which in a historian's memory propaganda moved to active ritual.[38]

The coincidence of the reign of Edgar's son Aethelred (the Unready: 978–1016), an ineffectual king, and the renewal of Danish invasions led to a new sort of propaganda proposed to the nation through law and sermon. It was based on a very old sort of propaganda. As early as Bede's writing of his popular *Ecclesiastical History* (in the early 930s) the perception of Anglo-Saxon and British history that had been proposed by the sixth-century British historian Gildas had been accepted into Saxon history: the pagan Anglo-Saxon invasions had been God's punishment of the wicked Christian Britons. When, in 793, Alcuin wrote back from Frankland both to King Aethelred of Northumbria and also to Bishop Higbald of Lindisfarne and his monks, he suggested that the Danish catastrophe was caused by the sins of the Christian English and that its remedy lay in reform. When in 1014 the English had collapsed before the Danes, with the end of the world approaching, Wulfstan, archbishop of York and bishop of Worcester, preached his "Sermon of the Wolf to the English," which summed up, in a masterful vernacular address, this whole interpretation of life and defeat and prodded the English to the new virtue. He enumerated with horror the sins that needed remedy; he recalled Gildas and said "take warning." But Wulfstan had preached through Aethelred's laws before he preached this sermon. Those laws had preached a return to the true faith, clemency, avoidance of slaving, clerical celibacy, ecclesiastical taxes, the keeping of feasts, fasting on bread and herbs and water, barefoot processions, confession, carrying of relics, the prostrate community's singing of the third psalm, the protection of sanctuary, that through God's help the English might find virtue and withstand their enemies.[39]

Under Aethelred (or over him) Wulfstan's message of propaganda to the English people, in law and sermon, was that their disasters were caused by their own vices; to win (in both worlds) they must become virtuous. Their own propaganda message to God was to be that by marching relicted and hungry through the countryside, by lying down to pray, by publicly behaving better, they were showing him their renewed virtue. When the king with whom Wulfstan had to deal was Aethelred's eventual successor, the victorious Dane Cnut (1016–1035), his message adapted itself and stressed the continuity of this king, who married the old king's wife, with the English tradition, his connection with Rome, with law giving and religion. He helped form the conventional English, Catholic Cnut of the

"Letter to the People of England." This Cnut could even move his more elaborately decorated messages, like his Winchester Charter, into a recognizably English royal-monastic pictorial style.[40] The English could accept the ordered peace of their new king's reign in virtue and with a sense of his visible, conventional Christian Englishness and rightness. Wulfstan was a master propagandist. But as with much other medieval propaganda, the expertness of Wulfstan's manufacture is more apparent than the effectiveness of its transmission to a broad audience. One of its major aims, the acceptance of a remodeled Cnut, was surely effected, but how much that was the result of Wulfstan's messages is not clear (although Wulfstan surely can take much credit for the shaping of Cnut himself).

The problem of how much of even the most magnificently contrived and complexly organized propaganda really found its way to its intended audience and affected that audience's behavior in the desired way is a recurring one. The rewriting of, or new way of writing and viewing, history (with its use of very old themes, such as "vengeance"), employed by the supporters of the new (fourteenth-century) Spanish Trastámara dynasty, seems really to have helped their acceptance and to have changed men's way of looking at things, or to have offered a shape for that change.[41] But, how much, for example, in its own time, did all the elaborate, again multimedia, Romanic and biblical contrivance around the court of Charlemagne really effect?[42] One can be moved deeply by the imperial power and resonance of the folios of a great Carolingian gospel book (like the opening page of Saint Luke or the portrait of Saint Mark in British Museum, Harley MS. 2788), by the imperial chapel of Aachen with its reminiscence of imperial San Vitale in Ravenna, by the silver Latin interplay of letters among the members of Charles's court, by the newly Roman script, by the ceremony of coronation, by Einhard's slightly later portrait, and much else besides. One can be thus moved, and be sure of this imperial propaganda machine's posthumous effect, without knowing how much immediate effect it had upon any large group of its contemporaries; and this is true even though one knows that one is at least dealing here with a court that had a sense of communication, of *missi* and capitularies and letters and grand assemblies. One can ask the same question of Ottonian propaganda, in spite of the Ottonians' monastic receivers. Even in small, resonant communities like England one cannot be sure of the continuity of communication between projector and broad audience.

The same question must be asked in the midst of very different artifacts and furniture (but still reminiscent of Charlemagne) in and of another blatantly propagandistic court (or at least circle), that of William the Conqueror. William's effectiveness is not open to doubt. Not only did he conquer England, but he accomplished · the almost inconceivable in the planning and execution of Domesday Book. The Conquest and Domesday were both, among other things, acts of propaganda. The Conquest pointed out to his difficult Norman warriors, William's leadership of them and his, at least partial, freedom from their parochial world. Domesday told Normans and English alike of the reality of William's rule in England. The Salisbury Oath seems to have been for William an act of pure propaganda. So, too, were William of Poitiers', chaplain to William, history of the Conquest, the *Deeds of William*, and the Bayeux tapestry, although the tapestry's connection with William himself is not so clear as its connection with his half-brother Odo and although in the tapestry's purpose the propagandistic and the decorative, and in the *Deeds* the propagandistic and the narrative, are pretty hopelessly intertwined—as in William's castles the defensive and the propagandistic are. Even when they are being considered solely as propaganda, the *Deeds* and the tapestry, straightforward and eleventh-century brisk as they may be made to seem, are both too richly complex to submit successfully to a quick description. But in both of them some very pointed propaganda elements are immediately apparent. Both works celebrate the accomplished victory; both, but particularly the *Deeds*, emphasize the particular importance of William himself in the action "Look at me well!''); both, among other pre-Conquest events, emphasize Harold's making and breaking his oath to William; both emphasize relics. The relics (and, in the event and the *Deeds*, especially the papal banner) make the Conquest more religiously acceptable, more crusade. The oath and oath-breaking appeal to one of the very central persuasions of eleventh-century warrior society in order that the campaign may seem a more thoroughly righteous one. The importance of William, drawn with wonderful wit and image in the *Deeds,* separates the duke from his men, makes him clearly their leader and properly their king. Each work has its own sharp peculiarities of taste: the flat, bright classical imagery applied to the identification of righteousness with success (as in the comparison between William and Xerxes) of the *Deeds;* the ironic border commentary, as if the Saxon seamstresses were fighting back in stitching the horrors of war and the vanity of pretension, in the tapestry (commentary —antipropaganda—that calls to mind the counterpoint of later mocking manuscript marginalia). Normans in Normandy and England could hear and see, nevertheless, the rightness of their successful cause, and the rightness of their being controlled by the epic-heroic but also prudent and smart duke-king who actually led what might mistakenly have seemed a joint enterprise (and whose power was in part shared by his brother, the bishop of Bayeux).[43]

These are excellently planned and executed pieces of propaganda in two media. But who actually heard and saw them? How many people could in fact have been affected by them? In spite of endless rebellion and war, and a desolate death, William was an extraordinarily effective king. But how much, beyond its helping him and his immediate followers to appreciate his position, beyond its making him and his government self-aware, did the propaganda really help with this effectiveness? It is a moot question.

However broad propaganda's effect, however helpful, it had become an attribute of kingship (as kingship was an example of it). So two great works explaining the government of William's great-grandson Henry II, "Glanville" and the *Dialogue of the Exchequer,* propaganda in their existence, included propaganda for a Roman interpretation of strong and governing kingship, as they enhanced Henry's constant propaganda of judging, writ-sending, voice-talking, eye-watching act. Henry's own great-grandson Edward I (son himself of an inefficient king but one who acted out the understanding of the propaganda of identification with an ancestor saint in rebuilding Westminster, even if in imitation of a much shrewder French contemporary) felt propaganda's necessity and naturalness in courtly act and gathered court. Edward's laws, which moved into his society's vitals and which had effective agents of dissemination in the courts in which they were heard and the cases they shaped, were acts of royal propaganda (propaganda for kingship), among other things, and were enhanced with words of propaganda that should have made them more acceptable—"'at the instance of the magnates of the realm.'' Less acceptably, Edward pressed his image of kingship upon his subjects in his *quo warranto* proceedings.[44]

Propaganda was a royal attribute, and all the smaller, specific royal attributes were its parts or contributed to it. Some monarchs, in fact, as one watches them, seem to have dissolved into or to have been shaped out of the attribute itself. Edward the Confessor, Otto III, Celestine V, Robert the Pious seem cut out of the very cloth of the propaganda of kingship and papacy.

The importance and continuity of the use of propaganda in western medieval Europe ought in no way to imply that it was an unchanging use. Such an implication or assumption would be absurdly false. The difference between the nature and use of propaganda at the beginning and at the end of the period, during the era of Beowulf and that of the Hundred Years' War, is, in fact, very dramatic. The two extremes should be seen together.

The growth of Christianity, the barbarian invasions, and the change in the political and social structure of the Roman world in the early centuries of the Christian era naturally produced propaganda of competition and defence (Pliny and Trajan, Constantine, Symmachus and Ambrose, Cassiodorus; the visual acts and symbols of Christian, Roman, and German, the fish and the cross, the statue of victory, the labarum, the dying hero, and the genealogies of god-sprung kings); they also demanded patterned explanation and explanatory propaganda of the sort they got from Zosimus and Augustine. But it is not this activity in the great world, centered around the Mediterranean empire, that is, for the comparison of early and late, particularly provocative; it is rather the world of the German north.

Happily, the first extensive verbal introduction to the oral, repetitive, active, epic-singing society of the Germans was written in one of the two late first-century tracts *(Germania, Agricola),* in which the Roman historian Tacitus examined the contrast between Roman and northern barbarian. Tacitus was not only a great master of artifice and persuasion, and of their careful observation, but he exposed, in his description of Roman propaganda (particularly in Britain) what German propaganda was not. He is thus the perfect introduction to the subject. Tacitus describes the establishment within, from a Roman point of view, the unformed society of the North of the Romans' great capturing instrument of propaganda, the city (and all its stone and tiled, inscribed, sculpted, walled parts and counterparts), forum and basilica, "arcades, baths, and sumptuous banquets," the features of "enslavement." These effects were promoted by Tacitus' hero, and father-in-law, Agricola, who "understood the feelings of a province," but who was nevertheless one of the Romans of whom Tacitus' perspicacious and articulate rebel within the *Agricola* says: "They make a desert; they name it peace."[45]

The place of Germanic propaganda, the propaganda of Beowulf, was, on the other hand, the gathering of warriors within the warm and lighted mead-hall or of the folkmoot beneath the accustomed tree (although it is hard to tell exactly how much the hall and the moot are emblematic memory and how much perceived reality—but this indecision itself is characteristically Germanic or at least characteristic of Germanic evidence). The Beowulf itself is the great example, although it must always be remembered that its greatness is known from its internal force, not from nonexistent external evidence of its widespread popularity. The Beowulf sings repeatedly "nonmaterial incentives for both individual and group discipline, loyalty. . . . "[46] Around the fire, over its mead, at its benches, in the hall, the small group heard the comforting, repetitive broad clichés, heard again of the glory of not deserting, and the shame and squalor of deserting, its leader; it heard again the honor it could share so that the utility of group loyalty became more than just utility, and stronger. The group had its propaganda sung to itself so that it might survive. This great central theme of Germanic propaganda, fame more cohesive than

death was destructive, was potentially disturbed, was questioned, by the intriguing difficulty of justifying Christianity within
the system and the system within Christianity, of reconciling a
new God to old customs of thought.[47] The answer to the problem (superficial as in the *Andreas,* deep as in the *Wanderer*) is
the great second theme of Germanic propaganda: to the man
bereft of the protection of his group, the wretched man alone,
must come the realization that the only true inclusion is within
God, the only eternal fame is celestial, the only true mead-hall
is, in its earthly guise, the church, and, in its heavenly, God's
paradise. Around the theme, in many media even within this
basically oral society, as in Wayland (offering to his victim's
daughter the cup of that victim's skull) and the Magi (offering
their gifts to the Child) on the whalebone of the Franks Casket,
Christian interpretations and Christian superiorities, but almost
always Christian analogies, proliferate (the new family, the new
hero, the new bravery, the new battle, the new loyalty, the new
generosity).

Next to this early, warm, bright enclosure, surrounded by a
dark, wet, hostile world, one can place the "flying rumours,
seditious bills, ballads, and prophesyings,"[48] the pamphlets,
broadsides, billboards, and graffiti, the mechanical contriv-
ances and pastries with messages that accosted the eye and ear of
the fifteenth-century pilgrim, tourist, as he fared abroad in his
travels through the world. The media had changed; and, in this
artificial juxtaposition, they seem to have exploded.

The many-copied pieces of vernacular French propaganda
against the English in the later stages of the Hundred Years'
War, with an appeal "felt at all levels of literate society," were
meant to keep or make the French loyal to France and hostile to
England, to reinforce "with reason the promptings of sentiment."[49] Henry VI's government (in England), less effective in
the end, still responded with its billboard genealogies, its dual
monarchy coins, and even pastry tableaux. And the masterpiece
of propaganda, for both sides, was the burning of Joan of Arc in
May 1431. Internal English propaganda supported the houses of
York and Lancaster against each other. The cult of the popular
saint, Richard Scrope, archbishop of York, executed under
Henry IV, prospered particularly "under the special aegis of"

Edward IV, when, for example, a chapel to him "was erected in the miraculous field where" he "had been executed."[50] The Lancastrians had had, before Henry VI, in Henry V, a propaganda machine who showed himself to his country in his tour of 1421, with his victories and their songs and poems, like the Agincourt carol, still, no doubt, in men's minds, and also his magnificently pageanted reception home from the wars and foreign victories. And the whole jangling effect of propaganda in artifact remained alive for Henry VII, who not only bound together the red and the white rose, but who, according to Polydore Vergil, had Richard's famous crown put on his head in the field at Bosworth.

The fifteenth century, and particularly noticeably in England, was a time of letters—business letters, love letters, news letters, letters of persuasion, artful or mistaken letters that told false stories of victory and defeat—a time in which the personal letter had become an instrument of propaganda. Through the flutter of letters and leaflets talked persuasive men and women, arguing and discussing until over them, as over Margery Kempe (for whom clothes also preached) and Archbishop Arundel, at Lambeth in 1413, "sterrys apperyd in the fyrmament."[51] And Archbishop Arundel preached persuasive politics to the people as we can still see (in Harley MS. 1319, fo. 12). In the century after John Wycliffe (and the Statutes of Provisors and Praemunire), men wrote persuading poems and books to each other in the vernacular. Bishop Pecok explained the faith, and Judge-Chancellor Fortescue the constitution, and the author of the "Libel of English Policy," in taunting, jingling verse, the problems, and their solutions, of English trade. (And in provincial towns people saw, again, vernacular plays.) In all this no propaganda campaign is more visible or persuasive than that launched to publicize for Canterbury the jubilee of the translation of Thomas Becket in 1420. For it, not only in prose but in verse, not only monks of Canterbury and a mysterious hand but also the schoolmaster of Faversham and a citizen of London posted sheets of propaganda in the church at Canterbury and on its doors, and at the hospice of Ospringe (near Faversham on the pilgrims' route), and on the doors of Saint Paul's in London.[52]

This is surely recognizably the world of printing that preceded the actual use of the printing press. It was already the actual world of paper, which had been increasingly used for the past century. It was a nationalist world; nations with their vernaculars (and their large reading audiences in the vernacular) were its particular categories. And it was preparing and retaining sentiments and vocabulary (Avignon-Babylon, for example) as well as media and audiences (the millers of Leicester, for example) for the Reformation's war of propaganda. But even in this atmosphere the particularity of this late propaganda must be kept in mind. In spite of the very general message of popular works like *Piers Plowman* or *The Cloud of Unknowing* (which survives in at least seventeen different texts), the essential purpose of much propaganda was no longer strengthening or adjusting the central bonds of society and its view of the world, but rather now the advocacy of certain specific positions or courses of action. In this sense propaganda had become "modern," and its modernity, again, clearly predates printing; the revolution had occurred before "the shift from script to print."[53] But once the press and this revolution had found each other, the press became the revolution's instrument, multiplied and preserved its effects, enlarged its audiences and allowed their members to read exactly the same words as each other.

The changed world of propaganda had not, of course, arrived suddenly. Since the thirteenth century particularly, larger audiences had been being provoked to life, and methods of publication had been expanding. Innocent III at the Fourth Lateran Council in 1215 had vigorously, if not untraditionally, broadcast his messages to the world. He himself was closely connected with the growing universities, institutions that shaped men's minds and thoughts and then released those men to go out to rule the world as its prelates, preachers, and civil servants. But it is Innocent's contemporary, Francis, whose name most normally suggests the nature of the change. The stories about his life were carried around the world and magnified his own perambulations. For him and his friars, and their confreres in other orders, there was a surprisingly broad listening world, which took its shape from the sermons it enjoyed hearing and formed its sense of narrative around the *exempla* of those sermons.[54] Even Francis' contemporary, Abbot Samson of Bury, built a pulpit in the abbey church and preached to the people in English, in his Norfolk dialect.[55] And even as the Franciscans were moving around England and annoying Matthew Paris (d. 1259), the rabidly xenophobic English monastic chronicler, he was composing in Latin, for his small, unknown audience, the sorts of nationalist and, in their way, anticlerical stories whose descendants, in message, would be carried by the Franciscans' descendants, in medium, into the world of propaganda of the later Middle Ages.

The change from early to late was also facilitated by, and at the same time it can be watched and measured in, the most notorious of all the medieval wars or series of wars of propaganda, the battles between pope and emperor and then pope and king of France, which stretched in their greatest intensity from the time of Gregory VII and Henry IV in the eleventh century to that of Boniface VIII and Philip IV in the late thirteenth and early fourteenth centuries. The long dispute has a particular importance in the evolution of the general nature of propaganda because its participants were so clearly interested in projecting both a general world view and also suggestions about specific behavior. Its propagandists were also, from the beginning, extraordinarily able—the Anonymous (or Anonymouses) of York-Rouen, Manegold of Lautenbach, and later Gerhoh of Reichersberg. But in the beginning their means of communication were somewhat limited: the tractate; the public Latin letter; the public excommunication, denunciation, and the like; the sermon; the public ritual act; the act of war. The barefoot scenes at Canossa and Canterbury, however, recall the imagination and effectiveness with which these limited means were exploited. By the time of Boniface VIII and his enemies, the means, and the language, had expanded. Philip IV not only had vernacular political sermons preached to his assemblies in Paris, but also, in a quite revolutionary way, he launched a massive campaign of controlled provincial propaganda, addressed to specific audiences, that elicited returns of stated, and sealed, agreement; and of these more than eight hundred have survived into the twentieth century. The movement of Jacopone da Todi's verses and the cult of Celestine V, and Boniface's machinations against the Colonna and his sowing their land with salt, and even the unsuccessful trial of Boniface, and particularly the genius of Philip IV's men moved the action to more various planes. New audiences and sentiments, motions, prejudices, and images were involved—to choose two: the sound and sight of Jacopone's dazzling verse could dance through the central Italian countryside on the friars' paths and ravish men's tastes to strong, despising suspicion of and hostility against their pope; and Philip's tale-mongers, catering to a taste that seems to have been curiously prevalent in his period (and to which he would appeal again against the Templars), created or published the figure of the grossly lecherous bisexual pope.[56]

These wars between the ecclesiastical and secular states with their differing interpretations of the descent of authority from God, and of its proper use, form again the central propaganda war of the Middle Ages. In it both sides repeatedly worked to establish in their audiences (sometimes, as in Manegold, envisaged audiences) the belief that their side's interpretation was what, on the basis of common and accepted old belief, any sensible man, properly guided, must accept. They were thus, as wise propagandists usually are, superficially conservative. And they were, at that level at which it was safe (the Fathers, the Bible), authoritarian. When Henry IV, "King not by usurpation," wrote to Gregory VII, "whose accession was tainted by such great perjuries," he could use Saint Paul, "who gave no quarter to an angel from heaven should the angel preach heterodoxy" and who thus did not except from condemnation Gregory as a teacher of heterodoxy.[57] Both sides backed their arguments, sometimes discreetly, with their own brands of force. And their arguments were cumulative, and appealed to a growing body of established prejudices and images.

In one of the later stages of the war there appeared a specific figure who, from the point of view of propaganda, is particularly interesting, the Emperor Frederick II. One of the things that makes him particularly interesting is his strenuous use of the propaganda of old Rome. When he captured the *carroccio,* the municipal war carriage, of Milan, at Cortenuova in 1237, as "victorious Caesar, after the manner of the ancient Emperors" he "laid" it "at the feet of Rome"—"the city," "the fountainhead of our power." In the words of his great historian, he wooed the Romans "with rhythmical high-sounding phrase."[58] He specifically recalled the Roman Caesars, and at Capua he built himself a Roman gate. The pageant was magnificent, but the audience was inadequate, too narrow, and perhaps confused. Again the problem of communication appears; it is surely, at least before Philip IV, the central dilemma of medieval propaganda and propagandists.

Communication in rather another sense, however, changed drastically within the medieval period. It can be seen happening in quite a short span of time. In the *Song of Roland* the Moslems are, for the most part, merely evil, dark reflections of the Christians; they have no real life, or language, or society, or religion of their own. They are unimagined; they are merely inverted. Inasmuch as they do not exist, they cannot, of course, be communicated with. The *Roland* is a poem and fiction, so that it may stylize beyond the wont of its society; but Robert the Monk's contemporary version of Urban II's speech gives no more sense of Moslem reality. The hard shell of action, the hard crust around people, the Turpin structure, has begun to loosen and weaken a bit by Odo of Deuil's mid–twelfth-century account of the disastrous, swarming, too slowly moving Crusade of the leper-visiting Louis VII. Odo has become experienced, sadly experienced. He knows about different peoples and places, about the Germans, the Greeks, and the Turks, for instance: "Let no one think that . . . I am inventing a Greek whom I have not seen." Odo knows the problems of language: " . . . he . . . by mixing with his own language certain words we knew and by repeating his own name often, made known his identity," and later, the emperor, "with the bishop of Metz as interpreter, . . . had moved the hearts of all to tears." Odo describes the horrible scene of drunken Germans, confused, tearing to bits the juggler who does not know their language. Not only does Odo see that there are real people there, to be interpreted; he also lives to see and write, in his terrible seventh book, of the Turks moved to give alms to the Franks.[59]

In Richard of Devizes' imaginative chronicle of the third Crusade, built around his hero, Richard the Lion-Hearted, the noble Safadin, brother to the noble Saladin, emerges, "with his cheeks all wet with tears"; and again the problem of language is realized as Queen Eleanor sees the horrors of interdict written on the faces of the people in the dioceses of Ely: "there was no need for an interpreter."[60] And, amusingly, the contemporary Jocelin of Brakelond lets his Abbot Samson tell his story, of the time when clerks carrying letters to Pope Alexander III were being seized in Italy, and when he, Samson, pretended to the Italians that he was a Scot by behaving bizarrely after the manner of Scots and shouting to the Italians, "Ride, ride, Rome, turne Cantwereberei." Only half a century later, William of Rubruck knew in the East that if he "had had a good interpreter" he could have had "an opportunity of sowing much good seed." And Jean de Joinville, writing another half-century later, but remembering the time of William's king, Louis IX, could see the opposing warriors as humans and acknowledge the generosity of a sultan; but his was neither so impressive nor so eccentric a communication as Francis'.[61]

A century after Joinville wrote, Margery Kempe, who could speak only English, found no national barriers but her language. When that was removed, as by a miracle of tongues or an interpreter, she could communicate with anyone anywhere in Europe or the Holy Land. It seems a very long way from Gregory of Tours' ambiguous attitude toward Frankish thought and values, for whom language was the one means of, or barrier to, communication that seems to have caused no trouble. The long, crooked road from Gregory to Margery, with the quick pace of its center piece, the change in, in this sense, communication, is inseparable from, but not identical with, the change in propaganda.

The changing propaganda with which medieval Europe, again, drenched itself variously—"semiheraldic prophecy," Joinville's windows at Blécourt, heads on poles and hangings like that of the thieving Fleming on Louis VII's Crusade or the 1249 robbers' accomplices at Winchester, the forgeries of Canterbury and many other places, the elaborate guidebooks with which by stitching together the Christian and classical pasts and monuments of the city Rome tempted money-spending tourists to the city, the seductive summonses to settle new towns—was not always successful. In spite of the successfully broadcast Christian ideas that had softened an eighth-century

Lombard king's faith in the duel, he could not eliminate it, "because of the custom of Our Lombard race." Nor could the women of Southwark, drenched by centuries of propaganda in favor of rights of sanctuary, be kept from stoning to death the foreign murderer of a widow as he passed her house on his way from sanctuary to emigration.[62] More tragically, perhaps, the losers of the second Crusade came home to face the fact that the propaganda that had promised them victory had been misleading, to wonder and to question and to write about what Bernard of Clairvaux, the man most responsible for the Crusade, called a judgment of God "so deep that I could almost justify myself for calling him blessed who is not offended thereat."[63]

In finishing, it seems wise to recall some major kinds of medieval propaganda. One may consider the epitaph of Alcuin, Northumbrian scholar at the court of Charlemagne, which calls its reader to remember death's end to life, for reader as for Alcuin, to remedy the health of his, the reader's, soul and pray for Alcuin's.[64] Alcuin evokes the great comparison, transitory human life and everlasting God. His elegant verses reinforce the values and answers that his Christian society has chosen in dealing with one of its, and everyman's and every society's, great problems. Alcuin's lines seem at first immobile, lying only on his tomb, and forming a procession through time with other tombs bearing essentially the same message. But the tomb is not really still; its verses go with the wayfarer who reads them, and into the collections that copy them, and move, if rather sedately, out of their local time and place. Against Alcuin, one may consider John Ball, bush-priest, preaching in the Peasants' Revolt of 1381. He marched around preaching his unanswerable sermons about the equality of Christian men. His voice, alive, was his medium, and the repetition of other men and women; and he preached active revolt.

In a way, though, the most distinctly medieval mode of propaganda is, I think, not either Alcuin's or John Ball's, but the mode of William of Malmesbury, writing in what may be in the end the finest and most compelling of all medieval chronicles and histories, his *Historia Novella*. William is trying, as he says, to make understandable order out of the superficial chaos of his time, but he is also wrestling with the problem of true political, social, and personal integrity seen against the kept and broken oath. He must explain why his protagonist, Robert of Gloucester, who does not seem to keep faith, is in fact acting according to the dictates of a higher faith, a higher social integrity.[65] In his important job, important partly because it offers a model for proper behavior in times of change and for the proper understanding of society, William is, on the whole, because of his intelligence and understanding and skill as both writer and historian, successful. He thus produces an unfinished but major piece of propaganda in depth, one that protects the reputation of a great man and offers society a pattern of adaptation that need not include the abandoning of its central persuasions. Major propaganda, indeed. But who did William think would read the great work he left? His patron? The monks of his monastery? It is, really, propaganda without audience, or with only, really, the audience of the imagined reader in posterity whom William would share with Bede.

From beginning to end, with different shadings, medieval propaganda existed within the thick, implicating texture of a semiliterate, a partially literate, society, in which observation had not been channeled and limited to specific media for specific purposes, but in which observation had been made sensitive by the specific allusion of the reading and writing of the literate within society, sensitive to the connection between written words and ideas. Here with full resonance sprang up the "rioall rich rede rose" of Lancaster. Here the legend of the Kyffhäuser developed around the not dead but sleeping Frederick II. Here the propaganda for Santa Maria Maggiore in Rome was spread through the west to observers of Franciscan calendars through the festal celebration of the remembered or invented miracle of an August snow.[66]

In the beginning, in the north, the purpose of propaganda, oral and redundant, had been, particularly, to reinforce the necessary social bonds of the small group (and the larger group of which it increasingly formed a part) and to adjust its bonds' clichés to include the precepts of a new and variously helpful religion.[67] The group was then small, but it was very like many other small groups, so that a world-system was preached to it and its counterparts. By the end of the Middle Ages the groups were both larger and more particular; their type is quickly illustrated by the group within the similarly vernaculared and royally ruled nation-state or, in another direction, by geographically spread but similarly intentioned recipients of commercial propaganda like pilgrims to Canterbury or tourists to Rome. The message was often more specific, and intended to produce a more specific action, than earlier propaganda; but often the particular subsystems (like England and France) were in many ways similar to each other (although, as invader and invaded, for example, not identical) and so could be approached with differently named but similar symbols and messages—the lily and the rose.

While the song of the king and the picture of the crown (like the saint and the nimbus) continued to be sung and painted (in differing styles), the change from early to late had been announced by the development of the subsystems of secular and ecclesiastical state during and around the investiture controversy. This controversy had produced a model of propaganda (and change within propaganda), and in no way more a model than in its appeal to "true past," to a variously viewed "convention," and in its moral and intellectual justifications of previously adopted political positions, of previous and expected material gratifications. The sequence could, of course, vary, early and late: "The permanence of victory," P. S. Lewis has written of the Hundred Years' War, "made valid for the French the 'national sentiment' the propagandists had so long asserted."[68]

Although medieval propaganda sometimes had a specific audience in mind and could reach it through effective and well-understood channels (as did Urban II and Peter of Oporto or, later, a king in parliament), its limitations were particularly limitations of communication, but also limitations of understood purpose, in an atmosphere redolent with echoing rhetoric, with a panoply of symbols of various authorities and traditions, with waves and counterwaves of subliminal information. The roads were too bad, and the air was too alive. Still, it was a setting (and sometimes a piazza setting) fitted superbly to produce certain sorts of propaganda, particularly mobile multimedia propaganda. This pageant propaganda could be to very specific effect, as it was in the false message with which Mortimer's adherents (in this presaging the activities of the parties in the Wars of the Roses, with their frightening false propaganda of defeat) trapped Edmund, Earl of Kent, the dead Edward II's brother. At Corfe, in 1329, according to Geoffrey le Baker, they set up a repeated nocturnal royal masque with dancing on the walls and turrets and with tapers and torches, so that the word would spread about that royal entertainments were being held at Corfe and the old king's sympathizers would believe him to be still alive and there and would be drawn to show themselves. Kent sent a disguised Dominican friar to Corfe, and to him was shown a man ''sitting splendidly at supper'' acting the king. The earl heard and believed, and he indiscreetly exposed his intention to release his brother and so was himself ensnared. The trap depended upon a ready visual vocabulary of kingship available to propaganda.

A more magnificent and central scene, and one that employed symbols richer in specific propaganda, was acted out at Anagni in September 1303 when Boniface VIII was attacked by the Colonna and the French. In what might have been merely a sordid scene, Boniface, according to the description of an eyewitness writing back to England, recalled to his contemporaries what to them was the most politically significant and magnificent of martyrdoms, Becket's, and one that other men, like Geoffrey of York, posing against a wall in Dover, had used previously. Boniface ringing the changes of the rich propaganda of the ''free church,'' available to him and his audience in this resonant world, redeemed the ambiguous behavior that had led him to Anagni with his Becket scene, crying out, as a public and observed, although condemned, martyr, to his attackers, ''Ec le col! Ec le cape!'' ''Here is my neck, here my head.''[69]

Boniface was member and product of a society encased in a rich miscellany of functional, usable symbols and echoes of icons and attributes, a society with a liturgical heart, and one that taught in procession (as well as disputation) and signaled with lighted candles, a society led by priest, king, and historical martyr. Boniface on the stage at Anagni remembered his part. He sent signals to whatever audience could hear; and the letter to the diocese of Lincoln, the reaction of Anagni and Rome, and our own recognition, all show that his message, at least in a limited way, carried. And although one's first impression is the Boniface's last pageant of propaganda failed, that it did not benefit significantly either *ecclesia* or himself, this may in fact be a misleading impression. The strength that Boniface's two successors had, their notion of their role, as well as the revived Roman fortunes of his own family, argue the compelling power and effectiveness of Boniface's last significantly remembered, sane scene.

The medieval West rang with propaganda, and echoes of propaganda. But, although at times medieval propaganda is concentrated in messages, incidents, scenes of clear and analyzable purposefulness and effect, like Clermont or Oporto or gardens of the Louvre, in general it stubbornly resists just that analysis which in another way it demands. This is most particularly true in the early Middle Ages and of those groups that can be seen to be sustaining themselves, facilitating their social survival, by chanting to themselves their great cohesive commonplaces about bravery and loyalty and "law." We can see these people telling themselves, and being told, the things they should be told in order to function socially. We can see in the telling the relation between speaker, preacher, singer, king, priest, bishop, and his audience, see at the same time both mutual dependence and the desire of the group to have a center, a leader, a token, a relic, an authoritative dictum, even, as at Sutton Hoo, a buried treasure and the memory of a dead king.[70] We watch king and bishop sitting, decorated, in amplifying councils, made potent in office as law-givers and patrons. They sit holding the Bible, genealogical history, and Germanic song, and point toward external battle.

They point, too, although less obviously, toward the plough, the kitchen, and the choir. Because, although much dominant propaganda does not explicitly distinguish among the classes and sexes who will hear it, much does, implicitly, because of its message (for example, "be loyal in battle"); and some propaganda is specifically directed toward keeping people (satisfied and virtuous) within their proper estates (for example, Alfred's description of a healthy tripartite society, Wulfstan's preaching against inverted values). In the mid–Middle Ages the highly propagandized figure of the knight was, as direct model, applicable to a single sex and a specific and limited range of classes; similarly, the propagandized figure of the monk was applicable only to men of one estate. By the time of Margery Kempe there was a different sort of flexibility, but many messages were directed to specific audiences. The keenness of Margery's hearing and the peculiarity of her position as an eccentrically loud, vocal, and inspired woman from an East Anglican upper oppidan class, allows us to perceive their particularity. But the particularity is colored by a prevalent tone in late medieval communication and propaganda, blankly demagogic and nationalistic, broad enough to affect classes and a sex relatively recently provoked to attention. Throughout the Middle Ages, however, and especially in the early Middle Ages, the most important guiding messages tended to be general, and each member of their audiences was expected to interpret "loyalty," for example, in a way appropriate to his own position. In the mead-hall, the assembly, the sermon crowd, we see the speaker figuratively surrounded by a general audience with its most important members closest to the speaker, his companions, with a surrounding, descending dependence of people to whom the message might in part sift, as Christianity often in fact did, through the linking, influential warrior magnates.

To return to the most difficult problem—although we can clearly see why the words of propaganda that, particularly early, medieval leaders and audiences chose to tell and be told were in fact effective, insofar as they were, we generally do not know, cannot see, how self-conscious the tellers as propagandists were or how understandingly, or even how, they actually chose the images and attitudes that they chose, except of course that they chose from a traditional and venerably authoritative repertory and used a conventional vocabulary. By the end of the Middle Ages the situation had changed a great deal; the propaganda there to which we are at first attracted is of a very different sort—relatively superficial, specific, self-conscious, at the exact level of French against English on posters. Europe had gone a long way in its return from the warring Germanic desert to the trading city. But underneath the surface, even on the eve of the Reformation, the most interesting and important, and most difficult fully to understand, propaganda is still that with which society reinforced its major cohesive values, the constantly and variously projected ideas, clichés, and commonplaces that allowed men to live in society and, in some way, to accept their lives.

## NOTES

1. Bede, *Ecclesiastical History of the English People,* ed. Bertram Colgrave and R. A. B. Mynors, Oxford Medieval Texts (Oxford: Clarendon Press, 1969), pp. 182–185; for a work concerned with "old chaos," see, for example, *The Life of King Edward,* ed. Frank Barlow, Medieval Texts (London, Edinburgh: Thomas Nelson and Sons, 1962), p. 16. For purposes of these notes I have tried to use easily available editions and translations of sources.

2. David Storey, *Radcliffe* (Harmondsworth: Penguin Books, 1965), p. 273.

3. R. H. Hilton, *A Medieval Society: The West Midlands at the End of the Thirteenth Century* (New York: John Wiley & Sons, 1966), p. 7. For a different and much more open sort of medieval society, see the essays that deal with Sicily and Catalonia in Helene Wieruszowski, *Politics and Culture in Medieval Spain and Italy* (Rome: Edizioni di Storia e Litteratura, 1971).

4. C. Grant Loomis, *White Magic* (Cambridge, Mass.: Mediaeval Academy of America, 1948), pp. 90–93; A. R. Myers, ed., *English Historical Documents,* vol. 4 (London: Eyre & Spottiswoode, 1969), p. 1217.

5. Bede, *The Ecclesiastical History of the English Nation With the Life and Miracles of St. Cuthbert and the Lives of the Abbots of Wearmouth and Jarrow,* Everyman's Library (London: J. M. Dent & Sons; New York: E. P. Dutton & Co., 1951), pp. 361–365; *Epistolae Cantuarienses* (vol. 2 of *Chronicles and Memorials of the Reign of Richard I*), ed. William Stubbs, Rolls Series (London: HMSO, 1865), p. 63; Jocelin of Brakelond, *Chronicle,* ed. H. E. Butler, Medieval Classics (London, Edinburgh: Thomas Nelson and Sons, 1949), p. 48; generally helpful in this connection is *Medieval Trade in the Mediterranean World,* ed. Robert S. Lopez and Irving W. Raymond, Records of Civilization, Sources and Studies (New York: W. W. Norton, n.d.).

6. John of Salisbury, *The Metalogicon,* trans. Daniel D. McGarry (Berkeley and Los Angeles: University of California Press, 1955), p. 142; *Mission to Asia: Narratives and Letters of the Franciscan Missionaries in Mongolia and China in the Thirteenth and Fourteenth Centuries,* ed. Christopher Dawson, Harper Torchbooks (New York: Harper & Row, 1966); *The Book of Margery Kempe,* ed. Sanford Brown Meech, Early English Text Society (London: Oxford University Press, 1940); Galbert of Bruges, *The Murder of Charles the Good, Count of Flanders,* trans. James Bruce Ross (New York, Evanston, and London: Harper & Row, 1967), pp. 113–114.

7. C. A. J. Armstrong, "Some Examples of the Distribution and Speed of News in England at the Time of the Wars of the Roses," *Studies in Medieval History presented to Frederick Maurice Powicke,* ed. R. W. Hunt, W. A. Pantin, and R. W. Southern (Oxford at the Clarendon Press, 1948), pp. 439, 447, 448; see, too, *The Cambridge Economic History of Europe,* vol. 2, ed. M. Postan and E. E. Rich Cambridge: Cambridge University Press, 1952), p. 264; and L. F. Salzman, *English Trade in the Middle Ages* (Oxford at the Clarendon Press, 1931), pp. 186–190.

8. Gregory of Tours, *The History of the Franks,* vol. 2, trans. O. M. Dalton (Oxford at the Clarendon Press, 1927), p. 321.

9. Claude Jenkins, "Christian Pilgrimages, A.D. 500–800," *Travel and Travellers of the Middle Ages,* ed. Arthur Percival Newton (London: Routledge & Kegan Paul, 1949), p. 63.

10. Beryl Smalley, *The Study of the Bible in the Middle Ages* (Oxford: Basil Blackwell, 1952), pp. xi–xii.

11. Charles W. Jones, "Some Introductory Remarks on Bede's Commentary on Genesis," *Sacris Erudiri* 19 (1969–70): 15–198, 135–147, 159–160.

12. Felix, *Life of Saint Guthlac,* ed. Bertram Colgrave (Cambridge: University Press, 1956), pp. 80–87, 112–113; Gregory of Tours, *History of the Franks,* trans. Ernest Brehaut, Records of Civilization (New York: W. W. Norton, 1969), p. 147.

13. D. C. Munro, ed., *Translations and Reprints,* vol. 1, no. 2 (Philadelphia: University of Pennsylvania Press, 1902), pp. 5–8; August C. Krey, *The First Crusade: The Accounts of Eye-witnesses and Participants* (Princeton: Princeton University Press; London: Oxford University Press, 1921), pp. 13, 30–33.

14. C. W. David, *De expugnatione Lyxbonensi: Conquest of Lisbon,* Records of Civilization (New York: Columbia University Press, 1936), pp. 68–85.

15. J. N. Hillgarth, ed., *The Conversion of Western Europe, 350–750* (Englewood Cliffs, N.J.: Prentice-Hall, 1969), pp. 35–63; this is an extremely helpful and important collection for the student of propaganda.

16. W. A. Pantin, *The English Church in the Fourteenth Century* (Cambridge: University Press, 1955), p. 255, for a sermon prepared but not delivered because a more important preacher arrived.

17. Myers, *English Historical Documents,* vol. 4, p. 415.

18. E. F. Jacob, *Essays in Later Medieval History* (Manchester: University Press; New York: Barnes & Noble, 1968), pp. 13–14, 19; Armstrong, "Examples of the Distribution," p. 443.

19. Robert Brentano, *Two Churches: England and Italy in the Thirteenth Century* (Princeton: Princeton University Press, 1968), p. 228.

20. Adolf Katzenellenbogen, *The Sculptural Programs of Chartres Cathedral* (New York: W. W. Norton, by arrangement with the Johns

Hopkins Press, 1964), pp. 13, 23–24, 63, 75; Peter Brieger, *English Art, 1216–1307*, Oxford History of English Art (Oxford at the Clarendon Press, 1957), p. 132 n. 2.

21. Carlo Bertelli, "L'Enciclopedia delle Tre Fontane," *Paragone* 20, no. 235, Arte (1969): 24–49.

22. See, for example: Victoria and Albert Museum, *Gospel Stories in English Embroidery* (London: HMSO, 1963); and F. Harrison, *The Painted Glass of York* (London: SPCK, 1927). For Italian cities, see particularly Helene Wieruszowski, "Art and the Commune in the Time of Dante," *Speculum* 19 (1944): 14–53, reprinted in *Politics and Culture*, pp. 475–502; the quoted phrases are from p. 487.

23. Myers, *English Historical Documents*, vol. 4, p. 1169.

24. *York Civic Records*, vol. 1, ed. Angelo Raine, Yorkshire Archaeological Society, Record Series, 98 for the year 1938 (Wakefield: for the Society, 1939), pp. 153–159.

25. Odo of Deuil, *De profectione Ludovici VII in orientem: The Journey of Louis VII to the East*, ed. Virginia Gingerick Berry (New York: W. W. Norton & Company, n.d.), pp. 16–19; *Memoirs of the Crusades by Villehardouin and de Joinville*, trans. Frank T. Marzials (New York: E. P. Dutton, 1958), pp. 149–50.

26. Galbert of Bruges, *Murder of Charles the Good*, pp. 79, 87–89, 91–92, 111–113.

27. Ernst H. Kantorowicz, *Laudes Regiae*, University of California Publications in History (Berkeley and Los Angeles, 1958), p. 4.

28. Hillgarth, *Conversion*, p. 22.

29. Irving Lavin, *Bernini and the Crossing of Saint Peter's*, Monographs on Archaeology and the Fine Arts (New York: Archaeological Institute of America and College Art Association of America, 1968), pp. 33–35.

30. Dorothy Whitelock, ed., *English Historical Documents*, vol. 1 (New York: Oxford University Press, 1955), pp. 746–747.

31. Dawson, *Mission to Asia*, pp. 118, 120.

32. F. M. Stenton, *Anglo-Saxon England* (Oxford at the Clarendon Press, 1950), p. 210.

33. Brentano, *Two Churches*, pp. 291–324.

34. Whitelock, *English Historical Documents*, vol. 1, p. 844.

35. Ibid., p. 846.

36. Ibid., p. 308.

37. Ibid., p. 387.

38. See particularly, *Regularis Concordia: The Monastic Agreement*, ed. Thomas Symons, Medieval Classics (London: Edinburgh: Thomas Nelson and Sons, 1953); Stenton, *Anglo-Saxon England*, p. 364.

39. Whitelock, *English Historical Documents*, vol. 1, pp. 775–779, 854–859, 405–411.

40. Ibid., pp. 414–416; and see, for example, Francis Wormald, *English Drawings of the Tenth and Eleventh Centuries* (New York: Frederick A. Praeger, 1953), p. 41, and pl. 15.

41. The theme of the propagandistic rewriting of Spanish history will be fully developed in forthcoming publications of Professor Helen Nader, from whom my information comes.

42. The best introduction to the many media of Charlemagne's machine is probably Donald Bullough, *The Age of Charlemagne* (London: Elek Books, 1965).

43. David C. Douglas and George W. Greenaway, eds., *English Historical Documents*, vol. 2 (London: Eyre & Spottiswoode, 1953), pp. 232–278, 217–231, 226; Lilian M. C. Randall, *Images in the Margins of Gothic Manuscripts* (Berkeley and Los Angeles: University of California Press, 1966).

44. T. F. T. Plucknett, *Legislation of Edward I* (Oxford at the Clarendon Press, 1949), p. 103; Donald W. Sutherland, *Quo Warranto Proceedings in the Reign of Edward I, 1278–1294* (Oxford at the Clarendon Press, 1963).

45. *Tacitus on Britain and Germany*, trans. H. Mattingly (Baltimore, Maryland: Penguin Books, 1967), pp. 70, 72, 80 (I have changed slightly the translation of the last quotation). For Zosimus and Augustine, see Walter Goffart, "Zosimus, the First Historian of Rome's Fall," *American Historical Review* 76 (1971): 412–441.

46. The words are taken, for comparative effect, from Hans Rosenberg, *Bureaucracy, Aristocracy, and Autocracy: the Prussian Experience, 1660–1815* (Boston, Mass.: Beacon Press, 1966), p. 92.

47. Compare Richard E. Sullivan, "Khan Boris and the Conversion of Bulgaria: A Case Study of the Impact of Christianity on a Barbarian Society," *Studies in Medieval and Renaissance History*, vol. 3. (University of Nebraska), pp. 54–139, particularly p. 136.

48. Armstrong, "Examples of the Distribution," p. 434.

49. P. S. Lewis, "War Propaganda and Historiography in Fifteenth-Century France and England," *Transactions of the Royal Historical Society*, 5th ser., 15 (1965): 1–21, 4–5, 6–7, 9, 21.

50. J. W. McKenna, "Henry VI and the Dual Monarchy Aspects of Royal Political Propaganda, 1422–1432," *Journal of the Warburg and Courtauld Institutes* 28 (1965): 145–162, pl. 58; and the same author's "Popular Canonization as Political Propaganda: the Cult of Archbishop Scrope," *Speculum* 45 (1970): 608–623, 621.

51. *Book of Margery Kempe*, p. 37; and see Myers, *English Historical Documents*, vol. 4, pp. 214–216, 229, 346; K. B. McFarlane, *John Wycliffe and the Beginnings of English Nonconformity* (New York: Macmillan, 1953).

52. Raymonde Foreville, *Le Jubilé de Saint Thomas Becket* Paris: S.E.V.P.E.N., 1958), pp. 127–137.

53. Theodore K. Rabb and Elizabeth L. Eisenstein, "Debate: The Advent

of Printing and the Problem of the Renaissance," *Past and Present*, no. 52 (August 1971), pp. 135–144, 144; Elizabeth L. Eisenstein, "The Advent of Printing and the Problem of the Renaissance," *Past and Present*, no. 45 (November, 1969), pp. 19–89, 19; *The Cloud of Unknowing and the Book of Privy Counselling*, ed. Phyllis Hodgson, Early English Text Society (London: Oxford University Press, 1944), p. ix.

54. *Scripta Leonis, Rufini et Angeli sociorum S. Francisci: The Writings of Leo, Rufino and Angelo Companions of St. Francis*, ed. Rosalind B. Brooke, Oxford Medieval Texts (Oxford at the Clarendon Press, 1970); *Liber exemplorum ad usum praedicantium*, ed. A. G. Little (Aberdeen: British Society of Franciscan Studies, 1908).

55. Jocelin of Brakelond, *Chronicle*, p. 40.

56. For Phillip IV and the revolution in propaganda in the thirteenth and early fourteenth centuries, see Helene Wieruszowski, *Vom Imperium zum Nationalen Konigtum* (Munich and Berlin, 1933), particularly pp. 121–140 and, within them, here, pp. 134, 138–139. I think that the best introduction to the investiture controversy is through Brian Tierney, *The Crisis of Church and State* (Englewood Cliffs, N.J.: Prentice-Hall, 1964); readers may also find Karl F. Morrison, *The Investiture Controversy: Issues, Ideals, and Results* (New York: Holt, Rinehart and Winston, 1971), as well as *The Correspondence of Pope Gregory VII*, trans. Ephraim Emerton, Records of Civilization (New York: W. W. Norton & Company, 1969), helpful. The most important collection of investiture records is in *Libelli de lite imperatorum et pontificum* (Hanover: Monumenta Germaniae historica, 1891–1897); for Gerhoh, see Peter Munz, *Frederick Barbarossa: a Study in Medieval Politics* (London: Eyre & Spottiswoode, 1969), pp. 379–382; for Phillip, see particularly, Joseph R. Strayer, *Medieval Statecraft and the Perspective of History*, eds. John F. Benton and Thomas N. Bisson (Princeton: Princeton University Press, 1971), pp. 305–306 and Pierre Dupuy, *Histoire du differend d'entre le pape Boniface VIII et Philippes le Bel* (Paris, 1655); for an introduction to Jacopone, John Moorman, *A History of the Franciscan Order* (Oxford at the Clarendon Press, 1968), pp. 265–266.

57. *Imperial Lives and Letters of the Eleventh Century*, trans. Theodor E. Mommsen and Karl F. Morrison, ed. Robert L. Benson, Records of Civilization (New York and London: Columbia University Press, 1967), pp. 150, 149, 151.

58. Ernst Kantorowicz, *Frederick the Second*, trans. E. O. Lorimer (New York: F. Ungar, 1957), pp. 448, 449, 451.

59. Odo of Deuil, *Journey of Louis VII*, pp. 28–29, 24–25, 42–43, 56–57, 36–37, 140–141.

60. Richard of Devizes, *Chronicle*, ed. John T. Appleby, Medieval Texts (London, Edinburgh: Thomas Nelson and Sons, 1963), pp. 75, 59.

61. Jocelin of Brakelond, *Chronicle*, p. 48; Dawson, *Mission to Asia*, p. 133; Villehardouin and Joinville, *Memoirs*, p. 220.

62. Hillgarth, *Conversion*, p. 108; Myers, *English Historical Documents*, vol. 4, p. 547.

63. Giles Constable, "The Second Crusade as Seen by Contemporaries," *Traditio* 9 (1953): 213–279, 275.

64. *Mediaeval Latin Lyrics*, ed. and trans. Helen Waddell (Harmondsworth: Penguin Books, 1952), pp. 104–105.

65. This interpretation of the *Historia* is the result of much class discussion and is as much my students' as my own.

66. S. J. P. van Dijk and J. Hazelden Walker, *The Origins of the Modern Roman Liturgy* (Westminster, Md.: Newman Press; London: Darton, Longman & Todd, 1960), pp. 376–377; Munz, *Frederick Barbarossa*, pp. 3–8, 14, 18.

67. The extreme difficulty of understanding the process through which the group learns to define and accept the clichés that can prove helpful to its survival is best approached, I believe, through Clifford Geertz' stimulating essay, "Ideology as a Cultural System," *Ideology and Discontent*, ed. David Apter (Glencoe: Free Press, 1964), pp. 47–76.

68. Lewis, "War Propaganda," p. 21.

69. Myers, *English Historical Documents*, vol. 4, pp. 50–51; "Relatio de Bonifacio VIII," ed. F. Liebermann, *Monumenta Germaniae historica*, Scriptores 28 (Hanover, 1888): 621–626, 623.

70. See Dorothy Whitelock, *The Audience of Beowulf* (Oxford at the Clarendon Press, 1951), for a probing, if rather indirect, study of the relationship between message and audience.

# CONTRIBUTORS

ROBERT BRENTANO received a Ph.D. in medieval history from Oxford University in 1952. He is professor of history at the University of California, Berkeley, and the author of *The Early Middle Ages* (1964), *Two Churches* (1968), and *Rome before Avignon* (1974).

S. N. EISENSTADT received his Ph.D. from Hebrew University, where he has taught since 1948, serving as professor of sociology, chairman of the Department of Sociology, and dean of the faculty of social sciences. His works include *Political Systems of Empires* (1963), *Essays on Comparative Institutions* (1965), *Modernization, Protest and Change* (1966), and *The Protestant Ethic and Modernization* (1968).

JOHN FERGUSON taught at the University of London, the University of Ibadan, and the University of Minnesota before becoming dean and director of studies in arts at The Open University in 1969. Among his works are *Moral Values in the Ancient World* (1958), *Foundations of the Modern World* (1963), *The Heritage of Hellenism* (1973), and *Utopias of the Classical World* (1975).

JACOB J. FINKELSTEIN (1922–1974) received a Ph.D. in Assyriology from the University of Pennsylvania in 1953. He taught at the University of California, Berkeley, and Yale University, where he was professor of Assyriology. He was the author of *Late Old Babylonian Documents and Letters* (1972).

CHARLES W. FORMAN received a Ph.D. in history from the University of Wisconsin in 1941, and divinity degrees from Union Theological Seminary in New York. He is professor of missions in the Department of Religious Studies at Yale University, and the author of *The Nation and the Kingdom* (1964), *Christianity in the Non-Western World* (1966), and other books and articles on the history and practice of Christian missions.

TALAT SAIT HALMAN has taught at Princeton University since 1966. In 1971 he served on a national coalition cabinet in Turkey, becoming the first minister of culture in Turkish history. His works include collections of his poems in Turkish and in English, *Modern Turkish Drama, The Humanist Poetry of Yunus Emre,* and the forthcoming *Contemporary Turkish Literature.*

GEORGE KIRK taught in Jerusalem, London, and Beirut before joining the Center for Mid East Studies at Harvard University. He is currently professor of history at the University of Massachusetts, Amherst, and the author of *A Short History of the Middle East* (1948), *The Middle East in the War, 1939–1945* (1952), *The Middle East, 1945–1950* (1954), and *Contemporary Arab Politics* (1961).

BRUCE MCGOWAN is a specialist in the field of Ottoman economic history and has taught at San Francisco State University and the University of Michigan. Formerly director of the American Research Institute in Turkey, he has spent several years in Turkey, Yugoslavia, and Greece laying the groundwork for his latest work, *Southeastern Europe in the Seventeenth and Eighteenth Centuries,* now in press.

ŞERIF MARDIN received a Ph.D. in political science from Stanford University in 1958. He has taught at the University of Ankara and Boğaziçi University, where he was head of the Department of Social Science and currently is dean of the faculty of administrative sciences. He is the author of *The Genesis of Young Ottoman Thought* (1962) and other studies of the intellectual history and sociology of the Ottoman Empire.

MARGARET MEAD (1901–1978), one of the few anthropologists to reach a wide popular as well as professional audience, was the author of *Coming of Age in Samoa* (1928), *Growing Up in New Guinea* (1930), and *Sex and Temperament* (1935). Until her death, she was adjunct professor of anthropology at Columbia University and curator emeritus of ethnology at the American Museum of Natural History in New York City. Among her last works are a volume of autobiography, *Blackberry Winter* (1972); and *Letters from the Field, 1925–1975* (1977).

A. LEO OPPENHEIM (1904–1974) received his Ph.D. from the University of Vienna in 1933. He was John A. Wilson Professor of Oriental Languages at the University of Chicago and editor in charge of the Assyrian dictionary project. His works include *Ancient Mesopotamia* (1964) and *Letters from Mesopotamia* (1967).

R. S. SHARMA received his Ph.D. from the University of London in 1956, and has served as University Professor and head of the Department of History at Patna University in India. His works include *Aspects of Political Ideas and Institutions in Ancient India* (1958), *Light on Early Indian Society and Economy* (1966), and *Indian Society: Historical Probings* (1974).

MAX WEBER (1864–1920), author of *The Protestant Ethic and the Spirit of Capitalism* (1905), has been one of the most influential social scientists of this century. His work is of awe-inspiring breadth, from economic and social history to comparative studies of law and religion; in addition, he wrote on methodological problems in the social sciences, the origins of urbanization, the sociology of music, and contemporary political life, including the Russian Revolution of 1905 and developments in Germany prior to and during World War I.

JOHN A. WILSON (1899–1972) received his Ph.D. from the University of Chicago, where he became director of the Oriental Institute, chairman of the Department of Oriental Languages and Literatures, and Andrew MacLeish Distinguished Service Professor of Egyptology. After his retirement in 1968, he served as president of the American Research Center in Egypt. Among his works are *Ancient Near Eastern Texts* (1951), *The Burden of Egypt* (1956), *Signs and Wonders upon Pharaoh* (1964), and *Thousands of Years* (1972).

ARTHUR F. WRIGHT (1913–1976) received a Ph.D. in history from Harvard University in 1947. He taught at Stanford University and Yale University, where he was Charles Seymour Professor of History. His works include *Buddhism in Chinese History* (1959), *Confucian Personalities* (1962), and *Perspectives on the T'ang* (1973).

# INDEX

Aaron the Just, Caliph. *See* Hārūn al-Rashīd.
ʿAbbās, 356
ʿAbbāsids, reign of, 356–360, 366, 371, 542
Abdal, Pir Sultan, 496, 513, 524
Abdulhamid II, Sultan, reign of, 384, 389, 402, 423, 434n, 441n, 526; administration, 410, 427, 428; curbs on free expression, 421–422; printing, 404, 406, 407, 408; road and rail construction, 408, 409; schools established, 410, 412–413
Abiathar, priest, 310
Abu Bakr, Caliph, 351, 352
Achaemenid, 542
Acropolis, 259
Actions, public, 267–273
Active values, 156, 162
Adab dynasty, 76, 103n
Adad-nirari I, 69–70
Adams, Samuel, 17
Adcock, F. E., 269
Address, forms of, 195
Administrative processes, 425–427, 461, 491n. *See also* Bureaucracy
Aegina, 277
Aeneas, 264, 275–276
*Aeneid,* 294
Aethelbald, King, 568
Aethelred, King, 570–571
Afghanistan, inscriptions in, 178
Africa, 43, 261–262, 264, 341–342. *See also* North Africa; West Africa
Afterlife, promise of, 166, 169–170

Agade, 104n. *See also* Akkad
Age grades, 34, 35
Age of Absolutism, 542–543
Agency principle, 446
Agincourt carol, 578
Agricola, 576
Agricultural ritual, 244–245
Agriculture: Egyptian, 154; Indian, 200
Agum II, 75, 103n
Ahab, 312
Ahmed III, Sultan, 401, 402
Ahmet I, Sultan, 508
Ahmet Hasim, 518, 527
Ahmet Midhat Efendi, 408, 419–420, 441n
Ahmet Yesevi, 522
Ājīvikas, 201
*Akh's*, 150
Akkad: city of, 77–78; dynasty, 60, 77–79, 81, 91; kings, 62, 63, 69, 105n; territory of, 59–60, 61
Akkadian language, 79, 105n; inscriptions in, 76, 115, 119; *narū*-literature in, 82, 106n; terms in, 89, 96n, 97n, 143n
Akyüz, Kenan, 419, 441n, 442n
Albanians, 451, 479
Alcuin, 571, 584
Aleppo, 368
Alevi sect, 510
Alexander, 184, 271–272; actions as propaganda, 267–268; coins of, 277, 279; empire of, 446, 454
Alexander III, Pope, 583

Alexandria, 12, 297, 339, 341
Alfred, King, 569–570, 588
*Al-futuwwa*, 364, 372, 379n
ᶜAli, Caliph, 353–354, 358, 363, 420
Ali Sir Nevai, 508–509
Alien contact, 42–43
Allahabad inscription, 185
Alland, Alexander, Jr., 21
Allegiance, unfixed, 33
Allport, Floyd, 32
Almohad dynasty, 371
Almoravid dynasty, 371
Altar of the Gens Augusta, 264
Altar of Zeus, 262
Amarna Revolution, 165
Ambition, national and personal, 259, 260
Ambrose, Father, 285, 556, 563, 575
Amenemope, 174
American Revolution, 17
Amnesty, edict of, 230–232, 251
Amon, 167
Amos, 299, 303–304, 313, 317, 322, 326; background of, 309, 328n; in Beth-el, 301, 314, 315; in ecstatic state, 319; and kings, 301, 312; on sacrifice, 315, 316
Anagni, 587–588
Anatolia, 470, 473; cavalry in, 448, 482; poets from, 518, 530; towns and villages in, 470, 480; Turkish language in, 447, 499; unrest in, 510, 520
Anaxagoras, 297
Ancestors: identification of king with, 574–575; promised return of, 43; valor of, 559, 561; veneration of, 216, 246–247, 249
Anday, Melih cevdet, 519
Andelibi, 513
Anglo-Saxon Chronicle, 569
Anglo-Saxon history, perception of, 571
Anglo-Saxon invasions, 571
Annals, royal, 72, 73, 102n, 120
Animals, injury to, Buddhism on, 200
Anonymity of authors, 179–180
Anthony, Saint, 556
Anthropology, 22
Antioch, 341, 342, 366
Anti-chrematistic tradition, 318
Antirational antinomianism, 542
Antisocial acts, prevention of, 241, 242
Antony, Marc, 269, 282, 286, 293
Anu, 93
*Anuśāsana Parva*, 180
*Anuṣṭupa chanda*, 179
Aphoristic attitudes, 285
Apocalyptic ideas in rebel ideologies, 253–254

Apocalyptic literature, 80, 88
Apochryphal stories, 76–78
Apochryphal testamentary confession, 81–83. *See also* Inscriptions, royal
Apollo, 764
Apollodorus, 261
Apologies, written Christian, 334–337, 347n
Apologists, 345–346
Apostles, Christian, 311, 324, 332, 338–339; missionary, 343–344; preaching of, 332–333
Apotropaic representations, 113
Ara Pacis Augustae, 263–264
Arab: garrison troops, 353, 354, 359; provinces, 454, 455; tribal society, 349. *See also* Tribal warriors
Arabia, 320, 342
Arabic: alphabet, 413; culture, 358, 423, 499, 522, 523; language, 373, 391–392, 393, 434n, 435n; literature, 385, 505, 509; script, 355, 413, 502; vocabulary, 456, 500, 502
Arabic-Persian literature, 502, 522
Arad-Enlilla, King, 105n, 106n
Aramaean dynasty, 95
Aramaean language, 16, 119, 127
Arapesh society, 32–34; communication in, 24, 27–28; innovation in, 38–39, 40; public opinion in, 36–37
Architecture, 147, 202. *See also* Buildings
Arik-den-ilu, reign of, 102n, 120
Aristophanes, 265, 274, 284, 292
Aristotle, 290, 497
Arjuna, 192
Ark of Covenant, 315
Arkell, A. J., 380
Armenia, Christianity in, 342–343
Arnulfings, the, 556, 566
Art, Islamic, 355
Art as propaganda, 183, 564–565. *See also* Sculpture
Artemis, Temple of, at Ephesus, 258
*Artha*, attainment of, 194
*Arthaśāstra*, 180, 186–189, 202, 204n
Articulatory apparatus, human, 21
Artifact, propaganda of, 578
Artisans, regulation of, 362
Artist, prerogatives and obligations of, 497, 531
Arts and Sciences, Imperial Academy of, 413–414
Arundel, Archbishop, 578
Ascetics, 363
Ascher, Robert, 21
Asclepius, 272
Ascriptive ties, 547, 549

Ashur. *See* Assur
Ashurbanipal. *See* Assurbanipal
Ashur-uballit, 69
Asia, Central, as intermediate culture, 206. *See also* Southeast Asia
Asia Minor, 81; Christianity in, 341, 342
Asiatics in Egypt, 152–153, 163, 164
Asik Pasha, 500
Aśoka, King, 181, 199, 201, 219n; and Buddhism, 208, 214; inscriptions of, 177, 178, 184, 185, 189–190
Assemblies, participation in Hellenic, 302
Assur, city of, 134–135, 139n, 140n, 141n, 306; Essarhaddon's letter to, 5, 125, 129–133; literary findings at, 72, 141n; Sargon's letter to, 124, 133
Aššur, the god, 110n, 122, 144n; communication with, 123, 124, 125, 131, 143–144n; enemies of, 120, 130
Assurbanipal, King, 92, 113, 133, 141n, 144n
Aššur-nirari VI, King, 142n
Assyrian Empire, 71–72, 95, 101n, 109n, 111, 124, 127–130, 306, 308; body politic, 134–136; economic structure, 121; imperialism of, 120, 142n; internal dissent, 123, 131–133; interregnum, 90, 108n; kings, 55, 97n, 133–137, 300; literary achievement, 69, 72, 73, 126–127, 129–130; military threat of, 69, 104n, 119–120, 120–121, 133–134, 164, 299, 305
Assyrian King List, 59, 63–64
*Aṣṭādhyāyi*, 178, 179
Astrologers, royal, 109n, 184, 188–189, 387
Astrology, political and social roles of, 197–198
Astronomy, Babylonian, 317
Atatürk, Mustafa Kemal, 503–504, 519
Atatürkism, 495
*Atebet-ül Hakayik*, 522
Athanasius, 295
*Atharva Veda*, 176, 181
Athelstan, King, 570
Athene, 276, 277
Athene Promachos, 262–263
Athens, 12, 128–129, 304; buildings and sculptures of, 259, 262–263; coins of, 276–277; drama of, 291–292; oracles, impact of, 273–274
Attalus I of Pergamum, 258, 262
*Aṭṭhakathās*, 179
Atticus, 297
Atrahasis, 56–57
Audience: attributes of, 7, 8; for pro-
paganda, 53–54, 585, 586; for published work, 579; of royal inscription genre, 115–116, 117
Augurinus, C., 278–279
Augustine, St., 285, 295–296, 557, 563, 569, 575, 593n
Augustus, 203, 286; buildings and sculpture of, 260, 263–264; in coins, 279–280, 281, 282; description of by Suetonius, 265–266; portraits of, 266; propaganda action of, 270–271; treatment of literature, 293–294, 298
Aurelius, Marcus, 259, 271
Australia, 42, 45
Autarchy, 153; theocratic, 162
Authority: acceptance of, 64; breakdown of, 153; consolidated basis for, 135–136; competition for, 163; dramatic expression of, 268; medieval symbols of, 586
Autobiography of Marduk, 84–87
Autonomy, institutional, 549–550
*Avadāna* literature, 200
Averroes, Ibn Rushd, 371, 379n
Avicenna, Ibn Sina, 371
*Azhar, al-*, 365
Aztec empire, 542

Baal, worship of, 311, 315
Babylon, 108n, 139n, 172, 300, 314, 542; First Dynasty of, 74–75, 76, 85, 94, 100n, 108n; Jeremiah on, 301, 304, 306–307, 308, 313; kings of, 58–59, 62, 67–69, 88, 119–120, 141n; primacy of, 94–96, 110n; rise and fall of, 58–59, 85, 87–88, 100n, 104n, 110n
Babylonia, 61, 69, 71; geographical outlines of, 137n; as international power, 95, 111; kings of, 59, 101n, 300
Babylonian Epic of Creation, 91–95, 102n, 109n, 110n
Bactria, 185, 278; Greeks of, 193
Baghdad, 357, 366, 372; caliphate, 359, 364, 365, 366, 368; as center of communication, 490; slave soldiers in, 359–360
*Bahasa* Indonesia, 203
Baki, 512
Bali, 32; villages of, 24, 36–38, 39–40
Balkans, 426, 473
Balkhi, Abu Shukur, 533
Ball, John, 584
Bāṇabhaṭṭa, 185
Banquets, royal, 119, 141n
Baptism, instruction for, 340
Barbarians, 262, 575

Bards, Ottoman, 394, 495
Barnet, battle of, 555
Baruch, 325
Basilica Aemilia, 260
Basilica Julia, 260
*Basiret,* 408
Bateson, Gregory, 25, 26, 34, 35n, 36, 39
Bauer, Wilhelm, xi
Bayeux tapestry, 573–574
Baynes, Norman, 272–273
Bayrami sect, 510
Becket, Thomas, 566, 578, 587
Bede, Venerable, 260–261, 552, 556, 569, 571, 585, 590n
Bedouins, 351, 470
Behavior, conventional, 26, 27
Behavior, standards of, 149, 212, 445
Bektashiism, 481, 492n, 510
Belief: literalness of, 43; unofficial, use of, 243–244
Beowulf, 575, 576
Berbers, 342, 365
*Berith* 313–314, 326, 327–328
Berkes, Niyazi, 436n, 437n, 438n, 440n
Bernard of Clairvaux, 584
Berndt, Ronald M., 43
Besiktas Circle, 415
Beth-el, sacrifice in, 314, 315
Beyatli, Yahya Kemal, 518, 527
*Bhagavad Gita,* 192, 196
*Bhagavata Purana,* 195
*Bhavisyat Purana,* 197
Bhisma, 182
Bible, 15, 41, 71, 289–290, 556, 567–568
Biblical prophecy, 83–84, 107n, 108n
*Bibliopola,* 12
Biographies of Chinese generals, 207
Birdwhistell, Ray L., 22, 30
Birgeri, Kadi, 403
Birth stories, Buddhist, 194, 199
Blood line, continuity of, 212
Bodhisattva, 208, 213, 246
Boethius, 569
Bonanno Pisano doors, Pisa, 564
Boniface, missionary, 567
Boniface VIII, Pope, 580–581, 587–588
de Bonneval, Marquis, 409
*Book of Changes,* 230
*Book of History,* 230, 231, 239
*Book of Proverbs,* Hebrew, 285
*Book of the Covenant,* 327
*Book of the Lyre,* 499
Book trade, 297–298
Books: as Christian instrument, 567–568; publication of, 296–298; scarcity of in Ottoman Empire, 434n. *See also* Ottoman Empire, printing in

Booty, 120, 122; king's distribution of, 130, 132, 142n
Borger, R., 107n, 108n, 110n, 142n
Bosnia, 451, 479
Bosquet, Alain, 497
Boudicca, 262
Bourgeoisie, modern, 15
Bourget, Paul, 422, 442n
Bouwsma, W. J., 14
Bowen, Harold, 380n, 432n, 436n
Brady, Mathew, 18
Brahma, 182, 183
*Brahmanas,* the, 176, 178
Brahmans, 201; in Bali, 40; beliefs in rebirth, heaven and hell, 198, family property, sanctity of, 193–194; relation to Buddhism, 195, 200, 207; and the social order, 191, 192–193, 195; use of astrology, 197
Brain, growth of, 21
Bravery, value of, 420–421
Breasted, James Henry, 147, 157, 162, 170, 173n, 174n
Brethren of Purity, 361
*Brhatkatha* of *Gunadhya,* 195
Brinkman, J. A., 107n, 110n, 137n, 139n, 140n
Britain: Christianity in, 342, 571; history of, perception of, 571; Roman presence and propaganda in, 261, 262, 576. *See also* England
Brown, John, 43
Brown, Roger, 22
Bruegel, Pieter, 9
Brutus, Marcus, 286
Buddha, the: communication of with various classes, 195; miracles of, 200; use of teaching of, 243. *See also* Gautama Buddha
Buddha Maitreya, 217; incarnation of, 229, 253
Buddhism, xiii, 36, 199, 201, 545, 546; and Brahmanism, 207; development of into world religion, 207–208, 210–211, 217; on family and property, 193–194; followers of, 195; and legitimacy of ruler, 181–182, 213, 247; literature of, 194, 199, 204; nirvana, 198; religious assemblies, 176–177
Buddhism in China, 205, 207–210, 218; Chinese symbolism, adding to, 253; divinities, introduction of, 216–217; economic effects, 215–216; propagators of, 209; temples and institutions in, 217, 246–247
Buffaloes, return of, 43
Buildings as propaganda, 257–262; as emblematic of a city, 258; as

memorials of events, 258–259; as symbols of royal power, 112–113, 114. *See also* Inscriptions, building
Bukhāra, 360
Bulaq press, Egypt, 403, 438n
Bulgarians, 479
Bunai village, 41
Bureaucracy: European, 425; Mesopotamian, 52, 111–112
Bureaucracy, Ottoman patrimonial sultanic, 383–384, 402, 417, 421, 424, 430; communication in, 381–383, 384, 429; middle level, 410, 419, 420, 428–429. *See also* Civilian administration
Burke, Kenneth, 534
Burrus, 282
Byers, Paul, 31
Byron, Lord, 261
Byzantine Empire, 352–353, 366, 367, 542; as administrative model, 354; court pageantry in, 272–273; emperor's appeal to pope, 367; legal precedent of, 356; techniques of, inherited by Ottomans, 447

Cadmus of Thebes, 298
Caesarea, 339, 343
Cahit Yalçın, Hüseyin, 420–421, 423, 442n
Cairo, 147, 365, 368
Calendar, institution of, 157, 244
Calendrical expert, 37
Caligula, 271, 281, 298
Caliph, 351–352, 362
Caliphate, 357–358, 360; Baghdad, 364, 365, 366; legitimacy of, 358, 361, 373
Call of prophets, 323
Calligraphy, 393, 435n
Cālukya, 184
Calvin, John, 13
Camus, Albert, 532
Candra, a god, 183
Candra, a king, 185
Candra Gupta II, 185
Canossa, 580
Canterbury, 554, 578, 580, 583
Capital: celebration of, 248; corps, 451; ritual enactments centered on, 244–245
Capitoline Wolf, 276
Caracalla, 261, 262, 271–272
Caravanserai, 473
Cargo Cults, 43–44
Carthage, 262
Cassian, 556
Cassiodorus, 575
Cassius, 286
Caste, 194; mixed, 193; purity, importance of, 191–192; religious and political, 545; status, Buddha on, 200
Castro, Fidel, 364
Catechists, 340
Cattle wealth, 199, 200
Cautionary stories, 76–77, 81–82
Cavalry, 451
Celestial pivot, 229
Celestine V, 575, 580
Celsus, 337–338
Censorship: imperial Roman, 285, 293, 298; Ottoman, 407, 421–422, 439n
Centers, autonomous political and social, 540, 543, 544–545, 546; relation to periphery, 546–547
Centrality, symbols of, 544, 547–548
Ceremonial: hostility, 35; writings, 118, 119
Ceremonies: in battles, 143n; binding religious and governmental establishments, 467; Buddhist, introduction of, 217; rejection or omission of, 25, 39; royal, 113, 114, 119, 223–224, 228, 565–566
*Ceride-i Havadis*, 405–406, 407, 415
Cevdet Pasa, 413
Chaldean dynasty, 95
Chang Ch'ien, 207
Change, impetus to, 501, 522–532
Chaos, primeval forces of, 92–93
Character, afterlife assessment of, 160–161
Charisma: of ʿAli and Husain, 354; Muhammed's, 351, 352; prophetic, 318
Charlemagne, 13, 559, 572–573, 584, 593n
Charles of Anjou, 553
Charles the Good, 555
Chartres, sculptural program at, 564
Ch'en dynasty, 232–233
Ch'en Shu-pao, 233
Ch'ien-lung, Emperor, 223–224
Ch'in, empire of, 221, 240
China, 205–219, 220–256; Buddhist cultural transformation of, 205, 210, 212–217, 218; communications in, 224; economy of, 215–216; education, classics in, 435n; elites of, 211, 217, 245; ideas and practices of, reasserted, 218; Indian influence on, 205–207; mass rising in, 209–210; reunification of, 232–234
China, Imperial, 220, 542; geography of, 221; reintegration of, 217; the royal progress in, 248–252; transitions of power in, 252–254
Chinese Communist Party, 240
Chinese rationalism, 172

Ch'ing dynasty, 241, 542
Chingiz Khan, 372
Chivalry, 565
*Chokma,* 317
Chou dynasty, 229, 239, 246
Chresmologists, 302
Christ. *See* Jesus
Christian: church structure, 339, 343–344, 546; community, 324, 333, 335, 338, 345–346; conquests in eleventh century, 371; controversy, 295–296; era, 179, 180, 181, 186, 190, 200, 203; faith and doctrine, 43, 44, 333, 334–336, 339–340; graffiti, 288; Holy Places, recovery of, 367; saints and relics, 558, 567
Christian communication, xiii, 330, 334, 344–346, 589; agents of, 337–338; of faith, 330–331, 334–336, 343; medieval gap in, 373; oral, 336–337; private, 337
Christian missions, 330–347; in church structure, 339, 340; division of labor in, 332; message of, 332–333; responses of various regions to, 341–343; scope of, 330–331
Christian missionaries, official and unofficial, 338–339, 343–344
Christian society: traditions of, 538–539; values of, 584; world view of, 563–564
Christianity, 284, 330–347; in favor in Roman Empire, 343; in Germanic propaganda, 577; and propaganda of competition and defense, 575; receptivity of ancient world to, 344–345
Christians, 350; Armenian, 479; Coptic, 342, 375; English, 571; in Muslim empire, 356; Oriental, 363, 375; Orthodox, 479; sacred states among, 329n
Chrysippus, 265
Chrysostom, Dio, 258, 563
Chu Hsi, 240
Chu Yüan-chang, 235–236, 239
Churchill, William, 28
Cicero, 268, 297
Circumcision, 316
Cities, old privileged, 134–135, 136
City-states, 52, 54, 59–60, 73, 80–81, 97n, 543, 546
City wall dialogues, 126–129
Civil engineering, school of, 410
Civil Medicine, Faculty of, 410
Civilian administration, 221, 401; separation from military, 399, 436n, 440n. *See also* Officials
Class, social: alienation, 431; conflicts, 197; development of, 536; distinction in propaganda, 588–589; intermediate, 399. *See also* Two-class system, Ottoman
Classic crimes, 233
Classic of Filial Submissiveness, 238–239
Claudius, 260, 262, 271, 279, 281, 282
Cleopatra, 265, 274–275
Clergy, secular, 387
Clermont, Urban II at, 558
Clichés for social survival, 595n
*Cloud of Unknowing,* 579
Clovis, 567
Cnut, 571–572
Coded messages, 24
Coinage, 276–284; as deification of Indian kings, 183; history of, 276; as propaganda of kings and states, 277, 282–283, 567, 568; of Roman Empire, 278–284
Colonial empires, European, 543
Colonna, the, 580, 587
Colossus of Rhodes, 258
Columbus, Christopher, 16, 555
Comedy, 513–514
Commedia dell'arte, 513
Commerce. *See* Trade
Commerce, school of, 410
Commentary: on ancient Indian texts, 179, 180–181; as social function of poetry, 504, 505, 506–522
Common people: effect of ritual enactment on, 251; gulf between urban elite and, 509
Communication, 4, 5–6, 10, 28, 31, 51, 257, 537; centers, 471–473, 541, 549, 550n; history of, xii, 9–15, 21, 51, 397–398, 580; limitations of, 553–554, 580, 582, 586; modernization of, 381, 397, 399–401, 408–409, 409–413, 429– 431, 444; patterns of, changes in, 382, 539, 541, 582–583; privileged, 491n; process, 1, 3–4, 5, 6–11; systems, 137, 372–373, 383, 390–391, 399–400, 433n, 459–460, 478, 547, 550; technology of, 12–13, 16–18, 19, 20, 22, 29, 31–32, 40, 42–43; types of, 538, 539, 550–551n
Communication channels, 7, 8, 382, 394–396, 445, 539, 547, 552–553; bureaucratic, 112, 383, 394, 423, 425–426, 428–429, 454, 456, 471–472, 473–475, 483, 484
Communicators, 5, 7–8, 429, 548, 549
Communism, 380n, 527, 529
Community action, 32
Conceptualization, capacity for, 31
Conformity, 169–170, 237–238

Confucianism, 210, 545; on classic
    crimes of ruler, 233; Classics of, 212,
    222, 223, 240; elite critique of, 210;
    imperial, 212–213, 221–222, 231,
    241; principles of, 221, 237, 238,
    243; schools of, 540
Confucius, 248–249, 254n
Consensus, 18, 176, 377n, 436n
Consent, 221; winning, 220, 221, 233,
    241
Constable, Giles, 595n
Constantine, 259, 266–267, 342, 343,
    557, 575
Constantinople, 368, 439n, 446–447,
    559
Constitutions: Ottoman, 408; Turkish
    Republic, 502, 530
Consubstantiality, 149
Contact culture, 42–43, 43–44
Content, manifest or latent, 7
Continuity and cohesion, 501–504
Coptic language, 342
Copyists, 297–298, 400
Cordova, 360
Corfe, 587
Coronations, 181, 566–567
Corvée, 55, 56–57, 470
Cosmic house, 229
Cosmic order, 544, 545
Cosmology, Mesopotamian, 92, 109n
Council of elders, 54. *See also* Imperial
    Council, Ottoman
Counterelites, 12
Counterprophecy, 304, 305
Couriers, 52, 487–488
Court, royal, 59–73, 318, 360–361;
    literary genres of, 116–117, 118, 140–
    141n, 196
Court chronicles, 102n, 185–186
Court prophets. *See* Prophets of the
    king
Courts, legal, 42, 313
Craft guilds, 362–363. *See also* Guilds.
Crafts, transmission of, 201–202, 204
Cratinus, 265
Creation: in Babylonian epic, 56, 92,
    109n; stories in cuneiform, 109–110n
Cresilas, 265
Crimea, the, 483, 485, 488
Crimean War, 427
Crusaders, 368, 372, 375, 562
Crusades, 582–583, 584; from Islamic
    view, 367–368, 369; Urban II's call
    to, 558–561
Cryptography, 1
Cthonian gods, 313
Cult practices, 127, 314–316
Cult shrines, 76–77, 88

Cultivated mind, value of, 392
Cults and political alliances, 313
Cultural: elitism, 382, 398, 421; expec-
    tations, departures from, 27; identity,
    537, 549; order, 538, 545, 549–550
Cultural Revolution, 255n
Culture: hostility, 310–311, 317; items
    of, 40. *See also* Contact culture; In-
    termediate culture
Cumali, Necati, 520
Cuneiform writing, 51; inscriptions,
    299; literary, 71, 72, 78; religious, 72,
    87
Curse of Akkad (Agade), 77–78, 80,
    103–104n, 106n, 109n
Custom, institutionalization of, 28–29
Cyrus the Great, 58, 100n, 308
Czech Reform, 14

Dadaloglu, 524
Daglarca, Fazil Hüsnü, 493, 520–522,
    531, 535n
Dalmatia, 342
Damascus, 353, 354, 368
Dance, 23, 565
Daniel, Book of, 290
Danish invasions, 569–571
Danton, 18
Danube, 488
Darius, 308
Dašaratha, 181
David, 309, 312, 566; lineage of, 333,
    556
Davut, Kara, 420
Death: in battle, Chinese fear of,
    214–215; denial of, 151, 162, 163; as
    release, 155–156
Debates, 175–176; rules of in Buddhist
    assemblies, 177
Decentralization, progressive, 153
Decius, 284
Dede Korkut tales, 522
*Deeds of William,* 573–574
Defoe, Daniel, 398
Deification of kings, 183, 272, 276
Deity: houses, 183; identification of
    king with, 115–116, 134, 184; patron,
    monarch's obeisance to, 86, 107n;
    tutelary, 66–67, 98n, 115, 116, 216,
    249. *See also* Kings, divinity of; Royal
    divinity
Delphi, oracle at, 27, 300, 308, 322
Demagoguery, 303–304, 305, 320, 589;
    war peotry as, 302
Democracy, 150, 162
Democratic: ideals, 310; procedures, 177
Democritus, 285
Demon, use of, 186

Demonstration as communication, 23
Demosthenes, 259
Denationalization, 333
Denniston, J. D., 291
Dervish: culture, 399; orders, 395, 480–482, 492n; sheikhs, 492n
Desert times, 317
Determinism, 168
Deuteronomic movement, 306
Deuteronomy, 311, 315
Deutsch, Karl W., 381, 442n, 443n
*Devānāṃpriya,* 181
*Devaputra,* 181–182
*Dharma,* 185, 194, 198
Dharmapāla, 185–186
*Dharmaśāstras,* the, 176, 179, 181, 196
*Dharmasūtras,* the, 178
*Dialogue of the Exchequer,* 574
Dictionaries, printing of, 404
Diocletian, 261
Diodorus, 171–172
Diogenes, 286–287
Dionysius the Areopagite, 290
Diplomacy: modern, 11, 26; Ottoman, 401, 489
Disguised communication, 24
Dissent, discouraging, 131–133, 241
Dissidents, use of representations by, 252–254
Distance, coping with, 32, 482–488
Distribution mapping, 23
Divan, responsibilities of, 461
Divan literature, 419, 432n, 435n, 507–509; genres, 510; poetry, 503, 505–506, 509, 512, 516, 523, 525
*Divan-i Hikmet,* 522
*Divan ü Lugat-it Türk,* 500, 501, 522, 523, 535n
Divination, 88–91, 121, 122, 143n; communication between priests and people, 197–198; influence of on statecraft, 89–90, 108n; literature, 58
Divine capital, 229
Divine determinative, 79–80, 105n
Divine names, Sufi repetition of, 355
Divine revelations. *See* Prophet, the
Diviners, positions of, 90, 91, 109n
Divinity, royal. *See* King, divinity of
Dobuans, 41
Documents, written, 51; carrying notion of rule, 568; legitimating, 384; as signs of power, 113
Dodds, E. R., 344
Dodona, 300
Dome of the Rock, 354
Domesday Book, 573
Domitian, 261, 298
Domus Aurea, 260
Donation of Constantine, 103n

Donatives, 271
Donkey Story, 514–515
Donne, John, 558
Drama, 196, 495, 524
Dramatic: dialogues, 126–129; propaganda actions, 267–268
Dreams in battle depiction, 122, 143n
Drum signals, 24
Druze, 375
Dutch colonial government, 36
*Dvārapaṇḍita,* 177
Dynasty: continuity, Augustus' determination for, 263–264; foundings, 225–226, 228, 229, 235; length of rule and of genealogies, 140n; name of, 225

Ea, 92–93
Eannatum, King, 62
Early man, communication in, 22–32
East, associations with, 249
Eastern Europe, public figures in, 25
Ebabbar, 75
Ebeling, E., 101n, 102n, 141n
Economic activities, communication in, 6
Economic rights and privileges, 55, 74, 75, 97n
Economy of effort, Ottoman, 485
Ecstasy: apathetic, 320; of calling, 326; direct, 321; external stimulation of, 323–324; as legitimation of prophecy, 327; prophets' states of, 318–319, 321, 322–323; solitary, 324–325
Edessa, 342
Edgar, King, 570
Edib Ahmet, 522
Edicts, imperial, 225, 226–228; copying of, 233, 234; style of, 234. *See also* Sacred edict
Edmund, Earl of Kent, 587
Education, 540; Chinese indoctrination in, 238–239; contribution of to language reform, 502; control of state over, 388, 430–431, 539–540; elite, 369, 387–388, 398, 399, 465, 540; modernization of, 409–413, 420–421, 422, 440n; oral, in India, 178; Ottoman general law on, 410; of primitives, 45; public, institutionalization of, 411, 431; view of in Enlightenment, 15; Western medieval, 394, 435n; Western-modeled, 402, 410–411, 417
Edward I, 574–575
Edward II, 564, 587
Edward IV, 555, 565, 578
Edward the Confessor, 575
Edwin Smith Surgical Papyrus, 148

Egypt, 127, 128, 149–150, 163, 352, 485, 546; art in, 122, 166; Christianity in, 341– 342; cultural communication with pre-Islamic Arabia, 349; dynasties in, 148; Empire of, 164–172, 542; intellectual contribution of, 172; Israelite alliance with, 308, 312–313; kings of, 183, 299; literature in, 154–156, 165–166; Middle Kingdom, 157–163; Old Kingdom, 147–149, 150, 152–154, 157–158, 160, 165, 166, 168; partisans of, 307–308; place of priest in, 314; power of, 69, 306; prophecy in, 320; Second Intermediate Period, 163; Tamil language in, 203; trade of, 366, 489–490; unity of, 163–164; water routes in, 488

Egyptian: ethos, 163–172; philosophy, 157, 172; psychology, 170; values, 145–146

Eight admonitions of Wang Mang, 238–239

E-kur, 77–78

El Djem, 261

Elam: invasion by, 85, 86, 107n; oracle against, 108n

Eleanor of Aquitaine, 583

Elections, interpreters for, 42

Elegies, 498, 503–504

Eliakim, 299–300

Elijah, 301, 312, 314

Elisha, school of, 310, 314

Elite, 453–468, 481; antagonism toward Naram-Sim, 91, 105n; control over communication and knowledge, 386–387, 390, 538–539; coup by, 58; culture, 206, 391–393, 432n, 457, 505; education and training, 385–388, 411–412, 420, 430, 445, 456–458; function of manipulating representations, 225–226, 228; microsystems within, 458; poetry criticizing, 511; problems for with social change, 537, 542; urban, chasm between rural people and, 509. *See also* Literati; Military class

Ellis, R. W., 140

Eloquent peasant, 161–162, 168

Emperor: alliance of with elite, 221, 224–226, 543–544; apotheosis of, 229, 263, 272; as god's vice-regent, 230, 264; portraits of on coins, 279; as religious leader, 246, 248–249; symbolic roles of, 244–245, 248, 547–548. *See also* Kings

Empires, centralized bureaucratic, 536–551; structural differentiation, 536–537, 541, 544, 546. *See also*

Centers, autonomous political and social

Emrullah Efendi, 430

Encomia, persuasive powers of, 505

Endowment text, 75–76

Enemies of the state, internal, 187–188

England, 554, 558, 573, 582–583; Conquest of, 573–574; importance of letters in, 578; medieval propaganda in, 556–558, 565–566, 569–572, 574–575, 577–578, 579, 584–585, 586–587; medieval sermons in, 563–564, 580; popular literature in, 398. *See also* Britain

English translations of Latin classics, 569

Enlightenment, the, 15

Enlil, 56–57, 61, 94; abode of, 77, 94, 104n; wrathful punishment of, 78, 104n

Enlil-nirari, 69

Ennin, diary of, 226–228, 244, 246, 255n

*Enuma Elish*, 92–95, 102n, 109n, 110n. *See also* Babylonian Epic of Creation

Epaminondas of Thebes, 259

Epics: ancient Indian, 179, 193, 196, 198; Assyrian, 69–72, 140–141n; Turkish, 494, 498, 503

Epicureanism, 286–287, 293

Epigrams, 285

Epitaphs, 286

Eponyms, 101n, 135

Equality, 159, 160, 162

Era-names, 225, 253

Ersoy, Mehmet Akif, 518–519

Esad Efendi, 392

Esagila, 86

Esarhaddon, 101n, 109n, 127, 129, 142n; letter of, 5, 123, 124, 125, 126–129, 129–133, 144n

Eskimo, 29

Esref, 517–518

Eternal life, 157, 159, 160, 161

Ethics: of Buddhism, 208, 213; Egyptian contribution to, 172; Ottoman books on, 503

Ethnic group of extraction, separation from, 457

Ethnic variety of Ottoman Empire, 446, 479

Etiquette, practical, 151–152, 166–167

Eucharist, interpretation of, 564

Eulogies of king, 184, 185–186

Eumenes II, 262

Euripedes, 292, 297

Europe: bureaucratic communication in, 425; centralized states of, 542–543, 550; effect of printing in, 437n; literary genres of, 422, 523–524; Ot-

toman, 480, 482, 486; Ottoman cultural contacts with, 401, 407; special police force in, 487–488. *See also* Eastern Europe; Western Europe
European alphabet, 413
Euthydemus, 297
Evil in Islamic thought, 373–374, 380n
*Exempla* of sermons, 579
Exemplary stories, 76
Exhortations, Christian, 334
Exorcism, 336–337
Exposition Pavillion, 242
Extispicy, 89, 90
Ezekiel, 299, 321, 322; ecstatic states of, 318, 319, 320, 322, 329n; ideal state, theological construction of, 307, 310; priestly outlook of, 309, 314; supporters of, 311

Fairs, seasonal, 473
Faith-healing, 252
Fakih, Hoca Ahmet, 511
Familialism and Buddhism, 215
Family: of coreligionists, claims of, 452; patriarchal, 196–197, 203–204, 212, 238; pedigrees for kings, 184; sanctity of, 193–194; trees, solar and lunar, 183–184
Fasting as ecstasy evocation, 324
Fasting month of Ramadān, 351
Fatalism, 169
Fate, god, 168–169
Fātima, 364
Fātimid dynasty, 364–367, 368, 542; subversion, 367, 371; tolerance of, 365–366
Ferentillo, 564
Fertile Crescent, 349
Fertility, land, observances for, 216
Fertility cults, 311
Festivals, purpose of, 274
Feudal systems, 543; reciprocal obligations in, 384; rituals of lords in, 246
Fez, court at, 360
Fiction, 81, 83, 495
Film, 18–19, 20, 29–30
Finances, imperial, 462. *See also* Fiscal administration
Fine Arts, School of, 410
Fiore, Quentin, 30
Firdausi, 533
Fiscal administration, 134; budget, publication of, 15; records, 51; survey as Ottoman instrument of, 448
Five Element System, 222, 253
Five teachings, 237–238
Flavian dynasty, 259, 260, 283
Flood, the, 63, 95, 98n, 110n

Flood waters, access to, 159, 160
Florence, party struggles in, 304
Folk literature, 419, 421, 435n, 502; poetry, 503, 506, 509–510, 524; poets, characteristics of, 509; tales, 194–195, 204
Folk religion, 243–244
Foot runner, 52–53
Foreign investment in Ottoman Empire, 427
Foreign politics, 58, 114; discussed in Turkish newspapers, 408; internal religious ramifications of, 307–308; and prophets, 305–307
Forgery: of messages, 24–25; of monuments and documents, 74–76; of validating material detail, 27
Fortescue, Chancellor, 578
Fortune, Reo F., 41
Fortune, worship of, 345
Fostlus, Sextus Pompeius, 178
Foundation documents, 118–119, 141n. *See also* Inscriptions, building
Fourth Lateran Council, 579
France: kings of and laudes regiae, 566–567; literature of, 443n; lycees of Second Empire, 411–412; of the past, 559, 561; vernacular propaganda of, 577
Francis, St., 556, 579, 583
Franciscans, 564, 579–580
Franks, 367–368, 371; addressed by Urban II, 559–560, 561; thought and values, 583
Frederick II, Emperor, 581–582, 585
Freethinkers, Islamic, 371
French language, 412
French Revolution, 14, 17–18
Freuchen, Peter, 29
Friars, preaching orders of, 564
Frisians, 556
Frontinus, 261
Fuad Pasa, 413
Future, prediction of, 567
Fuzuli, 507–508, 512

Gabriel, 349
Gaeta, 564
Gaius, 279
Galba, 282–283
Galbert of Bruges, 566, 590n, 592n
Gandhi, Mahatma, 534
Gaṅgā bath, 193
Gaul, 342
Gautama Buddha, 200, 211
Gautamīputra Śātakarṇi, 183
Gazi, Battal, 395, 420
Gazi Giray, 512

Geertz, Clifford, 595n
Gelb, I. J., 74, 102n, 103n, 144n
Genesis, Book of, 110n
Genteel intellectuals: educational level
 of, 318; and gratuitous oracles, 311
Gentiles, Christian mission to, 330–332,
 333–334, 341
Geoffrey le Baker, 587
Geoffrey of York, 587
Geography in Ottoman Empire,
 390–391, 402–403
*Georgics,* 293–294
Gerhoh of Reichersberg, 580, 594n
German society, 575–576; propaganda
 in, 576–577
Gernet, Jacques, 215–216, 255n
Gerontocracy, 29
Gesture behavior, patterned, 22–23
Ghazālī, al-, 370, 371
Ghost Dance movement, 43
Gibb, E. J. W., 494–495, 535n
Gibb, Hamilton A. R., 357, 369–370,
 376, 377n, 378n, 379–380n, 432n,
 436n
*Gibborim,* 310, 313, 318, 327
Gildas, 571
Gilgal, sacrifice in, 315
Gilgamesh, dynasty of, 79
Gilgamesh, Epic of, 102n, 106n
Glanville, 574
Global village, 30
Glossolalia, 324, 329n, 338
Gnomic poetry, 503
Gnostic theories, pre-Islamic, 364
Goa, 184
God, 178, 304, 305, 577; approval of,
 127, 128; descent of authority from,
 581; kingdom of, 331; man's relation
 to, in Qur'ān, 373; oneness of, 333,
 334, 349–350; propaganda message
 to, 571; propaganda of, 567; ritual
 repetition as communication with,
 355; satire against, 516; sultan compared to, 507–509
Gods, 81–82, 92–93, 124, 125, 168,
 169; assessment of character by, 159,
 160, 161; association of king with, 63,
 67, 100n, 112, 113–114; 150, 164,
 171–172, 181–184, 188–189; communications with king, 122, 143–
 144n; creator-god, 150, 159–160;
 favor of, 123, 135–136, 164–165; national, 164, 170; personal relationship
 with, 149–150, 170; royal submissiveness to, 82; role of in wars and
 fortunes, 60, 71, 87–88; sun-god,
 161; supreme god, 149, 150,
 159–160, 161

Goitein, S. D., 379
Gökalp, Ziya, 527
Goldhamer, Herbert, 11
Good deeds, 159, 160, 316
Government: control of communication,
 471–472, 474, 475; good, as theme of
 poetry, 504–505; service, higher
 education for, 369; visibility of in
 *Tanzimat,* 425–426
Graffiti, 287–288, 394
Grammars of ancient India, 178, 179
Grant, Michael, 275
Great Mosque, 354
Great Pyramid of Gizeh, 147, 157
Great Traditions, 546
Greece, ancient, 545; book trade in,
 297; Christianity, response to, 341;
 coins, 276, 278; culture of, 275–276,
 522, 538–539; monuments of, 258;
 philosophy of, 172, 370–371; prose
 in, 291; public records in, 288–289
Greek texts: of wall-of-city dialogues,
 126–127, 128–129; of Tutulki story,
 71
Greeks: appreciation of Egyptian
 wisdom, 172; of Egypt, 203;
 mercenaries, 139n; as minority group,
 479
Gregory, St., 569
Gregory VII, Pope, 580, 581
Gregory the Illuminator, 343, 344
Gregory Thaumaturgos, 339–340, 341,
 343, 344
Gregory of Tours, 555, 557, 583, 591n
*Gṛhyasūtras,* the, 178
Group memberships, 34–36, 37; concen-
 tric, 36. *See also* Social groups
Gudea, reign of, 63, 98n
Guilds: dervishes' association with, 481;
 diviners organized into, 89; Ottoman
 system of, 475, 476–478, 479–480,
 492n; schools attached to, 540; in
 West, 436n
Gulhane Rescript, 495
Gupta: kings, 183, 185, 192; period,
 180, 185, 193, 197, 542
Gutenberg, Johan, 16, 17
Güterbock, H. G., 103n, 106n, 108n,
 140
Guthlac, St., 556–558
Guthram, the Dane, 570
Gutians, 59–60, 78, 79, 98n, 104n,
 105n

Habib, İsmail, 434n, 435n, 441n
Hacib, Yusuf Has, 499–500, 504–505,
 511
Hadrian, 261, 262, 283–284

Haldia, god, 125
Halit Ziya, 422
Hall, Edward T., 30
Hallo, W. W., 99n, 100n, 101n, 105n, 140n
Halveti sect, 510
Hammurapi, 61, 62, 94, 97n, 108n, 140n; code of, 56, 65, 97n
Han dynasty, 219n, 232, 234, 542; Buddhism in, 209; collapse of, 209, 210, 213; elites' moral guidance in, 219; ideology of, 213, 221–222, 246, 249, 253; imperial Confucianism in, 212; and Wang Mang, 228, 229; Yellow Turban revolt against, 252, 253
Hananiah, 304, 305
Handsome Lake movement, 43
Handwriting analysis, 30
Hanging Gardens of Babylon, 258
Harappa period, 177
Hardedef, 156, 171
Harem, sultan's, 458–460, 491n
Hariṣeṇa, 185
*Harname*, 514–515
Harold, 573
Harsa, King, 184, 192, 197
*Harṣacarita*, 185, 191
Harṣavardhana, 185
Hārūn al-Rashīd, 357, 359
Hattusas, 81–82
Hayreti, 511
Headhunters, tribe of, 34, 35
Hebrew texts, 126–128, 335
Hebrews, ancient, 16, 172
Hedonism, non-moral, 154, 155, 156–157
Hegira, 351
Hell and heaven, belief in, 198
Hellanicus, 275
Hellenistic states, 542; oracles in, 308, 313, 320, 322; prophets in, 326, 327, 328; view of ecstatic and political prophecy, 302, 303, 320
Hellenistic world, forms of communication in: coins, 277–278, 279; cuneiform writing, 51; participation in, 302; recitatio in, 285. *See also* Greece
Henry II, 574
Henry III, 564
Henry IV, 577, 580, 581
Henry V, 578
Henry VI, 564, 577, 578
Henry VII, 565–566, 578
Hepatoscopy, 89–90
Heracles, 272
Heralds, 28, 29, 52
Hermodorus, 297
Hermogenes, 298

Herodian, 272
Herodotus, 125, 171, 273–274, 285
Hesiod, 285
Heterodoxy, 92, 94, 541
Hezekiah, 127, 128, 138n, 309, 315
Hieroglyphic taboos, 24
Higbald of Lindisfarne, Bishop, 571
Hillgarth, J. N., 591n, 592n, 595n
Himalayas, 205
Hindu: caste structure, 191, 193, 374; culture in Bali, 36; doctrine, 198, 200; reformers, authority used by, 199; sanction of divine origin of king, 182; sects, rituals of, 363; states, 542, 545; use of Vedic hymns, 178; values, 180, 195
Hindu Kush, 205
Hipparchus, 273–274
Hippolytus, 340
Hishām, 356
Hiss, Alger, 26
*Historia Novella*, 584–585
Historiography, 405
Historiosophic compositions, 78, 108n
History, 2–4, 27; allusions to and divination, 90–91; in China, 207; in India, 207; intelligibility of, 345, 346; of mankind, in Old Babylonian epic, 56; meaning of, 127, 129; as reference for statesmen, 290; rewriting of, 29, 572, 593n
Hitler, Adolf, xii, 12
Hittīn, battle of, 368, 369
Hittite language, *narū* tales in, 82, 106n
Hittites, 69, 85, 102n, 164
Hizir Pasha, 513
*Hizmet*, 407
Hoca Tahir Efendi, 517
Hockett, Charles F., 21
Holmberg, Allan R., 24
Holy Cities, 485
Holy Land, Crusade to, 562
Holy Spirit, 333, 339
Homer, 290, 297, 298, 302
Horace, 257–258, 293, 294
Horns of Hittīn, 368
Horologists, 188–189
Horoscopes, 184
Horse, introduction of, 53, 96n
Hosea, 301, 310, 312, 315, 318, 322, 325, 328n
Hsiao Kung-chan, 242, 255n
Hsüan Tsang, 177
Hsüan-tsung, reign of, 246, 249–252
Huang-ti, the Yellow Emperor, 223
Hulāgu, 372
Humility and the Egyptian, 170
Hūnas, 185
Hu Shih, 207, 218n

Humanism: in poetry of criticism,
510–511, 513; in West, 14, 390
Hundred Years' War, 575, 586
Hungary, 454, 488, 490
Hunt, rituals of, 498
Hurufi sect, 510
Hus, John, 14
Husain, martyr of Shīca, 353–354, 363
Husrev, Molla, 403
Hussite revolt, 13
Hyksos, the, 163, 164
Hymns: royal, 118; in royal inscription,
115; sacred, 67–68, 100n; to Tiglath-
Pileser, 72, 101–102n; to Tukulti-
Ninurta, 70
Hyperbole, 285

Iatmul society, 26, 32, 34–36, 37, 39
Iberia, 558
Ibn Khaldūn, 371, 453
Ibn Rushd, 371
Iconography, 113, 202, 208
Ideologies, competing, 53
Ideology, unity of, 412. *See also* Im-
perial ideology
Idols, 333, 334
Ihsan, Ahmed, 417, 439n, 440n, 441n,
442n
Ihsani, Asik, 530
*Ikdam*, 406, 408
Ilkhamids, 447, 482
Illiteracy, 202, 276, 475
Imam, 365
Imhotep, 156, 171
Imperial: centers, 544–545; ideology,
221–222, 246; power, psychological
basis for, 271; propaganda, 241,
263–264; symbols, 548–549; system,
221–222, 546, 548–550
Imperial Council, Ottoman, 459,
461–465, 477, 491n; delegated powers
of, 463–465; replication of in prov-
inces, 483, 484; viziers in, 461–462,
465
Imperial Rescript, 226–228
Imperialism, 129, 131, 133
Impersonal pattern, preservation of,
36–38
Importation of institutions, 40
İnalcik, Halil, 386, 437n, 443n, 490n,
492n
Inanna, 67, 78, 104n, 105n
Incan empire, 26, 542
Incarnations, 207, 211–212
Incest, 37–38
Incorporation principle, Ottoman, 445
India, 36, 175–204; ancient, literature
of, 179, 196–197; apathetic ecstasy in,
320, 325; Christianity in, 342; in-
fluence on China, 205–207, 210; in-
fluence on Persia and Greco-Roman
world, 206; political structure, 545,
550; salvation, path to, 326, 327;
state use of superstition, 186–189. *See
also* Buddhism; Hindu
India, social orders of, 191, 195, 196,
200, 203–204; preserving, 191–194,
198–199, 203, 204, 588
Indians, North American, 43, 103n
Individual and community, 172
Individualism, 150, 153, 154, 162, 163,
165, 166
Indo-European literature, 180
Indo-European peoples, 175
Indo-Iranian culture, 208
Indoctrination, popular, 240–244
Indonesia, 36, 45
Indra, 182, 183
Industrial revolution, English, 397–398,
420
Inequities, 192, 211–212, 514–515, 518,
521–522
Information: accumulation of, 537;
bearers of types of, 541; control of,
430, 540; dissemination of in early
Mesopotamia, 52–53, 139n. *See also*
Knowledge
Initiation ceremonies, 35, 39
Innocent III, Pope, 579
Innovation, process of, 541
Innovation among the Arapesh, 38–39
İnönü, Ismet, 519
Inscriptions, 75, 103n, 177–178, 185,
285–287; apochryphal, 76–77, 80–81,
83, 108n; building, 118–119; Bull-
inscription, 142–143n; as communication to subjects, 189–190; form and
style of, 76, 116, 124; formal
dedicatory, 115–116, 140n; as
historical evidence, 71, 117–118, 120,
123; of King Aśoka, 181, 184, 185,
189–190, 201; as literary genre,
116–118; royal, 51, 103n, 117, 229;
as temple weapon, 83; themes of, 57,
59, 72, 115, 121–123, 185–186, 192;
votive, 190
Inspiration, auditive character of, 321
Integration: commercial and urban, 390;
of values and behavior of elite, 445;
vertical to horizontal, 383
Integrity, 584–585
Intellectual: alienation of the, 506–507;
criticism, control of, 537, 538; ferment in China, 209–210; reorientation, 522–532
Intelligence gathering, 136, 488, 489; as
function of royal inspection, 248,
251–252

Intelligentsia, 415–417, 427, 545;
changing social values and literary
genres, 393, 417–418, 419; and com-
munication changes, 382, 423;
replacement of literati by, 383, 415;
Russian, 417; Westernized, 382, 421
Intermarriage, ceremonious act of,
267–268
Intermediary political control, 475, 477,
478
Intermediate cultures, 205, 206, 208
Intoxicants, prophets' curse on, 323–324
Invention, process of, 541
Investiture controversy, 586, 594n
Ionian philosophers, 291
Iran, 352–353, 359–360, 368, 372,
377n, 542; law of, 356; state religion
of, 354
Iranian: conversion of educated to Islam,
356, 359; secretary class, 358–359;
sects, rituals of, 363
Iraq, 352, 366
Irish Republican Army, 364
Iron technology, 201–202
Isaiah, 301, 318, 335; calling of, 326; in
ecstatic state, 318, 319; form of
prophecies, 322; Immanuel prophecy
of, 312; as pamphleteer, 299–300;
political views of, 306, 309, 312, 314;
relation to Jerusalem priests, 314; on
sacrifice, 316–317; social origins of,
309
Isaiah, Book of, 134, 138n
Ishbi-Erra, King, 61
Ishme-Dagan, 64
Ishtar, 75, 87, 103n, 105n
Isidore, 563
Isin dynasty, 56, 61, 63, 65, 67, 79,
98n, 99n
İskit, Server, 410, 437n, 438n, 439n,
440n, 442n
Islam, 16, 348–380, 545; as basis for
ʿAbbāsid authority, 357; chasm between upper and folk variety of,
391–392; conversion to, 352–353,
451, 465, 499, 523; dissemination of,
xiii, 362, 532, 533; meaning of, 352,
375, 377n; militant secessionist
movements within, 364; revival of,
526–527; scriptures of, 364–365;
values of as basis for Ottoman system,
455–456
Islamic: art as communication, 355;
community, 351–352, 353; culture,
388–389, 395–396, 426, 431, 503,
546; doctrine, inculcation of, 362;
education, 388–389, 391–392; empire, social diversity within, 357–364;

faith and ruling classes, 375, 455,
499, 505; literature, 404, 503, 522;
mysticism, 507; -Persian language,
359; religious establishment, 376,
466, 481; sciences, 378n, 433n, 451;
society, 348, 357, 372, 375, 379–
380n; values, 371, 376, 408, 456,
503, 509; view of Crusades, 367–368
Islamic Law, 358, 377n, 385; Doctors of,
384, 389, 391, 395, 432n, 433n
Isocrates, 292
Isolation, preservation of, 40
Israel: Christian mission in, 330, 331;
literature of, 299; political policies,
300, 313–314, 328n; prophecy in,
300, 302, 305–306, 320; workaday
ethic of, 327–328
Israelite Confederation, 299, 300
Istanbul, 427, 446–447, 488, 518; as
communication center, 484, 485, 487,
490; ecumenical patriarchs in, 478,
479; intragovernmental relationships
at, 483, 484; publishing in, 403, 404,
416
Italy, 342, 366, 490, 564
Ithaca, 302
Itur-Ashdu, 90
İz, Fahir, 431n, 432n, 434n
Izmir, 427–428
Izzet Molla, 496, 515–516

Jacobsen, Thorkild, 59, 60, 96n, 97–98n
Jacopone da Todi, 580–581, 594n
Jade Gate, 208
Jainism, 193, 199; literature of, 184,
199, 204
Janissaries, 451, 452–453, 481, 512
Japan, 20, 550
Jatakas, 199
Javanese aristocracy, immigrant, 36
Jehu, 310, 320
Jeremiah, 108n, 305, 316, 317, 329n;
capital trial, 311, 314–315; conflict
with priests, 309–310, 314–315;
criterion of true prophet, 327; on
Deuteronomy, 315–316; in ecstatic
state, 318, 319; form of prophecies,
300, 301, 304, 321, 322; life of, 309,
311, 318, 325, 326; and politics, 299,
306–307, 308; relation to kings, 303,
306, 312, 313, 314
Jeroboam II, King, 301, 303
Jerome, 296, 563
Jerusalem, 314, 368; conquests of,
127–128, 129, 304–305, 308, 319,
333, 368, 559; prophecy in, 300, 301,
303; seductions of for Crusaders, 560,
562; as spiritual center, 315, 556, 567

Jerusalem, Temple of, 315–316
Jesus, 104n, 559; in art, 266–267, 564; in Cargo Cults, 43; communication of, 331, 563; the historical, 348; as mediator between God and man, 374; as messiah, 333, 334–335; ministry of, 330–332
Jews, 290, 350; and Christian mission, 330–331, 332, 341; Exile of, repression of prophecy during, 300; in Muslim empire, 356, 479
Joan of Arc, 577
Jocelin of Brakelond, 583, 594n, 595n
John, 324, 332
John of Salisbury, 555, 590n
Johnson, Samuel, 398, 532
Johnson cult, 43
Joiakim, King, 303, 305, 312
Joinville, Jean of, 566, 583, 595n
Jourdain, M., 291
Journalism, Turkish: circulation of, 406–407; content of, 416–417; emigré, 423; free-floating, 415; genres of, 494, 524; history of, 405–408; recruiting of, 414, 415; as social mobilizer, 416, 421
Judah: god of, 127, 128, 129; prophecy in, 301, 313, 315, 317
Judaism, xiii, 299–329, 333–334, 372
Judea, 283–284, 538–539
Judges: duties of, 189, 448; poetic denunciation of, 513; training of, 387
Judgment Day, 350
Judgment of the deceased, 160–161
Julian, 295–296
Julius Caesar, 263, 268–269, 293, 297, 298, 360
Julio-Claudians, portraits of, 265–266
Justice: demand for in Old Kingdom, 162; meaning of in Middle Kingdom, 158, 161–162; in pre-Islamic epic, 504. *See also* Social justice
Justinian, 258, 271
Juvenal, 271

*Ka*, the, 149, 150, 154–156, 161, 168
Kaadiri sect, 510
Kaliṅga war, 185
*Kāma*, attainment of, 194
Kāmandaka, 194
K'ang-hsi, Emperor, 241–242
Kanik, Orhan Veli, 519–520, 535n
Kaniśka, 208
Kantorowicz, Ernst, 566–567, 592n, 594n
Kanuni Süleiman, 508
Karal, 424, 439n, 440n, 441n, 442n, 443n

Karatay, Fehme Ethem, 438n, 440n
Karma accumulation, 211–212, 247
Kashtiliash IV, 69, 70–71
Kassite dynasty, 69, 70–71, 75, 85, 95, 96n, 100–101n
Kathā system, 195
*Kathāsaritsāgara*, 195
Kâtip Çelebi, 386, 389, 390, 432n, 434n
Kātyāyana, 194
Kauṭilya, 180, 186–189, 202, 204n
Kaygusuz Abdal, 516
Kees, Weldon, 22
Kemalism. *See* Atatürkism
Kempe, Margery, 555, 578, 583, 589, 593n
Kent, England, laws of, 569
*Kharāj*, 352–353
Khufu-onekh, 147
King, 58, 61–62, 64–73, 88, 98n, 569–572; aversion to title of, 98n, 135; and Buddhism, 208, 211, 213–214; denotation of, 96n; divinity of, 115, 116, 122, 142–143n, 144, 181–186, 188–189, 197, 204; functions of, 65, 191, 194, 204, 223; future as audience of, 118, 141n; glorification of, 67–69, 73, 115, 116–117, 120–121, 124; great, defensive alliances against, 34; and high officials, 135; obeisance of to patron deity, 86, 107n; power of, 112–114, 135, 181–186, 188–189, 204, 566–567; relation to prophets, 311–313; responsibility for defeat, 66–67; restraints on, 54–55, 57, 58; restrictions on knowledge, 537–538; role as mediator between gods and man, 82, 223–224; as secular authority, 52, 54, 58–59, 96n, 123, 150, 191, 194, 204; self-predication of, 116; services of, 134, 136, 184–186; as protector of people, 57–58, 123, 134. *See also* Emperor
King, communication of: with enemies, 119–123, 133–134; with god, 143–144n; with subjects, 52–53, 125, 134, 189–191
King Berra, 43
King lists, 59–63. *See also* Sumerian Kings List
King of the Four Regions, 60, 61, 62
Kings, Book of, 108n, 138–139n
Kingship: attributes of, 96n, 566, 568, 570, 574, 575, 587; communication of, 111–112; divine patrimony of, 99n; institution of, 111, 154, 569; prophets' quarrel with, 310, 311–312,

327; Roman interpretation of, 574; single legitimate, ideology of, 59, 60, 62, 63
Kish, 78, 80, 98n, 105n, 106n
Knight, propagandized figure of, 588–589
Knowledge: access to, 382, 538; attitudes toward, 388–391, 433n; authoritative, religiously grounded, 389, 390; class restrictions on, 384, 388, 411, 431, 540; control of, 390, 431, 538,539; production of, 59, 405, 548; propagation of, 386–387, 390, 411, 414, 433n; specialized types of, 537–539, 541
Kobelen, village of, 39
Komindimbit, village of, 39
Köroglu, 510
Koran, 41, 385, 393, 478, 522. *See also* Qur'an
Kramer, S. N., 97n, 99n, 100n, 104n
Kremlin, 458
Kṛṣṇa, 192
Kshatriyas, 176, 191, 192, 195, 196
Kubera, 183
Kurdish sheikdoms, 485
Kurigalzu, King, 75
Kuṣāṇa kings, 181, 183
*Kutadgu Bilig,* 504–505, 522

Lacedaemonians, 129
Lactantius, 334, 336
Laenas, C. Popillius, 268
Lagash, 66, 98–99n, 99–100n, 107n; kings of, 62–63, 65, 98n, 99n, 103n
Lambert, W. G., 93, 97n, 101n, 105n, 107n, 110n, 140n, 141n
Lakṣmī, 183
Lancaster, house of, 566, 577, 578, 585
Land: charters, 190, 198; grants, 75, 103n, 192–193; reclamation, 215
Langer, Susanne, 497
Language, 6, 41, 479, 498–499, 582–583; learning foreign, 203, 489; literary, 384; origin of, 31, 257; among primitive peoples, 23; reform in Turkey, 393, 416, 422, 435n, 502, 522. *See also* Official language
Lao-tzu, 231, 243, 249
Lapidus, Ira Marvin, 375, 380n, 491n, 492n
Larsa dynasty, 61–62, 79, 98n
Latin: alphabet, 502; grammar, 394; as international language, 435n; replacement of by vernaculars, 14–15; Silver, 285
Latin Christianity, 374; literature of, 342
*Laudes regiae,* 566–567
Law: books, ancient Indian, 179, 191,

192, 193, 198; codification of in China, 239; as Islam's religious science, 379n; Mesopotamian "codes," 65; of Muslim empire, 355–356; old English, 569, 571; Ottoman printing on, 403, 404; pre-Islamic customary, 359; as responsibility of religious establishment, 465, 466; sacred, instruction in, 366; school, Ottoman, 412. *See also* Islamic law
Learned institution, 389, 426. See also *Ulema*
Learning: access to, 394–396; capacity, 31; centers of, 548; institutions, Islamic, 379n; in medieval speech, 562; parade of in *recitatio,* 285; traditions based on, 538–539
Lebanese Republic, 375
*Lectisternium,* 274
Legislation of Muhammed, 355–356
Legitimacy, 53, 54–55, 271, 361, 399, 489, 547; elites' support of, 224, 225–230, 454, 466; of kings, 60, 62, 63–64, 104n, 120–121, 228, 229, 232–234, 247; of prophets, 318, 325–326; symbols of, 213, 221, 387, 414, 426–427
Lenin, Nikolai, 365, 527
Letter, open, prophecy as, 304
Letters: in classical civilization, 289–290; in England, 578; in Pelagian controversy, 295–296; among primitive peoples, 41
Levant coast, 368, 372
Levend, Agâh Sirri, 432, 434n, 435n
Levite exhortation, 309, 310
Levite Torah, 326–327. *See also* Torah
Lewis, Bernard, 377n, 378n, 379n, 432n, 440n, 491n
Lewis, P. S., 586, 593n, 595n
Li Yüan, 235
Libanius, 295
Libel of English Policy, 578
Libertarian mysticism, 510
Libraries: at Alexandria, 297; for bureaucrats, 402, 438n; private, 297, 434n; public, development of, 297; suppression in, 298
Libyans, 164
Life, appreciation of, 170–171
Life as illusion, 207
Linton, Ralph, 43
Lipit-Ishtar, 56, 65
Lisbon, siege of, 561–562
Literacy, 13, 14–15, 16–17, 53, 276, 441n, 585; in Manus, 41, 42; spread of, 240, 241, 413, 438n
Literati, 80, 105n, 220, 252, 388, 399,

414; concept of, 441n; and modernization of communication, 390, 400, 437n; and power structure, 221-222, 223, 241, 251, 387, 414, 415; salons of Ottoman, 414-415; values of, 224, 418. *See also* Elite
Literature, 12, 291-296, 522, 556-558; classical, 442n; genres of, 80, 140-141n, 383, 495; mythological and epical, 56-57, 102n, 104n; oral, 194-195, 285, 500; popular, 199, 204, 394-395, 418-420, 441n; semibiographical, 185-186; and technology, 202. *See also* Divan literature; Folk literature
Litterateurs, 416, 417, 443n
Livery, propaganda of, 565
Livia, 283
Livy, 274, 294, 298
Logic, ancient Indian, 177
Logos, 364
Lomax, Alan, 23
Louis VII, 566; Crusade of, 582, 583
Louis IX, 566, 567, 568
Louis of Toulouse, bishop, 564
Love ideals, domesticated, 39
Love poems, neoclassical, 518
Loved one in Divan literature, 507-508, 509
Loyalties, cross-cutting of, 36
Lucullus, 297
Ludi Saeculares, ceremonies of, 270-271
Lugalannemundu, King, 76, 103n
Lugalzagesi, King, 66-67, 99-100n, 107n
Luther, Martin, 13, 15
Lycée of Galatasaray, 411-412
Lyceum, work of the, 290
Lycurgus, 297
Lydia, 276
Lyrics, Turkish, 494, 501
Lysias, 292
Lysippus, 265

*Ma'at,* 158, 161
Macer, L. Clodius, 282
McFarlane, Charles, 392, 434n
MacLeish, Archibald, 504
McLuhan, Marshall, 30, 284, 298
*Madrasa,* 366, 367, 368, 369-370, 375, 379n. See also *Medrese*
Maecenas, 293
Magic as a force, 158, 168
Magical strategems, 189, 211
*Mahābhārata,* the, 179, 180, 183, 184, 196, 197
*Mahāyāna,* 181-182, 200
Mahmud of Kashgar, 500, 501, 535n
Mahmud II, Sultan, 384, 413, 432n

Mahremi of Tatavla, 502
Malherbe, Abraham J., 334, 347n
Malik Shah, 367
Mallarmé, Stéphane, 532
Mamlūks, 372, 374-375
Ma'mūn, al-, reign of, 357-358, 377n
Man: independence of, 150-151; purpose of, 97n; relation of to God, 526
Manasseh, King, 301, 312
Manchus, 241, 255n
Manegold of Lautenbach, 580, 581
Manifesto: of Chu Yüan-chang, 235-236, 255n; as form of propaganda, 234-237, 252
Manipulations, symbolic, 228, 230-232
Manishtusu, 74, 79; Cruciform monument of, 74-75
Mansfield, John, 531
Mansium, 77, 106n
Manu, law books of, 182, 191, 192, 193, 194
*Manu Smṛti,* 182
Manus people, 26, 27, 41-42, 44
Mao Tse-tung, 30, 100n; distribution of works of, 255n; memorization of Sayings of, 240
Maori, 29
Maps in Middle Ages, 555-556. *See also* Geography in Ottoman Empire
Marat, 18
Marduk, 75; autobiography of, 84-88, 95, 108n, 109n; cultic statue of, 69, 85, 95, 110n; priesthood, 86-87, 100n; supremacy of, 92, 93-94, 109n
Margaret, Queen, 555
Mari, kingdom of, 98n; archives of, 54-56, 97n, 101n, 106-107n, 108n; banquets in, 141n; diviners in administration, 90; palace of, 139n
Maritime knowledge, Ottoman, 489-490
Market controller, 471-472
Market for print, 14, 15, 17, 579
Markets as communication centers, 471-472, 474, 480
Maronites, 375
Martin, Saint, 556
Martin of Braga, 563, 564
Martin of Tours, 567
Marx, Karl: proletariat communication network, 397; view of art, 497
Marxism, millennium in, 44
Mass influence, emotional, 325, 326
Mass media. *See* Media
Mass movements, 209-210, 224
*Mas'ūl,* 373
Material culture, 45
Material world, contempt for, 344-345
Materialism, 158, 528
Matrilineal groups, 34

Matthew, gospel of, 331, 340, 563
Matthew of Janov, 14–15
Maurya, 181, 193, 542; kings, 186, 190, 201
Mausolus of Halicarnassus, 258
Mawlawi sect, 500
*Mawlids,* 522
Mecca, 349, 350, 351, 354
Media, 15–16, 382, 541; control of, 12–13, 382–383, 431; in fifteenth-century Europe, 577; modern, 18, 19; Ottoman expansion of, 402–408, 426, 429
Medicine: Buddhist use of , 211; Ottoman books on, 403
Medieval propaganda, Western, 552, 553, 554, 556, 558–564, 584–585, 586, 588, 589–590; changing use of, 575, 579–581, 583–586, 589, 594n; multimedia, 569–570, 572, 573–574, 586–587, 593n; reporting of, 589; transmission of, 554, 572, 574; wars of, 580–581
Medina, 350–351, 354, 355–356
*Medrese,* 387–388, 410, 435n
Megiddo, 304, 308
Mehmed the Conqueror, Sultan, 494, 508
Mehmet II, Sultan, 462–463
Mehmet Akif, 526–527
Melami sect, 510
Melian Dialogue, 128–129
Melos, 128–129
Memorization, 178, 179, 180, 340; enforced, 237–240, 252
Memphite Theology, 148, 157
Merchant clan in Mecca, 350
Merchant class, 361, 374
Mercia, 568
Merodach-baladan II, 138n, 143
*Mesnevis,* 513
Mesopotamia, 50–110, 139n, 148, 320; Christianity in, 342; cosmology of, 95; economy of, 56, 102n; expansionist policies of, 299; political structure of, 58–59, 78–79, 150, 307; reign of Nebuchadnezzar in, 86; uniting, 60, 62, 78–79
Message, 7, 27–28, 587–588, 589, 595n
Messenger: Muhammed as, 350, 374; reliance on human, 25–26
Messianic age, 317, 332, 333, 334–335
Messianic claims, 253
Mevlevi sect, 510
Micah, 304, 315, 322
Microanalysis, 30
Middle Ages, 552–595. *See also* Medieval propaganda, Western
Migration, mass, 209

Milíč, John, 14
Military: campaigns, 120, 486–487; class, 384, 448–449, 450, 454, 457, 466, 490n; commanders, 360, 363, 368, 373, 374–375; education, 385–386, 402, 403, 404, 409–410, 438n; justice, chiefs of, 466, 468; machine, 399, 424, 486; posts, 472, 480; rule, 209, 261, 361, 362; strategy, 122, 143n, 400, 436n; victory and defeat, 60, 70, 271; Western influence, 400, 436n, 489
Military Academy, 409, 410, 411, 412
Military Medical School, 409, 411, 412
Military preparatory school, 410, 411, 412
Millennial hope of primitive culture, 43–45
Millennialist: rebel propaganda, 253; traditions of Buddhism, 217
Millet system, 396–397, 436n
Milo, 271
*Mimāmsā,* 177
*Mimesis,* 497
Mimetic behavior, 22
Ming dynasty, 235, 239, 241, 252, 255n
Minotaur, myth of, 275
Minstrels, Ottoman, 495
Miracles as propaganda, 567
Mirrors of Princes, 537
Missionaries: Buddhist, 208, 210–211; Christian, 338, 340. *See also* Christian missions
Mitanni Empire, 69, 101n
Mithradates of Pontus, 268
*Mizan,* 408
Mobility: medieval, 553–554; in Ottoman palace services, 457–458; restricted channels of, 540
Moieties, totemic, 34–35, 39
Mnemonic devices, 24, 25, 340
Modernization, Ottoman, 382–383, 422; and education, 394; poets as conveyors of, 495; of politics, 392–393; and printing, 403–404
Mogul empires, 542
Mohammed. *See* Muhammed; Prophet, the
Monasteries, 215, 217; investments of, 215
Monastic reformers, 570
Mongols, 239, 371, 372, 375, 568
Monk, propagandized figure of, 589
Monophysitism, 149
Monotheism, 149, 349; ethical, 332, 346
Montague, Ashley, 22
Monuments, 112, 113–114, 258, 265. *See also* Buildings; Sculpture
Mooney, James, 43

Moors and siege of Lisbon, 562
Moral: changes, 199–201, 204; exhorta-
  tions, 243; law, 327
Morality, 242, 346
Mortimer, 586–587
Moses, 324
Moslem. *See* Muslim
Mosque of Omar, 355
Mosques, 354–355, 474
Mosul, 101n, 368
Mount T'ai, 249, 250–251
Mountains, sacred, 249–251
Movable type, 16, 17. *See also* Printing
Movies, 19
Mowinckel, S., 140n
Muhammed, 320, 321, 349, 351, 354;
  as historic figure, 348–349; as
  messenger of God, 350, 374. *See also*
  Prophet, the
Muhiddin-i Arabi, 423
*Mukallaf,* 373
Mu-tawakkil, al-, 358
Multilingualism, 13–14
Munif Pasa, 413
Musaşir, 125, 133
Music, 23, 228, 385
Muslim: -Arabs, 351, 352; derivation of
  word, 377n; doctrine, 374, 378n; em-
  pire, administration of, 355–356;
  *millet,* 396; religious establishment,
  465–468, 491n; -Turkish schism, 510;
  -Turkish vassals, 376; unorthodox
  sects, 475, 480–482. *See also* Islam
Muslims, 582; as exploiting minority,
  354; and government recruitment,
  451, 452, 490n; in military class, 449
Mussolini, Benito, xii
Mustafa III, Sultan, 508
Mu'tasim, Caliph Al-, 360
Müteferrika, Ibrahim, 399, 438n
Myckiewicz, Adam, 525
Myers, A. R., 590n, 591n, 592n, 593n,
  595n
Mystagogues, vaticinating, 302
Mystic experience, traditions based on,
  538
Mystic poetry, Ottoman, 506–509;
  subversive nature of, 510; tone of,
  507, 508, 509
Mysticism, literature of, 395, 396, 441n
Myth: of origin or migration, 27:
  political use of, 275–276; reliability of
  as source, 57
Mythography, patriotic, 276

Nabonidus, King, 59, 100n, 119
Nabopolassar, Chaldean dynasty of, 95
Naham, 322
Nālandā, university of, 177

Namik Kemal, 415, 418, 419, 441n,
  496, 517, 524, 525
Nanking, 232–233
Nārada, a lawgiver, 191, 192
Naram-Sim, 60, 77–78, 80–81, 105n; in
  *naru*-literature, 81–82, 87, 91, 106n,
  108n; omens for, 80, 91, 109n;
  polemic against, 79, 80, 91; use of
  divine determinative by, 80
Narrative, first-person, 76
*Narū*-literature, 81–83, 87, 106n, 140n
Nāsir, Caliph Al-, 372
Nation, concept of English, 569–570
National: consciousness, 60, 422; unity,
  274
Nationalism, 14, 95, 165, 397, 440n,
  495, 498, 527, 579, 589
Nativistic cults, 42–45
Naturalism, 423
Naval Engineering School, 409
Naval science, 391
Nazarites, 312, 314
Nazim Hikmet, 496, 518, 527–530
Nazimaruttash, 70
Nazism, xi, 12
Near East: geography of, 137n; shared
  hegemony over, 69
Nebiim, the, 312, 314, 323
Nebuchadnezzar I, 86–87, 95, 107n
Nebuchadnezzar II, 95, 315; conquest
  of, 305, 314; relation to Jeremiah,
  306; use of Yahwe believers' in-
  fluence, 308
Necho, 308, 328n
Necker, Jacques, 18
Nedim, 434n, 516, 523
Nef'i, 496, 500, 516, 517, 518
Neo-Assyrian Empire, 73, 87, 101n,
  106n
Neo-Babylonian period, 57, 74, 111–144
Neo-Melanesian, 41
Neoplatonism, 364
Neo-Taoist ideas, 211
Nero, 260, 283; coinage of, 279,
  281–282
Nero Drusus, 266
Nerva, 283
Nesati, 506–507
Nesimi, 420, 496, 516–517
New Guinea, 32, 33, 34, 40–41, 44, 45
New Testament, 290, 330, 332, 556
News, spread of, 284, 555
Newspapers, Ottoman, 404–405, 406,
  408; circulation of, 439n; privately
  owned, 405–406; Turkish, 407–408
Nike, 263
Nilsson, Martin, 273
Nimrod, 71
Nineveh, 92, 139n, 141n

Ningirsu, priesthood of, 66–67, 99–100n
Ninos, 71
Ninurta, temple of, 77
Nippur, holy city of, 57, 60, 61, 98n, 110n; excavation in, 104n; gods' building of, 94; kings of, 80, 106n; pillage of, 109n; primacy of, 94; scholarly community of, 61, 104n; temple organization of, 77–78, 104n
*Nirvāṇa,* 198
Nisaba, 67
Nizām al-Mulk, 367, 368, 370, 378n
Nizami of Edirne, 502
Nomadic values, 509
Nomads, 206, 470–471
Nomenclature, conferment of, 225–226, 228, 229, 233, 251
Nonelites: education of, 411; Ottoman coordination of, 468–482
Non-Muslim subjects, 352–353, 354, 356, 404–405, 438n, 475, 478–480, 490
Nonverbal behavior, 30, 31
Nonverbal communication, 31, 564–568
Norman Conquest, 573–574
North Africa, 352, 483, 485, 488
Novel: in Britain, 398; in Ottoman Empire, 418, 419; in *Tanzimat* period, 524
Nubia, 154, 375
Nūr al-Dīn, 368

Obedience, 167
Objects in communication, 23–26
Oceania, 43
Octavian, 293. *See also* Augustus
Odo of Deuil, 566, 573, 582, 592n, 594n
Offa, King, 566, 568
*Official Gazette,* 405, 415
Official style, Ottoman, 384, 391, 392–393, 394, 441n
Officials: control of, 442–443n, 488; desertion of, 125–126, 130, 131–133; duties of in India, 189–190; etiquette for Egyptian, 151–152; former, as journalists, 415; local, 234, 237, 241–244; Mesopotamian hierarchy of, 112, 137–138n; poetry critical of, 512, 513, 515–516; specialization of, 490–491; suspicion of, 318; training of, 384, 385, 386, 410, 448
Oguz Epic, 504, 522
Oktay Rifat, 519
Old chaos, 552, 590n
Old Testament, 121, 126–128, 134, 138–139n, 328n
Omar, 351, 352. *See also* ʿUmar

Omens, 58, 79, 80, 123
Onomacritus, 273–274
Opinion leaders, development of, 541. *See also* Public opinion
Oppenheim, A. Leo, 5, 97n, 99n, 100n, 103n, 105n, 108n, 109n, 111–144
Opportunity, circumscribed, 166
Oracles: in Hellenic states, 313, 320; during Israelite confederacy, 300–301; itinerant vendors of, 302; in political propaganda, 273–275; of prophets, 306, 310–311; as public event, 303. *See also* Delphi, oracle at
Oral communication, 10, 175–177, 284–285, 300, 301, 303, 304, 305
Oral examination for university admission, 177
Original sin, 380n
Origen, 334, 337, 338
Orosius, 569
Orphics, 302, 317–318, 326
Orthodoxy, 65, 224
Osiris, 151, 160–161, 329n
Osman, 454
Otho, 283
Ottar the Black, 570
Otto III, 573, 575
Ottoman Empire, 363, 375–376, 415, 416–417, 427, 505; administration, 399–400, 424, 542; communication in, 381, 383, 384–385, 391–393, 398, 430, 446, 448, 471–472, 474, 475; culture, 400, 404, 410–411, 412, 414, 416, 418, 422, 423, 447–448, 500; economic structure, 390–391, 396–398, 399, 430, 477; economy, foreign interest in, 427; education, 369, 389–390; history of, 348, 372, 410, 412, 453–454; knowledge in, 388, 390–391; language, 392–393, 413, 441n, 456; military machine, 399, 486; poetry on, 505, 510, 511, 513–518, 524; political system, 381, 383, 384, 402, 405, 408, 430, 444–447; population, 410, 440n; printing in, 400, 403–404, 437n; reform, 400–402, 413; religious establishment, 401; rulers/elites, 454, 457, 459, 499, 503, 509–510; size of, 446, 486; social structure, 374, 384, 396–397; understanding of outside world, 391, 423, 428, 434n, 488–490
Ou-Yang Hsiu, 210, 217, 219n
Ovid, 294
*Ozans,* 498

Paganism, 294–295, 349
Page, T. E., 293

Pageantry, 268, 565–567, 586–588
Paine, Thomas, 17
Palace. *See* Royal palace, fame of
Palace School, 385, 386, 388, 428–429
Palace services, 134, 136, 456–457, 457–458
Palatine, 260
Palermo, 360
Palestine, 341, 352
Pāli language, 199; canons, 179; texts, 195, 200
Palian, 44
Pallavas people, 193
Pamirs, the, 205
Pamphleteers, 299–300
Pamphlets: political, 292, 304; religious, 295–296
Pan Ch'ao, 207
*Pancatantra,* 194
Pāṇḍavas, 184
Pandyan king, 203
Panegyrics, 503–504, 505, 507–509
Panegyrists, 196
Pāṇini's grammar, 178, 179, 186
Pantheon, 260
Paper, use of, 579
Papua New Guinea, 41, 43
Papuan language, 33
Papyrus, surgical, 157
Paris, Matthew, 556, 580
Parliamentary institution, 563
Parthenon, 259, 263
Parthian Empire, 342, 542
Participation, 540; institutional, access to, 541; popular political, 13–15, 54, 382, 540
Past, editing the, 28. *See also* History, rewriting
Past as escape, 171
Pasternak, Boris, 497
Pastoral affairs in India, 176
Pastoral groups, 447, 470–471
Patanjali, 186
Path to the Great Peace, 253
Patrilineal clans, 33, 34
Patrimonial regimes, 383, 543, 544, 546
Patrimonialism, 384–385, 543
Patriotism, 61–62, 98n, 164
Patronage, 401
Paul, St., 332, 333–334
Paul the Apostle, 557
Peasants: and Buddhism, 211, 217; and the prophets, 311
Peasants' Revolt, 584
Pecok, Bishop, 578
Peisistratids, tyranny of, 302
Pelagian controversy, 295–296
Pelagius, 295–296

Peloponnesian War, 126–127, 128–129, 274
Penny press, 17
Pere village, 42
Pergamum, self-image of, 262
Pericles, 259, 265, 302, 558
Periodicals, publication of, 407, 439n
Periphery, 544, 545; relation to center, 546–547
Persepolis, 267
Persian, 53, 308; border, 485, 486; culture, influence of, 499, 522; Gulf as trade route, 366; language, influence of, 391, 392, 434n, 499; literature, 385, 500, 505, 509; pillage of Jerusalem, 559; politics, 300, 302; vocabulary borrowings, 456, 500, 502
Persuasion, 563; belief in efficacy of, 221; sermon as means of, 561–564; sultans' use of encomia as, 505; techniques of in China, 220–224
Pessimism, 155–157
Peter, bishop of Oporto, 561–563, 586, 588
Peter the Apostle, 332, 557
Petofi, Sanda, 525
Pfeiffer, John, 21, 23
Pharaohs, 153; divinity of, 145, 150, 160
Pharos of Alexandria, 258
Phidias, 258, 262–263
Philip IV of France, 580–581, 582, 594n
Phoenicia: Christianity in, 320, 341; Egyptian trade with, 154
Phoenicides, 259–260
Physicians, training of, 387
Pidgin English, 41
*Piers Plowman,* 579
Piety, acts of, 374
Pilgrimage: as medieval gesture, 554; places of, 473
Pindar, 291
Pir Mahmut, 512
Pisarev, D. I., 533–534
Pisistratus of Athens: actions as propaganda, 267; manufacture of own oracles, 273; use of myth, 275
Plato: and the academy, 303; dialogues, 196, 297; public performance of, 285
Platonists, 290
Plays: religious, 565–566; shadow, 513; vernacular, 578. *See also* Drama
Pliny, 575
Pluralism, development of, 537
Plutarch, 259, 274, 284
Poetry, 77–78, 159; of criticism and protest, 501, 504, 524–525, 533, 534; engaged, 519–520, 524, 530–531,

532–533, 534; as entertainment, 495; importance of in Turkish history, 496, 497–498, 504, 533–534; new genres, 422; in Ottoman high culture, 494–495; patriotic, 525; of pessimism, 155–156; political content, 504, 517–520, 520–522, 524–525; as propaganda, 502–503, 504, 522, 523, 533; as subjective or objective reality, 497; thaumaturgical function of, 498
Poets, 140n, 291; and dissemination of Islam, 503; as eulogists of kings, 116–117, 185–186, 503, 505; pre-Islamic tribal, 349; roles of in society, 495–496, 523, 524, 525–526, 527, 530, 531, 532; Turkish, manifesto of, 519–520
Poland, lesser nobility of, 490n
Polemic, 54, 359, 533; of kings, 59, 64; of temple, 59, 74, 76–77, 79, 83
Police forces, special, 487–488
Policy, social, 3, 4, 9, 264, 291
Political: authority, upholding, 53, 181–183, 197–198, 203, 384; communication, 28, 131–133, 449–450, 469–482; issues among the Arapesh, 33–34; management, 446, 491n, 544; movements, 44, 495–496; parties, and prophets, 306, 307–308; partisanship, 306–308; programs, 44, 310, 328n; revolution, 16–17, 164–166; systems, 111, 134–135, 221, 399, 543, 546
Political Science, School of, 410, 411, 412–413, 417
Polybius, 290, 292–293, 294
Polycrates, 292
Polynesia, 28
Polytheism, 333, 334, 336, 344, 350
Pompeii, election graffiti in, 287–288
Pompey, 271
Pompey's Theatre, 260
Pons Fabricius, 260
Pontus, 278
Pony express, 53
Population increase, effect of on indoctrination effort, 241
Porta Praenestina, 260
Portraiture, 265–267
Portuguese navigation, 391
Position as a value, 158, 166, 167
Positivism, 441n
Postal systems, Ottoman, 408, 409, 424; mail traffic in, 409
Posture, external, as propaganda, 553
Pottery, Turkish, 494
Poverty, view of, 194
Power: communication of, 112, 248, 267, 268; and competence, 460; consolidation of, 224–232, 239, 482; distribution, 29, 539; holders, and prophets, 303–304, 305, 313; nature of, 127, 128, 129; relations, 307, 386–387, 445, 461, 491n
Prajāpati, 181
Prākrit language, 185, 196, 199; commentaries on texts in, 179
Prayer leaders, training of, 387
Prayers, ritual daily, 354
Prayers for success in *samiti,* 176
Preaching: itinerant, 338–339; missionary, 334, 347n; postapostolic, 334–335, 347n; reformist, 13, 14
Prefectural capitals, 247–248
Pre-Homo sapiens, 30
Preliterate societies: coherence of, 32; editing the past in, 28; power distribution of, 29; validating a myth in, 27
Premack, David, 22
Press, the Turkish, 438n, 502. *See also* Journalism, Turkish
Priests: and astrology, 197; attacks on rulers, 66–67, 78, 99–100, 105n; divining powers of, 197–198; of Egypt, 170–171; eulogies of rulers by, 184–185, 196; and land charters, 190; literature of, 196, 202, 203; and nationalism, 95; oracles of, by lot, 300; propaganda of, 94–95, 197; prophets' relationship to, 314–316, 318; ritual primacy of, 194
Primitive communities, 23, 31
Princes of ancient India, 189–191; political education of, 180
Printing, 13, 289, 397, 578–579; history of in Ottoman Empire, 390, 399, 401, 402–405, 437n; invention of, 16–18, 240, 296–297; in Rome, 297–298
Private communication, 337–338
Proletarian cause in literature, 527–528
Propaganda: anonymity in, 290; of competition and defense, 575; definitions of, 4, 5, 7, 51, 53–54; effectiveness of, 84, 365, 583–584, 589; etymology of, 257; in literature, 69–72, 91–92, 291–296; modernity of, 15, 579; promotional, 202; -within-propaganda, 556–558; role of in technology development, 202; use of by dissidents, 199–201, 224, 252–254, 292. *See also* Medieval propaganda, Western
Property: private, 203–204; sanctity of, 193–194; as a value in Egypt, 152, 156, 157, 158, 166, 167

Prophecy: apochryphal, 87; classical, 299, 320–321; divine, 83–88; form of, 84–86, 304, 321–322, 323; free, 301, 314; industry of, 310; interpretation of, 321–323, 329n; of Jesus, 331, 333, 350; as literary genre, 80, 83–84, 88; from mass influence, 323–324, 329n; oracular, 87; poetry of, 322; political, in Hellenic states, 302–303. *See also* Oracles

Prophet, the, (Muhammed) 350; dictation of Qur'ān by, 358; divine revelations of, 355–356; emphasis on Friday midday prayers, 354; kinship with, 353, 356, 358; life of, 503, 522; religious community of, 478; rule of equity of, 353; succession of, 361, 503

Prophets: attacks on, 303–304, 315; background of, 309, 317–318, 363; Christian, 335, 338–339, 343–344, 350; ecstatic states of, 318–319, 320–321, 322–323, 325, 328n; independence of, 310–311; Jeremiah's criterion for, 327; of king, 300–301, 310, 314; message of, 301, 310–318; political orientations of, 299–302, 305–306, 307, 308, 309–310; psychology of, 318–328; public appearance of, 301, 302–303, 305, 324, 325; relations with kings, 301, 303–308, 313; religious motivation of, 301–302, 307, 308, 314; self-legitimation of, 326; sources of support for, 311–312

Propylaea, 259–260

Prose: development of Turkish, 495; psychological analyses in, 422, 423; style, 178– 179, 291

Protest: in poetry, 497, 504, 506; public, 56–57; terms for, 59, 97n

Protestantism, 16, 207

Provinces: in collapse of Egyptian Old Kingdom, 153–154; communication with, 234–235, 483–486, 487–488, 580; effect of slave system on power of, 452; officials of, 139n, 484, 485; ritual enactments in, 244, 245–248; toleration of variety in, 485–486

Psalms, 335; First, 167; Twenty-third, 97n

Pseudochronicles, Babylonian, 88

Psychological warfare, xi, 254n

Psychopathic states, holiness of, 320

Ptah, 169

Ptolemies, the, 320

Public notices, 25

Public opinion, 54–58, 64, 97n; defined, 32, 38; importance of among primitive peoples, 33–34, 35–36, 36–37; mobilization of, by media, 408; restraints of, 54–55, 97n

Public well-being, 57–58, 59

Punic population, 342

Punic Wars, 274

*Purāṇas,* 179, 193, 195, 196, 197, 198, 201

Puzur-Sin, King, 64

Pyramid Age, 150

Pyramids, 258

Pythagoras, 302–303, 326

Pythia, 323

Quakers and prophecy, 329n

Quasimodo, 532

*Quipu,* 26

Qur'ān, the, 349, 358, 362; decorative repetition of phrases from, 355; God's relation to man in, 373; government based on, 357; as guide to righteous living, 353; legislation for social justice in, 355–356; verses from, on Byzantine art, 354. *See also* Koran

Rabbis, 311

Rabirius, 261

Radio, 18, 19, 20, 29–30, 40

Railroads, 409, 442n

Raine, Angelo, 565–566, 592n

Rāma, horoscope of, 184

Rāmacandra, King, 183

*Rāmāyaṇa,* 179, 180, 183, 184, 193, 196–197

Ramsey, Paul, 497

Rē, 161, 163

Reading: aloud, 285; relation to writing, 41

Realism in prose, 422–423

*Rebabname,* 500

Rebellion, in divination literature, 58

Rebirth, belief in, 198, 214

Rechabites, 310, 317; Puritan, 326

*Recitatio,* 285

Recitation of Vedic texts, 180

Record of Rites, 223

Records, 100n, 177–178; of events, 28, 124; of India, 177–178, 206–207; keeping of, in China, 206–207, 224; in Ottoman political system, 446, 461; preservation of, 288–289; purposes of, 68–69, 100n, 425

Recruitment, 544; of Ottoman staff, 385, 386; of native-born Moslems, 490n

Red Sea, 366

Reform, social, and role of poets, 495–496, 523, 524–531

Reform edicts, 56, 57–58
Reform text of Urukagina, 65–67, 73
Reformation, 13, 17, 579, 589–590
Reformist preaching. *See* Preaching, reformist
Regimes, anomalous, 485
Registers of Important Affairs, Ottoman, 491n
Relationships with others, 21–22, 166–167
Relics, 567, 573
Religion: popular, in China, 216–217; precepts of, adjustments to, 585; rules of, 190; search for support of, 171; sociology of, 311; state, 342–343, 354
Religions, world, xiii, 16, 545
Religious: assemblies, 176–177; assurance, need for, 344, 346; community, 323–324, 329n, 351, 478; establishment, 395, 465, 466–468; imperialism, 93; law, 310, 387; learning, 387, 390, 537; literature, 72, 80, 179–181, 403, 503, 522; movements, popular, 210; minorities, system of, 479–480; observances, 27, 187, 192–193, 216, 351; officials, 396, 433n, 454; personnel, training of, 387–388, 432n; political value of, 263–264; primacy, transfer of, 94–95, 110n; propaganda, 187–188, 284, 370, 563–564; reform, 14–15, 16, 127–128, 274; symbolism, 388, 548; tolerance, of conqueror, 308
Relocations after conquest, 120, 142n
Remigius, baptism of, 567
Renaissance, Western, 14, 15, 222, 390
Replication of form, 483–484
Representations, manipulation of, 220–224, 224–228, 229
Reputation, concern for, 155
*Res Gestae Divi Augusti,* 286
Resources, control and distribution of, 538
Re-Turkification, 502
Revenge, medieval, 561
Revolts, popular, Buddhist-inspired, 217
Revolution, *Tanzimat* poets' call for, 524–530
*Rg Veda,* the, 176, 180, 191, 193
Rhetoric: patterns of medieval, 553; and *recitatio,* 285; royal, 65–66
Rhone Valley trade routes, 342
Richard II, 565
Richard III, 578
Richard I the Lion-Hearted, 582
Richard of Devizes, 582–583, 594n
Richardson, Samuel, 398
Riding, Laura, 497

Rimush, 79
Rites, disappearance of, 35
Ritual: devaluation of, 316–317; enactments, 244–252, 570; primacy, 194; traditions based on, 538
Roads, 408–409, 424, 440n, 554
Robert of Gloucester, 585
Robert the Monk, 558, 559, 562, 582
Robert the Pious, 575
Robert the Wise of Naples, King, 564
Roe, Ann, 21
Roelker, Nancy L., 13
Rolle, Andrew, 5
Roman: aqueducts and roads, 261; city-states, 545; expression of achievement, 268–269; federation, concept of, 373; imperialism, 271; literature, 12; myth, invention of, 275–276; monuments, 258–259; propaganda, 258–259, 278, 576; settlements in India, 202–203; temples of kings, 183; trade, 202–203; values, 293
Roman Catholicism, 16, 257
Roman Empire, 375, 542, 575; and Christianity, 320, 339, 342–344; coinage of, 278, 279
Romanian principalities, 485
Romanians, 479
Rome, 261, 555, 567; book trade in, 297–298; Christianity in, 342, 345; goddess, 264; in Jubilee Year, 554; propaganda of, 581–582, 583; public buildings in, 260–261; public records in, 289; Republican, patricians in, 543
Romulus and Remus, 264, 276
Rotation in office, 483, 484–485
Rouen, 567
Roxelana, 459
Royal: budget, 18; bureaucracy, tyranny of, 65, 66; duties, 180; names, 116, 140n; palaces, fame of, 114, 139n; position, self-defined, 568; posts relays, 555; privileges, 114, 135, 139n; progress, 244, 248–252; propaganda, 58–59, 69–73, 79, 142–143n, 184–185, 573–574; testaments, 65, 102n; titularies, 115, 116; treasury, 113–114, 138–139n, 186–187. *See also* King
Ruesch, Jurgen, 22
Ruhsati, 518
Ruhi of Baghdad, 512–513, 515
Rules for Subjects, 239
Ruling class, 544, 545. *See also* Elite
Rumi, Mawlana Djalal al-Din, 500
*Rusdiye,* 410, 411
Russia: role of poet in, 530–531; *samiz-*

*dat* literature in, 528–529; the university in, 417
Ryle, Gilbert, 285

*Sabah,* 404–405, 406, 408
Sabbath, observance of, 316
*Sabhā,* 175–176
Sacred Edict, 241–243
Sacred numbers, 317
Sacrifice, 207, 216, 316–317
Safavi Iran, 375
Saharan tribes, 470–471
Said Pasha, 408–409, 416, 435n, 441n
St. Paul's Cathedral, 258, 564
St. Sophia, 258
Saints, converting, 567
Saints, pantheon of Buddhist, 208
Śaivas, 204
Śaivite Purānas, 196
Śakas people, 193
Salāh al-Dīn, 368–369, 371, 375
Salih Efendi (Hekimbasi), 417
Salisbury Oath, 573
Sallust, 261
Salonika, 427
Salvation, 331; path to, 326–328, 332
Samarqand, 360
Sami Pasa, 415
*Samiti,* 175, 176
Samoa: ceremonies in, 25; letter writing in, 41; official heralds in, 28, 29
Samson, Abbot, of Bury, 579–580, 583
Şanizâde Ataullah, 386–387
Sanskrit, 190, 196, 199, 203; literature in, 179, 193–194
Santa Maria Maggiore, 585
*Śānti Parva,* 180, 182–183, 191
Saphan, 306
Sargon of Akkad, 74, 77, 78–79, 99n, 104n, 105n, 107n; as subject of *narū*-literature, 81, 87, 108n
Sargon II, 113, 133, 142n, 143n; letter of, 124–125, 131, 143n; palace decorations of, 113–114
*Sarim,* 313
Sartach, 568
Sassanid empire, 542
*Śāstrārtha,* 177
*Śatapatha Brāhmana,* 181
Sātavāhana ruler, 183, 192
Satire, 513, 514–518
Savior-king, 85–86
Say, J. B., 403
Sayings of Mao, 240
Sayings of the Seven Wise Men, 285
Scaurus, 271
Schacht, Joseph, 376, 377n, 378n, 380n

Scholar-jurists, 373. See also *Ulema*
Scholiasts, 179
Schools, Ottoman, 382, 410, 417; intermediate, 410; and mathematics, 409; middle, 440n; normal, 410; primary, 393, 394, 410; secondary, 410; for training of officials, 384, 385–386. *See also* Education; Trades School, Ottoman
Schools, medieval municipal, 394
Schools, use of for propaganda purposes, 240–241
Schwartz, Theodore, 28, 43, 44, 45
Science, 2, 423; applied to communication analysis, 3–4; books on, published by Ottomans, 402–403, 404; compendium of, 361; Egyptian achievements in, 148, 157; natural, 360–361; suspicion of, 361
Sciences, Ottoman Academy of, 416
Scientific Society, Ottoman, 413
Scipionic circle, 292
Scribal: activities, 384–385; centers, 74; class, 386, 390, 400–401, 432n, 437n; code, 386; protocol, 385, 432n; schools, 51, 59, 116
Scribes, 124–125; competition among, 116–117; historic traditions of, 117; literary discretion of, 115–116; number and competency of, 437n
Script, 40, 41
Scrope, Richard, archbishop of York, 577–578
Sculpture, 157, 162, 202, 262–264
Sea exploration, 16
Sea Peoples, threat of to Egypt, 164
Sea routes, 554
Sects, unorthodox, 510
Secularism, 526, 527
Security, psychosis for, 163–164
Seer, Homeric, 302. *See also* Prophets
Seibert, Ilse, 143n
Seleucid dynasty, 101n, 277–278
Self-government, right of, 15
Self-help groups, protective, 363–364
Self-immolation, 43
Self-instruction, secular, 390
Self-reliance, 150, 168
Selim I, Sultan, 480–481, 486, 508, 511
Selim III, Sultan, 432n, 438; as poet, 508; reforms of, 384, 437n
Selim Nuzhet [Gerçek], 400, 437n, 439n
Seljuq sultanate, 366–367, 368, 372, 379n; patronage to *'ulāma,* 371; techniques of, 447, 482; unity, dissolution of, 367, 370
Semachiah, 300

Semaphoring, 24
Şem'i Efendi, 395
Semitic Dynasty of Akkad, 98n
Semitic names, kings with, 98n
Senatorial responsibility, illusion of, 264
Seneca, 282, 283, 285
Sennacherib, 101n, 110n, 127, 306, 307
Separatism, 153, 412
Serbs, 479
Serdari, 518
Sermon of the Wolf to the English, 571
Sermons: Franciscan, 579; as instrument
    of propaganda, 558, 563–564, 571;
    on Koran, 436n; mosque, 421; po-
    litical, 395–396, 580; undelivered,
    563, 591n. *See also* Peter, bishop of
    Oporto; Urban II; Wulfstan
*Servet-i Funun,* 417
Servet-i Funun school, 422, 441n
Services, public, 424, 430
Seven Wonders of the World, 258
Severan dynasty, 262
Severus, 259, 284
Sex distinction in directing propaganda,
    588–589
Seyh Galib, 501, 523
Seyli, 514–515
Seyrani, 518
Shamans, 216, 217
Shamash, 70, 74–75
Shamshi-Adad, king, 55, 63–64, 97n
Shang dynasty, 248
Shaw, Stanford J., 432n, 437n
Shebna, 299
Sheol, agreement with, 312–313
*Sheyhulislam,* 465, 467–468, 481
Shiʿa, 356, 358, 363, 364, 368, 375
Shiʿat, 353–354
Shiite segment of Moslem-Turkish
    population, 510
Shiloh, 314, 316, 329n
Shintoism, xiii
Shulgi of Ur III dynasty: apochryphal
    prophecy of, 87; divine determinative
    of, 79–80, 105n; narrative, 107n;
    priestly adulation of, 80; self-praising
    hymn of, 67–68, 100n
Shun-chih, Emperor, 241
Sibylline Books, 274
Sibylline Oracles, 274–275
Sicily, 558, 590n
Sign-producing systems, 111, 112–114.
    *See also* Symbols
Signs: arrangement of as style, 7; de-
    fined, 4; linguistic and nonlinguistic,
    112–113
Śilāhāras, 184
Silence, 167–168
*Śilpaśāstras,* 202

Silvester, Pope, 557
Simple Turkish movement, 502
Simpson, George G., 21
Sin, consciousness of, 169. *See also*
    Original sin
Şinasi, Ibrahim, 418, 419, 441n, 524
Sippar, 74–75
Śiva, 196
Sivan, Emmanuel, 269, 279n
Six Classics, 228
Six Maxims, 241
Skepticism: concerning divination, 143n;
    Egyptian, 154–157
Slave: bureaucracy, 385, 386; establish-
    ment, 466; troops, 373, 451–452. *See
    also* State slave system
Slaves as communication source, 490
*Ślokas,* 179, 180
Smoke signals, 24
*Smṛtis,* 179
Social change, 158, 201, 537, 541, 542;
    advocated by poets, 522, 523,
    524–531
Social cohesion, 394, 552, 585
Social control, 240, 241
Social criticism, 423, 506, 507, 520–522,
    541
Social forms, transmission of, 29
Social groups, 544, 585–586, 588
Social justice, 64, 355–356, 534
Social mobilization, 421, 422
Social order, 204, 214, 232, 243–244.
    *See also* India, social orders of
Social stability, 194–195, 224
Social survival, facilitating, 588, 595n
Socialization, 398, 421
Socioeconomic condition, 117, 536, 540
Socrates, 295, 297; portraits of, 265; war
    of pamphlets over, 292
Soldiers-administrators, 373, 374. *See
    also* Military
Solitary withdrawal, 349
Solomon, 312
Solon, 291, 302
Song, 23, 501; of Akkadi, 140n
*Song of Roland,* 558, 559, 561, 582
Soothsayers, employment of, 188–189.
    *See also* Oracles
Sophocles, 292
Southeast Asia, 203, 206
Spain and Christianity, 342, 371, 563
Spanish-American empire, 543
Spanish history, rewriting of, 572, 593n
Spanish Trastámara dynasty, 572
Specialization, 537
Specification of function, Egyptian, 148
Speech: capacity for, 31; development
    of, 23; divine, 321–322; freedom of,
    519; origins of, 21

Spies, king's use of, 188, 189
*Śrautasūtras,* 179
*Śrutis,* 178, 179
Ssu-ma Hsiang-ju, 234–235
Stalin, Joseph, xii, 528
Statecraft and divination, 89–91, 108–109n
State slave system, 450–453, 454, 455, 460, 465
Statesmen, training of, 384, 438n
Statutes of Provisors and Praemunire, 578
Stelae, 139n; erection of by kings, 114, 135, 251; inaccessibility of, 118, 119; inscriptions on, 115, 119, 140n
Stesimbrotus, 292
Storytellers, 188–189, 495
Stuart bureaucracy, 427
Style, defined, 7
Su Ch'o, 237, 238, 239, 255n
Su Wei, 237, 238
Subcultures, segregated, 383
Subjects: as class, 448, 449; communication with, 53, 114, 190–191, 468–469; Ottoman word for, 476
Sublime Porte, the, 416, 517–518
Submissiveness, 167–168, 237–238
Subriya, 126, 129–130, 132, 144n; king of, 129–130, 131, 132, 133
Success as value, 151–152, 154, 157, 162
Sudras, 191, 195
Suetonius, 260, 265–266, 293, 298
Şūfis, 355, 363, 364–365, 369, 370
Sui dynasty, 233, 237–238, 246
Sui Wen-ti, Emperor, 232–234, 237, 247
Suicide, 154–156
Süleyman I the Magnificent, 458, 460, 463, 486, 511; and governing, 459; as sultan-poet, 494
Süleyman Pasa, 412, 440n
Süleyman Sudi Efendi, 417
Sultans, 459, 465, 467, 488; harem influence on, 459–460; military activity of, 459, 463; in panegyrics, 507–509; as poets, 494, 508, 535n; portraits of, 438n; role in governing, 459, 461, 462–463; view of in poetry, 506, 511, 513, 517–518
Sumer, 51, 59–60, 61, 77, 98n; kings of, 62, 63, 67–69
Sumerian King List, 61, 76, 78, 98n, 103n, 105n; compilation of, 59, 60, 62; and legitimacy for Isin kings, 63; omissions from, 62–63, 98–99n; possible parody of, 63; programmatic nature of, 62
Sumerian language, 76, 96n, 97n, 103n, 105n, 115, 140n

Sumerian Renaissance, 60, 79
Sun-god, 87, 97n, 266–267
Sung dynasty, 236
Sunni Islam, 363, 366, 368, 370, 510; theology, 358, 365; *ʿulāma,* 375. *See also* Islam
Supernatural forces, control of, 253
Superstition, 186–189, 204
Suphi Pasa, 415
Surya, 183
Sutherland, C. H., 279
*Sūtras,* 178–179, 199
*Suttanipāta,* 200
Sutton Hoo, 588
*Suvarṇabhāsottamasūtra,* 181–182
Symbol system, 222, 391, 396, 536
Symbolic behavior, 119–123, 226–227
Symbolist poems, 518
Symbols: central, 538, 547; local, 538, 547, 548; in medieval society, 587–588; power of, 383; public, 278–279
Syme, Sir Ronald, 294
Symmachus, 295, 575
Syncretism, promotion of, 339–340, 344
Syracuse, 277, 278, 303
Syria, 299, 352, 353, 366, 368, 372; Christians in, 341, 342, 354

Tacitus, 576, 593n
Tagore, Sir Rabindranath, 534
Taib, Osmanzade, 512
Taine, Hippolyte, 497
T'ai-p'ing Rebellion, 242
T'ai-shan, sacred mountain, 223–224, 249–251, 252
T'ai-shang huang, title of, 235
T'ai-tsu, 239–240, 241
*Ta-kao,* 239–240, 241
*Takvīm-i Vekayi,* 405
Talip Apaydin, 530
Tamil kings, 202
Tamil language, 202–203
T'ang dynasty: agricultural ritual in, 244–245; Buddhist temples established by, 246; consolidation of, 230–232; founding of, 235; imperial rescript of, 266–268
T'ang Meng, 234–235
T'ang T'ai-tsung, Emperor, 230–232
*Tanzimat* era, 402, 424–427; administrative structural changes, 425–427; effect of on education, 411, 413, 416; effect of on poetry, 495, 517–518, 523–526
Taoism, 209, 210, 252
Target groups of propaganda, 224, 237–238, 252, 588–589. *See also* Audience

Tarhan, Abdülhak Hamit, 527
*Tarka*, 177
*Tasavvuf*, 510
*Tasvīr-i Efkar*, 407
Tax collection, Ottoman, 424
Tax exemption of Babylon, 86
Teachers, training of Ottoman, 387
Teachers of Christianity, 339, 340–341, 343–344
Technical ability of Egyptian Old Kingdom, 157
Technical assistance as millennium, 44
Technology: of communication, 8, 11–13; defined, 16; development of, 202, 204, 489, 541
*Tekke* poetry, 506, 510
Telegraph, 409, 442–443n
Television, 18, 20, 30, 40
Temple, Archbishop William, 344
Temple organization, 73–96; economic power of, 73, 74, 102n; economic role in conquest, 164–165; at Nippur, 77–78; in prophecy, 315; relationship with ruler, 58, 59, 66, 73, 83; revolt led by, 78–79
Temples, 77, 115; forged offerings to, 75–76; as investment in empire, 164–165; as part of king's ''services,'' 65, 134; rebuilding of, 85–86, 88
*Tercuman-i Ahval*, 406, 407
*Tercuman-i Hakikat*, 406, 408, 419
Terrill, Ross, 220, 255n
Tertullian, 335–336, 336–337
Tevfik, Ebuzziya, 418, 441n
Tevfik Fikret, 412, 525–526, 527
Textual criticism, 1
Thana, 184
Theatre, Western, 418. *See also* Drama; Plays
Theocratic establishment, poetry opposing, 506
Theocratic leader, Mesopotamian, 52, 96n
Theognis, 285
Theologians: plebeian, 302; satire of, 516–517
Theology: instruction in, 366, 379n; in verse, 504
Thersites, 302
*Thousand and One Nights*, 357
Thrales, 303, 318
Three Dynasties of China, 210
Three Treasures, emperor's, 247
Thucydides, 126–127, 128–129, 290
Tiamat, 92, 93; myth of, 309
Tiberius, 260, 266, 279, 280–281, 298
Tierney, Brian, 594n
Tiglath-Pileser I, 72, 73, 95, 101–102n, 120

Timgad, 262, 297
Timur Leng, 376
Titulary, phraseology of, 120
Titus, 259, 271
Tolls, Ottoman, 424
Tombs, Egyptian, 145–146, 157, 173n; building and maintaining, 158–159; physical decentralization of, 150; plundering of, 153; themes of, 163, 165–166
Tools of early man, 23
*Torah*, 316, 317
Torah, the, 327. *See also* Levite Torah
Town god, Egyptian, 150
Towns, Ottoman, 474–482, 492n
Towns, Roman, 261
Toynbee, Arnold J., 374
Trade: Assyrian, 121, 143n; Egyptian, 154; Indian, 202–203, 204; Ottoman, 427
Trade school, girls', 410
Trades School, Ottoman, 410
Tradesmen, associations of, 492n
Traditional societies, 542–543, 551n
Tragedy, 513–514
Trajan, 261, 264, 271, 283, 575; Column of, 259
Transhumance, 470
Transistors, 11, 19, 20
Translations, publication of, 403, 404
Transportation, difficulty of, 553–554, 554–555
Transylvania, 485
Tre Fontane, 564
Tregear, G., 29
Tribal: assemblies, Vedic, 175; federations, 543, 546; obligations, 350; pride, 359; warriors, 352, 353, 373
Tribute, 136
Trimingham, J. Spencer, 378, 379n, 380n
Triumphal arch, significance of, 259
*Trivarga*, 194
Troubadors, 12, 495
Tukulti-Ninurta I, 69, 71, 72, 85, 101n, 133; Epic, 70–71, 72, 101n, 102n
Tulip Age, 523
T'ung-chih Emperor, the, 243
Tun-huang, 208
Tūran, pre-Islamic rivalry of, with Iran, 359–360
Turco-Mongol rulers and Buddhism, 213
Turkey: modern, 382, 383, 390, 393–394, 430, 502; reform policies in, 398; Seljuq rule in, 368, 372
Turkish: identity, 498, 499–500, 501, 509; Moslems, 447, 452; national literature, 498, 501–502, 504, 509; nationalism, 504; slave-soldiers, 359,

360, 451, 452; solidarity, 501, 527; tribal confederacy, 366–367
Turkish language: effect of printing in, 437n; in instruction, 435n; literature of mysticism in, 395; maritime jargon, 490; as official language, 441n; Ottoman, 392, 393, 456; pride in, 499–500, 501–502, 523; reform of, 393, 413–414, 498, 500–502
Turkish Language Society, 502
Turkish poetry, 493, 494, 496, 500, 522; epics, 522; folk, 500–501; as a forerunner of social action, 497, 534; lyrics, 494, 501; and nature of Turkish society, 534–535; and roles of poet, 534; social commitment in, 520–522; social criticism in, 501, 510, 520–522
Turkish Republic, 503–504, 518, 527
Tutelary deities. *See* Deities, Tutelary
Twenty-four filial sons, 238
Two-class system, Ottoman, 448–450, 490n
Tyrtaeous, 302

ʿUlamā (Ulema), 386, 391, 432n, 448, 465, 491n; and the common man, 370, 372–373; as communication line, 387; dependence on ruling institution, 391; educational network of, 366, 387, 388, 389; endurance of de facto ruler, 361–362; as Islamic apologists, 362, 371, 374; in Muslim army, 369; political power of, 466, 491n; relation to Sufis, 363, 370; suspicion of independent thinking, 371
Ülken, Hilmi Ziya, 441
ʿUmar, Caliph, 351–353, 363
Umayyad: caliphate, 353, 354, 356, 357, 366, 370; clan, 353, 359
Umma, city-state of, 66, 80, 99n; kings of, 80, 105n, 106n; tutelary deity of, 67
Unat, Faik Reşit, 432n, 433n, 434n, 435n, 440n
*United States* v. *Alger Hiss,* 25–26
University: admission, 177; European medieval, 370, 379n; Ottoman, 410
Unseen forces, Chinese belief in, 216, 223–224
*Upaniṣads,* 178
Upshukinna, 93, 110n
Urban II, sermon on Crusade, 558–560, 582, 586, 588
Ur, city of, 60, 61, 99n, 105
Ur III dynasty, 63, 98n, 99n, 100n, 104n, 108n; administration of, 79; cautionary stories from, 77; hymns to

kings of, 67, 68; and purpose of Sumerian King List, 60; reform laws during, 56; rhetoric of founder, 65; royal inscriptions in Sumerian, 103n; Shulgi of, 67, 68, 87
Urartu, 125, 132–133; refugees from, 130, 131, 132
Uria, 305, 312
Ur-Nammu, 56, 65, 67, 99n, 100n, 105n
Uruk, city-state of, 60, 79, 80, 99n, 105n
Urukagina, 65, 66–67, 99n
Usuli, 513
Usurpers, claims of, 543–544
ʿUthmān, Caliph, 353, 359
Utopian construction, 310
Utopian exhortations, 313
Utu-Khegal, 60, 78, 98–99n

Vacuum tubes, technology of, 18, 19
Vahid Mahdumi, 501
Vaiṣṇavite: Purānas, 195, 196; use of literature to promote change, 204; vegetarianism, 201
Vaisyas, 191, 192
Validating material detail, 27
Vālmīki, 180
Value outcomes of communication process, 6, 9
Values: critique of social, 504; of Egyptian Old Kingdom, 151–152, 154, 157; instilled by folk literature, 195; memorization of, 237–238; modernist-secularist, 408; transformation of, 212–213; unity of, 237, 455–456, 589–590
Varna system, 191–193, 194, 199, 200
*Varṇa-dharma,* observance of, 195
Varuṇa, 183
Vassals in Assyrian power structure, 135
Vedas, 196
Vedic literature, 178, 180, 181, 196
Vedic period, 175–176, 180, 181, 184, 193, 199; astrology in, 197; public debates in, 175–176; tribal assemblies in, 175–176
Vegetarianism, 200–201
Veled, Sultan, 500
Vergennes, Comte de, 18
Vergil, 290, 293–294, 298
Vergil, Polydore, 578
Vernacular, 577, 578, 579; as requirement for political participation, 14
Verse: Indian literature in, 178, 179, 180, 196; uses of, 495. *See also* Poetry
Verse Account, by priests of Marduk, 100n
Vespasian, 260, 271, 283

Victoria, Queen, 197
Victory: importance of, 120–121, 122; realization of, 122–123
Victricius, 567
*Vidatha,* 175
Vīdyādharas, 184
Vikramāditya IV, 184
Vilification literature, 201
Village, Balinese, 36, 37–38, 39–40
Villages, Ottoman: communication characteristics of, 473; compared to towns, 475–476; contacts of with government, 469, 470; isolation of, 469, 470; social contacts in market, 469–470; specialized, 487
*Vinaya Piṭaka,* 177
Vindex, C., 282
Viṣṇu, 182–183, 196
Visual propaganda, 564–567
Vitellius, 283
Viziers, Egyptian, 145–146, 173n
Viziers, Ottoman, 461–462; grand, 458, 461, 462, 491n
Vocational preparation, 540
Voluntarism, 169, 170
von Grunebaum, Gustave E., 359, 360–361, 377n, 378n, 379n, 380n, 433n
Vyāsa, 120

Wallace, Anthony F. C., 48
Walter, Gerard, 269
Wang Lien, 255n
Wang Mang, 228, 229; admonitions of, 238–239, 241, 246
War: Akkadian word for, 143n; arts of, teaching, 385; Assyrian attitude toward, 142n; as basis of Ottoman system, 455–456; Chinese view of, 214–215; ideology, dramatic dialogues on, 127, 129; machines, maintaining, 136, 486; Mesopotamian attitude toward, 142n; as symbolic behavior, 119–123, 445
War-prophecy, free, 300
Wards in Ottoman towns, 474–475
Warlords, 211
Warring states, period of, 210, 221
Wars of Roses, 587
Watt, Ian, 398, 436n, 441n
Watt, W. Montgomery, 371, 376n, 377n, 378n, 379, 380n
Wealth, protection of, 194
Wei dynasty, 213, 219n
Weidner, E. F., 141n, 142n, 144n
Weld-Blundell Prism, 98n
Wessex, laws of, 569
West Africa, 24, 285

West Germany, 102n
Western civilization: depiction of rulers in, 122; influence of on Ottoman journalism and modernization, 416–417; literature of, access to, 423; military superiority of, 400, 436n; modernization of communication in, 382; scientific advances of, 422; scientific rational thought of, 418; values, 419, 420
Western Europe: age of mercantilism in, 397; central authority in states of, 424; Christianity in, 342; constituted bodies in, 384; cultural elitism in, 398–399
Westernization, 395–396, 427, 524
Westminster, rebuilding of, 574
Wheel of lives, doctrines of, 243
White man, destruction or eviction of, 43
Wieruszowski, Helene, 590n, 592n, 594n
Wife, obligations of, 194
William of Malmesbury, 584–585
William of Poitiers, 573
William of Rubruck, 567–568, 583
William the Conqueror, 573–574
Wilton diptych, 564–565
Winchester, 583; Charter, 572
Wisdom, worldly, prophets' view of, 318
Wisdom literature, 166–167, 171
Women: evidence given by, 42; in politics, through harem, 460; social seclusion of, 363
Word equivalents, 4
Word, written: as an aesthetic object, 222; in classical civilization, 289–296; efficacy of, 222–223; as a means of communication, 289–291. *See also* Writing
Words: emblematic force of, 222–223; reiterated, power of, 238; as signs, 4
Worker religiosity, 435n
World domination, hope of, 313
World politics, 307–308, 312–313
World War II: and free speech in Turkey, 519; technology of, 19
World's end, Jesus' announcement of, 331
Worship, 312, 329n, 351. *See also* Religious observances
Worsley, Peter, 43
Wren, Christopher, 258
Writing, 11, 177–179, 203, 204, 289, 290
Wu, Emperor, 234
Wu, Empress, 229, 239, 246

Wulfstan, archbishop of York, 571–572, 588
Wycliffe, John, 14–15, 578

Xenophon, 292, 297

Yagcioglu, Halim, 520
Yahya of Taslica, 512
Yahya, Sheikh-ul Islam, 517
Yahwe: *berith* with, 314; calling prophets, 323, 326; commandments of, 301, 307, 315, 316, 318, 327; divine speech, 321–322, 323; instruments of, 104n, 306, 312, 314, 318; revelation of, 320–321; voice of, 305, 320, 322, 323, 325–326, 327
[Yalman], Ahmed Emin, 438n, 439n, 440n
Yama, 183, 229
Yasmakh-Adad, 55
Yásodharman of Malwa, 185
Year dating, 68–69, 100–101n
Year of the Four Emperors, 282–283

Yellow Turbans, Revolt of the, 209, 252–253
Yemen, Ottoman military in, 483
Yesevi sect, 510
*Yin-yang* theory, 222, 230–231
York, house of, 577, 578
York-Rouen, Anonymous(es) of, 580
Young Turk movement, 412; Committee of Union and Progress, 373
Yüan dynasty, 236, 252
Yunus Emre, 501, 510–511
Yurdakul, Mehmet Emin, 527
Yü-wen T'ai, 237, 239

Zachariah, 319
Zedekiah, 301, 306–307, 309, 311, 319
*Zekenim,* 311
Zephaniah, 309, 322
Zion, 315
Ziya Pasa, 414, 441n, 518, 524
Zoroastrian clergy in Iran, 377n
Zoroastrians in Muslim empire, 356
Zosimus, 575, 593n
Zwingli, Huldreich, 317